HISTORY
BEHIND THE
HEADLINES

HISTORY BEHIND THE HEADLINES

The Origins of Conflicts Worldwide

VOLUME **2**

Meghan Appel O'Meara, Editor

GALE GROUP

Detroit
New York
San Francisco
London
Boston
Woodbridge, CT

Editor

Meghan Appel O'Meara

Gale Group Staff

Editorial: Bernard Grunow, Project Editor; Kathy Droste, Nancy Matuszak, Allison McNeill, and Gerda-Ann Raffaelle, Contributing Editors; Jason Everett, Associate Contributing Editor; Rita Runchock, Managing Editor.

Permissions: Maria Franklin, Permissions Manager; Debra Freitas, Permissions Associate.

Composition: Mary Beth Trimper, Manager, Composition and Electronic Prepress; Evi Seoud, Assistant Manager, Composition Purchasing and Electronic Prepress.

Manufacturing: Dorothy Maki, Manufacturing Manager; Rhonda Williams, Buyer.

Imaging and Multimedia Content: Barbara J. Yarrow, Imaging and Multimedia Content Manager; Randy Bassett, Image Database Supervisor; Dean Dauphinais, Senior Imaging Specialist; Dan Newell, Imaging Specialist; Pamela A. Reed, Imaging Coordinator.

Product Design: Kenn J. Zorn, Product Design Manager; Pamela A. E. Galbreath, Senior Art Director; Michael Logusz, Art Director.

ISBN 0-7876-4952-X
ISSN 1531-7307
Printed in the United States
10 9 8 7 6 5 4 3 2 1

TABLE OF CONTENTS

Contents by Subject viii

Advisory Board x

About the Series xii

Preface xiii

A

Algeria's Post-Colonial Civil War 1

Algeria's civil war has been characterized by extreme brutality.

Angola: Civil War and Diamonds 9

Angola's civil war—and cold war politics—have devastated the country since it won independence in the 1960s.

Austria's Shunning by the Global
Community 25

Western nations withdrew their ambassadors and sanctioned Austria when the ruling government merged with a controversial right-wing party.

B

The Basques: The ETA and Separatism 34

The Basque region is fighting a guerrilla war for separation from Spain.

C

China and Religious Protest: The Falun
Gong 42

The People's Republic of China has maintained strict control of its people's religions. The Falun Gong, an order devoted to the teachings of Li Hongzhi, has been declared illegal by the Chinese government and suffered violent suppression in the practice of its belief.

China and the World Trade Organization:
Values in Conflict 51

The People's Republic of China's application for membership in the WTO is a controversial one due to its economic and human rights policies.

The Colombian U'wa Indians: Sacred
Land and Oil 64

The U'wa Indians of Colombia have sued Occidental Petroleum Corporation in an effort to stop the company's exploration of territory they feel belongs to "Mother Earth" alone. The Colombian government must decide between its people and its profits.

Cyprus: An Island Divided 75

Ethnic and religious tension and the long-standing conflict between Greece and Turkey keep the island of Cyprus divided.

E

East Timor: The Path of Democracy for the
World's Newest Nation 88

In 1999 East Timor erupted in bloodshed following a vote for independence.

The Ecuadorian Indigenous People's
Movement: Autonomy and the
Environment 99

Indigenous people in Ecuador overthrew the president in January 2000, leading to the establishment of a *junta*, a small military government.

European Union Conflict: The British Beef
Controversy 112

The recent ban on the import of British beef highlights the economic conflict in the European Union.

G

Guatemala: Indian Testimony to a Genocidal War *122*
Rigoberta Menchú sued Guatemala's former leaders in Spanish court for human rights abuses. She stands for the thousands of Indians that suffered under the brutal dictatorship of the former Guatemalan government.

I

The Iranian Revolution: Islamic Fundamentalism Confronts Modern Secularism *132*
Recent attempts at secularization in Iran have been met with resistance from Islamic fundamentalists.

J

Jerusalem: Divided City *141*
A holy city for three religions, Jerusalem is of core importance in the Arab-Israeli conflict.

K

The Korean Peninsula: A Fifty-Year Struggle for Peace and Reconciliation *149*
The recent summit between North and South Korea, as well as the brief reunions for families separated for fifty years, provides hope for the resolution of a seemingly intractable conflict.

Kosovo: Ethnic Tensions and Nationalism *157*
In 1999 the United Nations and NATO occupied Kosovo, a province in the former Yugoslavia, in an attempt to protect the Muslim Albanian population from the Serbian military.

M

Mexican-U.S. Border Relations: Opportunities and Obstacles *169*
Tensions between Mexico and the United States are exasperated at its shared border because of the smuggling of illegal goods, drugs, and immigrants.

Mozambique: Independence and a Dirty War *179*
Mozambique has been attacked both directly and indirectly by its African neighbors in an attempt to destabilize a black-led government.

Myanmar: The Agony of a People *188*
Rebel groups battle the government for self-determination in Myanmar.

N

Native Americans: Centuries of Struggle in North America *198*
The plight of Native Americans is an enduring conflict of self-determination and occupation, protection and discrimination.

Nigeria and Shari'a: Religion and Politics in a West African Nation *214*
The Zamfara state repudiated Nigeria's constitution and adopted Islamic law.

Northern Ireland: The Omagh Bomb, Nationalism, and Religion *221*
The region of Northern Ireland has endured six hundred years of ethno-religious strife.

P

Peru's Shining Path: Revolution's End *236*
The Shining Path taught a philosophy of violent agrarian revolution in a country where the Indians feel marginalized.

R

Romania's Cyanide Spill *246*
In 2000, a cyanide spill polluted rivers and drinking water in affecting five countries.

S

South Africa's Truth and Reconciliation Commission *253*
South Africa formed a commission to investigate—and grant amnesty—for crimes committed under apartheid.

Sri Lanka: Civil War and Ethno-Linguistic Conflict *262*
The Sri Lankan civil war has emphasized the ethnic, linguistic, and religious differences between the Sinhalese and Tamils.

T

Tibet: Struggle for Independence *271*
Tibet, land of Buddhists seeks independence from the ruling People's Republic of China.

U

United Nations Peacekeeping Forces: Peace and Conflict *283*
U.N. peacekeeping efforts are challenged regarding their efficacy and neutrality.

U.S. Immigration: Sanctuary and
Controversy *292*
Immigration of foreigners into the United States has been a long-debated and very controversial topic among those who are already citizens of the country.

Zimbabwe's Land Reform: Race and
History *302*
Zimbabwe, attempting to rebound from enormous economic difficulties, struggles with the issue of land redistribution from white farmers to underemployed blacks in a racially-charged atmosphere.

Contributors *317*

General Bibliography *320*

Index *323*

CONTENTS BY SUBJECT

ECONOMIC

Algeria's Post-Colonial Civil War 1

Angola: Civil War and Diamonds 9

China and the World Trade Organization:
Values in Conflict 51

Cyprus: An Island Divided 75

The Ecuadorian Indigenous People's
Movement: Autonomy and the
Environment 99

European Union Conflict: The British Beef
Controversy 112

Guatemala: Indian Testimony to a
Genocidal War 122

Mexican-U.S. Border Relations:
Opportunities and Obstacles 169

Native Americans: Centuries of Struggle in
North America 198

Peru's Shining Path: Revolution's End 236

Romania's Cyanide Spill 246

U.S. Immigration: Sanctuary and
Controversy 292

Zimbabwe's Land Reform: Race and
History 302

ENVIRONMENTAL

The Colombian U'wa Indians: Sacred
Land and Oil 64

The Ecuadorian Indigenous People's
Movement: Autonomy and the
Environment 99

Romania's Cyanide Spill 246

ETHNIC

Angola: Civil War and Diamonds 9

The Basques: The ETA and Separatism 34

Cyprus: An Island Divided 75

Kosovo: Ethnic Tensions and Nationalism 157

Mexican-U.S. Border Relations:
Opportunities and Obstacles 169

Myanmar: The Agony of a People 188

Native Americans: Centuries of Struggle in
North America 198

Nigeria and Shari'a: Religion and Politics
in a West African Nation 214

Northern Ireland: The Omagh Bomb,
Nationalism, and Religion 221

Peru's Shining Path: Revolution's End 236

Sri Lanka: Civil War and Ethno-Linguistic Conflict 262

Tibet: Struggle for Independence 271

U.S. Immigration: Sanctuary and Controversy 292

POLITICAL
Austria's Shunning by the Global Community 25

China and the World Trade Organization: Values in Conflict 51

European Union Conflict: The British Beef Controversy 112

The Korean Peninsula: A Fifty-Year Struggle for Peace and Reconciliation 149

Mozambique: Independence and a Dirty War 179

United Nations Peacekeeping Forces: Peace and Conflict 283

RACIAL
South Africa's Truth and Reconciliation Commission 253

Zimbabwe's Land Reform: Race and History 302

RELIGIOUS
Algeria's Post-Colonial Civil War 1

China and Religious Protest: The Falun Gong 42

East Timor: The Path of Democracy for the World's Newest Nation 88

The Iranian Revolution: Islamic Fundamentalism Confronts Modern Secularism 132

Jerusalem: Divided City 141

Kosovo: Ethnic Tensions and Nationalism 157

Nigeria and Shari'a: Religion and Politics in a West African Nation 214

Northern Ireland: The Omagh Bomb, Nationalism, and Religion 221

Sri Lanka: Civil War and Ethno-Linguistic Conflict 262

Tibet: Struggle for Independence 271

TERRITORIAL
Jerusalem: Divided City 141

Kosovo: Ethnic Tensions and Nationalism 157

Native Americans: Centuries of Struggle in North America 198

Northern Ireland: The Omagh Bomb, Nationalism, and Religion 221

ADVISORY BOARD

Jerry H. Bentley is professor of history at the University of Hawaii and editor of the *Journal of World History*. His research on the religious, moral, and political writings of Renaissance humanists led to the publication of *Humanists and Holy Writ: New Testament Scholarship in the Renaissance and Politics and Culture in Renaissance Naples*. More recently, his research has concentrated on global history and particularly on processes of cross-cultural interaction. His book *Old World Encounters: Cross-Cultural Contacts and Exchanges in Pre-Modern Times* examines processes of cultural exchange and religious conversion before the modern era, and his pamphlet "Shapes of World History in Twentieth-Century Scholarship" discusses the historiography of world history. His current interests include processes of cross-cultural interaction and cultural exchanges in modern times.

Ken Berger received his B.A. in East Asian Studies at Eckerd College and his M.A. in Asian Studies and M.S.L.S. from Florida State University. He has been a librarian at Duke University since 1977, with almost all of his time spent as a reference librarian and bibliographer, including the last several years as head of reference. He is currently the Project Manager for the Library Service Center. He has written hundreds of reviews in East Asian studies, military affairs and history, and library and information science.

Frank J. Coppa is Professor of History at St. John's University, Director of their doctoral program, and Chair of the University's Vatican Symposium. He is also an Associate in the Columbia University Seminar on Modern Italy, and editor of the Lang Series on Studies on Modern Europe. He has published biographies on a series of European figures, written and edited more than twelve volumes, as well as publishing in a series of journals including the *Journal of Modern History* and the *Journal of Economic History*, among others. He is editor of the *Dictionary of Modern Italian History* and the *Encyclopedia of the Vatican and Papacy*.

Bill Gaudelli received his Ed.D. in Social Studies Education from Rutgers University in 2000. He dissertation was on "Approaches to Global Education." He teaches at Hunterdon Central Regional High School (winner of the National Council for the Social Studies Programs of Excellence Award) and Teachers College-Columbia University. Publications include "Teaching Human Rights through Conflict-Resolution" in *Social Science* and "Global Education: a Viable Framework for an Issues-Centered Curriculum" in *ERIC Documents*. He is a member of the National Council for Social Studies and the American Forum for Global Education.

Paul Gootenberg is a Professor of Latin American History at SUNY-Stony Brook. A graduate of the University of Chicago and Oxford, he specializes in the economic, social, and intellectual history of the Andes and Mexico, and more recently, the global history of drugs. He has published *Between Silver and Guano* (1989), *Imagining Development* (1993) and *Cocaine: Global Histories* (1999). Gootenberg has held many fellowships; they include Fulbright, SSRC, ACLS, Institute for Advanced Study, Russell Sage Foundation, the Rhodes Scholarship, and a Guggenheim. He lives in Brooklyn, New York, with his wife, Laura Sainz, and son, Danyal Natan.

Margaret Hallisey is a practicing high school library media specialist in Burlington, Massachusetts. She is a graduate of Regis College with a B.A. in English and of Simmons College with a M.S. in Library and Information Science. A member of Beta Phi Mu, the International Library Science Honor Society, she serves on the executive Boards of the American Association of School Librarians (AASL), the Massachusetts School Library Media Association (MSLMA) and the New England Educational Media Association (NEEMA).

Patricia H. Hodgson is the District Librarian for the Aspen School District, in Aspen, Colorado. She is a member of the American Library Association, the American Association for School Librarians, and the World History Association. She received her M.L.M. from the University of Colorado at Denver.

Donna Maier has been with the Department of History at the University of Northern Iowa since 1986. Her research interests are in nineteenth century Asante (Ghana), African Islam, and traditional African medicine. Her extensive lists of publications include "The Military Acquisition of Slaves in Asante," in *West African Economic and Social History, The Cloths of Many-Colored Silks* (1996), and *History and Life, the World and Its Peoples* (1977-90, with Wallbank and Shrier). She is a member of the African Studies Association and the Ghana Studies Council.

Linda Karen Miller, Ph.D., teaches American government, world history and geography at Fairfax High School in Fairfax, Virginia. A twenty-nine year veteran, she has received several national and state teaching awards such as the National Council for the Social Studies Secondary Teacher of the Year in 1996, the Organization of American Historian Pre-Collegiate Teacher of the Year in 1996, the Excellence in Teaching Award from the University of Kansas and the University of Virginia, and the Global Education Award from the National Peace Corps Association. She has traveled to Russia and Armenia under grants sponsored by the U.S. Department of State. She has published several lesson plans and articles for PBS and, most recently, Turner Learning's "Millennium 1000 Years of History." She also serves as a consultant to Newsweek magazine and the Wall Street Journal Classroom Edition, as well as the GED testing service.

Philip Yockey is Social Sciences Bibliographer and Assistant Chief Librarian for Staff Training and Development at the Humanities and Social Sciences Library at The New York Public Library.

ABOUT THE SERIES

In 1991 the world witnessed a political change of great magnitude. The Union of Soviet Socialist Republics (USSR) crumbled, ushering in a new era of democracy and the official end of the Cold War. East and West Germany had reunited just two years earlier; for many people formerly behind the Iron Curtain, now seemed to be a time of unbound freedom and autonomy. Yet ten years later, newscasts and newspapers report of a six year war between Russia and Chechnya, a former state within the USSR. After so much optimism about the future, what caused this instability and unrest? Was the cause based in a fundamental flaw of the initial break-up of the USSR or perhaps from something much further back in the regions' histories? How did the international community react to the USSR's collapse and the strife that was to follow?

History Behind the Headlines (HBH), a new, ongoing series from the Gale Group strives to answer these and many other questions in a way that television broadcasts and newspapers cannot. In order to keep reports both simple and short, it is difficult for these media to give the watcher or reader enough background information to fully understand what is happening around the world today. *HBH* provides just that background, giving the general public, student, and teacher an explication of each contemporary conflict from its start to its present and even its future. This thoroughness is accomplished not just by the in-depth material covered in the main body of each essay, but also by accompanying chronologies, textual and biographical sidebars, maps, and bibliographic sources.

Not only does *HBH* provide comprehensive information on all of the conflicts it covers, it also strives to present its readers an unbiased and inclusive perspective. Each essay, written by an expert with a detailed knowledge of the conflict at hand, avoids taking any particular side and instead seeks to explain each vantage point. Unlike television and newspaper reports, which may only have the time, space or even inclination to show one side of a story, *HBH* essays equally detail all sides involved.

Given the number of conflicts that beg such explication as *HBH* provides, an advisory board of school and library experts helps to guide the selection process and narrow down the selection for each volume. They balance the topic lists, making sure that a proper mix of economic, political, ethnic, and geographically diverse conflicts are chosen. Two volumes, each written in an accessible, informative way, will be released each year.

PREFACE

Selection and Arrangement

This volume of *History Behind the Headlines* covers thirty conflicts—including ethnic, religious, economic, political, territorial, and environmental conflicts. The topics were chosen following an extensive review of the conflicts covered in newspapers, magazines, and on television. A large number of potential conflicts were identified. Advisors—including academic experts, high school social study teachers, and librarians—prioritized the list, identifying those conflicts that generate the most questions. Topics were then selected to provide a regional balance and to cover various types of conflicts.

The conflicts covered are complex. Each essay discusses multiple aspects of the conflict, including economic and social aspects to religious conflicts, the interests of other countries, international organizations, and businesses, and the international implications of the conflict. The entries are arranged alphabetically by a major country, region, organization, or person in the conflict. Where this might not be clear in the table of contents, the keyword is placed in parentheses in front of the title.

Content

Each essay begins with a brief summary of the current situations as well as some of the major factors in the conflict. Each essay contains the following sections:

- **Summary of the headline event.** An overview of the contemporary conflict that has brought the issue to public attention. For example, violence in East Timor in 1999 and 2000 following the vote in favor of independence from Indonesia or the recent negotiations regarding the disposition of Jerusalem.

- **Historical Background.** The "Historical Background" is the heart of the essay. The author provides the historical context to the contemporary conflict, summarizing the arc of the conflict through history. Each essay tells the "story" of the history of the conflict, capturing important events, transfers of power, interventions, treaties, and more. The author summarizes the changes in the conflict over time, describes the role of major figures whether individuals, political organizations or religious organizations, and provides an overview of their positions now and in the past. Where appropriate the author may draw comparisons with similar situations in the country or region in the past. In addition, the author often attempts to put the conflict in the context of global politics and to describe the impact of the conflict on people around the world. Finally, the author may touch on how historians' understanding of the conflict has changed over time.

- **Recent History and the Future.** The final section brings the conflict up-to-date, and may offer some projections for future resolution.

Each essay is followed by a brief bibliography that offers some suggestions of resources for further research. In addition, brief biographies may accompany the essay, profiling major figures. Sidebars may provide statistical information, a quote from a speech, a selection from a primary source document (such as a treaty), a selection from a book or newspaper article that adds to the understanding of the conflict, or may explore an issue in greater depth (such as the role of the Internet in dissent or the issues involved in the dollarization of an economy). Images may also accompany the essay, including one or more maps showing the area of conflict.

A selected bibliography providing suggestions for background information and research on the nature of conflicts and a comprehensive index appear at the back of each volume.

History is to be Read Critically

Each of the talented writers (mostly academic authorities) in this volume strived to provide an objective and comprehensive overview of the conflict and its historical context. The nature of contemporary conflict, however, makes it difficult to wholly accomplish this objective. Contemporary history and, indeed, all history, should be read critically.

Acknowledgements

Many thanks for their help to the excellent advisors who guided this project—their attention and feedback was greatly appreciated. Many thanks, also, to the thoughtful and dedicated writers, who lent their expertise to help others understand the complex history behind sound bites on the news. Thanks to Bernard Grunow and the team at the Gale Group that made the manuscript a book. Finally, thanks to my family and friends—especially B.B. Sela—for their support and encouragement.

Comments on this volume and suggestions for future volumes are welcomed. Please direct all correspondence to:

Editor, *History Behind the Headlines*
Gale Group
27500 Drake Rd.
Farmington Hills, MI 48331-3535
(800) 877-4253

ALGERIA'S POST-COLONIAL CIVIL WAR

Since the early 1990s Algeria has gained increased notoriety in the Western media because of a violent civil conflict ostensibly between supporters of the government and organizations who wish to establish an Islamic state. This conflict has become well known for its bloody massacres of villages and, in particular, its harsh treatment of women. Rebel groups battle paramilitary organizations and the government, and civilians are often among the first victims.

Beginning in 1991 Algeria entered a prolonged period of bloodshed and social instability, stemming from national elections. The democratic elections were voided by the military when it became apparent that an Islamic political movement would emerge the winner. This was a major turning point for Algeria, which until this time had enjoyed a reputation as one of the Arab and African worlds' most progressive and forward-thinking states.

HISTORICAL BACKGROUND

Algeria is located in the northwestern portion of Africa in the region known as the Maghrib. The word Maghrib is a form of the Arabic word *gharb*, which means west. This is a reference to the fact that the region of Tunisia, Algeria, and Morocco is traditionally the western-most limit of the Islamic world. As part of the Mediterranean world Algeria has been part of major cultural movements for over three thousand years. Initially Algeria was part of the hinterland of the Carthaginian Empire (from about 800 B.C.) and was later incorporated into the Roman Empire when Rome destroyed Carthage in 146 B.C.

The advance of the Arabs and the introduction of Islam around the year 650 A.D., however,

The Conflict
Since the early 1990s Algeria has been involved in a harsh civil war, characterized by, among other things, the brutalization of its civilians.

Political
- The Islamic Salvation Front was the likely winner in an election; it was subsequently cancelled by the military government, causing disillusionment with the political system.

Religious
- The Islamic Salvation Front has the support of a significant portion of the population. The Front advocates the establishment of Islamic law, *shari'a*.

Economic
- The drop in oil prices in the 1980s increased the migration of people from rural areas to the city and increased poverty and social dislocation, adding to discontent and furthering violence.

CHRONOLOGY

650 Islam is introduced to Algeria.

711 Algeria invades Spain and Portugal (Spain and Portugal remain part of the Islamic world until 1492).

1518 Algeria is ruled by the Ottoman Empire.

1930 Algeria loses its independence and becomes a French colony, and later a *department* of France.

1954 The National Liberation Front (FLN) fights against France.

1991 The Islamic Salvation Front (FIS) wins a free election. The FLN, dissatisfied with the results, cancels the election.

1992–97 Civil war. The Islamic Salvation Arms (AIS) and the Armed Islamic Group (GIA) are formed.

1994 Algerian president General Lamine Zeroual begins discussions with the FIS.

1997 The AIS declares a cease-fire.

1999 Adbel Azziz Bouteflika is elected president. The AIS renounces violence.

have had a longer lasting impact on the area than any earlier outside influence. Although Algeria eventually became a nation in which the majority of people identify themselves as Arabs, a significant minority—especially in mountainous regions—still maintain the older Berber language and culture. Contemporary Algeria, along with Morocco, is distinguished from other states in North Africa by the retention of a prominent Berber community.

By 711 Islamic identity had grown strong enough that local North Africans or Berbers, under the leadership of Tariq ibn Ziyad, led an invasion into the Iberian peninsula of Europe. The invasion resulted in modern-day Spain and Portugal being part of the Islamic world until 1492.

By 1518, after the decline of various local political governments, Algeria came under the control of the Ottoman Empire. The Ottoman Empire, an Islamic empire based in Turkey, ruled a large portion of southeastern Europe and the Middle East from the fourteenth to the twentieth centuries. After the death of the Sultan Suleiman, the leader of the Ottomans in 1566, the Ottoman

Empire entered a long period of decline. As the empire declined, coastal rulers of what is now Algeria began to reassert its independence. In Western history these rulers are often known by the title of "Barbary Pirates" because of their habit of demanding tribute from ships that passed through their waters. Despite their description as pirates, the Algerians were respected by Western powers, and by the early nineteenth century the West and Algeria had signed a series of treaties, including one with the United States in 1815.

Colonization by France

By 1830, however, Algeria lost its political independence to its Mediterranean neighbor, France. There were many reasons behind the French conquest of Algeria. The France of Charles X and later Louis Phillippe was looking for a way to reclaim the greatness that France once held during the Napoleonic era of the 1800s, which included drastically expanding the country's empire. The invasion of Algeria also reflected a growing arrogance on the part of Europe toward the people of Africa and Asia stemming from Europe's readily apparent military superiority. The immediate cause for the invasion was a dispute between the governments of Algiers, capital of Algeria, and Paris, capital of France, over money the French owed for grain shipments. The French accused the Algerians of insulting them and France invaded the country in 1830. The initial French invasion had only limited success because of the spirited resistance of the Algerian people, led by the Berber Abdel Kader. However, by 1848, the French had subdued the country sufficiently to begin a process of colonization that would eventually result in one million Europeans living in Algeria by 1960.

Algeria was formally incorporated as a *department*, or province, of France in 1848. By the early twentieth century Algeria, like other colonial countries, had developed a cadre of Western-educated intellectuals who began to develop the argument for Algerian independence or, at least, enhanced rights for indigenous Algerians within the French system. Although the French responded by increasing the number of Algerians who could become citizens, the number was too small to significantly change the political dynamics of the colonial society.

After World War II Algerian nationalists began to agitate for independence, but they were violently repressed. The result was that by 1954, the National Liberation Front (FLN) of Algeria embarked on a full-scale war against France. This became the first successful indigenous war against

MAP OF ALGERIA. *(© Maryland Cartographics. Reprinted with permission.)*

colonial rule in Africa, and it became a benchmark in the struggle for political independence in the Third World. Despite the loss of two hundred fifty thousand people in the protracted struggle, Algeria emerged from the conflict as one of the undisputed leaders in the Pan-African, Pan-Arab, and non-aligned movements. The Pan-African movement included all of Africa; the Pan-Arab movement included all Arab states. The non-aligned movement included all states that were officially not aligned with either the United States or the Soviet Union or other communist countries.

Independence and Authoritarianism

After gaining independence Algeria's political development moved down a path similar to that of many other African and Arab nations of that period. Starting with the first independent leader, Ben Bella, Algeria was led by a series of authoritarian governments with a firm foundation in the country's military establishment. This type of leadership resulted in an ineffective political culture. In international matters Algeria was a major supporter of progressive political efforts from the African National Congress (ANC) in South Africa, to Afri-

AHMED BEN BELLA

1918– Algeria's first president was born in Marnia, Algeria, on approximately December 25, 1918. Ben Bella grew up speaking French and Arabic, and worked for his father's farm and business while attending the local French school. When he moved to Tlemcen to continue his education, he was subjected to racial discrimination by the French colonialists who controlled the government and the school. Bella soon joined the Algerian Nationalist Movement.

Ben Bella was conscripted into the French Army in 1937, and served with distinction during World War II. On his return to Marnia, he learned that the French had confiscated his farm. After a sham election in 1948, he lost hope in achieving independence democratically. He co-founded the Organisation Speciale, later the National Liberation Front (FLN), to combat the French militarily. In 1950 Bella was imprisoned, but was able to escape to Egypt.

In 1956, as insurrection divided Algeria, he was arrested by the French military while negotiating peace terms with the French premier. Released upon Algerian independence in 1962, Bella ran the socialist Bureau Politique and was elected president of the Algerian republic in 1963. He was deposed by the head of the army in a 1965 coup and imprisoned until 1980. Bella spent ten years in exile, but was allowed to return to Algeria in 1990.

can American activists like the Black Panthers in the United States, to international Marxists like Che Guevara. In internal matters the government found itself becoming increasingly authoritarian. Algeria failed to create political structures allowing its people an effective voice in government and it also failed explain its policies in a way that made common people feel that they had a stake in the continued development of the country.

In addition to an ineffective and authoritarian political culture, Algeria also suffered from problems that virtually all other countries in the developing world faced: namely, a fast growing population that was leaving the countryside and moving to the cities, only to find itself unemployed or underemployed. In this kind of climate it is not surprising that the government would eventually exhaust its political capital—the people's respect and goodwill—as a revolutionary force, and that people would begin to look to other authorities and organizations to address their problems.

By the early 1980s a number of problems had developed for the Algerian government. First, oil prices had declined. This had a huge impact on Algeria because petroleum products were and are its major source of revenue. The decreasing availability of money from oil meant that the government was less able than ever to handle the continuing influx of rural people into the cities. Of equal importance were events in the heartland of the

Islamic world. Specifically, in 1979, Iran, under the leadership of the Ayatollah Khomeini, proved that a revolution could be achieved without the use of Western-based ideology. Whereas the Algerian revolution had been intellectually shaped by Western-educated leaders and had even been supported enthusiastically by Western radical intellectuals, the movement of Khomeini was based solidly on the Shi'a Islamic traditions of Iran. The success of the Iranian revolution sent a clear signal to millions of Muslims that their own religious tradition could provide the spark for revolution as mighty as any other belief system.

Denial of Victory

By the late 1980s demonstrations were being held in Algeria to demand the end of one party government and the end of the National Liberation Front's (FLN) domination. By 1991 Algerian president Chadli Benjedid agreed to these demands and allowed free elections to take place. Once the first round of elections occurred, it soon became clear that the most popular party was the Islamic Salvation Front (FIS). The FIS believed in the foundation of a traditional Islamic state that would be ruled under the *shari'a* or traditional law of Islam. The FLN and the Algerian middle class, which were profoundly secular and Western-influenced, found the idea of an Islamic state unacceptable and cancelled the second round of elections rather than see the FIS win.

ALGERIAN WOMEN, HOLDING PICTURES OF THEIR MISSING RELATIVES BELIEVED TAKEN BY THE POLICE, DE-
MAND THE GOVERNMENT'S HELP TO FIND THEM IN ALGIERS, ALGERIA. *(AP/Wide World Photos. Reproduced by permission.)*

The denial of the FIS's legitimate victory is at the heart of the current conflict in Algeria. The worst period of fighting was between 1992 and 1997. During this time the Islamic Salvation Army (AIS), the armed division of the FIS, was formed and engaged in battle with the government. In addition to the AIS, another organization, the Armed Islamic Group (GIA), also came into being. The war in Algeria developed into a protracted and bloody conflict in which common people found themselves at the mercy of both the insurgents, or rebels, and the government.

During the period of the heaviest fighting, people in isolated villages were often approached by Islamic insurgents and asked to pay a tax to the rebels. If they could not or would not, the people might then find themselves being attacked. Often entire families were killed. One of the most unpleasant aspects of the Algerian conflict has been the degree to which violence against women has been used as a tactic of the combatants. In particular, insurgents have been accused of kidnapping and raping women and using them as sex slaves. This is an especially devastating fate for a woman

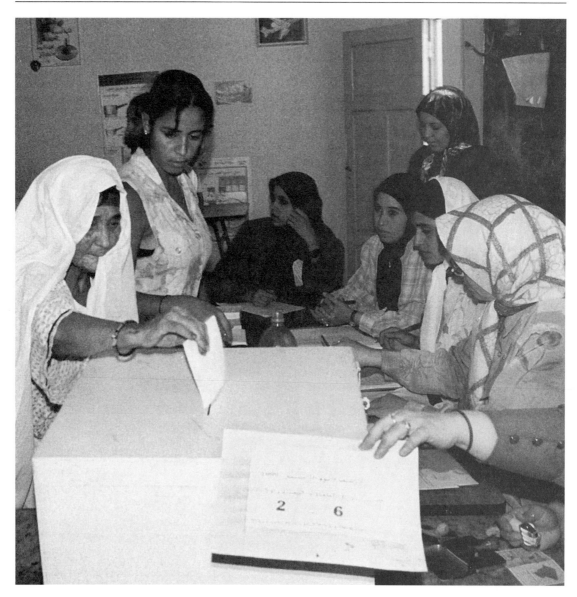

A WOMAN CASTS HER BALLOT ON A PEACE PLAN REFERENDUM, WHICH WILL HOPEFULLY END THE BLOOD-
SHED IN ALGERIA, BUT WHOSE SUCCESS IS DEPENDENT ON ISLAMIC MILITANTS. *(AP/Wide World Photos. Reproduced
by permission.)*

in a rural, conservative community. In many traditional communities, a woman having sex outside of
marriage, whether or not the sex is voluntary, is
seen as having shamed her family and she can be
subject to ostracism or, in some cases, death. In addition to sexual violence against women, insurgents
have been known to threaten female celebrities in
order to dissuade them from public life. For instance, female singers were threatened with death
if they performed, and female athletes were threatened with death if they appeared in public in athletic shorts, an action that, under *shari'a*, would be
a violation of the law.

In this kind of environment it is not surprising that people began to look toward vigilantism
for protection. Vigilantism is when citizens take up
arms to capture and punish suspected criminals, often without proper adherence to the law. Groups
known as *les patriotes*, the patriots, began to form
in order to protect their villages against those who
were suspected of complicity with Islamic rebels.
Les patriotes gained the de facto support of the government and combined resources to fight against
the rebels.

In 1994 General Lamine Zeroual became the
new president of Algeria, and he began to engage

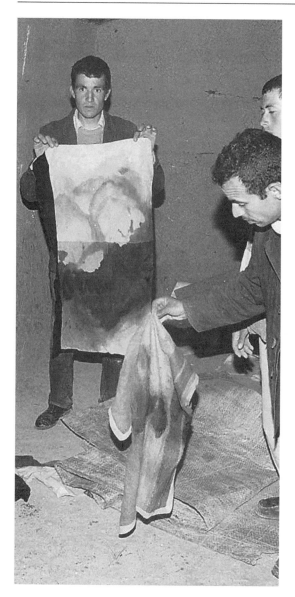

ALGERIANS EXAMINE BLOOD-STAINED CLOTHING AFTER ARMED ATTACKERS, THOUGHT TO BE ISLAMIC MILITANTS, KILLED SIX PEOPLE IN HATTATBA. *(AP/Wide World Photos. Reproduced by permission.)*

ABDELAZIZ BOUTEFLICKA

1937– Abdelaziz Bouteflicka was elected president of Algeria in April 1999. He won the popular vote, but under Algerian law the military is allowed to vote early. When these early results showed Bouteflicka leading, the other candidates dropped out of the popular election.

Bouteflicka was born in 1937, and gained prominence as a fighter in the National Liberation Front (FLN) against the French. He served in Algeria's first government cabinet as minister of sports, and was promoted after the 1963 coup. During his tenure as Algeria's foreign minister from 1965–78, he also served as a spokesperson for non-aligned nations groups, and, in 1974, as president of the twenty-ninth United Nation's General Assembly. In 1978, after being demoted by the military, Bouteflicka lived mostly in France. He continued to live in France even after being given a seat on the FLN's central committee in 1989.

Bouteflicka's 1999 presidential campaign focused on solutions to the on-going insurrection. In July 1999 he launched a general amnesty for members of militant Islamic militias, collectively called the Armed Islamic Group (GIA). Through the amnesty agreement President Bouteflicka invited all fighting units to disband, in exchange for a full pardon, by a deadline of January 13, 2000.

RECENT HISTORY AND THE FUTURE

In April of 1999 Abdelazziz Bouteflika was elected president of Algeria. Although many political activists and observers called the elections unfair, Bouteflika's experience as a foreign minister and his charisma appealed to a wide number of people. With the rise of President Bouteflika, the violence in Algeria has declined significantly. By June 7, 1999, the leader of the AIS, Madani Medrag, publicly renounced violence and urged his followers to lay down their weapons. Bouteflika has responded by developing an amnesty program for those insurgents who did not engage in the worst acts of violence, such as rape and murder.

Additionally, it appears that the stage may be set in Algeria for an official loyal Islamic opposition party to be formed, perhaps based somewhat on the model of similar parties in Turkey. The loyal opposition is a party that recognizes the right of the government to exist, though it disagrees with

the FIS in discussions. Although the talks did yield some results, the emergence of the GIA as an even more determined foe seemed to mitigate the progress that Zeroual achieved. Eventually, the government's use of harsh measures against the insurgents began to bear some results. By 1997 the AIS had declared a cease-fire, which it has since maintained. The GIA also agreed to the cease-fire, but has instead concentrated its forces more effectively.

its policies. The loyal opposition uses the political system—not violence—to try to gain control of the government. President Bouteflika released over twenty-three hundred Islamic activists from prison in July 1999, and stated that those who were not implicated in the violence will be allowed to establish political organizations.

Violence has clearly declined in Algeria but it is important to note that many of the underlying sources of friction in the society remain. Algeria in the late twentieth century had an unemployment rate of sixty percent, and many young men have simply fallen out of or have never joined the formal economy. One indicator of fundamental dissatisfaction has been a sharp increase in the number of suicides reported in the late 1990s. Despite these problems, it appears that armed resistance to the government is no longer an attractive alternative for many people. The violence may finally be coming to an end.

BIBLIOGRAPHY

"Abdel Azziz Bouteflika a President-Elect for Algeria." http://www.arabicnews.com (17 April 1999).

Canadian Broadcasting Corporation. *News in Review.* March, 1998.

Malley, Robert. *The Call From Algeria.* Berkeley, Calif.: University of California Press, 1996.

"Most Violent Crime in Algeria Since Bouteflika's Elections." http://www.arabicnews.com (16 August 1999).

Quandt, William B. *Between Ballots & Bullets.* Washington, D.C.: Brookings Institution Press, 1998.

Willis, Michael. *The Islamist Challenge in Algeria.* Ithaca, N.Y.: Berkshire UK, 1996.

Anthony Q. Cheeseboro

ANGOLA: CIVIL WAR AND DIAMONDS

The United Nations Security Council sanctions committee on Angola set off a storm of controversy in March 2000 with its report implicating African presidents in helping the National Union for the Total Independence of Angola (UNITA) rebels to buy weapons. The committee charged that rebels bought weapons from Eastern Europe, primarily Bulgaria, and had them shipped via other African countries in exchange for diamonds. The report charged that the rulers of Togo, Burkina Faso, the Ivory Coast, Gabon, and Rwanda helped ship weapons, spare parts, and fuel to Angola's rebel movement. Belgium was accused of having such lax standards at its Antwerp diamond market that rogue dealers were able to trade UNITA gems virtually without obstacle. The governments of Bulgaria and the various African states denied the allegations. Belgium's U.N. ambassador criticized the committee's failure to mention recent improvements in procedures at Antwerp, one of the world's diamond trading centers. The controversy represented the latest round in the effort to put an end to one of Africa's longest lasting conflicts, for control of the desperately poor but potentially rich country of Angola.

HISTORICAL BACKGROUND

Geographical Setting

Angola consists of two blocs of territory along the Atlantic coast of Africa. The larger of the two, Angola proper, lies south of the Congo River. Cabinda, a much smaller territory, lies north of the mouth of the Congo River and is separated from Angola proper by territory of the Democratic Republic of the Congo, formerly called Zaire.

THE CONFLICT

A civil war has brutalized Angola, raging since the 1960s fight for independence from Portugal. Over the years, other countries, including Cuba and South Africa, have funded the rebels or fought in Angola. Currently, the government is fighting National Union for the Total Independence of Angola (UNITA) rebels.

Ethnic

- The FNLA is predominately Kongo and anti-communist.

- The MPLA is predominately Mbunda and Creole, or Mestiço, and communist.

- UNITA is predominately Ovimbundu and was a major anti-colonial force.

- During colonization, Creoles were more likely to speak Portuguese and be educated; Africans of the interior—predominately the other ethnic groups—were more likely to be poor and uneducated.

Economic

- During colonization, ethnic divisions were made larger through increased economic differences. Creoles were developed by Portuguese rulers as an elite and were intermediaries in the slave trade. Kongo and Ovimbundu were more frequently agricultural laborers.

- Rebels, especially UNITA, have exploited diamond resources and support from abroad to fund their fighting.

- The United Nations has banned the sale of diamonds from Angola, because money from diamond sales funds the rebels.

CHRONOLOGY

1956 The Popular Movement for the Liberation of Angola (MPLA) is founded.

1961 The MPLA and the Union of Populations of Northern Angola (UPNA) begins a series of unco-ordinated attacks against the colonial Portuguese government.

1963 The Caninda Enclave Liberation Front (FLEC) is formed.

1964 Members of the Kongo ethnic group form the National Liberation Front of Angola (FNLA).

1966 Savimbi defects from the FNLA to found the National Union for the Total Independence of Angola (UNITA).

1974 President Caetano is overthrown in a coup d'état. General Spinola assumes power.

1975 Angola achieves independence from Portugal with the Alvor Agreement. The FNLA attacks the MPLA headquarters, leading to civil war. Cuban troops ar-rive in Angola in support of the MPLA. The first large shipment of arms from the Soviet Union arrives in Angola.

1976 The Angolan war ends. Cuban troops remain to enforce peace.

1981 South African forces carry out military actions against Mozambique, Zimbabwe, Zambia, and Angola.

1985 The U.S. Congress repeals the Clark Amendment and resumes aid to UNITA.

1988 An agreement is reached regarding Namibian in-dependence, a major issue for Angolan peace.

1991 Cuba withdraws troops from Angola. UNITA and the MPLA decide to merge and hold elections. Savimbi, UNITA's leader, is dissatisfied with the elec-tion results. Civil war resumes.

1994 The Lusaka Protocol establishes a cease-fire. The U.N. Security Council sends in U.N. peacekeeping troops.

1997–98 Angola intervenes in conflicts in Congo-Kinshasa and Congo-Brazzaville. Civil war re-erupts within Angola.

2000 United Nations' reports implicate various African presidents of helping rebel groups, such as UNITA, to buy weapons, thereby prolonging the war.

The country is largely agricultural, although its economy has been devastated by twenty-five years of civil war. Two main extractive industries provide most of Angola's revenues and provide the focus of the fighting in the civil war. The first is petroleum. There are major reserves along the coast of Cabinda and the northwestern corner of Angola, as well as along the forty kilometers, or twenty-five miles, of Congolese coastline that separates the two pieces of Angolan territory. The second major mineral deposit is diamonds, found in large quantities on the Lunda plateau of northeastern Angola.

Angola has a population of about ten million. There are dozens of ethnic groups speaking dis-tinct languages, but just three groups account for about three-fourths of the population. These are the Ovimbundu of central Angola, thirty-seven percent of the population according to a recent es-timate; the Mbundu of western Angola, from Luanda eastward, twenty-five percent of the pop-ulation; and the Kongo of the northwestern cor-ner, thirteen percent of the population. The pop-ulation of Cabinda, about one hundred thousand people, also belongs to the Kongo cultural cluster but tends to think of itself as "Cabindan." Because of the deaths and disruptions caused by decades of warfare, these figures and percentages should be treated as rough estimates. There are hundreds of thousands of Angolan refugees in neighboring countries, especially in the Democratic Republic of the Congo.

Reference books often cite statistics as to reli-gions practiced in Angola. For example, the *CIA World Factbook* for 1999 lists that forty-seven per-cent of the population expresses indigenous beliefs, thirty-eight percent Roman Catholic, and fifteen percent Protestant. This fails to take into account the fact that many Angolans are practicing Chris-tians–Catholic or Protestant—yet also retain some indigenous beliefs and practices. Christian evangelizing began among the Kongo people of the north-west. Later missionary efforts covered all areas of the country, but the north and the coast are still more heavily Christian than the interior and the south of the country.

All of these factors of physical and human geography—mineral resources, regions, ethnic groups, and religions—have their impact on politics. In the case of minerals, the connection is direct. The military activities of the government and its UNITA adversaries are financed largely by oil and diamonds, respectively.

Factors of human geography such as regional, ethnic, and religious identities matter a great deal as well. Each of the major parties has been identified with a particular region and ethnic group. Religion has also been important, although no party has been specifically Catholic or Protestant. To understand the impact of human geography on politics, it is important to look at Angola's history.

Forty Years of War

The current civil war in Angola, which the U.N. diamond ban is attempting to stop, is the continuation of fighting that has raged with few interruptions since 1960. The "peace" of the 1950s was, in fact, order imposed by oppressive colonial rule. Angola had been assigned to Portugal when the Europeans divided Africa in the 1880s. However, armed resistance to Portuguese rule continued until 1930. In 1959-60, when other African colonies were moving rapidly toward independence, there was no plan for the de-colonization of Angola or "Portuguese Africa."

Two uncoordinated uprisings, in Luanda and in the north, inaugurated a period of armed liberation struggle. In February 1961 members of the Popular Movement for Liberation of Angola (MPLA), led by Antonio Neto, attacked the São Paulo fortress and police headquarters in Luanda. At about the same time, in northern Angola, a series of attacks against Portuguese coffee planters led to a broad-based, anti-colonial revolt led by an organization known first as the Union of Populations of Northern Angola (UPNA). As the label suggests, the UPNA was a regional party, with an ethnic base among the Kongo people. Led by Holden Roberto, it underwent a series of mutations, first taking the non-regional name Union of Populations of Angola (UPA). Then it joined with a smaller party to form the National Liberation Front of Angola (FNLA).

Both the MPLA and the FNLA claimed to be struggling for the independence of the entire colony

JONAS MALHEIRO SAVIMBI

1934– Dr. Jonas Savimbi was born in 1934. After attending school in Angola, Savimbi continued his education in Europe. He studied medicine at the University of Lisbon (Portugal), and obtained a second doctorate in political science at the University of Lausanne (Switzerland), before he returned to Angola. In 1961 he joined the Popular Union of Angola (UPA), which later merged with a smaller party to form the National Liberation Front of Angola (FNLA), one of several factions fighting for liberation from Portugal.

In 1966 Savimbi left the FNLA to form the National Union for the Total Independence of Angola (UNITA). UNITA had grown into an army of thousands by the time Angola became independent in 1974. Savimbi was included in the hastily assembled interim government, but resigned and returned to guerrilla war when a Marxist government was established.

Throughout the 1980s the United States, China, and South Africa supported Savimbi and UNITA in the civil war against the Soviet- and Cuban-supported Popular Movement for the Liberation of Angola (MPLA), which controlled the central government. In 1992 Savimbi signed a United Nations-brokered peace agreement with the MPLA, which led to a cease-fire and multi-party national elections, in which Savimbi was a presidential candidate. After rejecting the results of the elections Savimbi re-armed UNITA and resumed the civil war.

of Angola. Each movement remained marked, however, by its regional origins. African and mixed-race intellectuals in the capital founded the MPLA, while members of the Kongo ethnic group in the north founded the FNLA. The FNLA moved beyond its ethnic origins in 1961 by recruiting Jonas Savimbi from the Ovimbundu ethnic community of central Angola. Savimbi's defection in 1964—and his founding of UNITA in 1966—left the FNLA a largely Kongo party.

In 1963 a new organization arrived on the scene. A number of people from Cabinda met at Pointe Noire, Congo-Brazzaville, and formed the Cabinda Enclave Liberation Front (FLEC). FLEC has since splintered into two rival military wings, FLEC-FAC and Renewed FLEC, or FLEC-Renovada. The FNLA operated from bases in Congo-Kinshasa, which shares long borders with Angola proper and the Cabinda enclave. The MPLA, excluded from Congo-Kinshasa, was able to operate from Congo-Brazzaville, which borders on Cabinda, and later from Zambia, which borders on eastern Angola proper.

From the early 1960s until 1974, the three main Angolan movements—FNLA, MPLA, and UNITA—fought against the Portuguese and each other, with no clear results. However, the cumulative effect of the colonial wars in Angola, Guinea-Bissau, and Mozambique turned the army against Portugal's undemocratic government. In 1974 a coup d'état, or rebellion, against President Caetano brought General Spinola to power. By 1975 power had passed from Spinola, who was relatively conservative, to younger leftist officers. The coup d'état of 1974 opened the door to independence for Angola and other Portuguese colonies in Africa.

Despite fighting between MPLA and FNLA forces in late 1974, African heads of state succeeded in convincing the three Angolan movements to join in negotiations with Portugal on an orderly transfer of power. These negotiations led to the Alvor Agreement of January 15, 1975, in which November 11, 1975, was set as the date for Portugal to hand over power to an Angolan coalition government. None of the parties took this last attempt at avoiding civil war very seriously, and sporadic fighting continued. The Alvor Agreement also was undermined by outside forces, which increased their support for their respective Angolan allies. China and the United States aided the FNLA, and later UNITA, while Cuba and the Soviet Union aided the MPLA. All parties were interested in Angola's natural resources, and the country was thrown into turmoil during the height of the Cold War.

In March 1975 the FNLA attacked MPLA headquarters and later gunned down fifty-one unarmed MPLA recruits. These incidents led to a full-scale civil war, with UNITA aligning itself with FNLA against MPLA. The scheduled elections never took place.

By early summer 1975 the FNLA had mounted limited offensives against the MPLA in northern Angola and along the coast. As another African-brokered attempt at negotiations broke down, the MPLA counterattacked. By the middle of July MPLA forces were in control of Luanda and had begun attacking FNLA strongholds in the north. Cuba resumed aid to the MPLA in July. About the same time, the U.S. Central Intelligence Agency (CIA) provided almost $50 million to train, equip, and transport anti-MPLA troops. In August, South African forces crossed the border into southern Angola, while troops from Zaire

joined FNLA forces fighting in the north. By mid-August 1975 Neto's forces were retreating.

The first Cuban combat troops arrived in Luanda in late September and early October and immediately took charge of much of the fighting. But the MPLA continued its retreat, pressured by Zairian and mercenary-led FNLA troops in the north and by UNITA forces and South Africans in the south. Savimbi could now use his substantial support among the Ovimbundu of central and eastern Angola. The MPLA controlled only its core areas of support in Mbundu country and in the cities, and continued to lose ground.

As Neto declared independence in Luanda on November 11, the MPLA was fighting for its existence only a few miles to the north. In the battle of Quifangondo Valley, Cuban artillery units armed with Soviet-supplied rocket launchers smashed the FNLA-Zaire forces and sent them fleeing toward the Zaire border. This in turn freed the MPLA and the Cubans to face the UNITA and South African forces approaching from the south. The first two weeks of independence saw the rapid advance toward Luanda of the UNITA army, led by about six thousand South African troops. By late November these forces controlled most major ports south of the capital as well as the Benguela railway. Savimbi began setting up his own civilian administration in Huambo, in cooperation with the FNLA.

The Soviet Union transported some twelve thousand Cuban troops to Angola and provided the MPLA and the Cubans with hundreds of tons of heavy arms, including tanks, anti-tank missiles, and fighter planes. By the end of November the Cubans had stopped the South African-led advance on Luanda. In two battles south of the Cuanza River in December the southern invaders suffered major setbacks. South Africa then decided to withdraw towards the Namibian border, partly because of its military problems and partly because the U.S. Senate voted on December 19 to block all funding for secret operations in Angola.

The Angolan war was over by March 1976. Huambo fell to MPLA forces on February 11. Roberto had already returned to exile in Zaire, and the FNLA had abandoned armed struggle. Savimbi returned to rural southeastern Angola with about two thousand troops and their U.S. and South African advisers. Savimbi's rebellion would rise again, in response both to conditions within Angola and to renewed external backing.

The Cuban expeditionary force, which eventually numbered at least forty-thousand soldiers, re-

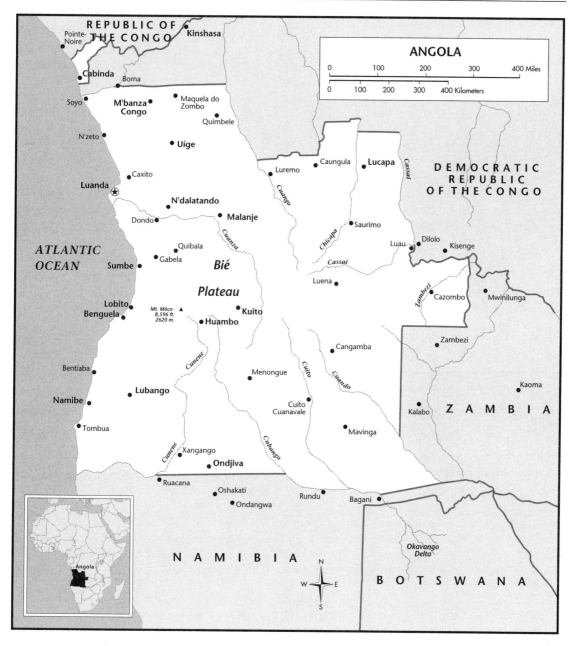

MAP OF ANGOLA. (© *Maryland Cartographics. Reprinted with permission.*)

mained in Angola to pacify the country and to ward off South African attacks. In 1977 the MPLA crushed an attempted coup by one of its leaders, and after a thorough purge turned itself officially into a Marxist-Leninist party. MPLA attempts to collectivize agriculture along communist lines, combined with attacks by South Africa and UNITA, led to the collapse of commercial agriculture, though it is difficult to distinguish the negative effects of the collectivization of agriculture from the effects of the attacks by South Africa and UNITA. The government came to depend almost entirely on the petroleum industry. An ironic situ-

ation arose in which Western companies—notably Gulf Oil—operated under the protection of Cuban troops, who were protecting the companies' installations from attack by UNITA forces.

With the assistance of strong South African support, UNITA reorganized itself as an effective guerrilla force. South African aid to UNITA and military intervention in Angola were partly motivated by the MPLA's support for the South West Africa People's Organization (SWAPO) fighting for independence of Namibia. American military aid to UNITA, via Zaire, resumed in 1985. War-

FORMER UNITA REBEL LEADER GENERAL ZACARIAS GREETS ONE OF THE FIRST CHILD SOLDIERS TO OFFICIALLY LEAVE ARMY RANKS IN LUANDA, ANGOLA. *(AP/Wide World Photos. Reproduced by permission.)*

fare engulfed the entire country. But in 1988, South African troops were defeated at Cuito Cuanavale in southern Angola. They were confronted with numerically superior Cuban and Angolan troops, and backed down rather than risking the loss of a large number of white troops. Following the defeat, South Africa promised to grant independence to Namibia and to stop supporting UNITA, while the Cubans agreed to withdraw their troops by mid-1991.

The MPLA's initial response to the South African withdrawal was to attack UNITA bases. The failure of this campaign, combined with increasingly effective UNITA attacks on oil installations and the collapse of communism in Eastern Europe, combined to lead the MPLA to adopt a more conciliatory posture. In mid-1990 the MPLA Central Committee decided to abandon Marxism-Leninism, communism, and the one-party state. Negotiations with UNITA proceeded rapidly and agreement was reached in May 1991 on a cease-fire and on a new constitution guaranteeing human and political rights. The two armies would be merged and multiparty elections would be held in 1992.

Elections were held under the supervision of the United Nations, which certified them as free and fair. The results gave the MPLA the most votes—but not enough to appease UNITA, which came in second. Savimbi rejected the results, and civil war resumed. Since 1993 the war has raged off and on, despite an international environment more favorable to the MPLA government than had been the case earlier. In 1993, the Clinton administration recognized the Angola government. That same year, the U.N. Security Council imposed an arms and fuel embargo on UNITA.

The Lusaka Protocol

In 1994 the United Nations brokered a peace agreement between the rebels and the government, called the Lusaka Protocol, and in February 1995 the Security Council decided to send seven thousand "blue helmets," or U.N. troops, to the country to verify the cease-fire. Fighting resumed the following month.

In July 1995 the Angolan parliament amended the constitution, creating two vice-presidencies—one of them reserved for Savimbi. However, UNITA allegedly refused to allow him to accept the post. In December 1995 fighting resumed in northern UNITA-controlled towns.

In 1997 the government reached an agreement with UNITA to form a government of national unity. UNITA deputies, elected in 1992, took their seats in the parliament, and a very large government was formed, including some UNITA ministers. As if to remind the authorities of their existence, forces of the Front for the Liberation of the Enclave of Cabinda (FLEC) clashed with the Angolan army. The portion of UNITA remaining loyal to Savimbi failed to disarm its troops, and in October, the U.N. Security Council approved sanctions against UNITA for non-respect of the peace agreement. The following year, the sanctions were expanded to include a ban on diamond exports by UNITA. The government recognized UNITA as a political party, but by July 1998 there were violent clashes between the army and UNITA troops in diamond-rich Lunda-Norte province. The war soon spread; by December, after the north and the east has succumbed, the center of the country was the scene of fighting.

In 1997–98, Angola's civil war became part of a network of wars throughout the region. Angola intervened, along with Uganda, Rwanda, and Burundi to help Laurent-Désiré Kabila overthrow Mobutu Sese Seko in the Democratic Republic of the Congo, as Zaire became known as once again. Later, Angola intervened in Congo-Brazzaville to help overthrow President Pascal Lissouba. Finally, in August 1998 Angolan troops supported Kabila against rebels backed by Uganda and Rwanda. These interventions hindered UNITA's access to supplies.

In 1999 the Angolan government won a series of triumphs over UNITA and victory appeared near. By the end of the year, however, UNITA had retaken several areas lost earlier. It was in this context of renewed UNITA success, financed by diamond sales, that the U.N. sanctions committee on Angola released the report accusing the presidents of Burkina Faso and Togo of helping UNITA with arms and fuel shipments in exchange for diamonds.

The United States, the Cold War, and Angola

U.S. policy toward Angola was made in the context of the Cold War—when the United States countered what it saw as threats of communism around the world. The policy toward Angola reflected lessons supposedly learned in Angola's neighbor to the north, the former Belgian Congo. The Belgian Congo became independent in 1960. It often was referred to as Congo-Leopoldville, after its capital, to distinguish it from the former French Congo, known as Congo-Brazzaville. When Leopoldville was renamed Kinshasa, the country was called Congo-Kinshasa until President Mobutu Sese Seko changed it to Zaire. When Laurent Kabila overthrew Mobutu, the country's name was again changed, to the Democratic Republic of the Congo. Fearing that the Soviet Union would exploit the chaos that followed Congolese independence in 1960, the United States had supported United Nations intervention to maintain Congolese unity while at the same time intervening covertly in support of non-communist forces. American intervention led both to the assassination of Patrice Lumumba, the first Congolese prime minister, and to the rise to power of one of Lumumba's former aides, later known as Mobutu Sese Seko.

At about the same time, the MPLA and the FNLA began armed struggle against Portuguese rule in Angola. One lesson that the United States had drawn from the Congo affair was that premature independence could lead to chaos, which the Soviet Union could exploit. A second lesson was that the United States should be prepared for independence. These lessons led to a contradictory policy. On the one hand, the United States cooperated with its NATO ally Portugal, which was attempting to hold onto its colonies. On the other hand, since Portugal would be unable to hold retain Angola indefinitely, the United States tried to ensure an acceptable successor regime. The MPLA was considered Marxist due to the beliefs of some of its leaders, and thus hostile to American interests. The Central Intelligence Agency therefore decided to support Roberto and around 1961 he began receiving small subsidies from the United States.

In fact, the MPLA, the FNLA, and UNITA each sought aid from whatever source would provide it. Neto, for example, went to Washington, D.C., in December 1962 to put his case before the U.S. government and its press and emphasize the misleading notion that the MPLA was a communist organization. During the following two years, Roberto appealed for aid to the Soviet Union, Cuba, China, Algeria, and Egypt. Later, Savimbi of UNITA approached the same countries, with the exception of the Soviet Union, as well as North Vietnam, and accepted military training for his men from North Korea and China.

The CIA chose to support Roberto, though the American diplomatic corps showed no such preference. A State Department cable to its African embassies in 1963 stated that U.S. policy was not to discourage an MPLA move toward the West "and not to choose between these two movements."

Even in 1975, when a congressional committee asked CIA Director William Colby what the differences were between the three contending groups, he responded that they were all independent organizations in support of independence and determined not to be exploited by industrialized, capitalist nations. When asked why the Chinese were backing the FNLA or UNITA, he stated that China backed these groups for the same reason the United States did—because the Soviet Union was backing the MPLA. This type of position taking was typical of the Cold War. The Soviet Union backed one group and the United States would usually back the other, each in an attempt to increase their influence in a region.

Choosing on this basis, the United States opted badly. Ted Galen Carpenter of the Cato Institute writes:

> When a new revolutionary government in Lisbon sought to jettison Angola and other remnants of Portugal's once extensive empire, three competing left-of-center Angolan factions maneuvered for political and military dominance. The U.S. government, with customary acumen, backed the weakest organization—the National Front for the Liberation of Angola (FNLA)—led by Holden Roberto, who was a relative by marriage to Zairian dictator Mobutu Sese Seko, a longtime American client.

Roberto's status as a Mobutu in-law symbolized his dependency vis-à-vis one of Africa's most notorious dictators, himself considered a dependent of the United States. The FNLA was the weakest Angolan organization largely because of Roberto's weakness as a leader.

It is typical of the Cold War that U.S. decision-makers concentrated on Soviet activities in Africa and paid little attention to Cuban interests in the region, which would prove more important in 1975 and thereafter. Cuba was active in Algeria until 1964, then focused on the two Congos in 1965–66. Most importantly, Cuba participated in the long struggle of the African Party for the Independence of Guinea-Bissau and Cape Verde (PAIGC) to overthrow Portuguese rule in Guinea-Bissau. Its ties to the MPLA dated from 1965, when Argentinean revolutionary leader Che Guevara met MPLA leaders in Brazzaville.

Before the Portuguese coup of April 1974 the aid given to the Angolan resistance movements by their various foreign patrons was sporadic and insignificant, essentially a matter of the patrons keeping their hands in the game. For example, beginning in 1969, Roberto was on a $10,000-a-year CIA retainer. The Alvor Agreement of January 1975 led the United States to up the ante. The National Security Council in Washington, D.C., authorized the CIA to pass $300,000 to Roberto and the FNLA. The funds were tagged for "various political action activities, restricted to non-military objectives," but the support could make additional money available for military uses.

In March 1975 the first large shipment of Soviet arms reportedly arrived for the MPLA. According to a congressional investigation, "Later events have suggested that this infusion of U.S. aid [the $300,000], unprecedented and massive in the underdeveloped colony, may have panicked the Soviets into arming their MPLA clients." Blum suggests in *Killing Hope* that the Soviets may have been influenced also by the fact that China had sent the FNLA a "huge arms package" and over one hundred military advisers.

The CIA made its first major weapons shipment to the FNLA in July 1975. Thus, like the Russians and the Chinese, the United States was aiding one side in the Angolan civil war on a level far greater than it had ever provided during the struggle against Portuguese colonialism. When the initial FNLA/Zairian advance into northern Angola was stopped by the MPLA, the United States faced a difficult choice. Unwilling to allow the MPLA and the Soviets an easy victory, President Gerald Ford gave the CIA almost $50 million to train, equip, and transport anti-MPLA troops.

In November 1975, as independence arrived, the MPLA was caught between Zairians and FNLA troops, led by white mercenaries, in the north and by UNITA forces, supported by South

HISTORIANS' CHALLENGES TO UNDERSTANDING CONFLICT

The greatest challenge to historians in dealing with Angola—as with many other conflicts—is to understand the participants as real human beings, making choices, not just moved by outside forces, including, in the case of Angola, colonial Portugal and the Atlantic slave trade. For the period since the late 1950s the outside forces certainly include the international political system, especially the Cold War, and the international economy, including the markets for minerals and the multinational corporations that sell and process those minerals.

It is undeniable that Angola's struggle for independence and civil war took place in the shadow of the Cold War. Some accounts of the struggle, however, fail to examine the internal dynamics of the conflict. Once a scholar has said that the MPLA was aided by the Soviet Union and Cuba, and that UNITA received support from the United States and South Africa, has one exhausted the topic? Were these organizations only pawns on the chessboard? In fact, each of them and their various leaders and factions correspond to social strata, regions, ethnic groups, and interests within Angola, which must be taken into account if one is to gain a real understanding of Angolan politics.

Terms like "allies," "patrons," "dependents," and "surrogates" imply greater or lesser equality between outside backers and inside groups and greater or lesser degrees of control of the latter by the former. A closer look—for example, as taken by Odd Arne Westad in his study of Soviet archival documents, "Moscow and the Angolan Crisis, 1974–1976: A New Pattern of Intervention"—reveals more complicated relationships. Furthermore, there is a difference of opinion as to the importance of ideology in the Angolan movements. William Blum, author of *Killing Hope: U.S. Military and CIA Interventions Since World War II*, minimizes the differences whereas scholar Patrick Chabal sees the MPLA as committed to a communist revolution in Angola. Further research may shed additional light on this problem, which cannot be resolved at this point.

Angola indeed seemed to have been a square on the chessboard for most decision-makers in Washington, D.C., and in Moscow. By the early twenty-first century the Soviet Union had ceased to exist and South Africa has made a rather successful transition to majority rule. The West "won" the Cold War—both in general and in southern Africa in particular. But looking at Angola, one is led to ask, to what extent did that "victory" cause the present tragedy? UNITA, previously aided by the United States and South Africa, now fights on with the proceeds from smuggled diamonds. The Angolan government fights UNITA by spreading thousands of landmines, financing its efforts from oil money that could be put to better use. To the extent that Angolans were, in facts, pawns in game of chess, millions of Angolans continue to pay a heavy price for the Cold War.

Africans, in the south. Yet timely Cuban and Soviet aid enabled the MPLA to defeat its enemies. A further U.S. response was blocked by a vote of the U.S. Senate, the Clark Amendment. Coming only a few months after the fall of U.S.-supported Saigon to communists in the East Asian country of Vietnam, the Angolan war presented the danger of another open-ended commitment in the eyes of many in the U.S. Congress.

The United States had concluded, from its success in defeating the Lumumbist rebellion in Congo in 1964–65 that African troops, reinforced by mercenaries, offered a useful alternative to direct intervention. In fact, the invasion of Angola by troops from South Africa, coupled with the participation of white mercenaries in the FNLA-Zaire forces attacking from the north, aroused the indig-

nation of leaders and the public in many African states. In this context, heavier backing by the Cubans and even the Soviets became acceptable.

The United States and South Africa in the 1980s

U.S. President Jimmy Carter (1977–81) announced that human rights would constitute the number one priority of U.S. foreign policy and consequently dissociated the United States from South Africa's apartheid government. Only a few years later, however, under U.S. President Ronald Reagan (1981–89) the fight against terrorism replaced human rights as the top priority of American foreign policy. Ending Carter's policy of hostility to South Africa, the United States adopted a policy called "constructive engagement."

A DISPLACED PERSON RIDES PAST A BUILDING BOMBED BY UNITA FORCES IN THE GOVERNMENT-HELD TOWN OF KUITO, ANGOLA. *(AP/Wide World Photos. Reproduced by permission.)*

and other pressures against the Front Line States. But the United States and South Africa were demanding more than the Front Line States were prepared to give, even under pressure. What began as coercive diplomacy, therefore, became a full-scale secret war. Throughout 1981 South Africa carried out military action against Mozambique, Zimbabwe, Zambia, and, especially, Angola. In August of that year South Africa mounted a major invasion of southern Angola, established a permanent military presence there, substantially increased its support for UNITA, and began to extend its own raids further and further to the north of that country.

The Reagan administration blocked the implementation of the United Nations plan for the de-colonization of Namibia by linking it for the first time to a withdrawal of Cuban troops from Angola. After South Africa had occupied a large area in southern Angola the United States vetoed a Security Council resolution condemning its actions.

In August 1982, during a major military effort by South Africa to extend its control of southern Angola, Reagan sent a "secret" letter to President Nyerere of Tanzania, Chairman of the Front Line States, urging him to accept the "linkage" of a Namibian settlement to the withdrawal of Cuban troops from Angola. Reagan suggested that if linkage were not accepted soon, the United States would cease to press for implementation of the United Nations plan for Namibia.

In mid-1983 South Africa sent its troops nearly two hundred miles into Angola. This third invasion was a harsh blow to a country already suffering from drought and disorganization of the rural economy. South Africa's UNITA "surrogates"—scholar Sean Gervasi's term suggesting that UNITA was fighting for South African interests and not its own—were extending their military actions into the center of the country.

As the war escalated in late 1983 U.S. diplomats pressed hard for a series of "non-aggression" agreements between South Africa on the one hand, and Angola and the other Front Line States on the other. Behind their diplomatic overtures there was the threat of increasingly harsh South African power. Charles Lichenstein, Deputy U.S. Ambassador to the United Nations at the time, told the *Johannesburg Financial Mail* that "destabilization will remain in force until Angola and Mozambique do not permit their territory to be used by terrorists to attack South Africa." Angola continued to insist that it would not accept "linkage."

That is, the United States would seek "to encourage peaceful evolutionary change" in order to forestall "mass revolutionary violence" within South Africa. Beyond South Africa's borders, the United States would seek "to counter Soviet influence in the region" and "to foster regional security." To pursue these objectives, the U.S. president approved specific lines of action, including assisting South Africa in resisting the international efforts to isolate it, especially at the United Nations; helping "end the guerrilla warfare that has continued in northern Namibia and southern Angola for 15 years;" seeking the removal of Cuban troops from Angola; and seeking a "peaceful solution" of the Namibian question.

South Africa began an undeclared war on the "Front Line States," neighboring states, in 1981. Its minimal objective was to put an end to attacks on South Africa and its dependency South West Africa, later Namibia, from those Front Line States. The maximum objective was to replace the socialist regimes of the Front Line States—including Angola—with regimes more to South Africa's liking.

By the summer of 1981 the United States and South Africa were working together to apply increasing military, economic, political, diplomatic,

In mid-1985 the U.S. Congress repealed the Clark Amendment. Savimbi visited Washington, D.C., and was hailed as a "freedom fighter." U.S. aid to UNITA was resumed, putting the Angolan government under greater pressure. There are some allegations that U.S. aid to UNITA continued before 1985, and that the aid was simply once again acknowledged in 1985.

Namibian Independence

Eventually, a deal was struck respecting the logic of linkage, refused earlier by Angola and the other Front Line States. In 1988 Angola, Cuba, and South Africa signed the treaty that granted independence to Namibia. The treaty called for a one-year transition period, beginning on April 1, 1989, that included U.N.-supervised elections of an assembly later in the year to draft a constitution. As part of the agreement Cuba was required to withdraw its fifty thousand troops from Angola by early 1991. The transition was temporarily disrupted when UNITA rebels from Angola crossed the border into Namibia and battled with U.N. peacekeeping forces.

Namibian voters went to the polls during U.N.-supervised elections in November 1989, and gave the South West Africa People's Organization (SWAPO) a majority in the constituent assembly. The new Republic of Namibia gained its independence on March 21, 1990, with SWAPO's Sam Nujoma as president. Angola held its own U.N.-supervised elections in 1992. As in Namibia, the left-wing nationalists won, but unlike the case in Namibia, the South African-backed right-wing party refused to accept the results.

Clearly, a Cold War perspective governed American decision-making regarding Angola, with the marginal exception of the Carter administration (1976-1980). While there are many critics of the U.S. Cold War policy toward Angola, particularly the policies under Reagan, South Africa made a successful transition from apartheid to majority rule and Angola abandoned the Soviet-Cuban model of single-party rule and command economy. Yet Angola paid a heavy a price for the policy, which took little account of its own needs and wants.

Cold War: The Soviet Role

Recently declassified documents demonstrate that the Soviet Union wanted both to install a Soviet-style regime in Angola and also to score a victory over the United States in the Cold War competition. The U.S. defeat in Vietnam made Moscow's increased involvement in Africa and Asia more politically threatening. Improved naval, air, and communications capabilities made possible an activist foreign policy that had been impossible earlier, such as during the Congo crisis of 1960.

The Soviet Union initially paid little attention to Angola. It provided some aid to the FNLA in the early 1960s, but switched to the MPLA in 1964, arguing that Roberto had helped Moïse Tshombe in the Congo and curtailed his own guerrilla operations in Angola under pressure from the United States. The amount of the aid, first to the FNLA and then to the MPLA, was very small.

In 1970, however, Soviet leaders endorsed a new African strategy developed by the KGB, the Soviet intelligence service. Due to the feeling on the part of southern African nationalists that their efforts to gain American aid had failed, the KGB saw an opportunity for Soviet gains. It also saw a danger that China, which was targeting countries and movements that already received Soviet aid, might come to control large parts of Africa in a loose alliance with the United States.

The new Soviet policy was immediately put into practice regarding Angola, where early contacts had shown the Soviets that the MPLA was a "possible adherent to Soviet ideas of state and society." Although the MPLA had been founded with help from the Portuguese Communist Party, it was a loose coalition of trade unionists, "progressive" intellectuals, Christian groups, and large segments of the middle class. In Soviet eyes, it badly needed restructuring. The MPLA, whose appeals for increased aid had been rejected only months before, was offered substantial military hardware, logistical support, and political training.

The Soviets found the MPLA poorly organized and divided into many factions. In early 1974 Soviet diplomats spent much time trying to reunify the MPLA and create some kind of alliance between it and Roberto's FNLA. However, the Soviet ambassador in Brazzaville reported that the MPLA had practically ceased to function and the only bright spot was a few pro-Moscow "progressively oriented activists."

Following the April 1974 coup Moscow decided to strengthen the MPLA under Neto and make it the dominant partner in a post-colonial coalition government. Soviet embassies in Brazzaville, Lusaka, and Dar-es-Salaam, Tanzania, were instructed to "repair" the damaged liberation movement, but Neto and his supporters refused to cooperate. When the FNLA and UNITA grew stronger, the Soviets responded by increasing their support for Neto, despite their misgivings. Late in

1974 the MPLA was able to establish a presence in Luanda and other cities, and to take control of most of the Cabinda enclave, which suggested to Moscow that it had made the right move.

Aware of increased CIA support for the FNLA, starting in January 1975 the Soviets concluded that Roberto would soon make an all-out bid for power. There was little they could do to help the MPLA resist the initial FNLA attacks, but they hoped that an alliance with UNITA might rescue their Angolan allies. By July 1975 when the MPLA was successfully counterattacking, Moscow still expected that the rival movements, or at least UNITA, would join an MPLA-led coalition government. Moscow did not believe that the United States or South Africa would intervene on a large scale but was worried about increased Chinese aid to the FNLA.

In August the tide turned again, thanks to large-scale U.S. aid to anti-MPLA forces and the intervention of South African and Zairian troops in Angola. When Congo-Brazzaville refused to allow increased Soviet aid to the MPLA to pass through its territory, Moscow asked Cuban leader Fidel Castro to intercede with the Congolese. Castro, however, used the Soviet request as the occasion to promote his own plan to send Cuban forces to Angola, with the aid of Soviet transport and Soviet staff officers, both in Havana and Luanda, to help direct military operations. Yet, Moscow—worried that such aid before independence would damage its already strained relations with the United States and upset more African countries—refused to transport the Cuban troops or to send Soviet officers to serve in Angola. Despite the refusal, Castro sent troops on his own.

Soviet policy and the MPLA were saved by South Africa's intervention, which was unacceptable to other African countries. Seeing the new anti-MPLA operations as a joint U.S.-South African effort, Moscow decided to assist the Cuban operation in Angola immediately after Independence Day on November 11. The aim was to put enough Cuban troops and Soviet advisers into Angola by mid-December to defeat the South Africans and assist the MPLA leaders in building a socialist state. Preparations for the airlift of Cuban troops to Angola intensified in early November and Soviet ships were sent to areas off the Angolan coast.

Just enough of just the right kind of aid arrived by Independence Day. Cubans used Soviet-supplied rocket launchers to defeat FNLA-Zairian attackers a few miles from Luanda. During the previous week large groups of Cuban soldiers started arriving in Luanda on Soviet aircraft. Moscow insisted that the primary objective of these forces was to contain the South Africans along the southern border and that the troops should not be used for general purposes in the civil war.

Soviet general staff officers started arriving in Luanda on November 12. At the same time—immediately after independence—the Soviet general staff took direct control of transporting additional Cuban troops to Africa, as well as providing advanced military equipment. By the end of November the Cubans had stopped the South African-led advance on Luanda. Defeats in southern Angola, together with the Clark Amendment, led South Africa to then withdraw.

Just as it had opened the gates for African acceptance of Soviet-Cuban aid to the MPLA, the by now defunct South African intervention also paved the way for African diplomatic recognition of the MPLA regime. Soviet diplomatic efforts contributed significantly to this development, for instance in the case of Zambia, where President Kenneth Kaunda switched to the MPLA side after substantial Soviet pressure.

To the Soviet leaders Angola proved that they could advance socialism in the Third World during a period of détente with the United States. The United States could be defeated in local conflicts under certain circumstances. First, the Soviet armed forces had to be ready to provide, at short notice, the logistics for the operation needed. Second, the Soviet Union had to be able to organize and control the "anti-imperialist" forces involved, in this case its local allies. Soviet personnel in Angola were very satisfied with the way both Angolans and Cubans had respected Moscow's political dominance during the war. Neto realized that he depended on Soviet assistance and that Moscow, not Havana, made the final decisions regarding assistance.

The Soviets had also learned from their Angolan experience that the Soviet Union could and must rebuild and reform local anti-capitalist groups in crisis areas. They believed that the MPLA had been saved from its own follies by advice and assistance from Moscow, which not only helped the organization win the war, but also laid the foundation for the building of a Soviet-style "vanguard party." A vanguard party leads the country in the formation of a communist system. Due to Soviet guidance, the "internationalists" were in ascendance. These new leaders understood that the MPLA was part of a Moscow-led international revolutionary movement and that they, therefore, depended on Soviet support. Taking the lead in reorganizing the MPLA, they would become the future leaders of the Marxist-Leninist Party in Angola.

In fact, Neto's independence of mind and his claim to be a Marxist theorist made it increasingly difficult for the Soviets to control and transform the MPLA. Differences between Soviet and Cuban perceptions of the political situation in the MPLA complicated Moscow's task. Castro considered Neto a great African leader as well as a personal friend. Neto asked for Cuba's assistance in building a Marxist-Leninist Party and Castro spoke of Angola, Cuba, and Vietnam as "the main anti-imperialist core" of the world. The nature of the Moscow-Havana-Luanda relationship may have been illustrated in May 1977, when Soviet favorite Nito Alves found his bid to oust Neto in Angola blocked by Cuban tanks.

Soviet leaders consistently overestimated their ability to impose their view on foreign leftists. In reality, the Angolans and Cubans were able to shape Moscow's actions. As early as 1975 Fidel Castro initiated armed support for the MPLA without Moscow's knowledge, calculating correctly that he could force Moscow's hand. The belief of many Soviet leaders that they could control domestic political developments in Third World countries was a misperception with fateful consequences for Soviet foreign policy and contributed significantly to the Angolan intervention. The supposed victory in Angola encouraged further Soviet "limited interventions" in Africa and Asia, culminating in a devastating war in Afghanistan.

The Weight of History: Ethnic and Other Divisions

The Cold War perspective pays too little attention to internal aspects of Angola's forty-year war. Some scholars, however, overemphasize one or another internal aspect. Typically, the war is explained by rivalry between the three main "tribes" or ethnic groups. It is true that three groups—the Kongo, Mbundu, and Ovimbundu— make up about three-quarters of Angola's population and that the three main political parties since 1960 correspond to these three ethnic groups. The FNLA was predominantly Kongo, the MPLA predominantly Mbundu and Creole or Mestiço, and UNITA predominantly Ovimbundu. The pre-colonial and colonial history of Angola, as well as more recent events, have made the ethnic divisions deep.

There is considerable continuity between the colonial period (1880s–1975) and the previous period, which began with the arrival of the Portu-

12-YEAR-OLD FENDER EMERGES FROM A SEWER IN LUANDA, ANGOLA, WHERE HE HAS LIVED FOR THREE YEARS WITH 15 OTHER CHILDREN. *(AP/Wide World Photos. Reproduced by permission.)*

guese. Since the sixteenth century, Angola had been linked with Brazil through the slave trade. There developed in Luanda a commercial and administrative Creole or Mestiço elite—Portuguese-speaking, mixed race, Catholic, and cosmopolitan—involved in the Atlantic trade. This Creole society lived in Africa but its connections with the interior of the continent were limited to trade—mainly the slave trade.

The effects of the slave trade on inland African communities varied enormously, between those that raided and traded slaves and those that were raided. Africans sold the slaves to traders acting as

AFTER A PEACE ACCORD WAS SIGNED IN ANGOLA, IN-
TERNATIONAL CHARITY GROUPS CLEARED THOU-
SANDS OF LANDMINES, LIKE THE ONE WHICH IN-
JURED THIS WOMAN WHO IS MAKING HER WAY
HOME FROM THE MARKET IN ANGOLA. *(AP/Wide
World Photos. Reproduced by permission.)*

Under colonial rule Africans were legally compelled to work if they wanted to avoid forced labor. They could become farmers in the colonial
economy or hire themselves out as laborers in
Portuguese agricultural or commercial concerns, of
which the most successful were the coffee plantations in the Kongo area. The Ovimbundu, of the
central highlands, had to seek employment on the
coffee plantations, since their agricultural economy
was not strong enough to sustain their relatively
large population. Those Kongo who did not work
as agricultural laborers were chiefly associated with
the business and trade that had developed in the
Belgian Congo to the north. Some of them became
substantial businessmen, a few owning plantations
in northern Angola.

Angola was a settler colony but—except for the
coffee plantation owners—most whites remained
relatively poor and unskilled. Their presence was a
barrier to the progression of Africans into the sort
of jobs that they might have had in other colonies
and was conducive to an atmosphere of racism and
petty discrimination that affected the ordinary
Africans and the Creoles of the cities. In addition,
colonial rule reinforced the separation between
Creoles of Luanda and Africans of the interior. The
Mbundu living east of Luanda interacted more often with the Creoles.

Such divisions were sharpened by social, cultural, and religious factors. As the Portuguese-
speaking Catholic Creoles lost ground to the newly
established colonial elites, they sought to maintain
their superior status by stressing the characteristics
that set them apart from other Angolans. Though
less prominent than they had been in the nineteenth century they remained at the heart of the
colonial order. Their world remained Portuguese—
in culture, language, and outlook. Inland things
were different. Influences from foreign Protestant
and Catholic missionaries and from other colonies,
either Belgian or British, where many worked, were
more important than those coming from Luanda.

By the 1950s there were two deeply frustrated
social groups: the Creole elites, and the Africans
of the interior, who were poor, uneducated, and
neglected at the bottom of a highly stratified social order. It is no coincidence that each of the first
generation of nationalist leaders—Neto, Roberto,
and Savimbi—came from Protestant mission
schools. Nor is it a coincidence that each was profoundly suspicious of the other. The Angolan nationalist movement was divided from the start. But
a number of internal and external factors explain
the perpetuation of this division, from the 1960s
to the present.

intermediaries for Luanda's Creole merchants.
Scholar Patrick Chabal writes that it "can be assumed that a number of Africans would, long before the colonial period, have viewed these city
based creoles as quite 'alien.'" Formal Portuguese
colonization led to the enforced decline of the
Luanda Creole community. The Creole elites became mere adjuncts to the new Portuguese colonial masters, while colonial rule created other
elites—both Mestiço and African—who challenged the supremacy of the older Creole society.

Apart from the Cold War, in which the MPLA and FNLA were backed by the two opposing superpowers, there are three other external factors that are identifiable: the key neighboring country—Congo/Zaire—supported the FNLA and opposed the MPLA; both the MPLA and FNLA had networks of support among other African countries; the FNLA was able to get early endorsement by the newly created Organization of African Unity (OAU). In fact, in Patrick Chabal's analysis, laid out in *Angola and Mozambique: the Weight of History*, internal factors were even more significant. The FNLA and MPLA represented two long-separate sets of interests: the Kongo "African" elites of the north versus the Luanda Creole community and its regional Mbundu supporters.

A second internal factor was a sense of racial difference. The FNLA considered the MPLA Creole leadership as a "non-African" group disconnected from the "real" Africa, even though several of the MPLA leaders were Black Africans.

Third, ideology separated the groups. The MPLA asserted itself as a Marxist organization rooted in communism. Though the FNLA and UNITA also had leftist leanings, they did not claim Marxism as part of their platform. Ideologically, the groups were more difficult to distinguish from one another, but they clearly did not share a similar vision to bind them together in their efforts in Angola.

Another important factor in the conflict is leadership. The MPLA and FNLA were in the hands of leaders with little taste for compromise. After the failure of an attempted merger in 1962, there was little chance that either Neto or Roberto would ever work with the other. Savimbi's decision to leave the FNLA and his rejection by the MPLA led directly to his decision to create UNITA, thus adding to the mix a third leader with traits similar to the others.

Angola's rival nationalists not only had to contend with competition from one another, but also from within their organizations. This contributed to disorganized strategies and led to difficulty capitalizing on successes. Thus, though the MPLA controlled Angola's capital on the country's day of independence, the group was never granted the legitimacy it claimed, and it did not have the power to gain full control of the country. As governing party, the MPLA remained split both personally and ideologically. Its declaration of itself as a Marxist-Leninist party was not merely taken to please external donors and to launch a "socialist" development program. It was an attempt to make a clear distinction between the MPLA and its competitors.

In its struggle to retain power the MPLA took an increasingly hard line stance. Three factors contributed to this change—Angola's economy, its position in regional and international relations, and the nature of the armed opposition. The Angolan government exploited the country's rich resources in oil and diamonds to fund the civil war and to keep the economy afloat. When UNITA took control of the diamond mines the government was still able to maintain military expenditures through its hold on the oil industry. UNITA quickly began financing its own efforts through the mining and sale of diamonds. Angola's vast resources, which should have been used to help enrich all of its people, were instead being turned against it.

The character of UNITA had the greatest influence on the evolution of the civil conflict. Born a genuine anti-colonial political organization, it became a military machine under the strong grip of power exercised by Savimbi. UNITA's access to foreign support and its control of Angola's diamond resources were used toward one end—to make Savimbi the undisputed ruler of Angola. Efforts toward this end are similar to MPLA conduct in that they reflect the inability of Angola's elites to form a broad anti-colonial coalition.

RECENT HISTORY AND THE FUTURE

The years since the inconclusive elections of 1992 have seen a continuing civil war, punctuated by agreements to stop fighting. The fortunes of the MPLA-dominated government and the UNITA rebels have risen and fallen. In 1999, for example, government forces claimed a number of regions from UNITA. The rebels seemed to be on the run. Later that same year UNITA struck back, and it became clear that the government hopes of an early victory were unfounded. Government forces have been stretched very thin by the need to defend the Cabinda enclave against separatists, as well as defending Angola proper against UNITA. The government intervened in the civil wars in Republic of Congo (Brazzaville) and in the Democratic Republic of the Congo (Kinshasa) in large measure to deprive the rebel groups of safe havens in these countries. In so doing, particularly in siding with Laurent Kabila in Congo-Kinshasa, it linked its own fate to that of the host regime. Angola was allied with Rwanda for Kabila and against Mobutu;

when Rwanda turned against Kabila, Savimbi and UNITA needed little encouragement to channel part of its diamond trade through Rwanda.

Early in 2000 South Africa suggested that Angola negotiate with Savimbi. Angola's reply, that it had tried negotiation time and again without success, was not without warrant. After years of fighting, the opposing sides are entrenched firmly against one another. The United Nations attempt to force UNITA to compromise by cutting off the flow of diamonds, and thus of funding, is unlikely to succeed, as there are many markets abroad willing to deal in the "blood" diamonds mined by the rebels. The most likely outcome is more warfare.

BIBLIOGRAPHY

Angola Unravels: The Rise and Fall of the Lusaka Peace Process. Human Rights Watch, 1999.

Blum, William. *Killing Hope: U.S. Military and CIA Interventions Since World War II.* Monroe, Maine: Common Courage Press, 1995.

Campbell, Horace. "The Military Defeat of South Africa in Angola," *Monthly Review* April 1989.

Carpenter, Ted Galen. "U.S. Aid to Anti-Communist Rebels: The 'Reagan Doctrine' and its Pitfalls," *Policy Analysis* 74 (1986).

Chabal, Patrick. "Angola and Mozambique: the Weight of History," *Working Paper,* 1998.

Cortright, David and George A. Lopez, eds. *Economic Sanctions: Panacea or Peacebuilding in a Post-Cold War World?* Boulder, Colo.: Lynne Rienner, 1995.

Crocker, Chester. *A High Noon in Southern Africa: Making Peace in a Rough Neighborhood.* New York: W. W. Norton & Co., 1992.

Duffy, James. *Portuguese Africa.* Cambridge, Mass.: Harvard University Press, 1959.

Fisher, Ian and Norimitsu Onishi. "Armies Ravage a Rich Land, Creating Africa's 'First World War'," *New York Times,* 6 February 2000.

Fisher-Thompson, Jim. *Angola Mired in Military Standoff, Human Rights Expert Says: Citizens are Losers, Alex Vines tells NDI.* U.S. Department of State, 4 April 1999/2000.

General Board of Global Ministries, The United Methodist Church. *Angola: A Country Profile.* http://gbgm-umc .org/africa/angola/aprofile.html (9 September 2000).

Gervasi, Sean. "Secret Collaboration: U.S. and South Africa Foment Terrorist Wars," *Covert Action Quarterly,* Fall 1984.

Gleijeses, Piero. "Havana's Policy in Africa, 1959–76: New Evidence from Cuban Archives," *Cold War International History Project Electronic Bulletin,* 8–9, 1997.

Maier, Karl. *Angola: Promises and Lies.* London: Serif, 1996.

Marcum, John A. *The Angolan Revolution.* Vol. 1. Cambridge, Mass.: MIT Press, 1969.

Minter, William. *Apartheid's Contras. An Inquiry into the Roots of War in Angola and Mozambique.* Atlantic Highlands, N.J.: Zed Books, 1994.

Ohlson, Thomas. "Strategic Confrontation versus Economic Survival in Southern Africa." In *Conflict Resolution in Africa.* Washington, D.C.: The Brookings Institution, 1991.

Prendergast, John. *Angola's Deadly War: Dealing with Savimbi's Hell on Earth.* Washington, D.C.: United States Institute of Peace, 1999.

Rupert, James. "Africans Flex Their Might. Now Angola Joins the Interventionist Mood," *International Herald Tribune,* 22 October 22: 1, 10.

Schatzberg, Michael G. *Mobutu or Chaos? The United States and Zaire, 1960–1990.* Lanham, Md.: University Press of America, 1991.

Westad, Odd Arne. "Moscow and the Angolan Crisis, 1974–1976: A New Pattern of Intervention." *Cold War International History Project Electronic Bulletin,* 8–9 Winter 1996/1997.

Thomas Turner

AUSTRIA'S SHUNNING BY THE GLOBAL COMMUNITY

In the fall of 1999 in Austria, the Austrian People's Party—led by Wolfgang Schuessel—invited a right-wing party to participate in ruling Austria. Specifically, in order to hold onto power, the Austrian People's Party invited the right-wing Freedom Party, led by the charismatic and controversial Jörg Haider, to join with the Austrian People's Party to establish a majority by which to control the parliament. The Freedom Party had won more than a quarter of Austrian votes in the October 1999 national election.

The world community was shocked by this turn of events, which seemed to be the beginning of Austria's reversion to its dark past of fascism. Politicians in many Western countries reacted swiftly and strongly. The United States recalled its ambassador to Austria and Secretary of State Madeleine Albright warned Austria that the United States would be monitoring the situation. Israel withdrew its ambassador from Austria indefinitely. Antonio Guterres, the Portuguese prime minister, warned of diplomatic isolation for Austria, as did Norway.

The Belgian foreign minister, Louis Michel, encouraged his countrymen to cancel their ski holidays in Austria; a significant act, given the amount of money tourism contributed to Austria's economy. Australia considered suspending the credentialling of its ambassador-designate to Vienna, Austria's capital. As quoted in the February 4, 2000 edition of *The Age*, Guentner Verheugen, a German member of the European Commission, said, "The message from the world is clear. The participation of a radical right-wing party in a democratic country in Europe will simply not be accepted. Those times are over, and I'm glad they're over." Such condemnation has its roots in Austria's past.

THE CONFLICT

In late 1999, the right-wing Freedom Party was invited to join the Austrian government. In response, Western nations, including the United States, withdrew their ambassadors and the European Union sanctioned Austria.

Political

- Austria's far-right Freedom Party espouses views that are anti-Semitic and anti-immigrant.

- The views of the Freedom Party cause fear and remind much of the world of the Holocaust.

- World opinion has never resolved whether Austria was a victim of Adolf Hitler's Germany or a willing participant in the Holocaust.

- Western nations, including the United States, the European Union and Australia, used sanctions, economic treats, and the removal of diplomats to register disapproval of Austria.

CHRONOLOGY

1920 The Republic of Austria is formed.

1938 The Anschluss takes place: Austria is forcibly incorporated into Hitler's Germany.

1945 Austria is occupied by Soviet Union, British, U.S., and French forces.

1955 Soviet Union troops withdraw from Austria and Austria is recognized as an independent and neutral state (though it remains within the Soviet bloc of influence).

1956 The Freedom Party of Austria (FPÖ) is formed.

1986 Jörg Haider becomes the leader of the Freedom Party of Austria.

1995 Austria joins the European Union.

1999 Haider's Freedom Party of Austria makes an impressive showing in the general election in Austria.

2000 The Freedom Party is invited to join the government. Sanctions and expressions of concern from around the world follow. Austria's chancellor signs a "democracy pledge" to ease concerns. Haider resigns as the FPÖ's leader.

HISTORICAL BACKGROUND

The Anschluss

The twentieth century has been tumultuous for Austria. The country began the century at the center of the six-hundred-year old Hapsburg Empire—an empire that once covered most of what has become Eastern Europe and ended up a prosperous but relatively insignificant modern republic. The Treaty of Versailles, drawn up in 1919 following World War I, essentially saw the final dissolution of this once-great imperial force. As a result of the treaty, Austria nearly lost its autonomy when it fell under the governing jurisdiction of Italy, and as the Nazis gained increasing power in Germany during the interwar years, it became apparent that Austria's course would change again.

The Nazi Party had several reasons for wanting to claim Austria as their own. Adolf Hitler, *Führer* (leader) of the Nazi Party, was born in Austria at Braunau-am-Inn in 1889, and had lived in Wien (Vienna) from 1907 to 1913. Indeed, Hitler did not relinquish his Austrian citizenship

to become a German national until 1932. Austria clearly held a special place in Hitler's heart. Furthermore, ninety-six percent of Austrians were German-speaking and were therefore culturally inclined toward their German neighbors and the Austrian Nazi Party had steadily gained support throughout the period. Thus in his seemingly endless appetite for *lebensraum* (living space) for Germany, Hitler decided to gain control over Austria by whatever means necessary.

As in many other parts of Europe, there had been a degree of unrest during Austria's interwar years. In the early 1930s, these sentiments began to come to a head. Austrian chancellor Engelbert Dollfuss had only a one-vote majority when he took power in 1932. His hold on power was made increasingly tenuous not only by pressure and threats from opposing political parties such as the National Socialists (Nazis) and the Social Democrats but also by Austria's perilous economic situation—in July 1932 Austria was forced to take a loan from the League of Nations of three hundred million schillings. In order to keep control of the country, Dollfuss introduced several restrictive measures that curbed the civil liberties of his countryfolk. Freedom of speech was suppressed, as was the freedom of assembly and freedom of the press. Political parties, such as the Austrian Nazis, were outlawed, and the Austrian parliament fractured into disarray. These actions only served to further agitate Dollfuss's opponents and convince them of his inappropriateness for office.

Civil unrest erupted early in 1934 and a series of incidents culminated in a *putsch* (revolt or uprising), made up mainly of Austrian Nazi supporters, on July 25, 1934. The Vienna radio station was occupied as well as a building that supposedly held a meeting of government ministers. Some ministers had been warned of impending events and had escaped. Dollfuss, nonetheless, stood firm against the rebels, remained in the building, and was assassinated. Kurt von Schuschnigg, one of the ministers who had managed to flee, took on Dollfuss's role, and a new government was formed. Many of the revolt's perpetrators were jailed, and Austria turned to Italy for support in its attempts to remain independent and for protection from German invasion. In response, Italian dictator Mussolini took his troops right up to the Austrian-German border in order to keep the Germans at bay. However, in tying themselves so firmly to the Fascist Italians, the Austrians were put in a difficult position when Italy aligned itself with Nazi Germany. Despite a short-lived silence in the aftermath of their abortive *putsch*, the Austrian Nazis once again became in-

ADOLF HITLER REVIEWS HIS TROOPS. *(Corbis. Reproduced by permission.)*

creasingly vocal in their support of their German allies, and the Austrian government again found itself losing control.

In 1938 a meeting was called between Schuschnigg and Hitler at the Berchtesgarden, Hitler's country retreat, at Obersalzburg, Germany. Schuschnigg and his secretary of state for foreign affairs, Guido Schmidt, were told by Hitler during their intense two-hour meeting that he had lost patience with Austria and intended to take action. According to Klauss P. Fischer in *Nazi Germany— A New History,* Hitler said, "I am absolutely determined to make an end of all this. The German Reich is one of the Great Powers, and nobody will raise his voice if it settles its border problems."

Schuschnigg was then presented with a document to sign that was essentially an ultimatum. It demanded the lifting of the ban on the Austrian Nazi Party and the release of all imprisoned pro-Nazi agitators. Further, Dr. Artur Seyss-Inquart, a staunchly pro-Nazi Austrian, was to be appointed minister of the interior with the power to enforce the above demands. Another pro-Nazi, Edmund von Glaise-Horstenau, was to become minister of war and help facilitate cooperation between the German and Austrian armies. Finally, pro-Nazi Dr. Hans Fischböck was to be made minister of finance to oversee the merging of Austria's economic system into Germany's. Austria, in short, would lose any sort of independence it may have

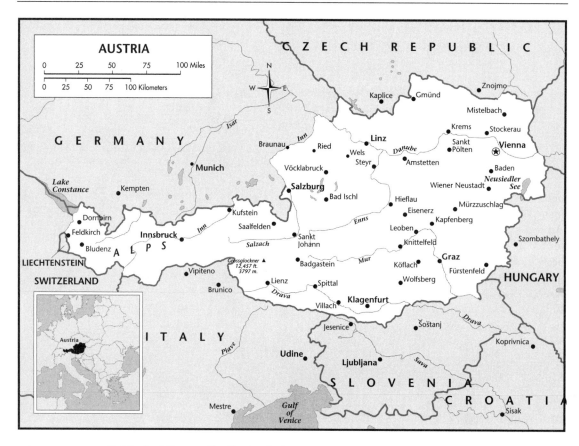

MAP OF AUSTRIA. (© *Maryland Cartographics. Reprinted with permission.*)

had and be subsumed under the German Reich. Protesting, Schuschnigg was once more shouted down by the *Führer*. Thus, under considerable duress and with grave misgivings, Schuschnigg signed the document.

Upon returning to Vienna, however, Schuschnigg hit upon a final, desperate plan. He announced that in March there would be a plebiscite (a plebiscite is a vote by an entire population, usually a vote of yes or no on a specific proposal). The people of Austria would decide for themselves if they wished to fall under the auspices of Nazi rule. If the majority voted against this notion, Schuschnigg would have a considerable trump card with which to undercut Hitler's assertion that most Austrians supported German control of their homeland.

Hitler was taken aback by Schuschnigg's initiative and decided he could not risk a plebiscite unless he could be completely assured of a favorable outcome. He demanded a postponement of the plebiscite, which Schuschnigg accepted. Then, realizing Schuschnigg's pliability, Hitler demanded Schuschnigg's immediate resignation and the appointment of Seyss-Inquart as chancellor. Schuschnigg gave in, and within hours, Austrian president

Miklas, upon whose approval the resignation of Schuschnigg and the appointment of Seyss-Inquart hinged, caved in also. The Austrian government had effectively fallen to the Nazis. Hermann Göring (a Nazi leader and founder of the Gestapo) appointed pro-Nazi ministers over the telephone from Berlin, and local Austrian Nazis settled themselves into the Austrian chancellery, cleaning out other people's desks and making way for the new order. Schuschnigg sadly recalled of that day, "One young man brushed past me without an apology. He turned around and looked me up and down with a purposely offensive, superior smile. Then he went and slammed the door as if he were at home. I stared after him, and suddenly I realised: Invasion! Not at the borders yet but here, in the Chancellery: the Gestapo." (Fischer, 1995)

Two days later Austria was proclaimed a province of the German Reich, and its name, Österreich—which Hitler hated—was changed to Ostmark. With the streets of Vienna lavishly adorned with flowers and swastikas, Hitler made his grand entrance. Austria's independence was conclusively pronounced dead and the *Anschluss* complete.

Austria During World War II

By association, Austria became a participant in many of the often-atrocious German prewar and wartime activities; virulent anti-Semitism became public policy shortly after the *Anschluss*. According to Barbara Jelavich's book, *Modern Austria: Empire and Republic, 1815–1986*, from 1938 to May 1939, the number of Jews in Austria dropped from 220,000 to 121,000 due largely to emmigration.

Likewise, when World War II was declared in September 1939, Austria was aligned with Germany and the other Axis powers, Italy and Japan. Austria vicariously shared in the victories gained for the Germans through Austrian troops who had been co-opted onto the Nazi side: Poland was conquered in three weeks, Norway and Denmark were taken in April of 1940; Holland, Belgium and France fell in May and June. However, thanks in part to the entrance of the United States into the war in 1943, the tide began to turn against the Axis powers. By the beginning of 1944, it was clear that the German war machine was in trouble.

As the war drew to a close, with an Allied victory becoming an increasingly likely outcome, where Austria stood in terms of allegiance and responsibility was a difficult question. Were the Austrians a conquered nation, along with the likes of Poland, Denmark, and France, or were they aligned with the enemy, no different than other German territories? Winston Churchill stated in a November 1939 speech that he regarded Austria as being among the nations taken forcefully by Germany. A meeting of foreign ministers in Moscow in November 1943 determined much the same but also indicated what would prove to be the contradictory nature of Austria's postwar status: Austria, though a victim of Hitler, would be held responsible for its part in the war.

Austria After the War

While Austria's civilian population did not suffer the severe food and fuel shortages that characterized their experiences during World War I, they were at the mercy of massive air raid attacks when the Allies invaded Italy in 1943. Factories and civilian centers were hit. Vienna suffered its first significant raid in April 1944, and subsequent attacks cost an estimated nine thousand Viennese their lives. The Soviet army made its way into Austria forcefully, bringing with it five days of fierce fighting, culminating in its arrival in Vienna on April 13, 1945. The war was finally over for Austria on May 7, with the cessation of this fighting. Hitler had committed suicide on April 30 in Berlin, and the Germans unconditionally surren-dered on May 8. Two hundred and forty-seven thousand Austrian members of the armed forces were dead, missing or had died in captivity; twenty-nine thousand civilians had died. More than 750,000 men were held in Soviet prisoner-of-war camps, some to return home as late as 1955.

Following the Second World War, Austria was divided between the four Allied powers—the Soviet Union, the United States, Britain, and France—in much the same manner that postwar Germany was, and this division was maintained until the mid-1950s. A degree of freedom was allowed the people of Austria, however. Moves were made toward the end of the war to reestablish the independent Republic of Austria and the first free elections since 1930 were held in late 1945. The Social Democrats and the Christian Social Party (now known as the People's Party) began their long-standing duopoly over Austrian politics during this period.

The Freedom Party of Austria

The political party that Jörg Haider led (until recently), the FPÖ (Die Freiheitlichen in Österreich or Freedom Party of Austria), was founded in 1956. It remained on the fringes of Austrian politics and made few inroads into the power held by the Social Democrats and the Christian Social Party. Two major strengths of the Social Democrats and the Christian Social Party were their ability to promote a healthy tourist trade that was vital to Austria's economy and to develop a progressive welfare state. However, when the 1980s recession and resulting claims of corruption blemished this untarnished state record and their long-held good public opinion plummeted, the FPÖ (Freedom Party) found an avenue through which to make their move towards power.

Jörg Haider was born in 1950 in the upper Austrian town of Bad Goisern to two enthusiastic, long-term supporters of the Nazi Party. Haider's parents had been early champions of the far-right movement, even moving to Germany to become party officials. Following World War II, Haider's parents were punished for their allegiances and forced to take up menial work. Critics suggest that Haider's parents' views left an indelible mark on his own political philosophies. Haider did very well in school and studied law in Vienna. During his youth he belonged to a far-right sports club and a university *bruederschaft*—a fraternity of uniformed students run by former Nazis (Roxburgh 2000). Haider joined the Freedom Party in 1976 and in 1986 became the leader.

When Haider became leader, the Freedom Party could barely secure five percent of the national vote. In the fourteen years since his ascension to power, the support base has risen to twenty-eight percent. This is a considerable achievement, given the strong hold on power held by the ruling two-party coalition. A significant part of Haider's success lies in his personal charisma. Commentators on the BBC News remarked that he "works a room like [U.S. president] Bill Clinton, embracing supporters and using the familiar 'du' form of address." Further, he has captured elements of the youth vote with his fashionable, youthful appearance and seemingly refreshing alternative approach to the otherwise slightly stagnant and dull world of Austrian politics. One youthful supporter appeared on the Australian Broadcasting Commission's current affairs program *Foreign Correspondent,* and said of Haider, "He's a very charismatic person and he also has the touch of the young man . . . he still has the aura of a young one, a dynamic one . . . ." Indeed, Haider has succeeded in capturing forty percent of his support from the voters under thirty years of age.

Yet for all of his apparent savvyness, Jörg Haider has stirred up controversy by espousing some rather un-savvy and politically incorrect opinions. At about the time he became leader of the Freedom Party, Haider inherited a massive estate in the Austrian province of Carinthia that was reportedly illegally purchased during World War II by his great-uncle from an Italian Jew who apparently sold his home under extreme duress from the occupying Nazi forces. During his first term as governor of Carinthia, after he taking power in 1989, Haider stated during a parliamentary debate that the Third Reich had an orderly employment policy. The uproar that resulted from this remark led him to resign from his post. He attempted to apologize for the comment after it met with such an outraged response, but he did not deny his belief in his statement. Instead, as related by the BBC News, he said, "I unequivocally made the point that this remark was not made with the meaning understood by you. If it reassures you then I take back the remark with regret."

It is an apology loaded with double meaning, the sort of dual edged comment typical of Haider. his words have often been said to mean whatever his audience wants them to mean. Not suprisingly, Haider was not dissuaded from his opinions; several years later, he described Nazi concentration camps as "punishment camps" (with the inference that their inmates were there because they had committed a crime and deserved punishment). He

also stated that, "The Waffen SS was a part of the Wehrmacht [the German military] and hence it deserves all the honour and respect of the army in public life."

Further, while attending a reunion of old SS men, Haider described those gathered as "sound, decent men of principle" and has also drawn a link between the deportation of the Jews by the Nazis to the expulsion of the Sudeten Germans from Czechoslovakia after World War II. During the early 1990s, Haider seemed to many to be nothing short of a Nazi apologist. A German neo-Nazi reinforced the suspicions of many when he wrote of Haider and the Freedom Party that:

> . . . the far-right Freedom Party . . . founded largely by former Austrian Nazis . . . now led by the charismatic son of Austrian Nazis, a grinning yuppie who praised the 'labour policies' of the Third Reich . . . its antiforeigner rhetoric about the need to protect Austria's 'cultural purity' didn't seem to hurt [the German neo-Nazi cause] either, nor did its leaders' veiled praises of the Third Reich or their support of SS veterans groups . . . (Hasselbach 1996).

Having hit upon the abundant well of popular malcontent regarding the all-encompassing powers of the European Union (E.U.) and its moves to broaden Western Europe's borders to admit the less fortunate inhabitants of the war-torn Balkan region, Jörg Haider has touted anti-European Union and anti-immigration stances as major planks of the FPÖ's political platform. He has played upon the social anxiety a country that is the bulwark of Western Europe and whose neighbors are less affluent Eastern European countries. The proximity of these countries is threatening to Austria, whose population is ninety-five percent Germanic stock (three percent of the population are Croat, two percent Slovene, and one percent Turkish). Haider has described the European Union as a "bureaucratic monster" the E.U. border broadening plans as "a declaration of war against all working and upstanding people." He attempted to stop Austria from joining the European Union in 1995. He also tried to force a referendum on whether Austria should join the E.U.'s single currency. On both counts, he failed.

Toward Austria's (approximate) five percent population of immigrants, Haider is no more generous. During the October 1999 electoral campaign, he suggested that the austere nature of the country's budget could be blamed on the added burden of immigrants upon the nation's economy. Haider has said of the immigrant population of Austria:

> You have to provide housing conditions for them, you have to organise a school system where they can speak their traditional language . . . we have to pro-

vide jobs for them and if we have an increasing unemployment rate in Austria, I don't think it's responsible to accept so many . . . immigrants coming to Austria and asking for jobs.

Doron Rabinovici, the Jewish Austrian writer and part-organizer of many of Vienna's recent anti-Haider protests, laments that Haider's "policy is to make social problems into ethnic problems." Haider lays the blame for the country's woes at the feet of immigrants and those who are different. Further, Rabinovici notes that abuse and harassment of Jewish people in Austria has increased tenfold since the Freedom Party's election to power. Barbara Greinicher, a worker for Austria's Caritas charity, which assists mainly refugees and immigrants, states that since the success of Haider's party "you can express . . . in public that you don't like foreigners, that you prefer Austrian culture." Leon Zelman, the head of the Jewish Welcome Service in Vienna (which connects visiting or returning Jews with their Viennese heritage), spent his teenage years in Auschwitz. He spoke to a BBC correspondent about his feelings towards Haider as Zelman sat in his room above St. Stephen's Square and watched and listened to a Haider rally:

> The way he [Haider] manipulated the crowd, the way the people cheered, the whipping up of hatred and intolerance—that was what scared him [Zelman], and reminded him of Nazi rallies he had witnessed as a boy. He [Zelman] says he wept at the memory.

The question is whether Haider has the makings of another Hitler: is the world community right to be concerned about the Austrian situation, or is it overreacting? Haider refutes charges of his party's neo-fascism and xenophobia and blames the charges on political manipulation by Austria's other parties. Haider denies the charges—either through a genuine desire to correct public misconceptions about his party's aims or through a more studied, politically astute and rather disturbing attempt to make the FPÖ's policies seem publicly acceptable as they make a dash for power. Again, on the *Foreign Correspondent* show, Haider claimed that:

> We have been attacked as being a xenophobic and fascist movement. There is no reason behind it. There's only the question of having a strong battle in Austria between a block of two powerful parties which do not want to lose power. We have been too successful in the past so they use all the arguments they can put on the table to attack us.

Haider has backed away from, if not apologized for, almost all of the outrageous remarks that he has made. In an address made in Vienna in November 1999, following the Freedom Party's electoral success, Haider apologized to Austria's Jewish citizens for some of his comments:

> In the past, some remarks which have been attributed to me in connection with Nazism which were certainly insensitive or open to misunderstanding. I am personally sorry for this, firstly because I believe I hurt the feelings of people who were themselves victims of Nazism or whose relatives were, and secondly because the statements were not made in line with the personal values of tolerance and humanity which are the basis of my political work.

In the same address, he went on to say that:

> Where we in the Freedom Party have responsibility, no one needs to pack their suitcases and no one has to leave their home. Where we in the Freedom Party have responsibility, freedom and democracy are in good hands. (BBC News)

RECENT HISTORY AND THE FUTURE

In February of 2000, Haider, with Wolfgang Schuessel, signed a "democracy pledge" that committed the political parties of both men to uphold just values while in office. Haider also recently volunteered to visit a Jewish Museum in Montreal while on a visit to Canada (his request was refused). His latest and most significant attempt at improving the chances of his ostracized nation and political party was to resign his post as the FPÖ's leader in late February 2000, to be replaced by Susanne Reiss-Passer. He officially stepped down in early May.

However, as with many of his remarks, Haider's actions can be interpreted as having dual meanings. His resignation from the FPÖ leadership has been dismissed by many as a ploy; some believe he meant to lull the concerned European community into a sense of security and then launch the great leap forward into the chancellor's seat. Indeed, when talking on the *Foreign Correspondent* of his chances of the ultimate success in Austrian politics, namely chancellorship, he said "I am sure that it will happen." The FPÖ likewise appears to be in no doubt that Haider will return. According to the May 22, 2000 issue of *Time*, new leader Susanne Reiss-Passer confidently proclaiming after Haider's resignation, "This is still Jörg Haider's party!"

For now, the situation is improving for Austria. Sanctions, such as the freeze on bilateral political contacts, may be suspended. Attempts have been made now to thaw relations between Austria and the rest of the world community. Switzerland was the first to make a move toward this, when in March 2000 it received Austria's chancellor, Wolfgang Schuessel, on his first bilateral visit since tensions arose. Switzerland, which is not a member of

THOUSANDS OF DEMONSTRATORS CARRYING BANNERS GATHER IN FRONT OF THE HOFBURG PALACE IN VIENNA, AUSTRIA TO PROTEST AGAINST THE NEW COALITION OF CONSERVATIVES AND THE FAR-RIGHT FREEDOM PARTY. *(Corbis Corporation. Reproduced by permission.)*

the European Union, traditionally receives new Austrian ministers first and saw no reason to behave differently after the most recent election. Finland followed in April when the Finnish foreign minister, Erkki Tuomioja, argued that the ban is counterproductive and hampers the making of key EU policy decisions.

Germany's new opposition leader, Angela Merkel, has also criticized the European Union's decision to isolate Austria, stating, as Finland has, that Austria is a vital part of the EU community. Further, Merkel suggested, the European Union's actions have led only to greater notoriety for

Haider. Hungary has also joined the countries moving away from the European Union's hardline position on Austria by receiving Schuessel on his second bilateral state visit since the shunning of Austria.

In fact, the actions of the European Union regarding Austria are being questioned as having legally contravened E.U. powers. The E.U. treaties allow for the suspension of a member who consistently violates democracy and human rights but there is no provision in the treaty for members who may, in the future, create such problems. Austria is scheduled to vote in a referendum that will give an idea of their feelings about the sanctions, and, as a result, their feelings about the European Union in general. Indeed, there are some who suggest that the whole incident has played right into Haider's hands in creating anti-E.U. sentiment.

On the *Foreign Correspondent* television program, Anton Polinka, an Austrian professor in politics and history suggested that:

> Haider is not a second Hitler or even a second Hitler in disguise . . . he's the successful Austrian version of a new type of right wing politics.

It is this phenomenon of right-wing parties that really makes the other members of the European Union nervous and, indeed, it is what this entire incident has been largely about. Extreme right-wing groups are gaining ground throughout Europe; Italy, Switzerland, Belgium, and France, parties bordering on the neo-fascist are making parliamentary gains. Swedish prime minister Goran Persson, addressing an international Holocaust forum in Sweden made these widespread concerns clear, when he stated that, "Anti-democratic forces continue to gain our support. The danger lies in our failure to learn from history, our failure to see the connection." Prime Minister Persson decided to call the forum after research revealed the fact that ten percent of Swedish schoolchildren do not know about the Holocaust. If the world begins to forget about Nazism's horrors, the rise of far-right figures like Haider may not seem so troubling until it is too late.

No matter how much of Haider's platform one takes seriously at this early stage, the ghosts of the past are certainly stirring in one form or another throughout Europe. Austria, it would seem, is just the beginning. Shadows of Austria's dark past, which the country has thus far largely managed to evade, are coming back to it in a variety of ways. Some Austrian companies are facing compensation claims for the use of forced labor during World War II and one of Austria's most respected neuropsychologists and forensic experts, Heinrich Gross, has recently been on trial for his part in a Nazi program to experiment on handicapped children, an experiment that is believed to have resulted in hundreds of deaths.

As the fallout from this international diplomatic crisis continues to land, the outcome remains unclear. Has Austria learned the lessons taught by its past? Haider, in typically double-edged form during a recent interview with the German periodical *Die Zeit*, showed an alarming hint of his more malevolent intentions, stated "There is a lot of excitement in the European chicken pen—even though the fox hasn't even got in."

BIBLIOGRAPHY

"Europe has Little to Fear from this Goose-Stepping Austrian", *Seattle P-I.com*. 12 October 1999. http://seattlep-i.nwsource.com/opinion/austop.shtml (8 September 2000).

Fischer, Klaus P. *Nazi Germany—A New History*. New York: Continuum Publishing Company, 1995.

Foreign Correspondent. Television program. On Australian Broadcasting Commission, March 2000.

Hasselbach, Ingo with Tom Reiss. *Fuhrer-Ex—Memoirs of a Former Neo-Nazi*. New York: Random House, 1996.

Jelavich, Barbara. *Modern Austria: Empire and Republic, 1815–1986*. 4th ed. New York: Cambridge University Press, 1993.

Laqueur, Walter. *Fascism—Past, Present, Future*. New York: Oxford University Press, 1996.

Leuker, Angela. "The Haider Effect," *Time* 17 July 2000, 36.

Parkinson, F., ed. *Conquering the Past—Austrian Nazism— Yesterday and Today*. Detroit, Mich.: Wayne State University Press, 1989.

Pitney, Geoff. "Haider Signs to Guarantee Democracy," *The Age*, 4 February 2000.

Purvis, Andrew. "This is still Jörg Haider's Party!" *Time*, 22 May 2000.

Roxburgh, Angus. "Haider and the Auschwitz Survivor." *BBC News Online*. 29 February 2000. http://news6.thdo.bbc.co.uk/hi/english/world/from%5Four%5Fow n%5Fcorrespondent/newsid%5F628000/628728.stm (8 September 2000).

Sully, Melanie A. *The Haider Phenomenon*. Boulder, Colo.: East European Monographs, 1997.

Emily Turner-Graham

THE BASQUES: THE ETA AND SEPARATISM

THE CONFLICT

The Basque region is in Spain and small sections of France. The Basques, ethnically and linguistically distinct from their Spanish and French neighbors, have sought independence. The ETA ("Basque Homeland and Freedom" or Euskadi ta Azkatasuna) has been waging a terrorist campaign for independence from Spain.

Political

- Periodically, Spain has granted the Basques some autonomy within Spain, though they have also brutally suppressed the ETA and suspected sympathizers.

- Recently, France has reversed a long-standing practice of not arresting ETA leaders hiding in France. They have started arresting *Etarras* and returning them to Spain.

Ethnic

- The Basques, as represented by the ETA, want self-determination, and, ultimately, independence from Spain.

"Terrorism: violence turns green into red," wrote Rod Usher in *Time* magazine on March 13, 2000, when the weekly magazine drew parallels between the conflict in Northern Ireland and another situation in Spain. In Spain the Basque separatist organization Euskadi Ta Askatasuna (ETA) had killed an army colonel in Madrid in January and a Socialist politician and his bodyguard a month later. More terrorist attacks followed. The public and the media alike were horrified and puzzled, for ETA had declared a truce in late 1998, only to break it unilaterally fourteen months later. Although apparently similar to other European terrorist groups that struck in Europe from the 1960s to the 1990s, ETA differs on cultural and ideological grounds. Like the Irish Republican Army (IRA) in Northern Ireland, ETA professes a nationalist agenda and seeks the independence of the Basque region of Spain. It is, however, closer to the German Red Army Faction (RAF) and the Italian Red Brigades in its socialist leanings. To understand the evolution of this terrorist group and its place in the history of Basque separatism, one must also take into account the history of Spain and Basque nationalism, which dates back a century.

HISTORICAL BACKGROUND

The Basque region, also known in the original Basque language as Euskadi, lies in northern Spain along the Bay of Biscay, with a few smaller areas across the border in France. The region became part of the Spanish crown in the Middle Ages. Initially dependent on agriculture and sheep herding, the Basque region was one of the first to industrialize in Spain, and to this day it produces most of Spanish steel. However, the Basque region

CHRONOLOGY

1890s Sabino de Arana founds the Basque nationalist movement.

1930s The Basque Nationalist Party (PNV) dominates local elections.

1936 A brief Euskadi (Basque) government is established during the Spanish Civil War (1936–39), but is forced into exile a year later.

1959 In response to the failure of an aging PNV leadership to maintain Basque interest in the face of the Franco dictatorship, a younger group splits off from the party and founds the ETA.

1962 The first ETA assembly forms.

1964 The pamphlet *Insurrection in Euskadi*, which suggests the Basques are a colonized group who must rise against their Spanish oppressors, is published.

1968 Mass arrests of Basque separatists follow the assassination of police commissioner Melitón Manzanas.

1973 Spanish vice-president Carrero Blanco is assassinated.

1974 A tactical debate over the methods of armed struggle splits the ETA into the political-military (pm) and military (m) factions.

1975 Spanish dictator Francisco Franco dies.

1977–78 A series of amnesties granted by the Spanish government are reversed when the ETA initiates a new wave of violence.

1983 The Spanish government establishes the plan *Zona Especial Norte* (ZEN; Special Northern Zone), designed to fight ETA terrorists.

1985 The Basque autonomous government condemns the ETA's actions.

1986 For the first time since ETA members started using southern France as a refuge from which to launch their activities, French authorities begin to arrest *Etarras* and send them back to Spain for trial.

1987 In November, the Spanish government establishes the Madrid Pact against Terrorism, with the participation of the PNV.

1988–89 The first ETA-declared truce, for the purposes of negotiating with the Spanish government, fail.

1993 For the first time since they have been represented in parliament in 1979, Basque political parties receive less than fifty percent of the vote.

1997 Members of the Herri Batusana political party, an ally of the ETA, are jailed for attempting to broadcast an ETA political ad.

1998 In September the ETA announces that it would observe an indefinite truce pending further negotiations with the Spanish government.

2000 The ETA breaks the truce by murdering several members of the Spanish political, military, and religious elites. Further bomb attacks take place in public areas.

is subject to cyclical downturns and thus suffers from heavy unemployment.

As a result of the French Revolution and the Napoleonic wars between 1789 and 1815, all of Europe underwent a transformation whereby nationalist consciousness grew along the lines of language, culture, religion and ethnicity. Nationalism is a desire for national unity and independence and a belief that one's nation is important above all else. Regions long under the control of nations were also affected and expressed their separate identity through measures ranging from the resurrection of language and literature to open warfare. Thus, in Spain, the Basque region fought and lost two wars for independence (1833–39 and 1874–76 respectively) against the state. In response to these defeats Sabino de Arana (1865–1903) established a Basque nationalist movement in 1898. The formation of a Basque nationalist movement coincided with Spain's decline on the international scene, including the loss of the Philippines and Cuba in the Spanish-American War, as well as to the hardships traditional Basque groups—elites and farmers alike—had suffered following industrialization.

JOSÉ ANTONIO AGUIRRE Y LECUBA

1904–1960 José Aguirre was born in Basque Country, Spain, on March 6, 1904. His father, a lawyer who was well known for his defense of Basque nationalists, died when Aguirre was sixteen. Aguirre rapidly finished school, and graduated with a law degree from Deusto University in 1926. After two years of military service he opened a law practice in Bilboa in 1928.

Aguirre married and started a family, while becoming increasingly involved in Basque nationalist activities. In 1931 he was elected mayor of Guecho. In 1936 three out of four of the Basque territories voted for autonomy, which was granted by the Spanish government. In October of that year Aguirre was elected president of the first Basque government. His official acts of government included adoption of the Basque flag and the creation of the Basque Army and Basque University.

A few months later, as civil war violence escalated, Aguirre and his family were forced to flee to Paris, where he set up a government-in-exile. With the outbreak of war between France and Germany, the Aguirre family was trapped behind German lines. Aguirre managed to smuggle his family to New York, where he taught at Columbia University. After the war, Aguirre returned to Paris, from where he administered his government-in-exile until his death on March 27, 1960.

Due to the hardships caused by industrialization an anti-capitalist mood dominated the Basque nationalist movement from the beginning.

Initially, the Basque movement had little success because of its lack of unity. Some sympathizers argued for complete separation from the Spanish state while moderates preferred a negotiated autonomy, limited autonomy within the Spanish state. There were further divisions according to urban and rural backgrounds, in which the Catholic clergy played a role. The centrist Basque Nationalist Party (PNV) was able to dominate the political scene at first. Outlawed between 1923 and 1930, the time of the dictatorship of Primo de Rivera, it experienced a rebirth when the Spanish Republic was established in 1931. That year, the PNV came to dominate local Basque elections and participated as a political minority in the Spanish national parliament until 1936.

The Civil War and the Franco Dictatorship

Because the Basque region was so heavily industrialized, when the Spanish civil war broke out in 1936 between republicans and monarchists, both sides sought to control Basque resources. The PNV eventually sided with the republicans in exchange for the promise of autonomous local rule. During the war an autonomous government comprised of nationalists and republicans functioned for seven months. With the victory of nationalist leader General Francisco Franco, however, the situation was reversed and the Spanish government began to remove all expressions of cultural diversity within Spain.

The measures applied against Basque culture were quite severe. The Basque language Euskadi, for example, was banned and schools were required to teach only Spanish. The PNV government that had functioned for seven months in 1936–37 went into exile in France. While in France, PNV president José Antonio Aguirre and his supporters worked with the Allies, while Spain remained officially neutral in World War II. In Spain Basque nationalists were unable to effectively oppose the suppression of their culture because of the heavy military and police control that weakened all clandestine movements throughout the country, including nationalist, socialist, and monarchist groups.

After the World War II Aguirre went to New York to ask the United Nations for help, but the advent of the Cold War stifled his efforts. The United States, eager for Franco's support against what the United States viewed as the communist threat in Europe, effectively reversed the political and economic boycott that affected Spain. The PNV leadership felt that this meant that they would have to wait for a change of government in Spain before restarting negotiations for self-rule of the Basque region. However, a new wave of repression of the Franco regime led to a split within the PNV. A total of twelve states of emergency were declared between 1956 and 1975, eleven of which affected the Basque region. Younger members of the PNV, upset at the lack of active opposition to Spanish rule, established of the Euskadi ta Azkatasuna ("Basque Homeland and Freedom" or ETA) in 1959.

The Early ETA

The ETA's agenda was, from the start, different from that of the PNV. Whereas the PNV considered working within the framework of politics, the ETA advocated a form of guerrilla warfare—

A SHEPHERD GUIDES HIS SHEEP THROUGH A VALLEY IN THE NORTHERN BASQUE REGION OF SPAIN. *(AP/Wide World Photos. Reproduced by permission.)*

wars fought by small groups using hit-and-run tactics—as a means to assert political demands. Furthermore, unlike other forms of Basque nationalism, the ETA also rejected any involvement of religion in politics and wanted a socialist form of government for the Basque region. Finally, it rejected the notion of a separate Basque blood based on nineteenth-century interpretations of nationalism, favoring instead the advocacy of cultural unity. By focusing on culture instead of ancestry, the ETA ensured sympathy from locals who were not of Basque descent.

In the early 1960s different streams of thought caused a strain within the ETA. While the general goal of autonomy remained consistent among all *Etarras*, as members called themselves, disagreements over methods made the organization into a profoundly heterogeneous body. As a result of such differences, the first assembly of ETA in 1962, held in secret, led to an ambiguous expression of its social and economic goals. Some *Etarras* argued for a liberation movement similar to those in developing nations, while others preferred the model of Marxist revolution by the working class. Goals appeared a year later in the publication of Frederico Krutwig's *Asconia* in which the author, a member of the academy of Basque language, outlined a revolutionary strategy for the Basque country similar to the struggles of developing nations. By 1979 the book had reached a third edition. In 1964 a new document—based in part on Krutwig and entitled "Insurrection in Euskadi"—was approved by the ETA fourth assembly. Nevertheless, the ETA's subsequent assemblies would continue to suffer from splits between proponents of armed revolution and those who called for negotiation with the state.

Escalation in the Late 1960s

Meanwhile, ETA activities remained underground. Beginning in 1960 any violation of the law, including the formation of disallowed groups, resulted in the facing of a military tribunal. By the end of the decade some eighty percent of all acts of dissent heard in military courts would not have been considered crimes in a democracy. However, the ETA also carried out robberies and kidnappings in order to provide funds for the organization. Generally, the kidnapping victims were released unharmed following payment of a ransom. Yet, in 1968 the Guardia Civil, paramilitary police, killed an *Etarra* caught in a robbery attempt. In reprisal, the ETA shot and killed a Spanish police commissioner outside his apartment. The Spanish government imposed a state of emergency and arrested over two thousand Basque separatists, including many who were not members of ETA. Many of the captives were tortured or held without trial. Eventually, a list of sixteen suspects was drawn up, all of whom admitted to being members of ETA, yet denied involvement in the assassination. This situation combined with the internal divisions within the ETA to destroy the organization's morale. Another of the Franco regime's actions, however, actually rebuilt a semblance of ETA unity.

The Spanish government organized a public trial of the suspects, which took place in Burgos, Spain, in 1970. The foreign press was invited to attend and reported on the accuseds' plight, which included violation of due process by the military tribunal as well as violence at the hands of the police. In the wake of protests in 1968 in Europe and in the United States, such police abuse caused international outrage. Within the Basque region, despite heavy arrests, membership in the ETA soared, and new members joined in support the ETA's goals.

The new generation of ETA members prompted even greater dissension within the organization. The extremist wing carried out new kidnappings, this time targeting major figures of the Spanish elite, such as the industrialist Lorenzo Zabala in 1972. The latter's company paid the ransom and promised to rehire striking workers who had been fired. While this event increased the ETA's prestige, it also horrified the PNV, and did little to quell the wave of violence.

The culmination of ETA violence under Franco came in 1973 with the assassination of his vice president and heir apparent, Admiral Carrero Blanco. Initially scheduled to be a kidnapping operation to obtain both funds and the release of political prisoners, the ETA military cell responsible for the action determined that the admiral was too heavily guarded to allow for such an operation. Instead, after identifying the admiral's habit of attending the same church on a weekly basis, the terrorists placed explosives under the street and blew the admiral's car up in the churchyard. The death of Blanco showed the vulnerability of the Franco regime and, paradoxically, hastened the end of Francoism following the dictator's death.

The Post–Franco Years

The death of General Franco in 1975 caused a shift in the relationship of ETA to the Spanish state. Within days, King Juan Carlos ordered the release of all political prisoners with the exception of those accused of "blood crimes," terrorism or murder. While this freed many ETA members, the majority of those remaining in jail were *Etarras* too. Spain became a democracy, and several Basque parties sought representation. Some groups espoused the goals of the ETA, such as the Herri Batusana and the KAS, or the Patriotic Socialist Coordinating Council, but they denied any attachment to the terrorist group. This democratic shift was troubling for the ETA, as it had made no plans to establish a regime that offered democratic representation, and thus legal channels for change. The split that had begun within the organization in 1974 now became permanent.

While all ETA factions rejected the Spanish Reform Laws of 1976, which allowed the establishment of political parties, and the constitution of 1978, their strategy to fight these measures showed clear divergence. On one side stood the ETA-military (ETA-m), which stressed the primacy of military leadership and thus of armed struggle. On the other side stood the ETA politico-militar (ETA-pm), which argued for a combination of political and military strategies against the Spanish government, such as the threat of terrorism, unless negotiations ensued. The ETA-pm thought its strategy would be more in keeping with a democratic society in which various degrees of sympathy could be gained from outsiders. To the ETA-m, however, only terrorism could secure Basque independence.

Terrorist actions by the ETA in 1977 prompted the Spanish government to reintroduce anti-terrorist measures suspended after Franco's death. At the same time, the Spanish government granted complete amnesty to all ETA prisoners. This established a pattern that continues to this day, whereby the Spanish government offers of amnesty are withdrawn in the wake of increased violence by *Etarras*, who perceive the amnesty as a sign of weakness and an ideal moment to further press their demands.

Between 1978 and 1980 the creation of a new political organization, the Basque Autonomous Community, led by a coalition of Basque political groups, convinced the ETA-pm to dissolve, which it did in 1981. Concessions from the Spanish state, combined with the lack of majority among Basque organizations, played a role in this. Members who wished to carry on the armed struggle joined the ETA-m.

The ETA-m announced in 1978 that it would negotiate with the Spanish government only on the basis of the "KAS alternative," a five-point program that called for:

- Total amnesty for all political prisoners—at the time there were some fifty-nine Basques in Spanish jails;

- Legalization of all political parties;

- Expulsion of the Guardia Civil, the Spanish paramilitary police, and the Spanish police from the Basque region;

- Adoption of measures to improve the living conditions of the working class;

- An autonomy status recognizing the national sovereignty of the Basque region, Euskara as the principal language, and law enforcement and military units under control of the Basque government.

By 1980 several of these changes had in fact been carried out by the Spanish state, which negotiated with the PNV as the leading representative of Basque interests. Other conditions, however, were deemed unacceptable, partly because ETA continued to escalate the violence.

In 1981 the ETA-m became the main ETA group and evolved into small cells of three- to five-member armed commandos who maintained connections with members in French exile. This organization resulted in the ETA becoming an extremely violent organization dedicated to continued acts of terrorism until the goals it had set were achieved. While it is difficult to accurately estimate the number of ETA-m members, the Spanish police stated in the 1980s that there were some twenty cells with ninety activists. The ETA-m's capacity to strike despite its small number of activists occurred in part because members could take refuge in France without fear of arrest. This French policy of non-involvement was initially due to dislike of the Franco regime and, perhaps, fear that the terrorists would try and stir trouble in the French part of the Basque region.

THE REMAINS OF A CAR BOMB WHICH KILLED A POLICEMAN IS THOUGHT TO BE THE WORK OF THE ETA, AN ARMED BASQUE SEPARATIST GROUP, AND IS BEING REMOVED BY RESCUE WORKERS IN BILBOA, SPAIN. *(AP/Wide World Photos. Reproduced by permission.)*

Fighting the ETA

In the 1980s, however, policy changes in Spain and in France reduced the influence of the ETA. First, a shift occurred in the 1970s with the arrest of certain ETA members by French authorities. By 1986 France began systematically arresting *Etarras* and turning them over to the Spanish authorities.

The Spanish government also initiated a stronger policy to combat terrorism. In 1982 the newly elected socialist government of Prime Minister Felipe González established the plan Zona Especial Norte (ZEN; "Special Northern Zone"), designed to fight ETA terrorists. The Spanish gov-

ernment has been accused of supporting right wing, anti-terrorist units that struck at suspected ETA members. As many as twenty-eight people were murdered, including some who were murdered simply on suspicion of being ETA sympathizers.

A third policy contributed to reducing the ETA's influence. The Spanish government allowed militants to repudiate armed struggle and rejoin Basque society. By providing militants with a way to leave the ETA, the government further reduced the organization's ranks. Between 1982 and 1986, two hundred fifty of its members accepted the of-

CELEBRATING THE USE OF THE OFFICIAL BASQUE LANGUAGE, "EUSKERA," DANCERS HOLD TORCHES WHILE THOUSANDS OF BASQUES FILL THE SOCCER STADIUM AT BILBOA, SPAIN. *(AP/Wide World Photos. Reproduced by permission.)*

fer of amnesty. In the process, the smaller ETA became even more dangerous, since the most extreme and dangerous members remained involved.

Meanwhile, the Basque population continued to agree, at least in principle, with the ETA's goals. The escalation of violence, however, leading to the deaths of bystanders alongside Spanish officials, provoked a slow revulsion at the ETA's actions. In March 1985 the Basque government explicitly condemned the ETA's actions for the first time, and the Basque parliament demanded that the ETA put down its weapons.

By 1987 the Spanish government admitted that it had started to negotiate directly with the ETA

toward ending hostilities. The ETA responded by saying that violence could end only once negotiations concluded successfully. In protest of the signing by all political parties of a State Pact Against Terrorism, the ETA carried out an extremely violent bomb attack in Zaragoza in which eleven people died, including children. It was not until 1988, when the ETA announced that it would allow the participation of political party representatives in talks, that negotiations resumed and a cease-fire went into effect. The cease-fire did not last, however, and over the past decade sporadic cease-fires have alternated with vicious attacks on Spanish officials and civilians.

During this time the PNV has moved further away from the ETA, leading the latter to initiate a harassment campaign against the PNV. The burning of party offices has become a common occurrence. Other Basque separatist groups, however, have moved closer to the ETA. Herri Batusana, which denied support for the ETA in the late 1970s, became its de facto political wing. In 1997 several of its members were jailed for having sought to broadcast a political ad made by the ETA.

RECENT HISTORY AND THE FUTURE

Since its first act of violence in 1968, the ETA has killed an estimated eight hundred people. Although the group's attacks seemed to have abated in the early 1990s, a new wave of violence at the end of the decade suggests a new terrorist core has come of age. The tacit support ETA members could count on, however, has been on the decline, with popular demonstrations against terrorism occurring in Basque cities. This has also begun to affect non-ETA Basque separatist groups. Whereas between 1979 and 1991 Basque parties could expect at least fifty percent of the vote in their home region, starting with the 1993 elections, they no longer received a clear majority. Furthermore, the new generation of the ETA has developed goals only loosely related to those of the original ETA. Overall then, while the ETA may continue to exist, its motives for striking have moved away from its concern for the Basque people and toward the adoption of an ambitious and violent agenda.

BIBLIOGRAPHY

Clark, Robert P. *The Basque Insurgents: ETA, 1952–1980.* Madison, Wis.: University of Wisconsin Press, 1984.

———. *Negotiating with ETA: Obstacles to Peace in the Basque Country, 1975–1988.* Reno, Nev.: University of Nevada Press, 1990.

Douglass, William M. and Joseba Zulaika, "On the Interpretation of Terrorist Violence: ETA and the Basque Political Process," *Comparative Studies in Society and History* 32, no. 2 (April 1990): 238–57.

Jiménes, Fernando. "Spain: The Terrorist Challenge and the Government's Response," *Terrorism and Political Violence* 4, no. 4 (1992): 110–30.

Llera, Francisco J., et al. "ETA: From Secret Army to Social Movement; The Post-Franco Schism of the Basque Nationalist Movement," *Terrorism and Political Violence* 5, no. 3 (1993): 106–34.

Sullivan, John. *ETA and Basque Nationalism.* New York: Routledge, 1998.

Usher, Rod. "Terrorism: Violence Turns Green into Red," *Time,* 13 March 2000.

Zirakzadeh, Cyrus Ernesto. *A Rebellious People: Basques, Protests and Politics.* Reno, Nev.: University of Nevada Press, 1991.

Zulaika, Joseba. *Basque Violence: Metaphor and Sacrament.* Reno, Nev.: University of Nevada Press, 1988.

Guillaume de Syon

CHINA AND RELIGIOUS PROTEST: THE FALUN GONG

THE CONFLICT

A large religious movement called the Falun Gong has garnered a lot of attention in the People's Republic of China and around the world. China has determined that the organization is illegal, and has punished public practice of the religion with imprisonment.

Political

- China has a long history of violence and social discord associated with religious movements.

- The Chinese government views the Falun Gong as a cult and a threat to public order.

- Adherents to the Falun Gong regard the practice as a basic human right.

Religious

- The People's Republic of China does not recognize the right to religious practice and as a communist government does not support religious freedom.

The tension in Beijing's Tiananmen Square was palpable the morning of April 25, 2000. Plainclothes police officers milled around the square, anticipating a possible demonstration by adherents of the outlawed group known as Falun Gong. With prearranged precision, devotees of the group emerged from the crowds of tourists, lofted Falun Gong banners above their heads, and began practicing the organization's hallmark exercises. Other demonstrators chose simply to sit and meditate. The hodgepodge group included all types of people from middle-aged women to young children.

The demonstrators separated into small clusters throughout the compound. Patrolling police officers, expecting a more concerted gathering, were momentarily confused. Scattering to the different corners of the square, they descended on the protestors with determined force, punching some, muffling others, and eventually dragging them all away. Police forced those tourists who had witnessed the affair away from the square, but not before confiscating their film. Similar outbreaks continued throughout the afternoon. By day's end the police had forcibly removed approximately one hundred demonstrators from the courtyard.

For many international observers, the combative response of the police officers was extreme and disproportionate to the actual threat of the peaceful demonstrators. Why, they asked, did the government feel so threatened by a seemingly harmless group whose motto is "truth, compassion, and forbearance?" To understand the government's response to Falun Gong, it is necessary first to understand China's religious heritage.

HISTORICAL BACKGROUND

China's Religious Heritage

While Falun Gong claims to be an "advanced cultivation system of mind, body and spirit," officials in China's capital city of Beijing have derisively labeled it a harmful cult. Whether or not such a classification is appropriate it does reveal the government's attitude toward the organization and in part explains Beijing's recent reaction. Falun Gong, officials claim, is a modern version of the superstitious, anti-government religions that have colored China's past.

In the nineteenth century, China was home to many religions and philosophical traditions. The three most important, however, were Confucianism, Daoism, also known as Taoism, and Buddhism. Whereas Confucianism stressed social harmony and organization, Buddhism and Daoism focused on mystical, otherworldly pursuits. Government rituals and intellectual treatises helped define each of these belief systems, yet for most people, the three were not mutually exclusive. Instead, Chinese religion consisted of an amalgamation of Confucianism, Buddhism, and Daoism. Each contributed its own gods and saints to the limitless pantheon of deities. At various life-stages and in different circumstances, individuals would rely on one or more of these three traditions.

Not surprisingly, this fluid, malleable religious tradition was vulnerable to reinterpretation according to local needs and desires. At times, disgruntled individuals channeled popular religious conviction against the government. In other words, religion in China has often been the vehicle for mass dissent and rebellion. The nineteenth century was particularly rich in these types of religious movements. Often shrouded in secrecy, certain religious orders launched violent attacks against local officials and citizens. Two of the best known of these religious groups were the Taipings and the Boxers.

In 1850 Hong Xiuquan (Hung Hsiu-ch'uan) and his followers, known as the Taipings, attempted to establish the Heavenly Kingdom of Great Peace, or Taiping Tianguo. Hong claimed to be the son of God and the younger brother of Jesus Christ. He explained that God had instructed him to overthrow the imperial government, spread his religion, and establish heaven on earth. Though Hong couched his teachings in Christian terms, his theology was a conglomeration of both traditional Chinese and Western ideas. Hong's rebellion, which lasted well over a decade, eventually claimed the lives of millions of individuals and nearly toppled the central government.

CHRONOLOGY

1850 The Taipings attempt to establish the Heavenly Kingdom of Great Peace, leading to a decade-long rebellion that costs millions of lives and topples the central Chinese government.

1900 Boxers United in Righteousness attack and kill foreigners and other individuals deemed impure or unorthodox because of religious beliefs in the Boxer Rebellion.

1949 China's communist government is formed. "Unofficial" religions are outlawed and suppressed as deceitful and destructive.

1966–76 The Cultural Revolution, led by Mao Zedong, destroys temples and churches.

1992 The *Zhuan Falun*, the Fulon Gong bible, is published.

1999–2000 As the popularity and publicity of the Fulon Gong movement grows, the Chinese government asserts that it was a threat to order, as "cults" like the Taipings and the Boxers have been in the past. Arrests and imprisonment of Fulon Gong members increase.

In 1900 another group of devotees captured the government's attention. Known as the Boxers United in Righteousness, members of the group were frustrated over the growing influence of western missionaries. Drawing on supernatural powers, the Boxers believed they could rid China of Christianity and all foreign influence. Leaders of the movement claimed that with one hundred days of spiritual and physical training their followers would become immune to bullets, making them virtually invincible. Through an intricate program of rituals, incantations, and magic ceremonies the Boxers indoctrinated thousands into their ranks. The Chinese imperial court, frustrated over Western demands, gave implicit support to the Boxers, though the group was beyond the ability of the government to control. For several months during 1900 the Boxers attacked and killed any individual they deemed impure and unorthodox. Eventually, an alliance of Western powers militarily suppressed the group, but not until the Boxers had shown the immense influence of popular religion among the Chinese public.

MAP OF CHINA. *(© Maryland Cartographics. Reprinted with permission.)*

Suppression of Religion in China

In the early twentieth century Chinese intellectuals began attacking religion as irrational and superstitious. Founders of the 1922 Great Federation of Anti-Religionists promised "to sweep away the poison and harm of religion on behalf of human society. We profoundly deplore the fact that in human society religion has spread a poison which is, ten times, a hundred times, a thousand times worse than floods or ferocious animals." Not incidentally, the federation's membership included many future leaders of the Chinese Communist Party (CCP).

With the formation of the communist state in 1949, China's religious landscape changed drastically. Though the Chinese Communist Party claimed to protect freedom of religion, government leaders made a sharp distinction between "super-

stitions" and the more orthodox "integrated religious systems" including Buddhism, Islam, and Christianity. Officials believed the so-called superstitious folk religions not only wasted the resources of the nation but also attracted potential anti-government rebels such as occurred with the Taipings and the Boxers. As the Deputy Mayor of Shanghai explained in 1953, "Cults have been deceiving the masses under the cover of the burning of [incense], kowtowing before their shrines, living on vegetarian diets, and saying Buddhist prayers while in effect their organizations were actually engaged secretly in counter-revolutionary activities . . . ." For this reason, the government outlawed and suppressed all unofficial religions.

Besides outlawing "superstition" the new government allowed and even promoted the persecution of officially recognized "integrated religious systems." For instance, though the constitution guaranteed that "every citizen of the People's Republic of China shall have freedom of religious belief," the government also explained that "rural land belonging to ancestral shrines, temples, monasteries, [and] churches . . . shall be requisitioned." Believers were frequently harassed, interrogated, and blacklisted. At the same time, Beijing promoted the establishment of "loyal" churches, ministered by reliable supporters of the CCP, to replace congregations deemed too independent. In short, though the government theoretically allowed certain churches to exist, it sought to regulate and control them.

Nowhere was this policy more evident than in the Chinese province of Tibet. In 1959 one of Tibet's preeminent Buddhist leaders, the Dalai Lama, fled into exile to escape the persistent persecution of the Chinese government. Beijing responded by placing the other top Buddhist official, the Panchen Lama, under heavy surveillance. For the rest of his life, the Panchen Lama remained a virtual prisoner of the communist regime, unable to exercise complete authority within his religious community. When he died in 1989 leaders in Beijing quickly responded by selecting the new Panchen Lama. Besides controlling Tibet's leadership, the Chinese government has systematically destroyed approximately six thousand temples and killed several thousand Tibetans.

Catholics have experienced similar domination by the Chinese government. In an attempt to undermine the influence of the pope, Beijing established its own "patriotic" Catholic church in 1957. Within this church the government has final control over the selection and over the ordination of priests and bishops, despite the wishes of the Vatican. Meanwhile, the original pro-Vatican Catholic Church, known in China as the "church of silence," has secretly worked to maintain doctrinal control and influence over its followers. Nevertheless, members of both the "patriotic" and the "silent" Catholic churches have complained of persecution and been singled out as foreign spies working "under the cloak of religion." Not incidentally, in 2000 Pope John Paul II announced plans to canonize one hundred twenty Chinese martyrs of anti-Catholic persecution.

Opposition to organized religion reached a feverish pitch during the Cultural Revolution of 1966–76. The Cultural Revolution, led by Mao Zedong, was an attempt to reinvigorate Chinese communism and often included the destruction of cultural icons associated with the pre-communist era. Seen as a lingering remnant of the old society,

religion was a common target of the Cultural Revolution's zealous "red guards." These "guards," consisting of thousands of young men and women, destroyed innumerable temples, churches, and mosques throughout China. Centuries-old artifacts and relics fell victim to the unchecked enthusiasm of the "revolutionary" legions. The fact that any vestiges of religion survived this tumultuous decade is remarkable.

Current Religious Policy of the People's Republic of China

Following the 1976 death of Communist Party leader Mao Zedong, China underwent a rapid series of economic and political reforms. Simultaneously, Beijing began looking more favorably on organized religion. For the last two decades the government has encouraged the restoration of old temples and mosques. It believes such a change in policy, a significant departure from previous years, will encourage tourism and appease minority groups. Consequently, Daoism and other traditional Chinese religions have experienced a revival, and foreign religions, such as Islam and Christianity, have grown immensely.

Though the government has become more tolerant of major religions it has maintained its skepticism toward minor sects. Claiming that unofficial religions are frequently covers for anti-government forces and organized crime, officials have arrested and imprisoned various sect leaders. Although Beijing no longer sees religion as inherently bad, the government is still wary of religious-led disruption and possible rebellion.

The Emergence and Suppression of Falun Gong

Recently, adherents of the group Falun Gong have disturbed the ruling authorities in Beijing. Alternatively known as Falun Dafa or "Law of the Wheel," Falun Gong is an organization of individuals dedicated to the teachings of Li Hongzhi, founder of the movement. According to the group's publications, Falun Gong originated in prehistoric times, but was not widely understood until "Master Li" published *Zhuan Falun*—the Falun Gong bible—in 1992. Before establishing his organization Li had worked as a government grain clerk in relative anonymity. At the same time he became increasingly interested in the healing powers of traditional breathing exercises. By 1992 Li had begun teaching others his methods and assembling a group of followers.

Li claims that through a set of five exercises an individual can cultivate his or her mind, body,

MEMBERS OF THE BANNED SECT, FALUN GONG, STRUGGLE WITH POLICE DURING A PROTEST IN TIANANMEN SQUARE, BEIJING, CHINA. *(AP/Wide World Photos. Reproduced by permission.)*

and spirit. The exercises he advocates entail slow-motion martial arts movements that emphasize precision, fluidity, and breathing control. For example, the exercise known as "Buddha Showing Thousand Hands" requires the practitioner to "open all the energy channels and mobilize energy circulation in the body by stretching the body gradually and relaxing it suddenly." Another exercise, "Way of Strengthening Supernormal Powers," is "a sitting tranquil exercise to strengthen supernormal powers and energy potency." Li suggests that through these exercises the individual can cultivate the values of *zhen-shan-ren,* or "truth-compassion-forbearance." Furthermore, Li asserts that the practice of Falun Dafa will lead not only to physical and mental health, increasing one's moral standards, but also to spiritual enlightenment. The group's literature promises that, eventually, practitioners of Falun Dafa will acquire a small *falun,* or "wheel of law," in their lower abdomen. This wheel will continuously revolve and endlessly cultivate the powers of the devotee.

Since 1992 Falun Gong's popularity has soared. The organization claims to have one hundred million practitioners in more than thirty countries worldwide. While it is unlikely the actual number is that high, Falun Gong has clearly penetrated every level of Chinese society. Its adherents

are not radical political activists, angry minorities, or pro-democracy students. Instead, most are middle-aged men and women who represent China's middle class and who are attracted by the simple promise of enlightenment. Whether factory workers or housewives, they have been loyal supporters of the government and do not consider themselves a threat to society.

Though Falun Gong has attracted many adherents and shares much in common with other traditional Chinese belief systems the government does not see it as a mainstream religious movement. Instead, officials have highlighted the more eccentric aspects of the group. For instance, the government claims Falun Gong has caused the deaths of more than fifteen hundred individuals either through suicide or through the refusal of medical treatment. State television has issued reports on the murderous activities of some Falun Gong members. In one television program producers showed graphic pictures of a Falun Gong individual cutting open his own stomach with a pair of scissors hoping to find the "wheel of law" in his abdomen.

Yet the most offensive aspect of the organization, from the government's point of view, is its overwhelming popularity. Simply because it is influential, claiming a larger membership than the Chinese Communist Party, Falun Gong has the potential to challenge the government. As Wang Ruoshui, a former deputy editor-in-chief of the Communist Party's newspaper, explained, "[government officials] are emphasizing the Falun Gong's tight organization, as if this is really terrifying. The message they are sending is that any organization outside the system is illegal." Government leaders are also wary of the organization's use of the Internet, taking Falun Gong beyond the rigid control of party media. Most alarming, however, is the prospect that Falun Gong is winning followers among the highest levels of government. In 1999 President Jiang Zemin discovered that the navy had been printing copies of *Zhuan Falun.* He also found that several party members were active supporters of the movement. Some sources claim as many as seven hundred thousand members of the Chinese Communist Party belong to Falun Gong, including several high-ranking military leaders and at least one Politburo standing committee member. For these reasons the government has continued to target the organization in newspapers, television programs, and in official announcements.

Falun Gong members have not passively accepted government-sponsored misinformation regarding their organization. Following a 1998 television program critical of Falun Gong the group sponsored a large protest outside the television studio. In 1999, when an academic journal published an article outlining the dangers of cults, Falun Gong practitioners again launched a large demonstration. According to government sources Falun Gong was responsible for at least eighteen separate protests during 1998 and 1999.

Despite the frequency of such protests, most were limited in size and intensity. Consequently, the massive protest of April 1999, truly surprised the government. On the morning of April 25, approximately ten thousand Falun Gong practitioners descended on Zhongnanhai, the office and residence compound for most of China's top leaders. Participants remained calm as they sat and meditated throughout the courtyard. Instead of signs and placards, each carried a small cushion to sit on. Soon the line of demonstrators extended over two miles long. The police, caught off-guard and bewildered by the demonstrators' methods, allowed the protest to go on throughout the day and into the evening. As one participant quoted in the *New York Times* explained, "What we stand for is good for the nation and good for society, so how can we threaten anyone? [The government officials] don't understand us. We want understanding." Local residents were equally confused about the demonstrations. "They're crazy," said one such observer, "but there are a lot of them, so the government has to listen."

Not surprisingly, the government did listen. The response, however, was not what the protestors anticipated. Rather than sitting with the group's leaders for an open dialogue government officials responded by targeting Falun Gong members for increased attack. Shortly after the massive April protest the government sent a directive to various business, government, and factory leaders asking each of them to identify Falun Gong adherents within their organizations. Many work leaders, fearing unnecessary interruptions in business, were reluctant to do so. Nevertheless, by early summer those individuals partial to Falun Gong were increasingly on the defensive.

In midsummer the government stepped up its persecution of Falun Gong. On July 22, 1999, the Ministry of Civil Affairs issued a declaration that explained, "the Falun Dafa Institute, and the Falun Gong organization under its manipulation, is an unlawful organization that has to be outlawed." The declaration continued, saying, "No one may hang or post in any place . . . signs that advertise Falun Dafa. No one may distribute in any place . . . propaganda materials that advertise Falun Dafa. No one may assemble in any place people for promot-

FOLLOWERS OF FALUN GONG CELEBRATE THEIR EIGHTH ANNIVERSARY AS THEY PERFORM MEDITATION EXERCISES NEAR THE BANK OF CHINA, HONG KONG. *(AP/Wide World Photos. Reproduced by permission.)*

ing Falun Dafa activities. . . . Activities . . . for the purpose of protecting and advertising Falun Dafa are prohibited." It concluded with a final warning stating, "Those whose acts of violating the above rules constitute a crime shall be held accountable for their crime; and if their acts do not constitute a crime, they shall be disciplined or punished according to the law."

On October 31, 1999, the government completed the legal suppression of Falun Gong with a new anti-cult law. The law called on the judicial system and the police to be on guard for cult activities and be prepared to act against them. It also decreed jail sentences of three to seven years for cult members who disrupted public order, and sentences of at least seven years for the leaders of such organizations. Not surprisingly, many have accused the government of applying the law retroactively in the prosecution of Falun Gong leaders and sympathizers.

As the government passed such laws against Falun Gong the police began rounding up and arresting members of the organization. According to Falun Gong reports police have arrested more than thirty-five thousand followers since July 1999. At least five thousand of those were allegedly sent directly to labor-camps without trial. As Gail Rachlin, a Falun Gong spokesperson in New York, explained, "In the one year since [the April] gathering, we have come to witness the Chinese government execute one of the largest, harshest and most arbitrary persecutions in modern history." For their part, officials claim Chinese courts have tried 2,591 cases related to Falun Gong. Of the ninety-nine they have concluded, the judges have sentenced eighty-four individuals to prison—some for ten years or more. Human rights groups have been concerned over the number of people sent to prison and for the treatment they have received. According to the British Broadcasting Company (BBC), reports of torture have become common, including the use of cattle prods and drug injections. According to a Hong Kong human rights group, at least sixteen Falun Gong individuals have died in police custody since April 1999.

RECENT HISTORY AND THE FUTURE

Despite the efforts of the government and the police, protests led by Falun Gong supporters continue to occur in China. Though no accurate tally is available, the official Chinese news agency has admitted the protests have become a nearly uncontrollable problem. "Since July 22, 1999, Falun Gong members have been causing trouble on and around Tiananmen Square in central Beijing nearly every day," the agency reported. "Some of the troublemakers were practicing Falun Gong, some were protesting, banners in hand and shouting slogans, and some were even attempting to detonate explosives." In the days leading up to the one-year anniversary of the April 1999 protest, demonstrations increased in frequency and participants. On April 13, 2000, police arrested more than two hundred individuals in downtown Beijing, kicking and punching many of them. Less than two weeks later

an additional one hundred protestors converged on Tiananmen Square, again facing arrest and detention. Though these protests are less sizable than the ten thousand-member sit-in of 1999, they are nonetheless symbolic of the enduring strength of the Falun Gong movement.

What, then, is the future of Falun Gong in China? According to China's Foreign Ministry Spokesperson, Sun Yuxi, "[China's] struggle to combat the Falun Gong cult has registered a success." Sun explains that ninety-eight percent of the group's adherents have left Falun Gong, leaving a small minority to blame for "creating trouble." Such claims may not be simple bravado. A recent poll reported by *Voices of China* shows sixty-three percent of Chinese have a negative opinion toward Falun Gong and forty-seven percent believe it is harmful to Chinese society. Facing a determined government and an unsupportive populace, it may be safe to assume Falun Gong will simply disintegrate. Even Li Hongzhi has dropped from the public arena recently, living in secrecy in New York as his movement struggles to find new leadership. Falun Gong may soon join the Taipings and the Boxers in China's dustbin of history.

On the other hand persecution and martyrdom frequently lead to increased devotion and even public sympathy. For example, while sixty-three percent of Chinese have a negative opinion toward Falun Gong, only thirty-one percent agree with the government's handling of the situation and sixty-two percent feel the government banned the organization purely for political reasons. In other words, though they may not agree with the group's actions, many people apparently feel some degree of sympathy toward Falun Gong. Furthermore, as one journalist pointed out, "a lot of Falun Gong practitioners were not originally in opposition to the government, [but] they are now . . . . The government drew a line, and they were on the other side of it." The government's actions have also led to increased international attention on the group. Falun Gong study groups have sprung up worldwide, and the organization continues to grow. Many international adherents are supportive of their Chinese counterparts. Some have chosen to travel to China to publicly protest the government's actions. With their foreign passports, they know their jail sentences will be short and relatively painless. In fact, some view prison as part of their purification process.

Whatever the future of Falun Gong, the group's conflict with the Chinese government has highlighted existing tensions in China. Communism, it appears, no longer has a monopoly on the

THE QUESTION OF RELIGIOUS EXTREMISM

China is not alone in its efforts to suppress a minority religious movement. France, Germany, and Belgium have all created commissions that investigate newly created religious sects. France recently passed a bill giving the government the authority to dissolve religious groups identified as cults that foster a "state of mental or physical dependence." Pakistan has the Blasphemy Law, which imposes the death penalty for defamatory actions including the profession of belief in prohibited faiths. Russia's Religion Law imposes a complicated registration process on all religions that, according to its critics, was designed to squelch all but the Russian Orthodox Church. And, in Uzbekistan, over five thousand people have been imprisoned under provisions of the Law on Freedom of Conscience and Religious Organizations. Primarily targeting orthodox Muslims, the law forbids "ritual dress" in public, among other restrictions. These are only a few examples of laws currently enforced that were written to protect the public from the potential violence that most governments believe is the inevitable result of religious extremism.

What these governments fear is fanaticism, a devotion to faith so extreme that public order and safety are threatened. Legislators worldwide point to cults like the Aum Shinrikyo in Japan, the Buddhist splinter group in Japan responsible for releasing poisonous gas into the Tokyo subway system in 1995, as evidence that cults encourage violence. Also frequently cited are groups such as the People's Temple Christian Church, founded by Jim Jones, whose nine hundred members committed mass suicide in 1978, and Uganda's Movement for the Extreme Restoration of the Ten Commandments, which put to death nearly one thousand members in March 2000.

Even though these are widely acknowledged as extreme examples, they are still used as proof that the religious movements identified as cults—groups defined as an elite society that form around a self-appointed, dogmatic leader that may use psychological coercion to indoctrinate and retain members—are inherently dangerous.

As hazardous as some cult members have proven to be to themselves and to the public, the laws designed to guard against their excesses have resulted in the restriction of religious freedom and political voice that often accompanies a religious movement. Whether by design or by practice, laws that restrict religious expression often result in the politicization of the faith being repressed. As the United States Advisory Committee on Religious Freedom Abroad notes, "In societies where the government imposes strict political ideology and control over the populace, including on religious matters, many individuals and communities of faith operate underground and risk harassment, detention, and imprisonment." This in turn can lead to the very violence the laws sought to prevent as suppression almost inevitably fuels fanaticism.

This paradox led the United Nations to appoint a Special Rapporteur on the Elimination of all Forms of Religious Intolerance. While this recently-created office recognizes that the "question of religious extremism" is one of the fundamental issues it will address, it also notes that such extremism needs to be examined within the "larger context of the economic, social, and political conditions that foster it." By doing so, it hopes to discover the root causes of religious fanaticism and prevent its potentially violent expression.

people's loyalty, and individuals are looking elsewhere for sources of inspiration and relief. Falun Gong has also revealed the ruling party's determination to retain control over organized religion. Like Falun Gong practitioners, Christians, Muslims, and Tibetan Buddhists have experienced increased persecution since the Falun Gong protests of 1999, including arrest and imprisonment. While the government officially protects freedom of religion, the nation's leaders are still very much aware of the potentially rebellious power of popular spiritual belief.

BIBLIOGRAPHY

"Beijing Breaks up Falungong Protests." *Straits Times.* 14 April 2000. http://web3.asia1.com.sg/archive/st/5/asia/ea4_0414.html (17 April 2000).

"China Hopes for Improved Ties with Vatican." Agence France-Presse. 11 May 2000. http://asia.dailynews.yahoo.com/headlines/asia/afp/article.html?s=asia/headlines/000511/asia/afp/China_hopes_for_improved_ties_with_Vatican.html (11 May 2000).

"China Quickly Quashes Falun Gong Protest." Associated Press. 25 April 2000. http://deseretnews.com/dn/view/0,1249,165007380,00.html (22 May 2000).

"China's Rules." *Washington Post.* 26 April 2000. http://www.washingtonpost.com/wp-dyn/opinion/A15755-2000Apr25.html (26 April 2000).

Eckholm, Erik. "China Enacts Strict Law Aimed at Smashing Cult." *New York Times.* 31 October 1999. http://www.nytimes.com/library/world/asia/103199china-cult.html (8 May 2000).

Faison, Seth. "Ten Thousand Protesters in Beijing Urge Cult's Recognition." *New York Times.* web edition. 26 April 1999. http://www.nytimes.com/library/world/asia/042699china-protest.html (8 May 2000).

"Falun Dafa: A High Level Cultivation Practice of Mind and Body Based on Zhen-Shan-Ren (Truth-Compassion-Forbearance)," a printed informational packet on Falun Gong provided to David Kenley by Frank Q. Ye, a Falun Gong practitioner from the National Institutes of Health in Bethesda, Maryland.

"Falun Gong Mass Arrest." *BBC News Online.* 25 April 2000. http://news.bbc.co.uk/hi/english/world/asia-pacific/newsid_724000/724793.stm (25 April 2000).

"An Introduction to Falun Dafa." http://falundafa.ca/introduction/intro_index.htm (22 May 2000).

Holland, Lorien. "Breaking The Wheel." *Far Eastern Economic Review.* 5 August 1999. http://www.feer.com/9908_05/p16china.html (26 April 2000).

Human Rights Watch. *China: State Control of Religion.* New York: Human Rights Watch, 1997.

Lawrence, Susan V. "Faith and Fear." *Far Eastern Economic Review.* 20 April 2000. http://www.feer.com/_0004_20/p16china.html (22 May 2000).

———. "Stressful Summer." *Far Eastern Economic Review.* 19 August 1999. http://www.feer.com/9908_19/p16china.html (26 April 2000).

Li Hongzhi. *Zhuan falun.* [Turning the Wheel of Law]. Beijing: Zhongguo guangbo dianshi chubanshe, 1994.

Lu Mei. "The Controversy over Falun Gong: What Do Chinese People Think?" *The Voices of Chinese.* http://www.voicesofchinese.org/falun/surveyrpt.shtml (24 April 2000).

Luo Zhufeng, ed. *Religion Under Socialism in China.* Trans. by Donald MacInnis and Zheng Xi'an. Armonk, N.Y.: M.E. Sharpe, 1991.

MacInnes, Donald E. *Religion in China Today: Policy and Practice.* Maryknoll, N.Y.: Orbis, 1989.

———. *Religious Policy and Practice in Communist China: A Documentary History.* New York: Macmillan, 1972.

Munro, Robin, ed. *Syncretic Sects and Secret Societies: Revival in the 1980s.* Armonk, N.Y.: M.E. Sharpe, 1989.

Pas, Julian F., ed. *The Turning of the Tide: Religion in China Today.* New York: Oxford University Press, 1989.

Penny, Benjamin. "Qigong, Daoism and Science: Some Contexts for the Qigong Boom." In *Modernization of the Chinese Past.* Honolulu, Hawaii: University of Hawaii Press, 1993.

The People's Republic of China Ministry of Public Security. "Text of Notice Banning Sect." *BBC News Online.* 22 July 1999. http://news.bbc.co.uk/hi/english/world/monitoring/newsid_400000/400943.stm (11 May 2000).

"Report: China Arrests at least 10 Underground Christian Leaders." *Cnn.com.* 18 May 2000. http://www.cnn.com/2000/ASIANOW/east/05/17/china.religion.ap/index.html (18 May 2000).

Rosenthal, Elisabeth. "China Finally Admits It: Falun Gong A Problem." *Chicago Tribune.* web edition. 21 April 2000. http://chicagotribune.com/news/nationworld/article/0,2669,SAV-0004210195,FF.html (24 April 2000).

"Sect Member Dies in Police Custody." *South China Morning Post.* 26 April 2000. http://www.scmp.com/News/China/Article/FullText_asp_ArticleID-20000426031821300.asp (26 April 2000).

"Taipei Devotees Lend Support to Besieged Brethren." *South China Morning Post.* 26 April 2000. http://www.scmp.com/News/China/Article/FullText_asp_ArticleID-20000426031830784.asp (26 April 2000).

Yamamoto, Tatsuro and Sumiko. "The Anti-Christian Movement in China, 1922–1927," *Far Eastern Quarterly,* February 1953, 138.

Xu Jianguo, *Jiefang Ribao* [Liberation Daily], Shanghai, 8 June 1953, and Shanghai Radio. June 7, 1953 as quoted in Donald E. MacInnis, *Religious Policy and Practice in Communist China.* New York: Macmillan, 1972: 178.

Zhu Xiaoyang and Benjamin Penny, eds. *The Qigong Boom.* Trans. by Paul Lam and John Minford. Armonk, N.Y.: M.E. Sharpe, 1994.

David L. Kenley

CHINA AND THE WORLD TRADE ORGANIZATION: VALUES IN CONFLICT

The People's Republic of China seeks membership in the World Trade Organization (WTO). This wish has engendered debate within China, the United States, and throughout the world. Those opposing China's admission present a litany of grievances. China remains an authoritarian state with a communist leadership. Its people cannot vote for that leadership, opponents note, yet the United States wants to let China into an international organization formed under the principles of democracy and liberalism. The WTO is founded on the notion of fair competition, yet China engages in slave labor. American politicians speak of jobs for all Americans, yet China will surely take jobs away from the United States with the lure of its low wages.

Proponents of China's admission counter that such arguments are exaggerated and fail to examine the big picture. For example, while some jobs will be lost, others will be created, and prices for goods in the United States will fall. Moreover, supporters assert that while it is true that China is currently authoritarian, the best way to liberalize its society is to invite it into the community of nations, not to exclude it. WTO admission would serve to welcome China into the world. Finally an excluded, closed, and embittered China is a dangerous China. An isolated or ostracized China might start a war. Again, the best way to avoid this is to fully integrate China into the world's economy. To better understand this situation, a number of questions need to be answered in depth: What is the WTO? Why does China seek admission? What are the arguments for and against such admission?

HISTORICAL BACKGROUND

The WTO, an international organization established on January 1, 1995, was formed to main-

THE CONFLICT

The People's Republic of China has applied for membership in the World Trade Organization. As the application winds through the bureaucracy and politics of approval, proponents and opponents debate whether membership will discourage China from human rights abuses, harm the economy of the United States and other Western nations, and encourage China to move toward a more open and participatory system of government.

Political

- China has a long history of oppressing political dissidents and religious believers. Opponents to China's WTO membership believe that China should have to demonstrate acceptance of differing views and a meaningful democracy, as well as putting an end to human and civil rights abuses before joining the WTO.

- Proponents of China's WTO membership believe that the requirements regarding the law and open decision-making regarding trade will encourage China's liberalization.

Economic

- Opponents feel that cheap Chinese manufactured goods—produced with low-wage or slave labor with no concern for the environment—will unfairly undermine Western manufacturing, causing the loss of jobs and harming the economy.

- Others feel that increased Chinese trade may undermine the existing Chinese government-controlled companies, causing economic dislocation and a too-rapid transformation in China.

CHRONOLOGY

1944 The Bretton Woods Conference is held. Forty-four countries lay out rules and institutions to govern post-World War II international trade and monetary relations.

1948 The General Agreement on Tariffs and Trade (GATT) is established. Twenty-three countries sign the charter in Havana, Cuba, to reduce customs tariffs.

1994 A GATT ministers meeting in Marrakesh, Morocco, establishes the World Trade Organization (WTO).

2000 China is granted Permanent Normal Trade Relations status by the United States, a major hurdle to securing membership in the WTO. Protests regarding China's membership in the WTO take place at major trade conferences around the world.

tain and expand an open, liberal system of international trade. The WTO works to reduce barriers to free trade and open markets. It is an outgrowth of the 1947 General Agreement on Tariffs and Trade (GATT). GATT was developed in response to the closed international trading system, which reduces international trade by placing limits on imports and large tariffs, or taxes, on imports. Closed international trading exacerbated the Great Depression and helped lead to World War II. GATT was originally to be a temporary organization until the International Trade Organization (ITO) was approved. When the ITO failed to win ratification, however, GATT was itself used to maintain an open system of international trade among participants. This was far more than GATT was designed to accomplish.

Though GATT struggled for decades to maintain free trade, its flaws became more apparent as time passed. For example, GATT only covered goods, not services such as consulting and banking. Yet the world's economy has become increasingly service oriented, especially among more developed countries. GATT's dispute settlement system was subject to abuse by member states, who slowly made the system ineffective. GATT did not deal well with non-tariff barriers (NTBs), which are barriers to trade other than overt taxes at the border. All countries thus protected their economies from free trade using NTBs. Free trade was in-

creasingly undermined. A long series of negotiations, such as the Tokyo Round, failed to invigorate the GATT. Finally, after eight years of negotiations ending in 1994, the Uruguay Round succeeded in establishing the WTO.

The World Trade Organization

The WTO provides a framework for open international trade by setting rules for such trade, by settling trade disputes, and by providing for continued negotiations toward further trade liberalization. A revised GATT remains a part of the WTO, but the WTO is now a broader umbrella organization. It has 136 members as of April 2000, with more seeking membership; the United States and the European Union are very influential in determining membership in the WTO.

The World Trade Organization is founded on the idea that free trade creates growth because it allows people to specialize in what they do best, what economists call comparative advantage. The organization seeks to lower barriers to free trade so that people can profitably concentrate on what they do best in their economies. The WTO also encourages predictability in world trade by setting certain rules that all members must obey. When all members obey the same rules, international trade and investment are encouraged. The WTO achieves predictability through a "rules-based system." Market access will not change suddenly or arbitrarily. Thus, businesses can effectively plan and real gains from trade be achieved. The WTO also creates something of a level playing field inasmuch as discrimination cannot occur within a market.

In its operation, the WTO operates on a number of standards to help set the "rules." It does not forbid tariffs, a form of economic protectionism, designed to encourage the purchase of goods made within a country by making goods from outside a country more expensive. Rather, the WTO lessens the negative effects of protectionism through the application of certain of its principles. The first principle is "most favored nation" status, or MFN. MFN requires non-discrimination among trading partners. Any member state must treat all products from all other states equally. The best trade deal given to any single member state must be given to all other member states. Treatment can be no less favorable than that provided to the "most favored nation." So, for example, if the United States decides to allow Mexico to export shoes to the United States at a reduced tariff, all other states must also be granted the reduced tariff. All trading partners receive the same benefits.

One potential element of confusion is the difference between MFN and normal trade relations (NTR) or permanent normal trade relations (PNTR). NTR means the same things as MFN. NTR is simply the term used in U.S. domestic politics. Any state that has NTR with the United States has been granted MFN for purposes of the WTO.

China was a special case until the year 2000 because its MFN status had to be renewed every year in the United States. Title IV of the Trade Act of 1974, also known as the Jackson-Vanik legislation, barred MFN status to certain non-market, usually communist, countries. The U.S. president could waive this policy of withholding MFN status. Such a waiver could be overturned by a congressional vote, though Congress never overturned a presidential waiver to China. Instead, Congress used these votes to voice displeasure with various Chinese policies ranging from freedom of religion to human rights to weapons proliferation. The votes became convenient soapboxes for congressional members to complain about U.S.-China relations without ever having to actually harm U.S. economic interests by revoking the Jackson-Vanik waiver.

Most observers agree that Jackson-Vanik did not comply with the WTO requirement that all rights arising thereunder must be "unconditional." Consequently, once China joins the WTO, the United States would be in violation of the organization's principles because Jackson-Vanik creates a condition to MFN status. China's rights are not unconditional if the United States can revoke them each year, as allowed under Jackson-Vanik. Because of this conflict of law, China had to be granted PNTR by the United States. This occurred, with considerable debate, in mid-2000.

A second key WTO principle is national treatment. National treatment requires that, once a product enters any member state, it must be treated the same as all domestic products within that state. This means that, while tariffs are acceptable—though they must be applied equally according to MFN—foreign and domestic products cannot be treated differently once inside the country. Once imports enter a country, they must be treated the same as local products.

A third key WTO principle is transparency. If products are to be treated equally in a domestic market, it is important that the rules and regulations within that domestic market be available and accessible to all parties. It is important, in order to determine whether a state is complying with WTO

LIST OF ABBREVIATIONS

General Agreement on Tariffs and Trade (GATT)

Intellectual Property (IP)

International Trade Organization (ITO)

Memoranda of Understanding (MOUs)

Most Favored Nation (MFN)

Non-Tariff Barriers (NTBs)

Normal Trade Relations (NTR)

Permanent Normal Trade Relations (PNTR)

State Owned Enterprises (SOEs)

World Trade Organization (WTO)

rules, to be able to examine its domestic law. Clearly presented and accessible laws are necessary to determine the nature of domestic laws and to understand how they are being enforced. If the laws aren't transparent—clear and accessible—there is an opportunity for protectionism because local or domestic people can manipulate local rules to their own advantage. Clear rules reduce the opportunity for protectionism as well as provide predictability. Uncertainty, on the other hand, reduces opportunities for trade because of the greater potential for losses.

The fourth key WTO principle is that of "rule of law." The WTO relies on the rule of law in its member states. Rule of law broadly includes those elements of a liberal system of law designed to serve the people and limit government. In this regard, law should be applied fairly and equally to all; it should include due process, open knowledge of the law, the right to appeal, unbiased justice, and finally, the judiciary should be independent. Rule of law is important for enforcing the promises in the contract, for minimizing corruption, and for allowing a market economy to thrive. Moreover, the WTO dispute settlement system depends upon member states' legal systems to provide accurate information and to enforce WTO rulings.

A few additional points are important beyond these four key WTO principles. The WTO covers far more trade related issues that did GATT. While GATT mainly concerned itself with traded goods, the WTO also covers trade in certain services such as banking and finance, accounting, insurance, and distribution. Services make up the bulk of the U.S. economy and represent American "comparative advantage." Opening markets to services is thus important to the United States. Similarly, the WTO includes certain protections for intellectual property (IP). Intellectual property consists of patents, trademarks, copyrights, and other protections for ideas. It is important to reward and protect ideas in order to provide incentive for further innovation. The WTO seeks to reward creators and provide incentive for further creation.

In addition to these new subject areas the WTO has improved dispute resolution and enforcement of its rules. In brief, members can bring other members before dispute settlement panels for violating WTO rules or even for violating the spirit of the WTO. An appeals system also exists. If the guilty party does not comply with a decision, the victim can impose penalties similar to the violations committed by the guilty party. It is much more difficult to delay or evade dispute settlement under the WTO than it was under GATT. The WTO is a more legalistic system than was the GATT system, and it is more clearly designed to guarantee rights arising under its authority.

The WTO seeks increased market access, economic competition, and fairness, while lowering transaction costs. The organization was not formed from a single agreement as was GATT. It is instead a complex international organization designed to administer numerous agreements, including, but not limited to, GATT. The WTO includes various new areas, which were previously domestic issues, such as intellectual property. In this regard, the WTO represents a significant expansion of international law. The WTO is expected to enhance world income by as much as one percent per year—though this figure is almost certainly exaggerated and these gains will probably be unevenly spread and likely benefit industrialized countries disproportionately.

Procedure for Joining the WTO

To join the WTO, China, like other nations applying for membership, must follow specific procedures. First, China must enter into bilateral agreements designed to open China's markets, called market access agreements, with a variety of states, including the United States and the European Union (E.U.) which represents its members as a single entity in the WTO. Because of the MFN requirement, China must provide all members with access equal to the most generous bilateral deal to

which it agrees. Beyond this, China must engage in multilateral negotiations with a WTO working party in order to ensure China's compliance with WTO rules and regulations, including the key principles discussed above. These negotiations will specify how China will meet its WTO obligations. After the bilateral and multilateral agreements are concluded, the WTO General Council, which includes all member states, must approve China's admission by a two-thirds majority. The United States and China concluded their bilateral agreement in November 1999 under the U.S.-China Market Access Agreement. These concessions are generally to take effect one to six years after China becomes a WTO member. The European Union and China reached their bilateral agreement in May 2000. Other bilateral negotiations continue, as do the multilateral negotiations, and these should be concluded sometime in 2001. The WTO General Council would then presumably approve China. Six months thereafter China would officially become a WTO member.

China and WTO Admission

China's economy grew at a phenomenal rate since economic liberalization began in the late 1970s. This rapid transformation from a communist economic system, whereby the economy was directed by the government, to a mixed, though by no means market, economy is nothing short of amazing. A market economy allows prices and production decisions to be dictated by the market—by supply and demand for goods and services. A mixed economy has features of both a government-directed economy and a market economy. However, economic growth in China has begun to stagnate, while foreign investment has fallen off. China's leadership is looking for ways to renew economic growth, but it also fears social instability. China's reformers face challenges from hard-line Communist Party officials who feel threatened by having to give up the power inherent in a government-directed economy.

The hard-liners have allies in their opposition to free trade. Free trade is often opposed by groups seeking economic protection, and China is no different. Local people and the businesses for which they work fear international competition. Certain jobs, such as in farming, are threatened by more efficient foreign production. These local interests bring pressure on local authorities who, therefore, oppose further economic liberalization. It is a natural outgrowth then that a combination of hard-line communist officials at the national level, along with local officials, business managers, and their

A SHOE SHOP CLERK HOLDS UP A FAKE SHOE IN SHANGHAI, CHINA, AS JUST SEVEN WORLD TRADE ORGANIZATION MEMBERS HAVE YET TO APPROVE CHINA'S BID TO JOIN THE TRADE GROUP. *(AP/Wide World Photos. Reproduced by permission.)*

employees, oppose further economic liberalization in fear for their own positions.

Reform-minded Communist officials seek economic liberalization for a number of reasons. First, and most simply, economic growth is stagnating in China. Most particularly, two important sectors of the economy are ailing: state owned enterprises (SOEs) and the financial system, consisting of banks and other financial institutions.

SOEs are businesses owned by the Chinese state and have a reputation for gross inefficiency. Many are bankrupt, though the government will not allow them to fail and props them up with additional funding. China will not allow the failure of the SOEs because of their importance to the economy. Since, as Harry Broadman reports in "China's Membership in the WTO and Enterprise Reform: The Challenges for Accession and Beyond," SOEs account for perhaps "one-third of national production, two-thirds of total assets, two-thirds of urban employment, and three-fourths of investment;" they are very important to China's overall economy. Moreover, they provide a social safety net not provided by the government, including housing, schools, and medical services. Additionally, SOEs represent major economic sectors such as heavy industry and key services. They

are protected from international competition through a variety of non-tariff barriers (NTBs), subsidies, and easy credit. On the one hand, SOEs are dragging the economy down. On the other hand, immediate economic competition would kill many SOEs, creating millions of unemployed and angry workers who lack any sort of social safety net. Political and social instability could follow.

China's national government first attempted to deal with this situation by injecting competition into the SOEs. China decentralized political authority and allowed local government to supervise the SOEs in hopes that regional competition would follow. This only complicated the picture, however, as local authorities now have an even greater stake in SOE survival and therefore seek to prevent painful reforms that would threaten SOEs. The central Chinese government does not want large-scale privatization, which would help generate competition, because it is not willing to release its control on the economy.

The SOE problem is complicated by the fact that the Chinese government continually extends credit to the SOEs. China forces its banks, which are also state-owned, to make loans to the SOEs. Since the SOEs seldom make money, they seldom repay their debts. Thus the financial sector has

PROTESTING THE ONGOING WORLD TRADE ORGANIZATION CONFERENCE IN SEATTLE, WASHINGTON, DEMON-STRATORS RALLY OUTSIDE THE U.S. CONSULATE IN HONG KONG. *(AP/Wide World Photos. Reproduced by permission.)*

come under severe strain. As the financial sector has come under pressure, economic problems have arisen. Essentially, the entire economy is being stressed because it is forced to carry the SOEs. This, in turn, has driven away much foreign investment. Yet without foreign investment, China's economic growth cannot continue. Foreign investors demand sound macroeconomic conditions, which means ending SOE subsidies. But the subsidies are the only way many SOEs manage to stay in business. Unwilling to let the SOEs float or sink on their own merit, China is in a difficult position.

Reformers seek to resolve the SOE dilemma by feeding greater competition into China in a new way. Their plan is to join the WTO, slowly open markets, and thus force the SOEs to become more competitive. The WTO allows the central government to demand painful but necessary, domestic adjustments. Domestic forces in China that are threatened by these changes, such as local interests and hard-liners, will surely fight these reforms, and WTO membership. China needs continued economic growth for social and political stability, yet this very growth will, at least in the short-term, intensify the very instability it is designed to reduce.

China's membership in the WTO should promote investment, encourage competition and economic growth, and enhance the political position of the reformers. If it succeeds it should provide social and political stability. This, in turn, should enhance China's position as a rising world power. Competition, it is hoped, will strengthen the domestic economy and encourage investment. Greater efficiency brings lower prices, increases production, and benefits consumers who therefore provide stability. The SOEs, it is hoped, can become profitable, taking stress off the financial sector, freeing up funds for other investment, improving macroeconomic conditions, and encouraging foreign investment. At the same time, corruption and bureaucratic red tape are acute and must be reduced. All of these goals, in turn, are dependent on implementing rule of law in China. This is perhaps the most difficult adjustment because it threatens the Chinese Communist Party's power: The party would no longer be above the law; the law would no longer exist to serve the state.

China's economy is likely to be buffeted by the changes demanded by the WTO. In particular, SOE employees and farmers are likely to suffer extremely high unemployment, possibly in the hundreds of millions. The financial system itself will be sorely tested, potentially resulting in the sort of currency instability that rocked Asia and Russia in the summer of 1998. The WTO also requires that the government give up some of its power, a notion China's nationalists will be uncomfortable with accepting. The increasing inequality of incomes that occurs with economic competition is antithetical to communism and will cause fundamental questions to arise about the country's political system.

Much short-term hardship will likely occur, and it is not clear whether China's political system can withstand the stress. China will likely attempt to gain the benefits of WTO membership while minimizing the costs by engaging in continued protectionism. This route, however, has dangers as well. The WTO may not accept this or could undergo considerable internal conflict attempting to resist China's intransigence. If China were to refuse to comply with the decisions of the WTO, the WTO's authority and ability to make and enforce laws would be questioned. In such an environment, other members might begin to refuse to comply and the WTO itself could collapse. Alternatively, without real liberalization, China may not reinvigorate its economy. Clearly, domestic Chinese arguments exist on both sides of the WTO question. The debate over the wisdom of allowing China membership in the WTO also rages in the United States.

Arguments Favoring China's Accession to the WTO

Arguments favoring China's accession to the World Trade Organization are varied and sometimes inconsistent. Perhaps the most obvious, though by no means most convincing, U.S. argument asserts that allowing China to join the WTO will create American jobs, especially in higher-paying professions. Jobs should be created in high technology, professional services, and other areas where the United States has comparative advantage.

Perhaps a sounder argument is that U.S. corporate profits should grow as a result of China joining the WTO. U.S. companies will have a huge new market open to them. More U.S. firms should be able to sell products in China as tariffs drop. More U.S. companies, especially in banking and insurance will be able to do business in China. U.S. agricultural concerns should also benefit, with $1.5 billion in profits estimated per year. As profits rise so do the incomes of Americans holding stock in these companies. More Americans hold more stock today than ever before. Similarly, the protection of intellectual property envisioned by the WTO can only help U.S. firms, individuals, and the overall American economy. Still, if one only examines sales in China, it is not immediately obvious that America is a net-winner in terms of value derived from trade. However, if U.S. companies move some production to China, corporate profits should rise substantially as the costs of production decline. China's membership in the WTO, it is argued, also locks in all these economic benefits. Overall, the benefits of China's entry are an improvement over the current situation. It opens markets and keeps them open. Ultimately the entire world benefits from trade because more goods can be produced using comparative advantage.

Others favor China's accession in order to more fully integrate China into the world economy under liberal, free market rules and, therefore, the broader liberal world order. A host of benefits allegedly arise from China's integration. For example, if China abides by WTO rules it should rapidly expand economically after an initial adjustment period. The quickest way for China to develop economically is to take advantage of its comparative labor advantage. All sorts of benefits arise out of China's economic growth. For example, China's middle class should expand. A large middle class has been identified as a prerequisite to democracy. Similarly, this dispersion of wealth to new groups and areas should create groups autonomous from the Communist Party and, potentially, a more civil society. Civil society is also often identified as a prerequisite for democracy. One advantage to China's becoming a democracy is that democracies do not generally disagree ideologically and may be less likely to engage in violent conflict. Thus, the more democracies there are in the world, the less war. This is especially important among "great powers" such as China and the United States, where a war could become a nuclear one. Democracies also typically do not abuse the human rights of their citizens.

A richer, more liberal China, it is argued, is a more cooperative China. Hence, greater cooperation may be expeected in areas as varied as nuclear proliferation, the environment, and resolution of world disorder. A more cooperative China might peaceably resolve different issues such as the contested Spratly Islands and Taiwan. In the alternative, a China kept out of the WTO may be angry and bitter. Such a China has less invested in the status quo and may become an anti-status quo player, such as Nazi Germany or the Soviet Union. Such powers seek to change the status quo, often violently.

On a narrower level, membership in the WTO not only solidifies current reforms but also promotes the rule of law. More foreign investment is likely when the rule of law is present because the system becomes more predictable. The rule of law, in turn, grants certain rights, which incrementally improves human rights. For example, as Sylvia Ostry explains in "China and the WTO: The Transparency Issue," the WTO grants individual rights inasmuch as protection for IP demands protection of individual rights and the ability to assert those rights. Such a process ultimately yields increased human rights because individuals have been granted legal personality to use against the government.

China will gain more from integrating into the world economy by maximizing its comparative advantage: labor. To truly maximize its comparative advantage, however, China must allow others to maximize their comparative advantage. That is to say, for maximum gain China would make only what it is best at and trade for the rest. So the more efficient economic development will see China importing various goods, in turn more fully ensconcing China in the liberal world order. The process appears to be self-perpetuating. Reformers are also likely to be bolstered by success and therefore continue supporting integration. Success makes it more difficult and less likely for China to reverse reforms. The real question, claim proponents of China's accession, is whether the United States wants to support or fight reform in China.

Yet another positive arising out of China's accession to the WTO, some argue, is improved dispute resolution between China and its trading partners, especially the United States. Currently, China resolves economic disputes bilaterally. This allows China to play parties against one another. For instance, if the United States claims China is not playing fairly, China may simply take its business to another country. This method allows China to extract concessions out of its trading partners. Under the WTO, however, disputes will be resolved in a multilateral forum. In such a forum, it is more difficult for China to play one country against another. It is the rules of the organization that are important, not individual member states.

Proponents of China's accession do not ignore the arguments against accession. One argument against accession claims China's membership in the WTO will increase the current trade deficit the United States has with China. Supporters argue, however, that the U.S.-China deficit is simply a manifestation of a broader U.S. deficit with the world. China has simply taken some share of that deficit from other states that export to the United States. Job losses will thus be felt more heavily in those states already exporting to the United States. Supporters of China's entry also note that trade deficits are really caused by aggregate domestic spending, not trade. So trade is not to blame for America's deficit; rather the purchasing choices of the American public are to blame. Thus both the deficit and job loss arguments are overstated. Proponents of China's accession also note that the United States and China have agreed to various "safeguard" clauses designed to protect the United States from a flood of Chinese exports.

Many opponents assert that China is unlikely to comply with the WTO and that all of the alleged benefits are simply academic hallucinations. Supporters would agree that compliance would be exceptionally difficult. The alternative, however, is even bleaker. China must be brought into a liberal world trading system, the sooner the better. The WTO will assist in ensuring compliance far better than individual countries could force liberalization on China. The incentives of participation are clear. WTO enforcement mechanisms offer the greatest leverage over China and any attempts it may make at non-compliance. If China wants to reinvigorate its economy, attract more foreign investors, and improve the lot of its people, membership in the World Trade Organization is the way to do so. China's leadership, however, must be willing to make concessions and comply with the rules of the organization in order to take its place in the international community.

Arguments Against China's Accession to the WTO

Those in the United States and other Western nations arguing against China's accession to the WTO would chafe at the claim that the United States has a moral obligation to bring China into the WTO. China's government itself is morally repugnant, they would say. In fact, objectors argue the United States should use WTO membership to force political liberalization in China. To reward the government of the Tiananmen Square massacre (1989), to reward the country that holds Tibet against its peoples' wishes, to reward a destroyer of human rights, an opponent of religion, and a neglector of women's rights—it is this that is morally unacceptable to many objectors. China's workers are paid pennies per hour. China engages in child labor and in forced prison labor. Of course, opponents would say, China has comparative advantage, but it has been achieved by coercion. China has no unions; hence its workers are not paid enough to buy U.S. products. To think that China will provide a market for U.S. products is unreasonable.

As to the contention that trade will somehow improve China's human rights record, opponents of admission to the WTO point out that, since President Clinton decided to "de-link" trade from human rights in 1994, human rights abuses have actually increased in China. The real way to improve human rights, then, is to retain the ability to reject China's MFN status. China should not be allowed to join the WTO and PNTR should be rejected. The ability to withdraw China's MFN status through Jackson-Vanik is the only sanction the United States has against Chinese abuses. Congress also would prefer not to give up the valuable public relations tool of the Jackson-Vanik waiver debate each year. Critics contend that China abuses human rights, is hostile to religious freedom, threatens its neighbors, and abuses its workers. It is not, they claim, the sort of country that the United States should support for admission to the WTO. Indeed, Taiwan's move to democracy is far more deserving of reward than China's continued rejection of liberalism. U.S. support only legitimizes China's authoritarian regime.

U.S. labor unions are especially hostile to China's membership in the WTO. They argue two points. First, China allows no independent labor unions and thus artificially maintains comparative advantage. Second, U.S. labor stands to lose the most if China enters the WTO. Many U.S. labor unions are made up of blue collar and/or semi-skilled workers. These are the workers who are most likely to immediately lose their jobs to China. But others stand to lose as well. Increasingly, China is producing more sophisticated products such as computers and telecommunications equipment. Moreover, labor unions argue that the motivation of U.S. corporations supporting China's membership in the WTO is not to open its markets. It will be decades or more before the average Chinese citizen can afford U.S. products. Instead, labor unions allege that U.S. corporations will move production to China because of its lack of labor unions and lower wages. American corporations will benefit, say the opponents, but American workers will suffer. Some see hundreds of thousands of lost jobs in the United States. One group of American workers most likely to suffer is textile workers. Overall, U.S. textile workers may lose one hundred fifty thousand jobs. Indeed, textile workers all over the world will lose jobs to China. Light manufacturing across the board should suffer as well. Opponents of China's accession to the WTO argue that the trade deficit with China will balloon as a result of admission to the WTO, at a rate of perhaps ten percent per year. China already ships one third of its exports to the United States, but only accepts ten percent of its imports from the United States. Opponents claim that the benefits to the U.S. economy are vastly overstated and the negatives are understated.

Opponents also argue that China's government ignores environmental issues when making economic decisions. As an example they point to China's insistence on using unclean, coal-burning fuel plants. China's environment is severely degraded. It has very few environmental regulations, and those it has are routinely ignored, especially by the SOEs. This policy should not be rewarded and allowing China to join the WTO will only increase pollution in China. China also shows little, if any, interest in improving its environmental record.

Opponents of China's admission to the WTO find fault at every turn with China's government. For some, the fact that China is authoritarian is the problem. For others it is more specifically that China remains dominated by the Communist Party, though it is no longer strictly a communist state in reality. The anti-communists would have the United States reward Taiwan for becoming democratic rather than China for remaining authoritarian. They feel that the West, led by the United States, is sending the wrong signal around the world by considering China for membership. The reality for these opponents is that China is not democratic and is, in fact, hostile to democracy and to Western-style liberalism. Yet it is Western-style liberalism that underlies the WTO, a factor that seems irreconcilable with the Chinese government.

These opponents point out that China has consistently broken international agreements. China has entered three memoranda of understanding (MOUs) with the United States designed to protect IP rights, and has promptly violated each accord. Given that it has a poor record of complying with other international commitments, there is little reason to believe it will comply with the WTO. Indeed, China's legal advisors have stated unequivocally that China will protect its markets beyond the WTO-mandated time period requiring compliance. China is not reducing NTBs as required by the WTO, but instead is actually increasing them. It appears that China has chosen the Japanese model of protectionism through close interaction between government and business. Yet, given its non-market based economy, its authoritarian state, and its large state-owned sectors, China may be more adept at this game than even Japan. China is engaged in an export-led growth strategy that the United States cannot afford to support.

Opponents of China's membership believe that command, or government-directed, economies like China's are antithetical to liberal trade rules such as those promulgated by the WTO. Non-market economies are especially well suited to break WTO rules because of the incestuous relationship between the state and firms. State trading is itself essentially a non-tarrif barrier, and the WTO is not prepared to deal with such issues because its dispute settlement system is designed to deal with market economies operating under the rule of law. China's government has shown itself time and again to be a government of bad faith, repeatedly introducing politics into economic decisions. If the United States were to displease China politically, say, on the issue of Taiwan, China could turn around and revoke a Boeing contract. Such actions clearly violate the WTO principle of national treatment. Similarly, China frequently demands technological transfers in exchange for market access. This too violates WTO principles.

Opponents believe that another problem with China's government is that it remains hostile to democracy and thus a threat to both U.S. national and international security. China refuses to renounce the use of force against Taiwan. It proliferates nuclear weapons technology and missile technology to Pakistan and perhaps to other unstable states. In doing so, it remains a threat to the United States and to U.S. interests. Not only are China's government and its policies problematic for WTO accession, but the structure of China's society, as it currently exists, is also problematic. The government has established no security net for its citizens; thus the people rely on their employers for basic necessities such as housing and education. If the employer's business fails, the employees are also at risk.

In addition, opponents suggest that China lacks the underlying structural reform to support the general commitments it has already made to open markets. Promises alone are not enough. China lacks the ability to comply with WTO rules and regulations. Even if China wanted to comply with the WTO, opponents argue, it could not do so anytime soon because it lacks the trained administrators and regulators necessary to impose WTO rules upon its economy. It lacks the capability to meet WTO standards on assorted levels.

Critics of China's accession to the WTO argue many strong points against that country's membership in the liberal trading organization. As mentioned earlier, China lacks the rule of law. Its court system is not impartial or independent. It caters to Chinese citizens in general and Communist Party members in particular. It allows selective application of the law so as to protect local interests, to the detriment of outside interests. Foreigners are systematically held at a disadvantage in China's legal system. Contracts may sometimes be unenforceable, as the system is subject to political manipulation and corruption. Provincial leaders often see fit to ignore court rulings. The Chinese system of justice leaves a great deal of discretion to the state. All of these factors are inconsistent with the WTO principle of rule of law. Furthermore, the system lacks transparency, another WTO principle. Rules are unclear or even purposely hidden. Individuals sometimes do not know what is acceptable or unacceptable, when or how rules will be applied, or what outcomes are likely under the legal system. Thus the system is unpredictable, contrary to another WTO goal.

The lack of rule of law, naturally, encourages corruption and local politics reflect this. The Chinese government has been gradually lending greater authority to the local levels of government. In an attempt to inject competition into the economy, economic power has been decentralized and local/provincial governments have far more power than in the past. The devolution of power from the center to local authorities grants assorted local party officials the ability to prohibit almost any private project. Bribery is often employed to gain autho-

IN BEIJING, CHINA, TOP TRADE NEGOTIATORS FROM CHINA (R.) AND THE UNITED STATES MEET IN A ROUND OF TALKS ON CHINA'S ACCESSION TO THE WORLD TRADE ORGANIZATION. *(AP/Wide World Photos. Reproduced by permission.)*

rization for such projects. The rampant corruption within the government in regards to the economy runs counter to the WTO's operating principles.

Beyond China's internal structure, there are additional arguments against allowing China to accede to the WTO. Some, for example, argue that WTO dispute resolution takes too long and China may choose to ignore it. They argue that U.S. laws—unilateral threats and sanctions—are more likely to be effective against China because China needs the U.S. market to help spur its economic growth. Others argue that the bilateral and multilateral agreements leading up to China's accession are incomplete and that WTO members will be un-

able to force more concessions from China in the future due to its size and importance. Still others argue from a more nationalist position: China and the United States are bound for an eventual conflict; the United States should do nothing to strengthen China. Nationalists in both countries are uncomfortable with the WTO's assault on traditional notions of sovereignty.

To opponents of WTO membership for China, China appears unready for such a commitment. Most of the country still lacks market institutions and rule of law. One sees continuing state intervention throughout the breadth and width of the economy. It is not clear that the leadership, locally or centrally, is committed to market liberalization, upon which the WTO depends. China has not demonstrated the level of cooperation necessary to make the WTO work, and may not be able to demonstrate this due to internal, or local, constraints. An intransigent China in the WTO threatens that organization's credibility as both a "rule maker" and a "rule enforcer." The WTO stands as one of the most significant achievements of international law to date. Critics contend that China's membership is too big a potential threat to the WTO's existence when it is so young and vulnerable. China can wait, they say. It can demonstrate true liberalization and then be allowed to join.

RECENT HISTORY AND THE FUTURE

Notwithstanding the strident and sometimes convincing opposition to China's accession to the WTO, accession is likely and is likely soon. The United States and the European Union have completed their bilateral market access agreements with China. The remaining states still required to do so are likely to reach agreement shortly. The multilateral agreement with the WTO working party must follow. While there remain differences, agreement should be reached here as well in relatively short order. The WTO will then almost certainly approve China's admission. From there, accession is certain. The corporations of the world want this result, and the governments they influence are unlikely to withhold it. Indeed, there is a strong argument that China's growth can drive the world economy well into the twenty-first century. China needs that growth even more than does the rest of the world. The WTO allows China to make the painful economic changes necessary to attract investment and continue growth. However, China can also be expected to maximize its utility under the WTO. Judging from past agreements China has entered into, it will likely attempt to get all it can out of the international trade organization to take advantage of others' open markets, while opening its own markets as little as possible. China may demand compliance from others, while attempting to protect its own industries. In this, however, China is not alone. The United States, the European Union, Japan, and other countries do the same thing. Operating in respect to the WTO's principles, however, these actions are moderated and subject to restraint. Whether or not China would respect these boundaries is as yet unknown.

BIBLIOGRAPHY

Alexandroff, Alen. "Concluding China's Accession to the WTO: The U.S. Congress and Permanent Most Favored Nation Status for China," *UCLA Journal of International Law and Foreign Affairs.* (Spring 1998): 23–42.

Barfield, Claude and Mark Groombridge. "Two Sides to China's WTO Membership." http://www.freetrade.org/pubs/articles/mg-11-22-99.html (8 September 2000).

Bhagwati, Jagdish and Christopher Lingle. "Q: Should China be Allowed to Join the World Trade Organization?" *Insight on the News* (December 1, 1997): 24–7.

Broadman, Harry. "China's Membership in the WTO and Enterprise Reform: The Challenges for Accession and Beyond." In *China and the Long March to Global Trade: The Accession of China to the WTO.* London: Routledge Press, 2000.

"China Must Keep its Eye on the Prize," *Asian Business* (December 1999): 4.

"China's Entry into WTO: A Boom for U.S. Firms?" *Business in Thailand* (1 December 1999): 51.

"China's WTO Accession to Significantly Boost U.S. Agricultural Exports." *Economics Research Service.* 2000. http://www.econ.ag.gov/briefing/wto/china.htm (8 September 2000).

Corbet, Hugh. "Issues in the Accession of China to the WTO System," *Journal of Northeast Asian Studies* (Fall 1996): 14–33.

Evenett, Simon. "The World Trading System: The Road Ahead," *Finance & Development* (December 1999): 22–5.

Forney, Matt and Nigel Holloway. "In Two Minds," *Far Eastern Economic Review* (19 June 1997): 66–8.

General Accounting Office. *World Trade Organization: China's Membership Status and Normal Trade Relation Issues.* March 2000.

Gill, Bates. "Limited Engagement," *Foreign Affairs* (July/August 1999): 65–76.

Groombridge, Mark. *China's Long March to a Market Economy: The Case for Permanent Normal Trade Relations with the People's Republic of China.* Washington, D.C.: Cato Institute. April 2000.

Hahnel, Robin. "China & the WTO," *Z Magazine* (January 2000): 30–5.

Harner, Stephen. "Financial Services and the WTO: Opportunities Knock," *China Business Review* (March-April 2000): 10–5.

Holloway, Nigel and Trish Saywell. "Anxiety Attack: Asia Firms Brace for China's WTO Entry," *Far Eastern Economic Review* (June 19, 1997): 70–1.

Hughs, Steve, and Rorden Wilkinson. "International Labour Standards and World Trade: No Role of the World Trade Organization?" *New Political Economy* (November 1998): 375–89.

Kapp, Robert. "WTO This Time?" *China Business Review* (March-April 2000): 6–7.

————. "Letter from the President of the U.S.-China Business Council in Full and on Time," *China Business Review* (January-February 2000): 14–5.

Lee, Yong-Shik. "Review of the First WTO Panel Case on the Agreement on Safeguards: Korea," *Journal of World Trade* (December 1999): 27–46.

Maggs, John. "About the WTO Deal With Beijing," *National Journal* (4 December 1999): 1364–5.

————. "China Trade Deal: No Fortune Inside," *National Journal* (11 September 1999): 2569.

McConnell, Moria. "From Relationships to Rules: A Comment on China's Accession to the WTO in Response to Pitman Potter's Article 'China and the WTO: Tensions Between Globalized Liberalism and Local Culture,'" *Canadian Business Law Journal* (December 1999): 463–73.

Morici, Peter. "Barring Entry? China and the WTO," *Current History* (September 1997): 274–7.

O'Neil, Robert. "China Votes Loom Large After Siege of Seattle," *National Journal* (22 January 2000): 248.

O'Quinn, Robert. *Beyond the MFN Debate: A Comprehensive Trade Strategy Toward China.* Washington, D.C.: Heritage Foundation, May 1997.

Ostry, Sylvia. "China and the WTO: The Transparency Issue," *UCLA Journal of International Law and Foreign Affairs* (Spring 1998): 1–22.

Potter, Pitman. "China and the WTO: Tensions Between Globalized Liberalism and Culture," *Canadian Business Law Journal* (December 1999): 440–62.

Prybyla, Jan. "China in the WTO: Threat or Promise of Good," *Issues & Studies* (January 2000): 143–60.

Smith, Craig. "Joining the Club: Like Others China Will Try to Protect its Own Industries," *New York Times,* 23 May 2000, sec. A13.

Tan, Kong-Yam and Mun-Heng Toh. "Strategic Interests of ASEAN-5 in Regional Trading Arrangements in the Asia-Pacific," *Asia Pacific Journal of Management* (December 1999): 449–67.

Tkacik, Michael. "Post-Uruguay Round GATT/WTO Dispute Settlement: Substance, Strengths, Weaknesses, and Causes for Concern," *International Legal Perspectives* (Spring/Fall 1997): 169–91.

Wang, Lei and Edwin Vermulst. "China and the WTO: A Negotiating History," *International Trade & Law Regulation* (5 October 1996): 167–71.

"WTO Accession: China's Next Steps," *China Business Review* (January-February 2000): 34–8.

Zekos, Georgios. "An Examination of GATT/WTO Arbitration Procedures," *Dispute Resolution Journal* (November 1999): 72–6.

Michael Tkacik

THE COLOMBIAN U'WA INDIANS: SACRED LAND AND OIL

THE CONFLICT

The U'wa, a small tribe of Indians in northeastern Colombia, have sued Occidental Petroleum Corporation, because it is removing oil from their land—with the permission of the Colombian government.

Political

- The U'wa live on the land and object to the destruction of the land, pollution, and dislocation of the U'wa people caused by the oil drilling.

- FARC, a guerrilla group in Colombia, bombs pipelines and otherwise disrupts the oil production.

- Environmental groups around the world support the U'wa.

- The Colombian government supports Occidental, since the government wants Colombia to make money from one of its major resources.

- Occidental argues that FARC and other rebel groups oppose oil development because it increases government oversight of the area, interfering with their drug trafficking.

The global demand for new sources of oil has pitted the U'wa Indians of Colombia against California-based Occidental Petroleum Corporation. The tribe, which resides in the eastern foothills of the Andes Mountains two hundred miles northeast of Bogotá, has threatened to commit mass suicide if the oil company begins drilling on territory near its reservation. According to the *Guardian*, one of the tribe's leaders recently proclaimed, "We prefer genocide sponsored by the Colombian government rather than handing over Mother Earth to oil companies." The U'wa believe that "Mother Earth" is sacred—since time immemorial they have lived by a law that requires respect and protection for the earth. Occidental's interest lies in its claim that an area known as the Samoré Block outside the U'wa reservation holds between one and two and a half billion barrels of oil that it wants to extract. If these estimations are correct, the site is Colombia's largest oil field. Juan Myar, Colombia's minister of the environment, has indicated that the social and environmental consequences of the exploration and development within the Samoré Block are acceptable.

Since 1992 the opposing sides have waged their battle on a number of fronts, including the Colombian courts, Occidental Petroleum's headquarters, Washington, D.C., in the United States, and in the mountains of Colombia. Both sides have powerful allies. The U'wa are backed by vocal environmental groups in the United States and, some sources suggest, guerrillas, or rebels, in South America. Occidental Petroleum has the support of the Colombian government, which is eager to increase foreign investment in the country because of the profit it receives from its largest export—oil.

HISTORICAL BACKGROUND

The U'wa People: History, Beliefs, and Land

According to legend, a group of U'wa Indians, led by Chief Guaiticu, killed themselves during the seventeenth century rather than submit to Spanish *conquistadors* (conquerors) who planned to enslave them. U'wa oral history indicates that thousands of adults placed their children in clay pots and pushed them off a cliff. The adults then walked backward over the precipice and plunged to their death. Although historians and anthropologists have been unable to substantiate a mass suicide off the fourteen hundred-foot-high "Cliffs of Glory" in the Colombian Andes, the U'wa have announced their willingness to repeat the event if Occidental Petroleum removes "the blood of Mother Earth."

The U'wa Indians, one of Colombia's many groups of indigenous peoples, comprise a small but vocal segment of the country's thirty-seven million population. The tribe, comprised of four thousand to eight thousand members, inhabits a vast reservation in the northeastern section of Colombia that includes parts of five departments, or states. Most of the tribe's members live in inaccessible areas of the Sierra Nevada del Cocuy-Guican Mountains, part of the Andes range. Oil is only one of the land's natural resources, among which includes a vast array of plants and animals including toucans, jaguars, and spectacled bears. Their subsistence economy is based on agriculture, livestock, hunting, gathering, and fishing. In a statement to the press in 1999 the U'wa claimed, "Our law is to take no more than is necessary; we are like the Earth that feeds itself from all living beings, but never takes too much because, if it did, all would come to an end. We must care for, not maltreat, because for us it is forbidden to kill with knives, machetes, or bullets. Our weapons are thought, the word, our power is wisdom." Because of their tradition, which emphasizes avoiding war and the use of weapons, the U'wa became known as "the thinking people." Despite the changing world around them, the tribe has maintained many of its ancient traditions, including its social structures and language. Most tribal members speak U'wajka, the native language of the U'wa. They also continue to practice their traditional religion. The *Werjayás*, wise ancients, and *Karekas*, medicine people, are the tribe's spiritual leaders and serve as a link between the U'wa and their ancestors, as well as between the people and the natural order. The members of the tribe believe that the creator, Yagshowa, endowed the *Werjayás* with the power to communicate with the gods and spirits.

CHRONOLOGY

1992 Occidental Petroleum and Royal/Dutch Shell purchase the rights to search for oil within a portion of Samoré Block in Colombia. Guerrillas regularly attack the pipeline, spilling oil.

1995 The U'wa and Occidental reach a preliminary agreement on seismic testing. The agreement, however, is never finalized. Occidental begins exploratory initiatives. The U'wa file a lawsuit in Colombia's supreme court, which rules in favor of the U'wa.

1996 Occidental resumes activities. The U'wa tribe elders threaten mass suicide.

1997 Members of the U'wa, the Colombian government, and Occidental meet to discuss the situation, but fail to resolve their differences. The U'wa Defense Working Group is formed. The Organization of American States conducts an investigation; the U'wa are not satisfied with the OAS' findings.

1998 Colombia proposes Occidental develop a smaller territory; the U'wa oppose the agreement.

1999 Three U.S. citizens, U'wa activists, are murdered near the Venezuelan border. FARC, a rebel group, claims responsibility, threatening the peace talks taking place between the group and the Colombian government.

2000 Occidental announces plans to begin operation in a five-acre area. Rebel groups label the site a war zone.

The Controversy: The U'wa, Their Government, and Occidental Petroleum

Although Colombia's 1991 national constitution requires that the government protect the U'wa and their territory, the government in the capital city of Bogotá controls all rights to the country's oil and any other minerals that lie below the land's surface. Occidental Petroleum's initial contact with the U'wa came in 1988 when the Caño Limon pipeline, which runs near the reservation, was under construction. The current conflict between the tribe and Occidental Petroleum, however, dates to 1992 when the Los Angeles-based Occidental company, along with Royal Dutch/Shell, purchased the right to search for oil within an eight hundred-square-mile portion of the Samoré Block. Throughout 1993 and 1994 the company met more than thirty times with the U'wa. Occidental tried to gain permission to conduct seismic tests within the U'wa reservation, and the two sides arrived at a preliminary arrangement in January 1995. The agreement was to be finalized the following month, but the U'wa failed to appear for the meetings. The tribe claims that the officials did not meet with Indians authorized to speak on behalf of the tribe and discussed education and health issues rather than Occidental's development proposals. Occidental officials and other observers, including Colombia's largest newspaper, *El Tiempo,* believed that intimidation by guerrillas opposed to development of the country's land persuaded the tribe to change its mind and resist the company's operations. Supporters of the U'wa argue that the suggestion that rebel groups influenced the tribe is dangerous because it places the Indians in jeopardy of reprisals at the hands of the Colombian military. The lack of an agreement prompted Occidental to shift its focus to areas outside the U'wa reservation.

Occidental Petroleum developed the Caño Limón oil field in northeastern Colombia during the early 1980s and helped transform the Latin American country into a major oil exporter. Crude oil extracted by Occidental travels via the 483-mile-long pipeline to Covenas, where it is exported to the United States. Attacks on the pipeline have been a regular occurrence since its completion in 1985. Environmental groups estimate that the pipeline has been the target of more than six hundred attacks in fifteen years. The sabotage has resulted in the release of 1.7 million barrels of oil onto the land and into water sources. Environmental groups assert that that guerrilla attacks on pipelines throughout Latin America cause significant oil spills and contaminate land and water supplies. Activists also argue that the construction of roads and pipelines by multinational companies often force indigenous people to relocate. Occidental and the Colombian government believe that the Armed Revolutionary Forces of Colombia (FARC), the country's largest rebel organization, and the National Liberation Army (ELN), the country's second-largest rebel group, are the source of the attacks. With some fifteen thousand members, the FARC has waged a long civil war with the Colombian government. Since the group's founding in 1966 it has assassinated more than thirty thousand foreigners and Colombians. Nearly half of the global kidnappings each year occur in Colombia, many of them attributable to the FARC. During 1998 Colombian rebels abducted some forty foreigners. The guerrillas often target outsiders because they know that they can receive high ransoms for them. Groups such as the FARC use the ransom money to fund their activities.

The ELN claims that the nationalization of Colombia's natural resources is one of its primary goals and that it is opposed to the government's oil policies because they lead to environmental devastation. The group bombs oil pipelines to protest the presence of foreign companies in Colombia and is the most powerful group in the eastern part of the country where the U'wa live. Occidental Petroleum believes that both it and the U'wa are the guerrillas' targets, a charge that the Indian tribe denies. In response to the activity of the guerrilla groups, the Colombian government mobilizes right-wing paramilitary groups to protect the interests of the multinational oil companies, a service for which the companies pay a great deal of money annually.

In addition to their opposition to oil exploration in Colombia and to the presence there of multinational companies, many of the guerrillas focus on protecting the Colombian drug trade, especially heroin and cocaine. Occidental Petroleum argues that, while the rebels might claim to oppose oil development for environmental and cultural reasons, the guerrillas oppose them because the presence of multinational companies in Colombia results in greater government oversight in the areas that the rebels dominate.

The Courts and Regional Mediation

In early 1995 officials from the Colombian government met with U'wa representatives about Occidental's exploration plans. The company asked the government to give it an opportunity to discuss the issue with the tribe. The U'wa believed that their request was appropriate and within the bounds of the nation's 1991 constitution, which gives indigenous people the right to voice their opinions about the extraction of natural resources from their lands. The U'wa claimed that the territory targeted by Occidental was within their ancestral lands. During the summer of 1995 Occidental began exploration activity in the Samoré Block. The tribe was upset because Bogotá gave the oil company permission to conduct explorations before the U'wa had an opportunity to complete their deliberations. Colombia's public defender, acting on behalf of the Indians, filed a lawsuit against the Environmental Ministry in the capital's superior court. The action claimed that the government violated the U'wa's constitutional rights by granting the permit and requested that the court revoke Occidental's environmental license.

In September 1995 Bogotá's superior court ruled in favor of the U'wa. Occidental appealed to the country's Supreme Court of Justice, which overturned the superior court's findings. In the wake of

ABOUT COLOMBIA

- There are eight U'wa clans. The Traditional U'wa Authority, the official ruling council and voice of the entire tribe, is made up of *Werjayás* and *Karekas* from all of the clans.

- The Colombian government requires that each indigenous people group have a president, vice president, secretary, treasurer, public prosecutors, and speakers. This is known as a *Cabildo* system.

- Spanish conquistadors enslaved many Native Americans during the fifteenth and sixteenth centuries and forced them to work in gold or silver mines.

- Bartolomé de las Casas (1474–1566) was a Dominican friar who worked to end the enslavement of Native Americans. He convinced Spain's Emperor Charles V (1500–58) that the Indians in the New World were rational beings and therefore should not be enslaved. Under the New Laws (1542–43) the emperor abolished Native American slavery. Many Spaniards in the New World, however, resisted his decrees.

- The U'wa seek to respect what they believe is a natural law of conservation. By observing this, the tribe believes that it will help maintain a balance between the spiritual world and the physical world.

- The U'wa refer to outsiders as *riowa*.

- The *Werjayás* and *Karekas* consider all matters pertaining to outsiders and then advise the *Cabildos*. No decision by the *Cabildos* is legitimate, the U'wa believe, unless the *Werjayás* and *Karekas* have ruled first.

- Colombian guerrillas commonly receive income from three sources: "war taxes" levied on international companies, the drug trade, and ransom money.

- Occidental's oil field in the Samoré Block contains enough oil to supply the United States for three months.

- In Spanish, FARC stands for *Fuerzas Armadas Revolucionarias de Colombia*.

- In Spanish, ELN stands for *Ejercito de Liberacion Nacional* .

- Some sixty-five percent of Colombia's oil is exported to the United States.

- Trade between the United States and Colombia amounted to nearly $11 billion in 1998. U.S. exports totaled nearly $5 billion, or thirty-two percent of Colombia's imports.

- The United States is Colombia's largest investor.

- More than three hundred thirty thousand barrels of oil arrive in the United States each day from Colombia.

- Colombia produces more than eight hundred thousand barrels of oil daily.

- Oil accounted for about twenty-four percent of the Colombian government's income in 1999.

the verdict and the resumption of the company's exploration of the area in early 1996, the tribe's elders announced the suicide threat. Upon review of the case in February 1997, however, the Colombian Constitutional Court ordered Occidental Petroleum to suspend operations in the Samoré area because it found that the government did not consult with the tribe and that drilling in the area would threaten the Indians' ethnic, cultural, and economic integrity. The court also ruled that the U'wa be consulted within the following thirty days. In March, Colombia's Council of State, ruling on a separate lawsuit filed by the public defender, contradicted the Constitutional Court and found that appropriate consultation with the tribe had occurred and

that the company could proceed with its operations. The council's judges also ruled that their verdict took precedence over the Constitutional Court's order. At the end of May 1997, representatives from twenty-seven U'wa communities, the Colombian government, and Occidental Petroleum met to discuss the company's work in the Samoré Block. The participants failed to resolve their differences.

In the wake of the unsuccessful talks the U'wa made two moves to heighten international awareness of their cause. First, they took their case to the Inter-American Commission on Human Rights of the Organization of American States and asked it to investigate the matter. Second, Roberto Cobaria,

A POLICE HELICOPTER BRINGS IN RIOT POLICE IN LA CHINA, COLOMBIA TO CONTROL THE PROTESTS OF U'WA INDIANS WHO ARE TRYING TO PREVENT OCCIDENTAL PETROLEUM FROM DRILLING ON LAND SACRED TO THE INDIANS. *(AP/Wide World Photos. Reproduced by permission.)*

also known as Berito Kuwaru'wa, president of the Traditional U'wa Authority, traveled to Washington, D.C., New York, and Los Angeles on a trip sponsored by U.S. environmental groups. While in California, the chief met with Occidental officials and told them that oil is the blood of "Mother Earth" and therefore should not be extracted. The chief also voiced the tribe's concern that if the company developed wells on the land, the inevitable guerrilla attacks on Occidental's pipeline will harm the U'wa's fishing, hunting, and agricultural activities.

The tribe also fears the Colombian military, which searches for the guerrillas and commits violent acts to drive them out of foreign companies' operation areas. Often civilians are caught in the middle of the civil war. Cobaria claimed that in June 1997, after returning from his U.S. visit, hooded gunmen invaded his home, beat him, and tried to force him to sign an agreement that would allow Occidental to drill for oil in the Samoré Block. The attackers promised to hang him if he did not cooperate, but Cobaria stood firm. The men dumped him into a river and he nearly drowned.

The tribe's efforts to bring attention to its cause were successful. A number of environmental and human rights groups joined forces and formed the U'wa Defense Working Group, originally known as the U'wa Defense Project. Since coming together during the summer of 1997, the nine organizations that comprise the coalition have publicized the Indians' cause in the press, on the Internet, and through protests staged across the United States.

During the summer of 1997, in an attempt to mediate the ongoing dispute, the Colombian Foreign Ministry invited the Organization of American States (OAS) to conduct an investigation into the matter. The OAS, in cooperation with representatives from Harvard University's Center for Non-Violent Solutions, backed the tribe's claim that activity around its legal reservation would have an impact upon the U'wa. Occidental Petroleum agreed with some of the OAS' recommendations, including a suggestion that both sides decrease their public rhetoric, but it refused to commit unconditionally to suspend its exploration and development in the Samoré region. The U'wa were also dissatisfied with the OAS' findings because they believed that the suggestions were based on the assumption that Occidental's operations in the Samoré Block would eventually occur. Their response to the OAS' recommendations indicated that the U'wa demand the final say over any activity on their ancestral lands, a provision that the Colombian constitution does not allow.

Despite the findings of the OAS, in early 1998 Colombia proposed that Occidental develop a smaller section of the Samoré Block than originally planned in exchange for a more favorable profit arrangement with the government. Occidental agreed to abandon the eight hundred-square-mile oil field into which it had invested more than $12 million, but had never dug a single well. Royal Dutch/Shell backed out of the deal citing financial problems, but some observers suggest that the company ceded its control to Occidental because of the controversy surrounding the project. Occidental relinquished rights to seventy-five percent of the new area, but applied for permission to explore the remaining twenty-five percent. The U'wa opposed the agreement and claimed that the smaller parcel was a part of their ancestral lands as well. Once again, the tribe argued that it was not consulted and it continued to maintain that the Colombian government did not have the right to allow Occidental to extract natural resources from its land. The Indians' actions angered government and oil company officials, who claimed that the U'wa were harming the nation's economic interests. Unless exploration in oil-rich territories proceeded, they argued, Colombia would have to begin importing oil by 2004. Occidental Petroleum suspended its plans in the Samoré Block as the OAS continued to mediate the disagreement between the Indians and their government.

Violence Strikes

The U'wa and their cause remained out of the international spotlight until February 25, 1999, when Colombian rebels abducted three U.S. citizens near the Venezuelan border. Terence Freitas, Lahe'ena'e Gay, and Ingrid Washinawatok were returning from the U'wa reservation after spending about a week with the tribe. The U'wa had invited the group to consult with them about developing a tribal education program, because the Indians had recently decided that they did not want to participate in Colombia's educational system. Working under the auspices of Pacific Cultural Conservancy International, an organization based in Hawaii and interested in indigenous rights, the group was led by the thirty-nine-year-old Gay, a resident of Hawaii and the organization's director. Washinawatok, a forty-one-year-old member of the Menominee Tribe of Wisconsin, and Freitas, twenty-four, were New York residents. Washinawatok led the Fund for the Four Directions, a group based in New York that focuses its efforts on American Indian issues. Freitas was well known to the U'wa. He had worked with the tribe since 1996 and founded the U'wa Defense Working Group in an effort to publicize the Indians' cause and assist them in their struggle against Occidental Petroleum. Because of his involvement with the U'wa he had received death threats on his home answering machine and credited them to paramilitary groups in Colombia. Freitas believed that the groups were connected with Occidental. FARC rebels also warned Freitas during a 1998 visit to Colombia that it wanted him to stay out of the region.

Forces working under the sponsorship of the country's main right-wing paramilitary organization, the United Autodefense Groups of Colombia (AUC), have tried to exterminate groups like the ELN and FARC, as well as human rights activists and people it suspects of supporting Colombian rebels. During previous visits to Colombia, Freitas believed that members of paramilitary groups had followed him. The Colombian military once detained him and forced him to sign a statement that released it from responsibility for his safety. He suspected that this was done in an effort to intimidate him.

Freitas, Gay, and Washinawatok had met with the U'wa in an attempt to learn more about the tribe and to work toward preserving its cultural identity. After completing their research with the U'wa, the trio headed out of the remote area to catch a flight to Bogotá. Armed men in civilian clothing detained them at a roadblock, demanded that they explain why they were in the remote area, and forced them from their vehicle. The men abducted the activists but released Roberto Cobaria, who was traveling with them. The U'wa, as well as the American and Colombian governments, blamed FARC for the kidnappings and demanded the trio's release. The incident angered the U'wa, which claimed that the Marxist FARC often invaded its territory. "The indigenous authorities are very upset by this," Cobaria announced according to the *Associated Press,* "because our territory is not respected. We are humiliated. We are abused."

A week after the Americans' disappearance, their bullet-riddled bodies were found in a wooded area near the Colombian border in Venezuela. Each of the victims had been blindfolded, bound, and shot at point blank range in the face, head, and chest. Marks on their bodies indicated that they had been tortured. Raul Reyes, also known as Luis Eduardo Devia, a high-ranking FARC commander, maintained that his organization was innocent. The AUC also denied any involvement in the killings, as did the ELN, which has a significant presence in the region. In the days following the incident, a war of accusations ensued between the paramilitary groups and the FARC. The AUC wrote a letter to Colombian President Andres Pastrana, which was reported by the *BBC,* that stated, in part, "The AUC leadership declares that our anti-subversive organization is not guilty, in any way, of the deaths of the U.S. citizens . . . . [The indigenous people] know that the FARC are the only ones responsible for the regrettable and condemnable action." The kidnapping and execution of the Americans threatened to derail planned

U'WA INDIANS IN LA CHINA, COLOMBIA REST UNDER A TENT AFTER CLASHING WITH POLICE IN AN ATTEMPT TO PREVENT OCCIDENTAL PETROLEUM FROM DRILLING ON LAND SACRED TO THE INDIANS. *(AP/Wide World Photos. Reproduced by permission.)*

peace talks between Pastrana's government and FARC. Colombian officials were concerned about the country's international reputation as a dangerous nation for foreign travel, and wished to end the ongoing struggle with the guerrilla group. FARC believed that it, too, could benefit from an improved international reputation.

FARC finally claimed responsibility for the crime five days after officials discovered the bodies. Senior commander Raul Reyes announced that a guerrilla leader and three of his men abducted and murdered the Americans without the consent of their superiors. Cellular phone conversations intercepted by the Colombian military intelligence

between German Briceño, alias Grannobles, the commander of FARC's Eastern Bloc, and his brother, Jorge Briceño, alias Mono Jojoy, FARC's military leader, indicated the gravity of the situation in relation to the group's impending peace negotiations with the Colombian government. Jorge Briceño told his brother, "This is the biggest political screw-up of all. This is a mistake from hell." He suggested that his brother find someone to blame for the killings. Although Colombian military intelligence indicated that Grannobles gave the order to murder the pro-Indian activists, FARC blamed a lower ranking official identified as Commander Gildardo, alias Marrano. Despite the organization's efforts to pass the blame to Gildardo, by the end of May the prosecutor general's office issued an arrest warrant for Grannobles and Gustavo Bocota Aguablanca, an U'wa, claiming that it had sufficient evidence to implicate them in the murders. The government believed that Bocota coordinated the abduction.

Concerns raised in Colombia over the incident focused not only on the troubled peace process between the government and the nation's largest rebel group, but also on actions that the United States might take. Fabio Valencia Cossio, the president of the nation's congress, expressed concern that the United States had been looking for a reason to increase its military involvement in Colombia. Once FARC admitted that it was responsible for the murders, U.S. Representative Benjamin Gilman, a Republican from New York and chair of the U.S. House International Relations Committee, warned that the activities of the rebels "threatens the security of U.S. citizens and must be combatted as such." In April 1999 Colombia received a commitment for $240 million in military assistance from the United States.

Arguments Over Territory Continue

Tensions between the FARC and the U'wa continued to mount after the discovery of the bodies. A month following the murders, Roberto Cobaria fled Colombia as a result of intimidation by the FARC's 45th and 10th Fronts. He had cooperated with government officials in their investigation and had identified the kidnappers as FARC members, and he believed that his life was in danger. Cobaria appeared at Occidental's headquarters in California in late April 1999 and joined representatives of environmental groups in a sit-in protest against the company. They once again called on the company to abandon its plans in the Samoré region, but a company spokesman announced that Occidental would proceed with its operations as soon as it received approval from the Colombian government. In mid-May an appeals court overturned a moratorium, or suspension, on the company's activities in the Samoré Block. This action cleared the way for eventual government permission for Occidental to advance its exploration and drilling. Colombia's government granted the company permission in September to drill a single well. Occidental announced plans to begin the operation in mid-2000 in a five-acre area on private land not far from the U'wa reservation. The ELN promised to oppose Occidental's activity. One of the rebel group's leaders labeled the site a "war zone" and issued threats against the company's employees and equipment.

Good news for the U'wa also accompanied Occidental's victory in the courts. In an attempt to resolve the territorial dispute with the tribe, during the summer of 1999 the Colombian government dramatically increased the size of the tribe's reservation from 98,800 acres to 543,000 acres. Bogotá used a territorial map provided by the U'wa to expand the tribe's landholdings, and claims that it granted the Indians every acre of land indicated on the map. The U'wa agreed to the redrawn boundaries until they discovered that the government planned to allow Occidental to drill immediately outside the new borders of their reservation. They then asked Bogotá to redraw the boundaries. The government refused and the Indians vowed to continue their fight against the project.

RECENT HISTORY AND THE FUTURE

Although the Colombian government increased the size of the U'wa reservation substantially during the summer of 1999 the tribe continued to oppose Occidental's exploration and development in the Samoré Block. In an effort to halt the company's progress on land just outside the reservation, a group of two hundred men, women, children, and U'wa elders established a camp at Gibraltar 1, Occidental's twenty-seven-acre drill site, on November 16, 1999. In a move designed to keep land out of the company's hands the U'wa announced that farmers in the area could not sell to anyone but the U'wa. Backed by the ELN and its intimidation tactics the people around the drill site sold their holdings to the Indians for a fraction of what Occidental offered them. The U'wa purchased two farms on the drill site. Upon their encampment, they removed the company's boundary markers and erected a peace flag. Meanwhile, the tribe gained additional support for its cause when representatives from environmental groups held an international summit in Bogotá to demonstrate solidarity for the Indians' fight. Environmental groups have accused the company of establishing operations in a rainforest, a charge the company denies, citing a third party environmental impact report to support its claim.

While the U'wa fought Occidental in Colombia, the tribe's supporters in the United States once again attempted to persuade the company to cease its work near the tribe's reservation. As the U.S. presidential primary season got underway in early 2000, environmental activists attempted to pressure Vice President Al Gore to speak out against the company and to sell the shares of Occidental

Petroleum stock that he administers in a trust fund for his mother as executor of his father's estate. Senator Albert Gore, Sr., was a longtime member of the company's board of directors and some U'wa supporters claim that his estate holds as much as $500,000 in Occidental stock. At a January demonstration in Manchester, New Hampshire, activists challenged the vice president to use his influence with the company and "intervene in the situation" involving the U'wa. Despite protests against the vice president's ties to the oil company, the Gore campaign successfully avoided controversy over the issue during the primaries, in part because Gore does not personally own the stock, as activists originally claimed. Atossa Soltani of Amazon Watch, a U.S. environmental group, challenged Gore to take a stand on the Samoré Block issue, stating in *LA Weekly* that, "If he wants to be an environmental champion, he needs to make a statement on the issue. And he needs to take personal responsibility for his family's fortune." Occidental's opponents revealed further ties between the Democratic Party and the oil conglomerate that suggested that Gore might have influence with Occidental. They claim that Ray Irani, the company's chairman, donated $100,000 to the Democratic Party soon after spending a night in the White House's Lincoln Bedroom and contributing a total of $400,000 during Gore's vice presidency. Activists also targeted Boston, Massachusetts-based Fidelity Investments, which controls about thirty million Occidental shares worth approximately $700 million. The groups called on Fidelity to sell the stock or pressure the company to cease its operations in the Samoré Block. In early February, groups staged protests at Fidelity's Boston headquarters as well as at its offices in cities across the United States. Such protests continued throughout the spring.

By the end of January 2000, Ecopetrol, Colombia's government-owned oil company and Occidental's partner in the Samoré Block exploration project, finalized approval for the California-based company to begin drilling. A judge granted Occidental an eviction order against the Indians who were staging a sit-in at the drilling site because, under Colombian law, the minerals below the soil belong to the government, not to the property owner. Colombian military forces and the Colombian National Police surrounded the protesters on January 19 and prevented food and water from reaching them. On January 25, authorities removed twenty-six Indians and transported them by helicopter to a military base. The U'wa claimed that three children died when some of the demonstrators jumped

into a river to escape riot police, but the claim remains unsubstantiated.

Hundreds of U'wa subsequently established a human blockade on the main highway that provided access to the drill site. Police chased them away with tear gas. Fulfilling its threat to act against Occidental, the ELN forced drivers onto the site with earth-moving equipment to dump some of the construction vehicles off of a 200-foot cliff. Police used tear gas and bulldozers to break another roadblock on February 11. The U'wa once more claimed that three children died when the protestors were forced to escape into the rapidly flowing Cubojon River. They also said that eleven adults disappeared. Again, both claims remain unsubstantiated. Clashes between police and the U'wa demonstrators continued into mid-February when authorities reopened the highway and earth-moving equipment entered the drilling area. By the end of the month the Colombian government had more than three hundred soldiers in the area to protect Occidental's project. The U'wa again blockaded the road, but abandoned their act of civil disobedience on April 22 when they returned to the mountains for a spiritual retreat.

Late March brought a short-lived victory for the U'wa and their supporters. Representatives of the tribe confronted Larry Meriage, Occidental's vice president for public affairs, in Washington, D.C., when he arrived for a meeting with Representative Cynthia McKinney. Meriage requested a meeting with the Georgia Democrat because of comments she made about Occidental during discussions concerning a proposed $1.3 billion military aid package for Colombia. The House of Representatives approved the two-year aid bill in late March 2000 and sent it to the Senate. McKinney, who serves on the House International Relations Subcommittee on International Operations and Human Rights, organized a surprise encounter with Roberto Perez, president of the tribe's governing council, and members of U.S. environmental groups that back the U'wa. Following the meeting, the U'wa Defense Working group issued a press release that claimed that Meriage agreed that the U'wa had not been consulted about Occidental's plans to drill the Gibraltar 1 oil well. Occidental, however, claimed it had no reason to consult with the tribe about the operation because it was outside the reservation.

Within days, the 11th Circuit Court of Bogotá decreed that Occidental had to stop preparing the area for drilling. Occidental filed an appeal. In mid-May the Superior Court of Bogotá overturned the Circuit Court-ordered suspension of activity at Gibraltar 1. It found that Occidental had proceeded appropriately and was not obligated to meet with the U'wa. Roberto Calderon, Ecopetrol's president, announced that the site preparation would resume immediately. As quoted by the *Associated Press*, Calderon stated, "To not go ahead with this exploration when the country needs it so urgently would be enormously prejudicial for the country."

In April demonstrators supporting the U'wa appeared once again at the company's annual shareholders' meeting. Some activists who held stock in Occidental proposed a resolution calling on the company to employ an independent firm to assess the risks to the company's profitability posed by the Samoré Block project and the U'wa suicide threat. Despite pleas from Roberto Perez, shareholders soundly defeated the resolution.

Today the U'wa, Colombia, Occidental, and guerrilla groups remain locked in a struggle that has lasted for nearly nine years. Colombia desperately needs the revenue that the Occidental project would bring in order to reduce its deficit spending and work within the requirements of a $2.7 billion aid package from the International Monetary Fund. The drilling could net the country as much as $900 million annually, but, argue the U'wa and the ELN, at the expense of Colombia's environment. Occidental maintains that the quarrel in the Samoré Block is between the U'wa and the Colombian government, not between the Indians and the U.S. oil conglomerate. It also maintains that the guerrillas' stronghold on the area is at the root of the problem. The tribe firmly asserts that the rebel groups did not influence its actions. It is unclear whether the U'wa have set aside their suicide threat. It appears that they have chosen instead to fight the project in the courts, through the news media, and with civil disobedience. In recognition of the U'wa's efforts the Spanish government in 1998 awarded the tribe the Bartolomé de las Casas prize. It is given annually to people who defend indigenous values. That same year Roberto Cobaria received the Goldman Environmental Award. It is presented each year to grassroots environmentalists in each of the world's six continental regions.

In mid-2000 Occidental was constructing a 1.5-mile access road to the Gibraltar 1 site and planned to begin drilling later that year. If the company finds enough oil to extract, it will apply for another environmental permit. Although protests by the Indians have subsided, the ELN has declared war on Occidental. The rebels extort money from company employees to ensure their safety. Activists

BARTOLOMÉ DE LAS CASAS

1474–1566 Bartolomé de las Casas was a Spanish priest who first exposed European oppression of Native Americans and who called for the abolition of native enslavement. He was born in Seville, Spain, probably in August 1474. After serving as a soldier and studying Latin, las Casas sailed to the West Indies in 1502. He received a land grant, which included the native inhabitants, primarily Indians, as part of the property.

After his ordination in 1513 he took part in the subjugation of Cuba and received another allotment of enslaved natives. As he evangelized to the indigenous population, he began to sympathize with their plight. After several trips to Spain to lobby on behalf of Native Americans, las Casas developed a joint Native-and-Spanish colony in South America in 1520, which quickly failed.

Subsequently, las Casas retreated to religious life. He produced many writings about the enslavement and brutalization of indigenous Americans and the religious implications of colonialization. Eventually, his work led to new laws that somewhat limited native enslavement. To enforce these laws, las Casas was named bishop of Chiapas in Guatemala in 1544. His final religious treatise forbade absolution for slave holders. Father las Casas died in Madrid, Spain, on July 7, 1566.

in the United States continue to proclaim their support for the U'wa and their opposition to the oil company.

BIBLIOGRAPHY

"Battle for the Sacred Oil." *Guardian* (London), 9 February 2000.

Chang, Chris. "A Leap of Faith," *Audubon*, January-February 2000, 14.

"Colombia: Guerrillas Admit Killing Three U.S. Citizens," *NotiSur - Latin American Political Affairs*, 12 March 1999.

Del Pilar Uirbe Marin, Monica. "Where Development Will Lead to Mass Suicide," *Ecologist* 29 (January-February 1999): 43.

"FARC Releases Communiqué on the Killing of US Citizens," *BBC Summary of World Broadcasts*, 13 March 1999.

Gibson, Bill. "Where Is Al Gore?" *LA Weekly*, 31 March 2000.

Marchocki, Kathryn. "Gore Headquarters Sit-In Site for Anti-Oil Drilling Activists," *Union Leader* (Manchester, N.H.), 27 January 2000.

Meriage, Larry. "Misinformation Surrounds Controversy Over Occidental's Colombian Wildcat," *Oil and Gas Journal* 98 (17 January 2000): 29.

"Native Rights Advocates and NGOs Criticize *El Tiempo El Tiempo*, 1 March 2000.

Selverston-Scher, Melina. "U'wa Indians Fight Back," *NACLA Report on the Americas* 33 (January 2000): 47.

Semple, Kirk. "Colombian Tribe Battles Oil Firm's Incursion," *Boston Globe*, 13 February 2000.

———. "The U'was' Last Stand," *U.S. News and World Report*, 14 February 2000.

Jeffrey S. Cole

CYPRUS: AN ISLAND DIVIDED

The island of Cyprus, roughly two-thirds the size of the state of Connecticut or the Bahamas, has long assumed an importance out of proportion to its size and population because of its strategic location and its impact on the national interests of other nations. Since the earliest days of maritime history the island's location in the eastern Mediterranean Sea has made it easily accessible from Europe, Asia, and Africa. Cyprus lies about 480 miles southeast of Greece, forty miles south of Turkey, and sixty miles west of Syria. Consequently, Cyprus has often been at the center of power struggles of some of the world's great civilizations and subject to foreign domination of its land and people.

Cyprus gained its independence in 1960 but since the Turkish invasion of 1974 has remained a partitioned island, divided along a line running east-west and through Nicosia, its capitol. The Greek Cypriot community to the south, known as the Republic of Cyprus, is internationally considered the official island government. The northern area, the Turkish Republic of North Cyprus, makes up thirty-seven percent of the island and is home to the smaller Turkish Cypriot community. A tortured history of ethnic intolerance keeps the island divided in the year 2000. A quarter century of ongoing negotiations sponsored by the United Nations have yet to produce a solution. At the beginning of the twenty-first century hopes run high that a shrinking, electronically communicating world and the need to establish commercial connections will push Cyprus toward reunification.

THE CONFLICT

Christian, Greek-ethnic Cyprus was ruled by the Ottoman Empire from 1571 until 1914, during which time many Muslim Turks moved to Cyprus. Following independence in 1959 (and earlier under British rule), tensions arose between the majority Greek Cypriots and the minority Turkish Cypriots, resulting in the division of the small island and the occupation of half of the island by Turkish troops.

Ethnic

- Greek Cypriots resented the disproportionate influence of the Turkish Cypriots in the government. Many Greek Cypriots supported union of Cyprus with Greece.

- Turkish Cypriots fear that their rights will be trampled by the majority Greek Cypriots, especially if Cyprus unifies with Greece. They look to Turkey for protection and support.

Political

- Turkey and Greece both feel obligated to their ethnic brothers in Cyprus. Turkey has troops in the Turkish Republic of Northern Cyprus to protect the Turkish Cypriots and deter union with Greece.

Economic

- Turkey, Greece, the Republic of Cyprus, and the Turkish Republic of Northern Cyprus are under considerable pressure to resolve the conflict in order to join the European Union, with the resulting trade benefits.

- The Turkish Republic of Northern Cyprus cannot export goods to the European Union member states.

CHRONOLOGY

1100–700 B.C. Mass migration of Greek-speaking people to Cyprus.

800 B.C. Phoenicians from the present-day Middle East migrate to Cyprus.

1571–1914 A.D. The Ottoman Empire rule Cyprus. Turkish Muslims move to Cyprus.

1850s With the Ottoman Empire in decline, the British agree to administer Cyprus on behalf of the Ottomans. Greek Cypriots seek unification with Greece.

1914 When Turkey (the seat of the Ottoman Empire) joins with Germany in World War I, Britain annexes Cyprus.

1915 Britain offers Cyprus to Greece in return for support during the war. Greece turns Britain down and remains neutral.

1954–55 Following a United Nations' decision not to take action on the issue of Cypriot self-determination, Greek Cypriots riot. The National

Organization of Cypriot Fighters, or EOKA, is formed and fights against the British.

1959 The Republic of Cyprus is formed and the Treaty of Alliance permits small numbers of Greek and Turkish troops to be stationed on Cyprus.

1963 The Cypriot president Markarios proposes changes to the constitution that enflames the Turkish Cypriot community. Inter-ethnic warfare continues and the Turkish Cypriot community begins moving north of the island and the Greek Cypriot community begins moving to the south.

1974 Following a Greek-sponsored coup d'état in Cyprus, Turkey invades the island, ultimately occupying the northern part of the island.

1983 Northern Cyprus declares statehood as the Turkish Republic of Northern Cyprus, though they are recognized only by Turkey.

2000 After years of unsuccessful negotiations, talks continue, with renewed signs of progress.

HISTORICAL BACKGROUND

Early History

From ancient times, Cyprus' tumultuous history has been a story of invasion and domination. Human habitation dates back from before 6000 B.C. After 1400 B.C. traders from the Peloponnesus began regular visits. Mass immigration of the Greek-speaking peoples from Peloponnese occurred between 1100 and 700 B.C.

With this migration, the island's culture became distinctively Hellenistic, or Greek dominated, and present day Greek Cypriots point to this period in arguing for their culture's dominance of the island. About 800 B.C. Phoenicians (present-day Middle East) settled on the island and lent a distinctive eastern influence. Three thousand years later some Turks and Turkish Cypriots look to this settlement as proof of early eastern cultural influence.

About 700 B.C., Cyprus came under Assyrian (present-day Iraq) rule followed by successive Egyptian, Persian, Greek, and, in 58 B.C., Roman domination. The most important event during Roman rule was the introduction of Christianity

in 45 A.D. when the apostle Paul landed on Cyprus accompanied by native Cypriot Barnabus. In 395 A.D. when the Roman Empire divided, Cyprus remained part of the eastern half of the Roman Empire, known as the Byzantine Empire. The island's history was part of that empire for the next eight hundred years, a period when Cyprus developed its strong Greek-Christian character reflected in the present-day Greek Cypriot community. After a brief possession by Richard the Lion-Hearted in approximately 1191, Cyprus fell into the hands of Guy de Lusignan, a dispossessed king of Jerusalem. The Lusignan dynasty established a Western feudal system in Cyprus. (Feudalism is a system whereby someone can hold a piece of land given to them by a lord in exchange for their service.)

In 1473 Cyprus came under Venetian control and was formally annexed by Venice in 1489. This annexation marked the end of the three hundred year Lusignan rule. Through those three centuries and in the subsequent eighty-two years of Venetian rule, Greek Cypriot serfs and laborers, who made up the majority of the population, managed to retain their native culture, language, and religion.

Ottoman Rule

Throughout the eight decades of Venetian rule, the Ottoman Turks relentlessly raided and pillaged Cyprus' communities. In 1539 the Turkish fleet destroyed the harbor town of Limassol. Although the Venetians fortified Nicosia, Kyrenia, and Famagusta, the other towns and villages proved easy prey for the aggressive Turks. The raids foreshadowed the full scale Turkish invasion in 1570. On July 2, 1570, sixty thousand troops landed near Limassol then immediately proceeded to Nicosia. Two months later on September 9, 1570, the city fell to the Turks who in victorious plundering put to death twenty thousand Nicosians and looted every church and public building. Kyrenia fell without a shot being fired. However, the Turks were not able to wrest control of Famagusta, which put up a determined defense, until August of 1571. The fall of Famagusta marked the beginning of three centuries of Ottoman rule.

The Greek Cypriots who survived the invasion yet again had new foreign rulers. However, some of the early decisions of the Ottoman rule brought welcomed changes. First, the feudal system was abolished allowing the freed Greek serfs to acquire and work their own land plus retain hereditary rights to the land. The end of serfdom profoundly improved the lot of the ordinary people.

Secondly, with the imposition of Ottoman rule, the Greek Cypriots, who were Orthodox Christians, began to develop a strong sense of cohesiveness. The Ottoman practice of ruling the empire through millets, or religious communities, prompted this development. The vast Ottoman Empire had many different ethnic religious communities. Rather than attempting to suppress individual religious communities, the Turks generally granted them a great deal of authority as long as they met the demands of the sultan, by collecting and paying taxes. Governing through millets reestablished the authority of the Church of Cyprus. The heads of the church became the leaders of the Greek Cypriots. The structured hierarchy of the church gave even remote villages easy access to a central authority. The leaders were responsible for overseeing the political and routine administrative activities of their communities and to collect taxes. Both the Ottoman Turks and the Greek Cypriots benefited from this arrangement. The empire received revenues from the collected taxes without the nuisance of daily administration. Greek Cypriots saw their Orthodox Church regain a measure of authority in the Greek communities, thereby reinforcing the cohesion of the ethnic Greek population.

MAP OF CYPRUS. *(XNR Productions Inc.)*

One of the more significant consequences of Ottoman conquest was the resettling of Turkish Muslims on Cyprus. Land was granted to the thousands of Turkish soldiers and peasants who settled on the island and established the first Turkish Cypriot communities.

Through the seventeenth and eighteenth centuries, Cyprus became a poor undeveloped backwater of the Ottoman Empire. The island's economy declined, due both to the empire's commercial incompetence and because the most important commercial trade routes shifted from the Mediterranean Sea to the Atlantic Ocean.

The rule of Cyprus by the Ottomans was sometimes indifferent, occasionally oppressive, and always inefficient and corrupt, ever susceptible to the whims of the various sultans. High taxes were demanded from both Greek and Turkish peasants. Uprisings both by Greek Cypriots and, occasionally, by Turkish Cypriots against Turkish misrule proved futile. In 1821 during the Greek mainland War of Independence, Ottoman rulers feared the Greek Cypriots would again rebel. The Ottomans rounded up and murdered the archbishops, bishops, and hundreds of priests and important laymen of the Church of Cyprus. These massacres caused considerable resentment against the Turks and furthered nationalist feelings among the Greeks.

Various Cypriot movements in the 1820s and 1830s continued in an effort to gain greater self-government. Three centuries of neglect by the Turks, coupled with the unending tax collections that left most of the people in poverty, served to fuel Greek nationalism. The Ottoman Turks were clearly the enemy in the eyes of Greek Cypriots. The Church of Cyprus remained the most important Greek institution and openly supported Greek nationalism. Years of domination had not destroyed the Greek Cypriots language, culture, and

SPARKED BY AN ABORTIVE COUP OF SUPPORTERS FOR A CYPRUS UNION WITH GREECE, TURKISH PARA-TROOPERS INVADED CYPRUS, CAUSING THOUSANDS OF GREEK CYPRIOTS TO FLEE AS THE TURKS OCCU-PIED NORTHERN CYPRUS. *(AP/Wide World Photos. Reproduced by permission.)*

religion that bound them to the rest of the Greek world. By the middle of the nineteenth century, *enosis*—union, or the idea of reuniting all Greek lands with the now independent Greek mainland— had taken root.

British Rule

The mid-1850s found the Ottoman Empire in serious decline. As the Ottoman Empire weakened, Russia, to the north, increased in strength and aggressively pushed southward attempting to expand the czar's empire to warm water ports. Desiring a base in the eastern Mediterranean, Britain agreed with Turkey in 1878 at the Cyprus Convention to administer Cyprus and protect the Ottoman Empire against Russian expansion. Initially believing the British would facilitate the unification of Cyprus with Greece as the British had done with the Ionian Islands, the Greek population welcomed them.

From the very beginning of their administration, the British were confronted with the Greek Cypriot's desire for *enosis*. The initial welcoming of the association with Britain quickly turned problematic due to the "Cyprus Tribute," payment to the sultan of island revenues above what was needed by the British to administer Cyprus' affairs. In re-

ality the payments ended up in the Bank of England. The annual tribute became an unending source of agitation and synonymous with British oppression.

Additionally, the British appeared to turn a deaf ear to the Greek Cypriot demand for *enosis*. The Turkish Cypriots who had been living on the island since the Ottoman invasion in 1571, were adamantly opposed to living as a minority under Greek rule. Few Turkish Cypriots objected to British rule and the British used them in the island's political structure to block Greek Cypriot efforts for *enosis*. For example, due to the way the Legislative Council was set up, voting generally resulted in a stalemate between the representatives of the Greek Cypriots and Turkish Cypriots. Only the British high commissioner, who usually favored the Turkish Cypriots, could break the stalemate.

British Annexation

With the advent of World War I, Turkey joined with Germany in 1914 in open hostility toward Britain and its allies. Britain annulled the Cyprus Convention and annexed Cyprus. Britain in 1915 actually offered the island to Greece hoping to induce Greece to enter the war on its side. Ironically, in light of the Greek Cypriot's fervent desire for *enosis*, King Constantine of Greece turned down the offer and held to a policy of neutrality.

Turkey formally recognized the British annexation in the 1923 Treaty of Lausanne and Cyprus officially became a crown colony in 1925. Although formal British rule brought improved efficiency in administration of Cyprus, there was little progress toward reconciliation of the most contentious issues. *enosis* continued to be a focal point for many Greek Cypriots. The enlarged Legislative Council still produced the same stalemate. The British government continued to rebuff pleas from Cypriots to make amends for the large sums of revenues placed in British coffers.

Contrarily, the British government proposed raising Cypriot taxes at the beginning of the 1930s to help meet deficits brought on by worsening world economic conditions. This proposal provoked mass protests and a violent riot that resulted in deaths, injuries, and the burning of the British Government House in Nicosia. Rebellious incidents occurred in a third of the island's almost six hundred villages. The British reacted with harsh measures. Particularly objectionable to the Greek Cypriots were British actions against the church. Several bishops were exiled and when the archbishop died in 1933 a standoff between the British officials and remaining church authorities kept the office vacant until 1947. The British downplayed the rule of the clergy in nationalist movements, enacted laws governing the internal affairs of the church, and prohibiting Cypriots to form any nationalist groups.

Post-World War II

In spite of the unpopular British rule, Cypriots firmly supported the Allied cause in World War II. More than 30,000 had served in various locations under British command by the war's end. Cyprus was left physically untouched by World War II, except for an occasional air raid. Yet, despite the show of patriotism against a common enemy, the vision of *enosis* remained in the minds of Greek Cypriots. During the entire war, supporters of *enosis* remained active, especially in London where they hoped to influence friends and lawmakers.

In October of 1947 Makarios II, the fiery bishop of Kyrenia, was elected archbishop of the Church of Cyprus. He refused to support any British policy that did not actively support *enosis*. None of Britain's post-war proposals for greater Cypriot self-government came close to fulfilling Greek Cypriot's ambitious expectations. The slogan of "*enosis* and only *enosis*" became popular within the Greek Cypriot communities.

In January of 1950, a ninety-six percent favorable vote for *enosis* was recorded. Makarios II died in June, and was succeeded by Makarios III, the bishop of Kition who at age thirty-seven was the youngest archbishop ever elected to the Church of Cyprus. Pledging at his inauguration to not rest until Cyprus was united with "Mother Greece," Makarios III proved to be a charismatic religious and political leader. He appeared before the United Nations (U.N.) in New York in 1951 to denounce the British policies. However, Britain insisted the Cyprus problem was an internal issue not subject to U.N. intervention.

At the same time Colonel George Grivas, a Cypriot native who had served in the mainland Greek army, began a determined effort to achieve *enosis*. Grivas, an avowed extremist, met with Markarios. But Makarios preferred to continue diplomatic efforts as opposed to instigating guerrilla uprisings. Grivas was disappointed with the archbishop's more moderate approach and the uneasy feeling between the two never dissipated.

Intensification and Estrangement

In August of 1954 Greece's representative at the United Nations formally petitioned that self-determination for the people of Cyprus be put on the agenda of the next session of the General Assembly. Archbishop Makarios seconded that request. The British position maintained the entire problem was an internal issue and Turkey steadfastly rejected the idea of union between Cyprus and Greece. The Turkish Cypriot community, whose minority status and identity had been protected under British rule, had previously refrained from direct action although they staunchly opposed *enosis*.

The official attitude of the Cyprus Turkish Minority Association, completely ignoring the 1923 Treaty of Lausanne in which Turkey gave up all rights to Cyprus, was that Cyprus would simply fall back under Turkish rule if the British ever withdrew. However, the increasing violence of the Greek Cypriot *enosist* movement of the 1950s concerned the smaller community and a Turkish Cypriot nationalism intensified to the point of rivaling the Greek Cypriot's passionate espousals. Some Turkish Cypriots began to advocate *taksim*, partition of the island, as a way of preventing them from becoming a minority in a Greek state.

The progressively widening division of Cyprus' Greek and Turkish communities was new to the island. The two groups had lived in mixed villages or in separate villages close to each other for centuries since the first Turk settlers arrived in 1571. Inter-communal relations were harmonious. Though intermarriage was rare, the two groups lived in congenial compatibility with inter-ethnic violence unheard of.

Mounting pressure for *enosis* during the twentieth century was the major reason for an increasing rift between the communities. The number of mixed villages declined while the first instances of inter-communal violence occurred. Underlying complexities included the British colonial policy of "divide and rule" as exhibited in legislature stalemates. The two communities' interests were pitted against each other with the British high commissioners casting a deciding vote. This served to maintain London's hold on Cyprus and fostered inter-communal animosity and distrust. Scholars have often noted that failure of British rule to engender a sense of Cypriot nationalism unifying all of Cyprus' population left a fateful legacy that doomed the Republic of Cyprus from the start.

Yet another underlying cause of the increased estrangement between the Greek and Turkish Cypriots was the practice in schools of the two communities using textbooks from their respective motherlands. The books were full of examples of cruelty, greed, deceitfulness, and atrocities committed during centuries of conflict between the two traditional enemies, Greeks and the Turkish empire.

As a result of these various factors the stage was set for inter-communal violence that erupted in the winter of 1954–55. In December the U.N. General Assembly considered the Cyprus issue and announced a decision to not take any action on the problem. Greek Cypriots reacted swiftly and violently with the worst riots since 1931. Makarios returned to Nicosia from the United Nations in New York on January 10, 1955. The more rabid Colonel Grivas had also returned to Cyprus. Makarios agreed with Grivas to form the National Organization of Cypriot Fighters (Ethnic Organosis Kyprion Agoniston - EOKA). EOKA quickly became widely known.

Under the leadership of Grivas, EOKA launched a four-year revolutionary struggle. A campaign of violence against British rule targeted government installations in Nicosia, Famagusta, Larnaca, and Limassol. Turkish Cypriots were asked to stand clear and refrain from opposing the violence against the British.

A meeting in London between Britain, Greece, and Turkey in August of 1955 accomplished nothing and only served to polarize the nations' positions. Greece was disturbed that self-determination, now a keyword for *enosis*, was not offered; and the Turks were disturbed because it was not forbidden. For Turkey an insurmountable barrier to *enosis* was that it meant Greek forces would be on an island only forty miles from its shore. Turkey found this completely unacceptable. Shortly, Greece withdrew its representatives from the NATO headquarters in Turkey and relations between the two NATO countries became severely strained.

Britain attempted to follow a get-tough policy in Cyprus against EOKA. In January of 1954 Makarios was arrested, charged with complicity in violence, and along with the bishop of Kyrenia and two other priests exiled to Seychelles. This action only served to leave the less moderate Grivas in charge of EOKA. Meanwhile, the Turkish Cypriots formed an underground organization known as Volkan (Volcano). Volkan established in 1957 the Turkish Resistance Organization (TMT). TMT vowed to fight for Turkish Cypriot interests.

By early 1958 inter-communal strife plagued the two communities on the island. Grivas tried to enforce an island-wide boycott of British goods and EOKA carried out sabotage attacks. In response to the crisis, British Prime Minister Harold Mac-

millan proposed the Macmillan Plan. This plan would devise a seven-year scheme of separate communal legislative bodies and separate municipalities. Greece and Greek Cypriots rejected it, saying the plan in essence put taksim in place, partitioning the island as desired by many Turkish Cypriots. Although not accepted, the Macmillan Plan spurred further talks.

In Zurich in February of 1959 talks between Greece and Turkey yielded a compromise agreement supporting Cyprus as an independent state. Greece, although still supporting *enosis*, realized the compromise avoided partition and Turkey avoided having yet another island off its coast under Greek control. Britain had preferred a more gradual end to its rule. But given the armed violence in the second half of the 1950s it looked at the creation of an independent Cypriot republic as the only way out of a difficult situation. Britain's eastern Mediterranean military needs would be met by allowing two British military bases on the island's southern coast.

Representatives of the Greek Cypriots and Turkish Cypriots along with Markarios who had since left the Seychelles convened with officials from Greece and Turkey in London. When Greek authorities failed to back Makarios' objections to the proposals, he accepted the agreements as a pragmatic course to follow. Ratified by all parties, the Zurich-London agreements became the foundation for the independent Cyprus constitution of 1960. Three provisions were the Treaty of Guarantee, the Treaty of Alliance, and the Treaty of Establishment. The "emergency" was declared over on December 4, 1959.

Independence—the Republic of Cyprus
The Greek Cypriots regarded the London agreement for independence as unsatisfactory but an acceptable alternative. The goal for which they had fought so hard during the emergency years was not reached. Cyprus would not be united with Greece but their worst fear, partition, would also not come about. The Turkish Cypriots, having faired well in the negotiations, readily accepted the agreements.

The Treaty of Guarantee ensured that Greece, Turkey, and Britain would guarantee the independence and sovereignty of the republic of Cyprus. Cyprus would not unite with any other state or be subject to partition. The signers of the agreements were pledged to uphold the "state of affairs." According to Article IV of the treaty, if the "state of affairs" was in danger or violated, Greece, Turkey, and Britain must act together to restore it.

GREEK CYPRIOT MILITARY FORTIFICATION BEHIND THE "GREEN LINE" AND BUFFER ZONE SEPARATING TURKS AND GREEKS IN NICOSIA, THE WAR-DIVIDED CAPITAL OF CYPRUS. *(AP/Wide World Photos. Reproduced by permission.)*

If joint actions were impossible, these states could act independently.

The Treaty of Alliance established tripartite headquarters (Cyprus, Greece, and Turkey) on the island and permitted Greece and Turkey to station 950 and 650 military personnel, respectively, to protect the island and help train its own army. The Treaty of Establishment allowed Britain sovereignty over 256 square kilometers of land on the southern coast for two military bases, Akrotiri and Dhekelia. Between the signing of the agreements in early 1959 and independence on August 16, 1960, further negotiations produced a long and detailed constitution that included extensive protections for the rights of the Turkish Cypriot minority.

Immediately preceding the August 16 date, elections were held in accordance with the constitutional arrangements. Among other requirements, Cyprus was to elect a Greek Cypriot president and a Turkish Cypriot vice president, both having veto power over the other. Makarios returned to Cyprus on March 1, 1959, and was elected president. Fazil Kücük, leader of the Turkish Cypriots was elected vice president. A fifty-member House of Representatives was to have thirty-five seats allotted to Greek Cypriots and fifteen to Turkish Cypriots. At the head of the judicial system would be the Supreme Constitutional Court with one Greek Cypriot and one Turkish Cypriot and presided over

by a judge from a neutral country. Rather than having a combined government, perpetuation of the separation of the two communities continued with the strongly bi-communal structure and function of the new government. In September of 1959 the new republic became a member of the United Nations, and in 1961 of the European Commonwealth, the International Monetary Fund, and the World Bank.

Independence and peace proved not to be synonymous. From the outset, governing the island became a difficult, contentious challenge. Serious problems with the constitution arose immediately. Greek Cypriot's were disgruntled over the Turkish Cypiots having a larger share of government than would be dictated by the size of their population. Formation of a Cypriot army composed of both ethnic groups, posed another problem. Makarios insisted on completely integrated forces, while Kücük favored segregated companies. Plans for the national army ceased. These difficulties reflected the now sharp division between the two communities. Acrimony made a spirit of cooperation impossible.

Violent Outbreaks of the 1960s
Both the EOKA and TMT reorganized in 1961–62, began training, and smuggled in weapons from their respective countries, Greece and Turkey.

Growing contingents of Greek and Turkish soldiers from the mainland, far in excess of the Treaty of Alliance numbers, arrived and joined with their respective ethnic organization. Friction rose, each side accused the other of constitutional violations and the courts were unable to decide disputes. Many Cypriots believed the government under the complicated terms of the 1960 constitution could not function.

In late 1963 Markarios decided only a bold move could save his country. He proposed a thirteen point series of constitutional changes to remove the impediments to a properly functioning government. The proposals, abhorrent to the Turkish community, considerably lessened the political rights and powers of the Turkish Cypriots. The tense atmosphere on the island exploded into serious inter-communal violence. In March of 1964 the U.N. Secretary General U Thant ordered the first members of the United Nation Peace Keeping Force in Cyprus (UNFICYP) to the island. By May 6, five hundred troops were in Cyprus. Although authorized for only a three-month period, a considerable contingent remained in 2000.

As the worst fighting subsided, Turkish Cypriots, some voluntarily and others forced by the TMT, began moving from their isolated rural homes and mixed villages to Turkish enclaves, predominately in Nicosia, where they hastily erected tents and built shacks. Many who did not move into Nicosia gave up their farms for the protection of other Turkish enclaves. Fear of further Greek Cypriot violence precipitated the moves.

In June of 1964 the House of Representatives with only its Greek Cypriot members participating established a National Guard with Grivas returning to Cyprus as its commander. Turkish Cypriots and mainland Turkey charged that large numbers of Greek regular army troops were being added to the National Guard. Only a harshly worded warning from the U.S. president Lyndon B. Johnson to the prime minister of Turkey thwarted an invasion of the island by Turkey.

Inter-communal violence again erupted in 1967 when Grivas and the National Guard initiated patrols into Turkish Cypriot enclaves. Fighting broke out and ultimately twenty-six Turkish Cypriots were killed. The incident left Turkey and Greece on the brink of war. President Johnson again intervened by sending Cyrus R. Vance to Ankara to begin negotiations. After ten days Greece and Turkey withdrew troops back to the 1960 treaty levels, and Grivas resigned his command post and left Cyprus. The crisis passed.

However, in a move which would come back to haunt him in 1974, Makarios did not disband the National Guard.

Markarios Maintains Rule

In 1967 a coup d'état entrenched a military dictatorship in Athens, Greece, that lasted until 1974. Many in the Athens regime pushed for *enosis* for Cyprus and were even willing to cede parts of Cyprus to Turkey in exchange for uniting the rest of the island with Greece. Greek pro-*enosis*ts and rightwing Greek Cypriots pressured Makarios with their demands. But in 1968 Makarios who had been reelected president of Cyprus in an overwhelming victory, saw the victory as a strong endorsement of his leadership and of an independent Cyprus. President Makarios stated that the Cyprus problem could not be solved with force but only worked out under the auspices of the United Nations

Inter-communal talks in the United Nations began in 1968 with Turkish Cypriots emphasizing the importance of local government in each community instead of the central government. Taking a directly opposite position, Greek Cypriot teams stressed central governing authorities over local administrations. In essence the Turks demanded a bizonal federation with a weak central government—a plan the Greeks rejected. The talks would stretch until 1974 with no real agreements reached. Meanwhile, Cyprus was in fact operating as a partitioned country. Makarios was president but his command did not reach into the Turkish enclaves. Moreover, the House of Representatives was functioning only with the thirty-five Greek Cypriot representatives. The reality of Cyprus was that the partition sought for years by Turks and Turkish Cypriots existed. Inter-communal strife continued unabated.

Sometime in mid-1971 Grivas, who had called Makarios a traitor to *enosis* in an Athens newspaper, secretly returned to Cyprus. He began to rebuild EOKA, now called EOKA B, with funds from the Athens *junta* (rulers). EOKA B's goal was to overthrow Makarios. Although Makarios had once been a strong leader in the campaign for *enosis*, he was now seen by many mainland Greeks and Greek Cypriots to be content with Cyprus independence. Those angered with Makarios are assumed to have been behind an assassination attempt in 1970 on Makarios' life. Once EOKA B was in place, Grivas directed terrorist attacks and propaganda campaigns against Makarios. In 1972 three bishops of the Church of Cyprus demanded Makarios resign. Makarios, totally embroiled in the struggle for power within the Greek nationalist community, was in a perilous position. Even though mass demonstrations proved that most people of Cyprus remained behind him, Makarios did bow somewhat to Greek pressure and reshuffled his cabinet. His overall fame and popularity in both Greece and Cyprus prevented his removal. Suddenly in 1974 Grivas died of a heart attack, but terrorism continued as one hundred thousand mourners vowed to continue his pursuit of *enosis*.

Partition

Another coup d'état in Athens in November of 1973 made General Dimitrios Ioannides leader of the *junta* in Greece. Ioannides was convinced Makarios should be removed from office. In July of 1974 the military *junta* in Athens sponsored a coup to overthrow Makarios and take control of the island. The Cypriot National Guard, infiltrated with over six hundred Greek officers and led by extremist Greek Cypriots hostile to Makarios for his perceived abandonment of *enosis*, carried out the coup.

Makarios barely escaped with his life and fled to London. The EOKA terrorist Nicos Sampson replaced Makarios as provisional president. Obvious to Turkey that Athens was behind the rightist coup, on July 20, 1974, Turkish forces invaded Cyprus. The Turkish government cited the terms of Article IV of the Treaty of Guarantee to justify the invasion. Turkey pointed out Britain's reluctance to use military force and the impossibility of joint action with Greece. Therefore, they unilaterally had to restore the "state of affairs" established by the 1960 treaties. Within three days, the Greek *junta* collapsed in Athens and Sampson resigned in Nicosia. Glafkos Clerides, the then-president of the Cypriot House of Representatives automatically became head of state replacing the short-tenured Sampson. The Turkish army remained on Cyprus and mounted a second brief campaign in mid-August.

Meanwhile, the three guarantor powers, Britain, Greece, and Turkey, met as required by the Treaty of Guarantee in Geneva but were unable to halt the Turkish advance until August 16. By that time Turkey had occupied the northern portion of Cyprus, 37 percent of the entire island.

The consequence of the Turkish invasion, or "military action" as the Turks preferred to call it, was a de facto partition of Cyprus. At the cessation of fighting, about 7,000 people were dead or unaccounted for. Each side suffered enormously. As many as 165,000 Greeks fled from the north side of the island to the south leaving behind their property and possessions. Many lived for months in crudely erected camps in southern Cyprus. To escape bloody reprisals of Greek nationalists, approximately fifty-five thousand Turkish Cypriots fled to the north. In all approximately one third of the island's population had been forced to leave their places of birth. The island's economy was left in shambles.

Inter-Communal Talks Resume

The 1974 military action left Cyprus partitioned along a line, called the "Attila line," running from Morphou Bay in the northwest to Famagusta in the east. With the Turkish Cypriots to the north and the Greek Cypriots south of the line, each ethnic community rebuilt their government and economy entirely separately. Both communities undertook efforts to remedy the effects of the catastrophe. They built housing for the refugees and integrated them into their rebounding economies. Both soon developed stable political systems.

Makarios returned to southern Greek Cyprus as president. The Greek Cyprus government in the south was internationally recognized as the official, legal government of Cyprus and the southern region continued the title of Republic of Cyprus. In February of 1975 the Turkish Cypriots declared the northern occupied territory a self-governing region to be called the Turkish Federated State of Cyprus. A provisional government was set into place with Rauf Denktash elected president in July of 1975.

Inter-communal talks to bring the two communities together again resumed in Vienna in January of 1975. The Makarios government met with Denktash. Both declared support for an independent Cyprus but serious differences existed over the form of government, size of the area to be retained by the Turkish Cypriots, return of refugees with compensation for property loses, and the withdrawal of Turkish troops.

After intensive U.N. efforts, Makarios and Denktash met again in early 1977. On February 12 the two men agreed on several substantive guidelines. The most important was that Cyprus would be a bi-communal federal republic, a bi-zonal country where the two communities would live in two separate zones with separate governments, while a weak central government would be established for administrative purposes and to safeguard the unity of the country. The agreement raised hopes of Cyprus' foreign friends that a settlement could be reached. The hopes came crashing down when Makarios, long the central figure in the Greek Cypriot community, died of a heart attack in

GREEK CYPRIOT DEMONSTRATORS THROW STONES AT TURKISH TROOPS IN PROTEST OF THE TURKISH OCCUPATION OF NORTHERN CYPRUS. *(AP/Wide World Photos. Reproduced by permission.)*

August of 1977. Although he had just agreed to a bi-zonal Cyprus, personally Makarios had expressed extreme regret over his long support of *enosis* that he believed ultimately led to the partitioning of Cyprus. In his own words, partitioning had "destroyed Cyprus" and he died a tragic figure. The overriding issue of all talks through the end of the twentieth century would be how to deal with the partition of the island.

Spyros Kyprianou, Makarios' successor, pledged to follow the positions he believed Makarios would have taken. But it quickly became ap-

parent he did not have the political skills and maneuverability of Makarios. In early 1979 President Kyprianou met with Denktash and the two leaders agreed on several points calling for resumption of talks on all territorial and constitutional issues. Although the points were a tactical means to secure further negotiations, no substantive issues were resolved.

With the continuing stalemate in negotiations, on November 15, 1983, Denktash declared Turkish Cypriot statehood. Citing the United States Declaration of Independence, he declared the establishment of the Turkish Republic of Northern Cyprus (TRNIC). Denktash insisted the move was not intended to block progress toward creating the bi-zonal republic. Rather, it was an assertion of political identity and equality of the Turkish Cypriots that would enhance prospects for a new relationship with the Greek Cypriots. The people of TRNC approved a new constitution in a referendum in 1985 and elected Denktash as their president. Only Turkey recognizes the self-proclaimed state, and no other countries established diplomatic relations with the North Cyprus state.

In February of 1988 the Greek Cypriots elected George Vassiliou as president. Vassiliou had campaigned on a pledge to solve the Cyprus problem with new energy and ideas. The United Nations arranged for meetings between Vassiliou and Denktash in 1988 and 1989. Regretfully, the secretary general reported the gap remained wide. Talks collapsed in early 1990 and, entering the last decade of the twentieth century, Cyprus remained partitioned.

1990s—A Land Divided

At the end of the twentieth century approximately two thousand members of the United Nations Peace-Keeping Force (UNFICYP) patrolled the buffer zone surrounding the so-called "green line" which divides the Republic of Cyprus from the Turkish Republic of Northern Cyprus. The U.N.-monitored divide extends east-west across the island and through Nicosia. Turkish and Greek Cypriot troops face each other across this buffer zone. On the Turkish side is the Turkish Cypriot Security Force supported by an estimated thirty thousand soldiers of the mainland Turkey army. On the Greek side, the Cypriot National Guard maintains a force of approximately thirteen thousand active troops. Except for a violent clash in 1996 leaving two demonstrators dead, no violent conflict has occurred since 1974. There is virtually no movement of people, goods, or services across the line.

The official population of the entire island in 1997 was estimated at 838,000. The Greek area held 655,000 and the Turkish area 183,000. Greek Cypriots made up seventy-eight percent of the population, Turkish Cypriots eighteen percent, and Maronites, Armenians, Greeks, and other Europeans contribute four percent. Ethnic nationalism permeates the two regions further entrenching the divide. Turkish flags fly above many buildings in the north, just as the Greek cross of St. Andrew appears on all church and public buildings in the south. The Turkish Cypriots speak Turkish, practice the Islamic religion, and clearly look to the Turkish mainland for support. The Greek Cypriots speak Greek, practice the Greek Orthodox religion of the Church of Cyprus, and orient toward Athens and Europe. Linguistic and cultural barriers increase as time passes. The only Turkish Cypriots who speak Greek are a few older people who worked in Greek businesses before 1974. Most young adult Greek Cypriots have never even seen a Turkish Cypriot and vice versa.

The economic disparity between the Greek south and Turkish north is significant. The economy of the south is extremely prosperous, while the northern Turkish economy is much smaller and poorer. The flourishing Greek Cypriot economy creates a standard of living in the south superior to some western European nations. This achievement was made possible by a flexible and skilled workforce, a well entrenched entrepreneurial class, a sophisticated program of government planning including economic incentives and wise investments, and a highly successful tourist industry that welcomed over a million tourists, mostly from Western Europe by the early 1970s. The service industry employs 60 percent of the labor force. Most services are directly related to tourism, the mainstay of the economy. Greek Cypriot per capita income was $13,000 in 1997. Prosperity has permitted an expansion of the educational system. Although students must travel abroad for university studies, the Republic of Cyprus has one of the highest rates of university graduates.

The Turkish Cypriot economy also operates on a free market basis but has grown much slower. Economic obstacles include lack of private and government investment, a lesser trained work force, rampant inflation and devaluation of the Turkish lira, and a Greek Cypriot economic blockade. The Turkish Cypriot per capita income is $3,600. The largest economic hurdle making foreign connections difficult is the state's lack of international recognition. In 1994 the European Court of Justice ruled that European Union member countries could only import produce from Cyprus which bore the official Government of Cyprus certificate of origin, meaning produce from the south or Republic of Cyprus. Turkey is the TRNC's primary trading partner supplying fifty-five percent of imports and absorbing forty-eight percent of exports. Economic assistance from Turkey is the Turkish Cypriot economic mainstay. However, tourism has been expanding to upwards of 360,000 tourists yearly, mainly from Turkey and the Arab world.

The Republic of Cyprus and the TRNC both have entirely separate stable republic forms of government. The Greek Cypriots elected Glafkos Clerides, a seasoned politician, as president in 1993 and again in 1998. Clerides' party, the Democratic Rally (DISY), believes membership in the European Union could help bring a peaceful solution to the problem of partition.

Rauf Denktash, the only person to have ever been elected president of the TRNC, was reelected in 1995 for a third term. He is highly trusted by Turkish Cypriots and seen as the best person to find a fair solution to the problems of partition.

1990s Inter-Communal Negotiations

World leaders continue to consider the status quo of Cyprus as unacceptable and view U.N.-led inter-communal negotiations as the best means to achieve a fair and permanent settlement. Over the years, negotiations have consistently faced the same major stumbling blocks. Number one is the lack of consensus between the two communities over how to govern and administer the island. The Turkish Cypriot's focus is on bi-zonality, political equality between the two communities, and security guarantees. They envision a loose federation of two nearly autonomous societies and governments that have limited contact. They want both to be recognized internationally as separate entities. The Greek Cypriots seek more integration and a more powerful central authority that, by virtue of their greater numbers, they would probably control. Greek Cypriots worry that international recognition of the north as a separate "nation" would legitimize the 1974 "invasion" and perhaps lead to the secession of northern Cyprus or to its union with Turkey. The Greek Cypriots seek a right of movement within the federation so Greek Cypriots would be able to return to their homes in the north, property settlements, and the return of a portion of territory lost in 1974. Turkish Cypriots reject these demands, fearing they could quickly become a minority in their own sector. Greek Cypriots also demand a timetable for withdrawal of Turkish forces from the island. Turkish Cypriots want the Turkish military to remain to guarantee their security and political rights. One further problem involves the approximately eighty thousand Turkish settlers who arrived from mainland Turkey after 1974. The Greek Cypriots do not recognize them and there is swelling resentment against them from the Turkish Cypriots as well.

Inter-communal negotiations sponsored by the United Nations in 1992 worked with a set of ideas that included many hard-won compromises from earlier negotiations on the difficult issues. Optimism was greater than usual that these talks between Greek Cypriot President Vassiliou and Turkish Cypriot President Denktash would yield a settlement. Yet, hung up on the same major points, they ended unsuccessfully in November of 1992.

Face to face meetings occurred again between the two communities' leaders, Greek Cypriots President Clerides and Mr. Denktash in 1997 and 1998. U.N. mediation by American and Russian negotiators failed to end the stalemate. Illustrating how difficult and complex the issues are, Clerides and Denktash, longtime friends and London-trained lawyers with detailed knowledge of the problem, were unable to come to an acceptable solution.

RECENT HISTORY AND THE FUTURE

Next Big Push for Peace—2000

Under heavy pressure from Washington, European leaders, and the United Nations, Clerides and Denktash scheduled "proximity talks" (where a diplomat moves between two separate meeting rooms) in Geneva in January of 2000. Optimism ran high spawned by a remarkable thaw in relations between Greece and Turkey that perhaps would trickle down to the divided Cyprus.

At the beginning of the twenty-first century an outbreak of peace and goodwill seemed to be spreading across the Aegean. A series of recent incidents plus major national interests were driving the cooperation between the ancient enemies. First in February of 1999, Athens was embarrassed when the Greek Embassy in Kenya sheltered Abdullah Ocalan, head of the P.K.K., the Kurdish rebel movement responsible for terrorism in Turkey. An outcry in Greece forced the hardline nationalist Foreign Minister Theodore Pangalos, known to refer to Turks as "rapists and thieves," to resign. He was replaced by George Papandreou who wasted no time in finding common ground with Turkish Foreign Minister Ismail Cem. In early 2000 each visited the other country—remarkable in that a Greek foreign prime minister had not visited Ankara in forty years.

Second, in August of 1999, a massive earthquake struck Turkey killing seventeen thousand people leading to an outpouring of sympathy and aid from Greece for the victims. Then, when an earthquake shook Greece a month later, a similar response came from the Turks. Conceptions that the two peoples were permanently incompatible tumbled.

National interests were also driving the cooperation. Greece, to keep pace with Turkey, could no longer afford to spend a high proportion of its budget on defense. Greek businessmen were clamoring for access to the large untapped Turkish market. For their part, Turkey was eager to become part of the European Union (E.U.), a powerful organization of fifteen European countries promoting cooperation in economics, politics, and foreign policy issues. Greece had been a member since 1981. In December of 1999 Greece agreed to Turkey finally becoming a candidate member of the European Union. To become a full member, the European Union said Turkey must push to settle its disputes with Greece including the ethnic stand-off in Cyprus.

Amid this conciliatory spirit of at least the mainland countries and with hopes the two Cyprus leaders would be creative in their approaches, Clerides and Denktash met in January and again in early July of 2000. The latest rounds produced nothing except agreement to meet again. The two disagreed on the same sorts of issues that they had disagreed on for decades: a central government, or a "confederation" as Dentash now called it, of two independent states; how to make the Turkish Cypriot minority feel secure; the return of land to the Greek Cypriots. The European Union also entered the picture. Greek Cypriots had been making progress in an effort to join the European Union on behalf of all islanders. Looking for membership, the Greek Cypriots had been steadily investing in upgraded air and seaports, improved banking systems, and telecommunications. Denktash had steadfastly refused to take part in the E.U. talks saying Turkish Cypriots could have no part of European Union until Turkey joined. However, now not only was Turkey's full membership imminent but it appeared Cyprus could be let into the Union within five years if the fifteen countries of European Union would agree to accept a divided island. Denktash seemed to be less strident in dismissing the European Union. The next talks between Clerides and Denktash were scheduled for July 24, 2000.

Meanwhile, even if the warming relations in the Aegean had not reached the hearts and minds of the two elderly leaders, it had reached the people of Cyprus. Flustered by years of deadlock, people were no longer waiting for settlement to come from politicians and outside powers. Recently, low profile meetings between people of both sides were thawing relations considerably. The Internet had become an invaluable tool for contact. Young people who felt no animosity against those they had never met, kept in touch across the Green Line through electronic mail. While the old men negotiated in Geneva, the young people organized a bicommunal picnic at a neutral site near Pergamos within territory administered by one of the British military bases that straddles the dividing line in the southeast of the island. Not only did the young people meet but they brought together Greek and Turkish Cypriots who used to live together in mixed villages before the 1974 violence. Hundreds managed to attend the event. Many Turkish Cypriots brought photographs of the villages the Greek Cypriots were forced to leave twenty-five years earlier. It was reported that all got along well, they had no problems and most were at a loss to explain what had gone so wrong. It appeared the reunification of Cyprus might not lie with the leaders but with a grassroots groundswell of ordinary people communicating via electronic mail and lamb kebabs.

BIBLIOGRAPHY

Borowiec, Andrew. *Cyprus: A Troubled Island.* Westport, Conn.: Praeger Publications, 2000.

Bulmer, Robert. *Essential Cyprus.* Lincolnwood, Ill.: National Textbook Company Publishing Group, 2000.

Crenshaw, Nancy. *The Cyprus Revolt.* London: George Allen and Unwin, 1978.

Durrell, Lawrence. *Bitter Lemons.* New York: Marlowe, 1996.

Hill, George. *History of Cyprus.* 4 vols. London: Cambridge University Press, 1940–52.

Hitchens, Christopher. *Hostage to History: Cyprus from the Ottomans to Kissinger.* New York: Noonday Press, 1989.

Joseph, Joseph S. *Cyprus Ethnic Conflict and International Politics: From Independence to the Threshold of the European Union.* New York: St. Martin's Press, 1999.

Koumoulides, John T.A., ed. *Cyprus in Transition, 1960–1985.* London: Trigraph, 1986.

Markides, Kyriacos C. *The Rise and Fall of the Cyprus Republic.* New Haven, Conn.: Yale University Press, 1977.

Mayes, Stanley. *Makarios: A Biography.* New York: St. Martin's Press, 1981.

O'Malley, Brendon, and Ian Craig. *The Cyprus Conspiracy: America, Espionage and the Turkish Invasion.* New York: St. Martin's Press, 2000.

Panteli, Stavros. *A New History of Cyprus: From the Earliest Times to the Present Day.* London: East-West, 1984.

Rogerson, Barnaby. *Cyprus.* Old Saybrook, Conn.: Globe Pequot Press, 1994.

Rustem, K., ed. "Turkish Republic of North Cyprus." In *North Cyprus Almanack.* London: K. Rustem and Brother, 1987.

Sevcenko, Nancy, and Christopher Moss, eds. *Medieval Cyprus.* Princeton, N.J.: Princeton University Press, 1999.

Solsten, Eric, ed. *Cyprus: A Country Study.* Washington, D.C.: Federal Research Division, Library of Congress, 1991.

Stefanidis, Ioannis D. *Isle of Discord: Nationalism, Imperialism and the Making of the Cyprus Problem.* New York: New York University Press, 1999.

Stephens, Robert. *Cyprus: A Place of Arms.* New York: Frederick A. Praeger, 1966.

Streissguth, Thomas. *Cyprus: Divided Island.* Minneapolis, Minn.: Lerner Publications, 1998.

Richard C. Hanes

EAST TIMOR: THE PATH OF DEMOCRACY FOR THE WORLD'S NEWEST NATION

THE CONFLICT

In 1999 East Timor erupted in bloodshed following a vote for independence. East Timor had been ruled by Indonesia, and had voted in support of independence. Anti-independence militias attacked the people of East Timor.

Political

- During the Cold War, the West supported Indonesia's takeover of East Timor because of its emerging socialist regime.

- In 1999 the people of East Timor sought, campaigned for and won an election that would grant them independence from Indonesia.

Religious

- Indonesia is predominately Muslim. East Timor is predominately Catholic. The rebels who attacked the East Timorese were Muslims who did not want to see East Timor become independent from Indonesia. There has been some suggestions that the Indonesian army participated in or encouraged the killing.

In August 1999, the people of East Timor went to the polls to vote for their independence. After years of military occupation by Indonesia, the whole world watched what was to be a triumph of democracy for the eastern section of a small island four hundred miles north of Australia. The event became an international affair. To insure that the referendum was free and fair, a United Nations (U.N.) observer team registered voters and made sure polling stations were not tampered with. Members of the media from all over the world descended on East Timor to report the good news and more than seventy-five percent of the people of East Timor cast a ballot for independence. Then, in what seemed a bizarre turn of events, East Timor erupted in violence. A group of anti-independence militias attacked the people of East Timor, set fire to their homes, looted cities, and wiped out entire villages. The militias then turned their weapons on the outside media and the U.N. observers, forcing them to flee as well. The world was shocked by the chaos and devastation that followed. Images of cities and villages on fire, families fleeing violence and slaughter, and hundreds of thousands of refugees trapped in West Timor caught the attention of the world.

According to Seth Mydans in the October 31, 1999 edition of the *New York Times*, in the twenty-five years leading up to the referendum, it is estimated that over two hundred thousand died because of Indonesia's occupation. Yet, for many years, most of this bloodshed went unnoticed. Although painfully familiar to people in Australia and Indonesia, this tragedy never seemed to make it into international headlines. Only bits and pieces of horrendous stories about torture and unlawful imprisonment occasionally trickled out. Then in 1991, East Timor was thrust onto the world's stage.

CHRONOLOGY

1515 Portuguese land on East Timor; later, East Timor becomes a Portuguese colony.

1600s The Portuguese and Dutch fight for control of the island.

1859 The Portuguese and the Dutch divide the island in half.

1914 The division of the island is made legal by the International Court of Justice.

1920 An uprising in East Timor is suppressed. More than three hundred thousand are estimated to have died.

1942 Japan invades East Timor. After World War II the Portuguese return.

1975 FRETILIN, a rebel group, declares independence. Indonesia invades and subdues East Timor.

1979 Massive famine hits East Timor.

1980 FALINTIL and other rebel groups fight the Indonesians and control parts of the country.

1991 The Indonesian army massacres Timorese civilians in Dili, in the Santa Cruz Massacre.

1997 The Asian financial crisis causes economic turmoil.

1998 Indonesian president Suharto resigns.

1999 Indonesian president Habibie agrees to hold referendum on independence. East Timorese votes for independence from Indonesia. Violence follows, as militias attack people and loot cities.

Under the watchful eye of Western reporters, members of the Indonesian Army massacred Timorese civilians in capital city of Dili. However, soon after this event, the problems within East Timor and its relations with Indonesia again lost international attention. The people of East Timor often complained that they were "forgotten by the world." In similar cases, like China's relationship with Tibet and Russia's breakaway republic of Chechnya, the world watched the situation unfold slowly and tragically. This is not the case with East Timor. The international community only began to take notice again in 1999 and even then, the events were described by one reporter covering the story as "news from nowhere."

Although East Timor spent most of the time out of the international spotlight, it felt the presence of the world for years. For centuries, international politics—with its colonial history, world wars, Cold War, and growing emphasis on human rights—influenced life the eastern part of the island. East Timor's economic development and political stability were shaped by events in other countries. Overall, the situation has proven tragic for all parties involved. In addition to the cost of human life, this internal war has destroyed the economy, scarred social relations between Muslims and Catholics, and scattered people throughout the island, creating a serious refugee problem. Nor has

this been a success story for Indonesia as approximately twenty thousand military personnel died fighting for control of the province. Now, in a recent turn of events, East Timor's problems are relevant to the rest of the world. Recent evidence of years of Indonesia's military brutality on the people of East Timor now stains Indonesia's international image of peace, prosperity, and development.

HISTORICAL BACKGROUND

The Geography and People of East Timor

East Timor is situated in the eastern portion of an island between Indonesia and Australia over an area that is about 5714 square miles (a little larger than the U.S. state of Connecticut and a little smaller than Kuwait). The terrain of East Timor is dramatic, with high mountain ranges dropping down to large plains that reach to the sea. The Sea of Timor, located between the Island and Australia, holds vast oil reserves. The economy is largely based on agriculture. Before the Portuguese colonized East Timor, most people were farmers with a handful of isolated fishing communities near coastal areas. The majority of East Timorese live in isolation, far from towns and foreign influences. Despite this, the island of East Timor is not secluded. Even before the Europeans arrived, many maritime explorers from China and India visited the island.

Today, diverse ethnicity, language, religion, and history create a patchwork quilt of people living in East Timor. Most observers identify two primary ethnic groups, the Belu (descendants of Malays who are predominantly in the southern portion) and the Atoni (concentrated in the central highlands). There are also several smaller ethnic groups, like the decedents of African slaves brought by the Portuguese. East Timor is home to a kaleidoscope of culture with at least eleven different languages including Tetum, Timorese or Vaiqueno, Portuguese and Indonesian. The terrain, which isolates many of Timor's residents from each other, maintains the diversity of the population. At the same time, the presence of India, China, Indonesia, the Dutch, and Portuguese contributed to the society as foreign influences exposed the people to a rich variety of religions and cultural practices. In 1950 the population of East Timor was approximately 440,000; at present there are more than eight hundred thousand people living in East Timor. Although there is diversity in language and ethnicity, it estimated that over ninety percent of the East Timorese are now Catholic.

Colonialism

The contemporary story of East Timor begins when traders from Portugal landed on the Island of Timor around 1515. The territory became a colony of Portugal in the sixteenth century. At the same time, the Dutch, another colonial power, controlled parts of the island. Then, in the 1600s, as each European power wanted to expand its control over the sandalwood trade, a dispute arouse between the Portuguese and the Dutch. For over two hundred years, the two powers fought for control of the island. Then in 1859 they reached a compromise, the European countries divided the island in half with the Dutch controlling the western portion and the Portuguese directing the eastern section. This relationship was negotiated by the International Court of Justice and eventually became legal and binding in 1914. Since that time, there have been two Timors—East Timor with a Catholic Portuguese tradition and West Timor with a connection to the Protestant Netherlands.

In the early days of colonialism, relations were calm as the native people harvested sandalwood and exchanged it with traders. Aside from the presence of the missionary Roman Catholic church, Portugal treated East Timor with reserve. However, at the turn of the twentieth century the situation in East Timor began to change. In 1920 an uprising in East Timor gave one indication that its people wanted to be free from rule by an outside power. The Portuguese military forces were better equipped and easily squashed the insurrection—silencing dissent for several decades. This early rebellion provides a glimpse of the commitment that the people of East Timor have to their freedom.

World War II and Cold War Politics

East Timor was swept up into international events during the 1940s when the island became a battleground in the Pacific Theatre of World War II. The Western Allies looked at East Timor as a strategic point from which to block the Axis powers (Germany, Japan, and Italy). Australia, aligned with the Allies (the United States, England, France, and the USSR), set up a pre-emptive military post on the island. In response, the Japanese invaded East Timor in February of 1942, successfully took over, and banished the Allies. According to James Dunn, an Australian consul, in his book *Timor—A People Betrayed*, the three years of Japanese control that followed resulted in the death of more than sixty thousand East Timorese by Allied bombings, famine, and Japan's brutal occupation. After the war, the Japanese left and Portugal returned to administer the eastern portion of the island. For the next two decades, Portugal emphasized economic development. The Catholic church became key to converting the people to Catholicism and educating the East Timorese by teaching both the native Tetum language and Portuguese. Despite the efforts of the colonial power, economic development was slow and by 1974, eighty percent of the population of East Timor still depended on subsistence farming and lived in rural areas, according to Matthew Jardine's book *East Timor: Genocide in Paradise*.

In 1974 political changes in Portugal brought a new government to power that gave Angola and Mozambique their independence. With these developments, the door opened for discussion about the status of East Timor. The Portuguese appeared to support the idea of granting East Timor its independence. With high expectation of autonomy, several local political parties emerged and began the process of forming a government. One party, the Association of Timorese Social Democrats (ASDT), strongly advocated self-rule and wanted an independent East Timor to adopt a socialist form of government. Later, this same political party became FRETILIN (The Revolutionary Front for an Independent East Timor), an advocate of Marxist theory that actively campaigned for the redistribution of land and wealth. After a small-scale civil war with a competing political party, FRETILIN declared East Timor an independent country on November 28, 1975. Dunn wrote in *Timor—A People Betrayed* that the new government "clearly enjoyed widespread support or cooperation from the people . . . leaders of the victorious party were welcomed." Despite the declaration of independence, many countries did not recognize the new government and rejected East Timor as an independent country. The period of self-rule was brief and it would be decades before a government controlled by the citizens of East Timorese government would again gain control.

The Invasion

Indonesia, East Timor's northern neighbor, had its own ideas about the island and wanted to control the entire territory. When the Republic of Indonesia (once a colony itself) became independent from the Dutch, it absorbed West Timor into its country and had an eye on doing the same with East Timor. Again, international politics changed the path of history in East Timor. During this time, the United States and the Soviet Union were still engaged in the Cold War. The pro-socialist party FRETILIN and East Timor's declaration of independence caught the attention of the United States and Australia who were concerned that the new country would be Communist. The Unites States had fought Communist governments in Korea and Vietnam and the support for a pro-socialist party triggered great concern when separatists in East Timor adopted a pro-Marxist platform. American officials were worried that East Timor was part of a Communist wave sweeping over Asia and Indochina. At the time, the leader of the Indonesian government, General Suharto, came to power by defeating a formidable Communist party known as the PKI (Indonesian Communist Party). With General Suharto, the United States found a natural ally to help contain the spread of communism in Southeast Asia. In early December 1975, U.S. president Gerald Ford accompanied by Secretary of State Henry Kissinger traveled to Jakarta, the capital of Indonesia, to meet with General Suharto. Reports indicate that the U.S. delegation assured the Indonesian government of their support in integrating East Timor into Indonesia.

On December 7, 1975, only days after the departure of the American delegation, Indonesia invaded East Timor. Naval ships and warplanes brought Indonesian troops to the newly formed country. One witness, a Catholic bishop, described the events of December 8 in the *Tapol Bulletin*: "The soldiers who landed started killing everyone they could find. There were many dead bodies on the streets—all we could see were the soldiers killing, killing, killing." The assault was successful as the new government collapsed and hundreds of thousands of people fled to the mountains to es-

SUHARTO

1921– Suharto, the former president of Indonesia, ruled through a military regime for three decades. His long reign provided stability, which allowed Indonesia to prosper economically. However, military violence, nepotism, and unequal distribution of wealth contributed to his downfall in 1998.

Suharto was born June 8, 1921, on Java, then a Dutch colony. After graduating from high school, he fought first for the Dutch, then for the Japanese. After World War II, he joined the struggle for Indonesian independence. Indonesian independence was granted in 1950. By 1963 Suharto was a Major General. As head of strategic command, he is suspected of directing the massacre of hundreds of thousands of suspected leftists. On March 12, 1966, Suharto seized control of the government, and in March 1967 was sworn in as president.

He relied heavily on American-educated economists, and by the time Indonesia forcibly annexed East Timor in 1976, the economy was expanding steadily. By restricting civil rights and dissent, Suharto ran unopposed in six elections. His family and close friends controlled the economy and amassed personal fortunes. By the time economic crises swept Asia in the late 1990s, most Indonesians, including the military, no longer supported him. Amid civil unrest, he resigned May 21,1998.

Suharto, like many Javanese, uses only one name.

cape the killing, rape, and torture. Less than two weeks after East Timor's declaration of independence, President Suharto of Indonesia annexed the territory and proclaimed East Timor Indonesia's twenty-seventh province. While the United States was celebrating two hundred years of independence in July 1976, East Timor lost its hope for autonomy. According to a history on Indonesian government's website, the invasion was intended to "end to the bloodshed and instability that marked the years of civil war and political strife following the precipitous Portuguese abandonment of their colony."

Indonesia began its rule over East Timor by relocating many people from their mountainous homes to live in coastal villages. In an effort to promote economic development, Indonesia built many roads and schools. They government also implemented several integration policies designed to cre-

XANANA GUSMAO

1946– Xanana Gusmao is a poet, revolutionary, and the de-facto leader of the East Timorese. He is considered the national hero and few doubt he would be elected president of the new country if he runs in the 2001 elections.

Gusmao was born in 1946, outside the East Timor capital of Dili. As a teenager, Gusmao ran away from the Catholic seminary he had been attending. He taught Portuguese and worked as a civil servant in Dili, where he faced racial discrimination by the Portuguese colonialists. In 1974 Gusmao became a journalist, and reported on the transitions of that year: the Portuguese left after five hundred years of occupation and Indonesian troops quickly invaded and began a campaign of terror. By 1981 Gusmao was the head of the resistance to Indonesia rule, and the most wanted man in Indonesia.

Gusmao eluded capture until 1992. While imprisoned, his letters, reports, and poetry drew international attention to the plight of East Timor. In 1998, after the East Timorese voted for independence in a referendum, militias ravaged East Timor for weeks. When Gusmao was released in October 1999, Dili was in ruins. However, Gusmao has begun to organize the East Timorese to begin rebuilding their country.

ate a less diverse society. For example, Indonesia declared Bahasa Indonesian the national language and outlawed Portuguese. According to Peter Carey in an article written for *Current Studies,* an Indonesian official proclaimed years later that, "We have done more for East Timor in twenty years than the Portuguese did in four-and-a-half centuries" However, the people of East Timor were willing to fight for their independence and began an internal struggle against the Indonesian presence. In the five years following the invasion, the Timorese formed guerrilla organizations and launched constant attacks against the external security forces. Then, in 1979, a massive famine spread over East Timor and hundreds of thousands of people starved to death. Estimates are that one hundred thousand people were killed during the invasion and approximately forty percent of the population died between 1975 and 1980 from war-related famine. Although many Western countries did not blink an eye as Indonesia captured East Timor, the United Nations was opposed to these actions and called on Indonesia to withdraw from

East Timor. The U.N. Security Council passed Resolution 384 (1975) declaring that the organization was "Gravely concerned at the loss of life and conscious of the urgent need to avoid further bloodshed in East Timor..." and, "[c]alls upon the Government of Indonesia to withdraw without delay all its forces from the Territory."

The Resistance: Guerrilla Warfare in East Timor

The occupation presented quite a nuisance to Indonesia and the problems in East Timor were commonly referred to as "a pebble in Indonesia's shoe." Under the leadership of FRETILIN, the pro-socialist political party, FALINTIL (Forcas Armadas de Libertacao Nacional de Timor Leste) emerged to confront the Indonesian military. Hundreds of young men went to the mountains to join the resistance. The Timorese were determined in their quest for their own country and *"Pátria ou Morte!"* (Fatherland or Death!) became the anthem of the people of East Timor. One rebel, Jose Xanana Gusmao, organized the Revolutionary Council of National Resistance to bring together several groups that were fighting the Indonesians separately. Another urban-based group was organized by students to fight an *intifada* (rebellion) on the streets of the capital city. The result was a network of guerrilla fighters that offered a powerful force against the military presence. In response, the Indonesia government stationed between twenty- and forty-thousand troops to enforce its rule. The first several years of the resistance movement were marginally successful. The Indonesian military, a well-equipped organization, effectively dominated the guerrillas and isolated many of the fighters in the mountains. During the 1980s, a stalemate was reached as the guerrilla forces controlled portions of the east and southeast with sporadic ambushes against the Indonesian troops.

During this time, the events in East Timor caught the eye of the Vatican in Rome. Traditionally, the Catholic church held a position of power under the Portuguese government. However, the predominantly Muslim Indonesia government no longer welcomed it. The Vatican also took offense at the policies rejecting the use of the Portuguese and Tetum languages and attempts to convert the people of East Timor into Muslim Indonesians. The church in the province—once an extension of the colonial power—had gone native: it now associated with the people rather than the government. During the invasion in 1975, many Catholic priests fled to the mountains with the people and began protesting against the treatment of the people of East Timor. One leading religious figure, Bishop

A YOUNG GIRL WALKS BY A BURNING HOUSE IN THE VIOLENCE-WRACKED CAPITAL OF DILI, EAST TIMOR, INDONESIA. *(AP/Wide World Photos. Reproduced by permission.)*

Carlos Filipe Ximenes Belo, wrote in letter to the United Nations Secretary General "We are dying as a people and a nation." In October of 1989, Pope John Paul II traveled to East Timor and in his sermon expressed concern that "those who have responsibility for life in East Timor will act with wisdom and goodwill towards all." However, rather than creating peace, the Pope's visit increased tensions and immediately following a papal mass, anti-Indonesia demonstrations broke out and security forces clashed with student protestors.

The Santa Cruz Massacre

With support of the Vatican, the United Nations, and an increasing international presence in East Timor, the rebel forces within the country began to stir. Looking back, one event in particular revealed that serious problems were brewing in East Timor. In October 1991, a crowd of people gathered at the Santa Cruz Cemetery in Dili, for a funeral of a teenage boy who had died fighting the Indonesian forces. Reports indicate that as mourners placed flowers at the gravesite, several anti-Indonesia protests broke out in the crowd. Eventually, the Indonesia militias opened fire on the crowd. One source reported that 271 were killed, 382 wounded, and 250 "disappeared" after the incident. The Santa Cruz Massacre, perhaps more than any other, focused attention on the conflict in East Timor. Several members of the inter-

AN AUSTRALIAN PEACEKEEPER RUNS BY A BURNING GOVERNMENT BUILDING IN THE RAVAGED CITY OF DILI, EAST TIMOR, INDONESIA. *(AP/Wide World Photos. Reproduced by permission.)*

national media, including two American reporters, Alain Nairn and Ami Goodman, were injured in the violence. In addition, two British journalists, Max Stahl and Steve Cox, filmed the bloodbath and their video played all over the world. The Santa Cruz Massacre brought images of Indonesia forces killing women and children to the world. The event changed the face that East Timor and Indonesia presented to the world. Peter Carey, author of several books on East Timor, writes, "It was impossible, given this visual evidence, for the Indonesian authorities to deny that killings had taken place or that the Indonesian army had not been involved." This event put East Timor on the world's stage. In response to the brutality, several Western govern-

ments including Canada and Denmark stopped sending aid to Indonesia and the U.S. Congress placed a temporary ban on the sales of arms and small weapons to the country.

The 1990s were a difficult time for the people of East Timor as the decade began and ended with violence. In 1995, violence broke out between Muslim settlers and the Catholic East Timorese youth. Once again, the world was reminded of East Timor when the Noble Peace Prize was awarded to José Ramos-Horta, Vice President of the National Council of Timorese Resistance and Bishop Belo for their work towards peace in East Timor. In 1997 the Asian financial crises and economic turmoil shook the region and destabilized the government in Indonesia. Thousands of Indonesians protested for political reforms. In May 1998, Indonesia's President Suharto resigned under intense political pressure. With these developments, optimism for change in the twenty-seventh province increased. Again, students in Dili demonstrated against Indonesia and the Indonesian military clashed with the protestors. In the first few weeks of 1999, Indonesia's new President Habibie, faced with problems in his own country, hinted that the solution for East Timor might in fact be independence.

The Referendum

For years, the United Nations tried to negotiate a resolution to the conflict in East Timor urging Indonesia to 'take the shoe off' and release the pebble. Then, with violence spiraling the country into chaos, the new leadership in Indonesian government did a remarkable about face. In June 1998, the United Nations successfully negotiated an agreement from Indonesia that it would allow a "popular consultation" to determine whether the people of East Timor wanted to be independent of Indonesia. In January 1999, President Habibie agreed to allow a vote on independence. Six months later, in June 1999, the United Nations established the United Nations Mission in East Timor (UN-AMET) to oversee a referendum on independence. In the days leading up to the referendum, the city of Dili came alive with pro-independence parades and chants of 'Viva Timor Leste!' ('Long live East Timor!'). At the same time, international concern grew when Tito Batista (a top pro-Indonesian leader) threatened to initiate a guerrilla war if the referendum supported the separatists. Out of eight hundred thousand citizens of East Timor, UN-AMET registered 450,000 voters. According to the *Wall Street Journal,* on August 30, 1999, the referendum on independence was held throughout East Timor, ninety-eight percent turned out for the referendum and a powerful and determined 78.5 percent of voters declared their desire to be released from Indonesia's rule.

The results of the referendum were made public on September 4 and the response was instantaneous. Within hours after the official announcement on independence, East Timor was set ablaze by the pro-Indonesian militia forces. The rampage erupted with murder, arson, destruction of property, and forced deportations. Again, the world took notice. Many news organizations including the BBC and CNN broadcasted images of terrorized people with their homes set on fire, being shot at, and once again fleeing to the mountains for protection. Reports of attacks on refugees seeking asylum in churches also shocked the world. Eventually the militias turned their weapons on U.N. personnel and the international media who fled to Australia. Catholic priests and nuns were specifically targeted and Bishop Belo and many of his followers were emergency evacuated by air to Australia. The bloodshed forced six hundred thousand people to flee their homes and 130,000 actually fled into Indonesia-controlled West Timor. Once in West Timor, the carnage did not end, many were crowded into refugee camps where the militias attacked them once again. In addition, hundreds of thousands of people fled to the mountains hoping to secure shelter in areas controlled by the guerrilla organization FALINTIL. Conservative reports indicate that at least seven thousand people died in the first few days after the announcement.

The United Nations, as well as the rest of the world, was taken back by the level and intensity of violence. In a statement to reporters, Secretary General Kofi Annan replied, "If any of us had an inkling that it was going to be this chaotic, I don't think anyone would have gone forward." Although the Indonesia government claimed that its military could quell the violence, many accusations began to surface that the military was actually backing the militias. As reported in the *New York Times,* in response to these fears, U.S. Secretary of State Madeline Albright, sternly warned, "The government and armed forces of Indonesia should understand that what happens in West Timor and to East Timorese living elsewhere in Indonesia is as important to the United States as what happens in East Timor itself." The United States and other countries also threatened to implement military and economic sanctions. The outside influence convinced the government in Jakarta to allow a multinational peacekeeping force into East Timor to restore order.

In response to international calls to end the violence, the United Nations created a peacekeeping mission to bring peace and order back to East Timor and assist UNAMET in promoting the successful transition to independence. Australia headed up the International Force for East Timor (Interfet) and a delegation of 9,150 military personnel and 1,640 police officers entered East Timor on September 20, 1999, reported the *New York Times.* As *Newsweek* stated, the operation was authorized to use "all necessary measures" to "restore peace and security" and provide disaster relief. This mission changed U.N. policy as traditional peacekeepers who are usually only armed with binoculars and walkie-talkies were now authorized to carry weapons.

Although most of the responsibility for East Timor now lay with the international community, events within Indonesia continued to influence the situation. In October 1999, President Habibie was given a vote of no confidence in the Indonesian Assembly and Abdurrahman Wahid, a Muslim cleric, became Indonesia's fourth president. With a change in political administration came another change in the policy towards East Timor. Twenty-five years after the invasion, Indonesia's assembly reversed the 1975 decree annexing East Timor and recognized the 1999 referendum in favor of independence. Indonesia officially relinquished political control of East Timor to the United Nations and in early November, the last of over twenty-five thousand Indonesian military forces (TNI) left East Timor. After the military withdrew, thousands of East Timorese gathered in the streets of Dili to celebrate the end of foreign rule. The United Nations then created the United Nations Transitional Administration in East Timor (UNTAET) to administer the country and set up a government.

RECENT HISTORY AND THE FUTURE

In a historic move, on February 29, 2000, President Wahid traveled to East Timor's capital and apologized to the people of East Timor for twenty-five years of bloodshed and past abuses. He expressed Indonesia's commitment to rebuilding peaceful relations and declared, "I would like to apologize for the things that have happened in the past . . . for the victims, to the families of Santa Cruz, and those friends who are buried here in the military cemetery." The President of Portugal, Jorge Sampaio is now working to establish good relations with Indonesia and assist East Timor in its quest for autonomous peace and stability. An investigation was carried out in early 2000 formally examining the Indonesian military and its role in the violence in East Timor. In addition to his formal apology, President Wahid held several trials to determine whether members of the Indonesian military were responsible for the violence that occurred after the referendum. In shocking testimony, several Indonesian soldiers admitted to killing civilians in East Timor. The United Nations is still investigating the relationship between the Indonesian military, the militias, and the violence after the referendum. One chief military leader, a soft-spoken man named General Wiranto, is accused of organizing the militia violence that erupted in August of 1999. Six other high-ranking Indonesian generals are also under investigation for violation of human rights in East Timor.

East Timor: Finding a Path To Democracy?

Even with its independence, East Timor is still not stable. Almost half of the people that fled East Timor after the referendum remain in refugee camps in West Timor. Despite the international presence, peace and order have been difficult to establish. In October of 1999, there were border clashes between U.N. peacekeepers, Indonesian policemen, and anti-independence militias. The frequent fighting on the West Timor border indicates that, although the Indonesia military forces are gone, the militias are still on the island and are prepared to fight. In addition, the economy of the country is in shambles. Most of the country's infrastructure was destroyed in the fighting, leaving roads and communications systems unusable. The United Nations currently administers the country and is working towards reopening schools, providing health services, establishing economic institutions, and forming government agencies. To secure these goals, UNTAET plans to administer the country until late 2001. Japan and Portugal are financially supporting East Timor's effort to reestablish its economy. However, after domination by Portugal for over three hundred years, followed by three decades of intimidation by Indonesia, the people of East Timor are wary of outside assistance that may mask yet another threat to their independence and self-determination.

Former rebel Jose Xanana Gusmao, after serving twenty years in a jail in Jakarta as a political prisoner, is now president of East Timor. In a recent speech, he told his fellow East Timorese that both the country and people of East Timor were starting from zero. In a recent article in *Foreign Affairs,* James Traub explains: "East Timor lacks the most basic necessities: not just doctors, dentists, accountants, lawyers, and police, but also tables, chairs, pots, and pans. Even in Dili, the capital, stop signs, traffic signals, and streetlights are nowhere to be found." With high unemployment, many are left with little to do and within Dili and there have been several instances of gang violence. Another issue facing the country is the role that FRETILIN will play in the government. It remains to be seen how a rebel organization, trained in guerrilla warfare, can adapt to the day-to-day governing of a country. East Timor is beginning a long journey toward peace. Recently reports of violence by youth gangs and former independence fighters reveal how a society that was militarized for so long, must now learn how to live in peace.

The problems of East Timor have affected both the political and economic stability of Indonesia. What was once viewed as an insignificant pebble might destabilize the entire country. The scar of East Timor may hurt Indonesia as it recovers from a national banking scandal and economic turmoil. In light of the evidence of brutality, many international financial organizations and countries have threatened to end trade relations and economic support. Indonesia must now also mend its relations with the rest of the world as an international backlash may cripple its recovering economy. Many fear that the military, still an important component in the Indonesian government, will retaliate against the new Wahid government. In addition, Indonesia may also find other provinces like Aceh and West Papua following East Timor's lead and attempting to break free from external rule. Indonesia is also undergoing its own transition to democracy and observers still fear that the world's fourth most populous country may revert to an authoritarian government controlled by the military.

In the new international era that promotes human rights, the international community wanted to believe that the Indonesian government was promoting economic and political development in East Timor. The United States as well as other countries accepted Indonesia's claims that the military was not involved in the violence after the referendum. One U.S. diplomat explained that "The U.S. had a deep and desperate desire to believe that the military would solve the problem," then, "that became a deep refusal to see that the military was the problem." However, a few months later, investigations by the United Nations revealed horrific evidence that has devastated the belief in the Indonesian government. In many ways, the situation in East Timor resembles other ethnic-based violence and efforts to escape the remnants of colonial rule. In Chechnya, we find a similar situation as the Muslim Chechens are fighting for independence from Russia. Kosovo presents another example where ethnic and religious conflicts lead to chaos and international involvement. At the same time, both East Timor and Kosovo reveal that the international community is responding to violence and brutality in other countries and is willing to commit resources to relieve human suffering and promote democracy.

East Timor serves as a test case for the United Nations and the success or failure of UNTAET will influence future peacekeeping and nation-building missions. This is the first time the organization has undertaken the task of building a country and an economic system from scratch. East Timor has no history of self-rule, democratic institutions, or popular participation in governing. Although, the United Nations has committed one billion dollars

and almost nine thousand troops to East Timor, they continue to face groups of internal terrorists and militias roaming the country killing civilians. Although, international involvement increases the chance for stability it is still difficult to tell who are the "goods" guys and who are the "bad" guys and, the warring factions remain difficult to locate. East Timor continues to present challenge for the United Nations and the international community.

BIBLIOGRAPHY

Bartholet, Jeffrey and Ron Moreau. "The Hunters and the Hunted," *Newsweek* 134 (27 September 1999): 38.

Brière, Elaine. "East Timor: History and Society," In *East Timor: Occupation and Resistance.* Denmark: Narayana Press, 1998.

Budiardjo, Carmel and Liem Soei Liong. *The War Against East Timor.* London: Zed, 1984.

Carey, Peter and G. Carter Bentley. *East Timor at the Crossroads: The Forging of a Nation.* Honolulu, Hawaii: University of Hawaii Press, 1995.

———. "East Timor: Third World Colonialism and the Struggle for National Identity," *Conflict Studies* 293/294 (October/November 1996): 3

———. "Secede and We Destroy You," *World Today,* 55 (October 1999): 4–5

Crossette, Barbara. "Albright Addresses New Warning To Indonesia," *New York Times,* 27 September 1999, p. A6.

Department of Foreign Affairs, Republic of Indonesia Homepage, http://www.dfa-deplu.go.id/english2/political.htm (18 July 2000).

Dunn, James. *Timor—A People Betrayed.* Milton, Queensland: Jacaranda Press, 1983.

George, Alexander. "Genocide in East Timor," *Contemporary Review* 249 (1986): 119–23.

Gunn, Geoffrey C. *East Timor and the United Nations: The Case For Intervention.* Lawrenceville, N.J.: The Red Sea Press, 1997.

Haseman, John B. "Catalyst for Change in Indonesia: The Dili Incident," *Asian Survey* 8 (1995): 757–67.

"Indonesian Soldiers Testify That They Executed Civilians" *New York Times,* 10 May 2000, A5.

"Interview with Former Bishop of East Timor," *Tapol Bulletin* 59 (September 1983).

Jardine, Matthew. *East Timor: Genocide in Paradise.* Tuscan, Ariz.: Odonian Press, 1995.

King, Neil Jr. and Jay Solomon. "'We Are No Fools': Diplomatic Gambles At the Highest Levels Failed in East Timor—U.N. Was Warned of Chaos But Felt Constrained; Inside Kofi Annan's Office—'A Window of Opportunity,'" *Wall Street Journal,* 21 October 1999, A1

Kohen, Arnold S. *From the Place of the Dead.* New York: St. Martin's Press, 1999.

Krieger, Heike, ed. *East Timor and the International Community: Basic Documents.* New York: Cambridge University Press, 1997.

Mack, Alistair. "Intervention in East Timor–From the Ground," *RUSI Journal* 144 (December 1999): 20–6.

Mydans, Seth. "A Timorese Era Closes Quietly As Army Goes," *New York Times,* 31 October 1999, 1.

Pateman, Roy. "East Timor, Twenty Years After," *Terrorism and Political Violence* 10 (1998): 119–32.

Pinton, Cantancio and Matthew Jardine, eds. *East Timor's Unfinished Struggle.* Boston, Mass.: South End Press, 1997.

Pope John Paul II, "Speech in Taci-Tolu," 12 October 1989.

Salla, Michael E. "Creating the 'Ripe Moment' in the East Timor Conflict," *Journal of Peace Research* 34 (1997): 449–66.

Sidell, Scott. "The United States and Genocide in East Timor," *Journal of Contemporary Asia* 11 (1981): 44–61.

Taylor, John G. *Indonesia's Forgotten War: The Hidden History of East Timor.* London: Zed, 1991.

Traub, James. "Inventing East Timor" *Foreign Affairs* 79 (July/August 2000): 74–89

"U.N. Takes Over Control of East Timor," *Daily Report,* Foreign Broadcast Information Service, transcribed text, FBIS-EAS-1999-1026. 26 October 1999.

"Wahid Apologizes to East Timorese Victims" *Daily Report,* Foreign Broadcast Information Service, FBIS-EAS-2000-0229. 29 February 2000.

Weatherbee, Donald E. "Portuguese Timor: An Indonesian Dilemma," *Asian Survey* 6 (December 1966): 683–95.

Wren, Christopher. "U.N. Creates an Authority To Start Governing East Timor," *New York Times,* 26 October 1999, A8.

Alynna Lyon

THE ECUADORIAN INDIGENOUS PEOPLE'S MOVEMENT: AUTONOMY AND THE ENVIRONMENT

For the first time in the history of Latin America an alliance between elements of the military and an indigenous people's organization conspired to overthrow an elected president. On January 21, 2000, hundreds of thousands of Ecuadorians, mainly from the Confederation of Indigenous Nationalities of Ecuador, known by its Spanish acronym CONAIE, flooded the streets and squares of the capital, Quito, to protest the newly proposed dollarization of the economy. Dollarization is the adoption of the currency of another country—in this case the currency of the United States. The rebel leaders took over the congressional and presidential buildings. Antonio Vargas, leader of CONAIE, Colonel Lucio Gutiérrez, and former supreme court president Carlos Solórzano soon formed the *junta* of National Salvation. A *junta* is a group controlling the government following a violent overthrow of the government. Colonel Gutiérrez promptly deferred to his superior, General Carlos Mendoza, who took his place on the ruling council.

The military-civilian *junta* did not last long. Within a few hours the United States expressed its vehement disapproval of the non-elected government and most industrialized nations followed suit. At this point, General Mendoza announced his resignation from the *junta* and threw his, and the military's, support behind Vice President Gustavo Noboa. Noboa, upon assuming office from President Jamil Mahuad, announced that the dollarization program would continue as part of the government's economic reorganization plan. Hours later, the indigenous people went back to their highland towns, feeling betrayed by the military high command, and put the new government on notice that it was being watched and judged. They reaffirmed their right to return to the capital should the government's performance fall short of their expectations.

THE CONFLICT

Indigenous people in Ecuador overthrew the president in January 2000, leading to the establishment of a *junta*, a small military government.

Political

- The indigenous people want legal, constitutional acknowledgement of the multicultural and multiethnic nature of their society.

- Indigenous people want to fully participant in the political system of the country.

Economic

- An economic shift from rural to urban and from agriculture to manufacturing has impoverished many Indians and dislocated them from their culture.

- Indigenous people have sued Texaco over the use and ownership of land and oil.

CHRONOLOGY

1940s The Ecuadorian Federation of Indigenous (FEI) is formed.

1970s Many indigenous people migrate to the cities in response to changing economic conditions, including the corporate takeovers of their land.

1974 The Confederation of Quichua Communities in Ecuador (ECUARUNARI) is founded.

1980 The Confederation of Indigenous Nationalities of the Ecuadorian Amazon (CONFENIAE) is established.

1986 CONAIE organizes. The Institute of Indigenous Cultures is established.

1990 The first CONAIE uprising involves the takeover of a church and the disruption of roadways.

1993 CONAIE sues Texaco in U.S. federal court.

1995 Pachakutik, the political organization of the indigenous people, is formed.

1998 The Ecaudarian constitution is amended to recognize Ecuador as a state of many cultures and ethnicities.

1999–2000 The program for the dollarization of Ecuador begins.

2000 CONAIE-sponsored protests against dollarization result in the overthrow of the elected government of Jamil Mahuad and the brief takeover by a *junta*.

HISTORICAL BACKGROUND

The Origins of CONAIE

Ecuador is one of the smallest countries in South America. It is about the size of Colorado or a little smaller than Malaysia, and has 12.5 million inhabitants. Twenty-five percent of the population is indigenous—natives to Ecuador who pre-date the colonization by Europeans—and most can be found in the Ecuadorian highlands. Nevertheless, most of the population has some indigenous blood. Until the mid-twentieth century the indigenous people were seen as obstacles to modernization because of the difficulty of integrating them into the market economy. The indigenous people generally participated in the traditional economy of the *hacienda*—a large farm or ranch that is controlled by an elite family but worked by indigenous people—

in which they produced most of their own subsistence needs. A market economy is an economy in which the means of production, most notably land and labor, are sold in the market. The concept of selling their labor was foreign to the indigenous people. Most of the native people were poor and illiterate and were seen as not being interested in productive pursuits. The Catholic church, as well as the Communist party, were interested in organizing the indigenous communities to protect their rights. The Ecuadorian Federation of Indigenous (FEI) was organized in the 1940s and supported by the Communist Party. The communists taught them how to organize and showed them how striking could serve as a powerful tool of resistance.

The main issues affecting the indigenous people were the 1964 agrarian reform and a top-down project geared at integrating the indigenous population into the rest of the society. For the most part, the needs of the indigenous communities were neglected. In the late 1960s and 1970s the progressive wing of the Catholic Church became more active. It began to put into practice the preferential option for the poor, a doctrine of the Catholic Church's which grew out of the theology of liberation and held that the poor should be given more opportunities than the rich in order to help them escape their disadvantaged social position. The Church became involved in creating indigenous organizations based on the needs and aspirations of the communities.

At the same time, other organizations were being formed to address the needs of indigenous people. One of these organizations was the Federation of Shuar Centers. Its proximity to the Peruvian border made it susceptible to not only Peruvian border raids but also to being conquered and made part of Peru. As a result the federation fought in numerous border skirmishes to protect Ecuadorian territory and resources. In fact, since 1942 Ecuador and Peru had disputed a sizable area of territory. This border conflict was resolved by a peace treaty in 1998 in which, according to the Ecuadorians, they lost 14,300 square kilometers. The Federation of Shuar Centers, assisted by the Salesian missionaries, established a pattern that was followed by other indigenous communities such as Quichua, Siona/Secoya, Cofán, and Huaorani. The pattern consisted of the formation of a federation to resist the incursion of "foreign interests"—anything outside of the community, including the Ecuadorian state, foreign corporations, and religious missionaries. Resistance employed by the Centers consisted of emphasizing self-direction, bilingual education, attainment of title to traditional lands, and anything

DOLLARIZATION

At the start of 1999 Ecuador faced tremendous economic challenges. Petroleum prices had plummeted, El Niño had wiped out many of the banana and coffee plantations, shrimp had been afflicted with a disease known as *mancha blanca,* and tourists were being robbed more often. Ecuador was left with virtually no exports, and the trade deficit began to grow. Any economist could have predicted that the *sucre* was bound to depreciate under these conditions. Few could have predicted the extent of the depreciation and the negative impact this would have on the economy and, in particular, the banking sector. In 1999 the *sucre* depreciated 104.4 percent and in the first ten days of January 2000, another 24.9 percent—894.5 percent on an annualized basis—before President Jamil Mahuad announced his plan to dollarize the economy and fixed the exchange rate at 25,000 *sucres* to the dollar.

Dollarization of an economy means adopting another country's currency. In this case, Ecuador decided to adopt the U.S. dollar as its own legal tender. Everything in Ecuador is in the process of being converted to dollars. Bank accounts have been converted from being expressed in *sucres* to being expressed in dollars. Dollars are circulating in the economy and must be accepted as payment for any purchase. Prices are now expressed in dollars. An educational program is underway in which the citizenry is being taught what U.S. currency looks like and how counterfeit bills can be recognized.

By adopting the dollar as its currency Ecuador abandoned its ability to use monetary policy as a tool of economic stabilization. The supply of money in the economy will now be a function of the country's trade surplus and its ability to attract foreign capital in the form of loans and investment. External shocks, such as changes in the demand for Ecuadorian products and natural disasters, can no longer be combated by increasing the money supply in order to decrease interest rates. Ecuador also lost an important symbol of national sovereignty.

Many see the removal of monetary policy from the hands of political appointees as the answer to Ecuador's financial turmoil. They point to Panama, which also uses the U.S. dollar as its legal tender. Over the past twenty years Panama has had an inflation rate lower than the United States. Its interest rates are among the lowest in Latin America and significantly lower than Ecuador's. If Ecuador could achieve the same results it could lead to sustained economic growth. So far the results of dollarization are mixed. There is some evidence that faith has been restored to the badly battered banking system. Increased deposits are being recorded for the first time in months. Inflation, however, does not appear to be decreasing. Low inflation is the key to lowering interest rates and reactivating the economy.

else that created a counter-ideology in opposition to nationalist ideas and practices. Together they reached one hundred thousand people. In 1980 the Confederation of Indigenous Nationalities of the Ecuadorian Amazon, or CONFENIAE, was born as an organization to represent indigenous demands and pursue unity while respecting the diversity of the communities. In the highlands, the Confederation of Quichua Communities in Ecuador (ECUARUNARI) was formed in 1974 with the support of the Catholic church. ECUARUNARI's initial goal was geared toward land issues; in the 1980s, it began to emphasize the defense of indigenous cultures and promote more political participation.

CONAIE was organized in 1986. One of its main objectives was to gather all of the indigenous communities, which had previously been isolated, into one large, organized, and representative body.

Its goal was to claim for the indigenous people the political voice that they had long been denied. They were concerned not only with land reforms and labor issues, but with redefining, through legislative reforms, the national identity, bilingual education, and traditional medicine. CONAIE unified its efforts by including not only the highland communities of the Quichua, but also the Awa, Chachi, Tsáchila, and Epera of the Pacific Coast; and the Quichua, Cofán, Siona-Secoya, Shuar, Achuar, and Huaroni of the Amazon Basin.

CONAIE aims to provide democratic representation to the indigenous communities. One of the tools that it uses is the Institute of Indigenous Cultures, which was established in 1986—the same year that CONAIE was organized. One of the main goals of the institute is to teach courses to indigenous students, who then return to their com-

MAP OF ECUADOR. (© *Maryland Cartographics. Reprinted with permission.*)

munities to teach what they learned in the institute. The courses are in several fields, including law, economics, ecology, and indigenous cultures.

CONAIE has succeeded in preserving the unity of the three indigenous organizations that had previously represented the highlands (ECUARUNARI), Amazonian communities (CONFENIAE), and the Pacific Coast (COINCE). It has succeeded in doing this because of the similar goals that all indigenous communities have, chief among these being recognition of their political and legal organizations within the context of Ecuadorian society.

The most important achievement for CONAIE was the successful campaign to adopt, as the first article of the 1998 constitution, the recognition of Ecuador as a state with many cultures and ethnicities. Similar constitutional reforms had already been adopted by Guatemala (1985), Brazil (1988), Mexico (1992), Paraguay (1992), Peru (1993), Argentina (1994), and Bolivia (1994). These reforms reflect a shift of perspective in the conception of the nation state by Latin Americans.

The prevailing historical notion had been that indigenous people should be integrated into Western culture. The goal was a homogenous national culture in which indigenous culture was seen as little more than an embarrassing vestige of the past that would be eradicated. By acknowledging that Ecuador is a pluri-cultural and multiethnic state, the constitution acknowledged the existence of the indigenous people as both individuals and groups. This was seen as the first step toward a social recognition, which would give them the human rights that had been frequently violated in the past. Moreover, these reforms recognize the citizenship of indigenous people and by implication the affirmation of their separate identity as a group.

The acknowledgment of a pluri-cultural and multiethnic state was an outgrowth of extensive work in promoting bilingual education, established in 1988 by an agreement between the government and CONAIE. Language is believed to be one of the major components of redefining national identity. Since the conquest in 1492, Spanish has been the only official language of Ecuador, while Quichua and other Indian languages have been confined to use in the local communities. Quichua is the most common language of the highland indigenous people; however, since Quichua is an Indian language most Ecuadorians do not speak it, believing that it is beneath them. Languages are more than a means of communication; controlling a people's language is one way to control the people. By diminishing the use and therefore the value of Quichua, many indigenous people felt that Indian culture was relegated to an inferior status. Efforts to change this situation can be found in the 1945 and 1984 constitutional reforms, which allowed Quichua to be taught alongside Spanish, especially in areas in which the majority of the population was indigenous. The biggest step, however, was made outside of official state institutions. In the late 1960s Archbishop Leonidas Proaño of Riobamba launched a program called Popular Radio Schools, the goal of which was to organize literacy campaigns. The program was very successful, and in the following years the progressive wing of the Catholic Church offered bilingual education programs in order to extend the use of Quichua throughout the highlands. By the end of the 1970s the Catholic University was offering Quichua courses and had formed a Center for the Investigation of Indigenous Education.

The bilingual education program in the province of Bolivar is another success. This program, which originated in the School of Andean Education and Culture of the state financed Bolivar

INDIANS, PROTESTING AGAINST THE GOVERNMENT OF PRESIDENT JAMIL MAHUAD, OCCUPY THE CONGRESS BUILDING IN QUITO, ECUADOR. *(AP/Wide World Photos. Reproduced by permission.)*

University, began in 1992. Students can earn a bachelor of arts in bilingual education and community development. The two languages taught are Spanish and Quichua. While the majority of the students are indigenous, a third are *mestizos*, people whose ancestors were both European and indigenous. The goal of the students is to be able to teach in rural communities and, even more, to redefine a sense of indigenous pride that makes them feel like members of a distinct group.

Mobilization and the Agrarian Problem

Because CONAIE stressed the value of diversity in the indigenous communities, it has been able to maintain its initial unity. That unity has been reflected in major mobilizations to oppose and protest various issues. The first successful uprising since CONAIE was established was in 1990. This uprising began with a symbolic act: the occupation of the Dominican church, one of the oldest churches in Quito. It seems that this church was selected because it was the church staffed by the Domincan order of Catholic priests in Quito. The indigenous feel a special bond with the Domincans because of the famous Dominican priest and defender of the indigenous in the sixteenth century, Bartolome de las Casas. A few days after the occupation, indigenous people blocked highways with tree limbs or by digging big holes into roads so that transporta-

tion could not move smoothly. Though the police blamed CONAIE, they could not identify the leaders since the leaders had left by the time the police could get to the highways. This uprising introduced a new way of protesting; the protesters were peaceful and showed the unity of CONAIE. The influence of the progressive wing of the Catholic church was evident in the peacefulness of the uprising; Archbishop Proaño had preached a peaceful alternative method for demanding that the needs of the indigenous people be met. His work between 1954 and 1985, and that of his successor, Bishop Victor Corral, concentrated mainly on the struggle over land and community organization. Bishop Corral not only supported the indigenous uprising but also celebrated a victory mass when the uprising reached agreement with the government.

The indigenous uprising was a result of rising expectations generated by the incumbent president of Ecuador, Rodrigo Borja (president from 1988–92). Borja gave the indigenous people hope of solving their ongoing land conflicts. He even gave legal status to CONAIE a few days after he entered office. The indigenous people's expectations, however, were not fulfilled by Borja's government. Though he created offices for indigenous affairs, Borja did not adequately address the land issues that were the main concern of the indigenous people.

INDIANS, SUPPORTING STRIKING TAXI AND BUS DRIVERS, FACE SOLDIERS IN QUITO, ECUADOR, WHERE A STATE OF EMERGENCY WAS DECLARED TO GIVE POLICE POWER TO BREAK UP PROTESTS. *(AP/Wide World Photos. Reproduced by permission.)*

The 1970s presented the military regime with the possibility of completing a modernization project for the economy based on oil revenue. There were two agrarian reforms, in 1964 and in 1973 respectively, and since then the indigenous people, as both individuals and communities, have been involved in numerous unresolved land conflicts. Part of the military's modernization project was to complete the agrarian reform that began in 1964. The military regimes in the 1970s were interested in giving land back to the indigenous communities, and they created the National Development Bank to promote credits for small landowners and developed stores with controlled prices for basic products. The military governments of the 1970s gave the indigenous people an estimated thirty-five percent of the land and tried to subsidize the rest of the agricultural production, though the result was not very beneficial to the indigenous people. Instead of creating rural employment, the small plots consisted, for the most part, of poor-quality land that did not produce enough for a family's consumption, much less the community's. Therefore, the indigenous people migrated to the cities, and this created both unemployment and underemployment. Between 1970 and 1985 the land available for basic cultivation fell by approximately thirty-three percent, while the area for commercial pasture use grew by 136 percent.

Migration to the cities had several effects on indigenous communities. The people became more dependent on the market economy. Their diet and clothes changed. Before the 1970s they ate what the land provided, mainly potatoes and corn in the highlands. But in the 1970s the indigenous people began eating new foods ranging from bread, bananas and Coke, to rice and noodles. Before they wore ponchos and *alpargatas*, traditional sandals, that were produced in the community. In the 1970s they began wearing tennis shoes, jackets, and hats that could be bought outside the indigenous community. The result was that they became "modernized" and depended on buying more products from the market, instead of making these products for themselves.

When recession hit Ecuador in 1982 the price of Ecuador's main natural resource, oil, dropped. Not only did inflation result from the drop in oil prices, but the indigenous people also lost the employment opportunities in construction and manufacturing that they had become dependent on in the 1970s. The drastic decline in wages, almost thirty percent, left the indigenous people in dire straits. From 1982 to 1986, when CONAIE was established, the indigenous communities went through a process of organizing and began to develop a sense of the need to defend their own rights.

When President Borja seemed to recognize the indigenous people's needs, but failed to deliver the promised agrarian reform, the indigenous organization was mature enough to engage in its first important mobilization of the twentieth century.

With the 1990 indigenous uprising the majority of the *mestizo* Ecuadorians learned that the indigenous people were organized and willing to participate in a mobilization to demand their rights to the land and to protest against inflation. However, the 1990 uprising was more than a protest for land rights and inflation control. It was the beginning of indigenous demands for full participation in the political system of Ecuador. For the first time, they talked about changing the constitution so that Ecuador would become a plurinational and multiethnic state that recognized indigenous culture.

This 1990 movement also made the rest of Ecuador aware of the meaning of the land to indigenous people. The indigenous people believe that *pachamama*, "the land" in the Quichua language, represents the mother of everybody, and who gives and receives from her children equally. Since the land is sacred, it should not be exploited, and it should not be seen as private property. Therefore, when the indigenous people lost their land, part of them died and the link between the indigenous communities was weakened. This is the heart of the indigenous people's fight to reclaim their land. By the end of the Borja presidency, the Amazon indigenous had received approximately 1,116,000 hectares.

Texaco and the Land

In another effort to protect their land, the Ecuadoran indigenous people sued a U.S.-based international oil company in U.S. federal court. CONAIE and environmental groups sued Texaco Petroleum Company, a subsidiary of Texaco, which began operations in Ecuador in 1964. In 1993 CONAIE accused Texaco of being responsible for the decomposition of the indigenous communities, especially the Cofán, and thus the destruction of their culture and environment. Because the oil operations were taking place in the original Cofán community, the people had to be moved and this displacement caused deterioration in their basic living conditions. Moreover, the extraction of oil has contaminated the water, damaged the food supply, and caused disease—mainly skin and respiratory infections. Texaco claimed that it had complied with the regulations, but the water tested by the researchers from the Harvard School of Public Health found that the water contained dangerous

levels of carcinogens, cancer-causing agents. Texaco maintains that the environmental damage is due to the influx of people into the region; regardless, it is obvious thatto environmental observers and visitors that damage has been done. Reports note that a salty crust covers the soil in places and at times black particles fill the air, born from thick black pools that spot the soil.

The interesting issue in this trial is that CONAIE has insisted that Texaco be tried in U.S. courts, specifically in Manhattan, New York. The reason CONAIE is suing Texaco in the United States is that Texaco is headquartered in the United States and that is where the corporate decisions were made. Furthermore, CONAIE was interested in making the people of the United States aware that the indigenous people of Ecuador exist and that they have a different way of viewing the behavior of Texaco in the Ecuadorian Amazon. Finally, Ecuadorian courts do not have the experience or appropriate legal remedies in environmental disputes, so the largest fine in Ecuador could only amount to a few thousand dollars.

In response to CONAIE's charges Texaco claimed that even though, in 1964, when it entered Ecuador, there were no rigorous environmental regulations, they were firmly committed to protecting the people and the environment of the regions in which Texaco operated. The U.S. company maintained that it had not dumped toxic wastewater into the Ecuadorian Amazon. It explained that when the oil was produced it was done through a method in which water and oil, both of which were trapped in a geological formation, were brought to the surface together. The oil was then separated from the water, and at this point the water, which is called "produced water," was discharged into nearby rivers and streams. This process was approved by the company's Ecuadorian partner, Petroecuador, and had been examined by two independent international consulting firms, AGRA Earth and Environmental Ltd., and Fugro-McClelland. They produced independent environmental audits and concluded that there was no lasting environmental impact from this process, which is used in other parts of the world.

Other sources contend that Texaco has spilled around seventeen million gallons of crude oil in Ecuador, fifty percent more than was spilled by the Exxon *Valdez* in Alaska. The company has discharged twenty billion gallons of toxic brine wastewater into the waterways of the region and has abandoned around six hundred uncovered waste ponds. Only 139 ponds have been cleaned.

Regarding the claim by the indigenous people that they have contracted diseases, Texaco does not accept the study presented by the plaintiffs and published by the Ecuadorian Union of Popular Health Promoters of the Amazon. Texaco maintains that the study does not address issues such as "harsh conditions of the jungle, diet, the lack of medical care," colonization, and the development of other industries such as agriculture, mining, and logging. Moreover, Texaco relied on the opinion of one of the leading toxicologists in the United States who believes that the report, indicating increased rates of cancer among the population where Texaco drilled, was alarmist. The toxicologist pointed out that eight cases over ten years among people ages five to eighty-six does not constitute a cluster of similar illnesses in which it can be established that a common factor is at work. Based on this evidence and analysis, Texaco declined to conduct a comprehensive health monitoring and treatment program for oil-related illness. The suit was still pending in mid-2000.

Texaco believes that it worked hard to prevent oil spills and that when oil spills did occur the company responded quickly to remedy the situation. Texaco provided as an example of its quick response the actions following the damage to the Trans-Ecuadoran Pipeline during the earthquake of 1987. Additionally, Texaco conducted a forty million dollar remediation program that began in 1995 and concluded in 1998. This remediation program consisted of closing producing wells and pits, modifying produced-water systems, replanting cleared lands, and improving contaminated soil. The Texaco program was approved by the Government of Ecuador; Petroecuador was made responsible for the remaining sites.

The remediation program has not eliminated the problem. River-water samples from the areas where Texaco conducted the program, tested by Greenpeace Research Laboratories, continue to show high levels of hydrocarbon concentrations. The pumping stations will not be upgraded, so the toxic water will still be dumped each day into the rivers. While Texaco has accumulated $1.53 billion of reserves to cover these costs and has posted high and growing levels of profit, only 2.5 million acres of deforested area will be replanted.

Although petroleum exploitation has made Ecuador a minor oil exporter, the presence of Texaco has influenced not only the environment but also indigenous people's organizations. Texaco has given the indigenous people an incentive to organize, and their organization has gained worldwide recognition. In 1994 Dr. Luis Macas, a Quichua lawyer and first president of CONAIE, won the Goldman Environmental Prize for his negotiations to transfer three million acres of rainforest back to indigenous control.

International Influences

During this time period there was strong growth among international indigenous organizations. In 1989 the International Labor Organization (ILO) adopted Convention 169, the most comprehensive international document recognizing the rights of indigenous and tribal peoples. Convention 169 not only calls for respecting the culture, ways of life, traditions, and customary laws of indigenous people, but also supports the right of these people to decide their own economic, social, and cultural development. Some of the main issues that Convention 169 seeks to address are bilingual and bicultural education, self-direction of programs that affect indigenous communities, and land rights. Codifying these rights in the Ecuadorian Constitution of 1998 provides indigenous people equal opportunity based on respect for their cultures.

Before Convention 169, the U.N. Economic and Social Council and the U.N. Commission on Human Rights established a Working Group on Indigenous Populations in 1982. In 1995 this working group produced a draft Universal Declaration on the Rights of Indigenous Peoples. The council not only promoted the International Year of Indigenous Populations of the World (1993) and the International Decade (1995–2004), but introduced new concepts regarding indigenous rights.

One of the most controversial concepts was the term "self-determination." This term caused problems because many governments see it as an attempt by indigenous groups to secede, or withdraw, from the countries in which they live. However, self-determination can also mean the right for a group to develop its own culture, enrich its language, practice its medicine, and refine its artistic manifestations within the existing country. Under this definition, the state that recognizes self-determination accepts new forms of political organization that will give indigenous people not only the right to political participation but also to self-management.

Archbishop Proaño played an important role in promoting self-determination by restoring the moral codes of the indigenous—do not be lazy, do not steal, and do not lie. Aside from these codes, the indigenous communities started a process of understanding the meaning of having one God, father of everybody. For the indigenous people of

Ecuador having one god means that all are brothers and sisters and, therefore, everybody has the same rights and responsibilities. These rights are the citizenship rights that the indigenous people are entitled to as individuals and as communities. Understanding these citizenship rights caused the indigenous people to undergo a process of rediscovery of their own cultural roots and to build their own community identities.

Multilateral lending institutions, bilateral aid agencies, and private foundations have expressed interest in adopting polices regarding indigenous people. The World Bank is revising the lending operations and environmental analyses that concern indigenous groups. The Inter-American Development Bank has adopted principles of action for projects that affect indigenous people. The United Nations Development Program is working on guidelines to support native groups. One obvious aim of these international agencies is to provide indigenous people with basic human rights based on their own cultures and to avoid the earlier violations of their rights by being more sensitive to how projects and programs will affect their well-being.

A New Alternative: Pachakutik

Until 1995 CONAIE's political strategy was to boycott the electoral process by urging its members to invalidate their votes by spoiling their ballots. Voting is a legal duty of Ecuadorian citizens—it is illegal not to vote. One method of boycotting elections was to simply stay home, and the other was to invalidate the ballot by either drawing an "X" through it or by voting for more than one candidate for each office. In 1995 CONAIE helped form a political movement to run candidates for elected office. The new political movement was named Pachakutik, which means return of the good times, and signifies change, rebirth, transformation, and the coming of a new era. Pachakutik expresses changes in the conception of society and the state. It is based on three main moral principles—do not be lazy, do not steal, and do not lie—that are present in everyday life and which the indigenous people want to incorporate into political practice. In doing so, they revive the traditional beliefs of their ancestors and enforce their identity, actions that CONAIE believes will help build a new society in which diverse cultures will be respected and will share responsibilities.

In 1996 Luis Macas, the first president of CONAIE, won the office of national deputy in the National Congress. He ran as an independent candidate on the Movimiento Unidad Plurinacional Pachakutik-Nuevo País (Pachakutik-New Country

DR. LUIS MACAS AND CONAIE

Dr. Luís Macas, a Quiche Indian, is the founder of the Confederation of Indigenous Nationalities of Ecuador (CONAIE), and the first indigenous person elected to Ecuador's National Congress (Disputado Nacional). A lawyer by profession, he uses his knowledge of national and international law to support the human rights of indigenous people.

Dr. Macas founded CONAIE in November 1986, to promote the rights of indigenous people, foster unity among the indigenous nations, preserve native language and culture, and to promote a sustainable natural environment. Dr. Macas's work often focuses on the connection between social justice and ecology.

The indigenous inhabitants of Ecuador face widespread poverty and discrimination. As a colonized people, they have been subjected to forcible evacuation for centuries. Recent decades have seen the loss of much of their farming areas, as native homelands are sold to companies, such as mining and oil corporations, by the Ecuadorian government. As a result, one of CONAIE's main objectives has been to promote agriculture geared toward self-sufficiency through indigenous peoples' control of their own land. One of Dr. Macas' greatest successes was negotiating the transfer of three million acres of rainforest back to indigenous control.

Dr. Macas resigned the presidency of CONAIE after his election to the Disputado Nacional in May 1996. He is the recipient of prestigious international awards, including the Goldman Environmental Prize.

Movement of Multinational Unity) ticket. This was a coalition of popular organizations that included CONAIE, Coordinadora de Movimientos Sociales (Coordination of Social Movements), and other smaller political movements.

Aside from Macas' election, in 1996 and in 1998 Pachakutik won several positions ranging from town council to congress. In 2000, Packakutik held six seats in the 121-member congress. Four of these six deputies considered themselves to be indigenous. Nina Pacari, the first indigenous woman to participate in the reform of the constitution (1998) served as the vice president and was the best-known Pachakutik member of the congress.

In the election held on May 21, 2000, in which local offices where decided, Pachakutik won twenty-three mayor's offices out of 215. Six of the nine women who ran for minor local positions were victorious. These women, all of them Quichua from the highlands, attributed their success to the political training of the women's school, run by ECUA-RUNARI, a branch of CONAIE. This school was the brainchild of an illiterate Quichua woman, Dolores Cacuango, who fought for indigenous rights in the 1940s.

The outcome of this election helped solidify CONAIE's political base. As Miguel Lluco, the national coordinator of Pachakutik-Nuevo Pais, pointed out, the indigenous people are showing that they have the power not only to mobilize but also to win elections, without the expensive advertising that characterize the right-wing parties. Moreover, the indigenous people are proud that they have risen to the challenge that the current president, Gustavo Noboa, asked them to meet: to win power through elections.

CONAIE Flexes its Muscles

Two major political events have shown that the indigenous people's movement has come of age. By organizing mobilizations and establishing Pachakutik, CONAIE has demonstrated that it has become a major player in the country's political arena. This strength has led to its participation in the overthrow of two governments over the course of three years. The first was the government of Abdalá Bucaram in 1997. In this instance CONAIE was just one of many sectors of the society that joined forces to oust the sitting president. The reasons were complex, but a major point of contention was the neo-liberal program that Bucaram wanted to implement. The second case, the overthrow of Jamil Mahuad in January 2000, saw CONAIE take a lead role in the removal of an unpopular government. This second case is all the more impressive in that in the absence of a coalition between CONAIE and elements of the military, the government would in all likelihood have survived. In November 1999 CONAIE put the president on notice that conditions would have to improve or they would take to the streets. The military had also been pressing Mahuad to resign. In December 1999 several groups, including CONAIE, middle-ranking military officers, priests, and merchants gathered to discuss the situation. When Mahuad announced the dollarization of the economy, CONAIE and the middle-ranking military officers agreed to organize the mobilization that overthrew the president.

Each of the groups participating in the uprising had different motives. According to the newspaper *Hoy*, Colonel Gutierrez participated in the uprising because he learned Mahuad was going to cut the military expenses in the budget. Gutierrez, however, claims that he participated in the insurrection because he believed that the main role of the military was to defend the national sovereignty. Mahuad, according to Gutierrez, had demonstrated that he was not interested in the needs of the majority of Ecuadorians. Therefore, Gutierrez, as a representative of the military, believed he had to stop the planned dollarization of the economy. CONAIE and Gutierrez claimed that they were not interested in taking power and that their main concerns were more profound: They were interested in making Ecuador aware of serious societal problems that need to be changed. Gutierrez asserted that was the reason the *junta* of National Salvation, formed by Antonio Vargas, Colonel Lucio Gutierrez, and Carlos Solorzano lasted only a few hours. Gutierrez also stated that in order to maintain the military chain of command, he turned power over to General Carlos Mendoza, who claimed that he never intended to remain in power but only joined the triumvirate as a means of buying time to avoid bloodshed and ensure a peaceful return to constitutional order. The military transferred power to vice president Gustavo Noboa, who decided that dollarization would remain an ongoing project. The indigenous people left Quito, and they have since been talking of finding alternatives to dollarization.

RECENT HISTORY AND THE FUTURE

At this point, CONAIE and the communities it represents seem frustrated. They have endured a decade of economic stagnation in which their population has suffered. They have seen the subsidies for food and fuel upon which they depend disappear and the savings flow into the pockets of corrupt bankers who then fled the country. They are now faced with the conversion of their economy to a dollar-based system in which external shocks can only be met with increased unemployment and higher prices. Their patience is wearing thin, and they are watching the new president very closely. A major mobilization was planned for the middle of June 2000. The mobilization occurred but was not as large as expected. CONAIE has refocused its efforts on achieving a plebiscite that would allow Ecuadorians to vote on dollarization, dissolution of congress, and amnesty for the soldiers jailed in connection with the short-lived coup. This has been one of their demands since February 2000.

AN EDUCATED BIAS

In addition to founding the Ecuadorian Federation of Indians, Dolores Cacuango is remembered in Ecuador for establishing the first bilingual schools in 1944. It was a remarkable achievement, one still heralded by current Ecuadorian activists, because Cacuango's actions legitimized for the first time education for the indigenous population in their native tongues. Seeing the Quichua children struggle to learn in Spanish, Cacuango first lobbied the Ministry of Education to offer classes in Quichua. When they ignored her repeated requests, she founded the first of four schools that offered classes in both Quichua and Spanish. Cacuango, like many activists before and after both inside and outside of Ecuador, filled a need that the ruling government was incapable or unwilling to meet and, by doing so, gave a new generation of activists the skills required to be heard by those in power.

The education of children is accomplished in most countries largely through the efforts of national public education systems. In many instances, however, national systems are inadequate or disintegrate for a variety of reasons ranging from natural disaster to political turmoil. How each country deals with such a breakdown impacts the form and methodology of future instruction. EDU-CO, a communal education movement that was established in El Salvador, began when parents hired their own teachers for schools that had been closed during the country's 1980–92 civil war. Educators in South Africa created the non-governmental organization OLSET, the Open Learning Systems Education Trust, to rebuild the educational system devastated by the apartheid political system. Like Ecuador's Popular Radio Schools, OSLET also uses the radio to reach rural students isolated by distance. In Bangladesh, the Bangladesh Rural Advancement Committee runs parallel to the national education system and educates over one mil-

lion children annually. Community efforts such as these are often more successful because they respond to local, rather than national, needs and are flexible enough to adapt to the students at hand. However, because they are responding to local pressures, national education standards can become difficult to enforce, and content can fall victim to local bias.

The most dramatic example of this is currently in play in Afghanistan where the Taliban, an orthodox Muslim government, came to power in 1996. During Afghanistan's war with the former Soviet Union and the civil war that followed, the public education system collapsed, leaving open only private schools that were primarily religious. In addition to teaching a very strict interpretation of the Qur'an, the Muslim holy book, the schools advocated the creation of a radical Muslim government. The Taliban is a coalition of these students educated in south Afghanistan. Ironically, one of the Taliban's first moves after coming to power was to send the female students home. Though the United Nations got the Afghan government to agree to open separate schools for women, the curricula of these schools is strictly limited and many have been subsequently closed.

Most governments recognize how empowering education can be and the potential threat or benefit an educated populace holds for governments democratically elected or militarily imposed. Burma just reopened its colleges and universities after a three-year shut down because the government viewed them as breeding grounds for dissent. Political activity of any type is banned on the campuses of universities in Belarus; and in Ecuador, recently elected indigenous legislators credit the work of Dolores Cacuango and others with giving them the skills they needed to achieve political office.

The indigenous movement in Ecuador began haltingly in the 1940s as regionally fragmented organizations concerned mainly with local and land issues. It received guidance and support from both the Catholic Church and the Communist Party. With the formation of CONAIE, however, these fragmentary organizations began to unite around issues common to indigenous people regardless of their regional roots, yet land reform remained the priority.

Over time, however, CONAIE began to broaden its concerns and incorporate cultural preservation and promotion into its agenda. It was the driving force behind the bilingual education movement. As cultural issues became more important to CONAIE, awareness of these issues among the membership increased. Cultural preservation and promotion renewed pride among the indigenous people and led them to see the value contained within their customs and traditions.

ECUADORIAN INDIANS SYMBOLICALLY CLEANSE THEMSELVES WITH INCENSE DURING A CEREMONY TO CELEBRATE THE SPRING EQUINOX. *(AP/Wide World Photos. Reproduced by permission.)*

CONAIE began pressing for wider societal acceptance, and recognition of this value began to challenge the commonly held assumption that indigenous culture was something to eradicate in the name of assimilation and progress. This led to an increased need for indigenous people to participate in the political process. The movement slowly reversed its prior stance of non-recognition of and nonparticipation in the political process to become an active and increasingly powerful player in Ecuadorian politics. In keeping with its contemporary focus on cultural recognition it has succeeded in achieving changes to the constitution that acknowledged the indigenous people as both collectives and individuals and recognize the pluri-

national nature of Ecuador's society. Constitutionally, indigenous customs and traditions now stand on a par with those of European and *mestizo* culture.

Luís Macas, one of the founders of CONAIE and head of the Scientific Institute of Indigenous Cultures (ICCI) is now calling for the creation of an indigenous university. Until now CONAIE's leaders have been educated abroad or in the *mestizo* universities of Ecuador. Creating their own university would further strengthen the movement by reinforcing pride and expanding the ranks from which future leaders would be drawn. CONAIE's leaders believe the movement is expanding both its power and its objectives, and it will continue to gain strength. The perpetual state of economic crisis in which Ecuador seems to find itself will continue to provide fodder for the growth of this movement.

This increased political participation has resulted in indigenous candidates succeeding at the ballot box in races ranging from minor local offices to the national congress. The indigenous movement has been an important player in the overthrow of two recent governments. Now it has challenged the current president, Gustavo Noboa, to consider the needs and demands of the indigenous population. This challenge has been backed by warnings that what happened to the two previously elected presidents could happen to the current president as well. Noboa has returned the challenge by calling on the indigenous movement to gain power through the ballot box, not the street. The movement has shown its ability to do both. Which it chooses remains to be seen.

BIBLIOGRAPHY

Ayala, Enrique, et al. *Pueblos Indios, Estado y Derecho.* Quito, Ecuador: Corporación Editora Nacional, 1992.

Becker, Marc. "Una Revolución Comunista Indígena: Rural Protest Movements in Cayambe, Ecuador," *Rethinking Marxism* 10.4 (Winter 1998).

Black, Chad. "The Making of an Indigenous Movement: Culture, Ethnicity and Post-Marxist Social Praxis in Ecuador," in Research Paper Series 32, Latin American Institute of the University of New Mexico, May 1999.

Collins, Jennifer N. "A Sense of Possibility: Ecuador's Indigenous Movement Takes Center Stage," *NACLA Report on the Americas* (March/April 2000): 33(5).

Dandler, Jorge. "Indigenous Peoples and the Rule of Law in Latin America: Do They Have a Chance?" In *The (Un)Rule of Law and the Underprivileged in Latin America.* Notre Dame, Ind.: University of Notre Dame Press, 1999.

"An Interview with Luis Macas: Fueling Destruction in the Amazon," in Multinational Monitor, XV-4 (April 1994). Reproduced in http:// abyayala.native.org/ ecuador/amazon/oil/macas.html (20 September 2000).

Rosero, Fernando. *Levantamiento Indígena: Tierra y Precios.* Quito, Ecuador: CEDIS, 1991.

"Texaco and Ecuador," *New York Times,* 19 February 1999.

"Texaco and Ecuador Information Package-Response to Claims." http://www.texaco.com/shared/position/docs/ responsec.html (20 September 2000).

"What Texaco Management is Not Telling Shareholders About the Company's Activities in Ecuador." metalab.unc.edu/freburma/boycott/oil/texaco.html (20 September 2000).

"Texaco and Ecuador Information Package-Remediation" http://www.texaco.com/shared/position/docs/ responsec.html (20 September 2000).

Zamosc, Leon, "Agrarian Protest and the Indian Movement in the Ecuadorian Highlands," *Latin American Research Review,* (1994): 29–30.

Ximena Sosa-Buchholz

EUROPEAN UNION CONFLICT: THE BRITISH BEEF CONTROVERSY

THE CONFLICT

In March 1996, scientists discovered a connection between Mad Cow Disease (Bovine Spongiform Encephalopathy, or BSE) and Creutzfeldt-Jakob Syndrome, a debilitating and ultimately fatal disease in humans. The European Union (E.U.) banned the export of British beef to E.U. member states in an effort to contain the disease. Even after the ban was lifted, France continued to prevent the import of British beef.

Political

- The United Kingdom is a late and ambivalent addition to the European Union.

- France and other E.U. members fear being overwhelmed and bullied by the United Kingdom and worry that the United Kingdom's special relationship with the United States will allow the United States greater influence in the European Union

- Prior to England joining the European Union, France was the leading E.U. nation.

Economic

- U.K. participation in the European Union has undermined some British industry, due to increased competition.

- The United Kingdom resents its financial obligations to the European Union, in particular payments for agricultural subsidies to other nations.

Many observers of international affairs have identified the European Union (E.U.) as a rising center of power in the contemporary world. Since the end of World War II, the nations of Europe have made much progress toward laying their historical animosities to rest. By the 1990s, most of the continent had developed into a large free-trade zone, and a common currency, the euro, was introduced on January 1, 1999.

The process of European integration, however, has not been without problems. The March 1996 discovery of a connection between the infection of British cattle with Bovine Spongiform Encephalopathy (BSE, or "Mad Cow Disease," *vache folle* in French) and the fatal Creutzfeldt-Jakob Syndrome (CJS) in humans led the European Commission (the governing body of the European Union) and the European Parliament to ban the export of British beef to E.U. member states or to any other nation. BSE causes sponge-like holes to form in the brain, causing disorientation, lack of coordination, and, eventually, death. CJS is an extremely rare human disease. An increased occurrence of CJS in the United Kingdom led scientists to determine that the consumption of meat from an infected cow can transmit the disease to humans. France resisted the further sale of British beef most vociferously and continues its boycott even though British cattle farmers have instituted changes and culled herds, and even though beef production in Britain has been scientifically proven to be safe. By 1999 the British government threatened to sue France in the European Court over its decision to restrict Britain's access to its agricultural markets. The political controversy drew serious criticism from British farmers and their supporters against the sweeping powers of European institutions to influence their livelihoods.

HISTORICAL BACKGROUND

Europe After World War II

The contention over the export of British beef is only one symptom of larger problems in the economic and political relations of the member countries of the European Union. Despite much "goodwill" propaganda about the benefits of European unity for peace and democracy, underlying tensions have existed since the inception of an integrated Europe. These problems have contributed to the recent controversy over the trade in British beef and to other controversial issues relating to trade and political relations.

Perhaps the most important cause of this problem in modern international relations is that the European Union was much more the product of convenience and strategic thinking than it was of pacifism or simple goodwill. In the wake of World War II, most of Europe faced economic devastation and political uncertainty. The decisive wartime roles of the United States and the Soviet Union had radically altered the international political landscape. The multi-polar global system dominated by several competing European powers, which had existed for several centuries, had been eclipsed by the emergence of two new powers (the United States and the Soviet Union) whose relative positions in the world were dramatically enhanced by the war.

In harsh practical terms the two superpowers divided Europe between them without any significant challenger. Eastern Europe and half of Germany lay first under Soviet military occupation and then under Moscow's de facto political domination. Most of the western half of the continent had suffered absolute defeat at the hands of the Germans, years of exploitative German occupation, and then a painful and costly liberation by the United States and Britain. Western Germany and Italy had been devastated in the fighting and were conquered and occupied by Allied armies. Although Britain had emerged on the winning side of the conflict without having to endure German occupation, the physical destruction and financial strain it had to endure, along with continuing trends of relative economic decline, left it weak and vulnerable. Indeed, Britain was so weak that its postwar Labour Party government, led by Prime Minister Clement Attlee, could only conclude that the country could no longer afford many of its commitments overseas. In 1947 it granted independence to India, its largest and most important colonial possession and the chief source and symbol of Britain's world power status.

CHRONOLOGY

1951 France, West Germany, Italy, Belgium, the Netherlands, and Luxembourg establish the European Coal and Steel Community, the first major European trade organization.

1957 The trade agreement is expanded to provide for a free-trade zone for all commodities.

1956 The United States supports Egypt in a British/Egyptian conflict over the Suez Canal, undermining British confidence in a joint U.K./U.S. future.

1958 The European Economic Community (the Common Market) is created.

1961 Britain applies for EEC membership.

1963 French president Charles de Gaulle rejects the British application.

1967 De Gaulle rejects the second British application for EEC membership.

1969 De Gaulle dies.

1971 French president d'Estaing approves membership in the EEC for the United Kingdom.

1973 Britain enters the Common Market.

1992 The Maastricht Treaty establishs an even closer alliance within the European Union.

1996 Scientists discover a link between Mad Cow Disease (Bovine Spongiform Encephalopathy) and a similar, but rare, human disease, Cruetzfeldt-Jakob Syndrome. The European Commission and the European Parliament ban the sale of British beef.

1999 Despite scientific assurances that British beef is safe, France continues to refuse to import British beef. The British government threatens to sue France in European Court to ensure the access to France's market guaranteed by the Common Market.

From the earliest days after the war, it was apparent that the reconstruction of European stability would require tremendous efforts and considerable expense. In order to facilitate recovery and prevent the rise of extreme political movements, the United States invested more than $13 billion in direct economic assistance to the various nations of Western Europe. Launching what came to be called the Truman Doctrine, direct American aid also provided for resistance to coercive attempts by Communists to seize power in Greece and Soviet attempts to extract diplomatic and military concessions from Turkey. The U.S. military also stood up to Communist expansionism when it supplied the blockaded western occupation zones of the city of Berlin for more than a year in 1948–49. The conclusion of a trans-Atlantic military alliance, the North Atlantic Treaty Organization (NATO), in April 1949 established a permanent U.S. role in the defense of Western Europe.

Early Support for European Integration

Consciousness of their vulnerability led the leaders of many European nations to believe that their best hope for future success lay in putting aside past differences and working toward a common future. Indeed, a politically and economically integrated Europe offered many solutions. Since it was becoming rather obvious that individual European nations simply could not afford whatever global presence they had maintained in better times, early proponents of European integration argued that a synthesis of European interests across the continent could provide a vehicle for Europeans to continue playing a major role in world affairs.

The German question was another major problem that European integration could address. After having come close to winning two world wars, Germany had proven its potential to establish rule over the entire continent. Fearful European politicians, especially the French, believed that Germany's inclusion in a multinational political and economic bloc would "drown" its military capabilities and any future political aspirations to dominate the continent. The politicians also believed that economic cooperation would open contentiously-defended markets and defuse the intense competition over resources that had historically characterized European diplomatic relations. The leaders of the West German state, which evolved from the Western Allies' occupation zones of Germany in August 1949, believed that the best way to secure the reunification of their divided country was to join forces with the United States and its European allies against communism.

These factors created a situation in which the interest of the two largest and most populous continental nations, France and West Germany, coincided. Movement toward political union offered to keep German ambitions under control while both nations could recover through the low defense spending that was consequent to their rapproche-

ment and through free trade with each other and their neighbors. The first inter-European agreement, in fact, was the establishment of the European Coal and Steel Community (ECSC) in 1951. Developed by French foreign minister Robert Schumann, the agreement provided for free trade in these two basic industrial commodities among France, West Germany, Italy, Belgium, the Netherlands, and Luxembourg. In a shrewd strategic context all would have free and equal access to West Germany's much larger raw material reserves and prevent their monopolization by Germans. The creation of the European Atomic Energy Commission (Euratom) also established a pan-European organization to control the development and use of recently discovered nuclear power.

The European Economic Community

Enjoying economic success and rather impressive postwar recoveries, continental Europe moved closer toward political union. Beginning in 1952, the continental powers began to discuss plans for a common European defense alliance. European leaders saw military cohesion not only as a way to harmonize Europe politically and economically but also as a way toward the emergence of a united Europe as a world power. Although the plans for this European Defense Community (EDC) failed, mainly because French leaders believed that America's commitment to NATO would defend Western Europe while leaving it free to concentrate its own resources on domestic economic development, it was nevertheless indicative of the logic behind further integration. By 1957 the six member states of the Coal and Steel Community signed a series of treaties in Rome that created a free-trade zone among them in all commodities. Taking effect on January 1, 1958, the European Economic Community (EEC) created a common market, the importance of which was established by essentially the same arguments advanced in favor of the Coal and Steel Community. West Germany would remain stable and under control through favorable economic relationships while its resources and industrial potential would be freely available for the recovery of its partners.

With Eastern Europe under Soviet domination and Western Europe moving into the common market created by the EEC, the status of one crucial component of European politics and history remained unclear. While some of the economically marginal areas of the continent (Scandinavia, the Iberian Peninsula, Greece) remained outside the integration process, Great Britain's absence was very noticeable.

BRITISH BEEF PRODUCERS DEMONSTRATE AGAINST THE BAN ON BRITISH BEEF AT THE EUROPEAN PARLIAMENT IN STRASBOURG, FRANCE. *(AP/Wide World Photos. Reproduced by permission.)*

Great Britain Opts Out

Before World War II, Britain had a somewhat idealized self-image. The popular British view of the "sceptered isle" claimed that the country had developed the ideal system of government, one based on precedent and tradition, without suffering the periodic outbreaks of political violence that had plagued almost all of its continental neighbors at one time or another. Until relatively recently, academic geopolitics maintained that the United Kingdom was in fact as distinct from continental Europe as it was from any other geographic area of the world. Britain's emergence as the world's leading industrial power in the early nineteenth century and its amalgamation of colonial possessions (Queen Victoria ruled over twenty-five percent of the world's surface when she died in 1901) reinforced the view that Britain and its people were not merely distinct, but superior.

The devastation of two world wars, the resulting financial constraints placed on the British Empire, and the rise of challengers to Britain's global rule had still not disabused many British leaders of that notion in the years after 1945. Although there was some initial enthusiasm for European unity, exemplified by Winston Churchill's 1940 call for Britain and France to join in a political union to fight Hitler's Germany and in his 1946 call for a "United States of Europe," the lead-ership of the country remained by and large aloof from the idea of integration. Britain took no part in the ECSC, EDC, EEC, or any of the other early experiments in creating trans-European institutions. To do so would have been public recognition that Britain could not prosper in the postwar world without surrendering its protected markets and elements of its political sovereignty. In other words, participation in the Common Market (another name for the EEC) and even in less ambitious European organizations would have ended Britain's traditional and jealously guarded political and diplomatic independence from any continental neighbor or combination of continental neighbors. Britain's emphasis on promoting trade with its remaining colonial empire and former colonies, which had become independent members of the post-colonial Commonwealth of Nations, continued to direct the attention of its leaders away from Europe.

Britain's relationship with the United States was another source of concern. Although there had been underlying currents and occasional flare-ups of tension in Anglo-American relations since the British North American colonies won independence, relations between the two nations had been remarkably close during most of the nineteenth and throughout the twentieth centuries. After World War II, many British leaders were eager to have this "special relationship" continue. By the mid-1950s the same Winston Churchill who had called for a "United States of Europe" in 1946 authored his four-volume, Nobel prize-winning *History of the English Speaking Peoples,* which charted the common history of Britain and the United States and strongly suggested that the two had a common future. George Orwell's 1948 fictional novel *1984* foresaw a future in which the United States and the British Empire were amalgamated in a single political entity. While it was apparent that the United States had become and would remain the senior partner in the relationship, many British leaders argued that a junior role in an alliance with the United States was preferable to Britain's submersion into a supranational entity that would limit its independence.

Facts of international politics spoiled that vision, however. One of the most important problems between the British and American governments during the war and in the years that followed was U.S. insistence, on ideological and commercial grounds, that Britain divest itself of its colonial possessions. Prime Minister Winston Churchill not only demurred but also actually asked the United States for help in restoring British control of colonies occupied by Japan during the war. While Attlee's financially strapped postwar government had willingly let go of India and of Britain's strategically significant mandate in Palestine, his successors were increasingly reluctant to surrender other British interests around the world. This policy caused a serious problem in 1956 when Gamal Abdel Nasser's Egyptian nationalist government nationalized the British and French shares of the Suez Canal Company. (When a government nationalizes private property it takes over control and ownership on behalf of the state.) Although President Dwight Eisenhower lent his tacit support to the recovery of the canal through military means, at the crucial moment American support faded. In the United Nations General Assembly, the United States actually voted with the Soviet Union and against its two NATO allies in support of a cease-fire that called for the withdrawal of the invading troops.

Reluctantly, the British leaders who had opposed greater involvement with European integration began to accept that the United States would not automatically support British interests. The Suez Crisis of 1956 was especially instructive, since it proved that the United States was more interested in pursuing its Cold War competition with the Soviet Union for influence in the Third World than alienating developing nations from the United

States and American interests by supporting imperialism. Although the special relationship between the United States and the United Kingdom was by no means broken off, American attitudes during the Suez Crisis were instrumental in hastening France's decision to work for the treaties that created Euratom and the EEC.

The United Kingdom and the EEC

Although Britain stayed away from the Rome Treaties of 1957 and the Common Market that they created, it became increasingly apparent that the liabilities of its partnership with the United States far outweighed whatever economic benefits it might have. Indeed, even as Prime Minister Harold Macmillan campaigned for the 1959 general election by telling his people, "You've never had it so good!," the fact of Britain's decline in relation to other countries was unavoidable. Progressively, continental European nations that had suffered much more in the war than Britain were reaching and even exceeding Britain in industrial output, per capita income, and standard of living. Even the big losers of World War II—West Germany and Japan—overtook Britain's economy in size in the 1960s. Between 1958 and 1962, moreover, most of Britain's remaining colonial possessions achieved independence and, together with the colonies that had done so previously, their roles as British trading partners declined considerably. As domestic economic problems hindered British growth and trade with the prosperous continental economies increased, Britain began to see European integration as the best available option for a prosperous future. Accordingly, Macmillan's government made a formal application for EEC membership in 1961.

Just as its EEC membership had been controversial at home, so was it controversial throughout the rest of the continent. French opposition to British entry into the Common Market was especially strong. Benefiting from France's leading position among the six member states of the EEC, French president Charles de Gaulle was reluctant to endorse any change that would detract from his country's preeminence. The inclusion of Britain's roughly equal-sized population and economy into the free-trade bloc was perhaps the biggest possible threat he could face. Britain's continuing relationship with the United States also made British EEC membership appear to be a subtle way for the Americans to enhance their European role and limit independent European action, something which the integrationist European politicians had feared all along. Whatever circumstantial evidence of this had existed before was substantiated in

December 1962, when Macmillan agreed to the full subordination of his country's armed forces and nuclear arsenal to American leadership in NATO. Only a few weeks later, in January 1963, de Gaulle rejected Britain's membership in the EEC and quite explicitly identified the prospect of "American domination" as a leading factor in his decision. De Gaulle rejected a second British attempt to gain EEC membership in 1967 for the same reason.

After domestic problems forced de Gaulle's resignation in April 1969, his successors were much more reconciled to the idea of British EEC membership. By 1971 French president Valery Giscard d'Estaing agreed in principle to allow Britain to hold a referendum on the subject. Although the issue remained somewhat divisive in Britain, a majority of the voting population approved EEC membership the following year, and Britain, together with Ireland and Denmark, formally entered the European Common Market on January 1, 1973.

British Tensions with the EEC

If the tortured process of Britain's entry into Europe created tense relations between the United Kingdom and its new partners, Britain's arrival to the EEC brought with it a number of fresh problems. Contrary to many hopes and expectations, Britain's entry into the Common Market did not generate new economic prosperity. As British trade with the continent increased, British industry lost ground to more competitive products from the continental European economies. Rising trade deficits with continental nations led to inflation, and this was worsened by the rising price of oil after the Arab-Israeli War of October 1973. Under the Labour Party governments of Harold Wilson (1974–76; Wilson had also been prime minister in 1964–70) and James Callaghan (1976–79), Britain suffered so seriously from what other EEC leaders called the "English disease" that serious civil unrest set in. Under Callaghan, the British government actually came close to declaring bankruptcy and was saved only by loans from the International Monetary Fund (IMF). Rather than experiencing an economic boom, Britain's financial situation in the 1970s more closely resembled that of a Third World country.

European integration became an even more contentious problem for Britain at this time. Although not all of its economic problems were related to EEC membership, the effect of free trade with the continental members was noticeable. The intrusion of European financial obligations into British economic life was also a serious issue. Even as its economy worsened and came to rely on the

NICOLAS ROUTIER STANDS NEAR A FIRE SET BY THE FARMERS OF NORTHERN FRANCE TO PROTEST AGAINST A FEE THEY MUST PAY TO BRING DEAD ANIMALS TO THE KNACKERY, A FREE SERVICE BEFORE MAD COW DISEASE. *(AP/Wide World Photos. Reproduced by permission.)*

international financial community for support, Britain's mandatory contribution to the treasury of the EEC increased from 60 million pounds in 1973 to nearly a billion pounds in 1979. Agriculture became a central issue in these developments, especially since the EEC spent (and its successor, the European Union, spends) a significant percentage of its annual budget, ranging from twenty-five percent to sixty percent, on agricultural subsidies for its member states under the rubric of its Common Agricultural Policy (CAP). As the quality of their own lives worsened, British taxpayers were required

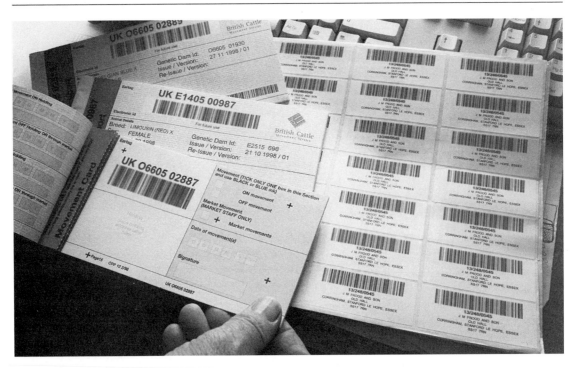

IN THE WAKE OF "MAD COW" DISEASE WHICH FORCED A GLOBAL BAN OF BRITISH BEEF, THE GOVERNMENT RE-QUIRES CATTLE PASSPORTS THAT MUST TRAVEL WITH EACH ANIMAL. *(AP/Wide World Photos. Reproduced by permission.)*

each year to pay more to support less efficiently run agricultural enterprises in France and other countries where farming lobbies had extracted numerous domestic concessions to support inefficient (yet cheaper and/or traditional) agricultural practices.

After Callaghan's government collapsed in a no-confidence vote in 1979, Margaret Thatcher's conservative government wasted little time in confronting this issue. In less-than-diplomatic language, Thatcher essentially accused Britain's European partners of having misappropriated British funds and quite simply, but no more diplomatically, demanded her money back. Thatcher's abrasive approach to negotiations with the EEC intensified as time went on. At one point, the French EEC president Jacques Delors cited one of Thatcher's diatribes as grounds for Britain's expulsion from the EEC.

As Thatcher wrangled with the leaders of other EEC members to reduce British contributions, she took a much less integrationist stance with regard to Britain's international position. The election of Ronald Reagan to the presidency of the United States in 1980 brought into office a man who shared many of Thatcher's political and philosophical principles more than any other world

leader. The two quickly developed a close personal and political relationship centered on confrontational opposition to the Soviet Union in the Cold War. This policy was an important European issue because the rest of the EEC had adopted official policies of rapprochement—the establishment of cordial relations—with Moscow. As early as 1966, de Gaulle had called for "detente, entente, and co-operation" with the USSR to enhance France's role as a world power. Beginning in 1969, his West German associates had developed a new strategy of *Ostpolitik*, or "Eastern Policy," designed to create lucrative trade relationships with Eastern Europe and the USSR and to ameliorate problems associated with the division of Germany. At a time when European integration pointed toward its emergence in an independent middle position in the Cold War, Thatcher closely cooperated with the Reagan administration's vehemently anti-Soviet policies. The renewal of the special relationship as the dominant feature in British foreign relations was further enhanced in 1982 when, with Reagan's full support and assistance, Thatcher successfully defeated Argentina's attempt to seize the disputed Falkland Islands, a British possession off the South American coast. Even as the Cold War appeared to be coming to an end, Thatcher thought largely in terms of British strategic interests and even initially opposed the reunification of Germany in 1989–90 because she feared the reemergence of German rule on the continent.

Domestically, Thatcher used her strengthened position after the Falkland Islands War to consolidate her combative approach to European integration. Prominent supporters of integration within her own Conservative Party, such as foreign secretaries Lord Carrington and Francis Pym, lost their frontbench ministerial positions and were replaced by right-wing supporters of Thatcher. Thatcher's economic and social policies did more to distinguish Britain from the other EEC nations than to harmonize the United Kingdom with them. Over the course of the 1980s, Thatcher steadily reduced the role of government in the economy, curtailed the power of activist organized labor, reduced taxes, and resisted social permissiveness in what was in many ways the opposite of the trend occurring on the continent.

The European Union

Although Thatcher's increasingly acerbic opposition to European integration and her political failures on other questions (notably the controversial poll tax, a local government tax reform passed in 1988) precipitated her resignation in 1990, the new decade was marked by continuing trends of contention in British-E.U. relations. Thatcher's successor as prime minister, John Major, relied on the "euroskeptic" wing of the Conservative Party for support but found that it was increasingly necessary to appease those who favored continued integration as well. Despite continuing controversy over Britain's financial contributions to the EEC, Major was willing to overcome serious opposition within his party in order to seek British ratification of the Maastricht Treaty (1992), which transformed the EEC into the more closely associated European Union. Although the British people approved the treaty in a referendum in August 1993, the victory was only possible because Major had been able to negotiate clauses that allowed Britain to opt out of the prospective European Monetary Union (EMU).

Britain's reluctance to engage in further unification created further problems. Major's government was partially responsible for the early failures to establish a common European currency and reacted strongly to the idea by withdrawing the British pound from the E.U.'s exchange rate mechanism (ERM). Major, like Thatcher before him, also strongly urged the further expansion of E.U. membership not because he believed in European

federalism, but because he quite shrewdly saw that as more and more nations joined, it would become increasingly difficult for his country's continental antagonists to build any definitive consensus on the future of the European Union. Diffusing the European Union would serve British interests by slowing down further economic and political integration. Accordingly, Britain favored the E.U. candidacies of Spain, Portugal, and Greece for entry in 1986 and those of Austria, Finland, Sweden, and Norway for entry in 1995 (though Norway voted not to join). Under Major, Britain also advocated the quick accession of former communist nations in Eastern Europe and other peripheral European states, including Turkey and Cyprus.

Another problem in the 1990s was that the enhanced powers granted to the European Commission under the Maastricht Treaty made many Britons feel that important domestic issues in their country would now be decided by self-interested and unaccountable foreign bureaucrats who sat in the commission's headquarters in Brussels, Belgium. These suspicions were exacerbated by the fact that the un-elected European Commissioners, who are in effect the European Union's cabinet ministers, were and remain in no real way responsible to the European Parliament, the elected body of representatives of the European Union's people, which sits in Strasbourg, France. In Britain as well as in other countries, this "democratic deficit" has created the impression that authority in the European Union is increasingly exercised in an undemocratic fashion. A spate of financial scandals reaching to the highest levels of the European Commission and the E.U. bureaucracy, including one that forced the resignation of the entire commission in March 1999, did little to improve the image of a prospective European super-state.

An additional recent concern in Britain has been that closer involvement in European supranationalism would erode Britain's cultural distinctiveness and its unique national customs and institutions. The decision of Tony Blair's Labour government to incorporate the European Convention on Human Rights into British law led to widespread speculation that the process would both concede more national sovereignty to un-elected foreigners and infringe upon national traditions. When Parliament approved the bill adopting the Convention in 1999, critics expected that the British criminal justice system would face humiliating changes dictated by European judges, and it was freely admitted that adherence to the Convention would force the abolition of capital punishment by bureaucratic mandate rather than democratic par-

JOSE BOVE

1953– Jose Bove is a sheep farmer and leader of the French "Peasant Confederation." In the business world, he is considered an important influence on the European economy: French leaders have consulted with him on agricultural issues such as genetically altered food. Many Europeans and North Americans considered him a hero.

Bove was born in Bordeaux, France, in 1953, but spent his childhood in Berkeley, California. After he returned to France, he immersed himself in activism, traveling to Tahiti to protest French nuclear tests and joining French farmers to protest the extension of a military base. He founded his political organization, the Confederation Paysanne in 1987.

In 1999 Bove and other activists were arrested for vandalizing a McDonald's restaurant in Millau, France. Bove drove a tractor and wagon through the not-yet-opened restaurant to protest the globalization of world economy, and its consequences on local farmers, diet, and traditional agriculture. Later that summer, he joined the protests that interrupted the World Trade Organization (WTO) conference in Seattle, Washington. Bove's core support group is comprised of other French farmers, who like Bove, have suffered from the affect of global economy since the United States, with the approval of the WTO, imposed one hundred percent tariffs on many French agricultural products following the European ban on hormone-treated beef.

liamentary vote. In the first months after the adoption of the convention, in fact, orders of the European Court forced certain procedural changes in British courtrooms and compelled the British government to allow open homosexuals to serve in the armed forces. The British press also speculated that the future of the country's Honours System, the uniquely British institution through which the monarch grants awards and aristocratic titles to distinguished subjects, might disappear because the process is not governed by the free and open competition mandated by the convention. One of the most dramatic protests against the Blair government's bill to remove hereditary peers (members of the upper house of Parliament who inherit their right to sit and vote) from the House of Lords in November 1999 argued that the measure was part of an E.U. attempt "drafted in Brussels" to harmonize the functioning of its member states' national legislatures.

RECENT HISTORY AND THE FUTURE

The British beef issue in many ways amalgamated one of the critical points of contention in the history of the European Union. After more than two decades of feeling burdened by their contributions toward the support of inefficient continental farmers, British farmers were told that their own produce, even after it no longer posed a health risk, was unacceptable for sale in certain continental countries. In addition to the direct cash subsidies they had provided, in other words, British farmers were required to suffer financially in what many saw as a trumped-up attempt to block their competition from domestic markets in other countries. That the relevant decisions on the question were made by a body which they neither elected nor which was accountable to them aggravated long-standing issues of national sovereignty and power relationships that had always characterized British-E.U. relations.

Britain's future role within the European Union remains uncertain. Although relatively few advocate the country's full withdrawal, substantial majorities of the population at large and of business leaders oppose Britain's accession to the common currency. In terms of national identity, public opinion polls have shown that Britons are less willing to identify themselves as "Europeans" than any other E.U. nationality. The relatively poor performance of the euro, the common European currency, since its introduction in January 1999, has done little to change these views. A growing industrial lobby even advocates British accession to the North American Free Trade Agreement (NAFTA), which created a free-trade zone in the Western Hemisphere in 1993. Proponents of further integration in the government and major political parties are finding it increasingly difficult to support steps in that direction without equivocation. Even Blair, the generally pro-Europe Labour prime minister since 1997, has no firm position on the common currency issue and has suggested Britain's withdrawal from the CAP. Although the war over British beef has ended, the issues that it symbolized remain at the core of the contentious politics of the European Union.

BIBLIOGRAPHY

Dinan, Desmond. *Ever Closer Union: An Introduction to European Integration.* 2d ed. Boulder, Colo.: Lynne Rienner Publishers, 1999.

George, Stephen. *An Awkward Partner: Britain in the European Community.* 2d ed. Oxford, England: Clarendon Press, 1997.

Kennedy, Paul. *The Rise and Fall of the Great Powers: Economic Change and Military Conflict From 1500 to 2000.* New York: Random House, 1987.

Major, John. *John Major: The Autobiography.* New York: Harper Collins, 1999.

Thatcher, Margaret. *The Downing Street Years.* New York: Harper Collins, 1993.

Urwin, Derek W. *The Community of Europe: A History of European Integration Since 1945.* New York: Longman, 1995.

Paul du Quenoy

Guatemala: Indian Testimony to a Genocidal War

The Conflict

Nobel Peace Prize winner Rigoberta Menchú sued Guatemala's former leaders in Spanish court for human rights abuses, including murder and torture. The charges stem from a time of brutal dictatorship in Guatemala.

Political
- The military repressed the people and rebel groups were formed to fight the military. To combat both government and rebel violence, paramilitary groups were formed. Military death squads emerged.

- Fear of the rise of communism in the western hemisphere and the wish to protect U.S. corporate interests encouraged the United States to support the military rulers.

Economic
- Coffee plantation owners (an oligarchy) and the United States wanted to keep control of the profits and land. Indians were moved off the land to make and expand the plantations.

- Rebels wanted to redistribute land and profits to the Indians.

On December 2, 1999, the 1992 Nobel Peace Prize winner Rigoberta Menchú Tum filed a lawsuit in Spain's Supreme Court against eight Guatemalans—three former presidents, three military officers, and two civilians—for their role in the repression launched by the state against Guatemalan citizens, primarily Mayan Indians, in that country's thirty-six-year civil war. Although the civil war that triggered the lawsuit has its contemporary roots in the Cold War, its beginning can be traced to the original conflict that emerged as a result of the Spanish conquest of the Americas five centuries ago. Spanish colonialism created an inequitable society divided along racial and ethnic lines in Guatemala. After the nation's independence from Spain, colonial political, social, and economic patterns survived into the modern national period.

HISTORICAL BACKGROUND

Colonial and Independence Period

The conquest of Guatemala by the Spanish created an initial division between the colonizers (the Spanish) and the colonized (the Indians) during the early contact period. Through three centuries of colonial rule the process of biological and cultural *mestizaje* (miscegenation, or the mixing of different races) produced three distinct social and ethnic groups that would dominate the nation's political and economic life: *criollos* (Creoles, or whites born in the New World), *ladinos* (term used in Guatemala for a person of biologically mixed European and Indian blood or a culturally Hispanicized Indian; in other Spanish-speaking nations the term *mestizo* is used) and Indians. After independence in 1821, the *criollos* came to dominate the political and economic system while the ladino population gradually increased its influence in these spheres. The Mayan Indians continued to hold a subservient political, social, and economic position. Economically, the Indians provided the labor and possessed the land demanded by the *criollos* and *ladinos* for their *haciendas* and plantations for the production of agricultural products for profit. The Indians, living in corporate communities, used their land for the production of subsistence crops (crops that provided food to feed the community). During the Spanish colonial period, Indian communities were legally recognized by Spanish law and could own land as a community, not as individuals. They sought to distance themselves from the national society that encroached on their traditional community life.

Rise of the Coffee Oligarchy

During the first fifty years of independence, provincial rivalries, internal struggles between liberals and conservatives, civil wars, boom/bust economic cycles, and foreign invasion and involvement rocked the nation and contributed to chronic instability. Until the 1850s, Guatemala's primary export was cochineal, a natural red dye. During the 1850s, coffee came to dominate as the primary export product in high demand on the world market. This demand contributed not only to the slow encroachment of *criollos* and ladinos on Indian lands for the creation and expansion of coffee plantations but also to the struggle for control of Indian labor. Indians were forcibly introduced to the rising market economy as their land was taken from them. After 1870, with the rise of the liberal coffee oligarchy (rulers), the loss of the Indians' land accelerated. Legislation was passed that facilitated the acquisition of land by the coffee oligarchy, provided labor through obligatory labor systems such as debt peonage (a system whereby debt is used to keep workers bound to the land) and the *mandamientos* (a forced labor draft that required Indians to work for planters), and created an infrastructure that benefited the export economy and not internal development. This assault on Indian lands contributed to periodic rebellions in the countryside as the Indians sought to defend their lands and way of life. Although the plantation owners had private armies, a professional military—composed largely of *ladinos* in its officer ranks—emerged during this period to ensure the continued domination of the *criollos* in the countryside. The expansion of the export economy contributed to urbanization and modernization that increased the separation of a "modern" urban sector and a "traditional" rural sector—largely populated by Indians. Economic and

CHRONOLOGY

1821 Guatemala wins independence from Spanish colonial rule.

1850 Coffee begins to dominate the Guatemalan economy and a coffee oligarchy begins to dictate policy in Guatemala.

1898 Spain loses the Spanish-American War, increasing U.S. influences in Central America.

1900s U.S.-based United Fruit Company begins to dominate Guatemala's economy with banana exports.

1944–54 The Guatemalan democratic revolution introduces reform measures to Guatemala, including some measures that the U.S. labels "Communist."

1954 A U.S.-backed and CIA-facilitated coup d'état topples the government leading to military rule.

1960–96 A series of rebellions are suppressed by the military (and paramilitary groups), resulting in thousands of deaths.

1968 Zacapa campaign occurrs, where an estimated ten thousand civilians are massacred by the military.

1996 Peace accords are signed.

1999 Rigoberta Menchú files a lawsuit in Spanish court to hold Guatemala's leaders responsible for their alleged crimes against the Mayan Indians.

political inequality increased during this period, as the Indians—the majority of the population—were marginalized from national life.

The Rise of the United Fruit Company and U.S. Influence

In the period from 1870 to 1920 economic development based on the use of the repressive apparatus of the state reached its zenith under the administration of Manuel Estrada Cabrera, who ruled the country from 1898 to 1920. At the beginning of the twentieth century, the U.S.-based United Fruit Company (UFCO) entered the country's economic life and it would come to dominate Guatemala's economy as one of the primary banana exporters. The government provided generous concessions of land for the creation of the company's banana plantations. Coffee and bananas became the leading export crops that dominated the nation's political and economic life. U.S. influence grew when it became the primary market for banana exports, which gave the United States' political and economic interests considerable leverage within Guatemala. U.S. supremacy in the Central American region increased overall as a result of Spain's defeat in the 1898 Spanish-American War. The United States developed its political and economic power in the country through investments, loans, and the U.S. embassy.

In 1920 with the overthrow of Cabrera, democracy interrupted Guatemala's authoritarian and repressive history. The dependence on two primary exports—coffee and bananas—made Guatemala vulnerable to the world market with its boom/bust cycles. From 1913 to 1938 these two products grew to represent seventy percent of Central America's exports and the trend continued until the 1960s. Guatemala's economy, however, could not withstand the drastic decline in demand for these products as a result of the Great Depression of 1929. The resulting economic crisis affected the internal social, political, and economic life of the nation as unemployment, bankruptcies, decline in wages, and other adverse economic consequences of the depression wracked Guatemala's fragile social and economic fabric. Strikes and labor mobilizations increased, with much of this activity directed against UFCO since the banana plantation workers were one of the most organized and radical sectors of the labor movement. A small Communist party participated in these actions. This instability and threat to national and foreign economic interests contributed to the rise of another dictatorial regime, that of General Jorge Ubico, a member of the coffee oligarchy. From 1931 to 1944 he ruled the nation with an iron grip as he went against those that he considered the enemies of the nation, especially those he considered Communists. He branded anyone who diverged from his particular ideological stance as "Communist," fearing that radical (Communist) elements would destabilize the country. His political power rested on three pillars: the military, the landowners, and foreign companies. Ubico found favor with the United States as he cooperated with it and its strategic, political, and economic interests.

The coming of World War II cut off European markets from Guatemala's primary exports. This situation contributed to a closer political and economic relationship with the United States since the U.S. market became the exclusive market for Guatemala's coffee exports. Other coffee producing nations also depended on the U.S. market, which could not absorb all of the surplus. Guatemala suffered continuing economic crises as unemployment increased and the state reduced social spending. Opposition to Ubico's regime emerged among the small middle class located in the cities. As a result of Ubico's economic development policies (that had created a modernized infrastructure for the export economy) a nationalistic middle class developed that challenged his administration. (Nationalism is a desire for national unity and independence, including meaningful control over your country and its resources.) This middle class emerged from the *ladinos* and was comprised of students, teachers, professionals, junior army officers, small shopkeepers, and others not allied with the politically and economically powerful upper class. The middle class sought to transform the political, social, and economic institutions that had characterized the nation since independence and establish a modern liberal capitalist system. Influenced by the Allied war against fascism—when the Allies, led by the United States, England, France, and the Soviet Union fought fascist Germany, Italy, and Japan—university students and military officers were the two primary groups that sought an alternative to Ubico's dictatorship and the creation of a democracy in Guatemala.

The Guatemalan National Democratic Revolution (1944–54)

Student demonstrations contributed to the overthrow of Ubico as other middle class sectors joined them in their struggle. The military refused to obey Ubico, ushering in the Guatemalan democratic revolution of 1944, which lasted until 1954. This move by the military would have lasting implications, since this was the first time that it acted as an organized group during a political crisis. During the next decades, the military would play an important role as a political and economic institution as it increasingly influenced national events. After Ubico's ouster, political parties were organized that participated in the first truly free elections, held in December 1944. Juan José Arévalo, a university professor and candidate of the National Renovation Party (Renovación Nacional, or RN), won the election. During his presidential administration (1945–51) the government quickly moved to transform the nation and put it on the road of capitalist modernity.

The reforms Arévalo's government enacted affected all sectors of Guatemalan society, especially those previously neglected groups, such as the workers, peasants, and Indians. Labor, a supporter of the revolution, benefited from the government as it abolished the onerous obligatory labor systems. The 1947 Labor Code provided other ben-

RIGOBERTA MENCHU TAM

1959– Rigoberta Menchú, recipient of the 1992 Nobel Peace Prize, was born into an impoverished Quiche Indian family in 1959. Her family, like most of the indigenous population of Guatemala, worked in virtual enslavement on plantations. Because citizenship was restricted to people of Spanish decent, indigenous Guatemalans had no protection under the law.

As a child, Rigoberta watched her brother die of pesticide poisoning, and other native people die of malnutrition, disease, and agricultural accidents. Her father, Vincente, became an activist for indigenous people's rights, and founded the United Peasant Committee. He and dozens of other people died in a fire at the Spanish embassy during a protest.

After her brother and mother were kidnapped, tortured and killed by the Guatemalan military, Menchú, wanted by the government at age twenty-one, fled to Mexico. There, she dictated her autobiography *I, Rigoberta Menchú,* which brought international attention to the conflict between the military government of Guatemala and the native population. (Some of the specific information in her autobiography has been questioned.)

Menchú continued her family's campaign, traveling and speaking about the plight of her people. She won the 1992 Nobel Peace Prize for her work, and used

RIGOBERTA MANCHU. *(AP/Wide World Photos. Reproduced by permission.)*

the monetary award to establish a foundation to continue the struggle for human rights for indigenous people. In 1999 she sued leaders of the Guatemalan government in Spanish court for human rights abuses, including the death of her family.

efits, such as guaranteeing decent working conditions, equitable wages, social security benefits, and the right to unionize. Utilizing their newfound freedom, urban and rural workers organized to better their daily lives. UFCO became a target of labor struggles as it represented what the workers saw to be the exploitation of the country by foreign interests. Arévalo, a nationalist, supported these efforts since his government, as well as the revolution, were characterized by their extreme nationalism.

With popular support, the RN's presidential candidate, Colonel Jacobo Arbenz, won the next free and fair elections held in 1950. He continued and intensified the progressive direction of the country by concentrating his attention on the nation's semifeudal agricultural structure. He implemented a sweeping land reform that alienated the

large landowners and foreign corporations with landed holdings—especially the UFCO with its large tracts of uncultivated land. The Constitution of 1945 declared *latifundios* (large-landed estates) illegal and had provisions for expropriating large-landed estates and redistributing the land to the landless. The aim of the land reform was the creation of a small farmer class that would have sufficient purchasing power for the expansion of the internal market. Through the creation of this internal market, national industry would find it profitable to engage in manufacturing consumer goods. The agrarian reform was an important step toward creating an economically independent capitalist nation.

During this period, two percent of the population owned seventy-four percent of the productive land. The democratic movement led to the

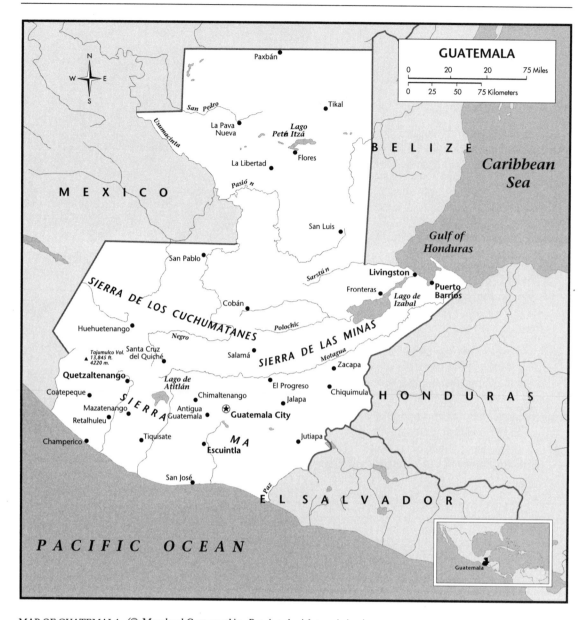

MAP OF GUATEMALA. (© *Maryland Cartographics. Reprinted with permission.*)

growth of the peasant movement and increased demands for land. The government acted by promulgating the Agrarian Reform Law of 1952, which provided for the expropriation of uncultivated lands in excess of 223 acres that would be distributed to landless peasants. The government compensated the owners by issuing them twenty-five-year government bonds. The state also provided credit and technical assistance to the new peasant owners in order to increase agricultural production. The Agrarian Reform Law brought the government into conflict with the UFCO, one of

the largest landowners possessing 550,000 acres. With only fifteen percent of this land under cultivation, it was subject to the provisions of the law. In 1953 the government expropriated 233,973 acres of this unused land, which was subsequently increased to 413,573 acres. The government also expropriated the unused lands of native Guatemalan large landowners. By 1954, one hundred thousand peasant families had benefited from this law. The national and foreign landowning elite labeled these actions as "Communistic" and the U.S. government in Washington, DC, soon agreed.

The Truncated Revolution: the CIA and U.S. Intervention

After World War II, the Cold War mentality reigned in Washington, DC, and the U.S. government viewed the events in Guatemala within the context of what Western officials saw as the Communist threat of expansion. Conflict emerged between the Guatemalan government and Washington as U.S. policymakers regarded these actions as "Communist." The weak middle class needed allies in its struggle against the traditional rulers and U.S. interests. The workers, an ally of the government in this struggle, increased their numbers in trade unions and demanded higher wages and other benefits. Pressure from the peasants and workers pressed the Arbenz government to the left, which alienated the government's supporters in sectors of the middle class frightened by the revolution's radicalization.

In the United States, the UFCO had allies in the U.S. State Department as Secretary of State John Foster Dulles had worked with the law offices that had drafted the UFCO's agreements with the Guatemalan government during Ubico's administration. Allen Dulles, John Foster Dulles's brother and the director of the Central Intelligence Agency (CIA), served as president of the UFCO. Other prominent U.S. government insiders, such as United Nations Ambassador Henry Cabot Lodge, owned stock in the UFCO. Also, the UFCO had lobbied Lodge when he was senator of Massachusetts, the home base of the UFCO. As opposition in the United States to Guatemala's actions increased, the stage was set for U.S. intervention in Guatemala. The U.S. government gave the CIA a green light to begin the destabilization of the country—seeking to create a situation that would force Arbenz to resign. Fearing an intervention from neighboring countries, the Arbenz government sought to acquire arms to protect the democratic revolution. When the U.S. prevented arms sales to Guatemala by creating an embargo (a restriction on trade), Arbenz turned to Poland, a Soviet ally, which complied with the request for arms. The U.S. State Department used this action as conclusive proof that Guatemala was in the Communist camp. Colonel Carlos Castillo Armas, a Guatemalan army officer chosen by the CIA and supplied with arms by the United States, used Honduras as a staging area for an invasion. Castillo Armas—with an army of 150 men—invaded Guatemala as planes supplied by the CIA and flown by U.S. pilots bombarded the capital city with propaganda fliers and incendiary bombs. The propaganda efforts were designed to make the invasion appear to have wider support than it did have and

caused the army to abandon the government. The government, refusing to arm the workers, quickly fell as Arbenz fled into exile and Castillo Armas was installed as president with Washington's approval. This event unleashed unprecedented repression and a series of military governments that dominated in Guatemala until 1996.

The many progressive reforms undertaken in the years from 1944 to 1954 were rolled back as the Castillo Armas government, ruling from 1954 until his assassination in 1957, attempted to reestablish the old order. One of the first actions by the government was the return of the UFCO properties that had been expropriated. Repression soon followed as those who had supported the previous government—workers, peasants, politicians, and others—were arrested as "subversives"; some were even executed. Castillo Armas repealed the 1945 constitution, centralized political power in his and the military's hands, refused the right to vote to more than two-thirds of the population and overturned the 1947 Labor Code and other legislation beneficial to workers, peasants, and Indians. After Castillo Armas's assassination, another military officer, General Miguel Ydígoras Fuentes, governed the country with the same ruthlessness from 1958 to 1963.

Military Governments and Civil War (1960–96)

In 1959 the Cuban Revolution gave hope to many in Latin America and contributed to the rise of guerrilla movements in the region. The Guatemalan Left had come to the realization that there could not be a political solution to the crisis in the country since it had been excluded from the political process by the military government. In 1960 a group of reformist army officers attempted a coup against Ydígoras that failed; many of the rebels were captured or killed in the fighting. Those officers who escaped organized the first of several guerrilla groups that operated in the country for the next thirty-six years, the Revolutionary Armed Forces (*Fuerzas Armadas Revolucionarias* or FAR) and the 13th of November Revolutionary Movement (*Movimiento Revolucionario de 13 de Noviembre* or MR-13). The groups attempted to follow the path of the Cuban Revolution by adopting a guerrilla war strategy. The United States, fearing a repeat of Cuba, supported the subsequent Guatemalan military governments by increasing U.S. military aid, which widened the conflict.

The continued repression of the populace by successive military governments contributed to the growing polarization of Guatemalan society be-

VILLAGERS WATCH FORENSIC ANTHROPOLOGIST
FRANCISCO DE LEON EXHUME SKELETAL REMAINS AS
PART OF AN ANALYSIS OF A MASSACRE PERPETRATED
BY REBEL FORCES IN THE 36-YEAR GUATEMALAN
CIVIL WAR. *(AP/Wide World Photos. Reproduced by
permission.)*

killing of a group based on ethnicity—because of actions such as the 1968 Zacapa campaign where an estimated ten thousand civilians were massacred in order to defeat the FAR. The repression from this period proved effective as the armed guerrilla movement was almost wiped out because it lost its rural base. From 1966 to 1970 a brief civilian interim, with the military still in effective control, reigned until Colonel Carlos Manuel Arana Osorio, known as "the Butcher of Zacapa," became president from 1970 to 1974.

In the 1970s, as the military ruled openly again, the guerrilla movement regrouped and new organizations emerged: the Guerrilla Army of the Poor (*Ejército Guerillero de los Pobres* or EGP) and the Organization of People in Arms (*Organización Revolucionaria del Pueblo en Armas* or ORPA). During the 1970s the United States continued to provide economic and military aid to successive military governments. The massacre of Mayan Indian villagers continued in the countryside. Amidst this terror, the Guatemalan economy grew under military supervision as it launched developmental programs that provided the military independent financial resources. Arana appointed General Eugenio Kjell Laugerud García as his successor, and he ruled from 1974 to 1978. Some of the repression lessened during this administration, but subsequently increased as the guerrilla movement gained in strength in the late 1970s. Heightened military repression and genocide against Mayan Indian villages characterized the administrations of General Fernando Romeo Lucas García (1978–82), General Efraín Ríos Montt (1982–83) and General Óscar Humberto Mejía Victores (1983–86).

The Lucas government dealt brutally with all whom dared oppose its rule. Death squad activities increased against union leaders, university professors, students, and others considered a threat to the government. Many of these individuals were either assassinated or "disappeared" (a term used throughout Central and South America for people who were taken by the military or paramilitary and never seen again). The FAR, which had staged a comeback since the repression of the late 1960s, and ORPA enjoyed considerable popular support in the countryside among the peasants and Indians. In response, the military stepped up its counterinsurgency activities in the countryside. The Peasant Unity Committee (*Comité de Unidad Campesina* or CUC) organized in the countryside. To protest the forced abduction of Indian boys and men into the army and the genocide occurring in the country, thirty CUC members and university students

tween an extreme left faction and right faction with no political center. This polarization contributed to the rise of right-wing death squads, such as the White Hand (*Mano Blanca*) that operated in the country, especially in the urban areas, against both reformists and leftists. In the countryside, the counter-insurgency campaign was especially brutal as the army, aided by police forces and irregular paramilitary groups (groups not officially affiliated with the military), waged a war against the indigenous population. This war has been called genocidal—representing the planned and systematic

peacefully occupied the Spanish embassy in Guatemala City on January 31, 1980. The army and the police massacred all of the occupants except for the Spanish ambassador and a CUC survivor, a Mayan Indian. Thirty-seven people died in the attack, including three Spanish nationals. As the ambassador left the country, the lone survivor was dragged from his hospital bed by the secret police, tortured, and his body dumped on the university campus.

The 1980s economic crisis exacerbated the political crisis in Guatemala as the military rulers' handling of the economy came under increasing attacks by the business community. A military coup by young officers brought Ríos Montt to power with the promise that he would pave the way for democracy and a return to civilian rule. Repression by death squads in the city lessened under Ríos Montt, a fundamentalist Protestant, but it increased sharply in the countryside as entire Indian communities were relocated or destroyed through extreme violence as part of the military's counterinsurgency strategy. These actions forced the Indian villagers off their land and many were forced into exile in Mexico and the United States as refugees. The director Gregory Nava captured this period in his feature film *El Norte* (1983), which presented the plight of a brother and sister seeking refuge in the United States as a result of a military massacre of their village. Increasingly isolated from the international community as a result of the extreme brutality of the regime, reformist military officers ousted Ríos Montt, who had failed to keep his promises, and replaced him with Mejía Victores. The transition to democracy began under his administration although the political repression and counterinsurgency campaign continued. In 1984 a constituent assembly was elected and the constitution rewritten in order to pave the way for elections. In 1985 national elections were held and the Christian Democrat candidate Vinicio Cerezo Arévalo won the election—the first civilian president elected in genuine elections after thirty years of military rule. Cerezo's administration (1986–91) did not bring an end to the civil war, which continued under the administrations of Jorge Serrano Elías (1991–93) and Ramiro de León Carpio (1993–96).

RECENT HISTORY AND THE FUTURE

The guerrilla forces, united as the Guatemalan National Revolutionary Union (*Unión Revolucionaria Nacional Guatemalteca* or URNG), realized that an armed victory was impossible, so it began to negotiate with the government for a settlement of the civil war. As long as the Cold War and conflicts in Central America continued, however, this negotiated settlement was impossible. The fall of the Soviet Union in 1991 and the end of the Central American conflict by 1992 contributed to talks with the civilian government that led to the signing of peace accords in 1996 under the administration of Álvaro Arzú Irigoyen (1996–2000), bringing an end to Guatemala's thirty-six-year civil war and initiating a new period of respect for human rights. The 1999 report by the Guatemalan Commission for Historical Clarification (CEH) estimated that two hundred thousand people, mostly Indians, were killed or disappeared during the conflict. Government forces were responsible for ninety-three percent of the atrocities while the URNG was blamed for three percent, leaving four percent of the case unresolved. The report laid the blame squarely on the United States for prolonging the war by supporting the Guatemalan military. In March 1999, U.S. president Bill Clinton apologized for United States complicity in these genocidal crimes.

Born in 1959, five years after the CIA coup, Rigoberta Menchú, a Quiché Indian woman, represented the human face of the Mayan Indian population that had been brutally repressed during the civil war. The genocide against the Indians touched her personally as she witnessed the slaughter of family members, including her brother, mother, and her father, Vicente Menchú, who lost his life during the Spanish embassy massacre. Leaving the country in 1980, she worked to expose the crimes of the successive military governments against the Mayan people. Her autobiography, *I, Rigoberta Menchú*, became a popular account of her life and how it intertwined with the brutal dictatorships and repression that her people suffered. Translated into numerous languages, it came under question in 1999 by U.S. anthropologist David Stoll in his book *Rigoberta Menchú and the Story of All Poor Guatemalans*, who questioned specifics contained in her account. Despite this, for her efforts on behalf of social justice and the search for peace in Guatemala, she was awarded the Nobel Peace Prize in 1992.

Influenced by the earlier case against Chile's ex-dictator Augusto Pinochet—when in 1998 a Spanish magistrate decided to put him on trial for murder, torture, and genocide—Menchú also decided to use the Spanish courts since she did not believe she could get justice in Guatemalan courts. Her 1999 lawsuit against eight Guatemalans— three former presidents (Lucas Garcia, Ríos Montt and Mejía Victores), three military officers (General Angel Aníbal Guevara Rodríguez, ex-Minister of Defense; General Benedicto Lucas Garcia, ex-army Chief of Staff; Colonel German Chupina Barahona, ex-chief of the National Police), and two civilians (Donaldo Alvarez Ruiz, governance minister during the Lucas Garcia administration; Pedro Garcia Arredondo, ex-chief of the National Police's 6th Command under Lucas Garcia)—was for alleged crimes of genocide, state terrorism, and torture. In particular, she based her charges on three specific cases: the Spanish embassy massacre, the murder of four Spanish priests—Faustino Villanueva, José María Gran Cirera, Juan Fernandez and Carlos Pérez Alonzo, and the torture and murder of other members of Menchú's family, including her mother. For her efforts she has been branded a traitor and has received death threats.

BIBLIOGRAPHY

Archdiocese of Guatemala. *Guatemala, Never Again!* Maryknoll, N.Y.: Orbis Books, 1999.

Americas Watch Report. *Messengers of Death: Human Rights in Guatemala, November 1988–February 1990.* New York: Human Rights Watch, 1990.

———. *Guatemala: A Nation of Prisoners.* New York: Americas Watch, 1984.

Banana Republic: The United Fruit Company: http://www.mayaparadise.com/ufc1e.htm (21 September 2000).

Black, George. *Garrison Guatemala.* New York: Monthly Review Press, 1984.

Booth, John A. and Thomas W. Walker. *Understanding Central America.* 3d ed. Boulder, Colo.: Westview Press, 1999.

Carmack, Robert S. *Harvest of Violence: The Maya Indians and the Guatemalan Crisis.* Norman, Okla.: University of Oklahoma Press, 1988.

Cullather, Nick. *Secret History: The CIA's Classified Account of its Operations in Guatemala, 1952–1954.* Stanford, Calif.: Stanford University Press, 1999.

Dosal, Paul J. *Doing Business with the Dictators: A Political History of United Fruit in Guatemala, 1899–1944.* Wilmington, Del.: Scholarly Resources Inc., 1993.

Draining the Sea: An Analysis of Terror in Three Rural Communities in Guatemala (1980–1984). http://hrdata.aaas.org/ciidh/dts/toc.html (21 September 2000).

Dunkerley, James. *The Pacification of Central America.* London: Verso, 1994.

The Experience of the Guatemalan United Fruit Company Workers, 1944–1954: Why Did They Fail?. http://www.lanic.utexas.edu/ilas/tpla/9501.html (21 September 2000).

Falla, Ricardo. *Massacres in the Jungle: Ixcán, Guatemala, 1975–1982.* Boulder, Colo.: Westview Press, 1994.

Gleijeses, Piero. *Shattered Hope: The Guatemalan Revolution and the United States, 1944–1954.* Princeton, N.J.: Princeton University Press, 1991.

Grandin, Greg. *The Blood of Guatemala: A History of Race and Nation.* Durham, N.C.: Duke University Press, 2000.

Green, Linda. *Fear as a Way of Life: Mayan Widows in Rural Guatemala.* New York: Columbia University Press, 1999.

Guatemala Memory of Silence: Report of the Commission for Historical Clarification. http://hrdata.aaas.org/ceh/report/english/toc.html (21 September 2000).

Handy, Jim. *Gift of the Devil: A History of Guatemala.* Cambridge, Mass.: South End Press, 1984, 1998.

———. *Revolution in the Countryside: Rural Conflict and Agrarian Reform in Guatemala, 1944–1954.* Chapel Hill, N.C.: University of North Carolina Press, 1994.

Harbury, Jennifer. *Bridge of Courage: Life Stories of the Guatemalan Compañeros and Compañeras.* Monroe, Maine: Common Courage Press, 1995.

———. *Searching for Everardo: A Story of Love, War, and the CIA in Guatemala.* New York: Warner Books, 1997.

Immerman, Richard H. *The CIA in Guatemala: The Foreign Policy of Intervention.* Austin, Tex.: University of Texas Press, 1982.

Jonas, Susanne. *The Battle for Guatemala: Rebels, Death Squads, and U.S. Power.* Boulder, Colo.: Westview Press, 1991.

La Feber, Walter. *Inevitable Revolutions: The United States in Central America.* 2d ed. New York: W.W. Norton & Company, 1993.

Manz, Beatriz. *Refugees of a Hidden War: The Aftermath of Counterinsurgency in Guatemala.* Albany, N.Y. : State University of New York Press, 1988.

McCleary, Rachel M. *Dictating Democracy: Guatemala and the End of Violent Revolution.* Gainesville, Fla.: University Press of Florida, 1999.

McCreery, David. *Rural Guatemala, 1760–1940.* Stanford, Calif.: Stanford University Press, 1994.

Menchú, Rigoberta. *I, Rigoberta Menchú: An Indian Woman in Guatemala.* Trans. by Ann Wright. London: Verso, 1994.

———. *Crossing Borders.* London: Verso, 1998.

Montejo, Victor. *Testimony: Death of a Guatemalan Village.* Trans. by Victor Perera. Willimantic, Conn.: Curbstone Press, 1987.

Perera, Victor. *Unfinished Conquest: The Guatemalan Tragedy.* Berkeley, Calif.: University of California Press, 1993.

Schirmer, Jennifer G. *The Guatemalan Military Project: A Violence Called Democracy.* Philadelphia, Penn.: University of Pennsylvania Press, 1998.

Schlesinger, Stephen and Stephen Kinzer. *Bitter Fruit: The Untold Story of the American Coup in Guatemala.* New York: Anchor Books, 1982.

Sieder, Rachel, ed. *Guatemala after the Peace Accords.* London: Institute of Latin American Studies, 1998.

Smith, Carol A. and Marilyn M. Moors, eds. *Guatemalan Indians and the State, 1540 to 1988.* Austin, Tex.: University of Texas Press, 1990.

Stoll, David. *Rigoberta Menchú and the Story of All Poor Guatemalans.* Boulder, Colo.: Westview Press, 1999.

Yashar, Deborah J. *Demanding Democracy: Reform and Reaction in Costa Rica and Guatemala, 1870s–1950s.* Stanford, Calif.: Stanford University Press, 1997.

Carlos Pérez

THE IRANIAN REVOLUTION: ISLAMIC FUNDAMENTALISM CONFRONTS MODERN SECULARISM

THE CONFLICT

Iran is an Islamic fundamentalist state that has repressed dissent for the last twenty years. There have been recent attempts at secularization—attempts to offer dissenting views and liberalize lifestyles.

Political

- Iranians have supported reform party candidates, and seem to want a country with meaningful political choices and participation, including multiple views and lifestyles.

- Many younger Iranians—who were not born when the Shah ruled Iran—are not as threatened by and hostile toward the West.

- Iran's leader, Ayatollah Khamenei, has warned against reformers and reforms and has threatened to nullify elections if reform candidates win.

Religious

- Some Islamic leaders believe that they must have an Islamic state, where all law is based on the Qor'an (also spelled Koran), in order to be moral and holy.

In 1997 the citizens of Iran elected Hojjatoleslam Mohammed Khatami president of the Islamic Republic of Iran. Despite his long association with the Ayatollah Ruhollah Khomeini and his support of the Islamic Revolution of 1979, most Westerners heralded his election as a move away from the strict Islamic regime of Khomeini and past presidents. This remarkable reception was due in large part to Khatami's own political journey, which moved him from Khomeini's camp toward a broader perception of Iran's role in world affairs.

Khatami is the son of a respected *ayatollah* (Islamic religious leader) and a graduate of the Qom Seminary, where he studied *ijtihad*, or the practice of religious leadership. Khatami worked closely with the Ayatollah Khomeini during the 1970s and was elected to the Iranian Parliament for the first time in 1980. It was during the Iran-Iraq War that Khatami began to change his political perspectives. Today, Khatami's government has made overtures to the United States and has engaged in modernization efforts many thought impossible only five years ago.

Khatami's election to the presidency in 1997 introduced a shift in power in the Islamic nation. Political observers considered Khatami's election to be a turning point and, indeed, the parliamentary elections held in February 2000 indicate a substantial change may have occurred in Iranian politics. The Islamic Iran Participation Front (IIPF), a reform party supporting increased secularization (secularization is a movement away from religious considerations) and increased contact with the West, won a majority of the Majlis (the Iranian parliament). This marked the first time since the Revolution of 1979 that the conservative Islamic Republic Party was not in control of the government.

CHRONOLOGY

1921 Reza Shah overthrows Qajar Dynasty, beginning the era of the Shahs.

1941 Reza Shah abdicates in favor of son, Mohammed Reza Shah.

1944 Muhammed Mossadeq enters Parliament.

1951 Iran begins nationalization of Anglo-Iranian Oil.

1953 Muhammed Shah is forced out of Iran.

1954 CIA stages a coup d'état to topple Mossedeq regime and restore the Shah.

1963 Ayatollah Khomeini is arrested in Iran.

1964 Khomeini is exiled from Iran.

1978 Khomeini organizes a revolution from France.

1979 Muhammed Shah comes to the United States for surgery. Ayatollah Khomeini returns to Iran. The Iranian Revolution begins. Iranian students capture the U.S. embassy in Tehran, taking fifty-three hostages.

1980 War with Iraq begins.

1981 U.S. hostages are released after 444 days in captivity.

1988 Iran-Iraq war is concluded.

1989 Ayatollah Khomeini dies. Position of leadership is taken by Ayatollah Ali Khamenei.

1997 Muhammed Khatami is elected president of Iran.

2000 Reformist parties capture Parliament.

The election was an astounding victory for reform party members. Not only did reform party candidates win twenty-nine of thirty seats in the capital city of Tehran, but ballot counts in mid-March indicate that various reform factions now control more than half of the 290 seats in the Majlis, giving President Khatami a powerful ally in his efforts to reform Iran. Reform party candidates currently control at least 165 seats, with fifty-two of those belonging to the Islamic Iran Participation Front. The IIPF's president is Mohammad-Reza Khatami, the brother of President Mohammed Khatami. The IIPF is one of several reform parties now active in Iran.

Having reform parties in control of the Majlis does not guarantee that Iran will moderate its strong anti-American, anti-Western rhetoric or policies, however. In accordance with the Iranian Constitution, Article 107, the Iranian government is composed not only of elected officials but also of a "Leader of the Islamic Revolution," a cleric appointed by the Assembly of Experts. This leader has broad powers to modify or overrule acts of the Majlis or the president. The current leader is Ayatollah Ali Hoseini-Khamenei (1939–), former president of Iran and a close follower of the Ayatollah Khomeini. He and his Guardian Council (a religious body overseeing Iranian government and politics) remain conservative and opposed to mod-

eration. Moreover, even though the Islamic Iran Participation Front is a "reform" party, it does not support the separation of church and state as does exist in the United States and some other democracies. The members of IIPF are still Muslim in political outlook.

Immediately after the election, Ayatollah Khamenei lashed out against reformists, warning Iranians that the reform party was no more than a tool to implement American-style political reforms and to end Islamic rule in Iran. Khamenei and the Guardians Council have threatened to nullify many reform candidates' victories. On May 8, 2000, the Guardians Council charged the Interior Ministry (a reform agency under the control of President Khamati) with vote fraud. Before this action the Guardian Council had overturned twelve reformist victories outside Tehran, giving two of those seats to unyielding candidates.

Khamenei's threat to annul election results has created a political crisis in Iran. The Islamic Students Association announced on May 13, 2000, that if the Guardian Council were to annul the reform victories in Tehran they would stage nationwide protests. The Islamic Students Association is a student movement supporting reform and claims to have more than ten thousand members. This would be the first time a large association like this actively opposed the hard-line regime in Iran.

MOHAMMAD REZA SHAH PAHLAVI

1919–1980 Mohammad Reza Pahlavi (the word *Shah* means King), the eldest son of Reza Shah Pahlavi, was born October 26, 1919, in Tehran, Iran. Mohammad Reza was educated in Switzerland, and returned home in 1935 to attend the Iranian military academy. After his father was exiled during the Anglo-Soviet occupation of Iran during World War II, Mohammad Reza became Shah on September 16, 1941.

By ignoring the parliament, the Shah exercised autocratic rule. Many considered the Shah a pawn of Western interests. The religious clergy denounced his social reforms, including promoting women's literacy, as anti-Muslim. In 1949 he escaped an assassination attempt. In 1953 he was briefly exiled after an uprising led by Prime Minister Mohammad Mossadeq.

The Shah was returned to the throne after a coup d'état facilitated by the U.S. Central Intelligence Agency deposed Mossadeq. As discontent grew in Iran in the 1970s, the Shah used his secret police, SAVAK, to silence opposition and murder dissidents. Amid civil unrest, the Shah fled the country January 16, 1979.

When Iranian students stormed the U.S. embassy in Tehran in October 1979, they demanded the Shah be returned to Iran to stand trial in return for the American hostages. The Shah refused to return; he died in Cairo, Egypt, on July 27, 1980.

What has brought about such a change in Iranian politics? Only ten years ago such support for reform would be impossible to imagine. Before 1997, for example, sources on Iranian politics failed to mention Khatami or the IIRP. Why has Iranian politics shifted so dramatically in what appears to be such a short time? The answer lies in the many changes Iran has undergone in the last half-century. Not only has Iranian politics changed, those who make such policies have changed as well. Many of those voting in the 2000 election are younger voters who did not live under the regime of the Shah of Iran. These are students who engage in dialogue with the West regularly through Internet communications, through study abroad, and through tourism. Today's youth of Iran are not the youth who waged the revolution in 1979.

HISTORICAL BACKGROUND

Geography and People

Iran is a relatively large Middle Eastern/South Asian nation bordering Iraq to the west, Afghanistan, Pakistan and Turkmenistan to the east, the Caspian Sea to the north, and the Persian Gulf to the south. The strategically important Gulf of Oman and Straits of Hormuz, through which millions of barrels of oil flow every day, are located just south of the Iranian city of Bandar 'Abbās. Iran is 1.65 million square kilometers (approximately 636,000 square miles) in size, making it slightly larger than Alaska or slightly smaller than Mexico. As of 1999, Iran has a population of more than sixty-five million people, making it about as populated as the Philippines. Roughly thirty percent of Iran's land is cultivated for crops or pastures. Most Iranians work as either agricultural (thirty-three percent) or industrial (twenty-one percent) sector workers. Unemployment is about thirty percent of the workforce, due to the long war with Iraq and due to international sanctions.

The people of Iran represent several distinct ethnic groups. Persians are the largest group, representing about fifty-one percent of all citizens. Azerbaijanis account for an additional one-quarter of the population, and the remainder are from such diverse ethnic groups as the Kurds, Arabs, Lur, Turkmen, and Balochi. The people of Iran speak several unique languages as well. Persian and Persian dialects are spoken by fifty-eight percent of Iranians, twenty-five percent speak Turkic and Turkic dialects, and the remainder speak Kurdish, Luri, Balochi, Turkish, and other languages.

The vast majority of Iranians are Muslim. Islam has two major branches of faith, the Shiite (often spelled Shi'a) and the Sunni. Eighty-nine percent of Iranians are Shiite Muslim and, as such, the Shiite control Iran. The Shiite believe that leadership in the Islamic community follows a dynastic succession (rulers from the same line of descent) from Imam Ali (a cousin of the prophet Mohammed) and his children. About ten percent of Iranians follow the Sunni faith. Sunni Muslims are "orthodox" Muslims. They are more willing than Shiite Muslims to interact with the West and are more likely to interpret the Qor'an (or Koran) broadly. Zoroastrians, Jews, Christians, and Baha'i represent about five percent of Iranians.

History

The modern history of Iran may be broken into four events: World War II occupation, the 1953 coup restoring the monarchy, the Revolution of

MAP OF IRAN. (© *Maryland Cartographics. Reprinted with permission.*)

1979, and the Iran-Iraq War and aftermath. Iran's role in World War II and the aftermath is a common story of a nation caught in a cold war between superpowers: the Axis (Germany, Italy, and Japan) and the Allies (the United States, Britain, France, and the Soviet Union). Iran engaged in constant efforts to avoid capture by either group and its strenuous efforts to pursue its own foreign policy make it a unique Middle Eastern nation.

World War II

Iran's importance to Allied plans in World War II is rooted in the fact that in 1941 the Allies were losing the war against Germany. The Allies needed oil and access to Africa, and Iran made an ideal base of operations for the African theatre. Unfortunately, the Shah (monarch) of Iran, Reza Khan, later known as Reza Shah and who reigned from 1926 to 1941, was sympathetic to the German cause. The Allies feared that Germany would ex-

pand its control over the Middle East and its vital oil supplies. Britain, Turkey, and the Soviet Union overthrew Reza Shah's regime in 1941 and jointly administered Iran until the end of the war. Reza Shah was deposed in favor of his son Mohammed Reza Shah Pahlavi in 1941 (who reigned from 1941 to 1979 and died July 27, 1980). (Throughout this essay, Reza Shah refers to the father; the Shah to the son.) From 1941 to 1951, the new Shah often faced strong opposition from the Majlis, which was led by Dr. Muhammed Mossadeq (sometimes spelled Mossadegh).

Mossadeq (1882–1967) was the prime minister of the Iranian government and a powerful opponent of Reza Shah. Mossadeq wanted to nationalize the Iranian oil industry and to remain neutral in the power struggles between the Soviet Union and the West. He successfully fostered a sense of Iranian nationalism until his efforts in 1951 to take control of the Anglo-Iranian Oil

AYATOLLAH RUHOLLAH KHOMEINI

1900–1989 Ayatollah Khomeini (sometimes called The Ayatollah) was born May 17, 1900, in Khomeyn, Iran. Born Ruhollah Musawi, he was the son and grandson of *mullahs* (Shiite clerics). After his father was murdered by the local landlord, Khomeini was raised by various family members, and attended Islamic schools.

As he became known as a scholar of Islamic law, Musawi took the surname Khomeyn (his hometown). In the 1950s, he was declared an *Ayatollah* ("chosen by God"), and by 1961 had become one of the most powerful religious leaders in Iran. After protesting the Shah's secularization policies as anti-Islamic, Khomeini was arrested, and then exiled from Iran.

Khomeini's call for a "pure" Islamic republic gained support within Iran as discontent with the Shah grew. After the Shah fled Iran in 1979, the Ayatollah returned to Tehran, the capital of Iran. Later that year, Khomeini was declared political and religious leader for life of the newly created Islamic republic. Under Khomeini's rule, Islamic law was reinstated, women were required to be veiled in public, and opposition was suppressed. The Ayatollah also denounced the United States, the USSR (Soviet Union), and non-Muslim influences. His death in 1989 caused millions to mourn in the streets of Iran.

Although the Shah was successful in creating a modern industrial state in Iran, he did it at tremendous social costs. Many Iranians opposed his secular views about government and called for the restoration of an Islamic government. Others called on the Shah to reform his policies and to rein in the power of his secret police forces. Overall, the Shah's vision of creating a global Iranian power failed due to poor administration and implementation of his modernization policies, poor management of the economy (inflation was very high during the 1960s and 1970s), increasingly strict control of political life, and his challenges to the ruling *ayatollahs* and other religious leaders in Iran. By ruling in such an authoritarian manner, the Shah managed to alienate almost every important sector of Iranian society except those in his family and court who benefited most from Westernization. By 1960 Iran's religious leadership, joined by many student revolutionaries, began a series of engagements that would result in the Islamic Revolution of 1979.

The Revolution of 1979

Despite the diverse factions who opposed the Shah, as late as 1978 there was no one spokesperson around whom these various factions could rally. Many *ayatollahs* had spoken against the Shah's regime, but it was not until 1978 that the Ayatollah Khomeini (often called The Ayatollah) rose to the leadership of the anti-Shah factions. In part, the Ayatollah's role in the revolution was a result of poor judgment on the part of the Shah and his followers.

The Ayatollah Ruhollah Mousavi Khomeini (1900–89) opposed the Shah's rule for many years. Khomeini was a respected elder clergy within Islam, but he was also a powerful populist speaker. His opposition to the Shah was primarily religious, but his attacks against the Shah's regime were based on religion, economics, and on gaining rights for the poor of Iran. His attacks against the government had led to many arrests and, in 1978, he was exiled to France. It was during this exile that Khomeini's power grew significantly.

The Shah wanted to undercut Khomeini's power. In the summer of 1978, the government printed a pamphlet attacking Khomeini and accusing him of certain religious indiscretions. Unfortunately for the Shah, the propaganda attack backfired and people rallied to Khomeini's defense. As a result of the attack, Khomeini became a central figure in the revolution and he began planning for a return to Iran.

Company (A-I). Iran had become a central supplier of crude oil for the West. The Anglo-Iranian Oil Company was an important producer of that oil, but most of the profits from A-I went to its British owners. Mossadeq's efforts to create an independent Iran, coupled with his pursuit of neutrality between the Soviet Union and the West led the U.S. Central Intelligence Agency (CIA) to sponsor a coup d'état (violent overthrow) that drove him from power.

The 1953 Coup

In order to prevent Soviet expansion into Iran and to secure continued access to Iranian oil, the CIA staged a coup in 1953 that toppled the Mossadeq government and restored the Reza Shah to power. The Shah then engaged in a series of reforms in Iran that modernized the nation, adopted many Western customs and practices, and promoted economic and commercial development.

The opportunity for his return came early in 1979, when the Shah came to the United States for treatment of cancer. While he was out of the country, the Ayatollah returned to Iran and quickly set about organizing an unusual cohort of religious leaders and young college students who then staged a series of revolutionary acts. By the middle of 1979 it was clear the Shah would not be able to return to Iran and that a revolution was under way. Charging that the Shah had been a tool of the "Great Satan"—the United States—Islamic forces stormed the U.S. embassy in Tehran and on November 4, 1979, took fifty-three American embassy workers hostage. U.S. president Jimmy Carter and his administration seemed at a loss to resolve this impasse.

Carter attempted to force the students to free the hostages by freezing Iranian assets, imposing economic and military sanctions on Iran, and finally by attempting a military rescue in April 1980. That rescue attempt failed and cost the lives of the rescue team. Three helicopters crashed miles outside of Tehran before the rescue attempt had begun and the rescue was aborted. It was not until January 20, 1981—the day President Carter left office—that the hostages were freed after being in captivity for 444 days. Carter's response to this crisis may have been one of the factors that cost him reelection in 1980.

The Shah left office in 1979, leaving Iran under the control of the Ayatollah Khomeini and his Islamic Revolution Party. By November 1980, the new regime found itself involved in a ten-year war against neighboring Iraq. This war led (on both sides) to some one million dead, two million wounded, and 157 Iranian villages of populations greater than five thousand destroyed. In the end, the war cost both countries close to $1 trillion. As with so many such conflicts, this terrible war could have been avoided.

The Iran-Iraq War

The conflict between Iran and Iraq seems to have been based on three Iraqi goals: the overthrow of the Ayatollah's regime, Iraqi desire to expand their territory and control in the Middle East, and the creation of greater oil reserves for Iraq by moving the borders between the two nations. Iraq's attacks against Iran created a serious political dilemma for the United States and for many Arab nations. The Iranian government hated the United States. Iraq's leader, Saddam Hussein, also opposed American involvement in the Middle East. No matter who won this war, American interests in the region were in jeopardy. Moreover, the gov-

THE THREE MOST PROMINENT ISLAMIC LEADERS IN IRAN, AYATOLLAH KHOMEINI, AYATOLLAH ALI KHAMENEI, AND PRESIDENT HASEMI RAFSANJANI, APPEAR ON A POSTER IN TEHRAN DURING A RENEWED CRACKDOWN TOWARD A MORE SECULAR, LIBERAL SOCIETY. *(AP/Wide World Photos. Reproduced by permission.)*

ernment in Iraq seemed to have close ties with the Soviet Union. An Iraqi victory could enhance the presence of the Soviet Union in this crucial oil-producing area.

At the outset of war, the two sides were relatively evenly matched. Iraq had a more technologically sophisticated army, but it was only about half the size of Iran's forces. Iran's military was also well-trained, due in large part to efforts by the Shah. Iran's population was roughly three times that of

MOHAMMAD KHATAMI

1943– Mohammad Khatami was born in 1943 in Ardakan, central Iran, the son of a well-known cleric. While obtaining university degrees in philosophy, theology, and education, he became politically active, writing pamphlets and organizing against the Shah. In 1978, Khatami taught briefly in Germany, but returned home after the revolution in 1979 to serve in Iran's national assembly, and as head of a government news group.

As minister of culture from 1982 until his dismissal in 1992, he was considered too liberal by the ultra-conservative *mullahs* (clerics), whom he defied by permitting concerts and female performers and by refusing to censor literature and film that some considered subversive. He served as director of the National Library until the 1997 presidential elections. Endorsed by a broad range of Iranians, Khatami swept the elections, receiving seventy percent of the vote.

Khatami's pledge to free the press and relax enforcement of Islamic law appealed to many Iranians, and especially to young people and women. As a Muslim cleric and direct descendant of the prophet Muhammad, he also appealed to many religious Iranians. President Khatami is married, and has three children. In addition to his native Farsi, he speaks fluent English, German, and Arabic.

Iraq's in 1980 (about thirty-six million to Iraq's almost twelve million). Both sides were equipped with American and Soviet military hardware.

The immediate consequence of the outbreak of war was severe economic disruption. Neither Iran nor Iraq could export oil—their main commodity—as long as the conflict continued. Policymakers in the United States and in the Middle East faced another dilemma. If either nation won the war, that nation would become a major player in Middle Eastern politics. Initially the United States attempted to negotiate a truce between the two belligerents, but as the war dragged on, American policy shifted.

United States president Ronald Reagan came into office strongly opposed to communism anywhere in the world. Articulating what is now called the Reagan Doctrine, the president and his advisors attempted to support internal anti-Communist insurgents (those revolting against the government) wherever they might have been operating. One

such place was in Nicaragua, where the Contra rebels were attempting to overthrow the government. In 1983 Congress passed the Boland Amendment, which prohibited U.S. aid to the Contras. At the same time, Middle Eastern forces in Beirut took seven hostages. The United States had intelligence sources who indicated that Khomeini's forces knew where the hostages were being kept.

Reagan recalled the hostage crisis of the Carter administration. He wanted to avoid a similar situation in his presidency and so he reversed the Carter arms embargo against Iran, hoping the sale of weapons would facilitate the release of the hostages. Moreover, administration officials saw the profits from the arms sales as a way to evade the Boland Amendment's requirements and continue to assist the Contra rebels in Nicaragua. Early in 1986, the U.S. Congress discovered what was going on and the whole program collapsed. Not only was the policy a political embarrassment to the Reagan administration, it was only partially successful in freeing the hostages. The policy also failed to change Iran's sentiments towards the United States.

The war dragged on until 1989, when Iran and Iraq signed a peace agreement. Why this conflict lasted as long as it did, especially since the Iraqi government of Saddam Hussein seemed willing to sign peace accords in early 1986, is a key question. Part of the answer lies in what the Iranian religious leadership gained from the conflict.

Most observers argue that there were three reasons the Iranian religious leadership pursued the war after 1986. First, the war allowed the religious leadership (the *ulama*) to eliminate political opponents in Iran, which permitted the Ayatollah and his followers to consolidate their control over Iran. Second, the *ulama* portrayed the war as a continuation of the struggles of Islam. Saddam Hussein and the Iraqis were Baath (or Ba'ath), a sect of Islam traditionally opposed to the Shiite sect. The Ayatollah Khomeini portrayed the war as a religious battle against the infidels—those who acknowledge no religious belief—of Iraq. Finally, the war effort allowed the Ayatollah's followers to promote Shiite followers to key command positions, thus gaining greater control of the military. In other words, the primary objective for the Ayatollah and his followers was to increase their control over Iran rather than to defeat Iraq.

Because Iran's population was so much larger than Iraq's, the leadership simply fought a war of attrition—everyone lost people, but Iraq had less people to lose. Iran agreed to peace terms in 1988, one year before the death of Ayatollah Khomeini. Khomeini was succeeded by the Ayatollah Khamenei, who is now the leader of the Islamic Revolution. Khamenei has served as president of the Islamic Republic of Iran and was a close ally of the Ayatollah Khomeini during the revolution. The end of the war opened a new era in Iranian politics, one the hard-line Islamic leadership could never have foreseen.

RECENT HISTORY AND THE FUTURE

The Iran-Iraq War involved almost forty percent of the adult male population of Iran. Many of those drafted into service were either wounded or killed. However, since 1989, a new cohort of Iranians has arisen. Like the cohort of 1979, these college students and activists desire more freedom, more opportunities, and more of the goods and services western nations have. They are connected to the outside world through study-abroad programs and the Internet. Many of those in the voting population (Iran has a universal right to vote for all citizens age fifteen or older) never lived under the Shah, and as much as one-third of those voting today never served in the Iran-Iraq War. Many of those who did serve in the war believe it should have ended before it did. One consequence of the war, then, has been an erosion of support for the Guardian Council and the Supreme Leader of Iran.

The young people of Iran have forged a successful alliance among themselves, the poor, and women's groups in order to bring about the moderate revolution making headlines in Iran. The ruling religious leaders promised these groups that the revolution and war would improve their lives. It did not. Most of these groups found themselves in worse situations politically and economically and many leaders of these groups became enemies of the state for calling for change.

The first real test of the reformers' power was the presidential election of 1997. The election of Mohammed Khamati signaled a change in popular sentiment in Iran, but the ruling religious leaders have so far refused to accept these changes. Parliamentary elections in February 2000 have intensified the division between older Iranians and the rising younger cohort. The Guardian Council has substantially weakened its position by threatening to nullify the February election. If the Guardian Council does overturn as many as twelve of the twenty-nine seats reformers won in Tehran, there is a very real chance of protests and demonstrations against the ruling Muslim leadership.

IN TEHRAN, IRAN, WOMEN IN WESTERN-STYLE CLOTHES AND THOSE IN THE TRADITIONAL MUSLIM "CHADORS" VOTE TO ELECT EITHER REFORMERS OR CONSERVATIVES TO THE PARLIAMENT. *(AP/Wide World Photos. Reproduced by permission.)*

This is not to say that these moderates desire a fully secular state with American-style separation of church and state. Many student leaders are calling for increased trade and access to the West, but deny that they want constitutional reforms. Nevertheless, the rhetoric of the Guardian Council is reminiscent of the language Ayatollah Khomeini used to attack and undermine the Shah's regime. Guardian Council members have charged reformers with attempting to undermine the Islamic state:

They [reformers] do not mean progress of the Islamic system, they mean removal of Islam and the position of the supreme leader. They promote American reforms. As long as I have responsibility and I'm alive, I will not allow these people to play with the country's interests. As long as the great principle of the position of supreme leader exists, conspiracies may create headaches but will not be able to destabilize this strong base. ("Iran's Khamenei," May 12, 2000)

Khamenei and his followers have attacked Iran's reform press as well. Khamenei accused the press of "portraying a distorted, unrealistic and disappointing image about the present and the future. It is portraying an atmosphere of tension in the society." These are the same kinds of charges Ayatollah Khomeini made against his enemies in 1978, before he began his crackdown against opposition parties and newspapers.

The future for Iran is uncertain. The Guardian Council's decision regarding the February 2000 elections will set the tone for the immediate future. However, the sweeping nature of the elections and the size of reformist control in the Majlis indicates that many Iranians support a secular reformist agenda. This is especially true since elections in Iran are non-partisan, meaning candidates do not run on a specific party label.

Whether the Guardian Council permits the results to stand or not, Iran's political culture is being changed by the same kinds of forces that created the 1979 Islamic Revolution: college students, poor urban workers, and farmers. They are changing Iranian politics for the same reasons as their fathers and grandfathers. The promises of the revolution have not been borne out by the government and these groups are trying to create the changes they believe will bring about those promises. For the short term, Iran's politics appear to be unstable and contentious, but the broad support for reform indicates that Iran is moving towards secularist reforms that will alter the structure of power in the Middle East.

BIBLIOGRAPHY

Amuzegar, Jahangir. *The Dynamics of the Iranian Revolution: The Pahvalis' Triumph and Tragedy.* New York: SUNY Press, 1991.

Baker, James A., III. *The Politics of Diplomacy: Revolution, War and Peace, 1989–1992.* New York: Putnam, 1995.

"Constitution of the Islamic Republic of Iran." http://www.uni-wuerzburg.de/law/home.html (1 May 2000).

Crabb, Cecil. *American Foreign Policy in a Nuclear Age.* New York: Harper and Row, 1983.

Dareini, Ali Akbar. "Reformers Sweep Iranian Elections," *Anderson Independent Mail,* 7 May 2000, 10A.

———. "Iran Students Warn of Vote Protest." 13 May 2000. http://wire.ap.org/APnews/center_story.html (13 May 2000).

"Iran." *CIA Factbook.* http://www.odci.gov/cia/publications/factbook/ir.html (8 May 2000).

"Iran's Khamenei Blasts Reformists." 12 May 2000. http://wire.ap.org/APnews (12 May 2000).

Keddie, Nikki, and Mark Gasiorowski, eds. *Neither East Nor West: Iran, the Soviet Union and the United States.* New Haven, Conn.: Yale University Press, 1990.

Kissinger, Henry. *Diplomacy.* New York: Simon and Schuster, 1994.

Lorentz, John H. *The Historical Dictionary of Iran.* London: Scarecrow Press, 1995.

McCormick, James M. *American Foreign Policy and Process.* Itasca, Ill.: Peacock Press, 1998.

Murphy, Richard W. "A Thaw in Iran," *Foreign Policy,* Winter 97–98.

Robertson, Charles L. *International Politics Since World War II: A Short History.* London: M.E. Sharpe, 1997.

Russett, Bruce, and Harvey Starr. *World Politics: A Menu for Choice.* San Francisco, Calif.: W.H. Freeman Company, 1981.

Sarbakhshian, Hassan. "Iran Ministry Denies Vote Fraud." 8 May 2000. http://wire.ap.org/APnews (12 May 2000).

Sharif, Taha. "The Price to Pay," *Iran Daily,* 16 May 2000, 1.

Weiner, Myron and Samuel P. Huntington, eds. *Understanding Political Development.* Boston, Mass.: Little, Brown and Co, 1987.

Workman, W. Thom. *The Social Origins of the Iran-Iraq War.* London: Lynne Rienner Publishers, 1994.

Michael P. Bobic

JERUSALEM: DIVIDED CITY

In June 1999 former mayor Teddy Kollek opened the Museum of the Seam in Jerusalem. The museum is unusual because it is situated on the west side of Route 1, the road that was built over the no-man's land that politically divided Jewish West Jerusalem from Arab East Jerusalem before the Six-Day War in 1967. It remains a symbolic division, since few Jews ever go east of Route 1 and few Palestinians go west, other than to work.

The museum itself is symbolically important, too. It is located in what had been the home of a member of the Palestinian elite before the formation of the State of Israel in 1948. From 1948 until the 1967 war it was a guard post for the Israeli Defense Force. For most of the period between 1967 and 1999 it had been a museum honoring the Israeli victory that unified the city of Jerusalem and brought Israel the West Bank and Gaza Strip.

In the mid-1990s, the German foundation that had largely funded the museum told its administrators that it was time to change. After a couple years of renovation, it reopened in its new form—to "raise awareness and provoke thought, encouraging dialogue and finding ways of coping with a multi-cultural society." In an hour's guided tour, visitors are shown powerful audio and visual vignettes not just about divided Jerusalem, but Sarajevo, Berlin, and Johannesberg as well. The guide and the exhibits encourage visitors to think about how they view the others, in this case how Jews see Palestinians and Palestinians see Jews. They are urged to reconsider their stereotypes and their hostilities so that the two communities can share this ancient and spectacular city, which visitors see at the end of the tour from the roof of the new museum.

THE CONFLICT

In 1947 the United Nations declared that Palestine, then under British mandate, should be split into separate Jewish and Palestinian states, and that Jerusalem—the holy city coveted by both groups—should be placed under international jurisdiction. In the fighting that following, both immediately and in the years to come, Jerusalem became increasingly divided and its disposition increasingly difficult to resolve. As Israel and the Palestinians move toward a potential settlement in 2000, the issue of Jerusalem remains as difficult as it was in 1947.

Religion
- Judiasm, Christianity, and Islam all regard Jerusalem as a holy place, central to religious expression.

Political
- The division of the city following the war and Israel's declaration of statehood has led to the politicization of all aspects of the city.

- After years of being unwilling to discuss any compromise, Israel, which regards Jerusalem as the capital and the core of Israel, has seemed willing to discuss ways to reach agreement.

- Israel has not agreed to Palestinian control of East Jerusalem, though they have offered the Palestinians some autonomy within Jerusalem.

- The Palestinians want East Jerusalem as the capital of a new Palestinian state. Jerusalem is the capital of Israel.

CHRONOLOGY

1400s B.C. King David and his son Solomon build the first Temple in Jerusalem (according to Judaism).

30–33 A.D. According to Christianity, Jesus Christ is crucified and resurrected.

600s The Muslims build the Al Aqsa mosque with the Dome of the Rock on top of the ruins of two Jewish temples that had been demolished centuries earlier.

1187–1917 Jerusalem is ruled by Muslims, primarily Ottomans (from Turkey), who provide considerable religious freedom for the local Christians and Jews.

1896 Theodore Herzl writes *The Jewish State*. Modern Zionism begins and Jews begin immigrating to Palestine (though in relatively small numbers).

1917 The Balfour Declaration suggests that the U.K. agrees to create an Israeli state in Palestine; at the same time, the British make promises to Arab leaders to establish a Palestinian state.

1917–48 Palestine is ruled by the United Kingdom in a mandate granted by the League of Nations, which later becomes the United Nations.

1947 The British announce that they would end their mandate, and the United Nations votes to divide Palestine into two separate states—Israel and Palestine—with Jerusalem being placed under in-

ternational jurisdiction (Resolution 181). Fighting breaks out.

1949 Israel declares Jerusalem the capital of Israel in violation of international agreements.

1967 Israel occupies all of Jerusalem following the Six-Day War. Israel begins to establish settlements on occupied land.

1987 The *intifada,* an uprising of Palestinian youth, is met with brutal repression by Israeli police.

1993 Talks begin in Norway, leading to a Declaration of Principles to solve the Palestinian/Israeli problem, called the Oslo Accords.

1995 Oslo II establishes agreements regarding more land and activities.

1999 The Wye River memorandum further extends the agreement.

2000 Israel withdraws from Israeli-occupied Lebanon. Discussions at Camp David in Maryland in the United States are unsuccessful, but, for the first time, Jerusalem is on the agenda. The Palestinians set September 13, 2000, as a deadline for declaration of a Palestinian state, regardless of whether agreement has been reached.

Yet despite the museum's attempts to encourage introspection and dialogue, in 2000, the Palestinians set a September 13 deadline: if no final agreement had been reached with Israel on the status of Jerusalem and a number of other issues, the PLO (Palestinian Liberation Organization) threatened to unilaterally declare a Palestinian state with East Jerusalem as its capital. Until May and June 2000, Israel had never been willing to talk about Jerusalem in discussions regarding political settlements. For Israelis, it was forever to be the capital of Israel, solely under their jurisdiction. In 2000, the fact that new Prime Minister Barak was willing to negotiate over Jerusalem was a sign of major progress, but the fact that the Israelis were still unwilling to cede East Jerusalem was and remains a major obstacle to reaching an agreement.

HISTORICAL BACKGROUND

Jerusalem is truly one of the world's most ancient cities. It is also one of the holiest sites in the world's three great monotheistic traditionsCJudaism, Christianity, and Islam.

The first references to what the Jews call *Yerushalayim* and the Arabs *Al-Quds* date from Egyptian tablets from about 1400 B.C. About four hundred years later, King David captured the heavily fortified city, making it the Jewish capital for the first time. Under David and his son Solomon, the Jews expanded their state and built the first temple in Jerusalem. The temple was then destroyed by the Babylonians in 586 B.C. and sent the Jews into exile. A half-century later, the Persians captured Jerusalem and allowed the Jews to return and rebuild the temple. It stood until the Roman emperor Vespasian destroyed it during a Jewish rebellion from 132 to 135 A.D. Jews were again banished from the city. Though it remained important to them theologically, it was not to be a major center of Jewish population for almost 2000 years.

Ancient Jerusalem was, of course, also the site of Jesus's crucifixion and, according the Christian theology, the city from which he was resurrected. Early on, therefore, Jerusalem also became a holy city for Christians with, for instance, the building of the Church of the Holy Sepulchre early in the fourth century.

To Muslims, Jerusalem is also holy because it is from there that the Prophet Muhammed is believed to have ascended to heaven. Once Muslims took control of the city in the seventh century, they began building religious shrines of their own. Most notably, they erected the Al Aqsa mosque (the third holiest site in Islam) with the Dome of the Rock sitting directly on top of the ruins of the two Jewish temples.

Jerusalem was the focal point of the Crusades. It was captured in 1099 during the First Crusade, in which an estimated thirty thousand people died, mostly Jews and Muslims. Saladin (Salah ad-Din) recaptured the city in 1187. In the thirteenth century, the walls were torn down to make it harder for the Crusaders to defend were they to capture it again.

Jerusalem Under the Ottomans

From Saladin's time until 1917, Jerusalem was ruled by Muslims, most notably by the Ottomans (Turks), who captured the city in 1536. They rebuilt and fortified the city walls, as they are today. They also allowed Christians and Jews to live in the city and even excavated much of the Western Wall of the second temple to provide Jews with a place to pray. Under their rule as well, the Via Dolorosa, supposedly the site of Jesus' walk carrying the cross, became a site of Christian devotion.

Under the Ottomans, the political and economic role of Jerusalem receded. It never was a major administrative center under Muslim rule, and by the beginning of the nineteenth century it only had about ten thousand inhabitants (roughly the same number as at the time of the Ottoman conquest). Its population was contained within the walls of what is today called the Old City. The population began to grow in the nineteenth century as a few Jewish pilgrims settled there and began building neighborhoods outside of the walls. Meanwhile, natural population growth led to the expansion of Arab villages in the outskirts of the city as well. By 1922 the population had grown to twenty-two thousand, with a very slight Jewish majority.

The Heart of the Israeli-Palestinian Conflict

Jerusalem became a political hotspot again in the twentieth century. Theodor Herzl and others founded modern Zionism in the late 1800s; soon, Jews began arriving in Palestine in ever-larger numbers, though, at first, relatively few of them settled in Jerusalem. At the same time, the Ottoman Empire had long been weakening, and finally disintegrated during World War I. The United Kingdom then officially took over Palestine as a mandate from the League of Nations (the precursor to today's United Nations). Historians rarely assess the British Mandate kindly. Even before it began, the United Kingdom sent mixed messages. The 1917 Balfour Declaration suggested that the British government was open to the creation of an Israeli state in what was then the Ottoman province of Palestine. At the same time, the British and French made promises for post-war autonomy to Arab leaders to get them to support the Allied war effort.

Post-war British actions frustrated both sides. The British limited Jewish immigration to Palestine, even after Adolf Hitler took power in Germany and began his campaign against the Jews that culminated in what it now known as the Holocaust. The British also did little to defuse tensions between the growing Jewish and Palestinian populations, both of which wanted to control Jerusalem.

During the U.N. mandate years (1917–48), tensions between the Jews and Palestinians (as well as tensions between both of the groups and the British) mounted. There were periodic clashes between Jews and Palestinians throughout the 1920s and 1930s. Thus, a 1929 dispute over access to the Western Wall led to a riot in which almost seventy people were killed. Sporadic rebellions against partition by Palestinians in the late 1930s claimed close to four thousand lives.

The conflict eased during World War II. Most Jews put their desire for statehood on hold and joined in the effort to defeat the Nazis, especially once extent of the Holocaust became clear. As the war ended, however, the demand for a Jewish state grew, and some Zionists engaged in terrorism, including the assassination of the United Nations representative in Jerusalem. The conflict over Israel's statehood was more between the Jews and

THOUSANDS OF MUSLIM WORSHIPPERS PRAY AT JERUSALEM'S TEMPLE MOUNT DURING RAMADAN. *(AP/Wide World Photos. Reproduced by permission.)*

the British than between the Jews and the Palestinians.

Resolution 181

In 1947 the British declared their intention to abandon their mandate over Palestine; the mandate had been transferred to the United Nations following the collapse of the League of Nations. In November 1947, the U.N. Special Committee on Palestine proposed Resolution 181, whereby the country be split into Jewish and Palestinians states with the city of Jerusalem placed under international jurisdiction.

Palestinians, who made up about two thirds of the population and owned most of the land, opposed the provisions of Resolution 181, and widespread fighting soon broke out. The fighters included what was by then a well-armed and trained Jewish army, plus troops from the neighboring Arab states. As would prove to be the case in later wars, the discipline, equipment, and training of the Israelis won out over the numerical advantage held by the Arabs.

Fighting raged through much of Palestine, yet Jerusalem remained the focus. Israel won just about all the land proposed for it in Resolution 181, as well as additional land. The war included ferocious fighting in and around Jerusalem that

left Israel in control of the western part of the city and Jordan in control of the old city, eastern neighborhoods (about eleven percent of the total land), and the West Bank as a whole. On December 13, 1949, Israel declared Jerusalem to be its capital; an action viewed as a violation of international agreements by most international lawyers—and most Palestinians. Subsequently, the United States and many other countries have refused to build embassies in Jerusalem; ironically, if the United States does build an embassy in Jerusalem, it will be located on land in the no-man's area set up at the end of the fighting nearby the Museum of the Seam.

The Catastrophe and Insecurity

Palestinians typically refer to their defeat as *al-nakhba*, the catastrophe. Thousands were killed. Hundreds of thousands fled (Palestinians claim they were forced to flee) their homes, launching a flood of refugees that remained at more than four million in mid-2000. Israelis looked at their new country and realized just how insecure they were: on a clear day, you can look from the campus of Hebrew University on Mount Scopus and see Jordan; at its narrowest point, Israel was only twenty-five kilometers (fourteen miles) wide. Disturbingly, all of Israel's Arab neighbors were pledged to its destruction.

Israel and the Arabs fought another war in 1956, largely over the Suez Canal, but it had little direct effect on Jerusalem. The biggest change and the most serious obstacle to peace today came with the Six-Day War of 1967, in which the Israelis won a decisive victory and occupied all of Jerusalem, the West Bank, and the Gaza Strip. Unlike the West Bank and Gaza, however, Israel formally annexed all of Jerusalem and even extended its traditional borders to include areas it considered strategically important. Despite the Security Council's passage of Resolution 242 and other documents that called on Israel to withdraw from all territory it occupied in 1967, Israel has consistently argued that Jerusalem is different and that the unified city is and will remain the capital of the Jewish state regardless of whatever agreements are reached on the West Bank or Gaza.

The Yom Kippur/October war of 1974 did little to affect the status of Jerusalem. The next major outbreak of tension influencing Jerusalem was the *intifada*, which began in Gaza in December 1987. The *intifada* (literally, a throwing off) was a mostly spontaneous uprising by young Palestinians who were, at most, loosely controlled by the PLO (Palestine Liberation Organization). The protesters often threw stones at Israeli police officers and other symbols of its authority. Hundreds of Palestinians were killed and thousands were arrested in a repressive reaction by Israel that, at least initially, showed shocking brutality.

Since the *intifada* died down, there have been fewer violent protests in Jerusalem and the rest of Palestine/Israel. However, there have been quite a few terrorist actions, though not by the traditional terrorist groups. On the Palestinian side, Hamas has carried out a number of attacks, including some deadly ones in Jerusalem's streets and open-air markets. Israeli extremists have also carried out attacks, including one on the al-Aqsa Mosque and another in which an ultra-orthodox Jewish doctor killed twenty-nine and wounded sixty-seven Palestinians who were praying at the Tomb of the Patriarchs in Hebron, just a few miles from Jerusalem.

Divided Communities

There are now serious divisions within the Jewish and Palestinian communities. Among the Jews, conservative ultra-orthodox and Sephardim (Jews of Middle Eastern origin) are resisting attempts to reach peace with the Palestinians. One ultra-orthodox Jew, Yigal Amir, assassinated the Israeli prime minister and leading peace advocate Yitzhak Rabin in 1995. The Palestinians are di-

vided, too, most notably between moderates in the PLO and militants opposed to reconciliation with Israel, such as Hamas.

In the third of a century since it occupied the entire city, Israel has solidified its political hold on East Jerusalem. Machine-gun-toting soldiers routinely patrol the Old City, including the entrance to the Temple Mount. The city has unified telephone, electrical, sewer, and other infrastructural systems. Israeli authorities try to tell Palestinians the organizations that can and cannot operate legally in the city, actions that most frequently have led it to limit the activities of Orient House, the unofficial office of the PLO in Jerusalem. An elaborate—and to Palestinians oppressive—system of rules, check points, and identity cards controls the number of Palestinians who can legally enter or live in the city. Whenever Israel deems it appropriate, it imposes closures, making it all but impossible for Palestinians who do have legal authorization to live in Jerusalem to work there.

For Palestinians, the most disturbing development since 1967 has been the construction of Israeli settlements on occupied lands. Some 160,000 Jews live in East Jerusalem, the West Bank, and Gaza in settlements built since the Six-Day War. Some of these are small, primitive outposts that will be relatively easy to dismantle. However, in East Jerusalem there are modern suburbs that are built on all the hills surrounding the city. The most recent and controversial is the one being built in 2000 at Har Homa/Jabel Abu Ghneim, about half way between downtown Jerusalem and Bethlehem. The current wave of construction will bring about thirty thousand Jews to Har Homa; eventually, the Israelis plan on a population of sixty thousand.

The difference between living standards in West and East Jerusalem is striking. Israeli authorities have done little to improve the quality of life among Palestinians—though they are better off than many others in non-oil-producing Arab states. For instance, Israeli authorities have built roughly forty thousand public housing units on land taken in 1967 but virtually none in East Jerusalem. Only 1.6 percent of Jewish Jerusalemites live in overcrowded conditions (defined as more than three people per room) but almost a quarter of Palestinians do. Classes in Jewish elementary and secondary schools average about twenty-five students; in Palestinian classrooms the figure is almost thirty. Between 1988 and 1998, over a thousand classrooms were built for Jewish students and less than three hundred for Palestinians.

MAJOR RELIGIOUS SITES OF WORLD RELIGIONS

Baha'i Faith

- Haifa, Israel
- Akka (Acre), Israel

Buddhism

- Lopburi, Nepal
- Bodh Gaya, India
- Sarnath, India

Christianity

- Bethlehem, Israel
- Nazareth, Israel
- Jerusalem, Israel
- Vatican City, Italy (Catholicism)

Hinduism

- River Ganges, India
- Gaya, India
- Varanasi (Beneres), India

Islam

- Mecca, Saudi Arabia
- Medina, Saudi Arabia
- Jerusalem (Al-Quds), Israel

Jainism

- Palitana, Gujerat, India

Judaism

- Jerusalem, Israel

Sikhism

- Amritsar, Punjab, India

The Peace Process

Until late 1992, it was illegal for Israelis to meet with members of the PLO. The United States, as well as Israel, refused to negotiate with the organization, even though it had been recognized by the United Nations as a legitimate voice of the Palestinian people and had largely renounced violence. However, that does not mean that there was no peace-process taking place. Israelis and Palestinians (supposedly non-PLO) had opened negotiations in Madrid, Spain, in 1991. However, these talks accomplished little.

Real progress came in an unexpected way, beginning in Jerusalem. Just inside East Jerusalem is the American Colony hotel. For years its bars, restaurant, lobby, and open-air courtyard have been a place where Palestinians, Jews, and foreigners gather together. As early as the late 1980s, informal groups of liberal-minded Arabs and Jews had been meeting at the American Colony and elsewhere. Organizations like Interns for Peace and Neve Shalom-Wahat al-Salaam (Oasis of Peace) found ways to bring people from the two communities together to begin finding common ground.

In early 1993, a then obscure Norwegian social scientist, Torje Rod Larsen, told people on both sides that his office and his government would be willing to facilitate talks. Thus began a series of secret sessions in and around Oslo, Norway. They began as informal talks between academics who had no official standing, though the leaders of both governments knew that these and other talks were taking place. Once it became clear that the professors were making progress, both the Israeli government and PLO sent top-level negotiators. Until the last moment, next to no one in the world knew the talks were occurring, including the administration of U.S. president Bill Clinton. Thus, virtually everyone was shocked when the Declaration of Principles was announced and formally signed at the White House on September 13, 1993.

The Oslo Accords

The Oslo Accords did not address the question of Jerusalem. In fact, the two sides understood that they could not reach an agreement on it at the time, and it was deferred until the so-called "final status" talks, which were due to be completed by mid-1999 but were still under way as of mid-2000. It did, however, bring formal recognition of Israel by the PLO and vice versa and started a gradual process transferring land and political control in Gaza and West Bank to the Palestinians. Since then, Oslo II (1995) laid out more land and functions to be transferred to the Palestinians. The memorandum also called for the resumption of the final status talks.

The assassination of Israeli Prime Minister Yitzhak Rabin in 1995 slowed the peace process dramatically. Following a few months of political uncertainty, hardliner Binyamin Netanyahu was elected prime minister of Israel. Netanyahu resisted all approaches from the PLO, the United States, and others. Even so, the two sides reached an agreement on the partial withdrawal from Hebron in 1997. Under pressure from the U.S. government in Washington, DC, Israelis (and the Palestinians) signed the Wye River memorandum in October 1998, which produced a further thirteen percent redeployment of Israeli troops, the releases of Palestinian prisoners, and changes to the PLO Charter's rhetoric on Israel.

The momentum regarding a settlement returned when Netanyahu was defeated at the polls in 1999 and replaced by retired General Ehud Barak. Barak was committed not just to peace with the Palestinians but with Syria and Lebanon as well. In June 2000, Israel ended its occupation of southern Lebanon.

Recent History and the Future

In July 2000, President Clinton brought the Israeli and Palestinian leaders together for what turned out to be a three week summit at Camp David, the presidential retreat in Maryland where an earlier agreement between Israel and Egypt had been formed. For the first time, Jerusalem was on the agenda. Ultimately, the talks failed in large part because the two sides could not agree on a compromise on the city's status. The Palestinians insisted that East Jerusalem had to be under their control and become the capital of their state as well. Israel was willing only to give Palestinians administrative control of part of the city and would only allow the capital to be in Abu Dis or one of the other Palestinian villages that have essentially become suburbs of Jerusalem. The two sides also could not agree on the status of what the Israelis see as legitimate suburban communities and the Palestinians see as illegal settlements inside the post-1967 borders of Jerusalem.

JERUSALEM GEARS UP FOR AN EXPECTED FLOOD OF PILGRIMS IN THE MILLENNIAL YEAR, 2000. *(AP/Wide World Photos. Reproduced by permission.)*

The PLO set September 13, 2000, as a deadline for reaching an agreement on final status talks, including not just Jerusalem but water rights, the status of refugees, and more. If an agreement is not reached, Chairman Arafat has threatened to unilaterally declare a Palestinian state. Not surprisingly, many observers have viewed Camp David as a failure. However, most participants see it as a step in the right direction, since Jerusalem and refugees both made it onto the agenda for the first time. There are rumors of new and creative ideas of sharing sovereignty for the city, and the prospects for some sort of settlement on Jerusalem are brighter than ever.

BIBLIOGRAPHY

Abu-Nimer, Mohammad. *Dialogue, Conflict Resolution, and Change: Arab-Jewish Encounters in Israel.* Albany, N.Y.: SUNY Press, 1999.

Gerner, Deborah, *One Land/Two Peoples: The Conflict over Palestine.* Boulder, Colo.: Westview, 1994.

Hiro, Dilip. *Sharing the Promised Land: A Tale of Israelis and Palestinians.* New York: Oliver Branch Press, 1999.

Horovitz, David. *A Little Too Close to God: The Thrills and Panic of a Life in Israel.* New York: Knopf, 2000.

PASSIA (Palestinian Academic Society for the Study of International Relations) *PASSIA Diary.* http://www.passia.org (1 September 2000).

Shlaim, Avi. *The Iron Wall.* New York: W. W. Norton, 2000.

Charles Hauss

THE KOREAN PENINSULA: A FIFTY-YEAR STRUGGLE FOR PEACE AND RECONCILIATION

In 2000, the announcement and subsequent inter-Korean summit between the South Korean president Kim Dae Jung and the North Korean leader Kim Jong Il in the North Korean capital of Pyongyang was historic: This was the first face-to-face meeting between leaders of the North and South, almost fifty years after the onset of the Korean War. The leaders bore the weight of all Koreans yearning for security, national reconciliation, and a peaceful resolution to the Korean War. The Democratic People's Republic of Korea (also known as North Korea) and the Republic of Korea (also known as South Korea) are still technically at war, since representatives of the United States and the Democratic People's Republic of Korea (but not the Republic of Korea) signed the Armistice Agreement that ended the fighting in 1953.

HISTORICAL BACKGROUND

Legacy of the Cold War

The origins of the inter-Korean summit lay in the political endgame of World War II. The division of the Korean Peninsula was an afterthought at the Cairo Conference of 1943. At the conference, China, Great Britain, and the United States agreed that Korea should become free and independent as soon as possible. The issue was further discussed at the Yalta Conference in February 1945 and the following Potsdam Conference and an agreement in principle was reached at the Moscow Conference in December 1945, in which it was tacitly agreed that the Korean Peninsula would be divided along the thirty-eighth parallel and that a four-power trusteeship of Korea would be established for a period of five years. The trusteeship would be followed by the formation of a Soviet-U.S.

THE CONFLICT

The Korean Peninsula has been divided for fifty years by political conflict, with the tensions occasionally resulting in military action. In 2000, North Korea and South Korea met for a legendary summit. The meeting of the leaders was followed by limited and temporary reunification of families separated by fifty years of war and political animosity.

Political

- At the end of World War II, the victorious Allies (the United States, the Soviet Union, France, and England), decided to temporarily divide and occupy Korea, formerly occupied by Japan. The United States occupied the south and the Soviet Union the north. As Cold War animosities between the West and the Soviet Union solidified, both South Korea and North Korea established their own governments, claiming the right to the entire Korean Peninsula.

- Cold War divisions between communist North Korea (supported by the Soviet Union and China) and Western-supported South Korea led to military actions, espionage, and the separation of families.

- North Korea, for several years in the midst of economic collapse and famine, needs to find a way to open itself to international trade and aid.

CHRONOLOGY

August 15, 1945 The Korean Peninsula is divided into communist North Korea and the U.S.-backed South Korea following the end of Japanese colonial rule.

June 25, 1950 Seventy thousand North Korean troops cross the thirty-eighth parallel.

July 27, 1953 The Democratic People's Republic of Korea (North Korea) and the United States sign the Armistice Agreement at Panmunjom. South Korean president Syngman Rhee refuses to sign the Armistice Agreement, threatening the entire accord.

April 26, 1954 The Geneva Conference on the reunification of the Korean Peninsula and other Asian matters opens.

January 21, 1968 A North Korean commando unit manages to infiltrate South Korea in an attempt to kill then-president Park Chun-hee. All but one of the commandos is killed before they can reach the Blue House.

July 4, 1972 North and South Korea issue a joint communiqué agreeing to achieve peaceful reunification of the Korean Peninsula.

September 4, 1980 The prime ministers of North and South Korea hold talks for the first time.

September 18, 1991 North and South Korea are admitted to the United Nations.

June 1994 Former U.S. president Jimmy Carter visits North Korea and proposes a summit with South Korean president Kim Young-sam.

July 8, 1994 North Korean leader Kim Il-Sung dies of a heart attack just before the North-South Korean summit.

April 1996 Washington and Seoul propose four-party inter-Korean Peninsula talks with Pyongyang and Beijing.

February 25, 1998 South Korean President Kim Dae-Jung proposes an inter-Korean summit in his inauguration speech. North Korea does not respond to this offer.

April 18, 1999 In Beijing, a meeting between representatives of the two Koreas collapses as North Korea refuses to discuss the reunion of families separated by the Korean War.

March 10, 2000 Kim Dae-Jung announces in Berlin that South Korea is willing to aid North Korea in rebuilding its moribund economy.

March 17, 2000 North and South Korea enter into secret talks in Beijing on an inter-Korean summit.

April 10, 2000 North and South Korea announce an agreement on a meeting between South Korean president Kim Dae Jung and North Korean leader Kim Jong-Il.

June 13, 2000 Kim Dae Jung arrives in Pyongyang to begin the historic inter-Korean summit.

Joint Commission that would be charged with the establishment of a provisional Korean government.

Following Japan's surrender and subsequent withdrawal from the Korean Peninsula on August 15, 1945, Korea north of the thirty-eighth parallel was occupied by Soviet forces, while south of the thirty-eighth parallel was occupied by U.S. forces. (The parallel indicates latitude and divides the country roughly in half.) The division of Korea emerged and became more pronounced since, immediately following the cessation of fighting, the Soviets and Americans went about establishing governmental and bureaucratic structures in their respective occupation zones. However, first each had to deal with the newly formed Korean People's Republic (KPR); an indigenous Korean movement that replaced the now disposed and disgraced Japanese colonial administration.

The Americans chose Syngman Rhee, a U.S.-educated expatriate, as the leader of South Korea, while the Soviets chose the veteran anti-Japanese guerrilla leader Kim Il Sung. In the North, the colonial bureaucratic and social structures were upset and collaborators were either imprisoned or driven off their land. Land reform was introduced; land was taken from landlords and redistributed to peasants. Key industries were nationalized. In the South, the American occupation forces set up

U.S. MARINES PATROL THE ICY HILLS NEAR NORTH KOREAN'S CHOSEN RESERVOIR DURING THE KOREAN WAR. *(AP/Wide World Photos. Reproduced by permission.)*

the United States Army Military Government in Korea (USAMGK) resurrecting the old Japanese colonial administrative structures, and dismissing the fledgling KPR.

No one had envisioned a divided Korean Peninsula but Soviet and American occupation policies all but ensured the polarization of politics in Korea and the emergence of ideologically opposed regimes. In February 1946, Kim Il Sung formed the Interim People's Council, while in the South, at about the same time, Syngman Rhee founded the Representative Council, the forerunner to the South Korean Interim Legislative Assembly. Ideological conflict between the North and the South continued when the United States submitted the Korea Question to the newly established United Nations in August 1947. As a result, the United Nations Temporary Commission for Korea (UNTCOK) was established. Resentments deepened on each side of the thirty-eighth parallel as preparation for separate elections progressed in each occupation zone. In the South, United Nations-sponsored elections proceeded in May 1948, and on August 15, 1948, Syngman Rhee declared the Republic of Korea (ROK) and claimed to be the sole legitimate government of Korea. The North countered by holding elections of its own and proclaimed the Democratic People's

MAP OF NORTH AND SOUTH KOREA. *(XNR Productions Inc.)*

KIM DAE JUNG

1925– Kim Dae Jung, president of South Korea, was the first opposition leader elected to the office. His "Sunshine Policy," liberalizing relations between North and South Korea, has allowed many Korean families to reunite after separation by years of war, and encouraged South Korean investment in North Korea.

Kim was born December 3, 1925, on a farm in Mokp'o, in what is now South Korea. After graduating from Mokp'o School of Commerce in 1943, he worked for a Japanese-owned company. In 1945 he took over the company, which prospered. Captured by the Communists during the Korean war, he was sentenced to death, but escaped to South Korea.

Kim became a pro-democracy advocate, denouncing the military government of South Korea. In 1961 he was elected to the National Assembly, and became renown as an orator, although many of his speeches were censored. As leader of the Korean Democratic Party, he unsuccessfully ran for president in 1971.

Throughout the next ten years, Kim was repeatedly kidnapped and arrested by the South Korean CIA. He was sentenced to death, although he was exiled to the United States instead. Allowed to return home in 1985, he continued to lead the democracy movement, and after several attempts, was elected president in 1997.

Republic of Korea in the following September. Korea now had two governments, each asserting its right to the whole of the Korean peninsula. Following the elections in the North and South, both the Soviets and Americans withdrew from their occupation zones, setting the stage for the Korean War.

Periodic confrontations ensued, each regime testing the military resolve of the other. Rhee began launching campaigns to suppress dissent within South Korea and increasingly called for the reunification of the Korean Peninsula. Beginning in the summer of 1949, the South launched raids across the border. In the fall of 1949 Northern forces responded with cross-border raids, initiating clashes against Southern troops. Sporadic cross-border attacks remained the norm; so much so that the U.N. secretary-general requested observers be placed along the thirty-eighth parallel to monitor the escalating tension between North and South.

The War Begins

There are conflicting reports as to which side initiated the Korean War, but it is generally acknowledged that the Korean War officially began on the morning of June 25, 1950, when North Korean troops poured over the thirty-eighth parallel. Within three days, Seoul, the South's capital, had fallen and the Rhee government fled in the face of the onslaught. South Korean troops were in full retreat. By the end of August 1950, the North's advance stalled along the so-called "Pusan Perimeter"

as the North's supply lines became susceptible to United States air offensives as well as the gradual build-up of United States/United Nations military personnel. The North's occupation of the South lasted for about two months until the United States and other Western nations; under the aegis of the United Nations mandate; intervened in support of South Korean forces. In September General Douglas MacArthur, commanding a combined U.N.-ROK force, staged a dramatic amphibious assault on the port of Inch'on, successfully landing troops behind the North's lines, cutting North Korean troops in two as well as cutting off supply lines. MacArthur quickly took Seoul from heavily outnumbered Northern defenders. Following the capture of Inch'on and Seoul, on October 7, 1950, MacArthur launched a counter-offensive, pursuing the disorganized North Korean army across the thirty-eighth parallel. Two hundred thousand U.S., ROK and U.N. troops quickly moved across the thirty-eighth parallel and drove toward the Yalu River, the North's border with the People's Republic of China. The war shifted again when, in November 1950, hundreds of thousands of Chinese troops crossed the Yalu River and launched a major offensive, driving U.S.-led forces back to the thirty-eighth parallel. A stalemate ensued, with fighting settling around the thirty-eighth parallel.

Armistice

Three years of fighting brought the sides no closer to resolving the political and military stalemate. Eventually, on July 27, 1953, the Democratic

People's Republic of Korea and the United States signed the Armistice Agreement at Panmunjom. The cost of the Korean War was staggering, the North's economic and transportation infrastructure having been completely destroyed, while in the South much of the industrial capacity was destroyed. Although precise figures are not available, it has been estimated that a combined three million people were either killed or wounded.

In the aftermath of the Korean War, North and South Korea became heavily militarized—with political leadership becoming dependent on the military to ensure regime stability. An additional consequence of the Korean War was the hardening of ideological and political attitudes between the North and South. The artificial and arbitrary division led to the separation of families as well as spurring political, ideological, economic, military, and diplomatic competition between the two Koreas that exists to this day. In the intervening years, antipathy developed between the rival regimes as each searched for advantage and supremacy over the other. Coupled with the antipathy was the fact that North and South Korean regimes were based on diametrically opposed principals and supported by Cold War adversaries.

During the 1950s and 1960s lip service was paid to reunification dialogue as each regime claimed to be the sole legitimate political entity speaking for the whole of the Korean Peninsula. To that end, each regime sought to assert independent political recognition, fiercely attacking the other through diplomatic channels, searching for advantage.

Rapprochement

Rapprochement (establishment of friendly relations) with the South came on August 6, 1971, when Kim Il Sung issued a surprise announcement indicating his willingness to establish contact with officials from South Korea, thereby reversing North Korea's long-standing position as the sole legitimate political entity on the Korean Peninsula. Soon thereafter, the South responded by proposing a meeting in the context of Red Cross emissaries—a proposal the North found acceptable, and on August 21, 1971, eighteen years after the armistice that ended the Korean War, representatives of their respective Red Cross societies met in Panmunjom for exploratory talks. Following months of stalled talks, South Korea proposed secretive and exclusive high-level talks. North Korea accepted the proposal and after months of negotiations, North and South Korea surprised the world by issuing a joint statement on July 4, 1972, providing a three-point de-

SOUTH KOREAN SOLDIERS PATROL DEMILITARIZED ZONE NEAR THE BORDER VILLAGE OF PANMUNJOM, SOUTH KOREA. *(AP/Wide World Photos. Reproduced by permission.)*

claration on the peaceful unification of the Korean Peninsula. Kim Jong Il had hoped to use the North-South dialogue as a means of politically and militarily isolating South Korea from its American and Japanese allies, as well as bringing about the withdrawal of the American troops stationed in Korea. The North Korean rapprochement failed when the North Korean delegation that visited Seoul miscalculated public opinion, offending a majority of the South Korean populace with inflammatory political rhetoric aimed at President Park Chun Hee and his American sponsors.

After this failed diplomatic foray, talks were suspended. Subsequent meetings during the late

KIM JONG IL

1942– Kim Jong Il, the Supreme Leader of North Korea, is the son of the former head of state, Kim Il Sung. Although "Dear Leader," as Kim Jong Il is called in North Korea, was once dismissed as incompetent, the 2000 summit of both Koreas' leaders, which he hosted, considerably changed his image.

Kim Jong Il (also spelled Kim Chong-il) was born in Siberia in the Soviet Union, on February 15, 1942, although his official biography claims he was born in North Korea. As a child, Kim frequently moved, and spent time in China as a Korean War refugee. While attending Kim Il Sung University, where he earned a political science degree in 1964, he began working for the Communist Party.

In 1969 he was named to the Politburo, and shortly thereafter became party secretary of propaganda. In 1974 Kim was officially designated to succeed his father and was groomed for the presidency. In 1980 he was named to the central committee, and in 1991 appointed supreme commander of the North Korean armed forces.

Upon the death of Kim Il Sung in 1994, Kim Jong Il became Supreme Leader; however, four vice-presidents functioned as heads-of-state until he was officially installed as president on September 5, 1998.

1970s and early 1980s yielded few results. Rapprochement with the South continued on a piecemeal basis with the North sending the South flood relief supplies in 1984, the reunion of families separated by the Korean War in 1985, and the establishment of economic ties in 1990.

International Influences

Since the collapse of the Soviet Union and China's embrace of capitalism "with Chinese characteristics," North Korea has lost its two major sponsors. In an attempt to integrate itself with the world system, North Korea and South Korea compromised and on September 18, 1991, both North and South Korea were admitted to the United Nations. North and South resumed negotiations and on a trip to North Korea in June 1994 former U.S. president Jimmy Carter visited North Korea and proposed a summit with South Korean president Kim Young-sam. Before the proposed North-South summit could commence, North Korean leader Kim Il Sung died of a heart attack. All plans

for the summit were postponed when Kim Jong Il declared a three-year period of mourning. North Korea became increasingly diplomatically isolated when, in 1998, it test-fired a missile that flew over the Japanese island of Honshu. Japan suspended foreign aid and halted diplomatic contacts with Pyongyang for two years. The United States followed suit.

During the latter half of the 1990s, North Korea remained both politically and diplomatically isolated, as economic conditions continued to worsen with successive crop failures. The U.N. World Food Program issued an alert on the conditions in North Korea, warning that food stocks were critically low and that the public distribution system was coming under strain. In June 1996 the United Nations launched an international appeal to help relieve the food shortages, and Japan, South Korea, and the United States all contributed. In addition, North Korea also leveraged the food shortage into an agreement with the United States to receive $2 million in return for the remains of 162 U.S. soldiers killed in the Korean War. North Korea continued to launch military incursions into the DMZ (de-militarized zone), and accidentally grounded a North Korean submarine off the coastal city of Kangnung in Kangwon Province. Since 1998 North Korea has continued to suffer widespread famine after five years of failed crops, as well as diplomatic isolation as a result of its nascent nuclear program.

Major Figures

The primary figures of the landmark inter-Korean summit are the South Korean president Kim Dae Jung and North Korean leader Kim Jong Il. Kim Dae Jung can be considered the architect of the inter-Korean summit. Long an outspoken advocate of reunification of the Korean Peninsula, Kim Dae Jung reversed the longstanding policy of nonengagement from previous administrations and consequently will be the first South Korean president to set foot in the North. Kim Dae Jung has called on the United States to lift economic sanctions and has played a major role in convincing former U.S. defense secretary William Perry to recommend that the United States engage North Korea diplomatically. Thus, the summit can be seen as a vindication for Kim Dae Jung and his "Sunshine Policy" with the North.

In the North, Kim Jong Il symbolizes the North Korean state. Since the 1970s, Kim Jong Il increasingly assumed a larger role in North Korean affairs of state. In 1984 his father, Kim Il Sung designated the younger Kim as his successor and was

NORTH KOREAN SOLDIERS WATCH THE SOUTH SIDE AT THE BORDER VILLAGE OF PANMUNJOM, NORTH KOREA. *(AP/Wide World Photos. Reproduced by permission.)*

given the name "Dear Leader." Upon Kim Il Sung's death in 1994 and the following three-year mourning period, Kim Jong Il assumed control of the North Korean state apparatus. Traveling outside of Korea for the first time since his father's death, Kim Jong Il has recently initiated bold diplomatic moves, visiting Beijing, China, to reaffirm the relationship between the two communist countries that fought together against the American and Southern troops in the Korean War. Some critics have argued that the summit is an attempt by Kim Jong Il to end North Korea's diplomatic isolation as well as ease the deteriorating economic conditions.

Although Kim Dae Jung and Kim Jong Il are largely responsible for the landmark summit, their allies—who are eager for peace, but want to see their interests protected—have supported both leaders.

RECENT HISTORY AND THE FUTURE

Buffer States and Borders

Reunification of the Korean Peninsula is of concern to China, Japan, and Russia, as well as the United States. As such, each has a vested interest in the outcome of the inter-Korean summit, stability of the Korean Peninsula, and avoiding problems of reunification. The political, economic, and social dislocation that will accompany reunification

will possibly have destabilizing effects. Although the prospect of a conflict comparable to the Korean War is unlikely, the possibility of regime collapse or political instability in the North is of concern. Political instability would undoubtedly create internal upheaval as well as the potential for mass migration southward, destabilizing the South's social and economic infrastructure. Another concern is that of the North's growing arsenal of weapons of mass destruction. The United States, South Korea and Japan would like to see an end to North Korea's suspected nuclear weapons program, as well as an end to the development of weapons of mass destruction. China is concerned that instability in the North would create the increased need for economic support and an outward migration of refugees from Northern Korean provinces. With the collapse of the Soviet Union, Russia has become marginalized in the intra-Korean affairs, but is still concerned about longer-term regional security and in the context of the unification process. For all powers, the prospect of reunification is filled with latent dangers and risks.

BIBLIOGRAPHY

Acheson, Dean. *The Korean War*. New York: Norton, 1971.

Cumings, Bruce. *The Origins of the Korean War: Liberation and the Emergence of Separate Regimes 1945–47*. Princeton, N.J.: Princeton University Press, 1981.

KOSOVO: ETHNIC TENSIONS AND NATIONALISM

THE CONFLICT

In 1999, NATO and the United Nations occupied Kosovo, a province in the former Yugoslavia, in order to protect the Muslim Albanian population from the Serbian military.

Political

- Serbia regards Kosovo as an integral part of Serbia.

- Albanians in Kosovo are worried they will be oppressed if Kosovo remains with Christian Serbia.

- NATO and the United Nations believe that it would show lack of moral resolve and strength if they did not prevent violence in Europe.

Ethnic and Religious

- Albanians (Muslims) feel that they would be suppressed by Serbians (Christians) and fear ethnic cleansing (the use of terror—including murder and rape—to drive an entire community from an area).

North Atlantic Treaty Organization (NATO) troops and the United Nations (U.N.) peace-keeping mission in Kosovo occupied Kosovo in the summer of 1999 with the intention of stopping interethnic conflict and promoting a peaceful multiethnic society in the province. Hardly a week has gone by since then without newspaper and television coverage of continued hostility between Serbs and Albanians—and of open conflict with peacekeepers by both groups. Clearly, restoring mutual trust after the NATO air war and Belgrade's attempts at ethnic cleansing will not be a short process.

Such a conclusion is reinforced by the fact that, while relations between the Albanian and Serb inhabitants of the region have not always been bitter, the Albanians of Kosovo (or Kosovars) have, throughout this century, disliked the incorporation of the province within modern Serbia and have periodically rebelled against it. But the historic counter-proposal to join Kosovo with Albania presents its own problems—essentially, the inclusion of the province in either state would leave a large, discontented minority.

Kosovo is thus quite typical of many areas of central and eastern Europe where two (or more) national populations are mixed together within borderlands. And just as typically, while there have always been conflicts between the two groups over issues such as resources or land owning, the most recent disputes are the result of the creation of national states (states based on an ethnic or "national" identity) in the region during the nineteenth century. Sadly, in most cases the solution to problems of ethnic intermixture has been ethnic cleansing—an activity not limited to the former Yugoslavia. Ethnic cleansing is the use of violence and terror

CHRONOLOGY

800s–1000s Kosovo is part of the Bulgarian Empire.

1100s–1300s Kosovo is part of the Serbian empire.

1389 Battle of Kosovo Polje (the "Field of the Blackbirds") is a major battle from which Serbs trace the downfall of greater Serbia.

1918–40 Serbs colonize Kosovo in an attempt to pacify the province.

1921–24 Albanians rebel against Royal Yugoslavia in the Kaçak Rebellion.

1944 The modern state of Yugoslavia is established under Josip Tito.

1974 The Yugoslav constitution is rewritten to declare Kosovo an autonomous province.

1980 Josip Tito dies.

1989 Serbian president Slobodan Milosevic strips Kosovo of autonomy. Protests begin.

1990 Troops are sent to Kosovo to impose control. Serbia dissolves Kosovo's government.

1991 Separatists declare Kosovo a republic.

1996–97 The Kosovo Liberation Army (KLA) emerges.

1999 NATO air strikes begin to prevent ethnic bloodshed in Kosovo.

to drive a people from a region. NATO intervention, if unintentionally, has caused hundreds of thousands of Serbs and Montenegrins to flee Kosovo and may have permanently changed the nature of the province.

HISTORICAL BACKGROUND

Conflicting Claims of Nationalism

Although relatively little has been written in English on the subject, the history of Kosovo has been the center of a long and politically charged debate between Serb and Albanian scholars. This is rather typical for regions of mixed population—for example, there is a similar debate regarding the history of Transylvania between Hungarian and Romanian scholars. In most of these debates there is a perceived link between historical presence in a region, and contemporary rights—the nationality that settled the region first, or has most densely or continually occupied it, has the better right to incorporate it in it into their modern national state.

This is not a phenomenon limited to eastern Europe, of course, but the strong linkage common in the region between medieval (and even ancient) history and modern nationality often strikes many—such as Americans or Australians—as somewhat strange. In part, this is probably because being an "American" does not entail a strict "national identity" in terms of ethnicity—any immigrant to the United States becomes an American despite ethnicity, but an immigrant to Serbia, for instance, does not so automatically become a Serb. Perhaps more importantly, the dominant theory of nationalism in the United States and western Europe is that the rise of national identity is fairly modern, dating to the time of the French Revolution. Before this, other forms of identity such as religion, family, profession, region of origin, or the village of birth were held more strongly than nationality: the average person living in France in the sixteenth century may have been little concerned (or just as likely, unaware) that he or she was "French." In central and eastern Europe, however, contemporary scholars tend to see national identity as extending centuries or even millennia into the past—the modern Greek nation, then, is the direct and unbroken descendant of the ancient Greek states.

The Serb-Albanian debate over who has the "right" to Kosovo is thus quite complicated and draws heavily upon history. It can, however, be simplified down to the crucial matters of "who was here first," and "who was here in larger numbers." Albanian nationalists tend to argue that the Albanians are descendants of the ancient Illyrian peoples and have lived in Albania and Kosovo for several thousand years, while the Serbs are relatively recent newcomers, arriving only fourteen hundred years ago. Serb nationalists counter that Albanians have only lived in Kosovo since the Ottoman conquest six hundred years ago and Albanians increased in numbers only as Serbs were forced to flee the terrible Turks. The Ottoman Empire, led from Turkey, ruled much of southeastern Europe and the Middle East from the fourteenth to the twentieth centuries. Some Serb nationalists go further to argue that the Albanian majority is even more recent, the result of mass immigration during World War II when the Germans and Italians favored their Albanian allies. A more objective historical analysis shows the issue to be somewhat more complicated than this.

ALBANIAN REFUGEES FROM KOSOVO ARRIVE IN BLACE, MACEDONIA IN APRIL 1999. *(AP/Wide World Photos. Photograph by Peter Dejong. Reproduced by permission.)*

Medieval and Ottoman Kosovo

Kosovo was a key province in the medieval Serbian Empire of the late twelfth to early fourteenth centuries, thus forming one of the critical components of Serb affection and claims to the province as a "heartland" of Serbia, or as the "Jerusalem of the Serbs." In fact, it was also part of the Bulgarian Empire of the mid-ninth to early-eleventh centuries, and of the Byzantine Empire before that, so while the Serb connection is undeniably strong, it is not unique. Despite some contemporary assumptions, it was not necessarily the political heartland of medieval Serbia. Czars relocated the political capital frequently as the borders shifted. But the center of the Serbian Orthodox

Church was always in Kosovo, which explains in part the high number and exceptional beauty of churches and monasteries there. The region's mines, particularly silver, were also an important element for the medieval Serbian economy. Finally, it seems clear that Kosovo's population was predominantly Serbian in this period. Although there is some evidence that an Albanian presence was in Kosovo this early, it was assuredly a minority.

This began to change after the Battle of Kosovo Polje in 1389. The Ottoman victory at the "Field of the Blackbirds" is often used as a barometer to show the fall of the Serbs and rise of the Turks; but in truth, the Serb Empire was already in decline with various Serb contenders fighting

THE FIELD OF BLACKBIRDS

The battle of Kosovo Polje, "Kosovo Field," in 1389 and its importance to contemporary Serbs has been widely noted in the media. Unfortunately, much of this attention has either been too uncritical of the current position or too critical, which makes it sometimes difficult to understand the issue.

In its "mythic" sense, the Field of the Blackbirds was the culminating event in which the Serb nation was shattered by an Islamic Ottoman Empire that proceeded to enslave and repress Serbs for four and a half centuries. Some see a religious or mystical meaning in this as well, with the enslaved and defeated Serbs to be redeemed after time; others see a national meaning of pride in resistance to a foreign conqueror. The assassination of Sultan Murad by the Serb noble Milosh Kobilich before the battle (who was himself killed by the Sultan's guard moments later) underscores this larger concept of resistance.

The historical "truth" is much muddier, at least in the eyes of American scholars. There were Serbs who fought on both sides of the battle (since, to preserve their positions, many local nobles in each region agreed to serve the Sultan as vassals), and the Serbian force included a number of non-Serbs (including Albanians). In addition, there is evidence that some peasants welcomed the Ottomans initially, since taxation was somewhat lower. And finally, Serbia itself was not directly annexed to the Empire until 1455—though an important

battle, Kosovo Polje was one part of gradual Ottoman conquest of the Balkans.

Historical "truth" does not by any means invalidate the "myth," however, and the importance of 1389 should not be dismissed as Serb nationalism or mysticism. Americans have their own myths about the history of the United States, which are often historically false but important to Americans today. The American Revolution is cherished as being a shining example of a war for liberty, human rights, and democracy and is enshrined as such in political rhetoric, in many popular histories and in the American mindset. But many historians have raised questions about how such mundane—even repulsive—interests such as anti-Catholicism (the British government's toleration for Catholics in Quebec angered many colonists), desire to seize Indian-held land (the British government sought to limit settlement in the Ohio Valley, at least partially to protect local tribes), and even tax evasion (the hated "taxes" were in large part intended to pay for the troops and naval forces used to protect the colonies) played a role in the war. Others have pointed to the status of women and black Americans to question the commitment to "rights" and "democracy." This is not to say that the American Revolution was not about representation and rights—but that things were not simple and should not be accepted at face value. The same can be said about the significance attached to the battle of Kosovo Polje.

amongst themselves, and the Sultan (the leader of the Ottomans) already in possession of most of Greece and Bulgaria. For that matter, Serb rulers continued to enjoy some independence until 1455 (and isolated fortresses held out until 1459), so the battle did not end Serb independence immediately.

Ottoman rule did result in gradual demographic shifts in Kosovo. Over time, the province had a growing Muslim population (much, but not all of which was Albanian) and a declining Christian one (much, but not all of which was Serbian). The reasons for the population shift are hotly debated, but are likely a mixture of immigration by Albanians, "Albanization" of Serbs who converted to Islam or took Albanian wives and husbands, and the flight of thousands or tens of thousands of Serbs from Kosovo (to northern Serbia and

the Krajina) after unsuccessful rebellions in 1690 and 1738. In any case, by the end of Ottoman rule in Kosovo the population of the province had shifted from a clear Serb majority to an apparent Albanian majority.

Kosovo and Royal Yugoslavia

By the beginning of the nineteenth century the Ottoman Empire was unable to keep the provinces in order; not only was banditry a widespread problem but also local warlords emerged, defying central authority. In such conditions political movements among the non-Turkish peoples in the Balkans (possibly inspired by the French Revolution's ideals of nationalism and enjoying a period of domestic national revival) were able to obtain increasing autonomy and then independence, beginning with Serbia in 1804. This gradual creation of national states was to transform local relations between ethnic groups into potential interstate conflicts, since the logic of nationalism demanded that all Serbs (or Greeks, or Bulgarians) be included in the new Serb state—even if a particular region included members of a different nationality. Such territorial questions were to loom large in the nine major conflicts—including the three most recent civil wars in the former Yugoslavia—fought in the region in the twentieth century.

Albanian interest in the creation of a national state came more slowly. Muslim Albanians were somewhat privileged under the Ottoman Empire and had less reason to resent it than did the various Christian groups. In addition, Albanians developed a sense of national identity more gradually, possibly because Albanian-inhabited regions had less contact with outside intellectual trends and influences, possibly because of relative poverty, and possibly because the strong identification with family and clan was still a viable alternative to a "national" identity. The turning point came in 1878, when the Treaty of San Stefano between Russia and Turkey awarded part of Albanian-populated Kosovo to Serbia. Although the Treaty of Berlin subsequently annulled this transfer the same year, Albanian leaders in Kosovo (united in the League of Prizren) protested the proposed transfer of Muslim inhabited lands to a Christian state.

Faced with an Ottoman government unable to protect it against the threat of Serbian annexation, the League increasingly pushed for an autonomous "Greater Albanian" province within the Ottoman Empire, which the Ottomans in Istanbul, Turkey, refused to grant—fearing this would lead to an independent Albania, as had happened with Serbia, Romania, and Bulgaria. Over time, and outraged over the failure of the reformist Young Turk regime in Istanbul to grant significant autonomy despite initial promises, Albanian leaders turned to open revolt in early 1912. After several engagements, the Ottomans—simultaneously fighting an Italian invasion of Libya—agreed to compromise with the rebels and grant most demands.

This came to naught, however, since the First Balkan War of that same year resulted in the Serb annexation of Kosovo (and the occupation of several parts of Albania by Serbian, Montenegrin, and Greek armies, in the hope to divide Albania between them). The Kingdom of Serbia, originally only a fraction of today's Serbia, had by the late nineteenth century established (or, as Serb leaders saw it, re-established) control over most of Serbia proper, and then began to push for the "liberation"

KOSOVO OR KOSOVA?

When events in Kosovo became headline news in 1999, there was some disagreement about which name to use for the region. The Serb form, Kosovo, generally prevails in English-language scholarship. In Albanian, however, the region is "Kosova" (or "Kosovî," in some grammatical situations). It is thus not uncommon to see journalists and scholars sympathetic to the Albanians use Kosova instead. "Kosovar" is increasingly being used to refer specifically to Albanians.

One added bit of confusion is that the Yugoslav government and many Serbs refer to the region as "Kosovo and Methoija" (or by the Communist-era acronym Kosmet) in the same fashion as "Bosnia" is more properly "Bosnia-Herzegovina."

of the Serb populations in Bosnia, Kosovo, the Hungarian Vojvodina, and Macedonia . The annexation of Kosovo (and part of Macedonia) in 1912–13 incorporated large, new lands where the local Serb population was outnumbered by ethnic groups hostile to Belgrade and which resisted the imposition of Serbian rule. An international commission created by the Carnegie Foundation found that Serb soldiers committed numerous acts of ethnic cleansing against both Albanians and Macedonians (crimes of which the Bulgarian and Greek armies were also found guilty).

Both Albanians and Macedonians sought to use World War I as a means by which to escape Serbian rule. Albanians hoped that a victorious Austria-Hungary, patron of the Albanian state newly established in 1913, would unite Kosovo with Albania. Though the Allies were ultimately victorious, Serbia was overrun by Austro-Hungarian, German, and Bulgarian armies in 1915 with much loss of life (possibly as much as one quarter of the Serb population died), while at the same time Serb troops fought guerrilla bands of Albanians in Kosovo. The open collaboration of Kosovars with the occupying powers—including Albanian military units who rose to support the Austro-Hungarians and anti-Serb persecution within Kosovo—was the justification for a new series of reprisals after the war.

The new Royal Yugoslavia created after World War I thus had a large Albanian component—nearly 450,000 Albanians in Kosovo and Mace-

IN BELGRADE, YUGOSLAVIA, A GIRL HOLDS UP A
PICTURE OF HER MISSING FATHER DURING A PROTEST
IN WHICH DEMONSTRATORS DEMAND THE RELEASE
OF SERBS STILL HELD BY ALBANIANS IN KOSOVO.
(AP/Wide World Photos. Reproduced by permission.)

Albanian and Turk estate owners. Many of these
colonists soon left the province, aghast at the rural
poverty of the region and alarmed by Albanian hostility.

The events of World War II followed the
precedent of World War I. The German invasion
of April 6, 1941, and the division of the country
placed most of Kosovo under Italian administration.
As the Italians had previously occupied Albania in
1939, Kosovo and Albania were united as a single
Italian colonial possession. As in World War I,
many Kosovars supported the Italians and Germans
and in return received various forms of limited autonomy, including Albanian-language schools.
Military auxiliary units were raised, including the
infamous SS Skanderbeg division. And again, local
Serbs were harassed and attacked, and tens of thousands fled to Serbia proper or were killed.

Considering the heavy Serbian losses during
the war and the disproportionate number of Serbs
who fought in the resistance to the Nazis, Albanian
collaboration with the Nazis is still bitterly regarded by many Serbs. Albanian collaboration
makes rather more sense, of course, if one accepts
that they considered it to be resistance to occupation by Serbia. It should also be noted that there
were Kosovar partisan detachments and resistance
to the Axis, if the intensity was less than in Serbia
proper (or in Albania, which was quite active in resisting the Italian occupation). In addition, there
were also Serb collaborators with the Germans. It
is clear that ethnic cleansing and atrocities by both
sides significantly altered the balance of population
in both wars and the interwar period. The Albanians continued to be a majority, but not an overwhelming one.

Tito's Kosovo

With the retreat of German troops from
Yugoslavia in the fall of 1944, the Communist
Partisans entered Kosovo and engaged in another
episode of guerrilla fighting with Albanian forces.
Some fighting even broke out between Albanian
and Serb partisan detachments, which made
Albanian loyalty to the new state particularly questionable. Although there were some initial possi-
bilities that Albania and Yugoslavia (and perhaps
also Bulgaria and Greece) would be united in a
larger federation, the early 1946 and 1953 constitutions of Yugoslavia created under the direction
of communist leader Josip Broz Tito did not grant
a republic or "national" status to Albanians. As relations with Albania worsened in 1948 after Yugoslavia left the Soviet bloc, official government repression of the Albanian population increased.

donia combined, and possibly larger—that fought
inclusion. The Kaçak Rebellion of 1921–24 saw
tens of thousands of Albanians rebel against the
new state, while similar rebellions raged in
Macedonia, Montenegro and Croatia against a
Serb-dominated central government. Faced with a
large Albanian population in Kosovo repeatedly
shown to be untrustworthy, Belgrade began actively
attempting to colonize Kosovo (and Macedonia,
also considered to be suspect) with Serb settlers.
Tens of thousands of Serbs were settled in Kosovo
during 1918-40, on land confiscated from local

KOSOVO, ALBANIA, AND GREATER ALBANIA

If a "Greater Albania" is created to join Albania, Kosovo, and western Macedonia into a single state, it is quite possible that unification would be driven by Kosovars. Greater Albania might, in many ways, be a Greater Kosovo.

Albania under the communist regime was one of the poorest countries in Europe, and since 1991 the country has been plagued by widespread corruption, abuse of power by ruling political parties, and economic malaise. The country reverted to near anarchy in March 1997 when much of the population lost its savings in a series of "pyramid schemes" and rioted in protest of the government's refusal to compensate the victims (in addition, there was suspicion that some members of the government had profited from the scheme) and of government corruption and repression in general. During the temporary collapse of government the military armories were looted and hundreds of thousands of automatic and heavy weapons were distributed among the people in general (many of which would be subsequently acquired by the Kosovo Liberation Army). A new government led by members of the opposition succeeded in re-establishing order, but was in turn shaken by an attempted coup d'état in September 1998. The government is still only partially able to oppose private vendettas (the notorious Albanian "blood feud"), the rise of organized crime in the cities (much of which claimed to be run by Kosovars), and outright banditry in rural areas. Vicious fighting between the two major political parties has also prevented order.

There are as many Albanians in Kosovo and Macedonia as in Albania, and most of the former enjoyed a standard of living and education much better than that available in Albania. The past decade has seen a rise of Kosovar influence among their co-nationals in both Tirana and in Macedonia, and the occupation of the province by peacekeepers may well increase this influence. If Kosovo does achieve independence, it may control the pace and path of future unification rather than Albania itself.

Interestingly, although relations between the KLA and the former government of Sali Berisha (which fell in 1997) were fairly close, the current government of Fatos Nano has distanced itself from both the KLA and pro-independence figures in Macedonia, likely in an effort to please both Greece and the FR Yugoslavia as well as the West—and attract badly needed investment and aid.

Any creation of a future "Greater Albania" would need to take into account the differing goals of the leaders of Albania, Kosovo, and the Albanian minority in Macedonia. What is good for Kosovars may well not be good for their co-nationals in Macedonia and Albania.

Agricultural land was collectivized, Muslim religious schools closed, and attempts were made to encourage Albanians to emigrate.

By the late 1960s, however, widespread Albanian discontent inspired Tito to change course. Alexander Rankovic, minister of the interior and creator of much of the architecture of repression in Kosovo, was purged and compromises were made with regard to Kosovar demands. Relations with Albania began to improve after 1961, when Albania left the Soviet bloc, and this resulted in some limited cultural and commercial exchange. In 1969 the University of Prishtina was established and classes were taught in both Albanian and Serbo-Croatian, with significant implications for Kosovo's later political history. Further, displays of Albanian nationalism were tolerated in an attempt to woo Albanians into becoming loyal supporters of federal Yugoslavia.

The most significant concession came with the 1974 constitution, which made Kosovo an autonomous federal province and provided it with equal representation within the federal government. Albanian cultural institutions were similarly encouraged and funded by the federal government. In addition, significant financial investment was directed towards Kosovo from the federal budget with the intention of creating a stronger economic base and providing employment opportunities for Albanians.

By Tito's death in May 1980, some of the effects of these policies of conciliation were becoming clear. Rioting broke out less than a year after his death, initially because of student demands for better food and housing (both of which were quite dismal). In fact, the university system well symbolizes some of the problems of Tito's later Kosovo policies. In 1980 over a quarter of the entire pop-

NATO JETS STRUCK TARGETS INSIDE KOSOVO NEAR THE ALBANIAN BORDER AS THOUSANDS OF REFUGEES, UNDER THE THREAT OF SERBIAN ARTILLERY, RELOCATED AWAY FROM THE BORDER. *(AP/Wide World Photos. Reproduced by permission.)*

ulation of Kosovo were students in elementary, secondary, or post-secondary facilities and, with government funding, very large numbers of Albanians were attending Prishtina University. At the same time, the university was relatively underfunded and was clearly inferior to the more prestigious universities in Ljubljana, Zagreb, and Belgrade. Nor could Kosovo possibly absorb the graduates of the university system: many new graduates found that their degrees (particularly in such fields as Albanian cultural studies) were of no use in finding them jobs. Nor had massive economic investment dramatically improved the situation in the province. Instead, the conciliatory policies had served to raise Kosovar expectations without providing the means by which they could obtain the standard of living they now expected. The result was a flurry of nationalist displays demanding an Albanian republic within Yugoslavia (or, in more extreme cases, union with Albania), demands seen as threatening by Serbs, Montenegrin, and Macedonians.

Chiefly because of the poverty of the region, Serbs had left Kosovo for the industrial cities of Serbia in large numbers during the 1960s and 1970s. But by the mid-1980s there was a widespread perception that Albanians were forcing Serbs to leave and that the Serb population was rapidly dwindling. Scattered vandalism, intimida-

tion, and violence against Serbs occurred and was exaggerated by the apprehension. The increasing Albanian presence in local political and economic life was also a form of pressure, and many Serbs began to feel that the Albanians were actively seeking to drive them out to create an ethnically pure state. By 1986 local Serbs began protesting the degree of "Albanianization" of Kosovo; Serb intellectuals, including members of the Serbian Academy of Arts and Sciences and several figures considered to be on the liberal left demanded that Kosovo be brought under the direct control of Belgrade to protect Serb interests there; and active debate was beginning about revoking Kosovo's autonomy among political figures.

Milosevic's Kosovo

By the late 1980s, the turmoil in Kosovo was not simply an Albanian-Serb conflict, but was seen by the other Yugoslav republics as a potential threat. Slobodan Milosevic's rise to power in 1987 as president of the Republic of Serbia was fueled by the support of Serbs angry over the abandonment of Kosovo to the Albanians. Massive demonstrations in response to Serb moves by Kosovar Albanians in late 1988 and early 1989 in support of autonomy and independence were seen by local Serbs as further hostile pressure, and counter-demonstrations were held in Belgrade, the capital of the Republic of Serbia. In response, the government of the Republic of Serbia imposed a state of martial law in the province, further polarizing sentiments in the region. At the same time, Milosevic and his political allies moved to eliminate the autonomy of Kosovo, and in March 1989 enacted amendments to the constitution of the Republic of Serbia to eliminate autonomy in Kosovo and, subsequently, the Vojvodina. In 1990 the Albanian members of the former parliament declared independence within Yugoslavia for a Republic of Kosovo, and Belgrade responded by eliminating the remaining vestiges of local government. The immediate effect of this period was to ensure widespread support for Milosevic, now widely perceived as a defender of Serb rights, and to frustrate Albanians who saw the gains of 1974 being illegally reversed.

All this was viewed with misgivings by the other republics. Slovenia and Croatia, long dissatisfied with Yugoslav economic policies, were unhappy at footing the bill for Serbia to regain control over a non-Serb populated region, however historically significant. Worse, Milosevic used federal troops and employed legally questionable moves. This raised the possibility that such moves might be made on behalf of the Serb minorities in Croatia and Bosnia. Further, by establishing control over Kosovo and the Vojvodina, Milosevic now controlled three of the seven votes within the ruling council of Yugoslavia, and controlling one more vote would give him control over federal policy. Although both Slovenia and Croatia had long pushed for reform and considered secession, the Kosovo crisis of the late 1980s helped push the two republics into the final steps that shattered Yugoslavia.

By 1992 Kosovo was divided into two spheres as Serbs dominated the government, police, education, and certain vital industries such as mining; and Albanians created their own shadow government, as well as dominating most economic life at the local levels. Ironically, as Albanians withdrew from FR Yugoslav institutions, they strengthened the position of hard-line Serbs in the government—it seems likely that Milosevic might have been defeated in the December 1992 elections if Albanians had not boycotted them and refused to vote. By the mid-1990s, large numbers of Albanians had left the province, chiefly because of the deteriorating economy and discrimination rather than as a result of violent ethnic cleansing.

Anxiety continued to grow among Serbs in Kosovo as events in Croatia and Bosnia played out over 1991-95; ultimately, Milosevic was unwilling to risk his own power base in order to intervene on the behalf of Serbs living outside Serbia, and the refugees from the Krajina that fled to Serbia were given only limited assistance (many, in fact, were pressured to settle in Kosovo as part of a new colonization program). Rather than inspire moderation on the local level, however, such fears led to active attempts to obtain weapons for protection against Albanians, since Belgrade was no longer to be completely trusted with defending them.

Albanian leaders for their part had gone on to proclaim an independent "Republic of Kosovo" in 1991 and conducted subsequent elections in 1992, appointing Ibrahim Rugova as the president. Despite certain provocative actions by his fellow Albanian political leaders, Rugova stressed nonviolent and passive resistance to Serb policies. International mediation was seen as the key to obtaining a peaceful solution, particularly as the horrors of the wars in Croatia and Bosnia came to light. Even as those wars raged, violence in Kosovo was generally limited to occasional rioting and protests.

Although there were isolated terrorist attacks against Serbian police officers as early as 1993, the emergence of the Kosovo Liberation Army (KLA) came relatively late, over 1996-97. Its emergence can be traced to several factors. First, passive resistance for five years had gained the Kosovars little and had not served to lessen Serbian repression. Worse, international recognition (though not by the United States) of the FR Yugoslavia came in 1996 without any provision regarding Kosovar rights, despite Rugova's expectations for international mediation. Finally, the anarchy in Albania in March 1997 made weapons available for nascent terrorists—as did the money made available by alleged illegal activities by some members of the KLA, such as drug smuggling. With many Albanians, particularly students, unhappy with Rugova's policies and with ready access to weapons, the emergence of a violent alternative may have been inevitable.

More vicious clashes between the FR Yugoslav police and security forces and the KLA broke out in September and November 1997 as police vehicles and barracks were attacked. By February 1998 Serb forces had realized the potential threat of the KLA and began to clamp down on the province more severely, driving more Albanians to support of the KLA. By the middle of the year, the KLA may have held as much as 40 percent of Kosovo. Large-scale Serbian offensives in August 1998 increasingly pressured the KLA, but also began to include attacks against civilian targets. The continued, escalating violence between the KLA and Yugoslav security forces in late 1998 led to international demands for mediation, and the threat of a new series of Yugoslav campaigns to the insistence of the International Contact Group on the Rambouillet talks of March 1999. When the talks broke down, to the NATO air campaign against the FR Yugoslavia and subsequent intervention.

RECENT HISTORY AND THE FUTURE

It is clear that the NATO and United Nations peacekeeping missions in Kosovo have changed the balance of power in the province. Most of the Serb population appears to have fled; media accounts in early 2000 suggest that nearly 250,000 Serbs, Montenegrins, and Roma (Gypsies) have left the province, and that about sixty thousand remain. The pretext for international intervention was to preserve and strengthen a multi-ethnic society, and the current missions in Kosovo still legally recognize the province as being part of the Federal Republic of Yugoslavia (Serbia and Montenegro). But Belgrade's power in and over the region has been crippled, and many Serbs have fled fearing reprisals from Albanians. At the same time, the rise of the KLA has undermined the more moderate Albanian parties and it is possible that any agreements undertaken by Albanian representatives might not be respected by all KLA factions.

In the short term, the future of the province is uncertain. Peacekeeping forces have been relatively unable to control widespread crime and corruption in the province, much of which is controlled by former KLA members. Disagreements between the United Nations and various Kosovar political factions have limited reconstruction efforts. And while elements of both the Serb and Albanian population are willing to collaborate in easing tensions, extremists and widespread bitterness on both sides have limited progress in creating a political dialogue. It is also uncertain how successful disarmament may have been, since large numbers of weapons (especially Kalashnikov assault rifles) were obtained by Albanian civilians from Albania, and were distributed to Serb civilians by the government of the Republic of Serbia. It seems unlikely that either NATO or the U.N. will be able to "disengage" from Kosovo in the near future.

Over the next five to ten years, it seems increasingly likely that many Kosovars will be unwilling to accept autonomy for the province within Serbia, particularly if the Republic of Montenegro were to secede—seen as a possibility in late 1999 and early 2000 if relations with Belgrade were to worsen. As Belgrade's influence continues to weaken, the Serb population dwindles and Albanians become increasingly confident in their ability to resist or delay integration, it seems increasingly likely that the province will simply declare its independence from Serbia—likely leading to political conflicts with the peacekeepers and potentially another round of war with the FR Yugoslavia.

A second possibility is partition of the province between Serbia and local political leaders, although both NATO and the U.N. have repeatedly opposed any division of Kosovo. Before 1999 it would have been difficult to draw a clear ethnic boundary in the province, but Serb flight has left only two large pockets of Serb settlements. The first, smaller pocket is in the southeastern corner of the country, bordering both the republic of Serbia and Macedonia. The larger pocket comprises part of the city of Mitrovica and surrounding areas to the north. This area is both almost exclusive Serb and borders Serbia; in addition, after less than a year it has become almost completely economically and politically segregated from the rest of Kosovo. The FR Yugoslav dinar is used as the currency, for example. The chief obstacle to partition would probably be the fact that the region holds access to much of the Trepca mine complex, crucial to Kosovo's economy and which Kosovars would be loathe to relinquish (and in which, prior to 1989, many Albanians worked).

In either of the three cases—renewed autonomy in the Republic of Serbia or Federal Yugoslavia, independence for the province, or independence for Albanian majority areas—it seems likely that the outcome will increase tensions to the south, in the Republic of Macedonia.

Macedonia—The Next Kosovo?

Kosovo is not the only part of the former Yugoslavia with a substantial Albanian minority. There are small numbers of Albanians in Montenegro and Serbia, and a much more substantial population in the Republic of Macedonia. While census figures from the 1991 and 1994 censuses in Macedonia are still an issue of dispute (many Albanians boycotted the first election, and claim the second census under-represents them) there are roughly 440,000 Albanian citizens in Macedonia, or one-quarter of the population—not counting either illegal immigrants or refugees from Kosovo, both present in considerable numbers.

As in Kosovo, birthrates among ethnic Albanians in the rural areas are higher than for ethnic Macedonians. There is also a similar trend of Macedonians leaving the rural countryside in favor of the cities; one result of this is that the total area of Albanian settlements is apparently slowly in-

HOUSES BURN AT MALISEVO, KOSOVO AS SERBIAN FORCES AND ETHNIC ALBANIAN MILITANTS CLASH IN ONE OF THEIR BIGGEST BATTLEFIELD ENCOUNTERS. *(AP/Wide World Photos. Reproduced by permission.)*

creasing, as Albanians settle in abandoned villages. The possibility that historic Macedonian centers, such as Ohrid, might be surrounded by Albanians disturbs many Macedonians, and there have been calls for the government to "resettle" Macedonian villages with ethnic Macedonians.

Unlike Kosovo, since 1991 there has been no official, open persecution of Albanians and Albanian political parties have been part of coalition governments—including the recent coalition government formed in 1998 by the Macedonian nationalist party VMRO-DPMNE. Albanians enjoy a number of rights as a minority, including the recognition of Albanian as an official language in state use and Albanian-language schools. Many

Albanians counter, with some justification, that there remains widespread unofficial discrimination against Albanians: Albanians have a lower standard of living, have their political influence minimized by gerrymandering (the manipulation of electoral districts), and are underrepresented in university admissions, the officer corps of the army, the police, and the middle levels of government. Allegations of police brutality against Albanians have been substantiated by the Helsinki Committee on Human Rights and Human Rights Watch, although there is less evidence that this is official government policy. Albanians have also protested certain articles of the Macedonian Constitution, which proclaims Macedonia as the state for the

Macedonians, endorses the Macedonian Orthodox Church as the official religion and initially declared Macedonian to be the only official language.

Albanian efforts to make the Albanian language completely equal to Macedonian in public use or to obtain more government jobs and funding have been greeted with hostility. Particularly contentious was the opening of the Albanian-language University of Tetovo in 1994, which the government declared to be illegal and has violently suppressed on several occasions. Ethnic Macedonian students have protested against both recognition of an Albanian university and against conducting classes in Albanian at the national university. Although the government softened on the matter over 1997–99, if Kosovo slides toward independence many Macedonians may draw parallels between the University of Prishtina and the University of Tetovo, and fear that the university may embolden secessionist demands. At the same time, some Albanian extremists see the university as too close to the Macedonian government and self-proclaimed members of the KLA have publicly threatened to kill the president of the university as a collaborator.

From the perspective of many Macedonians, Albanian demands for autonomy directly threaten the state's existence. Geographically, Macedonia is not large, and the loss of its western regions is alarming. The country has also suffered continued economic problems since independence, chiefly because of the loss of its Yugoslav trading partners (the routes through and to Serbia having been closed several times by U.N. embargoes), but Greek hostility and domestic corruption have not helped. Many Macedonians who have seen their standard of living decline from the Yugoslav era resent the increasingly assertive Albanian political movement, and suspect it may further weaken their livelihoods.

Most worrisome is that many Macedonians perceive their country to be surrounded by hostile states. Greece has engaged in a number of sharp diplomatic conflicts with Macedonia, chiefly over what many Greeks regard as the "theft" of Greek heritage—such as the term "Macedonia," which Athens refuses to acknowledge (and thus leading to the confusing practice of many international organizations referring to "the Former Yugoslav Republic of Macedonia," or FYROM). While recent Bulgarian policy has been extremely friendly, there is much dispute over the history of the Macedonians and lingering fears that the Bulgarians may actively seek to annex the country. And while many Macedonians have relatives in the FR Yugoslavia and have been somewhat sympathetic to the Serbs in the Croatian, Bosnian, and Kosovo conflicts, there are fears that Serbia could either seek to annex the Serb populated areas around Kumanovo in the northeast or (more likely) send troops into parts of Macedonia if the Kosovo conflict spills over into Macedonia if rebel Albanians attempted to escape to the south. In the face of external threats, possible Albanian secession has been interpreted as part of a potential repartition of the Republic of Macedonia.

All of this helps to explain why although government policy is much more tolerant than in much of the rest of the former Yugoslavia, domestic reaction can be so strong to events such as the Albanian mayor of Tetovo flying an Albanian (as well as a Turkish) flag in front of the city offices—an episode which ultimately involved fighting between Macedonian police sent in to confiscate the flags, at least one Albanian death, a seven-year jail sentence for the mayor (since amnestied), and widespread protests.

BIBLIOGRAPHY

Banac, Ivo. *The National Question in Yugoslavia.* Ithaca, N.Y.: Cornell University Press, 1984.

Jelavich, Charles and Barbara Jelavich. *The Establishment of the Balkan National States.* Seattle, Wash.: University of Washington Press, 1977.

Lampe, John. *Yugoslavia: Twice there was a Country.* 2d ed. New York: Cambridge University Press, 2000.

Macolm, Noel. *Kosovo: A Short History.* New York: Harper Perennial, 1999.

Manchevski, Milcho. Before the Rain. 112 min. Polygram Video, 1999. Videocassette.

Maras, Branka. *The Destruction of Yugoslavia: Tracing the Break-up 1980–92.* London: Verso Press, 1993.

Poulton, Hugh. *The Balkans: Minorities and States in Conflict.* 3d ed. London: Minority Rights Group Reports, 1998.

Rothschild, Joseph. *East-Central Europe Between the Two World Wars.* Seattle, Wash.: University of Washington Press, 1974.

Sugar, Peter F. *Southeastern Europe under Ottoman Rule.* Seattle, Wash.: University of Washington Press, 1977.

Troebst, Stefan "Macedonia: Powder Keg Diffused?" *RFE/RL Research Report* (28 January 1994): 33–41.

Vickers, Miranda and James Pettifer, eds. *Albania: From Anarchy to a Balkan Identity.* New York: New York University Press, 1997.

James Frusetta

MEXICAN-U.S. BORDER RELATIONS: OPPORTUNITIES AND OBSTACLES

A two-thousand-mile long border joins Mexico and the United States. This border was part of a dispute that sparked the Mexican American War (1846–48). That war was resolved under the 1848 Treaty of Guadalupe Hidalgo, which permanently excised from Mexican control the lands of present day Arizona, New Mexico, California, and Texas, as well as parts of Colorado, Utah, and Nevada. Since then, relations between the United States and Mexico have become more friendly. In 1994 the United States, Canada, and Mexico entered into the North American Free Trade Agreement (NAFTA), which encouraged free trade across their respective borders. The agreement brought renewed attention to the U.S.-Mexican border, particularly to the cheap labor, lower government restrictions on working and environmental standards, and the illegal trafficking of drugs and immigrants available from the Mexican side of the Rio Grande River.

Mexico's border towns are booming. For many years the U.S.-Mexican international border was considered a "no-man's land." Much of the border territory is arid and sparsely populated. Towns such as Tijuana, Tecate, Mexicali, Nogales, Piedras Negras, Ciudad Juarez, Nuevo Laredo, Reynosa, and Matamoros dominated life on the Mexican side of the border. Between 1940 and 2000 these towns experienced very rapid growth, and their importance to both Mexico and to the United States has increased. The towns are located in Mexico's six border states of Baja California, Sonora, Chihuahua, Coahuila, Nuevo Leon, and Tamaulipas. Over the last forty-five years the population of these states has increased dramatically from 3.7 million to 15.2 million people. During this same time period the thirty-nine towns along the U.S.

THE CONFLICT

Every year, thousand of immigrants, tourists, goods, and drugs enter the United States from Mexico or enter Mexico from the United States. Tensions over the border regarding the importing of illegal goods, including drugs, legal and illegal immigration, as well as the matter of cultural domination have made relations between the two countries challenging.

Political

- The immigration of Mexican workers—legal and illegal—causes considerable tension. Some Americans feel that Mexican workers take jobs that would otherwise go to U.S. citizens and depress wages; others believe that these are positions that would otherwise go unfilled and that the workers actually help increase U.S. economic growth.

- Many Mexicans who are living in the United States, including those who may hold U.S. citizenship, have relatives in Mexico, and feel an abiding affinity for their homeland. Some U.S. citizens are suspicious of what they perceive to be divided loyalty.

Economic

- Both Mexico and the United States are challenged in terms of addressing the flow of drugs from Mexico to the United States. Mexico has experienced considerable corruption of its political and law enforcement systems, undermining interdiction efforts.

- Labor unions and other groups in the United States are concerned that major manufacturing activities will move—or have already moved—to Mexico, where wages are cheaper and regulations are less stringent.

Cultural

- Border towns in Mexico, which cater to U.S. tourists, and Mexicans in the United States are concerned about being overwhelmed by U.S. culture and losing their own unique Mexican culture.

CHRONOLOGY

1822 The Federal Republic of Mexico is established.

1823 Texas, then a part of Mexico, is opened to immigrants from the United States.

1836 The United States becomes the first country to recognize Mexico's independence from Spain. Texas declares itself independent from Mexico.

1846 War breaks out between the United States and Mexico.

1848 The war ends and Mexico loses to the United States territory that today makes up New Mexico, Arizona, Nevada, Utah, California, and parts of Colorado.

1910–17 The Mexican Revolution takes place.

1920–33 During the Prohibition era in the United States, Mexican border town Ciudad Juarez becomes known for its growing number of bars and bootleggers who smuggle alcohol into the southwestern states of the United States.

1929 The National Revolutionary Party (which later becomes the PRI) forms in Mexico. It rules Mexico until 2000.

1940s The U.S. war mobilization in World War II helps to improve the Mexican economy.

1960–80 *Maquiladores* are established in Mexico in an effort to provide industrial development in Mexico to stabilize the populations on both sides of the border. *Maquiladores* are attractive to U.S. businesspeople because they offer cheaper, non-unionized labor. They attract Mexican workers as they provide a relatively high wage.

1969 U.S. president Richard Nixon launches "Operation Intercept" to prevent drugs from crossing the border from Mexico into the United States.

1990 A privatization program is initiated in Mexico.

2000 Vicente Fox, a PAN candidate who courts Mexican immigrants to the United States, is elected president of Mexico, ending the PRI's hold on the presidency.

border have grown more than twenty-fold. Their combined population today is close to five million people. Authorities on both sides of the international border have been forced to provide better water, housing, hospitals, and schools for the growing population. While the two countries cooperate on a number of issues, including environmental and natural resource matters, conflicts regarding immigration, culture, trade, and drugs continue to impact the border region and the relations between the United States and Mexico.

HISTORICAL BACKGROUND

Mexican immigrants have long been attracted to the border by job opportunities and higher than average wages. Historically, agriculture and livestock production supported the border populations, and industries that serviced these sectors thrived. In addition, Mexican border towns were initially seen as safe havens for fugitives from U.S. law. During the Prohibition era in the United States (1920–33), Ciudad Juarez became notorious for its growing number of bars and bootleggers who smuggled alcohol into southwestern states of the United States, a precursor to the prolific drug trade that would develop in the latter half of the twentieth century.

Throughout the Great Depression, from 1929 to the early 1940s, an economic slump created widespread misery and poverty on both sides of the border. In the early 1940s World War II created an economic boom. The U.S. government encouraged Mexican immigrants to cross the border to work in U.S. agriculture, as it needed this labor to replace that of U.S. citizens who were called to fight the war. With U.S. government support Mexican immigrants came to the aid of its northern neighbor. Throughout the 1950s and 1960s U.S. demand for Mexican labor continued. A mutually beneficial dependency developed. However, as U.S. soldiers returned from war looking for work, political pressure mounted to tighten immigration laws, and border crossing grew more difficult. Tighter border controls caused the population in Mexican border towns to swell.

Border cities catered over time to changing values, economic climates, and tastes. Handicrafts grew as tourism rose. Some U.S. citizens took day trips visit the foreign country so close to their native soil. Mexican border towns staged bullfights, horse races, cockfights, and exotic nightclub acts to attract U.S. dollars. "Quickie" divorces provided swift, cheap, reduced-trauma means for ending bad marriages. Many U.S. citizens came to Mexican border towns seeking such services, as well as medical cures that were not yet approved by the U.S. government but were available in Mexico. To the dismay of both U.S. and Mexican officials narcotics, gun running, and contraband traffic also increased along the border.

In the Mexican capital of Mexico City the borders were increasingly seen as a center for introducing U.S. values, morals, attitudes, products, and institutions—a threat to Mexican culture. Some Mexican women along the border, for example, believed that marrying a white American was a symbol of upward mobility. Values clashes have been a constant source of tension along the border, and U.S. influence has often been viewed as corrupting.

Many *fronterizos,* those living in the Mexican border towns, work in U.S. companies and visit the United States often, though most have not visited Mexico City or other destinations in central and southern Mexico. English words are mixed in with their Spanish when they speak, and street signs are often in English to help tourists. The *fronterizos* consume U.S. products, while tourist demand for Mexican food, music, and handicrafts does more to keep these alive than does local demand. The region's culture has become an amalgam of Mexican and U.S. cultures.

Community leaders in Mexican border towns resent the perception that they are less Mexican than residents in other parts of Mexico. On the contrary, they argue that they are "Mexicanizing" Americans. They blame Mexico City for any dilution of Mexican culture by arguing that not enough has been done for them by the federal government to integrate them with the rest of Mexico economically and culturally. They say that their links to the United States are matters of necessity, not of choice.

Much of the trade between the United States and Mexico goes through the border towns. The economies of the two nations at this juncture are firmly linked. In addition, the high level of traffic—be it in goods or humans—flowing across the border makes the area an appealing location for drug smugglers and illegal immigrants to take their chances in being overlooked in the mass of travel crossing the border each day. The increase in illegal immigration has strained U.S.-Mexican relations, while more drugs cross the border into the United States from Mexico than from any other location. With crime lords firmly entrenched, the border towns became rife with corruption. The Mexican government even produced a document entitled "Cartilla de paisano," or Brotherly Document, to inform Mexicans along both sides of the border how to deal with abusive or corrupt border officials.

Maquiladores

Between 1960 and 1980 it became apparent to U.S. officials that U.S. federal aid was needed on both sides of the border to stabilize populations and normalize relations. Federal money began flowing into common water projects, roads, schools, housing, and hospitals. To appease industrious Mexican shopkeepers who witnessed Mexican customers streaming across the border into places like Brownsville, Texas, to buy merchandise, Mexican officials gave permission to import duty free U.S. goods into Mexican border towns. U.S. legislation began to favor "in-bond" border factories in Mexico to provide alternatives to massive immigration into the U.S. for Mexican workers. These factories mushroomed on the Mexican side of the border, where such they became known as *maquiladores.* *Maquiladores* imported raw materials from the United States duty-free and exported finished products. U.S. tariffs were paid only on the value-added. These factories improved life along the Mexican side of the border and provided higher wages. The wages, relatively high in comparison to that available elsewhere in the country, attracted workers from throughout Mexico.

Non-unionized labor was part of the attraction of *maquiladores* for U.S. businesspeople. Organized labor in Mexico and the United States objected to the arrangement. Most laborers in the electrical assembly plants, textile factories, and fabrication facilities on the Mexican side of the border were young women—women formed ninety percent of the labor force in some factories. Male unemployment, however, increased. Labor organizers theorized that plant managers hired so many Mexican women because women were less likely than men to organize. Northern Mexico has a long history of anti-unionism, and U.S. companies operating in the border towns did not want unions involved in their work. As a result, unions suffered and wages were reduced. This attracted more U.S. investors, to whom the low wages and lack of organized labor appealed. Capital poured in, a trend that accelerated with the signing of the North American Free Trade Agreement (NAFTA).

Immigration

In addition to skilled labor, such as engineers, doctors, lawyers, and managers, many Mexicans crossed the border seeking jobs as maids and unskilled day laborers, including gardeners and janitors. Undocumented workers—those working without the proper paperwork to work legally in the United States—became a problem, as more people sought jobs than there were jobs available. Border cities began harboring business people who exploited workers' desires for higher U.S. wages by sneaking undocumented workers illegally across the border. Thousands of Mexican immigrants did and do arrive daily, hoping to reach the United States and the promise of a better life.

These immigrants were the frequent victims of crime along the border. The more that U.S. Border Patrols tightened the restrictions around illegal immigration, the more that would-be immigrants need guides to get into the United States. These guides grew to become part of vast organized crime syndicates which control stolen cars, gun running, drug smuggling, and, increasingly, the smuggling of illegal immigrants from Mexico, China, Guatemala, Russia, and elsewhere. Men known as *talons*, or claws, are predatory recruiters who lurk near bus stations and entice those seeking to cross the border to follow them to safe houses. There, the prospective immigrants wait to make the illegal trip across the border to the United States—usually for a steep fee.

Guides for undocumented workers are known as *coyotes*. *Coyotes* lead immigrants through the gullies and mountain passes along the border. Scouts, known as *checadores*, run interference and try to lead Border Patrols on wild goose chases away from real immigrants in order to increase their chances of success. The trek is often a dangerous one, and Border Patrols often find themselves rescuing illegal immigrants from dire situations, including freezing weather and injury from the harsh natural landscape.

Once on the U.S. side of the border, the new immigrants are turned over to *raiteros*, or daredevil drivers for hire, who take them north to Los Angeles, Phoenix, Albuquerque, Houston, St. Louis, Chicago, Virginia, or Boston. Smugglers often raise the price of passage upon reaching their destination or rape the women and rob the men. Smuggling often resembles kidnapping. As cries for restrictions on illegal immigration mount in the United States, so too does the danger associated with illegal entry into the country. The traffic in illegal immigrants across the U.S.-Mexican border is not restricted to Mexicans. Mafiosi charge $20,000 to smuggle Chinese into Mexicali, with its large traditional Chinese-Mexican population, and from Mexicali into San Diego, California. Border Patrols call such immigrants "OTMs," meaning "other than Mexicans." The high fees charged for the passage force immigrants into wage slavery in "sweatshops" for years to pay for their entry into the United States.

Immigration Issues

In an example of the negative feelings engendered by illegal immigration in the U.S. states most affected by it, California's electorate approved Proposition 187 in 1994. The law ended the state of California's efforts to provide education, housing, and health care for Mexican immigrants. A majority of the electorate obviously believed that such costs outweighed the benefits of cheap labor. Former California governor Pete Wilson denounced "Smugglers Canyon" south of San Diego, a high-traffic smuggling location, and called for a doubling of border patrols. Wilson called in the National Guard to stop illegal immigrants, charged border-crossing fees, and other measures to discourage the influx of Mexican immigrants.

Mexico's Congress retaliated to Proposition 187 and other anti-immigration measures in the United States by allowing Mexicans living in the United States to hold dual citizenship. Mexicans in the United States can now vote in U.S. elections without revoking their Mexican citizenship. Thus empowered, they can use their votes against U.S. politicians who oppose their interests, while still maintaining full political and legal rights in Mexico. The Latino population in the United States is growing at a rapid rate, and the political and social influences of this population are also on the rise. As its influence grows, so too will attention to issues such as immigration and measures such as Proposition 187.

The current immigration system along the U.S.-Mexican border is not meeting the needs of any of the interested parties. U.S. unions are troubled by the legal "guest worker" status of many Mexicans in the United States. They would like to negotiate a new immigration policy to normalize and rationalize labor between the United States and Mexico by increasing the number of permanent work permits issued annually and extending visas issued to Mexican workers who legally enter the

RENE CASTILLO (L.) AND GUSTAVO OLVERA PLACE A CROSS AT THE U.S.-MEXICAN BORDER FENCE BEFORE TAKING PART IN A 70-MILE MARCH TO PROTEST THE DEATH TOLL OF MIGRANTS ALONG THE BORDER. *(AP/Wide World Photos. Reproduced by permission.)*

United States. This is a measure aimed at encouraging legal immigration and cutting back on the number of illegal immigrants flowing across the border each year. Critics argue that this is a ploy designed to limit Mexican immigration and protect high U.S. union wages. Researchers estimate that Mexico must generate one million jobs annually to employ its youth, a rate which the government has not been able to meet. Some of the resultant overflow finds an outlet in the United States. Under NAFTA Mexico has become the tenth-largest exporting nation on earth; approximately two-thirds of its exports go to the United

States. Despite their differences, the two countries do benefit from one another.

The Drug Trade

In 1969 President Richard Nixon authorized "Operation Intercept." Vehicles crossing into the United States from Mexico were systematically searched for drugs. Traffic was stalled for days. Mexican officials were angry because the United States did not notify them of this operation before it went into effect. In addition, the Mexican government argued, the operation merely served to scapegoat innocent Mexicans by blaming the U.S.

LOWER PHARMACEUTICAL PRICES IN MEXICO HAVE ATTRACTED CUSTOMERS FROM THE UNITED STATES TO TIJUANA. *(AP/Wide World Photos. Reproduced by permission.)*

drug problem on its southern neighbor. Mexican officials argued then as they do now that the United States should attack demand, not supply, if it was serious about eradicating the drug problem. As fast as U.S. and Mexican law enforcement agents burned or destroyed Mexican marijuana and opium poppy fields, new ones emerged. Pro-marijuana legalization interests arose and portrayed Mexican drug barons as innocent victims of overzealous U.S. immigration patrols who mistreated and tortured them without probable cause. In 1976 both sides agreed to exchange prisoners to improve U.S.-Mexican relations. The exchange improved relations for a time, but a decade later drugs returned to the borderlands.

Cocaine processing labs appeared in Mexico. The United States had a major problem with Colombian drug cartels in Medellin and Cali, Columbia, whose primary port of U.S. entry for drugs was Miami, Florida. U.S. Drug Enforcement Agency (DEA) agents succeeded in disrupting the Colombian cartels, which served to shift the bulk of the illegal drug business into the hands of more than nine hundred Mexican drug gangs. Because they are so numerous, they are more difficult to monitor and control. These drug barons have turned the U.S.-Mexican border into one of the world's most violent, corrupt, and dangerous borders. Police on both sides of the border have tar-

geted the top five drug cartels because of their huge volume of business.

Once the Colombia-Miami, Florida, smuggling route diminished in importance, the Mexican-U.S. border rapidly transformed itself into the world's largest drug smuggling route. U.S. border officials estimate that seventy-five percent of all cocaine shipments entering the United States cross Mexico's border with the United States. Jeffrey Davidow, the U.S. ambassador to Mexico, and General Barry McCaffrey, the U.S. drug czar, provided a lower estimate of fifty percent. U.S. Senator Jesse Helms, head of the U.S. Foreign Relations Committee, alleged that drug barons operate with "virtual impunity" in border cities.

Mexico's drug cartels earn an estimated $30 billion annually. The drug trade within the United States is more than $150 billion per year. The mark-up of drug prices, both in transit and on U.S. streets, is enormous. Some feel that drug smuggling has polluted Mexico's legal and political system and turned Mexico into a "narco-democracy." According to a study conducted by the University of Guadalajara, drug kingpins spend $500 million a year bribing public officials. This is double the entire budget of the Mexican federal attorney general and the federal police. Mexicans argue that similar charges can be leveled against the United States.

Francisco Labastida, former Interior Minister of Mexico, increased spending by nearly $500 million over a three-year period on high-tech law enforcement equipment, planes, ships, and radar to intercept drug traffic. The federal police was known to be riddled with corruption, and Labastida created a new unit to fight drugs. The question then was, who would watch the new police force?

The Arellano Felix brothers dominated drug trafficking through Tijuana, Mexico. Tijuana in the early twenty-first century is the hub of U.S.-Mexican border drug smuggling, like Miami was in the early 1990s. Reynoso grocery stores in the United States order jalapeno peppers and other Mexican food items by the ton. An alliance between the Arellano brothers and the Reynoso brothers made it easy to import tons of cocaine and heroin disguised as peppers and other foods through legal ports of entry. Drugs were also smuggled into the United States through a variety of creative measures, which often slipped unnoticed by Border Patrols.

The nemeses of the Arellano brothers are Joaquim Guzman (Chapo, or Shorty) and Hector Palma (Guero, or Whitey), who form the Sinaloa cartel, also known as the Guzman-Palma crime family. The competition between the two cartels for dominance of the drug trade in their area is deadly and often terrorizes the towns around which the cartels are based.

Juan Garcia Abrego long dominated drug traffic along the Gulf of Mexico. Raul Salinas, brother of former Mexican president Carlos Salinas de Gortari, was in business with Abrego. While Carlos Salinas served as president of Mexico, Abrego sold drugs with impunity. After Ernesto Zedillo became president in 1994, both Abrego and Raul Salinas were arrested. In addition, allegations that the Arellano brothers contributed to political campaigns and used political pressure to have their rivals arrested, allowing them to expand, are widespread. Because drugs and politics are so closely aligned, despite the best efforts the Mexican police, many scholars, such as Jorge Castenada, consider Mexico a narco-democracy.

Corruption of Mexican law enforcement officers is a major problem. Drug money is quick and prevalent, while the salary of a Mexican police officer is paltry in comparison. Temptation helps lead to corruption, and not just for law enforcement. Politicians are tempted to get rich quick by helping drug barons launder billions of dollars. Mexican banks, resort hotels, shopping centers, and other organizations are used to "clean up" drug profits—

making the origin of the money unclear. When Cardinal Posadas Ocampo of Guadalajara spoke out against drug barons in 1993, he was killed. Allegedly, the politicians and gangsters in this region decided to make a statement about power and invincibility by publicly executing Bishop Posada. The message was that they could not be touched, no matter what they did. In 1985 drug dealers in Guadalajara killed Enrique Camarena, a DEA agent, causing a diplomatic crisis between Mexico and the United States. Some believe that drug barons were responsible for the murder of PRI presidential candidate Donaldo Colosio because, they claim, he had cracked down on Pacific Coast—primarily Tijuana—drug rings, while being soft on Caribbean or East Coast gangs. Colosio was killed in the West Coast border town of Tijuana.

The allure of drugs is overwhelming for many. Gangsters and police are seen as interchangeable, since many police work as guards and hitmen for drug lords. Cowboy boots, sunglasses, and assault rifles are cult icons. The Jeep Cherokee and Chevrolet Suburban are viewed as "war wagons." Both drug dealers and police use these vehicles. Their cargo space and durable rugged frames allow them to carry guns and drugs through the canyons and potholes along the border.

Camarillas and Corruption

To date, Mexico's political elite have been divided into *camarillas,* or political clans. The elites embark on joint business ventures, using their political leverage to secure contracts, licenses, favorable deals, and political protection from fellow members. Corruption at high levels was controlled by *camarillas.* The clans originated as groups of people who shared the same ideological values and interests. When the PRI held power, state-owned enterprises were promoted. Clan members were assured lucrative jobs, contracts, and other perks. Their children received the best possible education from the state; many of their children were educated at Harvard and Yale, as well as other U.S. universities.

When President Salinas and, later, his successor President Zedillo gained power, they used their position to sell off state-owned enterprises and to privatize the economy. Consequently, the PRI lost control of lucrative funds. The provision of funds based on friendship, kinship, and party loyalty continued, but the pie shrank. More and more *camarillas* were left out when favors were divided among the winners. Mexican presidents had based their power upon control of state resources. As the state

A MAKESHIFT HOME IN THE BORDER TOWN OF CIUDAD JUAREZ, MEXICO STANDS IN STARK CONTRAST TO THE URBAN NEIGHBORHOOD ACROSS THE BORDER IN EL PASO, TEXAS. *(AP/Wide World Photos. Reproduced by permission.)*

nal tensions would have to be managed if the state was to survive. This traffic is difficult to control within Mexico because 2,400 different police agencies are involved. These police must fight criminals who are clearly "bad guys," as well as fellow officers and corrupt units of privatized security companies who work for drug barons. Each police force is more or less a family-owned fiefdom that specializes in solving a particular type of crime; there are subway police, traffic police, bank police, forestry police, customs police, riot police, judicial police, town police, rural police, federal police, and others. Lured by the large amounts of money, internal corruption in some border town police forces is rampant.

Police units employ undercover agents known as *madrinas,* or godmothers. These secret cops are paid off the books to avoid detection. They carry guns and do "dirty work," such as killing opponents and stealing cars. Many human rights violations are carried out by *madrinas.* These police are often co-opted by drug barons; some become rogue cops or freelance agents who sell their services to the highest bidder.

Drug cartel baron Hector "*El Guero*" Palma of Sinaloa, routinely hired police officers as body guards, informants, look-outs, runners, and hit men. Palma, a former car thief, was one of Mexico's most violent gangsters. In 1995, when his private Leer jet crash-landed on his way to a wedding in Guadalajara, the pilot was killed. The pilot's body was stuffed into a sleeping bag, which was discovered by a local army unit not in Palma's employ. A massive raid on Palma's safe house was ordered by the military. They discovered that he was being protected by eight bodyguards and thirty-two judicial police officers. At Palma's trial it was revealed that he paid $40 million to top federal judicial police commanders in Guadalajara—more than the annual salaries for all federal judicial police for one month, nationwide. Palma admitted to bribing police in nearly every border town. He often was lodged by local police chiefs in their homes when he "inspected" his border smuggling operations.

In the bloodiest shoot-out in the history of Mexico's drug war, two groups of lawmen were pitted against each other. On March 3, 1994, teams of anti-narcotics agents from the federal judicial police were attacked near the U.S. border in Baja California. They were trying to arrest a local drug cartel boss. He escaped in the confusion of the shoot-out. His bodyguards included the Baja California chief of homicide and dozens of state judicial police from Baja California. This created a national scandal in Mexico. Many ethical policemen

shrank, their power diminished. Once unquestioned, their authority and power were now openly challenged, especially by presidential candidates from the pro-business PAN. Each *camarilla* had to fight for its life. Without state money, old alliances dissolved. Drug money began to provide new glue, a new source of largesse to replace lost state resources for the losing *camarillas,* as well as for the criminal class.

Salinas and Zedillo became resigned to the fact that privatization of the economy increased drug trafficking within Mexico. New internal and exter-

were embarrassed and ashamed of their fellow officers' outrageous behavior.

Army units have fallen victim to corruption too In Veracruz, regular army units were assigned antinarcotic duties at the airport. Drug barons corrupted the soldiers, who gunned down seven federal government agents who tried to seize a planeload of narcotics at the Veracruz airport on November 7, 1991, at the Tlatlixcoyan airstrip. By 1996 military personnel occupied top law enforcement in two-thirds of Mexico's states. About forty percent of Mexico's 180,000-person army worked on drug control. General Jesus Gutierrez Rebollo became Mexico's drug czar, yet in 1997 Gutierrez was arrested for selling protection to drug kingpins—the same people he was supposed to be working against.

By 1995 internal documents from the Mexican government estimated that fifty percent of the hired guns working for drug barons in Mexico were policemen, soldiers, or individuals who had retired from either service. Most law enforcement agencies are severely compromised, as are armed forces units involved in drug interdiction.

RECENT HISTORY AND THE FUTURE

There is reason for optimism in the border conflicts between the United States and Mexico. Law enforcement officers on both sides of the border are learning to respect one another, and cooperation is growing as many officers become acquainted with the laws and police cultures of both nations. Despite significant difficulties involved in fighting drug lords in Mexico and in the United States, as well as official corruption in both nations, progress continues. Efforts to reduce the U.S. demand for illegal drugs may reduce the flow of narcotics across the border, while the United States re-evaluates its immigration policy. Cooperation in these endeavors is enhanced by the closer relationship brought about by NAFTA. The trade agreement requires the two countries to work together on a number of issues, fostering greater understanding of where each stands on a range of issues.

Mexico's proximity to the United States will help it expand its service and information technology sectors. Border populations are assimilating selected elements of both national cultures. This will strengthen efforts to create a more democratic political culture in Mexico. Political reforms will increase U.S. investor confidence and increase the flow of funds into Mexico, helping to modernize its economy and encourage additional cooperation in other areas.

BIBLIOGRAPHY

Aguilar, Hector Camin. *Despues del Milagro.* Mexico City, Mexico: Editorial Cal y Arena, 1993.

Aleman, Velasco. *Las Finanzas de la Politica.* Mexico City, Mexico: Editorial Diana, 1995.

Anzaldua, Gloria. *Borderland/La Frontera. The New Mestiza.* San Francisco, CA: Apinters/Aunt Lute, 1987.

Baird, Peter and Ed McCaughan. *Beyond the Border: Mexico and the United States Today.* New York: North American Congress on Latin America, 1979.

Benitez, Santiago Perez. "Nueva Agenda Bilateral en la Relacion Mexico-Estados Unidos," *Voices of Mexico* 44 (July-September 1998): 110–1.

Castaneda, Jorge G. *The Mexican Shock: Its Meaning for the US.* New York: The New Press, 1995.

———. "New Policies on Immigration?" *Newsweek International,* 13 March 2000, 2–4.

Dettmer, Jamie. "Mexican Smoke and American Mirrors," *Insight on the News* 15 (22 March 1999): 6–7.

Dornbierer, Manu. *El Prinosaurio: La Bestia Politica Mexicana.* Mexico City, Mexico: Editorial Grijalbo, 1994.

Kandell, Jonathan. *La Capital: The Biography of Mexico City.* New York: Henry Holt and Company, 1988.

Madrid-Barela, Arturo. "Pochos: The Different Americans, An Interpretative Essay, Part I," *Aztlan* 7 (Spring 1976).

Martinez, Carlos Gonzalez. "Mexico and the North American Gateway to Globalization," *Voices of Mexico* 44 (1998): 43–7.

Martinez, Glenn A. "Mojados, Malinches, and the Dismantling of the United States/Mexico Border in Contemporary Mexican Cinema," *Latin American Issues* 14 (1998): 31–50.

Noonan, John T. *Bribes.* New York: Macmillian Press, 1984.

O'Meara, Kelly, and Jamie Dettmer. "Mexican Officials Aren't Mopping Up The Blood," *Insight on the News* 14 (2 November 1998): 6–7

Oppenheimer, Andres. *Bordering on Chaos: Guerrillas, Stockbrokers, Politicians, and Mexico's Road to Prosperity.* Boston, Mass.: Little, Brown and Company, 1996.

Paz, Octavio. *Labyrinth of Solitude.* London: Penguin Books, 1990.

Purcell, Susan Kaufman, and Luis Rubio, ed. *Mexico Under Zedillo.* London: Lynne Rienner Publishers, 1998.

Riding, Alan. *Distant Neighbors: A Portrait of the Mexicans.* New York: Alfred A. Knopf, 1985.

Rodriguez, Richard. *Hunger of Memory.* Boston, Mass.: Godine Publishing, 1982.

———. *Days of Obligation.* New York: Viking, 1992.

Roman, Richard. "Now You See It, Now You Don't: The Different Border Realities for Labor and Capital in the NAFTA Era," *Latin American Issues* 14 (1998): 77–90.

Romero, Elizabeth Gutierrez. "Hemispheric Free Trade: The Discussion in the United States," *Voices of Mexico* 44 (July-September 1998): 63–5.

Rotella, Sebastian. *Twilight on the Line: Underworlds and Politics at the U.S.-Mexico Border.* New York: W.W. Norton and Company, 1998.

Samos, Julian *Los Mojados: The Wetback Story.* Notre Dame, Ind.: University of Notre Dame Press, 1971.

Shain, Yossi. "The Mexican-American Diaspora's Impact on Mexico," *Political Science Quarterly.* 114 (Winter 1999): 661–97.

Shorris, Earl. *Latinos.* New York: W.W. Norton, 1992.

Valenzuela, Gabriel Estrella. "The New Millennium and Mexico's Northern Border Population," *Voices of Mexico* 44 (July-September 1998): 47–52.

Vaquera-Vasquez, Santiago. "Wandering in The Borderlands: Mapping an Imaginative Geography of the Border," *Latin American Issues.* 14 (1998): 107–32.

West, Woody. "The Two Faces of Dual Nationality," *Insight on the News* 14 (15 June 1998): 48–51.

Dallas L. Browne

MOZAMBIQUE: INDEPENDENCE AND A DIRTY WAR

Modern Mozambique has been shaped by many forces, chief among these being its thirty-year war. The war began in 1962 and ended in 1992. Aspects of the conflict continue to impact Mozambique. Throughout the country, more than ten million antipersonnel mines make it risky to farm the large, fertile tracts of land. The mines continue to kill and maim long after the battles of the Cold War have ended. In addition, man-made famine, resulting in thousands of deaths, is a very recent memory. The foreign-sponsored "civil war" is officially over, but its effects linger on the Mozambican people, who struggle to move beyond the violent past and carve out a future.

HISTORICAL BACKGROUND

Colonial Rule

Portugal was Africa's longest-standing European colonial power. Prior to their arrival on the continent, Arab princes had established minor colonial empires along East Africa's coast stretching from Mogadishu in Somalia, down to Sofala in Mozambique. When Vasco da Gama circumnavigated Africa on his way to India (1497–98), he was surprised to discover well-ordered Swahili towns with merchants who regularly held fairs to secure gold and ivory from African kings in the interior. Chinese and Arab ships filled these ports, and merchants from India were common visitors. Portugal supplanted the Arabs and established its rule over this lucrative trade in order to use African gold and ivory to buy spices in Goa, India, which they then sold in Europe.

Muslims invaded Spain and Portugal in 700 A.D. They ruled these areas until the early 1400s, when Portugal attacked the Muslims both in

THE CONFLICT

Mozambique was a colony of Portugal for more than two hundred years. Following Mozambique's independence from Portugal in the early 1970s, the white minority governments of Rhodesia, now Zimbabwe, and South Africa, began to fund and direct a campaign to destabilize Mozambique. Brutal warfare and massive destruction of the infrastructure left Mozambique impoverished.

Political

* Rhodesia and South Africa did not want successful black governments in neighboring states, because it undermined their claim that Africans could not govern themselves.

* FRELIMO turned to the Soviet Union for funding following independence, declaring itself to be a socialist organization.

* Some Western nations, including the Untied States, provided funding for the South African-sponsored RENAMO, as a way of fighting the socialist FRELIMO.

CHRONOLOGY

700 A.D. Muslims invade and colonize Portugal and Spain.

1400s Portugal attacks and gains independence from its Muslim rulers, and it supplants them in Mozambique.

1506 Portugal establishes a city at Sofala, Mozambique.

1962 The Mozambique Liberation Front, FRELIMO, is formed in support of Mozambican independence.

1962 FRELIMO attacks a Portuguese garrison at Chai.

1974–75 The Carnation Revolution in Portugal leads Mozambique to independence.

1975 Mozambique is granted independence and Samoa Moises Machel becomes president.

1962–92 Warfare erupts between FRELIMO and the Rhodesian and South African-sponsored Mozambique National Resistance (RENAMO).

1984 Mozambique and South Africa sign the Nkomati Accord. Machel agrees to oust African National Congress militants from Mozambique, and South Africa agrees to stop arming and funding RENAMO and destabilizing Mozambique. The South African military, however, continues to support RENAMO.

1986 Machel dies in an airplane crash. Joachim Chissano becomes president.

1992 Chissano and Afonso Dhlakama sign a peace accord.

Europe and in Africa to regain control of its territory. The Portuguese were aware of Christian African kingdoms known as the Lost Kingdom of Prestor John. They circumnavigated Africa to find these kingdoms, enlisting the support of African Christian allies and attacking the Muslims from the rear, as well as through frontal assaults in Europe. The conquest yielded an additional benefit of a shorter trade route to the spices of India and the Far East. Thus, Portugal replaced Mozambique's Arab and Swahili Muslim merchants as local powers.

Portugal established a base at the city of Sofala, Mozambique, as early as 1506. Portugal ruled Mozambique from its Indian Ocean stronghold in Goa, India, until 1752, when it finally set up a Mozambican administration. Portuguese adventurers known as *sertanejos*, or backwoodsmen, explored the African interior. The *sertanejos* made contact with the powerful African emperor known as Munhumutapa, who controlled the gold mines in the interior. They befriended him and helped him subdue his enemies. The king of Portugal was subsequently granted land by the Munhumutapa, which was leased to Portuguese settlers for three generations at a time. The leaseholder had rights over the labor of the Africans living on the land as well. The *prazero*, or leaseholder, was obligated to defend the king's land and to do so, he developed a slave army. Slave soldiers were known as *chikunda*. They protected mines and trade routes under the command of their Portuguese master.

The Africans produced the food that they consumed; the *prazos* only produced what was needed, while siphoning resources. No internal market for agriculture developed, since developing large agricultural plantations made no sense without lucrative markets. The *prazeros* made money by waging war against African chiefs. The *prazos* captured and sold so many Africans that, eventually, gold mines were forced to shut down for lack of labor. Even military functions were often contracted out to enterprising African chiefs.

The *prazeros* operated like African chiefs, often marrying local women and creating *mestico*, mulatto or mixed black and white, children, who inherited their leases. The king of Portugal tried to halt the Africanization of his subjects by decreeing that females of the family would inherit all property exclusively, on condition that they marry a white male. Few white Portuguese males took up the offers of these rich *mestico donas*, mistresses. Thus, most *prazeros* ignored the king and married into other *prazero* families or sought mates from Goa in India. The Europeans became Africanized, though the *prazero* was meant to introduce Portuguese blood, culture, and values into Mozambique's interior.

Portuguese colonialism produced little economic development. Instead, great emphasis was placed on teaching Africans to speak Portuguese and on converting them to Catholicism. Many Mozambicans converted to Roman Catholicism during the colonial era, yet only thirty percent of Mozambique's population in the late 1990s were Christian; ten percent were Muslim, and sixty percent continued to follow indigenous religions. Portugal defended its colonial legacy by arguing that its policies toward Africans were liberal and enlightened. Portugal claimed that any African who learned its language, accepted its religion, and earned academic degrees would be accepted as an equal of the Portuguese. Africans who thought like, behaved like, talked like, and shared Portuguese values and beliefs were known as *assimilados*. Lack of money, however, often kept Africans from attending schools to learn how to assimilate. Most Africans considered the Portuguese policy a sham or a hoax.

Not surprisingly therefore, at the time of independence in 1975, ninety-five percent of Mozambique's African population was illiterate. There was one black doctor in the entire country, and in a nation that depended on agriculture—an estimated eighty-four percent of Mozambicans are farmers—there was only one black agronomist. More damaging to Portugal's colonial record of African uplift is the fact that out of four thousand university students only forty were African at independence. Most airports, telephone lines, roads, dams, ports, and power lines supported export-oriented industries that primarily profited the tiny Portuguese minority who ruled Mozambique. Not a single railroad or road linked north and south Mozambique. Roads ran east and west and took people and goods from the interior to the sea and then to Portugal or to formerly white-ruled South Africa. No effort was make to link the country internally and to foster national development.

Anti-Colonial Unrest

Anti-colonial unrest began in the 1950s with peaceful protest. After World War II Portugal became a staunch member of the North Atlantic Treaty Organization (NATO), a mutual defense organization of Western European nations. Portugal gained membership in NATO despite its being ruled by a fascist government that brutally oppressed both the people of Portugal and the people in Portugal's colonies, including Mozambique. The country tried to hold on to its colonies throughout the 1960s, even after Britain and France granted independence to most of their former African colonies. Peaceful protests and petitions for independence were repeatedly ignored. Mozambique's African nationalists decided that they had to fight for freedom. Failure of peaceful challenge, not ideology, led patriots to launch guerrilla warfare in the 1960s.

Most of the leaders of the independence movement in Mozambique were *assimilados*. White liberals worked closely with both *assimilados* and many *mestico* Mozambicans who looked forward to independence. African resistance in Mozambique was unified, unlike in Angola where three African movements fought one another for control of the government. When unarmed farmers protested Portugal's African agricultural policies they were murdered in cold blood at Mueda in June 1960. Such atrocities were not reported in the international press, but they occurred with increasing frequency. This Portuguese "culture of violence" radicalized young Mozambican Africans. One member of the Mozambique Liberation Front (FRELIMO) was reported by Eduardo Mondlane in *The Struggle for Mozambique* as saying: "I saw how the colonialists massacred the people at Mueda. That was when I lost my uncle. Our people were unarmed when they began to shoot them. I was determined to never again be unarmed in the face of Portuguese violence."

Portugal's International and State Police (PIDE) infiltrated and destroyed all of the African independence organizations that formed inside of Mozambique between 1940 and 1960. As a result, most of the prominent leaders of Mozambique's independence movements lived outside of the country during the 1960s. Eduardo Mondlane lived in the United States and married an American wife before he and his wife moved to Tanzania. He headed FRELIMO from Tanzania's capital, Dar es Salaam, until a rival faction of FRELIMO killed him with a letter bomb supplied by PIDE. The current president of Mozambique, Joachim Chissano, worked and studied in the United States, as well as in eastern and western Europe. Likewise, Mozambique's first president after independence, Samora Machel, lived in colonial capitals and neighboring independent African nations while struggling to liberate his country.

The Mozambique Liberation Front (FRELIMO)

Mozambique's African émigré population supported independence across Africa throughout the 1960s. Most of Mozambique's exiles were intellectuals who talked of an independent Mozambique. Julius Nyerere of Tanzania gave the émigrés money, housing, arms, training, intelligence support, and encouragement. Nyerere and Mondlane encouraged the three largest Mozambican independence movements to unite, forming FRELIMO in 1962. Within FRELIMO there was considerable debate about objectives and tactics. Mondlane fought to make the movement multiracial, while others wanted a purely African movement. The success with armed struggle in Guinea-Bissau led to a debate over armed struggle versus peaceful change, and incidents such as the massacre at Muede tipped the balance in favor of armed struggle. Some FRELIMO leaders wanted a capitalist independent nation, while others favored socialism. With Mondlane's assassination in 1969

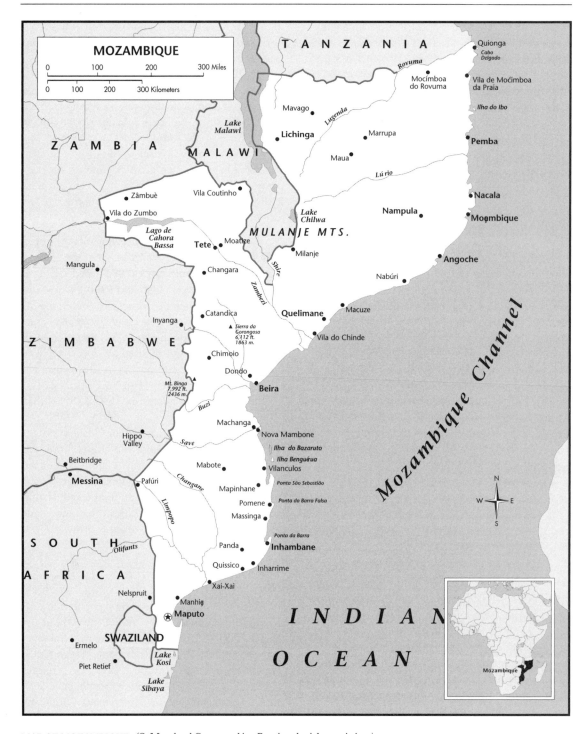

MAP OF MOZAMBIQUE. (© *Maryland Cartographics. Reprinted with permission.*)

and the rise of Samora Machel, FRELIMO committed itself to socialism.

On September 25, 1964, armed struggle exploded at Chai in northern Mozambique, when FRELIMO attacked an isolated Portuguese garrison. Portugal quickly rounded up and arrested over 1,500 FRELIMO insurgents in southern Mozambique, almost destroying the organization. At the same time, Portugal was fighting wars in Guinea-Bissau and Angola. FRELIMO took advantage of Portugal's thinly spread forces to launch attacks on Portuguese forces.

Portugal exploited the fact that most of FRELIMO's leadership was *mestico* originating in the south, turned the Makua and Makonde ethnic groups there against FRELIMO. Such divide-and-conquer tactics worked extremely well. A civil conflict, instigated by PIDE, broke out among Africans, and FRELIMO appeared weak in 1968 and 1970. To win over the African population, FRELIMO soft-peddled its socialist ideology and stopped criticizing African beliefs in witchcraft and other traditional practices; in the past these beliefs would have condemned Africans in FRELIMO-controlled zones to rigorous "re-education" programs. This new approach helped FRELIMO win over African peasants, many of whom FRELIMO's leaders considered to be superstitious and backward. FRELIMO even began to recruit witchdoctors as military commanders because many peasants had faith in the traditional healers and were willing to follow them.

Portugal responded by creating *aldeamentos*, or protected villages. Africans were rounded up and forced to move into fortified villages guarded by Portuguese soldiers. These villages were designed to stifle FRELIMO recruiting efforts, permit Portugal to provide social and other services to peasants inexpensively, and establish a defense perimeter around Portuguese-controlled areas. Portugal placed sixty thousand soldiers in the field to fight against ten thousand FRELIMO fighters. Of these soldiers, forty thousand were African troops under the command of white and *assimilado* officers. FRELIMO troops fought a hit-and-run war. They attacked Portuguese troops and African self-defense units. When large rockets, provided by the Soviet Union, were available FRELIMO used these to attack large Portuguese military bases and Portuguese-controlled towns.

FRELIMO pushed its troops further south, eventually threatening Vila Pery District and the white settlers south of the Zambezi. The war came close to Beira and major population centers. Portuguese troops were so thinly spread that they lost their effectiveness and FRELIMO stepped up attacks. They used sympathetic Africans to infiltrate farms, factories, and government installations. Portugal overreacted by destroying peasant villages and forcing people to move into *aldeamentos*. This led to a dramatic growth in FRELIMO membership in areas that previously had been indifferent.

Independence

The African guerrilla war put enough pressure on Portugal to contribute to the Carnation Revolution (1974–75). Many soldiers in the Portuguese army discovered that the African guerrillas were not demons, terrorists, or villains, but freedom-loving patriots and the Portuguese returned home and struggled against the rulers of Portugal, such as President António de Oliveira Salazar and his successor Marcello Caetano. The soldiers overthrew what they viewed as a common enemy and granted their African "fellow sufferers" their freedom. The guerrilla war was an important catalyst which made independence possible.

The European Community was another factor that contributed to Mozambique's independence. By 1970 Portugal had earned associate status membership in the European organization and was progressing toward full membership. Young Portuguese began directing their ambitions of economic development toward Europe. Youth began to view Portugal's colonies as failed enterprises that should be jettisoned. Moreover, full membership in the European Community demanded that Portugal divest itself of its colonies by granting them independence. High tariff barriers and protected colonial markets were not compatible with membership in the European Community. The vision of Portugal's leader, António de Oliveira Salazar, of an international Portuguese nation in which the colonies became states, died as Portugal integrated its economy with Western industrial nations.

Mozambique was granted independence on June 25, 1975, and Samora Moises Machel became its first president. Machel established a single party state ruled by FRELIMO. Machel was a pragmatist: He adopted socialism to please his patron, Julius Nyerere, of Tanzania. Nyerere had armed, trained, and supported Mozambique's fighters when few had faith in their ability to win their freedom. Machel's socialism also symbolized opposition to the continuation of colonial policy. In addition, Machel believed that to build and maintain modern institutions, such as schools, hospitals, banks, and corporations, that were needed to improve the lives of Mozambique's majority, the government needed to adopt socialism. The reality was that Machel needed money and the West would not fund Mozambique's development. By claiming to be a socialist he hoped to secure this money from the Eastern Bloc. The Eastern Bloc was the group of communist countries allied with the Soviet Union at that time. The Eastern Bloc's military support and the armaments it supplied delighted Machel, but he was disappointed that so little was offered for economic development.

Machel once observed that Britain sent members of its upper and middle classes to settle in and improve many of its colonies and thus British colonies thrived and flourished. These colonists were generally well educated, enterprising, and understood how to build successful businesses. By contrast, Portugal sent its lowest classes to Africa.

These Europeans often could not read and write themselves, so they did not see why Africans needed education. Moreover, they took not only top jobs, but also semi-skilled and even unskilled jobs, leaving only the lowest types of work for Africans. They were ignorant, wasteful, and often corrupt. Failing to understand or appreciate notions such as efficiency and forward planning, they left a terrible legacy for Mozambique's African majority. Mozambicans were bitter and discontent for good reason. Portugal offered them little beyond back-breaking, underpaid, under-appreciated work that resembled slavery. The African tradition of *cadonga,* or buying and selling on the thriving black market, was, and remains, a means of creating a second economy that met their needs and allowed them to express their entrepreneurial skills, despite being denied opportunities to become capitalists in the official economy.

Civil War (1972–92)

The second war was a Mozambican version of the Cold War, when the ideological conflict between Western nations and the Soviet Union led to conflict throughout the world. In Africa the Cold War was costly and deadly, as millions died in defense of ideologies that few truly understood. What Mozambicans really wanted was the right to determine their own futures and free themselves from the worst forms of exploitation. Instead, they found themselves ensnared in armies, fighting deadly, dirty "proxy wars." In the United States, Europe, and the former Soviet Union confrontation led to blustering and threats. In Africa and elsewhere, confrontation led to death, destruction of vital infrastructure, and suffering.

Apartheid—legalized racial segregation and separation—was the policy used by an Afrikaner white minority to dominate both the South African English and the African majority. The apartheid regime of South Africa clung to power. It feared that allowing an African regime to thrive next door in Mozambique would undermine its argument that Africans were incapable of self-rule. The Afrikaners therefore attempted to thwart African independence along their borders. When they failed to stop Mozambique's majority from gaining independence, they resorted to a deliberate policy of destabilization to discredit the regime. The main instrument of destabilization was the Mozambique National Resistance (RENAMO).

RENAMO was first created by Ian Smith's white minority rulers in Southern Rhodesia. Robert Mugabe and African freedom fighters used liberated areas within Mozambique as staging grounds for attacks against Ian Smith's white minority regime. Southern Rhodesia's army believed that its best defense was to divide Africans, create internal disputes, suspicion and doubt, destroy their confidence and African unity, and create a civil war that would turn Africans against each other. The Africans overwhelming numerical majority would thus be neutralized and cease to be a threat to continued minority rule in Rhodesia and South Africa. The key to this "dirty little war" was to turn the African peasants against the freedom fighters. After all, it was the peasants who made guerrilla warfare successful by feeding, housing, hiding, and sympathizing with freedom fighters.

In Mozambique, white Rhodesian army intelligence officers—like the Portuguese before them—discovered that FRELIMO sought to modernize agriculture in liberated zones. FRELIMO attacked selected aspects of traditional African culture that they felt kept Africans from advancing. They labeled traditional healers witch-doctors and ridiculed their practices. Many healers were so shamed that they went into hiding for long periods. Anthropologist Christian Gefray argued that FRELIMO alienated other peasants by forcing them to abandon traditional family homesteads and move miles away to live and work on state-owned collective farms. As the war became more violent these state farms were targeted and, therefore, often unsafe. RENAMO recruited among such disaffected peasants. As the civil war grew worse peasant living standards fell and RENAMO's recruitment rose.

The Rhodesian army recruited and trained this discontented, but influential, element. Rhodesia's chief intelligence officer, Ken Flower, claims that he created RENAMO to punish Mozambique for supporting Zimbabwean liberation forces. Zimbabwe was the name given to Southern Rhodesia after its independence. Flower hoped that RENAMO would force FRELIMO to cut off support for Zimbabwe's president, Robert Mugabe. The preferred technique was sabotage. Flower's goal, stated in Martin and Johnson's *Destructive Engagement: Southern Africa at War,* was,

> to disrupt the population and disrupt the economy which really comes under sabotage, to come back with decent recruits at that stage and hit FRELIMO bases they came across. And if they came across ZANLA [Zimbabwe African National Liberation Army] they were to take them on.

From the beginning RENAMO was thus a creation of white and black mercenaries. It was not a movement indigenous to Mozambique, and it lacked an ideology or purpose other than to frustrate the legitimate aspirations of black Africans. The leader of RENAMO, Afonso Dhlakama, sanctioned atrocities as a way of undermining the community. RENAMO would sweep through villages, killing the mature men and women and capturing young boys and girls. The children were forced to kill or they would face beatings, starvation, or even execution—they fought to stay alive. These child soldiers became tools of Dhlakama. Drugs were freely distributed to the child troops. Boy soldiers as young as twelve were recruited by force, then made to commit atrocities against their own families. Young girls were sexually exploited. RENAMO leaders used misleading information and outright disinformation to manipulate the children.

RENAMO decimated the country and its people by burning cooperative farms, destroying bridges and railway lines, killing educated doctors and teachers who worked with FRELIMO, and destroying schools, hospitals, and any institution that would advance Mozambicans. Factories were burned to the ground. No attempt was made by RENAMO to build a single bridge, school, hospital, or factory. Its Rhodesian and South African masters wanted to show Mozambican peasants that FRELIMO could neither protect them nor provide needed services. When Robert Mugabe won the war against Ian Smith for Rhodesian (now Zimbabwean) independence, white Rhodesian intelligence officers turned RENAMO over to BOSS, South Africa's intelligence service; the South African Defense Force and its Military Intelligence Department (MID) took over arms supplies and training for RENAMO in 1980. Right-wing elements in the United States and the United Kingdom also provided funding for RENAMO because they did not like FRELIMO's socialist stance and the fact that the Soviet Union financed FRELIMO.

Emboldened by Ronald Reagan's election to president in the United States, RENAMO attacked Nelson Mandela's African National Congress (ANC) offices in Mozambique. Such raids failed to weaken support for FRELIMO or the ANC. With South African and U.S. support, RENAMO's fighting forces grew from one thousand to eight thousand. Since FRELIMO needed railroads to export products and earn money from trade, RENAMO destroyed them. RENAMO destroyed eighteen hundred schools, preventing more than three hundred thousand children from receiving a basic education. RENAMO destroyed one out of every four hospitals and clinics. It looted and vandalized, and forcibly recruited Africans to serve as porters to carry their loot to safe havens in Malawi.

JACKIE D'ALMEIDA, DIRECTOR OF THE MINING CLEARING PROGRAM OF MOZAMBIQUE, LOOKS ON AS A MEMBER OF THE TEAM SEARCHES FOR MINES THAT RECENT FLOODS MAY HAVE DISPLACED. *(AP/Wide World Photos. Reproduced by permission.)*

Dhlakama is from the Ndau ethnic group, near Zimbabwe's border. In this area of Mozambique RENAMO was strong and set up "areas of control" where peasants were forcibly resettled to safe areas around RENAMO military bases. Peasants farmed their traditional family homesteads, but they were expected to feed RENAMO troops without compensation. Though Ndau was the language used widely by all tribes in this zone and many of RENAMO's most loyal foot soldiers were Ndau, RENAMO was not a tribal organization. Its leaders came from many different Mozambican ethnic groups. RENAMO did not make appeals to new recruits based on ethnic loyalty or identification, rather it offered new recruits opportunities to rob, loot, and make themselves wealthy.

RECENT HISTORY AND THE FUTURE

President Samora Machel and FRELIMO launched a diplomatic initiative. Machel visited British Prime Minister Margaret Thatcher in the 1980s, and Thatcher introduced Machel to U.S. President Ronald Reagan. Reagan was impressed with Machel and subsequently ordered the United States to oppose right-wing efforts within South Africa to overthrow the Mozambican leader. Mozambique, therefore, became an exception to Reagan's "constructive engagement" policy that normally supported the white minority apartheid regime then in power in South Africa and its efforts to influence politics in its surrounding area. Machel and South Africa signed the Nkomati Accord in 1984. Machel pledged to oust ANC militants from Mozambique, and South Africa promised to stop arming, training, and funding RENAMO and destabilizing Mozambique.

Right-wing South African soldiers, however, never intended to honor this agreement. They disagreed with the soft line taken by moderate South African diplomats. Documents uncovered in a raid on Casa Banana revealed what P.W. van der Westhuizen, head of MID for the South African military, was reported by James Ciment in *Angola and Mozambique: Postcononial Wars in Southern Africa* to have told Dhlakama, "We, the military, will continue to give them [RENAMO] support without the consent of our politicians in a massive way so they can win the war." Machel was hoodwinked and humiliated. Nyerere of Tanzania and other African presidents were angry and significantly increased military aid and training to FRELIMO.

Thousands of Tanzanian troops appeared in Mozambique to defend transportation corridors and support FRELIMO. The United States dropped its ban on bilateral aid to helped Machel, who was able to reschedule Mozambique's debt. The United States and the International Monetary Fund made Mozambique adhere to strict regulations. Its currency was devalued and efforts to make consumer goods available in the countryside were curtailed. Peasants wanted more consumer goods in return for producing more crops for consumption and export. As production rose, FRELIMO collected more taxes, which it used to step up military efforts against RENAMO. By 1990 Mozam-

bique was the world's poorest country with a per capita income of only US$80. In comparison, Somalia's per capita income was nearly twice as much. Aid programs that flooded Mozambique with free food undermined peasant farmers and reduced the country's sovereignty by making it dependent on foreign aid. In the midst of the chaos, non-governmental organizations (NGOs), especially aid organizations, moved into Mozambique to help. The NGOs hired the best and brightest people away from FRELIMO by offering higher salaries. Some analysts claimed that Western NGOs were "re-colonizing" Mozambique.

President Machel was killed in a mysterious plane crash in 1986. Joachim Chissano became president and he adhered closely to World Bank and IMF guidelines for Mozambique, resulting in Mozambique achieving the world's highest economic growth rate. On October 4, 1992, President Chissano, the head of FRELIMO, and Afonso Dhlakama, leader of RENAMO, signed a peace accord in Rome, Italy. The treaty was enforced by more than twenty thousand U.N. troops, who insured that all weapons were surrendered to the United Nations, and all armed groups were disbanded within six months. United Nations troops left Mozambique in January of 1995. The country became a model economic state until devastating floods in the late 1990s destroyed years of progress.

BIBLIOGRAPHY

Anderson, Hilary. *Mozambique: A War Against the People.* New York: St. Martin's Press, 1992.

Chan, Stephen, and Moises Vanancio. *War and Peace in Mozambique.* New York: St. Martin's Press, 1998.

Ciment, James. *Angola and Mozambique: Postcononial Wars in Southern Africa.* New York: Facts On File, 1997.

Finnegan, W. *A Complicated War: the Harrowing of Mozambique.* Berkeley, Calif.: University of California Press, 1992.

Hall, Margaret, and Tom Young. *Confronting Leviathan: Mozambique Since Independence.* Athens, Ohio: Ohio University Press, 1997.

Hume, Cameron. *Ending Mozambique's War: The Role of Mediation and Good Offices.* Washington, D.C.: United States Institute of Peace Press, 1994.

Huntington, Samuel. *The Clash of Civilizations and the Remaking of World Order.* New York: Simon and Schuster, 1996.

Martin, D. and P. Johnson, eds. *Destructive Engagement: Southern Africa at War.* Harare, Zimbabwe: Zimbabwe Publishing House, 1986.

Minter, William. *Apartheid's Contras: An Inquiry Into the Roots of War in Angola and Mozambique.* London: Zed Books, 1994.

Mondlane, Eduardo. *The Struggle for Mozambique.* New York: Penguin, 1969.

Nelson, Harold D., ed. *Mozambique: A Country Study.* Washington, D.C.: Foreign Area Studies. American University, 1984.

Nordstrom, Carolyn. *A Different Kind of War Story.* Philadelphia, Penn.: University of Pennsylvania Press, 1997.

Ramsay, F. Jeffress. *Global Studies: Africa.* Sluice Dock, N.Y.: Dushkin-McGraw Hill, 1997.

Shawcross, William. *Deliver Us From Evil: Peacekeepers, Warlords and A World of Endless Conflict.* New York: Simon and Schuster, 2000

Vines, Alex. *RENAMO: Terrorism in Mozambique.* Bloomington, Ind.: Indiana University Press, 1991.

Dallas L. Browne

MYANMAR: THE AGONY OF A PEOPLE

THE CONFLICT

Rebel groups have been battling the government of Myanmar, formerly Burma. The government has been criticized for its harsh suppression of rebels and protestors.

Political

- The government of Myanmar has been criticized for denying human and civil rights and for violently suppressing protestors, including lengthy imprisonment and torture.

- Rebel groups have used kidnapping and hostage taking to protest the government.

Ethnic

- Many of the minority ethnic and religious groups in Myanmar feel marginalized and oppressed.

Myanmar, better known to the rest of the world as Burma, is a strategically important country situated in Southeast Asia. For well over a decade, especially since 1988, the country has been in the news because of the military government's ruthless suppression of the democracy movement and its disregard for basic human rights. Politics, however, is not the only source of conflict in this land of Buddhist pagodas. Ethnic, linguistic, racial, economic, religious, and, perhaps, ideological reasons complicate the political situation there. Trafficking in illicit drugs through what is called the Golden Triangle—an area where the borders of three southeast Asian countries, Thailand, Myanmar and Laos meet—adds another dimension to the Burmese problem. As a result, Myanmar, once a prosperous, agriculturally self-sufficient country, has become one of the poorest countries in the world today.

The conflict in Myanmar has manifested itself in different forms at different times and places. In October 1999, a group of students, exiled from Myanmar, took over the Myanmar embassy in Bangkok, Thailand, and held forty people hostage. Thai officials described them as "student activists" and did not treat them as terrorists. Moreover, Thais, in order to secure the release of hostages, arranged safe passage for these students to an area of Myanmar border controlled by rebel groups. In response, Myanmar temporarily closed its borders with Thailand.

In February 2000, two ethnic Karen boys, Johnny and Luther Htoo, made international headlines. (Karen is one of the minority ethnic groups in Myanmar.) These twelve-year-old, cigar-smoking boys are the "generals" of God's Army, a Karen Christian guerrilla group fighting for independence from Myanmar. A group from the guerrilla organization took control of a hospital in neighboring Thailand. They held eight hundred patients and hospital employees as hostages for twenty-two hours. Thai security forces stormed the hospital and killed all ten members of the guerrilla organization. According to reports, some of the guerrillas had earlier participated in the take-over of the Myanmar embassy in Bangkok. The Myanmar forces have since then raided and destroyed their bases. In a recent filmed interview with Reuters (July 2000) the Htoos have denied any responsibility for this attack on the hospital. They maintained that the Burmese government soldiers, not the Thais, were their enemies.

Johnny and Luther Htoo represent one aspect of the conflict in Myanmar: that of ethnic minorities fighting for autonomy from the government in Yangon (formerly Rangoon). The Htoos represent one faction of the Karen rebels who have been fighting against the national government for more than five decades. The Htoos began their campaign as a reaction to a government raid of their village. The armed forces raped the women, killed men in front of their families, and then burnt the houses in the village. According to an Amnesty International report, government forces regularly mistreat people in rebel areas.

Aung San Suu Kyi, the daughter of the revered national hero Aung San, has been in the news ever since she returned home to Myanmar from London in 1988. Her struggle against the military government has resulted in her being placed under house arrest for more than six years. After her release, when she tried to visit her party's offices outside Yangon, in July and August of 1998, the government prevented her from going there. In July Burmese soldiers stopped her on a bridge outside Yangon. She sat inside her car for six days. Finally, unable to starve her into submission, one of the soldiers took control of the car and drove her back to Yangon. In August 1998 when she set out to go to Bassein to visit supporters of her party she was prepared to stay in the car for a while. The military government saw it as a calculated attempt on the part of Suu Kyi to embarrass it in the eyes of the international community. According to diplomatic sources the soldiers towed her van to the same bridge where she spent six days in July and later forced her to return to Yangon. The government was criticized for its handling of the situation. In April 1999 Dr. Michael Aris, Suu Kyi's husband, died of prostate cancer. The military authorities did not allow him to visit her in Yangon, and she could not go to London to see him for fear that the gov-

CHRONOLOGY

1886 Burma becomes a province of British India.

1937 Burma is separated from India.

1942 Japan invades Burma.

1945 The Anti-Fascist People's Freedom League, led by nationalist hero Aung San, turns against the Japanese and helps the Allies to reoccupy Burma.

1947 The Burmese win independence. Aung San wins the first election, but is assassinated before taking office.

1948 U Nu becomes the first prime minister. The Karen ethnic group begins its struggle for autonomy.

1976 Ethnic liberation groups continue to rebel, ultimately controlling much of the countryside.

1988 Thousands are killed by the military following student protests. Daw Aung San Suu Kyi, the daughter of Aung San, becomes a leader in the resistance movement and is ultimately imprisoned.

1991 Aung San Suu Kyi is awarded the Nobel Peace Prize but is not permitted to travel to receive it.

2000 Protests persist. Sanctions against the military *junta* in Myanmar continue. God's Army, an ethnic Karen rebel group led by Johnny and Luther Htoo, take control of a hospital in neighboring Thailand.

ernment would not let her back into Myanmar. When Dr. Aris died, he had not seen his wife since 1995.

Although the Internet and e-mail are the means of communication and information in many parts of the world, in Myanmar these media are prohibited for ordinary citizens. Owning a modem is illegal and can result in a jail sentence of fifteen years. A Burmese man, James Nichols, was imprisoned for illegally operating telephone and fax lines; he later died in jail. Today, modems are restricted to use only by foreigners, top government officials, and business people with close contact with the military government. In December 1999 the government banned private e-mail providers. The Ministry of Post and Telegraph is the only agency authorized to provide e-mail service in Myanmar. The military *junta* is afraid that the

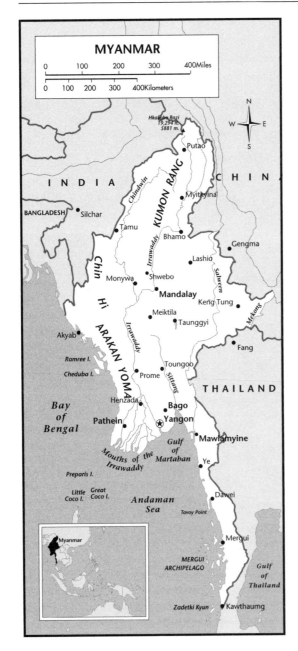

MAP OF MYANMAR. (© *Maryland Cartographics. Reprinted with permission.*)

Internet and e-mail will become dangerous tools in the hand of dissidents.

This continued repression of the people, their leaders and the opposition political parties caused U.S. President Bill Clinton on May 4, 2000 to suspend all economic aid to Myanmar. The president declared that Myanmar was ineligible for American trade and investment programs. He prohibited the sale of weapons to the country and declared his intention to block economic aid to Myanmar from international organizations. The United States

would also downgrade its diplomatic representation in Yangon to *chargé d'affaires* level and restrict visas for senior Burmese officials and their families.

HISTORICAL BACKGROUND

Geography and Climate

Between the two Asian giants of India and China, Myanmar is also bordered by Bangladesh in the west and Laos and Thailand in the east. The Bay of Bengal and the Andaman Sea form the southern and southwestern boundaries. Its situation on the main Indian Ocean shipping lines (extending from Australia to the Middle East), make Myanmar a strategically important nation. Almost the size of the state of Texas (768,500 square kilometers) or a little smaller than Namibia, Myanmar, according to 1999 estimates, has a population of more than forty-eight million.

The eastern coastal areas constitute lower Myanmar and the interior region to the north is called upper Myanmar. Its long coastline (1930 kilometers) is blessed with many excellent natural harbors. The Irravady is the most important river in the country. It originates in the Himalayan mountains and runs through the middle of the country. Most of the ancient cities and the capital of Myanmar are on the eastern side of the river. The mountainous regions in the west and the north form Myanmar's natural boundaries. The Arakan Yoma Range separates the country from the Indian subcontinent. The highest mountain peak, Mt. Hkakabo Razi (19,296 feet) is in the north.

Monsoons bring rains to Myanmar. Some areas receive up to two hundred inches of rainfall annually. Most of the monsoons come between May and September. During monsoon season, landslides, cyclones, and flooding are common. The hot, humid summer season lasts from March to May.

Geography has placed Myanmar and Thailand in the same region. The historic rivalry between the two is a source of continuing conflict and tension. The movie *Anna and the King* mentions this rivalry and shows how one domestic faction used it against the king and the country. In the north, China borders the country and the Mongols from China once attacked Myanmar. It shares a long border with India and that border is another area of concern for the Burmese authorities.

Ethnic Groups

Ethnic diversity is a source of conflict in Myanmar. It is the most ethnically diverse country in mainland Southeast Asia. Complicating this diversity is the fact that each ethnic group has its own language. People have lived in Myanmar since the Stone Age. The Mons were one of the first people to come to the country. They came from western China. Some scholars suggest that Indian emperor Ashoka had sent a Buddhist mission to the Mons. By the beginning of the Christian era, however, Mons were well established in lower Myanmar. It was during this period that the Indian religious, commercial and political influence began to take hold in Myanmar. Gradually there occurred a harmonious blending of Indian and Mon cultural elements.

The Pyus occupied the western side of Irravady. By the eighth century A.D. the Pyus were overrun by invaders. The descendants of these invaders are the modern day Karens. The Burmans migrated to Myanmar and established themselves in the country by the ninth century A.D. They conquered the Mons and drove the Karens to the east of the river. The Mons introduced the Burmans to Indian culture, which the Burmans gradually adopted.

Burmans now constitute the dominant majority population in the country. The most important ethnic minorities are the Shans, Karens, Mons, Chins, Kachins, and the Arakanese. The Karens live in lower Myanmar in the Kayah state. The Shans are found on the hills along the Thai border. The Mons can be found in the delta region of Myanmar. The Chins inhabit the mountainous regions in the northwest. Along the Chinese border live the Kachin people. Most Burmese people are related to the Chinese and the Tibetans. In addition, there are other ethnic groups of varying size and strength living in Burma, including large numbers of Chinese and Indians.

Religion

Complicating the problem of ethnic and linguistic diversity is the religious factor. Most Burmese are Buddhists. They follow mostly the Theravada branch of Buddhism, also known as Hinayana or the Lesser Vehicle. Theravada Buddhism is conservative and fundamentalist and uses Buddhist scriptures written in Pali, an ancient Indian language used by Gautama Buddha. In Theravada tradition, the individual is responsible for his/her own salvation. Good deeds make one an *arhat* or a perfect saint. In the other main branch of Buddhism, the Mahayana tradition, the person who becomes a saint or *bodhisattva* is ready for salvation or *nirvana*. However, the saint, rather than achieving nirvana, postpones it to help others to become *bodhisattvas*.

TWELVE-YEAR OLD JOHNNY HTOO SMOKES A CIGAR DURING A MEETING WITH THE ASSOCIATED PRESS AT THE JUNGLE BASE OF THE FRINGE REBEL GROUP, KAREN, IN MYANMAR. *(AP/Wide World Photos. Reproduced by permission.)*

Buddhism entered Myanmar from India, its land of origin. Although Burmese tradition suggests that Buddha himself had visited the region, Buddhism probably took root in the land only in the seventh century A.D. Compared to Hinduism, with its strict caste system, many gods, rituals, and Brahmin dominance, Buddhism was a much simpler religion. Buddhism was easy to join and practice.

Theravada Buddhism came from Sri Lanka and south India. Burmese Buddhism does not completely follow Buddhist scriptures. Elements of the Burmese animistic past are readily mixed with Buddhist teachings and practices in modern Burma. The mixing and mingling were not necessarily planned, but are also not easily noticed.

While an overwhelming majority (eighty-nine percent) follow Buddhism, there are other religions such as Christianity and Islam that are practiced by the ethnic minorities in Myanmar. Christianity and Islam each constitute about 4 percent of the total religious make-up of the population. While the Karens and the Shans are mostly Christian, the Arakanese are Buddhists and Muslims. During the British colonial rule, Christian

U AUNG SAN

1916–1947 Aung San was born in 1916 in Natmuak, Burma, into a family active in anti-colonial resistance. As a student at Rangoon University in 1936, he joined the nationalist student group *Thankin* ("Master," the term Burmese were required to use when addressing the British), and led a student strike. After graduating from the university in 1938, he joined the Dobaya Asi-ayone (We-Burmans Association), becoming its secretary-general in 1939.

During World War II, Aung San allied with the Japanese against the British. He was appointed secretary of defense, and raised the Burmese Independence Army, which took over local administration of Japanese-occupied territories. As the war progressed, Aung San grew to distrust Japanese motives, and in March 1945 joined the Allies (the United States, Britain, Soviet Union, and France).

After World War II, Aung San founded the Anti-Fascist People's Freedom League. When the British returned, Aung San was imprisoned as a traitor. The Burmese revolted, and he was released and given a cabinet position. In 1946 he traveled to London and negotiated Burmese independence. In 1947 Aung San's AFPFL party won 196 of 202 seats in the elections. On July 19, 1947, as the constitution was being drafted, Prime Minister Aung San and most of his cabinet were assassinated by political rivals.

missionaries converted large number of ethnic minorities to their faith.

Islam came to Myanmar during the fourteenth century, probably through Indian merchants who had already accepted the Islamic faith. It was relatively quick and simple to become a Muslim and the democratic and egalitarian nature of Islam was also attractive. Like other religions of Myanmar, Islam also contains elements from other religions and ancient practices of Myanmar. This religious diversity has caused serious problems for Myanmar. The fact that different ethnic groups practice different religions has greatly contributed to the intensity of conflict in Myanmar.

History

People have lived in Myanmar since the prehistoric times. The Mons, Pyus, and Burmans who came at different periods settled mostly in the delta regions (near the water). It was here that they built cities and kingdoms. These early kingdoms were greatly influenced by Indian Buddhist and Hindu ideas. Political unification, however, came only in the eleventh century A.D. Unification was achieved by the rulers of Pagan (Bagan) who conquered the Mons of lower Irrawady. The new Burmese rulers maintained close contact with the Ceylonese (now Sri Lankans) and the Indians from southern India. During the thirteenth century Mongols under Kublai Khan invaded and destroyed the Pagan kingdom. Two centuries later, the Burmese were reunited under the Toungoo dynasty (1546). Nevertheless, unhappy with their life under the majority, minorities were already setting up their own kingdoms within Burma. During this time, Europeans began to enter the country as traders.

During the middle of the eighteenth century, Burma was, once again, reunited. This unification was under the Konbaung dynasty (1756), which conquered the Shans and attacked Thailand. Having defeated the Thais, the Burmese enslaved thousands of them. Toward the beginning of the nineteenth century, Konbaug power began to decline. The British were a colonial power in India, and under Burmese king Bagyidaw, relations between the Burmese and the British in India worsened. Consequently, the two countries—Burma and British India—fought three wars between 1824 and 1885. As a result, Burma was gradually absorbed into the British Indian Empire; the absorption was completed in 1886.

The majority of Burmans were under direct colonial British rule and Burmese socio-economic and religious life suffered. The ethnic minorities, however, were allowed a certain freedom in managing local affairs and institutions. Minorities, therefore, developed a stronger sense of group identity during the colonial period. This helped to increase the rivalry between the majority Burmans and the minority groups. The British rulers recruited large number of ethnic minorities into the police and the army and these recruits were often useful in suppressing any sign of majority Burman rebellion.

In 1935 Myanmar received limited autonomy from Britain. Two years later, Myanmar was separated from the British Indian Empire. Gradually, there emerged a nationalist movement led by educated Burmans living in the cities. These nationalists emphasized Burmese language, religion, and culture; because of the lingual, religious, and cultural diversity of Burma, minority groups were uneasy about the Burman's intentions. The Burmans' nationalist movement was anti-Indian, anti-Chinese, and anti-capitalist, in response to the previous Indian and Chinese control of the economic

THE INTERNET: "A PLATFORM FOR TROUBLEMAKERS"

The Myanmar Computer Federation estimates that there are more than fifty thousand computers currently in operation in Myanmar. However, they are not networked and do not have access to the Internet, which officials have declared a "platform for troublemakers." The few hundred people in Myanmar who are allowed e-mail and Internet access must go through the server established in January 2000 by the government's information ministry. Among the ministry rules are prohibitions against posting any writing "detrimental to the state of the Union" and instructions on how to obtain permission to create Web pages. These regulations are likely to remain in effect as long as sites like BurmaNet and its accompanying e-mail listserv burmanet-l remain online. Created in 1995 by the Free Burma Coalition, BurmaNet has members in twenty-eight countries and is considered to be one of the most successful cyber-activist organizations currently in operation. It collects and distributes information from exile groups located in Myanmar's border regions and actively campaigns for international economic sanctions, selective purchasing laws, and tourism boycotts. Organizers credit their success to the power of the Internet, which allowed them the ability to rapidly create a community out of exiles scattered worldwide and to disseminate information to them quickly and cheaply.

Political activism on the Internet has blossomed in the last decade. Lauded in news accounts as "the greatest democratizer the world has ever seen" because it is "nonhierarchical, interactive, and global," the Internet has web sites for anyone and any organization with electronic access and an issue to publicize. This freedom, which has allowed for groups such as the Free Burma Coalition to lobby international organizations successfully, has also spawned cyber-hactivists. Also dedicated to social protest, hactivists target government and institutional Web sites for virtual sit-ins. One group, the Electronic Disturbance Theater of New York City, let users download software that repeatedly phone their

Web target and then search on the word truth, actions which seriously hampered a site's ability to function. Scorned by more traditional cyber-activists, who criticize such conduct as bad netiquette that could justify government censorship of the Internet, hactivists' future plans include more interactive programs that will permit users to virtually march on their targets.

These types of Internet protests and campaigns have caused many governments to impose Internet restrictions similar to those enforced in Myanmar. China established the Internet Information Management Bureau to stop the "infiltration of harmful information" to its nearly nine million Internet users. Its security certification process is aimed at cyber news services and other content providers and strives to insure that information published has the "correct orientation for public opinions." Internet use in Singapore, a country trying to exploit the commercial applications of the Internet, is monitored by the Singapore Broadcasting Authority, which searches for content published by individuals or organizations that would "tend to bring the Government into hatred or contempt." E-mail is regularly censored in Bahrain with offenders receiving jail time for e-mailing information considered to be politically sensitive to dissidents living outside the country. Cyber activists are concerned that any type of censorship will eventually hurt their causes and they worry about the growing trend of many governments, including the United States and Great Britain, to legislate the use of encryption technology. For governments interested in the e-mail of its citizens, encryption programs that allow for the private transmission of data such as credit card numbers can complicate interceptions.

In the meanwhile, Myanmar has gone on the Internet offensive. While it still restricts Internet use to a select few, it now sends daily propaganda sheets and newspaper summaries to the BurmaNet listserv.

---

life of the country. In addition, the movement emphasized Buddhism to the exclusion of all other religions, further offending minorities, especially the Burmese Christians.

During the 1930s and 1940s, Aung San and U Nu led the nationalist movement. Aung San had

formed a group called the Thirty Comrades, who were greatly attracted by Japanese anti-colonial propaganda. Hoping that the Japanese were serious about their anti-colonial stand, the nationalists tried to secure their help against the British. During the Second World War, Aung San and his associates worked with the Japanese for a while. When

AUNG SAN SUU KYI, OPPOSITION LEADER OF THE MYANMAR GOVERNMENT AND NOBEL PEACE PRIZE WINNER, ADDRESSES THE UNITED NATIONS COMMISSION ON HUMAN RIGHTS. *(AP/Wide World Photos. Reproduced by permission.)*

they realized that the Japanese had colonial and imperialist tendencies of their own, the Burmese nationalists broke their alliance with the Japanese. Instead they formed an Anti-Fascist People's Freedom League. The Thirty Comrades provided the leadership for the country during the post-colonial, post-war Burma.

Aung San's work against Japanese imperialism made him a national hero much like George Washington in the United States or Mahatma Gandhi in India. All segments of Burmese population opposed continued British rule in the country after World War II. In January of 1947, Aung San and his associates were able to persuade England to organize a convention to prepare a constitution for Myanmar. In the elections held in April, the Anti-Fascist People's Freedom League won with a clear majority. However, in July, Aung San and six of his cabinet colleagues were assassinated by their political rivals. On January 4, 1948 Myanmar became independent under the leadership of U Nu.

Independence and democracy did not bring political stability or economic recovery in Burma. Minorities, especially the Karens, were unhappy in the union and soon became rebellious. The concentration of power, with all positions in the army

and police in the hands of Burman majority, caused resentment among the minorities.

The democracy experiment in Myanmar was a failure, with rebellion, instability, inflation, and corruption in government undermining it. Taking advantage of the instability and fearful that the U Nu government might allow some minorities to secede from the unified country, the army, under the leadership of general Ne Win, overthrew the democratic government and took control of the country on March 2, 1962. The army formed a revolutionary council led by General Ne Win, one of the original Thirty Comrades, and would not tolerate any opposition to its rule. Many Burmese welcomed the military take-over, though students and Buddhist monks who opposed the army were mercilessly silenced. The new rulers created a political party, the Burmese Socialist Party and proclaimed a "Burmese Way to Socialism."

The new government moved quickly to get rid of all foreign elements in society; they turned against Indian and Chinese businessmen and Indian civil servants. Moreover, the government decided to cut ties with the outside world. Myanmar withdrew from the non-aligned movement. The non-aligned movement was a foreign policy position of many of the developing countries during the Cold War that did not align with either the Western or Soviet blocs. Prime Minister U Nu was a founding member of the movement. State socialism under the military rule did not solve the country's economic problems; in fact, the economic condition of the people steadily declined under the new rulers. This prompted the United Nations in 1987 to give Myanmar the Least Developed Nation status.

RECENT HISTORY AND THE FUTURE

The military's attempt to keep the diverse elements in the country under control did not work. Ethnic minorities continued to revolt and the government was unable to exercise its authority in rebel areas. Moreover, a black market came into existence, which was bigger than the state-operated economy. Opposition to the military rule and the state-controlled economy grew in strength and the army quickly turned against the troublemakers. Nevertheless, in 1981, Ne Win resigned as the president of the country, though he continued to be in charge as the chairman of the Burma Socialist Program Party. A retired general, San Yu, became president of Myanmar.

The anti-military feeling among all sections of Burmese population, especially students and Buddhist monks, finally gave expression to mass protests and violence in March 1988. The protests started as a dispute between some students and a teashop owner, though it soon it became a national movement. The government's efforts to stop the riots failed. The confrontation between the government and the protesters lasted several months, until the military coup d'état (violent overthrow) of September 1988.

In April 1988, while the anti-government protest was growing in strength, Daw Aung San Suu Kyi, daughter of the martyred national hero Aung San, returned to Myanmar to tend to her ailing mother. She soon became a strong critic of the government and its human rights violations. In July 1988, Ne Win resigned as the chairman of the party. On September 18, 1988 the military under the army chief-of-staff General Saw Maung took control of the government, though it was widely believed that Ne Win continued to be the real power behind the army takeover. Between September 18 and 21 the army killed several hundreds of civilians, including students and Buddhist monks, to stop the rebellion.

The military now formed the State Law and Order Restoration Council (SLORC). The new

AUNG SAN SUU KYI

1945– Aung San Suu Kyi, recipient of the 1991 Nobel Peace Prize, was born July 19, 1945 in Rangoon, Burma (now Myanmar). Her mother, Khin Kyi, was a diplomat. Suu Kyi's father, Aung San (Burma's first prime minister), was assassinated when she was two. Suu Kyi (pronounced Sue Chee) lived in Myanmar until her mother became the ambassador to India in 1960.

In the mid-1960s, Suu Kyi moved to England to study at Oxford. She married, had two children, and lived in the United Kingdom. In 1988 Suu Kyi's mother suffered a stroke, which prompted Suu Kyi to return to Myanmar. While in Myanmar, the slaughter of protesters by Myanmar's military dictatorship impelled her to speak out. She was chosen to lead the National League for Democracy (NLD).

Threatened by Suu Kyi's writings and activism, the military *junta* placed her under house arrest in 1989. In the 1990 elections, the NLD won a vast majority; but the *junta* refused to allow the elected parliament to take power. "Daw" (Lady) Suu Kyi was freed from house arrest in July 1995, although her communication and movements continue to be restricted. In September 1995, she provided the keynote address, via smuggled videotape, to the United Nations Fourth World Conference on Women. She continues her work for democracy and administers basic food and medicine services from her Yangon (Rangoon) headquarters.

government abandoned socialism and adopted a free market economy. It encouraged foreign investments in the country. The *junta* also changed the name of the country to Myanmar, a change many countries have not yet accepted. The capital Rangoon became Yangon.

The opposition parties formed a National League for Democracy (NLD) and Aung San Suu Kyi became one of the most important leaders of the movement. Suu Kyi, a charismatic leader and orator, drew large crowds to NLD meetings. Her role in leading the non-violent demonstrations made the military nervous. Finally, in July 1989, the government placed her under house arrest and thousands of NLD supporters and leaders throughout the nation also were arrested. The arrest only helped increase the fame and influence of Suu Kyi.

The international criticism of the *junta* continued. In response, the *junta* decided to hold elections in May 1990. The *junta* was confident that it could control the outcome of the elections. Aung San Suu Kyi was still under house arrest and her deputy, retired general Tin Oon, was in jail. However, the election results would be a surprise for the *junta*. The NLD got more than two-thirds of the seats in the parliament, winning 392 of the 485 seats. The military-backed National Union Party (formerly, the Burma Socialist Program party) managed to win only ten seats.

The military leadership was stunned by its defeat at the polls but was eager to blunt international criticism; at first, it welcomed the results. The government spokesman had at the time even invited the elected representatives to take power as soon as they could. Two months later, when the NLD tried to form the new government, the military government changed its mind and refused to hand over power to the elected representatives. The military decided that it would continue to rule under martial law until a strong and pro-military constitution could be put in place. The parliament was never convened. The NLD continued its demonstrations. In 1991 while still under house arrest, Suu Kyi won the Nobel Prize for peace. The *junta*, however, did not allow her to go abroad to accept the award.

The United States and other Western countries have been critical of the *junta* for its refusal to seat the legally elected parliament, as well as for the government's human rights violations. In April 1997, General Than Shwe replaced the ailing Saw Maung as head of the SLORC. In January 1993, the *junta* convened to draft a new constitution for the country. The convention consisted mostly of people selected by the military; the NLD was given only eighty-eight seats. In 1996 NLD delegates withdrew from the convention and the convention has not made much progress in drafting a constitution for the country since it began its deliberations in 1993.

On November 15, 1997 the military rulers dissolved the SLORC. They formed a new governing council called the State Peace and Development Council (SPDC). The SPDC also created a cabinet consisting of mostly military personnel. General Than Shwe became the prime minister as well as the chairman of the SPDC. This reorganization, according to some observers, was the result of a power struggle between two top generals and followed General Ne Win's visit to Indonesia, then an authoritarian state under the control of General Suharto. According to reports this reorganization was an attempt to imitate the Indonesian political model in Myanmar.

The NLD did not see any reason for optimism in these changes as its leadership came under increasing scrutiny and harassment. Suu Kyi, although released from house arrest in 1995, is not free to move as she pleases. The generals treat her as a traitor for marrying late British academic Michael Aris and for encouraging international sanctions against Myanmar. The global community has also not been impressed by the recent political developments in Myanmar. Canada, the United States and Japan among many others have imposed economic sanctions on Myanmar. U.S. president Bill Clinton in April 1997 formally banned all new American investment in Myanmar and many foreign firms have withdrawn from Myanmar, including Apple Computer, Oshkosh B'Gosh, Eddie Bauer, Reebok, Liz Clairborne, Levi Strauss, and Pepsicola. In May 2000, President Clinton imposed additional sanctions on the Burmese military *junta*. However, these sanctions and the disapproval of other nations have not yet been effective in encouraging democracy.

In 1998 the NLD formed a ten-member group and declared that it was the only legitimate parliament. In retaliation the government arrested scores of NLD supporters. The standoff between the military and the NLD continues. On May 27, 2000 the NLD celebrated the tenth anniversary of 1990 election—the election it had won. Speaking on the occasion, Suu Kyi demanded that the army surrender its power to the elected representatives of the people. She asserted that NLD would not accept any sham elections or a constitution developed by the military. The police had arrested more people in anticipation of the tenth anniversary celebration, and only about three hundred people attended the meeting because of police harassment. Most NLD leaders and supporters remain jailed.

The military government, it appears, is determined to control political power in the country at least for the foreseeable future. It is more powerful than ever before, with more people in its ranks and more modern weapons in its arsenal. It is able to concentrate on its political opponents because it has arranged at least an uneasy cease-fire with its ethnic rebels, including some who have been fighting against the government for almost five decades.

Economic liberalization has not improved the lives of most of the people. There is growing Chinese influence on the economy and the continuing Chinese economic and military presence in Myanmar is a source of concern for India and Thailand. The Buddhist monks in the country remain restive. The ethnic and religious minorities are weary of Burman dominance in all aspects of the country's life. Thousands of people were forced to flee the country because of continuing repression: there are Burmese refugees in both Thailand and Bangladesh. Unless or until the military shows willingness to hand over control of the country to its popular and elected leaders, Myanmar is unlikely to improve from its ranking as one of the poorest countries in the world.

BIBLIOGRAPHY

Aung-Thwin, Michael. *Pagan: The Origins of Modern Burma*. Honolulu, Hawaii: University of Hawai Press, 1974.

"Burma with National Anthems, Flags, Maps and its People, Economy, Geography, Government." *E-Conflict World Encyclopedia, 2000.* http://www.Emulateme.com/Burma.htm (30 April 2000).

Cady, John Frank. *Thailand, Burma, Laos and Cambodia.* Englewood Cliffs, N.J.: Prentice Hall, 1966.

———. *Southeast Asia: Its Historical Development.* New York: McGraw Hill, 1964.

Central intelligence Agency. "Burma." *The World Fact book 1999.* http://www.odci.gov/cia/publications/factbook/bm.html (21 May 2000).

"Country Profile: Myanmar (Burma)." *Facts on File World News Digest.* 31 December 1997. http://2facts.com/stories/index/c00125.asp (30 April 2000).

"Facts on Aung San Suu Kyi." *Facts on File World News Digest.* http://www.2facts.com/stories/index/b0004.asp (17 May 2000).

"God's Guerrillas or Evil Twins?" *New York Times,* 28 February 2000.

Husarska, Anna, "Lady in Waiting," *New Republic,* 12 April 1999, 16–8.

Kamdar, Mira. "Rangoon: A Remembrance of Things Past," *World Policy Journal,* Fall 1999, 89–109.

Kirshenbaum, Gayle. "Aung San Suu Kyi," *Ms.,* January 1996, 56– 7.

Markille, Paul. "Survey: Southeast Asia: The Agony of Other Lands," *Economist,* 12 February 2000, 11–4.

"Myanmar: Junta Reorganizes, Changes Name; and other Developments." *Facts on File World News Digest.* 31 December 1997. http://www.2facts.com/stories/index/1997 087990.asp (17 May 2000).

Steinberg, David I. "Burma/Myanmar and the Dilemmas of U.S. Foreign Policy," *Contemporary Southeast Asia,* August 1999, 283–311.

Thein, Myatt, and Maung Maung Soe. "Economic Reforms and Agricultural Development in Myanmar," *Asian Economic Bulletin,* April 1998, 13–29.

Toolan, David S. "Burma's Gandhi," *America,* 8 February 1992, 84–5.

U.S. Department of State, Bureau of East Asian and Pacific Affairs. "Conditions in Burma and US policy towards Burma for the Period September 29, 1999 to March 27, 2000." http://www.state.go/www/regions/eap (3 May 2000).

Williams, Lea E. *Southeast Asia: A History.* New York: Oxford University Press, 1976.

George Thadithil

NATIVE AMERICANS: CENTURIES OF STRUGGLE IN NORTH AMERICA

THE CONFLICT

Native Americans believe that they have been dislocated from their land by invaders—European colonizers—and demand independence for their nations. The U.S. government provides for limited independence within the context of the United States.

Political

- Native Americans believe they compose distinct nations who have not voluntarily joined the United States and should have sovereignty. They believe the United States has duplicitously broken treaties.

- Legal issues include forest management, mineral development, water rights, and reparations.

- The United States provides special rights, including limited autonomy, to Native Americans, which it does not provide to any other groups within the country.

Ethnic

- Ethnic discrimination has limited the achievements of Native Americans.

Economic

- Native Americans feel marginalized and impoverished by the United States and have been removed from valuable land.

- Native American organizations have sued the U.S. government's Bureau of Indian Affairs.

In *American Indian Policy in the Twentieth Century*, Vine Deloria, Jr. wrote: "The federal-Indian relationship . . . is like no other in the world . . . Indian tribes appear to have the same political status as . . . independent states . . . yet they . . . seem to be forever mired in a state of political and economic pupilage." During the last two decades of the twentieth century, Native Americans in the United States have experienced a cultural and economic renaissance after the devastation their culture experienced triggered by events brought about by the European colonization of North America centuries earlier. Despite the time that has passed, the issue of tribal political independence, or sovereignty, can still be seen in U.S. headlines in the year 2000 as it was during early seventeenth-century treaty negotiations with Dutch colonists.

The concept of tribal political sovereignty in 2000 is central to numerous natural resource management and economic development issues. By the beginning of the twenty-first century, tribal lands held much of the last remaining deposits of natural resources in North America. Ongoing legal issues involve water rights allocation, forest management, restoration of fish runs, reestablishment of an economic landbase, mineral development (including gold, copper, zinc, oil and gas, uranium, and coal), heavy-metal poisoning of waters clean-up, and flow management of major waterways including the Columbia, Snake, Colorado, and Missouri Rivers. Legal conflicts frequently pit the general public and state governments against tribal governments, with the federal government weighing in on various sides depending on the circumstances behind the particular dispute.

Economic issues involving casino development usually grabbed the public's attention, but

CHRONOLOGY

1787 The Northwest Ordinance, enacted by the Continental Congress, asserts ownership of lands gained from Britain that were not part of the original colonies, but also recognizes existing Indian right of possession to those lands.

1823–32 *Johnson v. McIntosh* (1823), *Cherokee Nation v. Georgia* (1831), and *Worcester v. Georgia* (1832) affirm the tribal right to occupy and govern their lands, tribal sovereignty from state jurisdiction, and defines a moral trust responsibility of the United States to the tribes. In contrast to these laws, President Andrew Jackson authorizes the removal of large numbers of Indians from their land.

1879 In the *United States ex. rel. Standing Bear v. Crook,* the Supreme Court asserts that Indians off-reservation were "persons" as defined in the Fourteenth Amendment.

1884 The Supreme Court rules that the Fourteenth Amendment of the Constitution does not automatically extend citizenship to Indians.

1887 The General Allotment Act, also known as the Dawes Act, authorizes the Bureau of Indian Affairs (BIA) to divide communal reservation lands into small, privately owned parcels, to encourage Indians to become small, "civilized" farmers. Between 1887 and 1934 Indian Country is reduced from 138 million acres to forty-eight million acres due to the allotment policy.

1924 The Indian Citizenship Act grants all Indians born in the United States citizenship. Although able to vote and hold state office, Indians are not subject to state law while on Indian land.

1934 The Indian Reorganization Act ends the allotment process and, among other things, encourages the formation of governments with U.S.-style constitutions, causing conflict between new tribal leaders and traditional leaders.

1953 The U.S. government policy again encourages assimilation through tribal termination—ending the special trust relationship and converting tribal reservation lands to private lands. Approximately one hundred tribes are selected for termination. Much Indian land is lost.

1968 Congress passes the Indian Civil Rights Act (ICRA), which extends most, but not all, of the Constitution's Bill of Rights to Indians, including free speech protection and free exercise of religion.

1970s The "Red Power" movement grows, including the American Indian Movement (AIM).

1974 The Supreme Court rules in *Morton v. Mancari* that American Indians can be treated differently from other U.S. citizens by the federal government because tribes are political—not racial—groups.

1988 The Indian Gaming Regulatory Act is passed by Congress. Within a decade, one-third of the 554 federally recognized tribes operate some form of gaming.

2000 Approximately two million Native Americans, including Hawaiian and Alaskan natives, live on 314 reservations or in cities throughout the United States.

---

tribes were also investing in other long-term business ventures during the 1990s, potentially involving billions of dollars. In addition, during the summer of 1999, a class-action lawsuit asking for tens of billions of dollars in payment was filed against the U.S. Department of Interior's Bureau of Indian Affairs (BIA) alleging over two centuries of misuse of Indian assets held in trust by the U.S. government.

HISTORICAL BACKGROUND

Native Americans Today

The term "Native American" is commonly used to refer to American Indians living within the United States. However, it also includes Hawaiians and some Alaskan Natives not considered American Indians. When referred to collectively, Native Americans often prefer being called by their tribal names, such as Nez Percé, Navajo, Sioux, or Oneida.

The social and legal position of Native Americans in U.S. society is complex, evolving incrementally over time. Indian Law is a special branch of law in the U.S. legal system. By definition, tribes are formally recognized sovereign nations located within the boundaries of the United States. Over forty-five million acres, or just over two percent of lands within the United States, are actually governed by these tribal governments. Lands under tribal jurisdiction, both owned by tribes or held in trust for tribes by the U.S. government, are formally referred to as Indian Country. It is estimated the peak Native American population was perhaps as high as ten million people five hundred years ago when Europeans first appeared in the Western Hemisphere. The population plummeted to three hundred thousand by the 1920s, at its lowest point. By 2000 the population had rebounded to approximately two million Indians and Hawaiian and Alaska Natives, who live on 314 reservations or in cities. More than 250 native languages are spoken in Indian Country. In 1800 the native population controlled three-quarters of what would eventually become the United States. In the 1990s Indian reservations had a thirty percent poverty rate, with unemployment six times the national average. Health and education needs are high. Almost sixty percent of American Natives live in substandard housing while twenty-nine percent are homeless.

Not all American Indians live in Indian Country today; in fact most do not. There is a long tradition of urban residence among native North Americans, such as the early large pre-contact settlements in the Southwest and Mississippi River Valley. With the establishment of European colonies, Indians became a key part of colonial villages. However, by the early nineteenth century the United States adopted policies to isolate Indian peoples away from the settlers who were moving west, often forcing the Native Americans to remote areas set aside for them. Despite many Indians seeking wage labor in newly established towns, most lived in rural settings into the early twentieth century. In 1930 only ten percent of Indians lived in cities.

However, with thousands of American Indians serving in the U.S. military abroad during World War II (1939–45) or working in defense plants, their exposure to mainstream society made life on poverty-ridden reservations less acceptable after the war. The GI Bill (a bill passed to offer special benefits to veterans in post-war years) also provided new educational opportunities. The population began to move to cities. The U.S. government adopted assimilation policies in the 1950s designed to integrate Indian peoples into mainstream U.S. society, adding further impetus to Indian urbanization. Government programs including the Adult Vocational Training Program and the Employment Assistance Program focused on urban relocation. From 1952 to 1972 the government sent over one hundred thousand American Indians from reservations to urban job placement centers. As a result, the percentage of Indians living in cities expanded from thirteen percent in 1950 to almost thirty percent by 1960. By 1990 the majority of American Indians, or fifty-six percent, lived in urban areas. Still, the reservations in Indian Country remained the focus of native pride and political identity.

History of U.S.-American Indian Relations

Tracing the long history of U.S.-Indian relations from the nation's early years dramatically illustrates how the present-day American Indian legal standing in the United States is not the result of a well-organized body of legal principles. Rather, it is a legal mosaic of accumulated laws and policies coming from many diverse sources over centuries. Although many similarities exist among them, each tribe has its own unique cultural and legal history. For over two centuries, U.S. Indian policy has shifted between periods of supporting tribal self-government and economic self-sufficiency to periods of forced Indian social and economic inclusion into the dominant society.

The basis for U.S. Indian law, which is actually U.S. law about Indians and not by Indians, was well established before American independence was achieved. During the seventeenth century European colonists settled along the Eastern Seaboard and began negotiating treaties with local indigenous groups, treating them as they would other politically independent nations. In return for peace and security for their settlements, the colonists recognized the Indian right of possession to lands they were occupying and using. The United States, following independence from Great Britain, inherited this age-old European international policy. As a result, tribal sovereignty was internationally recognized well before the United States gained independence and its own political sovereignty, and this recognition became the basis for future U.S.-Indian relations.

Fresh from victory over Britain in the American Revolution (1775–83), the fledgling nation made securing peaceful and orderly relations with American Indians one of its first items of business. The 1787 Northwest Ordinance, enacted by the Continental Congress, asserted U.S. ownership of newly gained lands from Britain that were not part of the original colonies but also recognized existing Indian right of possession to those lands. Consistent with the European doctrine of discovery used by early explorers in claiming New World lands, the United States inherited from Great Britain the exclusive right to negotiate with the native peoples who still occupied those lands relinquished by Great Britain. Attempting to end the practice of private individuals or local governments negotiating treaties with or buying lands directly from the sovereign Indian nations, the ordinance stated that only the federal government could legally carry out such activities.

Recognition of tribal sovereignty was directly addressed in the U.S. Constitution, adopted in 1788. Authority for the federal government's legal relationship with tribes was written into the Commerce Clause of Article 1 which reads simply that Congress has power "to regulate Commerce with foreign Nations and . . . the Indian Tribes." The U.S. Constitution also recognizes the legal status of Indian treaties in Article VI by stating, "This Constitution, and the Laws of the United States . . . and all Treaties made . . . shall be the supreme Law of the Land." Treaties ratified by the U.S. Senate hold the same legal force as federal laws and hold precedence over state laws. Further reflecting the significance of Indian relations to the new nation, one of the first acts passed by the first U.S. Congress was the Indian Trade and Intercourse Act of 1790. Exercising its new constitutional authority, Congress reserved treaty-making powers for the federal government and brought all interaction between Indians and non-Indians in the United States under federal control.

Not surprisingly, legal challenges to the concept of tribal sovereignty and exclusive federal authority over Indians soon arose. Strong proponents of states' rights attempted to gain control over Indian relations. As a result, U.S. Indian policy became further defined by three landmark Supreme Court decisions between 1823 and 1832. The legendary chief justice John Marshall issued three opinions related to American Indian issues that came to be known as the Marshall Trilogy. The cases were *Johnson v. McIntosh* (1823), *Cherokee Nation v. Georgia* (1831), and *Worcester v. Georgia* (1832), which affirmed the tribal right to occupy and govern their lands, tribal sovereignty from state jurisdiction in Indian Country, and defined a moral trust responsibility of the United States to the tribes. Marshall described tribes as "domestic dependent nations" essentially free of state control.

The trust obligations meant the United States was responsible for Indian health and welfare. The place of the Indian tribes on the U.S. political landscape was established. Unfortunately for the Indian peoples, these principles were not universally embraced. As early as the 1830s, President Andrew Jackson (served 1829–37) rejected Marshall's opinions and pressed on with Indian removal policies.

U.S. Indian policy—as directed by Congress using its constitutional authority—has proceeded from the 1790 Indian Intercourse Act to the year 2000 along a winding pathway of alternating goals. Policy swerved from "civilizing" the tribes (1780s–1820s) according to European ideas at the time, to isolation and protection on reservations (1830s–1870s), forced assimilation into American farming society (1880s–1920s), recognition of reorganized tribal governments and relations with the federal government (1930s–1940s), termination of trust status (1950s), and finally to support for tribal self-determination and integrity (1960s–2000). Despite early U.S. Indian policies from 1787 to 1830 that were seemingly protective of Indian rights, Indian peoples suffered catastrophic loss of economies, lands, and life from the relentless westward push of U.S. expansion.

Treaties, Removal, and Reservations

Based on the Indian Intercourse Act, between 1790 and 1871 the U.S. Senate ratified over 370 treaties with Indian nations. In the seventeenth and eighteenth centuries, the greatly outnumbered colonists pursued treaty agreements with American Indians to secure peace and regulate trade. Though outnumbered, the colonists carried forward the ethnocentricism that dominated Europe for centuries—that they would carry civilization to the rest of the world's populations. Added to this belief were humanitarian sensitivities brought on by the Age of the Enlightenment in the seventeenth century. As a result, an effort to "civilize" indigenous peoples predominated policy.

Following the Revolutionary War, treaties also served to acquire lands and gain Indian allegiance to the newly formed nation instead of to England. The United States signed its first formal U.S. treaty with the Delaware Indians in 1778. In 1789 the U.S. Constitution recognized Indian treaties as equivalent to federal law, thus enforceable in state and federal courts.

By the 1820s treaties began to focus on removal of Indians from their traditional homelands to lands away from expanding U.S. settlement. One of the more tragic examples of U.S.-government actions came in the 1830s removal policy directed by President Jackson. Under this policy, the United States forcefully removed the Five Civilized Tribes from the southeastern United States to the newly created Oklahoma Indian Territory. Thousands of deaths directly resulted from initial long-term detention followed by the 1,800-mile, six-month march, known as the Trail of Tears.

Following the acquisition of what is now the southwestern United States from Mexico and the opening of the Oregon Trail to the Pacific Northwest in the 1840s, federal treaty commissions sought out tribal groups throughout the West to acquire Indian lands and relocate them to reservations. Through treaties made with tribes in the American West, eastern U.S. Indian removal policies of the 1830s continued throughout the 1860s. The tribes exchanged land, water, and mineral rights for peace, security, health care, and education. The western treaties created a vast reserve system in which Native Americans could exclusively exercise their inherent rights within certain defined territories, called reservations. In 1871 Congress closed the treaty period with more than 650 treaties signed and 370 ratified into law.

Many northwest treaties and some in the Great Lakes region also reserved non-exclusive Indian hunting, fishing, and gathering rights outside reservation boundaries to help preserve traditional economies. The typical language of such treaties is exemplified in the 1855 Point Elliott Treaty of western Washington which states, "The right of taking fish at usual and accustomed grounds and stations is further secured to said Indians in common with all citizens of the Territory . . . together with the privilege of hunting and gathering roots and berries on open and unclaimed lands." Other off-reservation rights, depending on the treaty, also might include trapping, shellfish gathering, grazing stock, tapping trees for maple syrup, gathering wild rice, or cutting down trees for tipi poles. The allocation of these unique property rights to tribal members was the responsibility of tribal governments. State hunting regulations and limits were largely constrained by the exertion of tribal sovereignty and the supremacy of treaties over state law.

Besides economic issues, treaties also identified other rights for Native Americans including the right to self-government by recognizing the political sovereignty of tribes to manage their own affairs. The right to exclusive use of reservation lands also carried with it the property rights to subsurface minerals. Treaties also commonly contained provisions for health, education and other services, but these promises have not been considered rights.

The treaties paved the way for a cooperative coexistence between the United States and Native Americans but were not consistently upheld. Many believed that the dwindling native populations in the late nineteenth century would eventually cease to exist altogether. Consequently, treaties were considered temporary by some. Honoring these treaties also conflicted with the promotion of non-Indian settlement and economic development in newly acquired U.S. territories. But American Indian peoples persisted.

Fish and game occupied a central role in Indian spiritual and cultural life and defending hunting and fishing rights constituted defending American Indian cultural identity. Interpretation of treaty rights in the courts has a long complex history. In *Lone Wolf v. Hitchcock* (1903), the Supreme Court ruled that Congress has the plenary (absolute) power to unilaterally take away rights. However, the responsibility of federal trust requires careful exercise of this absolute power, meaning it should be used only when it would be beneficial to Indian peoples. The Court in *United States v. Winans* (1905) established the Reserved Rights Doctrine in which tribes retain inherent rights unless they are explicitly taken away by Congress. For example, the Court in *Menominee Tribe v. United States* (1968) held that a tribe retains its hunting and fishing rights even if its reservation is terminated by Congress, unless legislation specifically states the rights are no longer valid. The Court ruled in *Winters v. United States* (1908) that inherent to creation of reservations through treaties were water rights necessary to support residential and economic use of the reservation. The decision, known as the Winters Doctrine, remained central to water rights negotiations with states at the end of the twentieth century.

To resolve legal disputes over treaty interpretations, the "canons of construction" described in *Winters v. United States* (1908) state that courts should always interpret unclear treaty language from the tribal perspective. At nineteenth century treaty councils, Indians were usually the weaker negotiating party, often unable to speak or understand English and acting under duress.

In 1871 Congress ended the treaty-making era, closing a major chapter in U.S.-Indian relations. By this time, the Indian population had largely been relegated to remote areas, out of the way of U.S. expansion and settlements, and removal was considered essentially complete. Away from U.S. markets, prospects for Indian economic recovery were slim at best. Continued U.S. expansion along with the discovery of gold in the 1860s brought increased demand for natural resources.

The remote reservation lands to which Indian tribes had relocated became increasingly more attractive to settlers. Some of the last treaties forced on the tribes greatly reduced the size of reservations established by earlier treaties.

In contrast to rights of tribal governments, the legal rights of Indian individuals was not a major concern of the federal government or the courts throughout much of the nineteenth century. Tribal relations were largely guided by treaties rather than standard U.S. law, and legal dealings with individuals was generally avoided. A system for policing Indians developed largely outside of U.S. court jurisdiction. Indian agents, having ready access to the U.S. military, exercised broad authority. They readily detained numerous individual Natives for a wide range of alleged actions.

By the 1870s social reformers in the East shifted their attention away from slavery and began to focus on Indian issues. Demands for humanitarian action gathered momentum. An 1879 federal court ruling in *United States ex rel. Standing Bear v. Crook* asserted that off-reservation Indians were "persons" as defined in the Fourteenth Amendment, having the same constitutional due process and equal protection rights as U.S. citizens. The ruling meant that the U.S. Army could no longer exercise broad authority to detain Indians without full civilian constitutional protections. Nevertheless, much about the legal standing of Indian individuals still remained poorly defined. In 1884 the Supreme Court ruled the Fourteenth Amendment of the Constitution did not automatically grant citizenship to Indians.

Assimilation

By the 1880s, remaining groups of American Indians were coming under greater pressure to relinquish their lands to accommodate U.S. expansion. Many American Indians believed their only chance of survival was through integration into American society. A major period of forced cultural assimilation began with the General Allotment Act of 1887 and lasted into the 1930s. In a sense, this was a return to methods used during the colonial period to "civilize" Indian peoples. Many European settlers believed the indigenous tradition of communally owned property was creating a barrier to Indians adopting Western ways. As a result, Congress passed the Allotment Act, also known as the Dawes Act, authorizing the Bureau of Indian Affairs (BIA) to divide communal reservation lands held in trust by the federal government into smaller, privately owned parcels. The agency allotted 160-acre parcels to families and eighty-acre parcels to single adults over eighteen years of age. Indians receiving allotments also received U.S. citizenship to speed their assimilation. U.S. policymakers reasoned that if they owned their own property, Indians would most likely become farmers and adopt the U.S. farming lifestyles.

Given the high death rates among the Indian population before 1887, much reservation land was left over after every tribal member had received their allotment. Those unallotted lands were declared "surplus" and sold by the United States to non-Indians. In addition to the "surplus" lands, much allotted land went into forfeiture (was lost) when many Indians could not pay taxes on their often remote, unproductive desert properties. This land, too, went to non-Indians eventually. Even when land was productive, markets were usually still too distant. As a result, the allotment policy became an economic disaster for Indian peoples, reducing Indian Country in the United States from 138 million acres in 1887 to forty-eight million acres by 1934. In many cases, the more agriculturally productive lands on reservations passed out of tribal control.

As part of the assimilation effort, Congress granted American Indians born in the United States citizenship through the Indian Citizenship Act of 1924. The act also made Indians citizens of the states in which they resided. Although able to vote and hold state office, they were not subject to state law while on Indian lands. The Constitution's Bill of Rights, however, still did not apply to interactions between Indians and their tribal governments because of tribal sovereignty. As a result, tribal members could be subjected to harsher legal penalties from their own tribal governments than could non-Indians in U.S. society for the same crimes.

Reorganizing Tribal Governments

By the 1930s the tragedy of the allotment policy had become readily apparent to U.S. policymakers. Secretary of the Interior John Collier recommended an end to assimilation efforts and Congress responded. Stressing tribal sovereignty, the Indian Reorganization Act of 1934 ended the allotment process, stabilized remaining tribal land holdings, and promoted tribal self-government. The act encouraged tribal governments to adopt U.S.-style constitutions and form federally chartered corporations. Although many tribes elected to organize under the rules of the act, many rejected developing such constitutions. Rather, some of them organized new governments under their own tribal rules. Despite the seemingly supportive policy of encouraging the formation of modern tribal governments, the newly established, more modern governments and the new governments' tribal leaders often conflicted with the traditional tribal political leaders and structure.

As a result of the acts, though, some tribes with a sufficient land base and marketable natural resources, such as timber, developed an economic base and prospered during this period. The Supreme Court reaffirmed the federal trust obligation during this time in *Seminole Nation v. United States* (1942). The Court ruled the United States held a "moral obligation of the highest responsibility and trust" to be judged "by the most exacting . . . standards."

Termination

By 1953 U.S. governmental policy had shifted back to fostering assimilation. This time the government unveiled "termination" policies. The major component included provisions to terminate the federally recognized—and financially supported—status of those Indian tribes and reservations that seemed most ready for such a move. Termination legislation also included a relocation provision to move Indian people from reservation communities into major cities as a means of acculturating them more quickly into mainstream society. Termination of a tribe meant ending the special trust relationship and converting tribal reservation lands to private lands. Access to federal health and education services was curtailed. Approximately one hundred tribes were selected for termination. As in the allotment period, much Indian land—some very productive—was sold to non-Indians. The economic base for those Indian communities was devastated. As part of termination, Congress also passed Public Law 280 in 1953, which expanded state jurisdiction onto tribal lands in selected states, decreasing tribal sovereignty even further.

The welfare of urban Indians became an increasing concern of the federal government under its trust responsibilities as the Indian population shifted from reservations to cities. Urban Indians increasingly were victims of racial discrimination and poverty. Underemployment led to homelessness, rampant substance abuse, and unusually high injury, disease, death, and infant mortality rates. To provide support for the expanding Indian urban population, Indian centers, clubs, and churches appeared in many cities. However, sources of funding for these urban Indian social services became controversial, as tribal leaders did not want limited funds intended for reservation services diverted to non-reservation Indians. After considerable pres-

sure was applied to the government by the National Congress of American Indians and other Indian groups, by 1958 it became official government policy that tribes must consent to their own disbandment, and termination came to an end. Another factor was the civil rights movement of the 1950s and 1960s, which inspired the Red Power movement. Indian activism grew and spread during the early 1970s to the rural reservations through activities of various groups, including the American Indian Movement (AIM).

In 1976 Congress passed the Indian Health Care Improvement Act to address the urban Indian plight. Exposure to the civil rights movement of the 1950s and 1960s in the cities also inspired Indian radicalism and the Red Power movement. Such activism spread in the early 1970s to the rural reservations through activities of various groups, including the American Indian Movement (AIM).

An important socio-cultural result of Indian migration to the cities was the mixing of Indian peoples from many tribes. This growth of pan-Indian-ism further altered American Indian identity. Urbanization brought other changes: traditional lifestyles were lost, Native languages forgotten, and tribal connections often broken. Intermarriage with non-Indians became more common.

With the resurgence of tribal economies in the 1980s and corresponding growth in political strength, some urban Indians moved back to their rural tribal communities. There they applied their educations and skills to further propel Indian resurgence in America. Urbanization and reservation revitalization constituted conflicting trends in late twentieth century Indian life. Questions and issues related to tribal membership and rights, claims to Indian ancestry or tribal affiliation, and intellectual property issues (regarding who has the right to represent Indian interests to the mainstream society) became major concerns.

Tribal Self-Determination

With a decline in Indian well-being both on and off reservations by 1960 and the rise of the Red Power movement congressional support for termination policies did not last long. U.S. Indian policy again took a dramatic shift in the 1960s toward tribal government self-determination in which the tribes would govern their own internal affairs. The goal became to empower tribes to manage their own affairs free of government oversight or intrusion.

Influenced by the American civil rights movement, a series of congressional hearings in the 1960s focused on the lack of consistent civil rights protections offered by tribal governments to their members. As a result, Congress passed the Indian Civil Rights Act (ICRA) of 1968 which extended most of the Constitution's Bill of Rights to Indian peoples, including free speech protections, free exercise of religion, and due process and equal protection of tribal government laws. The act did not extend to Indians the right to a jury trial in civil cases, free legal counsel for the poor, search and seizure protections, and prohibition of government support for religion. Tribal governments were free to promote their own tribal religions. Issues such as gender discrimination in tribal laws still could not be challenged under federal law. The act also cut back some of the states' authorities granted in Public Law 280. In respect for tribal sovereignty, interpretation of ICRA was left to the tribes and tribal courts, not federal courts. Federal courts could only review tribal court decisions in certain types of criminal cases.

Other legal distinctions for Indians were also identified. Title VII of the 1964 Civil Rights Act explicitly exempted Indian hiring preference laws from due process protections in some instances. For example, the BIA could favor Indian applicants in filling jobs within the agency. The 1974 Supreme Court ruling in *Morton v. Mancari* affirmed that American Indians can be treated differently from other U.S. citizens by the federal government, despite anti-discrimination laws. Tribes may be treated as political—not racial—groups on occasions when the U.S. government is exercising its trust responsibilities to protect Indian interests and promote tribal sovereignty. If the Indian hiring preference laws were only designed to help Indians as individuals, they would be deemed illegal.

Because civil rights protections for Indians were different from other U.S. citizens, determining who was Indian and who was not had increasingly important legal consequences. Individuals can gain tribal membership through birth or marriage and may have substantial non-Indian ancestry. Conversely, a person of total Indian ancestry who never establishes a relationship with a tribe cannot claim legal Indian status. As an exercise of their tribal sovereignty, each of the over 550 recognized tribes in the United States determines the basis for membership in their tribe. Generally, an Indian can be anyone having some degree of Indian ancestry, is considered a member of an Indian community, and who promotes themselves as Indian.

The biggest boost in support of tribal sovereignty and self-sufficiency came in 1975 when Congress passed the Indian Self-Determination and Education Assistance Act, giving tribes much greater opportunity to administer federal programs benefiting Indian peoples that were previously administered by the BIA. Many of these programs provide health and education services.

For the next two decades Congress continued passing acts protecting tribal rights and interests, including the American Indian Religious Freedom Act (1978), the Indian Mineral Development Act (1982), the Indian Gaming Regulatory Act (1988), the Native American Graves Protection and Repatriation Act (1990), and the Indian Self-Governance Act (1994). The 1994 act amended the earlier 1975 Self-Determination Act making more federal government services to tribes subject to tribal administration. Though many tribes welcomed the trend toward greater political independence, some tribal leaders feared greater self-governance would also lead to a declining interest in fulfilling its trust obligations by the United States. The federal economic safety net could be largely lost. Nonetheless, the self-governance trend progressed through the 1990s. Legislation was introduced in late 1999 to further increase tribes' responsibility to run hospitals, clinics, and other programs overseen by the Indian Health Service. The self-governance requirement insists that tribes must demonstrate established financial and management skills.

During the self-determination era, tribal court systems expanded as many tribes gained greater economic and political power. Due to the broad diversity of tribal legal systems, however, the attrition of justice and the way it was applied differed from tribe to tribe. Aside from those court systems patterned after U.S. models, some tribes retained traditional systems and others had no systems at all.

By 2000 the resulting branch of U.S. law, commonly called Indian Law, was a very peculiar part of the U.S. legal system, with tribal governments and their peoples possessing a unique legal status. Under the sovereignty concept, tribes could form and reorganize their own governments, determine tribal membership, regulate individual property and manage natural resources in Indian Country, provide health services, develop gaming businesses, regulate commerce on tribal lands, collect taxes, maintain law enforcement, and establish tribal court systems. Members of federally recognized tribes were both U.S. and tribal citizens, simultaneously receiving benefits and protections from federal, state, and tribal governments.

Status of Indigenous Populations Worldwide

Similar health and welfare issues of Native Americans in the United States are shared with other indigenous populations worldwide. In late 1999, the World Health Organization (WHO), the United Nations' health agency, reported that the 300 million indigenous peoples around the world faced shortened life spans due to widespread disease and poverty. As demands on natural resources by the world's developed industrial nations have increased in remote areas, the WHO reported increases in the rates of diseases such as diabetes, malaria, yellow fever, and cancer, as well as alcoholism and infant mortality, coupled with decreasing life expectancies among those indigenous populations. Life expectancies were ten to twenty years less than the general population and infant mortality was three times higher. Suicide rates and domestic violence also rose as traditional values became increasingly lost. Even Arctic populations were increasingly exposed to industrial environment contamination. In the United States American Indians have higher rates of tuberculosis, liver disease, cancer, pneumonia, diabetes, suicide, and homicide than the general U.S. population. In many tribes amputations, blindness, and dialysis are a way of life as diabetes is rampant. In some cases, eighty percent of tribes are afflicted. The disease is blamed on lifestyle changes forced upon the Natives during the past two centuries. In Bolivia, twenty percent of indigenous children die before their first birthday, and 14 percent die before reaching school age.

A strong wave of attention to the plight of indigenous peoples has been sweeping Latin America. For the first time since 1821, a Peruvian Native ran a strong race in 2000 for the presidency of Peru. The president of Ecuador was toppled in January 2000 by an Indian rights movement. In December 1999, Venezuela became the fourteenth Latin American country in recent years to grant new constitutional rights to indigenous groups, allowing them to apply tribal law in their territories. In general, interest in cultural traditions, including medicines, clothing, ceremonies, and language was renewed in an effort to recapture cultural identities.

The Indian Health Services (IHS), a U.S. federal agency, provides health care for about three-fourths of the two million Native Americans in the United States. Treaties and other laws require that health care be provided in both reservation health centers and in urban clinics. Recognizing the hopelessness and despair still prevalent in much of Indian Country, in March 2000 the U.S. Commission on Civil Rights recommended formation of a federal task force to seek solutions. In April 2000 President Bill Clinton (served 1993–2001) visited the Navajo Nation to stress how the American economic boom of the 1990s had by-passed some communities. Almost forty percent of Navajo households are without electricity, seventy percent are without telephones, and unemployment is fifty percent.

Alaskan Natives

Experiencing a distinct cultural and legal history, Alaskan Natives struggled through the twentieth century to claim rights to their indigenous land base and participate in mainstream Alaskan society. Not until the 1940s did non-Natives actually outnumber Natives in the territory. Correspondingly, socio-cultural change came slowly until the end of World War II (1939–45). With the status of Alaskan Native land rights still awaiting resolution in the mid-twentieth century, many indigenous peoples continued a traditional subsistence lifestyle relatively unrestrained. The slowness of Alaskan Natives to assimilate into Western society and adopt white, middle-class values stimulated persistent white paternalism, negative stereotyping, and economic exploitation.

A collision course between Native Alaskans and U.S. expansionism erupted when Alaskan statehood occurred in 1959. Under the Alaskan Statehood Act, the new state could claim 104 million acres of public lands, much of it ancestral lands still used by Alaskan Natives. In reaction, Native Alaskan political organization, guided by the Alaska Federation of Natives, grew in strength through the 1960s. With the discovery of major oil fields in northern Alaska in 1968, Natives legally stalled construction of the Alaska pipeline, critical for transporting oil to the southern Alaskan coast. Industry, the state, and President Richard M. Nixon (served 1969–1974) joined the Alaskan Natives to lobby Congress for a comprehensive resolution.

In response, Congress passed the Alaska Native Claims Settlement Act (ANCSA) in 1971. Bargaining from an unusual position of political strength, Alaskan Natives received forty-four million acres of land and $962 million in exchange for dropping all claims to the remaining 335 million acres. ANCSA created twelve regional and almost two hundred village Native corporations to disperse and invest the funds and guide future Native economic development.

Representing the most important legislation to address land ownership and use in Alaska, the act

LEONARD PELTIER

1944– Leonard Peltier is currently serving a double life sentence for murder. However, many people in the United States and throughout the world believe he was wrongfully charged and is instead a political prisoner, convicted of murder on the basis of his beliefs and Native American activism.

Leonard Peltier was born September 12, 1944, and raised by his French- and Oujibwa-speaking grandparents, until he was sent to a Native American boarding school. As a young man, he became active in the American Indian Movement (AIM), a Native American civil rights organization. He came to national prominence after a June 1975 shoot-out on Pine Ridge Reservation near Oglala, South Dakota, which left two Federal Bureau of Investigation (FBI) agents dead.

The FBI quickly arrested four Native Americans. One was released for insufficient evidence and two were aquitted on the grounds of self-defense. Peltier, however, was extradited from Canada and convicted on two counts of murder. He has since been given an additional sentence for an escape attempt.

The FBI charges, and the courts have upheld, that Peltier was involved in the shooting that killed the FBI agents. However, the FBI has been accused by international human rights organizations of instigating violence against the Lakota community prior to the firefight and fabricating evidence afterward. Peltier has been refused a retrial, despite court findings that the FBI withheld evidence that may have exonerated him.

LEONARD PELTIER. *(AP/Wide World Photos. Reproduced by permission.)*

catapulted Native participation into Alaskan socio-political and economic life and reestablished Native Alaskan control over their own affairs. A major intent of ANCSA was to assimilate Alaskan Natives into mainstream American society, transforming them from a communal society to one of private ownership and free enterprise. A system of regional and village-level profit-making Native corporations was designed to provide better educational and economic opportunity and to guide economic development for increased independence.

The relative high incidence of poverty compared to the general population, poor access to quality health care, suppression of religious freedom, and complex subsistence issues persisted. By 1990 over eighty-five thousand Natives resided in Alaska, most still living in small rural villages. Becoming more of a minority in Alaska's booming economy and population growth, the Native population dropped from around twenty-five percent of the state population in 1950 to fifteen percent in 1990.

With chronic socio-economic problems still existing toward the end of the twentieth century, many Alaskan Natives sought to limit the role of the ANCSA corporations, strengthen tribal governments, and resurrect their traditional subsistence economies. Through tribal governments created to regulate Native affairs—including the establishment of tribal courts, taxation systems, and management of village assets—Native villages more aggressively asserted an inherent right to self-rule. Though some socio-economic gains were made by the end of the twentieth century, economic discrimination and exploitation persisted. The Alaskan state government has opposed formal recognition of tribal self-government. In 1998 and 1999 Alaskan Natives and sympathizers marched in the capital city of Anchorage, protesting the state's position. Regarding Native access to wild game, the state faced a choice of either instituting an unpopular subsistence priority system including the Natives and other non-Native resource users, or having the federal government take over management of fish and game throughout the region.

Hawaiian Natives

The first European contact with Hawaiian Natives was by British sea captain James Cook in 1778. Native Hawaiian sovereignty was threatened as internal Native political factions arose because of stresses caused by nineteenth-century colonization of the islands. By 1850 private property ownership driven by American business interests competed with the Native common lands policy. Finally, in 1893, Hawaiian Native leader Liliuokanani abdicated under hostile pressure from the United States, and a new constitution was adopted granting U.S. citizens the right to vote in Hawaiian elections. In 1898 Hawaii was annexed as a U.S. territory and Natives were forced to cede "all former Crown, government and public lands to the United States." With this final loss of an economic land base, Native Hawaiians faced difficult times. In response to the Native condition, Congress passed the Hawaiian Homes Commission Act in 1920. The commission was considered part of the federal trust obligation for the welfare of the natives and it was incorporated into the new state constitution when Hawaii gained statehood in 1959. The Office of Hawaiian Affairs (OHA) was established in 1978 to administer services for the Natives. It was established that only Native Hawaiians had the right to vote for the board of nine trustees who administer OHA. However, a non-Native successfully won a Supreme Court decision in early 2000 in Rice v. Cayetano when the Court ruled that Natives, constituting twenty percent of the islands' population, did not hold exclusive right to vote in trustees' elections. Natives felt this decision was a major blow to Native Hawaiian self-government. The Native Hawaiians were not considered a political group, as the mainland Natives were considered, but instead a race by the Court.

Natural Resource Use and Management

Tribal sovereignty has come into play in a number of late twentieth-century socio-political issues and legal actions. For example, in the 1980s Section 519 of the Clean Water Act gave tribes authority to establish their own water standards. As a result, in December 1997 the Supreme Court ruled in favor of the Isleta Pueblo in a case pitting the tribe against the city of Albuquerque located

upstream. Tribal water-quality standards established downstream of the city and upheld by the Court could force the city to add $400 million of improvements in its water systems to assure the higher standards downstream. The Confederated Tribes of Salish and Kootenai in western Montana won a similar water-standards case in federal district court in October 1998.

Treaty Rights

With increased competition over natural resources in the latter part of the twentieth century, tribes began winning favorable court rulings protecting off-reservation hunting and fishing rights granted by treaties of the previous century. An intense battle in the Northwest over fishing rights to the Columbia River resulted in a Supreme Court ruling in *Washington v. Washington State Commercial Passenger Fishing Vessel Association* (1978). The Court affirmed a lower court ruling that the treaty language "in common with citizens of the United States" means that Indians were entitled to half of the allowable take of salmon from the river.

The Mille Lacs band of Chippewa and seven neighboring tribes won a 1999 Supreme Court decision upholding their rights under an 1837 treaty, after eight years of negotiation and litigation against the state of Minnesota. In western Washington several tribes began asserting treaty rights to access ancestral shellfish beds across state and private lands. Such tribal harvests had effects on thousands of private property owners along two thousand miles of public and private tidelands as well as state and commercial shellfish growers. A lower court ruling in favor of the tribes stood as the Supreme Court refused to hear an appeal on the shellfish harvesting case. In 1999 the Makah Indian whale hunt off the Washington coast for the first time in over seventy years dramatized the exercise of treaty rights, drawing considerable international attention. The Makah's actions brought an increasingly familiar confrontation between the exercise of aboriginal traditional economic activities and environmental protection interest groups. Despite physical confrontations out on the water, the tribe did manage to capture a whale.

Other court actions sought to protect habitat. A district court victory in *Pyramid Lake Paiute v. Morton* (1973) blocked diversion of water from a lake in northwestern Nevada.

Economic Development–The Rise of Economies in the 1990s

Until the late twentieth century, Indian reservations were almost uniformly caught in a cycle of poverty, welfare, and hopelessness, which had persisted for generations. With economic success stories being few and widely scattered before 1988, a new era of tribal economics arrived when Congress passed the Indian Gaming Regulatory Act. Within a decade, one-third of the 554 federally recognized tribes in the United States operated some form of gaming, generating an estimated annual income of $6 billion. Due to tribal sovereignty, casino revenues are tax free, but agreements with the states required under the act often provide some compensation to states to pay for increased infrastructure needs of the community. Additionally, some tribes voluntarily relinquished some sovereignty to buy insurance for casinos and other business ventures. Immunity was waived against lawsuits to the limits of insurance coverage.

The most notable success in gaming was the Foxwoods Casino and Resort operated by the 500-member Mashantucket Pequots of Connecticut. Comprised of three-million-square feet plus a high-rise hotel and twenty-four restaurants, in 1998 it became the largest tribal facility in the country. Originally one of the more powerful tribes on the East Coast prior to colonial settlement in the seventeenth century, their size had shrunk to only thirty members by 1983. The Pequots built their casino in 1992 after finally receiving federal recognition. By 1998 the tribe was making over $1 billion a year through its casino and other businesses, and they had become the largest employer in New England and largest landowner in Connecticut.

Similar stories unfolded elsewhere in the country. The Coeur d'Alene Tribe of northern Idaho became the economic powerhouse for a four-county area through gaming. With their newfound income they built a $5 million wellness center and an eight-thousand-bed hospital. The Objibwa of Minnesota built two lavish casino and hotel complexes in the early 1990s, including the Grand Casino Mille Lacs. Unemployment fell from forty-six percent to less than ten percent, housing improved, and new lands were acquired. The Oneida of Wisconsin became the largest employer in the Green Bay area due to gaming and other business ventures.

Aside from gaming, another novel economic endeavor launched in 2000 with substantial income potential was the establishment of an "offshore bank" by the Blackfeet Tribe of Montana. The Glacier International Depository Ltd. was established on tribal land just east of Glacier National Park. Free of state regulation, the bank sought deposits of wealthy foreigners.

Other Effects of Economic Gains

Indian gaming successes have given rise to a new generation of Native American entrepreneurs. Many of these new business leaders see gaming not as an end goal of tribes, but a means to establish a long-term diversified tribal economy to support a lasting increase in quality of life. Gaming revenues first went into education, housing, health and elder care, and law enforcement. But as wealth accumulated, investments in a wide range of developments grew, as well as philanthropic donations to local non-Indian communities. Successful tribes sought by more land for development and business enterprises ranging from golf courses to industrial parks were sought. Unemployment rates in many areas plummeted. Examples of these successes include the Choctaws of eastern Mississippi who, in addition to a casino, by 1999 also operated a construction company, an electronics manufacturer, retail stores, and industrial parks; the Paiute of Las Vegas, Nevada, built a high-quality golf course.

Another key objective of many tribes who had culturally and economically rebounded was to reconstruct tribal identities by focusing on lost languages, songs, dances, and other traditions. For this purpose, the Mashantucket Pequot built a $135 million museum and a research center.

Modern Reaction to Tribal Sovereignty

The substantial economic gains some tribes had managed to achieve brought a backlash by the federal and state governments and the general public. Issues of economic development and tribal sovereignty became increasingly intertwined by 2000. As some tribes boosted their incomes, many opposed continued tribal tax-free and largely regulation-free status. Many complain that tribal businesses operating free of state taxes and regulations hold an unfair competitive edge against non-Indian businesses. The concept of sovereignty came increasingly under attack. Political initiatives were introduced in the late 1990s to weaken tribal immunity based on sovereignty. Tribal proponents responded that such efforts typically represented what tribes have endured for centuries: whenever Indians gain something of value, the dominant white society seeks to take it away.

One key issue among tribes and policymakers in 2000 resulting from casino wealth was how to redistribute limited federal funding support to tribes through the BIA. Tribes receive $3 billion annually directly from the federal government for tribal services as well as free legal representation from the U.S. Justice Department. The funding has

POLICE BLOCK ROUTE 438 TO PREVENT THE
CATTARAUGUS INDIANS FROM ACCESS TO THE NEW
YORK THRUWAY, WHICH THEY HAD BLOCKED IN
PROTEST OF THE STATE'S COLLECTION OF SALES
TAXES ON INDIAN LAND. *(AP/Wide World Photos.
Reproduced by permission.)*

Another reaction to gaming developments was
growing opposition to putting more land in trust
for tribes as more holdings were being acquired.
When lands are placed into federal trust they become exempt from local taxation and zoning requirements. However, trust also means the land is
not privately owned. Consequently, banks will not
accept land as collateral, so many Indians are shut
out of the conventional home-loan process. By
2000 the BIA opposed putting new land acquisitions into federal trust for tribes.

The local population feared new casino development would occur on these isolated parcels of
land within their communities. In reaction, tribes
are spending millions of dollars in donations to political parties and hiring lawyers, lobbyists, and
public relations firms. Some tribes have even
opened lobbying offices in Washington, D.C.

Legal Jurisdiction

When Indians commit crimes or civil offenses
off the reservation, they are subject to county, state
or federal courts. But on reservations, tribal jurisdiction extends to tribal members committing minor crimes, but not to non-Indians as ruled by the
Supreme Court in *Oliphant v. Suquamish* (1978).
Tribal members committing major crimes on reservations, such as murder or armed robbery, are subject to federal jurisdiction. Claims against tribes go
to tribal courts where tribes can invoke sovereign
immunity to limit damages.

The Supreme Court ruled unanimously in a
1998 Yankton Sioux case that the State of South
Dakota held legal jurisdiction over non-Indian, privately owned lands within reservation boundaries,
but not largely surrounded by Indian-controlled
lands. The Supreme Court also unanimously ruled
that the State of Minnesota held the right to tax
lands directly owned by the Leech Lake Indian
band and not held in trust status. Similarly, in
Montana v. United States (1980) the Court ruled
the Crow tribe of Montana could not generally regulate hunting and fishing of non-tribal members
on private lands within reservations. The Court
held that tribes can exercise civil authority on non-
Indians on private lands in reservations only when
conduct threatens tribal "political integrity, the
economic security, or health or welfare of the
tribes." By 2000 just how much jurisdiction tribes
have over privately held land within reservations
was still somewhat uncertain. Some circumstances
occur where tribal jurisdiction extends beyond
Indian Country. The 1978 Indian Child Welfare
Act recognizes tribal authority over child custody
cases involving tribal children off reservation.

been vital for health and welfare services and remains so for those still stuck in the poverty cycle.
Several proposals were offered regarding what degree of tribal wealth should affect the allotment of
federal aid. Tribes achieving greater economic self-
sufficiency feared that, along with decreasing federal support to their particular tribes, the federal
government would also tend to ignore its trust responsibilities leading to many other social and legal ramifications.

Major Figures

The struggle to maintain tribal sovereignty has included a wide-range of players. Key tribal individuals who stood against the onslaught of U.S. expansionism include many names now embedded into American history such as Tecumseh, Crazy Horse, Red Cloud, Geronimo, Standing Bear, Black Elk, Looking Glass, Plenty-Coups, Sitting Bull, Cochise, Joseph, and Black Kettle. These leaders defended their lands from the constant encroachment of American settlement. More recent leaders have included Ron Allen of the Jamestown S'klallam of western Washington, who served as president of the National Congress of American Indians—the largest Native American organization in the United States—through much of the 1990s. Kevin Gover, an Oklahoma Pawnee, became head of the BIA in 1997 under the Clinton administration. Other influential leaders have been: John Echohawk and Walter Echo-Hawk of the Native American Rights Fund, a nonprofit legal defense group based in Boulder, Colorado; Robert Coulter, executive director of the Indian Law Resource Center in Washington, D.C; Wilma Mankiller, Cherokee leader and national activist; Ada Deer, Menominee educator and activist who supervised tribal affairs under the Clinton administration; Ben Nighthorse Campbell, first Native American U.S. senator; and Suzan Harjo, Cheyenne-Arapaho activist who served in President Jimmy Carter's (served 1977–81) administration. Additionally, literature and academic studies by Native American authors have proliferated through the 1990s. A key scholar and author of this trend was Vine Deloria, Jr. of the University of Colorado. Among the many others are: Wendy Rose, Hopi poet; Alfonso Ortiz, San Juan Pueblo anthropologist; Jack D. Forbes, Powhatan author and scholar; Russell Thornton, Cherokee author and sociologist; James Welch, Blackfeet-Gross Ventre novelist.

Among non-Indians central to the sovereignty issues was President Bill Clinton, who opened the door to U.S.-Indian relations wider than any president since President Richard Nixon. For the first time since 1822, representatives of more than three hundred tribes met at the White House with the Clinton administration to discuss sovereignty and intergovernmental relations. Secretary of the Interior Bruce Babbitt, a former Arizona governor, was a central figure in carrying out Clinton's initiatives, however, Babbitt became embroiled in the legal dispute over the status of federal management of tribal assets. Another prominent figure and a key political opponent to tribal sovereignty has been U.S. senator Slade Gorton, Republican from the state of Washington. Many Indian people have considered Gorton their primary political foe since the 1970s. Similarly, Republican governor Tommy Thompson of Wisconsin has been outspoken on limiting tribal commercial business immunity from taxation and regulation, and on limiting tribal clean water standards to reservation lands only.

RECENT HISTORY AND THE FUTURE

Despite foreign incursions and the loss of a significant amount of their native lands over the past five centuries, Native Americans have endured. Though isolated on poverty stricken reservations and in inner cities for much of two centuries, the Native population has rebounded demographically, economically, and politically.

With the increased economic and political presence of tribes throughout the nation, legal skirmishes continue over Indian efforts to reassert tribal sovereignty. Bills in the legislature continue to attempt to question tribal sovereignty and self-determination and likely seek to curtail Indian gaming as well. The Supreme Court showed signs throughout the 1990s of restricting the concept of Indian Country. In addition, bills before Congress have proposed exempting all non-Indian land within reservations from tribal jurisdiction. Some tribes—not those enjoying the gaming boon—have offered their lands for nuclear waste storage. Considerable excitement and debate has resulted in this regard involving state governments and local publics. This issue promises to be sensitive throughout the coming years and central to the sovereignty question. As urban sprawl creeps toward once remote reservation boundaries, jurisdictional and sovereignty disagreements will undoubtedly further escalate.

The unique legal intergovernmental relationship between the federal government and tribal governments has been described as "measured separatism." Tribes have sovereign authority to exercise jurisdiction and decision-making authority over important aspects of tribal social and political life. Holding onto that authority has become a major focus as tribes become economically successful.

BIBLIOGRAPHY

Bordewich, Fergus M. *Killing the White Man's Indian: Reinventing Native Americans at the End of the Twentieth Century.* New York: Doubleday, 1996.

Burton, Lloyd. *American Indian Water Rights and the Limits of Law.* Lawrence, Kans.: University of Kansas Press. 1991.

Champagne, Duane, ed. *Chronology of Native North American History: From Pre-Columbian Times to the Present.* Detroit, Mich.: Gale Research, Inc., 1994.

———. *Contemporary Native American Cultural Issues.* Walnut Creek, Calif.: AltaMira Press, 1999.

Clark, Blue. *Lone Wolf v. Hitchcock: Treaty Rights and Indian Law at the End of the Nineteenth Century.* Lincoln, Neb.: University of Nebraska Press, 1994.

Cohen, Felix S. *Felix S. Cohen's Handbook of Federal Indian Law.* Albuquerque, N.Mex.: University of New Mexico Press, 1971.

Dahl, Kathleen A. "The Battle Over Termination on the Colville Indian Reservation." *American Indian Culture and Research Journal* 18 (1994): 29–53.

Davis, Mary B., ed. *Native America in the Twentieth Century: An Encyclopedia.* New York: Garland Publishing, Inc., 1994.

Deloria, Vine, Jr. *American Indian Policy in the Twentieth Century.* Norman, Okla.: University of Oklahoma Press, 1985.

———. *God is Red: A Native View of Religion.* Golden, CO: Fulcrum Publishing, 1994.

——— and Clifford M. Lytle. *The Nations Within: The Past and Future of American Indian Sovereignty.* Austin, Tex.: University of Texas Press, 1998.

——— and David E. Wilkins. *Tribes, Treaties, and Constitutional Tribulations.* Austin, Tex.: University of Texas Press, 1999.

Falkowski, James E. *Indian Law/Race Law: A Five-Hundred Year History.* New York: Praeger, 1992.

Getches, David H., Charles F. Wilkinson and Robert A. Williams, Jr. *Cases and Materials on Federal Indian Law.* 3d ed. St. Paul, Minn.: West Publishing Company, 1993.

Goldschmidt, Walter R., et al. *Haa Aani, Our Land: Tlingit and Haida Land Rights and Use.* Seattle, Wash.: University of Washington Press, 1998.

Harmon, Alexandra. "When is an Indian not an Indian? 'Friends of the Indian' and the Problems of Indian Identity." *Journal of Ethnic Studies* 18 (1990): 95–123.

Holford, David M. "The Subversion of the Indian Land Allotment System, 1887–1934," *Indian Historian* 8 (1975): 11–21.

Hoxie, Frederick E., and Peter Iverson, eds. *Indians in American History: An Introduction.* Wheeling, Ill: Harlan Davidson, 1998.

Johnson, Troy R. "Roots of Contemporary Native American Activism." *American Indian Culture and Research Journal* 20 (1996): 127–54.

Lewis, David R. *Neither Wolf Nor Dog: American Indians, Environment, and Agrarian Change.* New York: Oxford University Press, 1994.

Lieder, Michael, and Jake Page. *Wild Justice: The People of Geronimo vs. the United States.* New York: Random House, 1997.

Malinowski, Sharon, and Anna Sheets, eds. *The Gale Encyclopedia of Native American Tribes.* Detroit, Mich.: Gale Research, Inc., 1998.

McLaughlin, William G. *After the Trail of Tears: The Cherokees' Struggle for Sovereignty, 1839–1880.* Chapel Hill, N.C.: University of North Carolina Press, 1994.

Mitchell, Donald C. *Sold American: The Story of Alaska Natives and Their Land, 1867–1959.* Hanover, N.H.: University Press of New England, 1997.

Ortiz, Alfonso. "American Indian Religious Freedom: First People and the First Amendment," *Cultural Survival Quarterly* 19 (1996): 26–9.

Prucha, Francis P. *The Great Father: The United States Government and the American Indians.* Lincoln, Neb.: University of Nebraska Press, 1986.

———. *American Indian Treaties: The History of a Political Anomaly.* Berkeley, Calif.: University of California Press, 1994.

Quinn, William W., Jr. *Federal Acknowledgment of American Indian Tribes: The Historical Development of a Legal Concept.* American Journal of Legal History 34 (1990): 331–64.

Sorkin, Alan L. *The Urban American Indian.* Lexington, Mass.: Lexington Books, 1978.

Thornton, Russell. *American Indian Holocaust and Survival: A Population History Since 1492.* Norman, Okla.: University of Oklahoma Press, 1990.

Trope, Jack F. "Existing Federal law and the protection of sacred sites." *Cultural Survival Quarterly* 19 (1996): 30–5.

Vecsey, Christopher, ed. *Handbook of American Indian Religious Freedom.* New York: Crossroad Publishing Company, 1991.

Washburn, Wilcomb E., ed. *Handbook of North American Indians: History of Indian-White Relations.* Vol. 4. Washington, D.C.: Smithsonian Institution Press, 1988.

Weatherford, Jack. *Indian Givers: How the Indians of the Americas Transformed the World.* New York: Fawcett Columbine, 1988.

Wilkins, David E. "The U. S. Supreme Court's explication of 'Federal Plenary Power': An Analysis of Case Law Affecting Tribal Sovereignty, 1886–1914." *American Indian Quarterly* 18 (1994): 349–68.

———. "Indian Treaty Rights: Sacred Entitlements or 'Temporary Privileges?'" *American Indian Culture and Research Journal* 20 (1996): 87–129.

Wilkinson, Charles F. *American Indians, Time, and the Law: Native Societies in a Modern Constitutional Democracy.* New Haven, Conn.: Yale University Press, 1987.

Wilson, James. *The Earth Shall Weep: A History of Native America.* New York: Atlantic Monthly Press, 1999.

Wooster, Robert. *The Military and United States Indian Policy, 1865–1903.* Lincoln, Neb.: University of Nebraska Press, 1995.

Wunder, John R. *Native American Law and Colonialism, before 1776 to 1903*. New York: Garland Publishing, 1996.

———. *Constitutionalism and Native Americans, 1903 to 1968*. New York: Garland Publishing, 1996.

———. *Recent Legal Issues for American Indians, 1968 to the Present*. New York: Garland Publishing, 1996.

———. *Native American Cultural and Religious Freedoms*. New York: Garland Publishing, 1996.

———. *Indian Bill of Rights, 1968*. New York: Garland Publishing, 1996.

Richard C. Hanes

NIGERIA AND SHARI'A: RELIGION AND POLITICS IN A WEST AFRICAN NATION

THE CONFLICT

The Nigerian state, or province, of Zamfara declared in 1999 that it was repudiating Nigeria's constitution and adopting Islamic law, *shari'a*. Observers feared that Nigeria would dissolve into civil war. Violence broke out and many people fled their homes.

Political

- The Muslim population of Zamfara was enthusiastic about adopting *shari'a* to deal with crime that the state seemed unable to stop.

- The central government rejected Zamfara's right to establish a separate legal system and civil rights groups challenged the constitutionality of the system.

Religious

- Nigeria is comprised of roughly equal numbers of Christians and Muslims.

- Christians object to being forced to abide by Islamic law.

Economic

- In the 1980s the price of oil plummeted, causing economic dislocation, violence, and land disputes.

Beginning in the fall of 1999 American newspapers such as the *New York Times* and wire services such as the Associated Press and Reuters began to publish stories regarding the announcement by Nigeria's northern Zamfara State that it would implement *shari'a*. *Shari'a* is the Islamic code of law that for centuries has provided a complete guide to life for Muslims. Because Nigeria's population is roughly divided between Muslims and Christians, many sources feared that the move to establish *shari'a* would further divide the country or lead to violence and possibly civil war. For several months both sides argued the constitutionality of the issue. During this period, several other northern states declared that they, too, would seek to implement *shari'a*. In February 2000 widescale rioting between Muslims and Christians in the northern city of Kaduna led to hundreds of deaths, particularly of Christians. In the Christian-majority regions of the south Christian mobs took vengeance on the region's Muslim minority. Relatively silent up to that time, the Nigerian Federal Government, under the leadership of Olusegun Obasanjo, suspended *shari'a* in the northern states and convened conferences of governors and religious leaders to reach a compromise. On May 1, 2000, leaders from around Nigeria, including the northern states, agreed to "shelve" *shari'a* and return to the use of the Nigerian penal code. For the time being, at least, peace and tolerance won over religious conflict and bigotry in Nigeria.

HISTORICAL BACKGROUND

Located on the coast of West Africa, Nigeria is a very large country—it is roughly the size of the states of California, Nevada, and Utah combined, or almost twice the size of Spain. With a population of over one hundred million, it is the most populous country in all of Africa. There are over 250 languages spoken in Nigeria, a fact that highlights the country's incredible cultural diversity. Often referred to as "tribes" in the press—a term disliked by many scholars of Africa because it encourages images of Africans which are more based in myth than reality, these ethnic groups draw upon a variety of cultural and linguistic traditions. The largest groups include the Hausa in the north, the Ibo in the southeast, and the Yoruba in the southwest. Furthermore, Nigeria's north is predominantly Muslim, while other parts of the country, particularly the southeast, are predominantly Christian. In the southwest and the Middle Belt, as the central states are known, the population is almost evenly distributed between Muslims and Christians. Prior to the invasion and conquest of the region by the British in the early 1900s there was no political unit known as "Nigeria." In 1914 Britain combined its protectorates of northern and southern Nigeria into a single colony, which it ruled until 1960, forcing the various Nigeria ethnic groups to come together as a single political and economic unit. When the British left Nigeria they handed power over to a hastily organized, yet democratically elected government. The British had organized the new country into three semi-independent regions—the north, the west, and the east. The northern region, home to more than fifty percent of the new country's population, handily dominated the first elections in 1960 and gained control of the federal government.

In 1966, following a military coup d'état, or violent overthrow, that left many national leaders dead, the predominantly Ibo eastern region attempted to secede from the Federal Republic of Nigeria and establish its own country, known as Biafra. The Biafrans were motivated to create their own country both because of ethnic violence against Ibos in the north and because recent discoveries of oil in the southeast promised great wealth—so long as it did not have to be shared with the rest of the country. After three years of brutal civil war the Biafrans were defeated and the eastern region was forcibly reunited with the rest of Nigeria. In 1973 the Arab oil embargo of the United States led to a massive increase in the value of crude oil, and the economy of Nigeria underwent an oil boom. A huge influx of earnings and lavish government spending on public works such as schools, hospitals, and education helped to ease ethnic and religious tensions in the country.

In the 1980s, however, the price of oil dropped rapidly. As the oil boom turned to an oil bust, the

CHRONOLOGY

1900 British Protectorate of Northern Nigeria is established.

1914 The protectorates of northern and southern Nigeria combine to form Nigeria, still a British colony.

1960 Nigeria achieves independence from the United Kingdom.

1967–70 Eastern Nigeria secedes to form the new country of Biafra along ethnic lines. Nigeria fights a bloody civil war and the secessionists are defeated.

1973 The Arab oil embargo drives up oil prices, making Nigeria a relatively wealthy nation.

1980s The drop in the price of oil has a devastating effect on the Nigerian economy, leading to increased crime and violent.

1995 Political parties are permitted.

1999 Nigerians return to democratic rule. The Zamfara state announces it will set aside the Nigerian Penal Code in favor of *shari'a*, Islamic law. Other states follow suit.

2000 Riots—resulting in many deaths—break out all over Nigeria. After suspending the *shari'a*, the government convenes the National Council of State that recommends that Zamfara return to the Nigerian Penal Code, with some changes made to accommodate *shari'a*.

Nigerian economy collapsed. Nigeria went from being one of the world's twenty-five richest countries to one of the twenty-five poorest. The value of the *naira*, the Nigerian currency, went from two dollars to the *naira* to eighty *naira* to the dollar in just a few years. People's life savings were wiped out and those in the middle class could no longer afford imported goods. As competition for increasingly scarce state funds became more desperate, rivalries between different ethnic and religious groups became fiercer. Violence between religious groups, particularly in the north between southern Nigerians living in the *sabon gari's*, new towns, and the region's mostly Hausa indigenous population became increasingly common. Such conflicts were often sparked by disputes over land, trade, or national political struggles—but the lines of division were often along the lines of religioun and ethnicity.

Military rule has also been an important factor in Nigeria since 1966. Excepting a three-year

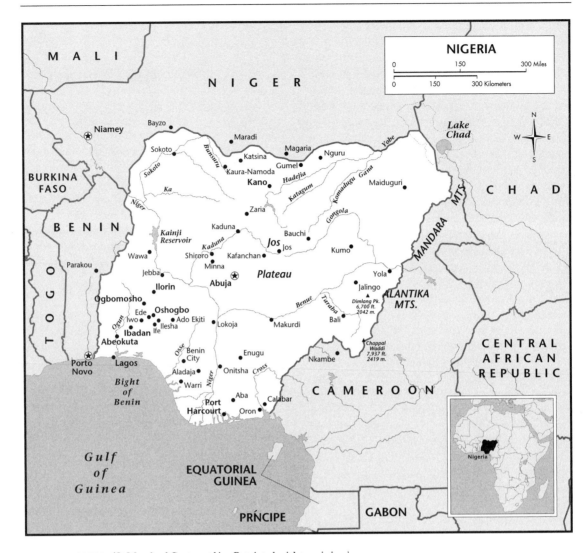

MAP OF NIGERIA. (© *Maryland Cartographics. Reprinted with permission.*)

period from 1980 to 1983, Nigeria has been primarily ruled by the country's military. Coups were common. As Africa's largest country, many hoped that a transition to democratic rule would help Nigeria lead by example and help reestablish democracy on the continent. In 1999, after the death of the military dictator Sani Abacha, Nigerians held elections and returned to democratic rule. Olesegun Obasanjo, a retired general and former head of state, was elected president. Interestingly, Obasanjo was the only Nigerian military ruler to have previously turned power over to a civilian government—which he did in 1980.

The *shari'a* controversy added yet another potential source of conflict into the complex ethnic, religious, and political environment of Nigeria. The newly elected governor of Zamfara State, Al-

haji Ahmed Sani, signed the *shari'a* bill on October 27, 1999, thus fulfilling a central promise of his campaign. The bill stated that *shari'a* would become the official law of Zamfara State on January 27, 2000, replacing the Nigerian penal code. As a result, the new civilian government of Nigeria was faced with a major challenge almost immediately after taking power.

What exactly is *shari'a*, and why would the Muslim population of Zamfara State desire such a religious system of law? *Shari'a* uses the holy Qur'an, also known as the Koran, and the *Sunna*— the example of the life of the Prophet Muhammad—to determine what is right and what is wrong. *Shari'a* thus involves all aspects of a Muslim's life, not just matters of criminal law, but also issues of how one should pray, the nature of family relations, and proper forms of personal conduct. Further, support of *shari'a* is a key factor by which Muslims judge the legitimacy of their governments. Some Muslims living in Nigeria's south declared that they would immigrate to northern states once Islamic law was established. In Islam, unlike in the American tradition of government, there is no desire for a division of church and state. Rather, it is the duty of the state to support the practice of Islam. This situation is similar to the call by many Christian fundamentalists in the United States for prayer in schools and the posting of the Ten Commandments in courtrooms.

The Muslim population of Zamfara State responded enthusiastically to the establishing of *shari'a*. In addition, Islamic nations such as Saudi Arabia and Libya sent word of their support for the move. Reports in the press stated that taxis in Zamfara State had segregated themselves to carry only men or women, since Islamic law stresses that men and women who are not related should not mingle in public. The consumption of alcohol was outlawed and physical punishments ranging from caning to amputation to death were instituted for theft and violent crimes. Many Muslim Nigerians and even a few non-Muslims believed that the implementation of *shari'a* would guarantee peace and safety for everyone. In the climate of poverty created by the oil bust, Nigerians have become increasingly concerned with crime and security. Just as many politicians in the United States have called for "get tough" policies on crime, Nigerian Muslims see *shari'a* as a way to protect their lives and property. Indeed, Governor Sani of Zamfara claimed that the implementation of *shari'a* would be a cure all not only for violent crime, but also for domestic disputes and civil crimes such as tax dodging. As he stated in an interview with the *Abuja Mirror* newspaper in February 2000, "the most important thing is the fear of God. With that, we don't even need the police."

Obviously not everyone agreed that *shari'a* would improve conditions in Nigeria. Christian minorities in the north and organizations in the south, such as the Christian Association of Nigeria (CAN), spoke out against the proposed move to implement *shari'a* in Zamfara. They feared that their rights would be violated, a charge denied by supporters of *shari'a*, and argued that Nigeria's 1999 constitution made such a move illegal. The Muslim leaders of Zamfara stated that since the constitution guaranteed freedom of religion to all Nigerians, and because their state was over ninety percent Muslim, they were within their rights to implement *shari'a*. Notably, not all Muslims in the

north agreed that Zamfara State's move was constitutional. The *Guardian* reported on October 21, 1999, that Sadiq Abdullahi Mahuta, the chief justice of Katsina State, declared the move unconstitutional. Perhaps more surprising was the comment by Sheik Ibrahim El-Zakzaky to *Compass Direct* on September 21, 1999. Zakzaky, who is often labeled as an extreme Muslim fundamentalist, declared that establishing *shari'a* at the current time "might end up creating an instrument of oppression and exploitation in the hands of the leadership, particularly when they lack commitment and discipline."

Despite such opposition and the danger of conflict, the state governments of Sokoto, Kano, Niger, and Kaduna states soon announced their plans to implement *shari'a*. While each of these states is in the predominantly Muslim north, some, particularly Kaduna, have very large Christian populations. Various Christian and civil rights organizations in Nigeria filed suits challenging the constitutionality of establishing a religious-based code of law. Just as in the United States and other Western countries, however, such lawsuits take months or even years to work their way through the court system before reaching the Nigerian Supreme Court, which would then judge the constitutionality of the issue. Further, some states in the southeast, including the predominantly Christian state of Cross-River, threatened to establish "Christian Law" in response. Many press reports suggested that Nigeria might go the way of Sudan in the 1970s—a north/south civil war along Muslim and Christian lines.

On February 21, 2000, the situation became violent. In the northern city of Kaduna, the CAN organized a protest march against the state's proposal to implement *shari'a*. At some point during the march, violence broke out. Each side blamed the other for the outbreak. Hundreds were killed as fighting spread throughout the city. A great deal of property, in the form of automobiles, homes, and businesses, was destroyed. Many southern immigrants to the north prepared to flee their homes for safety in the south. Condemning the riot, President Obasanjo declared it to be the worst outbreak of violence in Nigeria since the civil war of the 1960s. As mentioned earlier, such outbreaks of ethnic and religious violence are not unheard of in the north. What followed, however, was unusual. In southern cities such as Aba, Owerri, and Uyo, there were large reprisals against Muslim minorities—something that had never occurred before. Dozens more were killed and homes and businesses were destroyed. Sources outside of Nigeria feared the country was moving toward civil war. Inside Nigeria,

ACCORDING TO THE ISLAMIC LAW, SHARI'A, ALL FEMALE STUDENTS AT THE ISLAMIC PRIMARY SCHOOL FOR GIRLS IN ZAMFARA STATE IN NORTHERN NIGERIA MUST KEEP COVERED FROM HEAD TO TOE. *(AP/Wide World Photos. Reproduced by permission.)*

some suggested that the conflict was an example of the inability of a civilian government to keep the peace. Still others suggested that the violence was being incited by supporters of military rule simply to discredit the new civilian government.

Either way, it is true that Obasanjo's government had not taken many concrete steps toward resolving the issue. Up to the riots in Kaduna and the southern cities, Obasanjo and other federal government leaders had attempted to deal with the *shari'a* controversy through existing channels, such as the courts and personal contacts with state governors. Faced with the possibility of even wider outbreaks of violence, Obasanjo announced on March 1 that *shari'a* would be suspended in any state that had implemented the Islamic code of law. These states, particularly Zamfara, did not immediately accept Obasanjo's presidential order, arguing that he did not have the constitutional right to prevent them from implementing *shari'a*. On March 22, 2000, the Zamfara state government upset Nigerian human rights advocates by publicly amputating the right hand of a man named Bello Garki Jangebe for stealing a cow.

The debate over the constitutionality of the *shari'a* and over the relative balance between federal and state authority gave new life to another political debate. For years, many groups in Nigeria, particularly those sponsored by smaller ethnic groups in the Middle Belt and the south, have been calling for a Sovereign National Conference (SNC), which would bring together representatives from as many interest groups in Nigeria as possible to debate the very nature and organization of the Nigerian nation. As a sovereign body the conference would have the right not only to write a new constitution—the 1999 constitution being seen as faulty—but also to determine the very future of the Nigerian state. Many in Nigeria feared that such a conference might lead to a radical redistribution of state power and wealth or even a break-up of the country. Using the conflict over *shari'a* as an example of the failings of the current political structure of Nigeria, advocates of the conference bombarded national and regional newspapers and news programs with calls for the SNC.

RECENT HISTORY AND THE FUTURE

On April 3, 2000, under pressure from the federal government and numerous Nigerian organizations, the governors of all nineteen northern states met at Arewa House, the former home of the first premier of the northern region after independence, in order to discuss the issue of *shari'a*. The meeting was opened by the Sultan of Sokoto, who is the traditional leader of northern Nigerian Muslims. The meeting called upon the states of Zamfara, Niger, Kano, and Kaduna to put their move to *shari'a* on hold until a panel composed of Muslim and Christian leaders could be formed to investigate a compromise on the issue. In particular, the groups would be charged with finding a way to harmonize the penal code with the needs of Muslims. Named the National Council of State, such a panel did meet in early May 2000. The council was comprised of all northern and many southern governors, former heads of state General Yakabu Gowan, General Ibrahim Babangida, General Muhammadu Buhari, Earnest Shoinikan, President Obasanjo, and numerous Christian leaders. After extensive meetings, the council reached a consensus that the calls for *shari'a* should be set aside and the penal code once again put into force. Minor modifications to the penal code would be allowed, however, to make it more appealing to the Muslim population.

The debate over the place of *shari'a* in Nigeria is not a new one. In 1958 the northern region of Nigeria moved to replace the existing system of

THE BODY OF A MURDERED CIVILIAN LIES AMIDST THE RUBBLE OF KADUNA, NIGERIA'S BURNED-OUT DOWNTOWN AREA, AFTER DAYS OF ETHNIC RELIGIOUS CLASHINGS BETWEEN CHRISTIANS AND MUSLIMS. *(AP/Wide World Photos. Reproduced by permission.)*

shari'a—which had long been supported by the British colonial rulers—with a national penal code, thus establishing the roots of the modern system of the contemporary legal system in Nigeria. Even in the 1950s this was considered a very substantial move and was extensively debated by the Muslim population. Local *shari'a* courts continued to operate, but they only had jurisdiction over matters of civil and family law, not over criminal proceedings. The issue once again came to national attention during the constitutional convention of 1978, when, under Obasanjo's military leadership, the country was making the transition to civilian rule. There was a call for the establishment of a national

shari'a court of appeals. Extensive and often divisive debates continued until the motion was withdrawn. A similar issue was raised during constitutional proceedings in 1988. When the angry nature of the debates threatened to derail the constitutional process General Babangida, the current military ruler, declared the issue of *shari'a* to be a "no go" area, with that section of the new constitution to be authored by representatives of the military government.

Babangida's government was also sensitive to religious conflict in that it had sparked national controversy in March 1986, when Babangida declared that Nigeria had joined the Organization of

Islamic Conference, an international organization of Islamic nations. Protests by Christian groups and conflicts between Muslims and Christians led to Babangida's public withdrawal of Nigeria from the organization.

The nature of the Western press coverage of the *shari'a* controversy is worth examination. While quick to point out what is seen in the United States as Muslim fundamentalism, the media dedicated little to the discussion of why so many Nigerian's find *shari'a* appealing. Further, press coverage peaked when the conflict turned violent. Even news organizations that had largely ignored the issue suddenly ran stories, complete with color photos of burned cars, armed police, and angry crowds, that focused only on the loss of life and property and which described the conflict only in simple terms of Christian-Muslim violence. Africans frequently complain that the Western press pays no attention to their news unless it is bad. Such would seem to be the case in the issue of *shari'a* in Nigeria. There has been almost no coverage of the efforts by the Nigerian government to find a peaceful resolution to the issue, a resolution that was based on consensus rather than being forced by the federal government. Those who read about the violence from the Western press were missing important points of the issue and learned little about the Nigerian government's attempts to resolve the matter.

For the time being the immediate problem—the call for *shari'a* by northern states—has been addressed. The underlying challenges facing Nigeria, however, remain. Nigeria, like most African nations, is still faced with the huge task of forming a common consciousness between hundreds of ethnic groups who are divided by history, language, and religion. As citizens of a country forcibly created by outsiders and burdened by debt and poverty, Nigerians must also find a way to create a national identity and live together despite their differences.

BIBLIOGRAPHY

Aborisade, Oladimeji and Robert Mundt. *Politics in Nigeria.* New York: Longman, 1998.

Enwerem, Iheanyi. *A Dangerous Awakening: The Politicization of Religion in Nigeria.* Ibadan, Nigeria: IFRA, 1995.

Reynolds, Jonathan T. *The Time of Politics (Zamanin Siyasa): Islam and the Politics of Legitimacy in Northern Nigeria, 1950–1966.* Bethesda, Md.: University Press for West Africa, 1999.

Sanneh, Lamin. *The Crown and the Turban: Muslims and West African Pluralism.* Boulder, Colo.: Westview Press, 1997.

Jonathan T. Reynolds

NORTHERN IRELAND: THE OMAGH BOMB, NATIONALISM, AND RELIGION

On Saturday August 15, 1998, the small town of Omagh in County Tyrone in Northern Ireland became known throughout the world. At 3:10 P.M., a five-hundred-pound car bomb shattered the center of the town, killing twenty-nine people and injuring another 220. In the thirty-year history of the violence, euphemistically termed "the Troubles" in Northern Ireland, it might seem strange that this particular incident should cause such shock and uproar. The fact that it was the incident that caused the single greatest number of deaths in Northern Ireland was certainly a factor. However, the context of this horrific act was particularly significant in that it took place in the midst of a cease-fire called by the Provisional Irish Republican Army (PIRA) and adhered to by the loyalist paramilitary groups, such as the Ulster Defense Association (UDA), the Ulster Volunteer Force (UVF), and the Ulster Freedom Fighters (UFF). After twenty-five years of violence, peace of a sort had been brokered between the opposing factions, which could be broadly described as Catholic, nationalist, and republican on the one side, and Protestant, loyalist, and unionist on the other.

Hence, the shock of the bomb—which had been placed at the junction of Market Street and Dublin Road, in the center of a busy town at peak shopping time. There was no political or military targets singled out—the aim seems to have been to maximize the loss of life. A warning had been given to a Belfast news agency some forty minutes before the explosion, but this warning designated the Omagh Courthouse as the site of the bomb and was some four hundred meters from the actual explosion. Usually in the context of the violence in Northern Ireland, such bombs were part of an economic war, waged largely by the PIRA, and some smaller groups such as the Official IRA (OIRA)

THE CONFLICT

Northern Ireland, an area in the north of the island of Ireland that has been part of the British Empire for six hundred years, has experienced horrible religious strife for much of the last century. Bombings and shootings have targeted both Protestants and Catholics.

Political

- Many Catholics—or republicans—believe Northern Ireland should be independent or should be united with the Republic of Ireland.

- Many Protestants—or unionists/loyalists—believe Northern Ireland should remain part of the United Kingdom.

- Republicans charge gross human rights abuses have been committed by the United Kingdom and by the Protestant army in Northern Ireland.

- Unionists claim that republicans, especially the IRA (and PIRA), are terrorists that target civilians.

Religious

- Catholics assert past and continued religious oppression by the Church of England.

- Historically, Protestants have feared the influence of the Pope and of the Roman Catholic Church.

Economic

- Catholics believe they have been economically marginalized and discriminated against, including having their lands taken by a conquering British army. Catholics are generally poorer than Protestants in Northern Ireland.

CHRONOLOGY

1600s–1700s Encouraged by the English government, large numbers of Scottish Presbyterians settle in predominately Catholic Ireland. Much of the settlement is in the north.

1690 King James II of England is overthrown by his successor, and son-in-law, William of Orange. King James, a Catholic, retreats to Ireland to launch an effort to reclaim his kingdom. His army is defeated at the Battle of the Boyne, launching a violent retaliation against the Irish, who support James. Many of the Irish are forced off their land in favor of Protestant settlers.

1845–49 The Potato Famine devastates Irish crops, causing massive starvation and the deaths of 1.5 million Irish.

1905 Sinn Féin is founded.

1916 The Easter Rebellion, when Irish republicans fought for independence from Britain, is brutally suppressed and the leaders executed.

1921 Ireland is partitioned. The southern part of the island receives autonomy; the six northern provinces remain under British rule.

1922 The southern counties become the Free Irish State, later renamed Eire.

1968–69 Riots break out in Londonderry against British discrimination against Catholics.

1970–71 The Irish Republic Army takes up arms against the British. Protestant militias fight in retaliation. Over the next thirty years, hundreds die in sectarian violence.

1985 An Anglo-Irish Agreement provides Eire with a consultative voice in Northern Ireland's affairs.

1996 Peace talks begin.

1998 John Hume, a Catholic leader, and David Trimble, a Protestant leader, win the Noble Peace Prize for their efforts to end the violence in Northern Ireland.

1999 Issues over decommissioning arms remain, and tension continues, though peace accords were ratified in both Eire and Northern Ireland, including agreements about the claim of Eire on Northern Ireland and about requirements for Northern Ireland achieving independence.

and the Irish National Liberation Army (INLA), against unionist businesses and those that were part of the support-structure of the British Army in Northern Ireland. In this case, however, no such target was visible; instead carnage and the massacre of ordinary people were the only results.

Fears that this bomb was a sign that the PIRA had ended its cease-fire were ended when responsibility for the Omagh bomb was claimed by a hitherto unknown group—the Real IRA (RIRA). This group was formed when, at Provisional Sinn Féin's Ard Fheis (annual party conference), in 1986, the party agreed to end its policy of abstention from the taking of seats in both the Irish and British parliaments. This policy had long been a corner stone of militant republicanism, which refused to recognize the legality of the Republic of Ireland or of Northern Ireland. Those delegates who did not agree with this decision walked out of the conference, and ultimately, out of the party, and formed a new party, Republican Sinn Féin (RSF), which was led by Ruairí Ó Bráidaigh, former president of

Provisional Sinn Féin, and Dáithí Ó Conaill, former chief of staff of the PIRA. Two years later, in 1988, this RSF reaffirmed its support of the "armed struggle" and subsequently rejected the peace talks that had led to the cease-fires of 1994–96 and 1997 to date.

The reasons behind the planting of this bomb are imbedded in the history of the northern Irish state itself, in its constitution, and in the history of its different communities. However, the history of the northern Irish state is a long and tangled one, and needs to be seen in the context of the relationships of colonization and decolonization of Ireland by England over a period of some seven hundred years. The context of the violence in Northern Ireland over the past thirty years or so must bee seen within the context of the period from 1170 to 1600, as gradual English incursions into Ireland became more formally structured; the period from 1600 to 1800, a time when plantation and colonization set up the structural divisions that have existed in Ulster to the present day; the period from 1800 to 1922, when allegiances to Ireland and England became the defining factors in the creation of the northern Irish state; and the period from 1922 to the present, when Northern Ireland's endemic cultures of division and separation, along both religious and political lines, gave way to violent conflict.

HISTORICAL BACKGROUND

Remote Origins

The terms Northern Ireland and Ulster have often been used interchangeably, but in actual fact they are derived from different sources. Ulster is one of the original divisions of Ireland into five different sections, or provinces (the others being Munster, Leinster, Connacht, and Midhe), and there is evidence of the term's existence since 30,000 B.C. It was comprised of nine different counties, whereas the political term "Northern Ireland" was first coined in 1922, and referred to six of these counties. Hence, the early history of Northern Ireland is inextricably connected with that of the whole island, though there has been a long history of separation. In 100 B.C. a defensive rampart, called Black Pig's Dyke, was built by the people of Ulster as a fortification against invasion from the south of Ireland. From the earliest times, there was a strong Scottish influence in Northern Ireland, with clear divisions between the Ulster Gaelic families, led by the Ui Neill, and the more Scottish influences of the Cruithin. At the Battle of Moira, in 637 A.D., Congal Claen leading an army of Ulstermen, reinforced by Picts, Anglo-Saxons, and Britons were defeated by the Gaelic (Irish) families.

These remote battles and conflicts demonstrate a long connection between Ulster and Scotland, with an equally long history of conflict between the Scottish and Gaelic influences. Clearly emigration and immigration between Ulster and Scotland has long been a feature of Ulster's history, and predate the more formalized plantations and colonizations of the seventeenth century.

1170 to 1600: English Colonization of Ireland

In 1169 the first Normans arrived in Ireland at the invitation of Diarmad MacMurrough, the king of Leinster. Normans, a people from a province in northern France, colonized England, part of Wales, and Italy in the eleventh century. The Normans who arrived in Ireland were a mixture of Norman-English and Norman-Welsh and they were acting very much on their own initiative. In 1177 John de

MAP OF IRELAND. (© *Maryland Cartographics. Reprinted with permission.*)

Courcy marched into Ulster, killing the king of Ulster in 1200. The ongoing animosity between the Gaelic and Anglo-Norman factions in Ulster continued, with Belfast Castle being demolished by the O'Neills in 1476 and 1489. In 1522 the Irish Privy Council appealed for ships to patrol the coast and stem the Scottish settlement of Ulster. The ongoing friction between the Gaelic families, allied to some of the long-settled English families (Old English), and the "new" English settlers, was to be further reinforced by the reformation. After Henry VIII's repudiation of Catholicism, and the resultant rise of Protestantism, the lines of battle that have become so familiar to students of the Northern Irish conflict began to emerge.

In 1549 King Edward VI further altered the Church of England, following the example of Martin Luther, removing confession, processions, and the doctrine of transubstantiation. Many Irish refused to accept the changes both for religious reasons and because the changes were written in the English, as opposed to the Irish, language. Therefore Ireland remained Roman Catholic while England gradually became more overtly Protestant. Politically, this had important consequences for Ireland, as the Gaelic Irish, and their Old English allies, were almost completely Catholic in religion, whereas the New English were, conversely, practically all Protestant.

From an early stage, therefore, politics and religion were signifiers of different sides of the conflict. The connection of the political with the religious meant that each side had a strong sense of belief in the righteousness of their cause. The battle lines of native, Irish-speaking, and Catholic, as opposed to colonizer, English-speaking, and Protestant were being established even then.

Stung by incursions of the new English, and their replacement of the Gaelic and Old English in offices of state, Hugh O'Neill and his ally, Hugh O'Donnell, mounted a war against the Elizabethan English, winning a number of battles over nine years of war. O'Neill and O'Donnell adopted defensive postures inside Ulster, defeating whatever armies were sent against them, culminating in the defeat of Sir Henry Bagenal and six thousand men at the battle of the Yellow Ford. O'Neill attempted to make this war a national and religious one, calling on King Philip of Spain and the Pope for aid. The war culminated in the Battle of Kinsale, a battle which was to become one of the foundational moments in the history of Ireland. The war also led to the plantation of Ulster, a plantation which led directly to the presence of the unionist population in Northern Ireland, and by extension, to the ongoing conflict between English and Irish notions of identity in Ulster.

The plantation was the catalyst for the huge differences in identity, culture, and religion that characterize the northeast of Ireland. The very act of creating a plantation was an opportunity for the new settlers, but a tragedy for the natives who had been driven out from their homes. As these native people remained close by, a legacy of bitterness was sown that would grow over the years.

1600 to 1800: Plantation and Post-Reformation

In September 1601, O'Neill and O'Donnell received aid from Spain in the form of an army of thirty-five hundred men, who landed at Kinsale, on the south coast of Ireland. The Spanish army was attacked by the Lord Deputy of Ireland, Mountjoy, in October, and O'Neill and O'Donnell marched south to relieve the siege. O'Neill, O'Donnell, and the Spanish were defeated by Mountjoy on December 24, 1601, a defeat which broke the power of the Gaelic families in Ulster. The English government was determined to seize this opportunity and began an ongoing policy of plantation. For example in 1605, land in county Down was granted to Hugh Montgomery and James Hamilton. The first Scottish settlers arrived in 1605–06. Their first task was to build cottages and dwellings. By 1630 about five thousand Scots had settled in county Down.

By 1607 both O'Neill and O'Donnell had left the country, their lands being declared forfeit to the English rulers, and by 1610, a large-scale plantation of four million acres with English and Scottish settlers was undertaken. Different strategies were used, with counties Down, Monaghan, and Antrim being planted by private individuals, while counties Derry and Armagh were primarily planted by English settlers with more centralized organization. Counties Tyrone and Donegal were planted largely with Scots, while there was a mixture of Scots and English in counties Fermanagh and Cavan.

This plantation set out to lessen Gaelic influence and instead to incorporate an institutionalized sense of Englishness into the province. In 1613, for example, a charter was granted renaming Derry the city of Londonderry, and creating a new county of Londonderry. The government had learned from the earlier failures of Queen Mary's plantation of Laois and Offaly in Leinster, and of Queen Elizabeth's plantation of Munster. In both of these, the settlers had been isolated and were vulnerable to attacks from the Irish whose land had been taken. In Ulster, this problem was overcome by the construction of plantation towns, wherein most of the planters could take shelter. Defending huge tracts of land was often impossible, so three sizes of plantation were set out: 405 hectares, 607 hectares, and 810 hectares. Planters were expected to build fortified houses, called *bawns* on their land. These plantations proved popular, with an estimated twenty thousand Scots settling in Ulster between 1605 and 1609, bringing with them their Presbyterian religion, which was different from both Catholicism and the Church of England, although still being classified as Protestant.

The careful planning of these plantations led to their success. Given the fact that the planters were living on land that had been taken from the native Irish, high levels of animosity existed between both groups. The building of *bawns* testified to the fear and siege mentality that existed in the mindset of the planters.

In 1641 the displaced native Irish, many of whom had been evicted from their homes, rose in rebellion. Ten thousand to fifteen thousand planters were killed in a series of attacks, which drew the battle lines of the present conflict very clearly, as native, Catholic Irish attacked planted, Protestant Scots and English. In the following year, some ten thousand Scottish troops were sent to defeat this rebellion, and many of the Scottish soldiers remained in Ireland, taking up the land vacated by the earlier planters. Oliver Cromwell led the army during the war and sought to punish Ireland, and subsequently the planted areas were largely untouched, as parts of the rest of Ireland were planted by Cromwell's soldiers, a plantation again based on religious, as well as political criteria. The ongoing sense of religious, social, and cultural differences within the region continued to develop, and this development would come to a climax in 1687.

In England, the increasingly pro-Catholic policies of King James II, from 1685 onwards, began to make his Protestant subjects fear that he was going to reintroduce Catholicism as the state religion. To complicate matters, his daughter, Mary, had married Prince William of Orange, a Dutch Protestant, making the latter heir to the throne. Richard Talbot, Earl of Tyrconnell, began strengthening the Irish army with an eye towards future conflict. It was his attempted garrisoning of some Catholic soldiers in Londonderry in 1688 that was to set in motion a train of events that are commemorated to this day by the "marching season," in Northern Ireland. The marching season takes place during the summer months when unionists and the Orange Order celebrate the events of the Williamite war by a series of marches or parades through the cities and rural areas of Northern Ireland. In later years, they have become contentious as they often pass through nationalist areas, where they are perceived as being triumphant. The Protestant citizens of Londonderry were unwilling to appear openly hostile to the Catholic soldiers, and it was left to the Apprentice Boys of the city to bar the gates, an action that was repeated in Enniskillen, in County Fermanagh.

In 1689 William and Mary expelled James from England and were crowned in the Glorious Revolution, and re-established Protestantism in England. The Catholics in Ireland declared support for James, who landed in Ireland to begin his fight to recapture the throne later that same year. He had some early victories, going on to besiege the towns of Londonderry and Enniskillen. In August of that year, William landed at Carrickfergus, County Antrim.

In 1690 four thousand Danish troops from the European Grand Alliance troops arrived in Ireland to aid William, while Louis XIV of France sent troops to aid James. On July 1, 1690, the most significant battle of the war took place at the River Boyne, in County Meath. William won the battle, losing four hundred men to James's thirteen hundred, and this battle is still celebrated by unionists as their victory over the forces of Catholic Ireland. After the Treaty of Limerick, in 1691, the position of the Protestants was strengthened by the inception of the penal laws, which prohibited Catholics and Presbyterians from land ownership, voting, taking part in politics, and the ownership of weapons. The Toleration Act, in 1791, removed the stigma of illegality from being a Presbyterian. In the same year, the United Irish Society was founded in Belfast by Presbyterian radicals.

The United Irish Rebellion of 1798, led by Theobald Wolfe Tone, was influenced by the American and French revolutions, with high levels of involvement by Presbyterians in Ulster. Tone, influenced by the French Enlightenment, had little time for religion, and saw the aim of his organization, the United Irishmen, as the creation of a country where the terms Protestant, Catholic, and Dissenter (Presbyterians were known as Dissenters) would be subsumed under the common name of Irishman. However, economic, religious, and political differences were by now deeply set, and the rebellion was a failure. In Ulster, tensions between Catholics and Protestants still ran high, with competition for land in Armagh leading to the formation of the Peep o'Day Boys, a Protestant agrarian movement, whose counterpart was the Catholic Defenders. After a skirmish in County Armagh in 1795, afterwards known as the Battle of the Diamond, the Protestant Orange Society (later called the Orange Order) was founded.

The battle of the Boyne remains an icon of identity for Ulster Protestants. Much of the marching season that has caused confrontation by unionists parading through nationalist areas, recalls and celebrates events of this war, with "King Billy" (William) seen as a defender of Ulster Protestantism. Much of the vocabulary and symbols of the present conflict have their origins in this period.

1800 to 1922: Unionism and Nationalism

The 1798 rebellion was a prime cause of the Act of Union, in 1801, which set up the United Kingdom of Great Britain and Ireland, to be ruled from London, with the abolition of all regional parliaments. It is to this union that the unionists proclaim their loyalty, as it is a guarantee of their Britishness. With the industrial revolution and the expansion of the Irish linen industry, Ulster prospered. The disastrous effects of the potato famine (1845–48) on a mainly Irish economy of small farms were less severe in the increasingly industrialized northern province of Ulster. With the start of the union of Great Britain and Ireland, Irish politics became increasingly polarized along politico-religious lines. Daniel O'Connell appealed to Catholic nationalism in his attempts at repealing the union; the Irish Republican Brotherhood, also known as the Fenians, staged a rebellion in 1867, which was defeated.

The Act of Union was a polarizing factor in Irish politics, with a number of groups set up to oppose it, including the Home Rule League, which went on to became the Home Rule Party, led by Isaac Butt, and later by Charles Stewart Parnell. Home Rule would allow Ireland some autonomy within the British Empire. In 1886 Gladstone introduced the First Home Rule Bill, which was defeated in the House of Commons. Rioting broke out in Belfast (with fifty people being killed), a symbol that large groups of people in Ulster wanted little to do with Home Rule. The Irish unionists founded a group, the Irish Unionist Alliance, which gained support from the business community, and from the English Conservative Party, who felt that if Ireland broke away, then Scotland and Wales might wish to do the same. Randolph Churchill, playing what he called the "Orange Card," addressed unionists saying that "Ulster will fight, and Ulster will be right," thus assuring them of Tory (conservative) support. From 1886 to 1892, the conservatives were in power, and Home Rule was not pursued. In the meantime, Irish nationalism was emerging, with the foundation of the Gaelic Athletic Association (GAA) in 1884, to promote Irish sports, while in 1893, the Gaelic League was founded to promote the Irish language. These tended to further differentiate the Ulster unionists, who were now dissimilar in religion, political aspiration, and cultural and linguistic practices.

It is from the Act of Union that "unionism" in Ireland derives its name, its ideology, and its history. The Britishness that is enshrined in the Act was very much part of their own British identity, and any schizophrenia which they may have felt, as Anglo-centric Protestants planted in Ireland, was now dissolved in the overall sense of union. The connections between unionism and conservative politics were also laid at this period.

In 1900 the Fenians began to re-form as the Irish Republican Brotherhood (IRB), while in 1905, Arthur Griffith set up a new political party, called Sinn Féin, which, as a republican party, was against Home Rule, instead supporting full independence for Ireland. In the 1909 general election, the conservatives and liberals won 272 seats each. The Home Rule Party, under John Redmond, won eighty-four seats, thereby holding the balance of power. In return for Redmond's support in curbing the power of the House of Lords, the liberals introduced the third Home Rule Bill in 1912. By now, unionism, aided by the conservatives, had become highly organized in its opposition to Home Rule. In 1905 (ironically the year of the founding of Sinn Féin), the Ulster Unionist Council had been founded as a body that would unite unionist tactics. Sir Edward Carson and Sir James Craig emerged as leaders, whose argument was that the Protestant population of the northeast of Ireland constituted a separate nation, and should therefore be treated differently than the rest of Ireland. Their case was strengthened by the Curragh incident (also called the Curragh mutiny) in which fifty-seven of the seventy officers at the Curragh, under the command of Major-General Sir Hubert Gough, stated that they would resign their commissions before enforcing Home Rule against the loyal subjects of Ulster.

The unionist reaction to a third Home Rule Bill was to organize a week of demonstrations. On September 28, 1912, the Solemn League and Covenant was introduced by Craig, which some 450,000 people signed to voice their opposition to the Home Rule Bill, swearing to use "all means which may be found necessary to defeat the present conspiracy to set up a Home Rule parliament in Ireland." One of the suggested options was that the four counties with a Protestant majority—Antrim, Down, Londonderry and Armagh—could be left out of the Home Rule Bill. To reinforce their position, in January 1913, the Ulster Volunteer Force (UVF) was founded, organized along the lines of the British army, and claimed to have a membership of one hundred thousand. In late April 1914, twenty-five thousand rifles and three million bullets were illegally landed by the UVF from the *Clydevalley* at Larne, Bangor, and Donaghadee, under the direction of General Sir William Adair and Captain Wilfrid Spender. There was no police intervention, and the landings were successful.

The threat of violence to oppose political steps that were seen as threatening to the community in Ulster was first invoked in modern times with the formation of the UVF. The importation of guns, largely unopposed by the police, demonstrated the widespread sense of injustice that Ulster should become part of an Irish nation. This was also the first mention of the idea of partition, with a Catholic, Gaelic, southern Ireland partitioned from a Protestant, British, northern Ireland. The perceived connections between unionism and the British Army officer class would serve to contribute to nationalist fears throughout the conflict.

Stung by the success of this mobilization, nationalists founded the Irish Volunteer Force (IVF) and in July 1914, they landed fifteen hundred rifles and forty-five thousand bullets at Howth, near Dublin. The police did intervene here, and four people were shot at Bachelor's Walk in Dublin. With two armed camps in the country, civil war was a very real possibility, and the liberal government suggested that each county hold a plebiscite to decide whether it wanted Home Rule or union with Britain. If a county voted no, it would remain outside the Home Rule for six years. However, the debate was brought to a halt by World War I, with the bill suggesting the plebiscite being postponed until the war was over. Both unionists and nationalists felt that by joining in the war on the side of the British, their bargaining positions would be all the stronger when the war ended, with Redmond urging nationalists to "serve wherever the firing line extends." Thousands of nationalists joined the British Army's 10th and 16th divisions, while large numbers of unionists joined the 36th Ulster Division, which suffered fifty-five hundred casualties at the Battle of the Somme in the first two days of July in 1916.

That year also saw a sea change in nationalism, as a small group of the Irish Volunteers and the Irish Republican Brotherhood planned and executed a rebellion against the British in Easter week. Fifteen hundred men and women took part, and after five days of fighting, and 450 dead, the rebels surrendered. The rising was not popular at first, but the execution of seventeen of the leaders for treason was a watershed in terms of nationalist public opinion, with huge resultant gains for Sinn Féin, which established a policy of refusing to participate in the offices that they had been elected to in Westminster. The policy of abstention, or refusing to take the seats of office, was designed to show that the nationalists did not recognize the legitimacy of the government. Eamon de Valera, who had fought in the rising, ran in the Clare East election, on the platform of securing an independent Irish Republic. He was elected, but refused to take his seat. In terms of the situation of Ulster with respect to the rest of Ireland, he stated that, "if Ulster stands in the way of attainment of Irish freedom, Ulster should be coerced."

This split in the Irish Volunteers would mark a trend in republican politics with splinter groups having a large part to play in the politics of Ireland. The majority, who were in favor of the war with Britain, called themselves the National Volunteer Force (NVF) while the smaller group retained the original name. The year 1916 saw the beginning of republican violence, without any democratic mandate, a pattern that has since persisted in Northern Ireland. The threat of coercion, as voiced by de Valera, was an ongoing source of the unionist fear.

By the end of World War I, the Irish political scene had been "changed utterly," in the words of the poet W. B. Yeats. The British general election of 1918 saw Sinn Féin win seventy-three seats while the Home Rule Party had been reduced to six. The Irish Unionist Party won twenty-six seats, mostly in Ulster. All seventy-three Sinn Féin ministers of parliament (MPs) set up their own parliament in Dublin, called Dáil Eireann, on January 21, 1919. The Irish Volunteer Force renamed themselves the Irish Republican Army (IRA), and on the same day as the inaugural meeting of Dáil Eireann, two members of the Royal Irish Constabulary were killed at Soloheadbeg, in County Tipperary, an action which began the Anglo-Irish war, or war of independence.

Despite the ongoing conflict, the British government decided to implement Home Rule, and accordingly passed the Government of Ireland Act in February 1920. This act partitioned Ireland into two states, of twenty-six and six counties respectively, with parliaments in Dublin and Belfast, which were subordinate to that of Westminster. Northern Ireland, as a state, was agreed to comprise of the following counties: Londonderry, Tyrone, Fermanagh, Antrim, Down, and Armagh. Its first elections were held in May 1921, with the unionists winning forty seats, the nationalists and Sinn Féin six each. The unionist leader, Sir James Craig, became the first prime minister.

Elections were also held for the parliament in Dublin in 1921, with Sinn Féin taking 124 seats while the remaining four were taken by unionist candidates. The IRA, under the leadership of Michael Collins, continued the war against the British, making regular attacks on Northern Ireland. In July 1921, a truce was signed, which eventually resulted in the Anglo-Irish Treaty of December of that year. This gave greater measures of independence to the twenty-six counties, now called the Irish Free State, which was to remain in the Commonwealth. In terms of relationships with Northern Ireland, a Boundary Commission was to ensure that the border between the states would be fair to the allegiance of nationalist and unionist communities living close to the border. Also, a Council of Ireland was to be set up to ensure cordial relations between the two states, and to oversee the eventual unification of the country. This council never actually met, and the Boundary Commission report was shelved in 1925, with no changes made to the border. The period following the treaty was a turbulent one, with civil war between pro- and anti-treaty factions in the south, at the cost of four thousand to five thousand lives, and widespread violence in Northern Ireland with approximately 232 people killed and roughly one thousand injured. In 1932 Fianna Fáil, the anti-treaty patty in the civil war, joined the government, with Eamon de Valera as leader.

1922 to 1967: Unionism and Nationalism

In 1934 Lord Craigavon made a famous "Protestant Nation" speech, where he called Stormont (the parliament in Ulster) a "Protestant parliament for a Protestant people." In 1936 a Public Order Act was imposed on parades or marches that were thought to disrupt public order. In 1937 the Irish Free State changed its name to Eire in a newly-written constitution, which declared, in article 2, that Eire's boundary consisted of the whole island of Ireland, while article 3 claimed the right to pass laws for the whole island. Some northern nationalists founded the Anti-Partition League, in 1945, a group which gained a lot of support from the Irish Free State, which provided them with money in the 1949 Northern Irish election. De Valera's government stated that it would give unionists "reasonable constitutional guarantees" if they would agree to a united Ireland. Basil Brooke, the prime minister of Northern Ireland, responded by saying that "Ulster is not for sale," before looking for guarantees from the British regarding the permanence of Northern Ireland's United Kingdom status. The proclamation of Ireland as a republic (with another change in nomenclature from Eire to the Republic of Ireland) by Taoiseach John A. Costello, in 1949 was followed by the country's withdrawal from the Commonwealth.

The Ireland Act in 1949 guaranteed Northern Ireland's status within the United Kingdom while recognizing the status of the Republic of Ireland.

The Anti-Partition League was disbanded in 1951. In 1956 the IRA began a border campaign with attacks on areas of Northern Ireland. As a result, internment of those suspected of IRA activity was introduced in both Northern Ireland and the Irish Republic. The border campaign ended in 1962 due to lack of support. In the 1950s, Northern Ireland prospered, and with the advent of British funding for the Northern Irish welfare state, economic conditions were better than those of the Republic of Ireland. Discrimination against Catholics was charged against the unionist regime, with Protestants holding nintey-five percent of the top civil service positions in the Northern Irish government.

In 1963 Captain Terence O'Neill became prime minister of Northern Ireland, and a year later, the Campaign for Social Justice was formed, to protest against what it saw as discrimination against Catholics. In 1965 O'Neill met the Irish taoiseach (prime minister) Séan Lemass in Belfast, the first such meeting, which caused some disquiet among unionists, who felt that the power of the Catholic Church in the Republic (the 1937 constitution guaranteed its "special position," and it obliged Protestants who married Catholics to undertake that their children would be brought up as Catholics), represented a danger. In 1966 Ian Paisley, who had also founded the Free Presbyterian Church, set up the Protestant Unionist Party and began to oppose O'Neill's policy of *rapprochement* (lessening tensions). Nationalist celebrations of the fiftieth anniversary of the Easter Rebellion caused rioting with loyalist counter demonstrations. The IRA blew up Nelson's Pillar in Dublin that same year, but had become largely irrelevant in the increasingly prosperous Republic of Ireland.

1967 to 2000: The Troubles

The 1947 Education Act had opened third-level (university) education to a generation of nationalists, and in keeping with the *Zeitgeist* of the 1960s, the Northern Ireland Civil Rights Association (NICRA) was formed in 1967, looking for voting rights for all in local elections (only rate payers—property owners—had the vote until then), as well as an end to gerrymandering of constituency boundaries (the action of manipulating the boundaries of a constituency so as to give an unfair advantage at an election to a particular party or class). They also highlighted the reform of housing allocations and public sector appointments, the repeal of the Special Powers act, and the disbandment of the all-Protestant, paramilitary-style, B-Special police force. Because the NICRA did not inform the police of the planned marches, their marches were declared illegal. In 1968 the first civil rights march, from Coalisland to Dungannon, was held in August 1968, and was peaceful.

However another march, on October 5, was stopped by the Royal Ulster Constabulary, with a baton charge, leaving a number of the marchers injured. The march had been banned by the police under the Public Order Act. Two days of rioting followed, and this incident is seen by many as the beginning of the present "troubles." The whole incident was filmed, and drew the attention of the world's media to Belfast. Four days later, People's Democracy, a radical student organization, was formed, and in November, Terence O'Neill announced a five-point reform plan in the areas of voting, housing, and formation of a complaints commission. In late November, a civil rights march in Armagh was stopped by the police due to the presence of a counter-demonstration, led by Ian Paisley and Ronald Bunting (both of whom were subsequently imprisoned for illegal assembly). In December, O'Neill made a televised speech, stating that Ulster stood at a crossroads; the speech gained O'Neill considerable support. The NICRA called off its campaign.

On January 1, 1969, People's Democracy began a four-day march from Belfast to Derry, a notion borrowed from Martin Luther King Jr.'s march from Selma to Montgomery, Alabama. On the fourth day, the march was attacked by loyalists, including some off duty B-Specials, at Burntollet Bridge. The police were ineffective in preventing this attack. Again it was filmed and again these pictures went around the world. O'Neill announced an inquiry into the incident. An election was called for February, with O'Neill's policies dividing unionists into official (twenty-seven seats) and unofficial (twelve seats) groups. In April, "one man, one vote" was introduced by the unionist parliamentary party (by a vote of twenty-eight to twenty-two). James Chichester-Clarke resigned in protest. O'Neill, feeling his position had become increasingly untenable, resigned to be replaced by Chichester-Clarke. It was agreed to allow the Apprentice Boys parade (commemorating the barring of the gates of the city against James the Second in 1688) to go ahead in Derry. As the parade passed close to the nationalist Bogside area, serious rioting erupted. The Royal Ulster Constabulary (RUC), using armored cars and water cannons, entered the Bogside, to end the rioting. What was to become known as the Battle of the Bogside lasted for two days, and rioting spread throughout the north. In Belfast, streets of houses were burned down by rioters and over thirty-five hundred fam-

IAN PAISLEY

1926– Ian Paisley is the leader of the Democratic Unionist Party. Seen as an archetype of primal unionism, Paisley has actually been one of the main figures responsible for fracturing the once seemingly monolithic façade of unionism, thereby being influential in destabilizing the positions of Terence O'Neill, James Chichester-Clarke, and Brian Faulkner.

Strongly influenced by evangelical Protestantism, Paisley founded his own church, the Free Presbyterians, in 1951, and his religious fundamentalism, enunciated through booming, apocalyptic, anti-Catholic oratory, found a receptive audience in the hectic climate of the 1960s. His ideology is clear from the title of his first political party, the Protestant Unionist Party, later to become the Democratic Unionist Party, and his appeal has long been strong in rural and urban working class areas. In European elections—he has been an MEP since 1979—Paisley has proven a formidable vote getter. While opposing the Good Friday Agreement in principle, his party took its place in the Northern Ireland Assembly and also in its ministerial appointments.

ilies, mainly Catholics, were driven from their homes. Seven people were killed and one hundred wounded as the rioters began to use guns. The riots spread across Northern Ireland. The Irish Taoiseach, Jack Lynch made a television broadcast stating that the Irish government were setting up field hospitals along the border, and blamed the present situation on the "policies pursued for decades by successive Stormont governments." He went on to make the point that the Irish government could "no longer stand by and see innocent people injured and perhaps worse." So, on August 15, the U.K. prime minister Harold Wilson ordered the British Army into Belfast and Derry to support the RUC. Four days later he also ordered the Stormont government to introduce "one man one vote," disband the B-specials, and disarm and restructure the RUC.

In August 1970, a new nationalist party, the Social and Democratic Labour Party (SDLP) was formed, led by Gerry Fitt, with John Hume as deputy leader, to voice nationalist opinion. In March 1971, Brian Faulkner replaced James Chichester-Clark as prime minister. During these riots, the IRA demand for a united Ireland was

JOHN HUME

1937– John Hume is leader of the Social Democratic and Labour Party (SDLP). The key figure in constitutional nationalism in Northern Ireland, he came to prominence in the civil rights movement in the late 1960s. Hume served as minister of parliament for Foyle since 1969, and a minister of the European parliament for Northern Ireland in 1979.

He was a founding member of the SDLP in 1970, and has been seen as the architect of the Hume-Adams document which "aimed at the creation of a peace process," a process which ultimately led to the increasing politicization of Sinn Féin and the PIRA cease-fires. Ironically, the involvement of Sinn Féin in politics has created a strong rival to the SDLP within the nationalist constituency.

Hume has been seen as someone who can gain the trust of more moderate unionists, and he has remained a hugely popular figure in the Republic of Ireland. His appearance with David Trimble on stage at a U2 concert on May 19, 1998, as they campaigned for a "yes" vote in the Good Friday Agreement referendum heralded a sea change in the relationships between unionism and nationalism.

rekindled; this resulted in a split of the organization into the Official IRA and the Provisional IRA (PIRA) in December 1969. The more militant PIRA received arms and money from sympathizers in the Republic and in the United States. The PIRA targeted policemen and became increasingly involved in civilian demonstrations and riots. Twenty-five people were killed in 1970 and 174 in 1971. By mid-1970, the PIRA were believed to be around fifteen hundred strong, and there were 153 explosions in 1970, escalating to 304 explosions in the first six months of 1971. In September of 1971, a further splintering in the unionist community took place, with Ian Paisley and Desmond Boal founding the Democratic Unionist Party (DUP).

The violence in Northern Ireland worsened in 1972, with 467 people killed. The British government entered into secret negotiations with the PIRA, who called a truce for the duration. The PIRA's demand for unity was unable to be met by the British and the negotiations broke down. The PIRA response was to detonate twenty-six no-warning car bombs in Belfast on July 21, 1972, killing eleven people and injuring 130. The day is now known as Bloody Friday. The Ulster Defence

Association (UDA) retaliated by killing five Catholics. Ten days later Operation Motorman, the dismantling of the nationalist "no go" areas, was implemented. Overall twenty-one thousand British troops, nine thousand UDR members, and six thousand RUC took part in province-wide operations.

Given that in 1969, the slogan IRA was equated with "I Ran Away" in street graffiti, the birth of the PIRA, as well as using the term 'Provo' from the English language, was a response to what was seen as official repression, and collusion from the RUC. Internment and Bloody Sunday swelled their numbers, and many nationalists saw the PIRA as continuing the war begun in 1916. However, their campaign of bombing and murder alienated many in the Republic of Ireland, though republican strategists thought that the PIRA could bomb the British into negotiations.

The Irish and British governments wanted the unrest to end, and attempted to establish an agreement whereby power would be shared between unionists and nationalists in a new assembly. The role of the Irish government in the administration of these powers was a major sticking point for Brian Faulkner, the Northern Irish prime minister. However an agreement was brokered at Sunningdale in England, allowing for the establishment of a Council of Ireland, which would give the Republic some influence over Northern Ireland. The executive took office on January 1, 1974, and was composed of eleven voting members (six Unionist Party, four SDLP, and one Alliance Party), and four non-voting members (two SDLP, one Unionist Party, and one Alliance Party). However, in elections held in 1974, anti-Sunningdale candidates won twelve seats in Westminster to the pro-agreement side's eleven, and in May of that year, an umbrella group calling itself the Ulster Workers Council, organized a province-wide strike that effectively paralyzed communication, power, and industry in Northern Ireland. The Ulster Defence Association (UDA) manned barricades, which, when removed by the British army, were instantly replaced. The province ground to a standstill, and to further add to the tension, loyalist car bombs in the Republic of Ireland, in Monaghan and Dublin, killed thirty-three people. When the British government refused to negotiate with the strikers, all unionist members of the executive resigned, and Northern Ireland was again under direct rule.

Perhaps the most important feature of the strike was the grass roots support given to the strikers by ordinary Protestants, who clearly felt that their politicians were not giving them the leader-

STUDENTS PLAY NEAR GRAFFITI SUPPORTING THE IRISH REPUBLICAN ARMY'S REFUSAL TO DISARM, WHICH
COULD LEAD TO THE SUSPENSION OF THE PROTESTANT-CATHOLIC ADMINISTRATION IN BELFAST, NORTHERN
IRELAND. *(AP/Wide World Photos. Reproduced by permission.)*

ship they desired. It further fractured the unionist parties, and with the formation of Vanguard, another player was added to the political scene. Brian Faulkner resigned, and unionist control over the politics of Northern Ireland was superceded by direct rule from London.

During the 1970s, the PIRA campaign of terrorism and the loyalist responses continued, with 2,161 people being killed between 1970 and 1980. In 1976 the British Secretary for Northern Ireland, Merlin Rees, removed special category status from paramilitary prisoners, meaning that, in effect, they were being treated like ordinary criminals. Their

five demands included the wearing civilian clothes, free association in the prison, access to educational facilities, restoration of lost remission of sentences, and the right not to do prison work. At the Maze prison, a number of republican prisoners undertook what they called the "dirty protest," in that they refused to wash, or clean their cells, or to wear prison clothes. In 1980 there was a brief hunger strike, which was called off in December. However, the issue remained unresolved and in March 1981, a new hunger strike began, with wide nationalist support. The conservative government, under British prime minister Margaret Thatcher, refused to negotiate,

GERRY ADAMS

1948– Gerry Adams is president of the Provisional Sinn Féin (PIRA). He went from Belfast barman to reputed Irish Republican Army (IRA) leader between 1969 and 1973, although he has repeatedly denied IRA membership. In 1979 Adams spoke about the need for a political as well as a military dimension to the republican movement. He began talks with John Hume, of the Social and Democratic Labour Party (SDLP), in 1988 and in 1993, with a view to fashioning a pan-nationalist strategy. The resulting Hume-Adams document paved the way for IRA cease-fires in 1994 and 1997, with Adams being seen as a key architect of the PIRA cessation of violence.

Adams served as minister of parliament for West Belfast from 1983–92, and again since 1997. His claims to be a fully constitutional politician have been viewed with ambiguity by his detractors, notably referring to his "they haven't gone away, you know" remark about PIRA during the first cease-fire, and his carrying of the coffin of Shankill bomber Thomas Begley. His meeting with David Trimble on September 10, 1998, was the first such meeting between representatives of unionism and militant nationalism since that of Michael Collins and James Craig seventy-five years earlier. Gerry Adams has undoubtedly been responsible for the transformation of the republican armed struggle.

political rise of Sinn Féin, who, by June 1983 had some 13.4 percent of the vote in Northern Ireland as opposed to the SDLP's 17.9 percent. This could well be seen as the beginning of the politicization of Sinn Féin under its current leadership, with Gerry Adams being elected an MP in 1983.

In the 1980s, the violence and counter-violence continued. In 1984 four people were killed as the PIRA planted a bomb in the Grand Hotel in Brighton, where Margaret Thatcher was staying for the Conservative Party Conference. Political progress was also being attempted. The New Ireland Forum report, in 1984, was a debate on the future of Northern Ireland. Boycotted by the unionist parties, it was comprised of the Irish government and the SDLP (Sinn Féin's connection to PIRA violence precluded their presence), and it offered three possible political options: a united Ireland, a confederation of Northern Ireland and the Republic, and joint authority over Northern Ireland. In 1985 secret British-Irish negotiations resulted in the Anglo-Irish Agreement, wherein the British recognized the Irish Republic's right to make proposals concerning Northern Ireland, and the Irish government recognized the principle of unionist consent as a prerequisite to a united Ireland. Unionists were angered as they felt that a foreign government was being given a say in running their country. Sinn Féin was also aggrieved, as the agreement recognized the status of the Northern Irish state (something that Sinn Féin steadfastly refused to do). Unionists mounted an "Ulster Says No" campaign, but despite a petition with four hundred thousand signatures being sent to the Queen, the agreement remained in force.

The principle of unionist consent, and the *de facto* recognition of the right of the Republic of Ireland to have some say in Northern Irish affairs, signaled major shifts in the ground rules of the politics of Northern Ireland. The UVF and UDA began targeting RUC personnel, seeing them as traitors to the union by enforcing this agreement. It also demonstrated that the Irish and British governments were pursuing a long-term policy of diplomacy on Northern Ireland.

1987–88 was a particularly bleak time period for the Troubles, with eight PIRA men being shot dead by the SAS in Loughgall, County Armagh, and with an PIRA bomb exploding during Remembrance Day celebration in Enniskillen, killing eleven people. Three PIRA members were killed by undercover army agents in Gibraltar, in March 1988, and during their funeral, a loyalist gunman shot three of the mourners dead in Milltown cemetery. During the funeral of one of these people, two

and ten hunger strikers died before the strike was terminated, in October 1981. Thatcher went on to say, "We are not prepared to consider special category status for certain groups of people serving sentences for crime. Crime is crime is crime, it is not political." One of the strikers, Bobby Sands, was elected a member of Parliament during a election for the Fermanagh/South Tyrone seat, while two H-Block prisoners were also elected to Dáil Eireann in the 1981 general election. On Sands' death, Owen Carron, his election agent, won the subsequent election. On October 6, 1981 James Prior, Secretary of State for Northern Ireland, announced a series of measures which went a long way to meeting many aspects of the prisoners' five demands.

The main import of the hunger strikes was twofold. Firstly, the PIRA and INLA strikers became martyrs within their community, and created a wave of sympathy for their cause as they demonstrated an ability to suffer as well as to inflict suffering on others. Secondly, these strikes saw the

British army corporals drove into the cortege, and then were beaten and killed, presumably by the PIRA. In August of the same year, eight British soldiers were killed by a bomb attack on a bus at Ballygawley, County Tyrone. The need for some resolution was becoming all the greater. Between 1988 and 1992, attempts were made to initiate all-party talks in Northern Ireland. In an effort to make some progress, the talks were divided into three tracks: one dealing with internal relations, another with North-South relations, and the final one with Irish-British relations. The carrot was held out to Sinn Féin that it could be part of these talks if the PIRA called a cease-fire. This was the main sticking point, with the political parties reluctant to enter into talks with nationalist or unionist para-military organizations who still used terrorist methods. Of course, if some form of peace were ever to be found, then the people with guns would have to be part of the negotiations. The beginning of this process can be traced to a series of talks between John Hume and Gerry Adams, while the IRA was still pursuing its violent campaign, in 1988. A further significant development of this period was the inception of two new unionist political parties, the Progressive Unionist Party (representing the UVF), and the Ulster Democratic Party (representing the UDA). Now, paramilitaries of all sides had political adjuncts.

The significance of this period is the increasing randomness of the violence, led to support for negotiations. The gradual politicization of the paramilitaries proceeded, and all tracks of nationalist and unionist opinion were now being considered. Unlike Sunningdale, the necessity for inclusivity was very much at the core of this process.

In 1993 the Downing Street Declaration committed the British and Irish governments to setting up structures for talks, which would be inclusive. In 1994 the Declaration's perspective on arms was clarified: if a group "laid down their arms" they could be part of talks. After a visit to the United States, and at the urgings of U.S. President Bill Clinton, on August 31, 1994, the PIRA announced a "complete cessation" of military operations. On October 13, the UVF and the UDA followed suit. A debate began about the "permanence" of the cessation, and in 1995, the issue of loyalist parades in nationalist areas became important, with ensuing riots around the time of the marching season. The issue of decommissioning of arms prior to entry into talks was a sticking point, with the British prime minister, John Major, setting this as a prerequisite to Sinn Féin's entry into talks. U.S. senator George Mitchell's subsequent report brokered

SUPPORTERS CELEBRATE THE PEACE AGREEMENT WHICH PAVES THE WAY FOR A NEW PROTESTANT-CATHOLIC ADMINISTRATION IN BELFAST, NORTHERN IRELAND. *(AP/Wide World Photos. Reproduced by permission.)*

a compromise whereby phased decommissioning could take place during any talks. The PIRA felt that decommissioning should be the end of a process of negotiation, and not a prerequisite, and, on February 9, 1996, they ended the cease-fire. The same night, a one-ton bomb exploded in Canary Wharf, in London, killing two people and causing millions of pounds worth of damage. This was followed by another 1.5-ton bomb in Manchester. In July 1996, residents of the nationalist Garvaghy Road opposed an Orange Order march through their area from Drumcree church in Portadown. The RUC forced the demonstrators to allow the march to proceed, causing much nationalist anger. Earlier loyalist rioting and roadblocks were followed by a week's rioting by nationalists. In the Republic, on June 7, Detective Garda Jerry McCabe was shot dead during a post office raid in Adare, County Limerick, an action which was damaging to the PIRA in terms of support in the Republic, and subsequently a number of arms dumps were disclosed by disaffected supporters.

In 1997 a Parades Commission was set up to adjudicate on the routes of parades. Labour's Tony Blair became prime minister, with both Gerry

DAVID TRIMBLE

1944– David Trimble is leader of the Ulster Unionist Party (UUP). When an Orange Order march was forced down the Garvaghy Road, in July 1995, and David Trimble led that march arm-in-arm with Ian Paisley, few would have thought that this man was to transform the nature of unionist politics within the next three years.

Trimble was elected leader of the UUP on September 8, 1995. He was originally viewed as a hard-line unionist, but has directed a transformational change in unionist politics, finding common ground with the Social and Democratic Labour Party (SDLP), and being able to work with Sinn Féin, despite clearly expressed reservations on the decommissioning issue, which would require the rebels to give up their arms.

In sitting in government with Sinn Féin, he has faced virulent opposition, both from the Democratic Unionist Party (DUP) and from members of his own party. He has weathered internal criticism and is leading unionism toward a position of centrality in the development of inclusive political structures in Northern Ireland.

Adams and Martin McGuinness becoming MPs at Westminster. Portadown again became a flashpoint, with the march proceeding down the nationalist Garvaghy Road, and subsequent rioting involving more than six hundred petrol bombs thrown, two hundred car hijackings, and five hundred attacks on the security forces. Later that July, the PIRA announced a second cease-fire. Sinn Féin signed the Mitchell principles, though the PIRA did not. The Ulster Unionist leader David Trimble courageously led his party into negotiations, and later into government, with Sinn Féin and the SDLP, thereby breaking a logjam that had been an issue for thirty years. From March to April, negotiations were intense, and then, on April 10, the Good Friday Agreement emerged. The Good Friday Agreement was endorsed in referenda in both Northern Ireland (seventy-one percent in favor), and in the Republic of Ireland (94 percent in favor of constitutional change disavowing the Republic's claim to the whole island). The UDA's leader in the Maze prison went on record on the BBC saying, "the war is over."

The danger of regression into violence was clear throughout the peace process in the shape of the Drumcree standoff. The relative speed with which the agreement was reached was a sign that peace was clearly desired, but it also contained an indication that some items may have been rushed, and could still become a problem in the later stages of the process. The verbal ambiguities of the peace process, while allowing all sides to claim victory, would cause difficulty in the future.

In the elections for the Northern Ireland Assembly, the UUP got twenty-eight seats, the SDLP twenty-four, the DUP twenty, and SF eighteen, and on Wednesday, July 1, 1998, the first meeting of the Assembly took place, with all parties present. David Trimble, leader of the UUP, was elected First Minister Designate, with Seamus Mallon, deputy leader of the SDLP, elected Deputy First Minister Designate. Despite the widespread popularity of the agreement, hard-line loyalists and nationalist groupings were very much against what they saw, from their different perspectives, as a compromise. A further split in PIRA saw the formation of Republican Sinn Féin, and their military arm the Continuity IRA (also known as the Real IRA). It was this latter group that planted the Omagh bomb, hoping to create dysfunction within the peace process. However, the sheer pointlessness of the violence had the opposite effect, and the UUP and PUP entered into talks with Sinn Féin, who also made positive responses regarding decommissioning. Tony Blair and Bill Clinton visited Omagh, and the town's name became almost a rallying cry in the peace process. On September 10, 1998 David Trimble had his first meeting with Gerry Adams at Stormont. Decommissioning continued to be a stumbling block (PIRA seeing it as something to be negotiated, while the unionists saw it as a pre-condition for negotiation) and to the forming of an executive with Sinn Féin. Forming an executive is the term used in Northern Ireland to mean forming a government in parliament. On September 14, the Northern Assembly met for the first time since June 1998. However, differences over decommissioning caused a delay in the formation of an executive, and with the argument still raging, John Hume and David Trimble received their Nobel Peace Prizes on December 10. The decommissioning issue remained unresolved into 1999.

RECENT HISTORY AND THE FUTURE

Two important developments can be seen in the midst of the wrangling over decommissioning. The PIRA and Sinn Féin had clearly recognized the legitimacy of the Northern Irish state, a major development in republican thinking. The unionists, on the other hand, had clearly accepted the right of the government of the Republic of Ireland to have some input into the politics of Northern Ireland, a notion that had shattered the Sunningdale Agreement, and brought about the UWC Strike.

On July 15, 1999 an attempt to kick-start the Northern Assembly failed when the UUP and David Trimble did not attend the inaugural session, citing decommissioning. Seamus Mallon, of the SDLP, resigned as Deputy First Minister. To break this deadlock, George Mitchell, who had succesfully brokered the Good Friday Agreement, began a review of the agreement with the specific aims of solving the decommissioning issue, and obtaining an executive. On November 16, the PIRA said it would appoint a representative to the arms commission, a move that paved the way for Sinn Féin's participation in the Assembly. On Dec 2, 1999, power was devolved from London to Belfast, and all parties agreed to participate in this government. Devolving power from Westminster to Stormont meant that the people of Northern Ireland would have a say in the governing of their own society for the first time since direct rule from London was introduced in 1972. Power sharing, as a guarantee that the nationalist tradition would have a voice in government, was a central plank in the inception of this devolved government. However, in January 2000, the arms commission reported no progress on PIRA disarmament, and the unionists threatened to pull out of the executive. With no agreement forthcoming, the Northern Irish secretary, Peter Mandleson, suspended the executive after seventy-two days in power, and restored direct rule on February 11. Talks continued between Sinn Féin and Unionist Party politicians. On May 6, after much British-Irish governmental maneuverings, the PIRA offered to "put their arms beyond use," meaning that they will be put in storage, and subject to inspection by international arbitrators to ensure that they have not been used. Power was restored to the Assembly on May 30, 2000.

The formula for putting the PIRA arms beyond use looks to be the best hope of continuing dialogue between the parties. Hundreds of political prisoners have been released, with recent releases coming from the Maze prison on July 29, 2000. The constant collective decision-making that is a concomitant of parliamentary democracy may gradually encourage the parties to shed their mutual demonization of each other and begin the long and difficult process toward a more inclusive society. The Omagh bomb, if only as a catalyst in this process, has achieved a place in history that will be long remembered. It also remains as a signifier that there remain groups who refuse to follow the democratic wishes of the people of all communities in Ireland.

BIBLIOGRAPHY

Bardon, Jonathan. *A History of Ulster*. Belfast, Northern Ireland: Blackstaff Press, 1992.

Bew, Paul, and Gordon Gillespie. *Northern Ireland: A Chronology of the Troubles*. Dublin, Ireland: Gill and Macmillan Publisher, 1993.

———. *The Northern Ireland Peace Process, 1993–1996: A Chronology*. London: Serif Publisher, 1996.

Elliott, Sydney and W. D. Flackes. *Northern Ireland: A Political Directory 1968–1999*. Belfast, Northern Ireland: Blackstaff Press, 1999.

Hennessey, Thomas. *A History of Northern Ireland, 1920–1996*. Dublin, Ireland: Gill and Macmillan Publisher, 1997.

Hoppen. Theodore K. *Ireland Since 1800: Conflict and Conformity*. Harlow, England: Longman, 1987.

Hughes, Eamonn, ed. *Culture and Politics in Northern Ireland 1960–1990*. Milton-Keynes, England: Open University Press, 1991.

Jackson, Alvin. *Ireland 1798–1988*. Oxford, England: Blackwell Publisher, 1999.

Miller, David, ed. *Rethinking Northern Ireland: Culture, Ideology and Colonialism*. London: Longman, 1999.

Stewart, A.T.Q. *The Narrow Ground: The Roots of Conflict in Ulster*. London: Faber Publisher, 1977.

Whyte, John. *Interpreting Northern Ireland*. Oxford, England: Clarendon Press, 1990.

Wichert, Sabine. *Northern Ireland Since 1945*. London: Longman, 1999.

Eugene O'Brien

PERU'S SHINING PATH: REVOLUTION'S END

THE CONFLICT

In the 1980s in Peru, *Sendero Luminoso* (the Shining Path) was a feared and brutal revolutionary organization. Still known for kidnapping and murder in support of its cause, it no longer threatens to topple the Peruvian government. Leader Abimael Gúzman Reynoso, also known as Comrade Gonzalo, a charismatic scholar, believed and taught the Maoist philosophy of violent agrarian revolution.

Political

- The Shining Path is a communist (Maoist) organization and supports the radical redistribution of land and other resources.

- Many of Peru's Catholics embraced, for a time, liberation theology, which advocated on behalf of the poor and persecuted, using the Christian scriptures as justification.

- Opposition parties have been periodically outlawed in Peru, leading to increased radical political beliefs.

Economic

- The Peruvian government was unable to address issues of trade and agriculture, resulting in increasing impoverishment and dislocation, and disaffection with the government.

Ethnic

- The Shining Path was primarily comprised of Indians— natives to Peru prior to European colonization—who felt marginalized and discriminated against in contemporary Peru.

In May 2000, a small band of terrorists attacked the offices of the largest telephone operator in Peru in the town of Huancayo, less than one hundred miles outside of the capital of Lima. The Maoist organization Shining Path (*Sendero Luminoso* in Spanish) claimed responsibility for the attack. The attack burned some records and damaged the building, but there were no reported deaths.

In February 2000, Shining Path rebels made headlines on two occasions. On the second of February, Shining Path rebels killed three park rangers and robbed several tourist buses in the central Andes Mountains, which run through the middle of Peru. These terrorists were seeking money for their organization and were seeking to demonstrate that despite massive arrests of Shining Path members in 1997 and 1999 the organization still existed. On the ninth of February, rebels held in the notorious Yanamayo Prison deep in the Andes mountains outside of the province of Ayacucho released twenty-four hostages they had taken almost two months earlier and surrendered to prison officials.

Earlier, in October 1999, a Shining Path guerrilla force ambushed Peru's army, killing five soldiers. The attack came as two hundred members of the Communist Party of Peru (PCP) planned to surrender to government forces. Throughout 1999, Shining Path rebels carried out numerous attacks against government, business, and civilian targets in an effort to keep their dying movement alive. Shining Path rebels have been at war with the Peruvian government since 1980 when SP founder Abimael Gúzman Reynoso led a small band of rebels into the central Andes town of Chuschi to destroy election ballots and to disrupt national elections. While this action failed to create more than a small problem for the Peruvian government, it was a harbinger of almost twenty years of murder, violence and political unrest in southern Peru.

The Shining Path organization has been called "the most dangerous and violent terrorist organization in the world" by the Terrorism Research Center. Despite the arrest of Shining Path founder Abimael Gúzman Reynoso (also known as Comrade Gonzalo) in 1992 and second-in-command Oscar Alberto Ramirez Durand (known as Feliciano) in 1999, the organization has continued its guerrilla war against the Peruvian government. This war began officially in 1980 as an effort to topple the existing regime and establish an Indian-run socialist system emphasizing agricultural development and Marxist-style government. In the following twenty years of Shining Path's existence, it has murdered as many as twelve thousand Peruvians.

HISTORICAL BACKGROUND

Geography and History

Peru is a small South American nation of 496,223 square miles. It is slightly smaller than Alaska (586,412 square miles), and approximately the same size as South Africa (471,010 square miles). Peru is located on the western coast of South America and is bordered to the south by Chile and Bolivia. To the east is Brazil, the largest nation in South America. Peru is directly south of Colombia and Ecuador. The northern part of Peru is slightly below the equator, which means its weather is largely tropical. The Andes Mountains, which run all along the Western coast of South America, cover most of Peru.

Peru's population of approximately 26.6 million (1999 estimate) is primarily employed in agriculture or service industries. Most of the industry that exists in Peru is what is called First Sector industry—mining of metals, drilling for oil, producing raw textiles, and fishing. Peru's primary exports include copper, zinc, coffee, cocoa, and wheat and other grains. Most Peruvians are severely underemployed. Some figures indicate that since 1980 wages in Peru have dropped over seventy percent. This intense poverty played a significant role in creating support for the Shining Path rebels in the early 1980s and 1990s.

The people of Peru represent several distinct ethnic groups. Peru, unlike Mexico or Brazil, has a large indigenous population (forty-five percent), followed by the *mestizo* (thirty-seven percent). *Mestizos* are Latinos of mixed ancestry, often by intermarriage between native Indians and European

---

CHRONOLOGY

1826 Peru wins independence from Spain.

1948 Peru's president outlaws the liberal People's Party.

1968–80 Peru is governed by the military.

1980 Belaúde is elected president. Economic chaos ensues throughout the 1980s. The Shining Path conducts its first violent action.

1981 Shining Path guerrillas control much of Ayucucho.

1982 Shining Path guerrillas control most of southern Peru and some of the south-central Andes.

1985 Shining Path moves to the cities.

1987 Shining Path refocuses its efforts on educational programs. At the same time, the Shining Path becomes involved in controlling the drug business.

1992 Abimeal Gúzman (Comrade Gonzalo) is arrested and imprisoned.

1993 Gúzman, in prison, calls on the Shining Path to renounce violence.

1999 The Shining Path's second-in-command Ramirez (also known as Feliciano) is captured.

---

settlers. Those of European descent account for about fifteen percent of the population. Other nationalities account for about five percent of the Peruvian population. Despite this population distribution, those of European descent control most political and economic institutions. This disparity is responsible for much of the political conflict in Peru during the twentieth century.

The vast majority of Peruvians are Roman Catholic, although the Catholic church in Peru is split between traditional Catholics and those who follow liberation theology. Liberation theology is a merging of Marxist and Christian philosophies regarding governmental and individual obligations to the poor of Peru. Most Liberation Theologians generally advocate wider dispersion of wealth. In Peru's case, Liberation Catholics have called on the government to take the wealth of landowners and give that wealth to the poor native people. Peru's Catholicism is a result of Spanish conquest and settlement in the 1600s and 1700s. Peru did not gain its independence from Spain until 1826.

Peru's modern history may be broken into four broad sections: the period from 1936 to 1948, marked by the rise of the Peruvian Communist Party (PCP); the period from 1948 to 1968, marked by increased tension between socialist forces in Peru and the Peruvian military; the period from 1968 to 1980, marked by military rule and broad economic collapse; the period from 1980 to the present, marked by democratic reform and defeat of Peru's communist factions by government forces. This is the period in which Shining Path emerged as a distinct military and political force in Peru's politics.

From 1936 to 1948

Peru's independence from Spain in 1826 did not produce an immediate solution to its economic or political woes. Peru's (largely European) political leadership chose to develop the nation's international export trade rather than to develop domestic commerce. To that end, the Peruvian government created an export business for guano, the droppings from seabirds. This was an excellent fertilizer widely used by commercial farmers in the United States and Europe. Peru's decision to pursue this kind of trade distorted economic development in the small nation and left Peru vulnerable to international markets and trade. The economic downturns of the 1873 and 1893 depressions, coupled with a war against Chile to the south, led to serious political unrest in the mountainous nation. Only by agreeing to allow Great Britain to build a railroad in Junín, a department in south-central Peru ("departments" are like states or counties in the United States or Australia; Peru has twenty-four departments), was the government able to survive. The railroad was designed to allow Peruvian mining companies to extract important minerals and then ship them to the coast for transport to Britain and elsewhere.

This contract seemed to bolster Peru, but by 1920 over eighty percent of Peru's commercial and manufacturing enterprises were foreign-owned. This substantial foreign investment angered many domestic firms who could not compete against these international corporations. In order to attract foreign investment, the Peruvian government often offered tax incentives and profit sharing plans that overseas businesses found very appealing. By the mid-1920s, many small businessmen, university professors, and department governmental officials began to call for more "nationalistic" economic policies. Peruvian economic elites wanted Peru's international policies to emphasize domestic companies and products, not imported products. This conflict is a second component of Peru's political difficulties in the twentieth century.

One consequence of the political unrest caused by the government's inability to solve the trade and farm issues was the growth of national socialist and labor organizations. APRA (American Popular Revolutionary Alliance) was one of the earliest and largest of these unions. In its early years, APRA called for the inclusion of the indigenous and *mestizo* masses in the economic boom created in the 1880s. While extremely unpopular with the politically powerful Peruvian military, APRA followers (called *apristas*) demonstrated excellent political judgment. During the free elections of 1945, APRA won a majority of seats in the Peruvian legislature and three seats on President Jose Bustamante's cabinet. In this position of power APRA was able to implement some political reforms and to increase the power of labor unions in Peru.

Unfortunately, these reform efforts, coupled with continuing rumors that APRA intended to resort to political violence if its demands for faster reforms were not met, weakened APRA's popular support. In 1948, President Bustamante was forced by the military to outlaw the People's Party, a coalition of socialist and extreme liberal parties of which APRA was a key member. The military wanted more action taken, but Bustamante refused. A coup d'état followed, removing Bustamante from power and placing several military commanders in control of the Peruvian government.

APRA's efforts to cooperate with governmental officials created a split within the party in 1920. Those who followed Victor Raul Haya de la Torre (1895–1982?), APRA's founder, believed that they could best serve the native and poor of Peru by cooperating with government forces whenever feasible, but continually emphasizing Peruvian nationalism against the government's internationalist policies. The Marxists within the organization, led by Jose Carlos Mariátegui (1895–1930), advocated a strong position of militant opposition to the existing government. Mariátegui established the Confederacion General de Trabadores Peruano (General Confederation of Peruvian Workers) to advocate this Marxist line. The governments throughout the 1930s and 1940s suppressed the CGTP as well as the APRA.

The Period of Military-Civilian Government (1948–68)

Following the coup of 1948, General Manuel Odría seized control of the government of Peru. He allowed the legislature to continue to hold elections and to meet, but for all practical purposes he governed as a dictator. Odría had been a cabinet officer under Bustamante, but was disillusioned by the

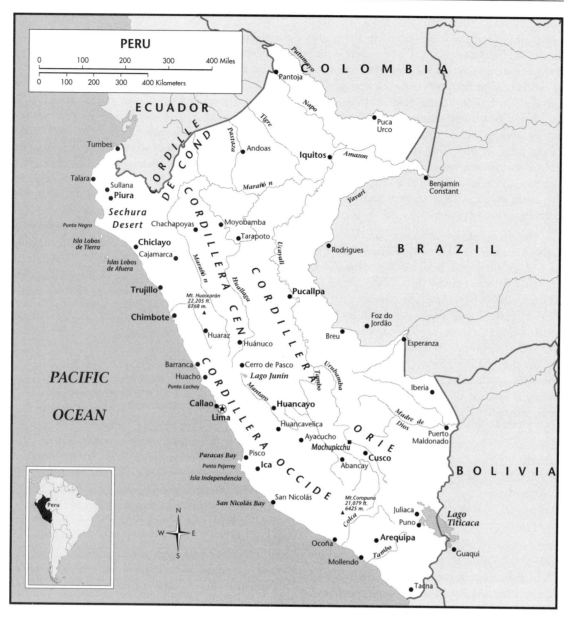

MAP OF PERU. (© *Maryland Cartographics. Reprinted with permission.*)

chaos and poor governance he believed lay at the heart of the conservative APRA coalition that had been in power since 1945. During his presidency, he outlawed the *apristas* and other communist organizations. Odría's rule was marred by political unrest, but it also created economic growth. Much of this economic development was due to the outbreak of the Korean War in 1950. During the course of the war, Peruvian mineral and metal exports increased tremendously, as did the price for these commodities. Peru entered a period of relative wealth and economic expansion. However, it was primarily Peru's European economic and military elites who prospered under these develop-

ments while the native and *mestizo* populations suffered greatly. This continued disparity between wealthy Europeans and poor native populations helped to strengthen the PCP (the Communist Party of Peru), which split from the CGTP during Odría's rule.

The importance of agrarian politics in Peru is rooted in its farm system. The farm structure in Peru was based on the *hacienda*, which was a large farm or plantation whose owner would rent out part of the land to sharecroppers. These sharecroppers would farm the land, and then give to the landowner the majority of their crops, keeping a small amount for their own subsistence. The land-owner would sell the crops and keep the profits. By the 1950s, the majority of landowners were of European descent while the croppers were native or *mestizo*. These croppers grew increasingly dis-gruntled with the inequitable distribution of wealth and power and during the 1950s hundreds of thousands of them seized *hacienda* lands and be-gan to farm illegally. Government efforts to con-trol these invasions were hampered by poor coor-dination and a pitifully small police force, so for the most part the farm owners and "squatters" came to an uneasy truce.

The events of the 1950s solidified a split that had occurred in the 1920s and 1930s in the APRA. As was already noted, in the 1920s, some Marxist *apristas* split off to create the CGTP. During the 1950s, the CGTP fractured again into several com-munist parties, including the PCP-Red Flag, which followed communist China, and the PCP-IU, which followed Stalinist, or internationalist communism. APRA's cooperation with Peru's gov-ernments continued to be a point of contention leaving it often at odds with the various commu-nist organizations in Peru. Many within the emerg-ing PCP advocated violent opposition to the re-gime, while others advocated a strategy of peasant education. These debates foreshadowed the actions of PCP-SL (Shining Path) would follow thirty years later.

Because of President Odría's policies, the CGTP gained strength among union workers and farmers, particularly in the southern part of Peru. Unrest led Odría to permit regular elections in 1956; these elections would mark the end of his rule in Peru. APRA cooperated with several ex-tremely conservative organizations to help elect Manuel Prado to office and to defeat PCP/CGTP candidates. In exchange for this support, Prado as-sisted APRA in gaining many seats in the legisla-ture. This cooperation exacerbated the split be-tween APRA and CGTP.

Prado's government, however, turned out to be a disappointment. Rather than chart a new course for Peru, Prado continued many of the controver-sial internationalist policies of Odría and other presidents. His policies created more economic growth, but failed to resolve the problems of in-come distribution on the farms. The demands for agrarian reform and land redistribution went largely unanswered. Peru's poor population placed much of the blame for this on the Peruvian legislature. Prado did not run for reelection in 1962.

The election of 1962 was a bitterly contested race between Haya de la Torres of the APRA, Odría

(who had formed his own party), and Fernando Belaúnde Terry. Belaúnde, an architecture profes-sor, appeared out of nowhere, but won election in 1963, after military intervention annulled the 1962 elections. While Belaúnde was a dynamic speaker and had tremendous public appeal, his government was marred by a legislature divided between *aprista* forces and those following Odría. Belaúnde was un-able to address agrarian reforms despite increasing numbers of hacienda invasions and increased vio-lence in rural areas. Belaúnde was also unable to chart an effective policy concerning Peruvian oil. Nationalists and socialists demanded that he take over the oil industry from the American companies that controlled oil production. Conservatives, many of whom received profits from the oil trade, op-posed such a move. Belaúnde's policies of a grad-ual nationalization or takeover, met with resistance from both groups.

Throughout this period agrarian unrest, par-ticularly among Peru's native population, grew. The PCP helped to foster this unrest. It was also dur-ing this time that a young college professor by the name of Abimeal Guzmán Reynoso began teach-ing at the newly opened University of San Cristóbal du Huamanga in the department of Ayacucho. Ayacucho is a department of Peru with a large number of native people. Guzmán, a life-long so-cial democrat, had become a Marxist during his years in college. During his tenure at the University of San Cristóbal, he would implement his own no-tions of Marxist revolution through classes and through close ties to the PCP. Guzmán founded the Shining Path branch of the PCP in order to foster a revolutionary spirit among the natives of Ayacucha and its surrounding areas.

It is not too much to claim that Shining Path was Guzmán's creation. During his tenure at the university, Guzmán began to build his organiza-tion. His program included offering extension classes on Marxist doctrine to the native popula-tion outside the university. He also began gather-ing together the intellectuals and students who would form the organizational core of Shining Path. Throughout the 1960s and early 1970s, Guz-mán continued to preach a Maoist doctrine of vi-olent peasant revolution and to call for the creation of a socialist government dominated by the native people of Peru. Sometime in the mid-1960s, Guz-mán took a trip to China, where he encountered many advocates of Maoism. This visit left its mark on Guzmán, whose writings were, from then on, often imitative of Mao's own works.

By 1968 events in Peru had reached a critical period. Negotiations with American oil companies had broken down. Landowners continually faced takeovers by sharecroppers, and an imminent coup by APRA threatened governmental stability. Into this volatile situation stepped the Peruvian military. Taking over the government in 1968, the military would rule Peru until elections in 1980. Military rule in Peru would be marked by many successes, but tremendous failures in promoting civil rights, in solving the agrarian problem, or in gaining popular support for its rule.

The Military Takes Charge (1968–80)

The military government in Peru faced three critical problems. First, of course, was growing peasant unrest over land reform. Coupled with this was the increasing power of the PCP among the peasantry and labor unions. Second, the government faced several international crises. The most critical issues were a show-down with the United States over oil exploration and sale, settlement of a dispute with both northern and southern neighbors about fishing off of coastal waters, and finally, Peruvian international debt, which was enormous. The military government's handling of these issues showed great energy and resolve, but the recession of the mid- and late-1970s, coupled with internal division about how the military should pursue reform, proved insurmountable obstacles.

Domestically, the military government began a program of massive expropriation of private farms. In 1968, ninety percent of farmlands were in the hands of only two percent of the Peruvian population. By 1975, the military regime had appropriated eleven million acres of land, turning much of it into farming cooperatives overseen by military officials. These co-ops employed thousands of farmers and sharecroppers and allowed them to keep the profits of their farms. These co-ops were not uniformly successful however. By the mid-1970s, four distinct economic cultures existed in Peru.

Most of Peru's major cities, sugar and cotton farms, and all her ports are on the coast. These coastal cities had enormous wealth. In the northern and central Andes, mining operations dominated the local economy until the recession of 1973 reduced the demand for metals. Many mines closed and thousands of workers were either laid off or underemployed. Farmland in the southern Andes is wind-swept, rocky and very dry. This has traditionally been a poor area of Peru. The standard of living in the southern Andes is among the lowest in Peru and in Latin America. The department of Ayacucho, the home of the Shining Path, is still noted for poverty despite many years of efforts to improve conditions. The last area, the jungles of Peru, contains only about ten percent of Peru's population. Other than a thriving cocaine business, this area was and is extremely undeveloped. Almost no governmental or infrastructure services exist, such as roads or water, and the population lives in extreme poverty.

This diversity presented the military government (and subsequent governments) with unique challenges. Attempts to solve the agrarian problem left over half the native population in poverty and without land. Particularly in Ayacucho, this oversight created more unrest and calls for reform and the PCP used this unrest to foment calls for revolution. The military government's successes in foreign policy were more clear. They successfully nationalized Peruvian oil and won exclusive fishing rights within Peruvian coastal waters, but these successes did not solve the poverty of much of the population. Although the government managed to renegotiate its foreign debt, this also failed to increase the military regime's popularity. When it opened the door for popular elections in 1980, few doubted it would be voted out of power.

During the 1970s, Guzmán was busy as well. He had organized Shining Path into two units. The first continued the educational programs among the native population around Ayacucho, while the second unit began plans for armed combat against the government. By 1977 Guzmán had determined that violence was much more likely than educational efforts to bring about the reforms he desired, and so in 1978 he established a military training school. By 1980 Guzmán and Shining Path were ready to begin a two-decade war against the government of Peru.

The Modern Era: 1980 to the Present

The military regime's efforts had brought some solutions to Peru's international and domestic problems, but once again international markets worked to undermine all the government had accomplished. Beginning in 1974 the international market for oil, sugar, and copper dropped drastically. Peru, which had built much of its prosperity on international commerce, found itself hard-pressed to repay the many loans it had taken to pay for progress. The military government faced an additional hurdle because of its earlier program of nationalizing industries. Many international lenders refused to make new loans to Peru. In order to cope with a growing economic crisis, the military government in 1977 began reversing many of its programs. It opened Peru up for increased foreign investment and involvement in the economy; it began

POLITICAL IDEOLOGIES IN PERU

Marxism: A political philosophy which states that all conflict is economic conflict. Marxists believe that the world is controlled by those who have economic resources. History indicates that at some point in the future, the workers (proletariat) will overthrow the bourgeoisie (owners of goods and businesses) and divide economic wealth equally or fairly.

Leninism: A development of Marxism which claims that the proletariat revolution will occur among agrarian people, not among industrialized nations. Leninism also calls for the export of revolution through the use of vanguard parties, or small groups of party loyalists who educate the workers to their condition of servitude to the bourgeoisie (owners of goods and businesses).

Maoism: An extension of Leninism that argues that peasants must be directed to revolution against the bourgeoisie by a vanguard of armed partisans. This armed revolution then converts itself to a ruling regime until the owners of goods and businesses have been defeated.

of the farmers. Belaúnde also attempted to develop lands to the south, to provide native and *mestizo* populations with free education, and to improve transportation systems in Peru.

Belaúnde's reforms angered most business owners in Peru. Foreign investors were leery of the new government and so the needed cash infusion never occurred. Moreover, the decade of the 1980s was a time of unusual weather patterns. These weather problems essentially destroyed Peru's agricultural market and brought the Peruvian economy to a state of near collapse. By 1985, sixty percent of Peru's industries were out of business. Wages dropped to one third of what they were in 1980.

The elections of 1985 marked a change in Peru's political power structure. Alan García won election to the presidency. García, a member of the APRA, planned to protect domestic businesses from foreign competition and increase the wages and living conditions of poor Peruvians. This was an aggressive agenda, which appeared to be working in 1986 and 1987. Inflation had been reduced from a pre-1985 high of 258 percent to 63 percent. In contrast, inflation in the United States for the same period was only about five percent; current U.S. inflation is about three percent. García attempted to stimulate the farm industry by allowing farm prices to rise substantially; however, he also capped wages. This meant that while prices were rising in Peru, wages were not.

President García made the economic situation worse by announcing a plan for the Peruvian government to takeover all private banks in 1986. He intended to use this as a means to stimulate investment in domestic industry and slow investment in overseas ventures, but what he actually did was create an economic panic. The fallout was that by 1988, inflation in Peru was at about 2000 percent. Real salaries declined by about half, which meant that workers were in one of the worst economic situations they had faced in more than thirty years.

García faced an additional problem. Shining Path rebels had been on the move since 1980, and by 1990 threatened to topple García's regime and take control of Peru. This turn of events was startling, considering how small Shining Path was and how slowly its rise to power had been.

Shining Path and Revolution

Guzmán's organization had been remarkably successful during the 1980s. Its first activity, an attack against a polling booth, had not indicated the power and success the organization would have. By 1981 Shining Path guerrillas controlled much of

to reduce subsidies to farmers and urban workers; and it changed a very popular job-security law, which had allowed workers to achieve tenure after three months of employment. After 1978 workers had to work for three years before gaining vested rights.

The people hit hardest by these reforms were, of course, the poor agrarian and urban populations. Scholar David Werlich stated in 1984 that these changes in policy resulted in "widespread malnutrition, dramatic increases in poverty-related diseases and a sharp rise in the rate of infant mortality." As protests mounted and demands for reform battered the government, the president called for elections, to be held in 1980.

The 1980 presidential elections were to be a time of great hope, followed by a time of great disappointment. Fernando Belaúnde Terry won the presidential election in 1980. Belaúnde was a conservative candidate committed to opening Peru to increased international trade. His government embarked on a series of tariff reductions, reduced governmental subsidies to domestic companies, and deregulation of gasoline and food prices on behalf

UNDER HEAVY SECURITY, SHINING PATH LEADER ABIMAEL GUZMAN WAS TRANSFERRED IN A CAGE TO A
MAXIMUM SECURITY PRISON ON A NAVY BASE IN CALLAO, PERU. *(AP/Wide World Photos. Reproduced by permission.)*

Ayacucho. The Shining Path organization was very
popular among the sharecroppers and poor of
Ayacucho and the surrounding departments in part
because it was able to create law and order and provide education for natives, something the government had been unable to do. Shining Path's growth
and control of various southern departments presented no real danger to the government at first.
By 1982 Shining Path rebels controlled most of
southern Peru and began making inroads to the
south central Andes. It was not until 1983 that
Belaúnde's government began to understand the
threat Shining Path represented.

RECENT HISTORY AND
THE FUTURE

In 1985 Shining Path changed its focus from
a primarily rural organization to one centered in
urban centers. This was due in large part to the
spread of Shining Path's revolution into the cities
and urban centers near Lima. At the same time,
Guzmán and his followers began to moderate their
calls for violence and political murder. Some commentators suggest that by 1987, murder and violence were secondary to educational programs as
Shining Path's primary revolutionary tools. Shining

CONSTRUCTION WORKERS PROTEST PRESIDENT ALBERTO FUJIMORO'S REELECTION BID IN FRONT OF THE GOVERNMENT PALACE, LIMA, PERU. *(AP/Wide World Photos. Reproduced by permission.)*

Path also began to deal and control the drug trade in 1987. This provided the organization with substantial resources with which to continue their revolution.

The election of 1990 spelled the end of Shining Path's power in Peru. Alberto Fujimori, an engineering professor and one-time talk show host, defeated all major party candidates for the presidency. Fujimori promised to rebuild Peru's economy, to privatize large corporations, and to pursue policies of free trade similar to those being pursued in the United States. Fujimori also made defeat of

Shining Path a major goal as well. To this end, he gave the police and military extraordinary power to pursue Shining Path rebels through informants, wiretaps, and other methods. These efforts paid off in 1992 with the arrest of Guzmán and two of his top deputies.

Guzmán's arrest seriously wounded Shining Path resistance. In 1993 Guzmán made a televised appearance calling for Shining Path rebels to renounce violence and cooperate with Fujimori's government and most rebels followed his call. However, a small cell of rebels continued to fight, following the leadership of Oscar Alberto Ramirez Durand, known as Feliciano. Those following Feliciano fought until Feliciano's arrest in 1999. After that, Shining Path largely ceased to exist.

All that remains of Shining Path's organization are perhaps a few hundred rebels working out of the Andes Mountains. While these rebels stage the occasional raid against government or police officials, Shining Path no longer controls even the territory around Ayacucho. Most scholars agree that Shining Path was a cult built around the personality of Guzmán and his ideals. Once he was captured and capitulated, the heart of the organization died.

This does not mean that resistance against Fujimori has subsided. The PCP remains an active organization in Peru, despite its many factions. Fujimori's reelection in 2000 was marred by questions of voter fraud and intimidation. Shortly thereafter, a scandal erupted and Fujimori stepped down. With leadership unresolved, opposition groups might resort to political violence again. What is clear is that, despite claims to the contrary by Shining Path members, the organization, which once controlled almost half of Peru, is now a small band of only a few hundred followers. The Shining Path no longer represents a threat to Peru's political stability.

BIBLIOGRAPHY

Alisky, Marvin. *Historical Dictionary of Peru.* London: The Scarecrow Press, Inc., 1979.

Cameron, Maxwell A., and Philip Mauceri. *The Peruvian Labrynth: Polity, Society, Economy.* University Park, Penn.: Pennsylvania State University Press, 1997.

Gorritti, Gustavo. *The Shining Path: A History of the Millenarian War in Peru.* Trans. by Robin Kirk. Chapel Hill, N.C.: University of North Carolina Press, 1999.

McClintock, Cynthia. *Revolutionary Movements in Latin America: El Salvador's FMLN and Peru's Shining Path.* Washington, D.C.: United States Institute of Peace Press, 1998.

Palmer, Monte. *Dilemmas of Political Development*. Itasca, Ill.; F. E. Peacock Publishers, Inc., 1989.

"Peru." *The World Factbook 1999*. http://www.odci.gov/cia/publications/factbook (2 June 2000).

"Peru: Shining Path Leader Captured." Reuters News Service report, 14 July 1999.

Roberts, Kenneth M. *Deepening Democracy? The Modern Left and Social Movements in Chile and Peru*. Stanford, Calif.: Stanford University Press, 1998.

Shafer, Robert Jones. *A History of Latin America*. Lexington, Mass.: D.C. Heath and Co., 1978.

"Shining Path." *Terrorism Research Center Report*. http://www.terrorism.com/terrorism/ShiningP.html (20 May 2000).

Weiner, Myron and Samuel P. Huntington. *Understanding Political Development*. Boston, Mass.: Little, Brown and Co., 1987.

Zirakzadeh, Cyrus Ernesto. *Social Movements in Politics: A Comparative Study*. New York: Longman, 1997.

Michael P. Bobic

ROMANIA'S CYANIDE SPILL

Water Contamination and Political Crisis
A gold mine—jointly owned by Romania and an Australian company—dumped cyanide-tainted water into a major river in Romania in January 2000, killing fish and endangering the health of people in several countries.

Political
- Countries weigh the need to encourage investment with the need to protect their environment and people. Strict regulations are often seen as a deterrent to investment.

Economic
- Who should pay for the clean up and help alleviate the economic impact?

- Fish were killed and water resources damaged, causing economic repercussions for years to come.

On January 30, 2000, a massive spill of water with a high cyanide content occurred at the Aurul gold mine, Baia Mare, in northwest Romania. A reservoir at the mine overflowed its dam as a consequence of heavy rain and winter snowfall, and an estimated one hundred thousand cubic meters of water, with cyanide concentrations as high as seven hundred times the maximum considered safe (0.1 milligrams per liter), was released. Much of this contaminated water entered the region's drainage systems, notably the Szamos and Somes rivers, which are tributaries of the River Tisza. The pollution entered neighboring Hungary through the rivers and polluted a reservoir supplying the city of Szolnok, eighty kilometers southeast of Budapest, Hungary. Some nine days after the spill, cyanide levels were still approximately 2.8 milligrams per liter—twenty-eight times the amount considered safe by the World Health Organization. The pollution subsequently spread to Serbia, though the contamination diluted as the Tisza joined the Danube; the cyanide concentration declined to less than 0.2 milligrams per liter. As a precaution, the Ukraine authorities put an embargo on the use of water from the Danube. This brought the number of countries affected by the cyanide spill to four. To make matters worse, another spill occurred on March 10, 2000, from another mine in the same region; twenty-two thousand tons of tailings (tailings are fragmented ore that is being processed) with high concentrations of heavy metals were released into the River Tisza's tributaries after a tailings dam failed following heavy rain.

HISTORICAL BACKGROUND

The Aurul mine incident in particular has drawn attention to several factors. First, there is the international context of the spill. The mine is jointly owned by Esmeralda Exploration, an Australian mining company based in Perth, Australia, and Remin, a Romanian state-owned mining company, a partnership that calls into question issues of responsibility. Furthermore, the pollution created by this (and other spills) does not respect national boundaries in terms of its impact. In this context, the incident reflects the hydro-politics of the region—the distribution, use, and control of water resources. Second, there is the ecological impact of the spill, which is related to the toxicity of the released water, notably the concentration of cyanide, and the regulatory control that is intended to safeguard ecological health. This is also related to human health in that safe concentrations of cyanide have been surpassed in reservoirs and, as a result, fish that people consume may be contaminated. Third, there is the economic context: the local and regional impact of the spill on river-based economic activities, especially fishing industries, as well as the adverse impact of such a widely publicized event on the share prices of Esmeralda Exploration. These characteristics are typical of other major spills that have occurred elsewhere in the world.

The International Context

The joint ownership of the mine means that, in principle, restoration and reparation should be funded by both Esmeralda and Remin. The concept that the polluter pays for restoration is widely accepted, though enforcement is difficult and disagreements about how much funding is required abound. Commissioner Margot Walstroem, in Szolnok to inspect the Tisza river, said to CNN that "there is great unanimity that the polluter pays" for damages. Serbia threatened to sue in international court for reparations.

It is, however, difficult to envisage how the partners, either singly or jointly, could finance the cleanup. The ramifications in terms of the spatial and temporal dimensions of the spill, such as its widespread impact and the time it will take for the river systems to recover, challenge the capability of any organization. Even with the promised assistance of the European Union the task is immense. In addition to promising funds for ameliorating the pollution in the Szamos, Tisza, and other affected rivers, the E.U. commissioner pledged to initiate legislation to improve safety measures, which should prevent similar accidents in the future. Such legislation could involve restrictions on the use of cyanide for gold extraction, a complete ban on cyanide use, or improved design for tailings dams.

CHRONOLOGY

January 2000 Cyanide from a gold mine was released and water supplies contaminated in Romania, Hungary, the Ukraine, and Serbia.

March 2000 A second spill of tailings was released, further contaminating the water supply.

Because the River Tisza is a tributary of the Danube, the pollution from the spill affected a large area of the river network, and spread into at least three countries. That the area affected is so large highlights some of the problems associated with shared water resources. In this case, water management became a challenge of international cooperation and the goal was to avoid not only ecological damage, but also the impairment of international relations. As Romica Tomescu, the Romanian environment minister, remarked, the incident has not been opportune in view of Romania's desire to become a member of the E.U. Moreover, confusion over the magnitude of the incident, its impact and its cause, which was widely reported in the media, upset Romania's affected neighbors.

The Ecosystem/Human Health Context

Cyanide compounds are often used in the mining of both precious and non-precious metals. Many cyanide compounds, such as potassium cyanide and sodium cyanide (chemical formulae is KCN and NaCN—carbon and nitrogen—plus either potassium or sodium) readily combine with metals and are thus useful for extracting metals from ores. However, cyanide also reacts freely with a wide range of other elements to produce many compounds that may be toxic to organisms, including humans. Cyanide's ability to combine with metals is an advantage for metal mining yet its capacity to produce a wide range of toxic compounds means that it can be hazardous unless its use is tightly controlled and adequate safety measures are established to safeguard both workers and the environment.

At the Aurul mine, cyanide solution, most likely sodium cyanide, a white solid that dissolves easily in water, was being used to extract gold. When placed in water, the two components of NaCN separate into a positively-charged sodium

MAP OF ROMANIA. *(© Maryland Cartographics. Reprinted with permission.)*

ion and a negatively-charged cyanide ion. The latter combines with the positively-charged hydrogen ions in the water to form hydrogen cyanide (also known as hydrocyanic acid or HCN). Hydrogen cyanide combined with any of the cyanide ions left in the water creates a particle called free cyanide. The amount of free cyanide that occurs in the water varies according to the alkalinity of the water. At high alkalinity there is a high volume of the negatively-charged cyanide ions, but as alkalinity decreases an increasing amount of ionic cyanide converts to HCN. The most efficient extraction of gold or other metals takes place when alkalinity is kept high to maintain high concentrations of ionic cyanide, which combines with the gold. Elevated alkalinity is achieved by adding lime or sodium hydroxide. The degree of alkalinity is usually considerably higher than that which normally occurs in nature. Consequently, the water used to extract gold is highly alkaline and contains high concen-

trations of free cyanide. It is confined to reservoirs that are isolated from drainage systems by a so-called tailings dam. In Aurul, the escape of cyanide-rich water was caused by the overflow of the dam.

The ecological impact was most marked in the vicinity of the mine and the Szamos and Somes Rivers, and spread to the River Tisza, the tributary of the Danube into which the Szamos and Somes flow. Media reports of the impact on aquatic life are varied but it is estimated that approximately one hundred fifty tons of fish were killed. Many of these were washed into the Danube, an occurrence with implications for the aquatic ecology of the affected rivers in Romania, Hungary, and Serbia. Undoubtedly, many other aquatic organisms and bird populations were equally affected and food chains disrupted. Bird populations, in particular, will be affected by eating contaminated fish and by the loss of their food sources as fish and other aquatic organisms die. In addition, there is concern that the impact of the spill will be long lasting because of the presence of heavy metals, such as cadmium and zinc, which may also have been released. This is certainly the case with the subsequent spill in March 2000 from another mine in the same area as the Aurul mine. The impact of the spill from the Aurul mine has been so great that it has been compared with the Chernobyl nuclear reactor disaster of 1986. While this may be an unrealistic comparison, there is no doubt that the Aurul spill has been serious.

Reports indicate that the incident may have affected the drinking water of as many as two million people, but because it was registered very soon after it happened its direct impact on human health was limited and no casualties have been reported. Citizens of Szolnok, southeast of Budapest, were warned not to drink tap water because of excessive cyanide concentrations in the water-supply reservoirs. Moreover, freshwater was transported by tankers to hospitals and schools. In the long term, it is possible that some contamination of groundwater may occur. Fishing has also been banned in the area, and restaurants throughout the affected area have been obliged to remove fish from their menus. These latter impacts not only reflect ecological impact but also the economic impact. Fears concerning poisoning through the consumption of contaminated fish stem from the fact that cyanide will be present in tissue. It does not, however, build up in tissue. If ingested in large quantities cyanide can cause breathing difficulties, cardiac problems, and enlargement of the thyroid gland; there is, however, no evidence to show that high concentrations of cyanide give rise to cancer and the role of cyanide in causing birth defects remains unknown.

The Economic Context

In addition to human health, the Aural spill has caused problems for the fishing, farming, and mining industries, and damaged the provision of domestic water supplies. The latter is the most short-lived since the pollution was diluted fairly quickly as the polluted water passed through the drainage system. Nevertheless, costs are incurred by local authorities whom provide domestic water. Because of the tailings spill two months after the cyanide spill, authorities with active mines in their regions, or even individuals living in the vicinity of mines, must be prepared to finance alternative water supplies on short notice.

Local and regional fishing industries, both recreational and commercial, experienced problems as a result of the spill. It may be a medium-term problem. Food chains and food webs within aquatic

IN THE DANUBE RIVER, ZDRAVKO MAZINJANIN COLLECTS DEAD FISH WHICH WERE POISONED WHEN A DAM OVERFLOWED AT THE BAIA GOLD MINE IN ROMANIA, CAUSING CYANIDE TO FLOW BY RIVER TO YUGOSLAVIA. *(AP/Wide World Photos. Reproduced by permission.)*

ecosystems do not recover immediately; new organisms need to be recruited and become established. The intricate web of life that characterizes river systems is particularly vulnerable to damage, and it, in turn, affects the range of species and populations of bird life that depend on it. It is impossible to estimate how long it will take before fish populations recover to economically viable populations. Local ecologists suggest that around eighty percent of river life could die as a result of the spill and that it could take many years to recover. Thus the prospects for the recovery of livelihoods based

AN EMPLOYEE RECEIVES INSTRUCTIONS TO FIX A DAM NEAR THE BAIA MARE GOLD MINE IN ROMANIA TO PREVENT FURTHER TOXIC CHEMICAL SPILLS INTO A NEARBY RIVER WHICH HAS CAUSED DAMAGE TO RIVERS IN HUNGARY AND YUGOSLAVIA. *(AP/Wide World Photos. Reproduced by permission.)*

on fishing are not encouraging. This is a particularly significant problem for a part of Eastern Europe that is struggling economically and that is recovering from the recent Balkan conflict.

The contamination may adversely affect other economic activities in the region. If the cyanide contamination spreads into groundwater and thus into wells, agriculture may be adversely affected. Local people interviewed after the incident from the Aurul mine now believe that the spill caused contamination of the area's wells, with cyanide levels reaching fifty times more than the acceptable level. This contaminated water may impair pastoral agriculture, notably cattle and horse production. As in the case of fishing, recovery and, equally important, confidence in products from such pastoral activities may take several years to recover fully. The short-term future, for many residents in the area engaged in farming, is no more encouraging than it is for those involved in fishing industries.

Although relatively few people are employed in the mining industry in this region of Romania, the closure of the Aurul plant following the spill, and the possibility of other mine closures, limits opportunities for employment and has repercussions for the local economy. Furthermore, the initial publicity surrounding the cyanide spill had economic repercussions for the Esmeralda Exploration Company. On February 9, 2000, the company's share price fell by approximately thirty-eight percent and dealing of shares was then suspended. As a result, Esmeralda's shareholders will have been considerably disadvantaged financially. Pollution is all encompassing; it is rarely confined within international boundaries—nor does it discriminate on the basis of human, ecological, or economic factors.

Alternative Methods of Mining

The potential toxicity of cyanide compounds means that their use in metal-extractive industries is potentially hazardous. Nevertheless, the method is still relatively widely used because it allows the extraction of low-grade ores, including those with as little as 0.02 troy ounce or 0.622 grams per metric ton. After the ore is extracted, it is crushed into fragments of approximately 1 to 3 centimeters in diameter. It is then heaped onto huge sheets of impermeable plastic, and diluted solutions of cyanide compounds (usually sodium cyanide) percolate slowly though the heap over several months. The gold is then recovered by heating. In addition, recent research has focused on the use of microorganisms, notably bacteria and fungi, to degrade cyanide salts and release the gold. This is one aspect of bio-mining, which is becoming increasingly important, though in this case it does not eliminate the need for the use of cyanide compounds.

In the future it may become possible to employ other organisms that concentrate gold in conditions free of cyanide or other toxic substances.

Other methods of gold extraction include the use of mercury, a metal that readily combines with gold to create amalgam. The addition of mercury to a gold pan results in amalgam production and allows the gold to be subsequently recovered by either heating the amalgam to vaporize the mercury (this can be recovered by immediate cooling which causes condensation) or by squeezing the amalgam through a fine cloth. Neither method is safe in terms of ecological or human health because mercury is easily lost during such operations and can cause nerve and brain damage to those who come into contact with it. For this reason, it is not recommended for gold extraction, though it is still used in many parts of the world, such as in the Amazon Basin, where it has become a serious pollution and health problem. Overall, the use of mercury for gold extraction causes more problems than the use of cyanide compounds.

RECENT HISTORY AND THE FUTURE

The Challenge of International Disasters

Contemporary ecological disasters often breech international boundaries and challenge methods for addressing them. International courts and relations are addressing new and complex issues in attempting to balance the many diplomatic, environmental, and commercial interests. As in the case of the cyanide spill in Romania, a company owned (at least partially) by individuals in one country (in this case Australia) may be held responsible for a disaster that happens in another country—and affects still other countries. Differing environmental and business regulations and challenges to management further complicate the situation.

In 1986 a nuclear reactor in Chernobyl, Ukraine, then part of the Soviet Union, was destroyed during a routine test. Radioactive material was released, causing death and illness in the vicinity of Chernobyl. Radioactive material rose into the atmosphere and covered most of the northern hemisphere.

The 1989 oil spill in Alaska's Prince William Sound, when the Exxon *Valdez* ran aground and spilled about eleven-million-gallons of oil, has yet to be resolved. Exxon spent about $2 billion on the project and another $300 million in compensation for losses; though is appealing a court order to pay $5 billion to those damaged by the spill. The court cases continue.

U.N. ENVIRONMENT PROGRAMME EXPERTS COLLECT WATER FROM A DAM NEAR THE BAIA MARE GOLD MINE IN ROMANIA TO ASSESS THE DAMAGE FROM A CYANIDE SPILL THAT HAS KILLED FISH IN HUNGARY AND YUGOSLAVIA. *(AP/Wide World Photos. Reproduced by permission.)*

And in 1984 in Bhopal, India, a Union Carbide chemical plant experienced a gas leak, releasing forty tons of methyl isocynate (MIC) into the environment. People asleep awoke gasping for breath; approximately seven thousand died within days, and five hundred thousand were affected. The Indian government estimates that—more than fifteen years later—several people die from poison-related illnesses a month. The leak has been traced to a disgruntled employee.

Every day governments attempt to balance environmental and labor regulations with attracting new businesses and jobs to the region. Every day courts weigh responsibility and penalties associated with disasters. In many cases there is not a single legal arbiter of responsibility—due to the complex ownership and impact of man-made environmental disasters, a corporation may be sued in numerous venues, including its host country, its own country, and international courts.

BIBLIOGRAPHY

Agency for Toxic Substances and Disease Registry. "Cyanide." 2000. http://www.atsdr.cdc.gov/tfacts8 .html (8 September 2000).

Craig-David, J.R., J. Vaughan and B.J. Skinner. *Resources of the Earth: Origin, Use and Environmental Impact.* Upper Saddle River, N.J.: Prentice Hall, 1996.

Korte, F. "The Dilemma of Processing Gold with Cyanide." *Fresenius Environmental Bulletin* 7 (1998): 141–228.

Moran, R.E. "Cyanide in Mining. Some Observations on the Chemistry, Toxicity and Analysis of Mining-Related Waters." 17 February 2000. http://www.mpi .org.au/rr/docs/bob_morans_cyanide_toxicity_paper .rtf (8 September 2000).

Antoinette M. Mannion

SOUTH AFRICA'S TRUTH AND RECONCILIATION COMMISSION

From the 1960s South Africa gained international notoriety for its policy of apartheid. However, the roots of apartheid—a system of racial segregation—began long before the twentieth century. Apartheid had existed early in the twentieth century, but it was only after the National Party, the party of Afrikaner nationalism, came to power in 1948 on a platform of apartheid that racial segregation was applied in ever more extreme forms. Before 1948 black Africans had been the chief sufferers of racial discrimination; after 1948 those designated "Coloureds" (mixed ancestry) and "Asians" found themselves subject to similar racially discriminatory laws. The provision that black African males should carry and produce on demand a "pass" document was applied to African women as well, and rigid barriers were set up against Africans moving from the rural areas to the towns. Under Hendrik Verwoerd, National Party Prime Minister from 1958, apartheid came to include the creation of separate small states for Africans (the Bantustans, or "homelands"), to which millions of people were forcibly relocated.

There was a long history of black protest against racial segregation in South Africa. The African National Congress (ANC) took the lead in peaceful, nonviolent protest in the 1950s, but that era came to an end when the police opened fire on unarmed protesters at Sharpeville, in Transvaal province, in March 1960. Shortly after the Sharpeville massacre, the ANC and a newly formed rival party, the Pan-Africanist Congress, were declared unlawful organizations. Both organizations continued to work in secret and began to organize armed resistance, though only the ANC's armed resistance achieved any measure of success, and that only after more than a decade. In the face of armed resistance, the apartheid state became even more re-

THE CONFLICT

South Africa was formerly ruled by a minority white population that denied political participation to the majority black population. During this time, black groups fought for recognition of their rights, including the right to self-government, and were frequently brutally oppressed. As part of the process of moving to majority rule, a commission to investigate human and civil rights violations was established.

Political

- Some view the commission and the exposure of past violence—including murders committed in support of apartheid—as the best hope for community healing for the future.

- Some criticize that the individuals who committed the violence should be tried and punished—not merely confess their crimes.

- Critics view the investigation as political and believe it will delay focus on the future. In addition, they believe the commission disproportionately focuses on crimes committed by white people and ignores crimes committed by the former rebel (black) groups.

- In addition, detractors allege that individuals should not be held responsible for crimes committed while representing the government.

CHRONOLOGY

1948 The National Party comes to power in South Africa on a platform of apartheid, which is severe and institutionalizes discrimination against non-whites.

1950s The African National Congress engages in non-violent protests of apartheid.

1960 A massacre of unarmed protesters occurs at Sharpeville. The ANC and other organizations begin to organize for armed resistance. Years of mistreatment, including deaths in police custody and disappearances, follow.

1976 Police fire on unarmed schoolchildren in Soweto township.

1990 South African president de Klerk lifts the ban on the ANC and other parties and announces plans to negotiate for majority rule.

1991 Negotiations for majority rule begin at the Convention for a Democratic State. The negotiations continue sporadically, finally leading to an agreement.

1994 Nelson Mandela is elected the first president of a democratic South Africa.

1995 The Promotion of National Unity and Reconciliation Act is approved by parliament.

1996 Hearings of the Truth and Reconciliation Commission begin.

1998 The Truth and Reconciliation Report is published.

pressive than before. Legislation was passed to provide for detention without trial and the police acted with ever-increasing brutality. When police opened fire on unarmed schoolchildren demonstrating in Soweto township outside Johannesburg in June 1976, resistance and repression both escalated. Armed guerrillas committed acts of sabotage and the police began to use such extreme measures as poison and assassination to get rid of political opponents. In the 1980s, many believed that this increasingly brutal conflict could only end in a racial bloodbath. To most people's surprise, such a bloodbath was avoided through a process that provided for the dismantling of apartheid and the transition to a democratic society.

One of the aspects of South Africa's transition from apartheid to democracy that has attracted most interest in the outside world is the establishment of a Truth and Reconciliation Commission. The Commission was created to investigate the truth about the long history of conflict brought about by the system of apartheid. It was hoped that this would aid the process of reconciliation of the races in the post-apartheid era. But, in fact, only certain aspects of the past were explored, with results that remain controversial.

HISTORICAL BACKGROUND

The Establishment of the Truth and Reconciliation Commission

The Truth and Reconciliation Commission (TRC) emerged out of the negotiated settlement in South Africa, and should itself be seen as an integral part of that settlement. In the mid-1980s, there appeared to be a stalemate: the National Party government refused to abandon apartheid, and its main opponent, the ANC, was committed to waging an armed struggle until apartheid was overthrown. In the course of the struggle, the ANC had become radicalized, and many of its members believed that apartheid was integrally part of the capitalist system in South Africa, and wished to overthrow both apartheid and capitalism. In the mid-1980s, therefore, it seemed unlikely that the two sides would be willing to compromise sufficiently for a negotiated settlement to be reached. Yet, both sides came to realize that neither could defeat the other, and that a continuation of conflict would bring the economy of the country to its knees and involve vast suffering. In the late 1980s, a series of talks were held, most of them in secret, between members of the ANC and people with links to the government. As a result, each came to some understanding of the other's position. South Africa's rulers had been concerned about the influence of communism in the ANC, but decided to alter course in part because of the winding down of the Cold War, and particularly the collapse of communism in Eastern Europe in late 1989. The ANC, for its part, presented itself as an organization not dominated by Communists, more pragmatic than ideological.

In February 1990, South African president F.W. de Klerk, though from a conservative Afrikaner background and heir to the apartheid traditions of his predecessors, decided on a bold move designed to seize the initiative. He announced that his government was un-banning the ANC, the Communist Party, and other organizations, and was now willing to enter into negotiations for a new democratic order. This paved the way for formal talks between the government and the ANC, which

MAP OF SOUTH AFRICA. *(© Maryland Cartographics. Reprinted with permission.)*

began some months later. In August that year, at one of its meetings with the government, the ANC agreed to suspend its armed struggle, and in December 1991 the first formal multi-party negotiations began at what was called the Convention for a Democratic South Africa, held at the World Trade Center near Johannesburg airport. The process of negotiating a new democratic constitution for the country broke down in mid-1992, but in the face of the threat of economic collapse and racial civil war, the parties decided to return to negotiations, which resumed early in 1993. They were successfully completed in November of that year, when an agreement was reached at the World Trade Center for transitional arrangements leading to a democratic election and for an interim consti-

tution that would come into effect when the founding election for the new South Africa was held.

Only through a series of compromises was agreement on the interim constitution reached. Most of these compromises concerned the form of government to be introduced in the new South Africa, but a crucial one related to the question of amnesty for political offenders—people, including the police, who had committed illegal or violent acts in support of or against apartheid. The National Party, which had already granted amnesty to some of its officials, wanted a blanket amnesty, of the kind that had been granted when Chile returned to civilian rule, or had been granted to South Africa's neighbors, Zimbabwe and Namibia, when those countries had become independent af-

STEVE BIKO. *(AP/Wide World Photos. Reproduced by permission.)*

ter long periods of bitter conflict. The National Party had relied upon the security forces—the police and the military—to support its rule, and could not now abandon those who had worked on its behalf. But the ANC would not agree to a general amnesty, arguing that amnesty would be to sweep under the carpet what had happened in the past, thus starting the new democracy off on the wrong foot. Under apartheid rule there had been a culture of secrecy, in which the security forces had become virtually a law to themselves: Many people had disappeared without a trace, and some had been murdered, but the circumstances of the disappearances and deaths had not been revealed. The case of the Black Consciousness leader, Steve Biko, who died in police custody in September 1977, was only the most notorious of these. Relatives of Biko wanted to know who had been responsible and for those responsible to be put on trial for their crime. Many other South Africans had seen their loved ones disappear, die under suspicious circumstances, or become the victims of torture and felt such atrocities could not just be forgotten. Indeed, many people feared that unless the secrets of the past were exposed the fragile new democracy would be undermined.

Ideally, all victims of human rights abuses would receive justice, and all perpetrators and those who gave them the orders to commit their crimes

would be punished. Some in the ANC wanted trials of apartheid officials similar to the Nuremberg trial at the end of World War II, in which the leading Nazis were charged and tried for their horrendous crimes (twelve were sentenced to death). But in South Africa, there had been no victory over a defeated enemy, and the very nature of the negotiated settlement precluded a Nuremberg-type trial. Some suspected there was even a secret agreement between the National Party and the ANC that the apartheid politicians should not be put on trial. So while some, such as the Biko family, continued to demand justice, others were prepared to accept that in the interests of national reconciliation, it was necessary to provide for a process by which people could obtain amnesty for past offenses. The ANC decided that if the perpetrators revealed what had happened they would be given amnesty for their acts, since the acts had been committed during a struggle that was now over. As part of the negotiated settlement founding democratic South Africa and paving the way for majority rule, it was agreed that a clause should be inserted at the end of the interim constitution of 1993 to deal with the question of amnesty. The clause stated, "in order to advance . . . reconciliation and reconstruction, amnesty shall be granted in respect of acts, omissions and offenses associated with political objectives and committed in the course of the conflicts of the past." In not speaking of a blanket amnesty, it left the door open to amnesty being granted on certain conditions, and out of that clause the Truth and Reconciliation Commission grew.

Nelson Mandela was elected the first president of a democratic South Africa in 1994. Dullah Omar, the Minister of Justice in Nelson Mandela's first government, introduced in 1995 legislation into the first democratic Parliament to establish a Commission to deal with "the conflicts of the past." The Commission would not only to find out what had happened in the past, but would grant amnesty from prosecution to those who made full disclosure of what had happened. The Promotion of National Unity and Reconciliation Act was approved by parliament after much debate in July 1995, after parliamentarians and others had studied truth commissions in other parts of the world, most notably in Chile. The South African commission bore certain similarities to previous ones, but there were also striking differences. Chief among these was that amnesty would only be granted on "full disclosure" of what had happened.

Some South African lawmakers wanted the TRC to follow the Chilean model and meet behind closed doors. But it was decided that the hearings should be in public unless there was a very strong reason not to (and few hearings were held in private). The Commission was designed to bring about a process of healing, and for that a public catharsis was needed. After the hearings, it was hoped, the country could "put the past behind it" and move into a new future, after the truth about the conflicts of the past had been revealed and a measure of reconciliation achieved.

President Mandela, in consultation with his cabinet, appointed the members of the Commission. Public nominations were called for and interviews held, after which the president decided on the final appointees. Archbishop Desmond Tutu was appointed as chair of the Commission, with Dr. Alex Boraine, an ex-minister of religion and parliamentarian, as his deputy. Critics of the Commission were later to allege that those appointed were mainly ANC supporters, and that flawed the entire process. It was certainly the case that the great majority of commissioners had a strong anti-apartheid background, but once appointed to the commission, they were required to be evenhanded. A panel of judges was appointed to decide on amnesty for political offenders.

The Commission had a complex structure. Separate committees were appointed, one on Human Rights Violations, another on Amnesty, and a third on Reparation and Rehabilitation, while a Research Department investigated human rights' violations and played a crucial role in drawing up the detailed five-volume report, which the TRC published in October 1998.

The Work of the Commission

The Commission was required to investigate "the conflicts of the past," and the first volume of its report did provide a general historical context to the events it investigated. But those events were necessarily specific and individual, and there were numerous aspects of apartheid and the resistance to it, which the Commission did not explore at all. Its life was to be only two years, for it was thought that the Commission's work should be completed before the second democratic elections, due in mid-1999. Yet, there were far more amnesty applications than had been expected and the amnesty hearings continued into 2000.

Given the limited time available to it, the Commission had to limit the scope of its work. The first important limitation to its work was that the period it was to explore was to begin on March 21, 1960, the date of the Sharpeville massacre, in which sixty-nine unarmed people had been shot by the

NELSON ROLIHLAHLA MANDELA

1918– Nelson Mandela was born July 18, 1918, in Trandskei, South Africa, and was raised to assume leadership of his tribe. Instead, he attended University College of Fort Hare until he was suspended in 1940 for political activity. After completing his bachelor's degree by correspondence, he earned his law degree in 1942 from the University of South Africa.

Mandela joined the African National Congress (ANC) in 1944. After his acquittal on charges of treason in 1961, Mandela founded Umkhotno We Sizwe (Spear of the Nation), the military wing of the ANC. While imprisoned for leading a strike, he was convicted of sabotage and given a life sentence in 1964.

Mandela was incarcerated until he was hospitalized in 1988, spending eighteen years of his sentence at Robben Island Prison. Under internal and international pressure, then-South African president de Klerk released Mandela on February 11, 1990. Mandela returned to leadership of the ANC, becoming its president in July 1991.

Mandela and de Klerk cooperated in transitioning South Africa to a non-racial democracy, and were awarded the 1993 Nobel Peace Prize for their efforts. After winning the first open elections in April 1994, President Mandela established the Truth and Reconciliation Commission (TRC), and introduced sweeping social reforms. In 1996 Mandela oversaw creation of a new constitution; the following year, he resigned his post with the ANC and did not run again in the 1999 presidential election. After leaving office, he retired from active domestic politics, though he has continued to work to establish peace throughout Africa.

police outside the Sharpeville police station when demonstrating against the pass laws. There was no doubt that the massacre was a major turning point in the history of apartheid rule, but apartheid rule had begun in 1948 and racial segregation in South Africa had an even longer history. The major piece of legislation dividing the land dated from 1913, for example. A full understanding of the conflict that had led to the military struggle of the last decades of apartheid rule would have required a detailed examination of the earlier period. In the event, most of the TRC's work concerned the years from the early 1970s. As apartheid had moved into a reform phase from the early 1970s it had also be-

DESMOND TUTU

*1931–*Anglican Archbishop Desmond Tutu is well known for his efforts to end apartheid in South Africa, for which he received the 1984 Nobel Peace Prize. Although he retired from church leadership in 1996, he continues to head South Africa's Truth and Reconciliation Commission, and to advocate for human rights throughout the world.

Desmond Mpilo Tutu was born October 7, 1931, in Klerksdorp, South Africa. He graduated from the University of South Africa in 1954, and taught high school until 1957. In 1960 he was ordained as a priest and moved to London, where he earned a master's degree from Kings College in 1966. He taught theology in Johannesburg until 1972, when he became assistant director for the World Council of Churches. He served as dean of St. Mary's Cathedral in Johannesburg from 1975–76, and as the Bishop of Lesotho from 1976 until he became general secretary of the South African Council of Churches in 1978.

Tutu repeatedly risked imprisonment for advocacy of non-violent opposition to apartheid, and for encouraging economic sanctions against South Africa. In 1986 he became the head of South Africa's Anglican Church when he was elected the first black archbishop of Cape Town. After South African independence he was appointed to lead the Truth and Reconciliation Commission in 1995.

come more repressive and human rights violations had greatly increased.

As the TRC hearings revealed, this repression was for complex reasons. In the aftermath of the Rhodesian bush war, which had failed to prevent the coming to power in Zimbabwe (formerly ruled by a white minority) of the radical (black African) Mugabe, many disgruntled whites returned to South Africa determined to do anything needed to prevent a similar development in South Africa. A number of men who had been involved in atrocities in South Africa's war against the South West African People's Organisation in Namibia—the most notorious was Eugene de Kock, who became head of the Vlakplaas unit—now returned to South Africa, and began to use the methods they learned in Namibia. Deaths in police custody in the 1970s had become almost routine until the Biko killing, and had led to inquests in which considerable evidence had emerged regarding police methods, even if culpability had not been assigned. The inquests led some

elements in the security forces to believe that it would be easier to assassinate people and cover their tracks. This led to the formation of death squads, begun at Vlakplaas. This was also the time when actions by Umkhonto we Sizwe (also known as M.K.), the armed wing of the ANC, increased dramatically, with high profile attacks on the gas-from-coal plant in the Transvaal (1980) and the Koeberg nuclear power plant outside Cape Town (1982). It appeared to the government that the war was escalating—a war against a revolutionary force determined to create a socialist South Africa. In such a climate, some elements in the security forces—as the police and military were now working closely together in the National Security Management System devised by President P.W. Botha soon after he took office in September 1978—came to accept the need to use assassinations and other human rights violations as weapons of war, to turn back the "revolutionary onslaught" on South Africa.

It was, however, with the township revolt that began in September 1984 that the use of such unorthodox methods reached the apogee. Behind the revolt that engulfed most of South African townships, lay a host of socio-economic and political factors, including issues such as high rents, poor housing, unemployment, and the deterioration of municipal services in the townships. It was a time of economic recession, and the introduction of the tricameral (three house) parliament that excluded black Africans; these issues and a new black local government system stirred the anger of the township masses. The rebellion followed a decade of political mobilization, beginning with the Soweto Revolt of 1976. From the late 1970s, numerous community-based organizations were formed, mainly to address issues such as rent increases, inadequate housing, and other material grievances facing the township residents. Unlike in 1976, in the 1984 revolt material grievances, rather than ideological ones, lay behind the rebellion. Students demanded the institution of Student Representative Councils, an end to corporal punishment, free books and school supplies, an end to sexual harassment, and age limits in classes. These demands meant almost continuous school boycotts, arranged by the Congress of South African Students, an organization of high school students founded in 1979. The United Democratic Front, a deliberately loose confederation of organizations sympathetic to the broad goals of the ANC, had been launched in 1983 to protest against the tricameral constitution and the Black Local Authorities Act.

The actions of the security forces—raids, teargas, beatings, and shootings in the townships—in-

THE TRUTH AND RECONCILIATION COMMISSION IN SOUTH AFRICA, SET UP TO EXAMINE HUMAN RIGHTS ABUSES UNDER APARTHEID, HEARS IT'S FIRST WITNESS. *(AP/Wide World Photos. Reproduced by permission.)*

flamed the situation, and in many of the townships the system of control by the state broke down. The banned African National Congress had called upon the people to "Make South Africa Ungovernable," and there was much talk of "people's power." Township youth sought to direct the struggle against those with links to the government and many youths lost their lives in skirmishes with the police and the army. Some police and informers were killed by the "necklace" method. Tires were put over the person's neck and set on fire. In an effort to regain control the security forces used a host of tactics or "dirty tricks." It was at this time, evidence before the TRC suggested, the government decided to launch, at considerable cost, a chemical

and biological weapons program, one of the purposes of which was to deliver an effective gas that could be used against demonstrators. This program would result in vast corruption—for which its chief architect, Dr. Wouter Basson would later be put on trial—and attempts to develop highly dangerous substances.

If the beginning date of the TRC's work was relatively uncontroversial, the closing date of its work did become bitterly contested. Initially the closing date was set at December 5, 1993, the date on which the transitional arrangements for the founding democratic election had come into force. Many argued that this marked the irreversible beginning of a process of democratization. But General Constand Viljoen, leader of the right-wing Afrikaner Freedom Front, which had not joined the process until early 1994, argued strongly for a later date, in part because some of his supporters had been involved in acts of violence after December 5, 1993. In the end, Mandela, in the interests of reconciliation, agreed to extend the final date to May 10, 1994, the day of his inauguration as president. This brought within the range of amnesty those who had been responsible for such crimes as the terrorist attack on the Heidelberg tavern in Cape Town, the Afrikaner Weerstandsbeweging (AWB) incursions into Bophuthatswana in March 1994, and the bombing campaign immediately before the 1994 election.

RECENT HISTORY AND THE FUTURE

The Hearings

The Human Rights Violations committee began in April 1996. Meetings were held at venues in different parts of the country. Victims of atrocities, or relatives of those who had suffered, testified to killings, abductions, torture, and other forms of severe ill treatment. Most witnesses told of security police brutality, and found it difficult to express any forgiveness for what had happened, though, occasionally, there were remarkable instances of reconciliation. According to *Looking Back, Reaching Forward*, the mother of one of those killed in the attack on the Heidelberg pub in a Cape Town suburb in December 1993 told the killers, when they applied for amnesty, "I am happy that you are well . . . You could not tell us here how you felt while killing innocent people, which indicates to me that possibly you have been trained to 'not feel' and I recognise how important that would be in a killing machine . . . I have no objection to the granting of amnesty for you . . . Thank you for being able to look me in the eye and for hearing my story."

Those who were granted amnesty did not have to express contrition, but merely had to make full disclosure of their actions, which had to have been done for a political reason. If granted amnesty—and only a small proportion of applicants were—they were then exempt both from criminal prosecution and from any civil action for damages. The families of some of the most prominent people killed by the security forces attempted to have this overturned in the Constitutional Court, on the grounds that they had a right to seek damages. But the Court rejected this, on the ground that the in-

tention was to encourage the guilty to apply for amnesty. The Reparations Committee of the TRC would eventually suggest a large sum be paid to the twenty thousand victims of violations and their families, but the matter was then referred to the government, which by mid-2000 had made no decision on the matter. In the meantime, only extremely meager payments in emergency relief were paid out to victims.

Towards an Assessment

Much new information has emerged from the TRC, including information regarding the scale of M.K. operations in the late 1980s and the way in which people—such as Steve Biko and Matthew Goniwe, a leading resistance figure—had been murdered. Because of its amnesty provisions, the policemen responsible for Biko's death identified themselves and sought amnesty. After giving their testimony, they did not receive amnesty, however, because they were found not to have made a full disclosure. They claimed that Biko had hit his head against a wall during a scuffle, a claim that, ironically, ruled out a political motive for their crime. At the hearings, the TRC heard much about the work of Vlakplaas, a farm near Pretoria from which "dirty tricks" operations of the security police had been conducted. The TRC learned of the way in which a number of key activists had been killed and their bodies disposed of, including Stanza Bopape, whose remains had been thrown into a crocodile-infested river, after which the police engaged in an elaborate cover-up of his murder. The TRC was able to identify the remains of some of those buried in unmarked graves and to arrange for their bodies to be reburied.

Alongside the TRC, a number of key apartheid criminals were put on trial. Eugene de Kock, head of Vlakplaas, received a sentence of more than two hundred years for his many crimes, and then applied for amnesty for a number of them. Because of the work of the TRC, Dr. Wouter Basson was put on trial for his role as head of the country's chemical and biological weapons program, in which he had allegedly assisted in the murder of hundreds of captured "terrorists." As the state did not have the resources to put on trial all the many apartheid assassins and torturers, however, it was only through the TRC that the stories of their crimes came out. Some of what now became general public knowledge had first appeared in the alternative press from the late 1980s, particularly the *Weekly Mail* and the *Vrye Weekblad*, whose courageous reporting was now vindicated and authenticated.

What did not come out before the TRC was the full story of the chain of command. How much had the leading politicians of the time known of what was happening? Former president P.W. Botha justified all his actions as falling within the prerogative of a head of government defending his country against a dangerous ideology, refused to admit any guilt, and would not appear before the TRC. Botha's successor, F.W. de Klerk, appeared before the TRC, but he continued to deny concealing any human rights violations. He did accept responsibility on behalf of his party for "cross-border raids against military bases and facilities, actions in terms of existing security legislation and propaganda actions," but not for "murder or assassination or the kind of criminal activities that organisations such as the Vlakplaas unit and the C.C.B [the Civil Co-operation Bureau, a military "dirty-tricks" unit] are alleged to have committed." He said that he acted to deal with such crimes as soon as knowledge of them came to his attention, and he refused to apply for amnesty, on the grounds that he had committed no crime. Many did not believe him.

Much of what the military had done in the apartheid years was not explored. There had been many raids on neighboring countries, and vast destabilization efforts, especially after P.W. Botha had come to office in 1978. But the generals were able to argue that they could not disclose what they had done in other countries, for they might then be prosecuted in those countries. Attempts to get the neighboring countries—Namibia, Botswana, Zimbabwe, Zambia, and Mozambique—to provide reciprocal amnesty failed.

The ANC's record did not escape scrutiny by the TRC, though it had itself begun to explore human rights violations in its camps in exile before the TRC was set up. A relatively independent Motsuenyane Commission had, in 1993, severely criticized the ANC's security department for brutality and the national executive for not having kept proper control over the camps. When Deputy President Thabo Mbeki appeared before the TRC in August 1996, he commented, "We should avoid the danger whereby concentrating on these particular and exceptional acts of the liberation movement, which could be deemed as constituting gross human rights violations, we convey the impression that the struggle for liberation was itself a gross vi-

olation of human rights." Yet many believe that the ANC could not claim that everything it did was moral just because of the morality of its struggle. When the TRC's report was about to be handed to Nelson Mandela in October 1998, the ANC wanted it stopped, because of the way it sought, in the organization's view, to criminalize the struggle, but neither Tutu nor Mandela accepted this position.

The Inkatha Freedom Party was much less ready than the ANC to come before the TRC and much of the violence that had occurred between its supporters and the ANC, especially in KwaZulu-Natal, went uninvestigated. Some critics pointed to this and other major gaps in the Commission's work and called it a failure; others pointed to the Commission's successes and believe that by uncovering the truth the Commission has helped set in motion a process of healing. Others claimed that by opening wounds, the TRC helped to keep the hatreds of the past alive. In the middle of 2000, the work of its amnesty committee was approaching an end. Only with the passage of time will it be possible to look back and assess to what extent its work did indeed promote reconciliation in what remained a deeply divided country.

BIBLIOGRAPHY

Davenport, Rodney and Christopher Saunders. *South Africa: A Modern History*. Johannesburg, South Africa: University of Toronto Press, 2000.

de Klerk, F.W. *The Last Trek*. London: Trans-Atlantic Books, 1998.

Krog, Antjie. *Country of My Skull*. Johannesburg, South Africa: Random House, 1998.

Truth and Reconciliation Commission. *Report*. Cape Town, South Africa: Groves Dictionaries, 1998.

Tutu, Desmond. *No Future Without Forgiveness*. London: Doubleday and Co., 1999.

van Zyl, Paul. "Dilemmas of Transitional Justice: the Case of South Africa's Truth and Reconciliation Commission," *Journal of International Affairs*, Spring 1999.

Villa-Vicencio. Charles and Wilhelm Verwoerd, eds. *Looking Back, Reaching Forward: Reflections on the Truth and Reconciliation Commission of South Africa*. Cape Town, South Africa: Zed Books, 2000.

Christopher Saunders

SRI LANKA: CIVIL WAR AND ETHNO-LINGUISTIC CONFLICT

THE CONFLICT

The violent civil war on the island of Sri Lanka off the Indian subcontinent reflects the tension between the ethnically, linguistically, and religiously different Sinhalese and Tamils. Nearby India is a major force in political perception in Sri Lanka and periodically intervenes. India's diverse population both mirrors and exacerbates some of Sri Lanka's tensions. From 1987–89 the Liberation Tigers of Tamil Eelam (the Tamil Tigers, or LTTE) fought the Indians and Janatha Virmukthi Peramuna (the People's Liberation Front, or JVP) fought the Sri Lankan army. With the JVP defeated and the Indians out of the country, LTTE and the army fought each other.

Religious

- The Sinhalese are mainly Buddhist; the Tamils are mainly Hindu. Tamils, in the minority, feel discriminated against. There are also other, smaller, religious groups, including Christians and Muslims.

Ethnic

- The Tamils, with a religious language and culture, are a minority within Sri Lanka, a linguistic majority within southern India, and a minority within all of India.

- The Sinhalese, a majority in Sri Lanka, are a linguistic minority in southern India, but a religious majority on the Indian subcontinent.

Political

- Since independence, the government has swung between the conservative UNP (United National Party) and the left-wing People's Liberation Front, though neither has consistently supported the Tamil minority.

- The majority is sporadically afraid that even minor concessions to the minority Tamils will result in the Tamils taking over the government and oppressing the majority.

In April 2000, the Liberation Tigers of Tamil Eelam (LTTE, Tamil Tigers, or Tigers) over-ran the Elephant Pass fortifications at the gateway to the Jaffna Peninsula. They seemed poised to capture the entire peninsula, including the city of Jaffna, capital of northern Sri Lanka, and to reconstitute the secessionist mini-state they had lost five years before. It was an amazing resurgence for the rebels. In contrast, the Sri Lankan army appeared on the brink of a major defeat, losing the gains that it had made nearly five years earlier, when it seized Jaffna. "The army is in a terrible mess and there is no easy way out," said the former Air Chief, Vice-Marshal Harry Goonethileke. The central government had poured in thousands of troops, fortified the bases and claimed it was winning the hearts and minds of the local Tamil population.

The Tigers, who had vowed to retake the peninsula, began an offensive late in 1999. In mid-April they launched a major assault to cut off the Elephant Pass complex that guards the main route linking the peninsula to the mainland. There were some fifteen thousand troops inside the complex, being attacked by one third that number of Tigers, but the troops were unable to hold on and the order came to withdraw. India, which had provided support to the Sri Lanka government at an earlier stage of the war, made it clear in May 2000 that it would not send its own troops to Sri Lanka; however, the Indian Navy would, if necessary, intervene to evacuate Sri Lankan troops from the Jaffna Peninsula.

In the following months, the military situation became stalemated. The guerrillas were apparently unable to seize Jaffna; the army could not defeat the guerrillas. Consequently, the war dragged on, with devastating effects for the economy and for

CHRONOLOGY

1948 Ceylon (now Sri Lanka) becomes a Dominion. The Ceylon Citizenship Act is passed and Tamils lose citizenship.

1956 Sinhala is declared the only official language. The Sri Lanka Freedom Party (SLFP) wins the general elections, and S.W.R.D. Bandaranaike serves as prime minister.

1959 S.W.R.D. Bandaranaike is assassinated.

1960 S.W.R.D. Bandaranaike's widow, Sirimavo Bandaranaike is elected prime minister. She continues the policies of Sinhala nationalism.

1965 The United National Party gains power. Sirimavo Bandaranaike loses power.

1970 Sirimavo Bandaranaike wins power again.

1972 Sri Lanka gains independence and a new constitution; the name is officially changed to Sri Lanka.

1977 R. Jayawardene becomes prime minister and makes some concessions to the Tamil minority, including the recognition of Tamil as a second national language.

1980 Sirimavo Bandaranaike is expelled by parliament for misusing her power while prime minister.

1983 Widespread violence (and anti-Tamil pogroms) is waged against Tamils following a LTTE ambush and the killing of thirteen soldiers.

1987 The short-lived Indo-Sri Lanka peace accord attempts to establish peace in Sri Lanka occur. An Indian Peace Keeping Force is established. When the peace accords do not hold, India attempts to disarm the rebels by force. For the next two years, the LTTE fights the Indians and the JVP fights the Sri Lankan army.

1989 After the Indians withdraw from Sri Lanka and the JVP leadership is destroyed, LTTE and the Sri Lankan army fight each other.

1991 Indian leader Rajiv Gandhi is assassinated by a LTTE assassin.

1993 Sri Lankan Prime Minister Premadasa is assassinated by a LTTE assassin.

1994 S.W.R.D. and Sirimavo Bandaranaike's daughter, Chandrika Kumaratunga, is elected president.

1999 President Kumaratunga is almost killed in a Tamil Tiger suicide attack that kills more than twenty people.

2000 The Tamil Tigers overrun the fortifications at the gateway to the Jaffna Peninsula. The army and the Tamil Tigers battle.

the living conditions of all Sri Lankans. Human rights violations by both sides continued.

Politically, there was a stalemate of another sort. Government efforts to defuse the conflict by decentralizing power failed to win sufficient support in parliament. The government's inability to fulfill its earlier campaign promise of ending the war appeared likely to lead the electorate to punish it at the polls, and perhaps even to elect a new government less willing to compromise.

HISTORICAL BACKGROUND

The Setting of the Conflict

Sri Lanka is a pear-shaped island nation in South Asia. From northwest Sri Lanka, the Indian mainland is just thirty-three kilometers (twenty-two miles) away. Sri Lanka's area is 65,610 square kilometers; thus, it is slightly larger than West Virginia and not quite twice the size of Portugal. The island occupies a strategic location near major Indian Ocean sea lanes.

Neutral background material is almost impossible to find concerning Sri Lanka. One group or another contests almost any "fact." Even the name of the country is contentious. Until 1972, Sri Lanka was officially known as Ceylon, an English word derived from the Sanskrit *Simhadaladivipa*, meaning "Island of the Sinhalese." The name of the country in Sinhala and in Pali (language of the Buddhist Scriptures) is Lanka, and the prefix Sri is an honorific. To the Tamils, however, the island is Ilam or Ilankai. (Ilam is spelled Eelam by the nationalists of the LTTE.)

The mere fact that a country has different names in different languages is not a cause or justification of civil war, of course. Europe provides several examples of countries with two names, including Suomi, also known as Finland. In Sri Lanka, however, Tamils saw adoption of the official name Sri Lanka as relegating them to perpetual domination by the Sinhalese.

Sri Lanka's population was estimated at 19,145,000 in 1999 but the precise figure is unknown, in part because of the war. Since the outbreak of hostilities between the government and Tamil separatists in the 1980s, several hundred thousand Tamil civilians have fled the island. As of late 1996, 63,068 were housed in refugee camps in south India, while another thirty to forty thousand lived just outside the Indian camps. More than two hundred thousand Tamils have sought political asylum in the West.

The composition of Sri Lanka's population is another politically charged question. There is a contradiction between the symbolically important binary opposition of Sinhala versus Tamil, and the real ethnic composition of the population, which is more complex. The *CIA World Factbook* (1999) presents three breakdowns—ethnic groups, religions, and languages—without explaining the linkages. According to the *CIA World Factbook*, there are three major ethnic groups: Sinhalese, who comprise seventy-four percent of the population, Tamils, eighteen percent, and Moors, seven percent. Three smaller minorities—Burghers, Malays, and Veddas—make up the remaining one percent. This breakdown also describes the native languages spoken in Sri Lanka. Under religions, the *Factbook* lists Buddhists sixty-nine percent; Hindus, fifteen percent; Christians, eight percent; and Muslims, eight percent.

In fact, there is a considerable degree of congruence between ethnic and religious identities. Thus, the Sinhalese are mainly Buddhists while the majority of Tamils are Hindus. However, the exceptions to this general rule are important. Most of the so-called Moors (Sri Lankan Muslims, as opposed to Malays) are Tamil speakers, yet they deny that the LTTE and other Tamil groups speak for them. Christians include Sinhalese, Tamils, and Burghers (who claim descent from the Dutch colonizers); their political importance is greater than their numbers suggest, since they tend to be of elite status.

Sri Lanka's crisis is particularly intractable because the Sinhalese, like the Tamil and Muslim communities, consider themselves to be a minority in some contexts and thus feel insecure. This is due to the close proximity of India, which often constitutes a frame of reference. Tamils feel that they are victims of discrimination as Tamil-speakers and as Hindus, in a state dominated by Sinhala-speakers and Buddhists. They identify with their fellow Tamils of southern India who constitute a minority within the Indian subcontinent dominated by speakers of Hindi and other Indo-European languages.

From a Sinhalese point of view, however, the Sinhalese constitute a linguistic minority in relation to the much more numerous Tamils of northern Sri Lanka and southern India. In religious terms, the Buddhist Sinhalese are a minority in relation to the Hindu majority of the subcontinent.

As for the Muslims, they are a minority among Tamil speakers and within Sri Lanka as a whole. On a regional level, the hundreds of millions of Muslims of Pakistan, India, and Bangladesh are outnumbered by the Hindus. As stated by scholar Kenneth Bush, the situation in Sri Lanka and India of interlocking minorities recalls the situation in the British Isles, where Catholics are a minority in Northern Ireland, a majority in the Republic of Ireland and in the island as a whole, but a minority in the British Isles.

Overview of the Conflict

The inter-ethnic civil war in the 1980s and the high level of violence since then are rooted in Sri Lanka's transition to independence. Sri Lanka was led to independence by the conservative United National Party, which had been formed prior to the elections of 1947 by representatives of a variety of nationalist and communal parties. Sri Lanka achieved Dominion status in 1948 and independence in 1972. The Sri Lankan constitution conformed to the "Westminster Model,"—the English model—in that the chief of government was the prime minister, whose party held a majority in parliament, and the head of state was the British monarch, represented in Sri Lanka by a governor-general. Although the UNP was dominated by English-educated leaders and included people from all of the island's ethnic groups, the first version of the Tamil question arose under its rule. The issue was the status of the so-called Indian Tamils, who had been brought to the island by the British. Among the earliest acts passed by the House of Representatives were measures denying citizenship to the majority of the Indian Tamils, and disenfranchising them. The political motive behind these acts was the fear by Sinhala leaders of the electoral strength that could be exercised by the

Tamil plantation workers, who supposedly sympathized with a communist party.

Economic and cultural grievances fused in the first years of independence to produce a populist Sinhalese nationalism that swept aside the UNP. The economic grievances included falling prices for Sri Lanka's cash crops and rising unemployment for the educated. In the cultural sphere, the UNP was felt to be out of touch with traditional language, art, and religion. In 1956 a left-wing coalition led by the Sri Lanka Freedom Party (SLFP) won the general elections by capitalizing on this populist nationalism.

S.W.R.D. (Solomon) Bandaranaike of the SLFP served as prime minister until 1959, when he was assassinated. His government made Sinhalese the sole official language and took measures for state support of the Buddhist faith and of Sinhala culture. Nationalism was linked to socialism in that the state was given a major role in economic development and promotion of social equality.

Bandaranaike's ethnic nationalism provoked unrest. The small but influential Christian community was alienated by his educational reforms. Far from uniting the Sinhalese community, his religious and cultural reforms alienated various factions. And the violence of the 1980s was foreshadowed when Tamil opposition to the Official Language Act (or Sinhala Only Act, as it was popularly known) led to counter-demonstrations in Sinhala areas. The prime objective of these demonstrations was to oppose any concessions to the Tamils. Tension erupted in the May 1958 communal riots, the first of a series of Sinhala-Tamil riots and the first major violent conflict in Sri Lanka. The predominantly Tamil Federal Party was outlawed.

Bandaranaike was murdered in 1959. Press accounts have attributed Bandaranaike's murder to a "crazed Buddhist monk." What is more to the point was that Bandaranaike, who had exploited Sinhalese chauvinism to win election, was seen by some as betraying that cause by making conciliatory moves toward the Tamil community.

The premier's widow, Sirimavo Bandaranaike, rode a wave of public sympathy to a landslide victory in the 1960 elections. Her government continued to implement the policies of Sinhala nationalism. All private schools were nationalized, and state-subsidized private schools were abolished because of the dominant position of Christian missions in the educational field. The state pursued the nationalization of economic enterprises.

By 1965 issues of language and religion apparently were less important to Sinhalese voters, and economic issues (unemployment, high prices, and shortages of consumer goods) caused them to turn to the UNP. Minorities, alienated by the Sinhalese nationalism of the Bandaranaikes also supported the UNP. The UNP came to power and Sirimavo Bandaranaike lost her position.

After five years of rule by the conservative UNP, Sirimavo Bandaranaike won the 1970 elections in alliance with Marxist (socialist) parties. Some have attributed Sirimavo Bandaranaike's subsequent move to the left to her personal ties with the Chinese leadership and with the Indian prime minister Indira Gandhi. According to scholar Peter Kloos, it is more plausibly a response to domestic pressures, in particular those arising from unemployment among educated youth. In 1971 these domestic pressures would lead to a major insurrection by a predominantly Sinhalese left-wing group, the People's Liberation Front (Janatha Virmukthi Peramuna, or JVP), which nearly toppled the government.

In 1972 Sirimavo Bandaranaike developed a new constitution for the country. The Sinhala name "Sri Lanka" replaced Ceylon. The country became a republic, committed to promoting socialism and the Buddhist religion. Tamil activists charged that the minorities lost rights that had been protected since independence. Young Tamils began to turn to secession (withdrawal from the state) as a goal and armed struggle as a means. Scholar Peter Kloos points out the similarities between the JVP and the LTTE, which he calls "violent youth movements."

Sirimavo Bandaranaike enacted reforms that restricted private enterprise and extended nationalization to a number of private industries and foreign-owned plantations. Imports were banned and many Sri Lankans still remember the long lines for bread and rationing of basic necessities, such as rice and cloth. At the same time that she enacted leftist policies, Sirimavo Bandaranaike used the military to ruthlessly crush the JVP revolt. With the crushing of the rebellion, the small Marxist parties who had been part of Bandaranaike's coalition government began to desert her.

Bandaranaike responded to loss of support by restricting the independent press and by postponing elections for two years. When they were finally held in 1977, her party was reduced to a mere eight seats in the 157-member Parliament, down from ninety in 1970. Bandaranaike managed to win her own seat from her hometown. But in 1980, parliament expelled her, accusing her of misusing power while prime minister, and banned her from holding public office for seven years. In 1977 R. Jayawardene of the UNP became prime minister. In the aftermath of the elections, widespread anti-Tamil rioting took place.

In 1978 Jayawardene pushed through a new constitution, changing the parliamentary form of government to a French-style presidential system, whereby the popularly-elected president is the head of state, chief executive, and commander-in-chief of the armed forces. Sinhala remained the sole "official language," but Tamil was recognized as a second "national language" that could be used in parliament or in provincial assemblies, as well as in administration in the northern and eastern provinces. Citizens had the right to education in either national language. Jayawardene also banned the LTTE but was unable to end the radical Tamil movement.

The country had been sliding toward civil war since the 1970s, but 1983 stands out as a pivotal point. In that year, the return of the bodies of thirteen soldiers, killed in an ambush by the LTTE, led to an anti-Tamil pogrom in Colombo. (A pogrom is an organized massacre.) Far from trying to stop the pogrom, government officials encouraged the killing and destruction. The result of the violence was to weaken the position of moderate Tamils and to reinforce the claim of the LTTE that only it could defend Tamil interests.

By 1987 the escalation of the war was causing large-scale civilian casualties and a flood of refugees to India. The Indian government decided to coerce the Sri Lankan government into halting its offensive by sending supplies to the LTTE. According to Subramanian, instead of easing the crisis, India was drawn into a large-scale military intervention that failed to achieve its objectives.

The Indo–Sri Lankan Peace Accord and War, Again

Under the pressure of Indian aid to the LTTE, the Jayawardene government negotiated the Indo–Sri Lankan accord of July 29, 1987, to establish peace in Sri Lanka. Order was to be maintained by an Indian Peace Keeping Force (IPKF). In the first phase, the IPKF was to supervise the surrender of arms by the various militant groups, followed by the formation of the Interim Administrative Council. The council was to include representatives of various groups but the LTTE wanted to dominate the council, and Tamils from rival groups were murdered, as were Sinhalese.

The peace agreement completely collapsed when a group of captured LTTE militants supposedly committed suicide in the custody of the Sri Lankan army, giving the LTTE a pretext for resuming armed struggle. An IPKF post was shelled, a convoy was ambushed, and five unarmed Indian para-commandos were brutally killed. The Indian authorities decided to disarm the LTTE by force. They ordered Operation Pawan, designed to cripple the LTTE by capturing its headquarters in Jaffna City (the Sri Lankan army had been unable to capture LTTE headquarters). The Indians did not use artillery or air support, so as to minimize civilian casualties and material damage. Yet, thanks to sophisticated equipment, including radios capable of intercepting Indian messages and sniper rifles with infrared sights, as well as their ability to mingle with the civilians, the LTTE resisted effectively. It took two weeks of bitter fighting, and many Indian casualties, to capture Jaffna and other northern cities. However, the capture of the cities did not defeat the LTTE, many of whose fighters were able to regroup in the jungle.

The decision of the Jayawardene government to allow Indian intervention caused a surge of patriotism among the Sinhala, which in turn facilitated a revival of the JVP. Thus, from 1987 to 1989, Sri Lanka was the theater of two parallel wars. In the Tamil-speaking areas, the LTTE fought the Indians, while in the Sinhala-speaking areas, the JVP fought the Sri Lankan army. Civil order disappeared. When the JVP threatened to kill wives and children of soldiers and policemen, "secret death squads" began killing JVP members and sympathizers. "Official and unofficial government violence, LTTE and JVP violence, and violence perpetrated to settle private quarrels or for material gain became indistinguishable," according to Kloos. In January 1989, Jayawardene was forced to step down, in favor of his prime minister, Premadasa, who moved to end the intolerable situation.

The JVP leadership was killed in November 1989, which put an end to the war in the south. Premadasa then forced the Indian army to leave. With the JVP and the Indians out of the picture, the two wars became one, pitting the LTTE against the army. And despite the apparent disparity in strength, the LTTE soon succeeded in carving out a mini-state in the north.

In the aftermath of the Indian intervention, both Indian leader Rajiv Gandhi, who had sent Indian troops to restore order, and Premadasa, who had forced out the Indian troops, died at the hands

THE BANDARANAIKE FAMILY

The Bandaranaike family has been part of the Sri Lankan leadership for almost seventy years. S.W.R.D. Bandaranaike (1988–1959) and his wife Sirimavo Bandaranaike (1916–) both served as prime minister. Their daughter, Chandrika Bandaranaike Kumaratunga (1945–), is the current Sri Lankan president.

Solomon West Ridgeway Dias Bandaranaike was born into a prominent Ceylonese family on January 8, 1899, in Colombo. He was educated in Britain at the University of Oxford. In 1931 Bandaranaike was elected to the State Council, which consisted of British-educated Ceylonese. In 1940 he married Sirimavo Ratwatte, and they began a family. Daughter Chandrika was born in 1945, followed by their son, Anura, in 1949.

Bandaranaike was elected to the new House of Representatives in 1947, as a member of the United National Party (UNP), and appointed as minister of health and local government. After Ceylon's independence in 1948, he grew dissatisfied with the Western-oriented UPN, and resigned his positions with the party and the government in 1951. He founded the nationalist Sri Lanka Freedom Party and was re-elected to the legislature in 1952. Over the next few years, Bandaranaike formed a coalition party, the Mahajana Eksath Peramuna (People's United Front, or MEP), which won a landslide victory in the next elections. He became prime minister April 12, 1956. As prime minister, he promoted socialist economic policies, neutrality in international affairs, Sinhalese nationalism, and Buddhism, to which he had recently converted. On September 25, 1959, Bandaranaike was shot by a disgruntled monk and died the next day.

Following her husband's assassination in 1959, Sirimavo was chosen to lead the Sri Lanka Freedom Party. Following the July 1960 elections, she became the world's first female prime minister. Her policies continued her husband's socialist economic programs, nationalization of resources and schools, and international neutrality. She continued to promote Buddhism and Sinhalese nationalism, which alienated the island's Tamil population. An economic recession eroded her political support, and she was voted out of office in 1965.

She returned to office in 1970, when a socialist coalition government regained power. During this tenure, she introduced a new constitution that renamed Ceylon as Sri Lanka, and created an executive presidency. She also introduced land reform and further nationalized industry. However, once again the country suffered from economic stagnation and mounting ethnic strife, and she was removed from office in 1977. In 1980 she was stripped of her political rights by the Sri Lankan parliament, but these were restored by executive pardon in 1986. She returned to parliament in 1989, and served again as prime minister from 1994 until her retirement in 2000. She died several months later.

Chandrika Bandaranaike Kumaratunga is the current president of Sri Lanka. She was born in Colombo in 1945, and educated in Europe; she earned her doctorate in political science at the Sorbonne in Paris. After graduation, she returned to Sri Lanka but dropped out of political life after she married actor Vijaya Kumaratunga in 1978. Vijaya Kumaratunga was assassinated in 1988, which prompted Chandrika's return to politics. She took over leadership of the SLFP, which frustrated the aspirations of her brother, Anura, who left the party to join the rival UNP. Kumaratunga was first elected prime minister in 1990. She won the presidential election of 1994, at which time her mother was appointed prime minister. Throughout her tenures as head-of-state, Sri Lanka continued to suffer violent ethnic strife, which erupted into civil war by the mid-1990s. Although she once proposed a new constitution that would grant more political power to Tamils, her narrow reelection in 1999 was based on a platform of ending negotiations with the Tamil separatists and continued military spending. Her brother Anura, who serves in the legislature, continues to lead the UNP and is considered one of her chief political rivals.

---

of LTTE assassins. Gandhi was killed in 1991. That same year, Premadasa survived repeated moves to impeach him by members of his own party (the UNP) as well as by the opposition, on charges of corruption, wiretapping, and authoritarianism. The struggle left the UNP weakened and divided. Premadasa was assassinated on May 1, 1993, by a suspected Tamil separatist suicide bomber who rode a bicycle into the president as he watched a May Day parade in Colombo. On May 7, parliament unanimously elected Prime Minister Dingiri Banda Wijetunga, an ally of Premadasa, president; Wijetunga then appointed Ranil Wickremasinghe as prime minister.

The new president made fresh peace overtures to the LTTE but little progress was made. A parliamentary committee appointed to find a solution to the decade-old ethnic conflict recommended two separate councils for the north and east and a quasi-federal system to meet the rebel demand for an independent homeland. The rebels rejected the offer, and in September nine thousand government troops mounted a major offensive against them. A Tiger sea base in Kilali on the Jaffna Peninsula was captured on October 1, 1993, and the government troops destroyed 120 boats. Despite the loss of Kilali, most of the Jaffna Peninsula remained under LTTE control.

In 1994 Chandrika Kumaratunga, daughter of Solomon and Sirimavo Bandaranaike, was elected president. Her mother became prime minister once again, a post she occupied until August 2000.

Kumaratunga came to power on a platform promising a negotiated settlement of the civil war, increased accountability for past human rights abuses, and an end to government corruption. In January 1995, a cease-fire was declared between the government and the LTTE and the two sides began negotiations. But in April the LTTE broke the cease-fire, sinking two patrol boats and shooting down two troop transport planes. By the time the government unveiled its proposal for a political settlement in August, featuring a plan to devolve central control to regional councils determined in part along ethnic lines, the war was again in full swing. In December, the army captured the city of Jaffna, stronghold of the LTTE. In 1996 the war continued, accompanied by numerous civilian casualties caused by both government forces and the LTTE. Both sides engaged in extra-judicial killings, as did Sinhalese and Muslim guards armed by the Sri Lankan government, and members of Tamil groups opposed to the LTTE.

The government launched a military offensive, nicknamed "Sure Victory," in 1997. Despite the name, the offensive failed to achieve a decisive victory over the LTTE. The Tamil movement responded by a bomb attack in a parking lot in the center of Colombo, in which eighteen people were killed and more than one hundred wounded. As a result of the bomb and the decline of civilian morale, the government offered to stop the military offensive if the LTTE was willing to discuss proposals involving increased autonomy for the regional councils administered by Tamils and Muslims. The government, however, also maintained its basic position regarding the LTTE. The guerrilla group would need to lay down its arms first and agree to arrive at a settlement within a stipulated time frame. These requirements were unacceptable to the LTTE. In April the government and the main opposition, the UNP, agreed to present a common front in negotiations with the LTTE.

Kumaratunga was herself almost killed in an attack by a suspected Tamil Tiger suicide bomber on the final day of campaigning for elections in December 1999. The bomber blew herself up just five meters (sixteen feet) from President Kumaratunga at a rally in Colombo, killing more than twenty people. The president was blinded in her right eye, and used the occasion to address the nation twice—first on radio and then on television where she appeared with a white patch on her eye. She went on to be re-elected for a second successive term as Sri Lanka's president.

RECENT HISTORY AND THE FUTURE

In August 2000, with the war apparently stalemated, the Sri Lankan government turned to constitutional revision as a means of ending the conflict with the Liberation Tigers of Tamil Eelam. The draft constitution would have devolved powers to the regions, including one administered by minority Tamils, in an effort to give the Tamils a political alternative to the separatist LTTE rebels. An interim council would have administered the north and east, which the LTTE claims as a Tamil homeland.

Unfortunately for the cause of peace, the attempt to revise the constitution failed, at least for the time being. President Chandrika Kumaratunga's ruling People's Alliance needed a two-thirds majority—150 votes in the 225-member parliament—to push through its new constitution. The government expressed confidence that it could muster the two-thirds vote, even without support from the main opposition United National Party. A government minister said the UNP's full support was not needed, as several of its members of parliament were ready to break away and back the government proposal. Several small, moderate Tamil parties also were supporting the new constitution.

Once the reform was approved, the government would then approach the LTTE for negotiations, even though the rebels have said in the past that they would not agree to talks until they recaptured their former stronghold of Jaffna. Kumaratunga told parliament, "I have a little hope that the LTTE will finally understand the realities of the situation and agree to talks." She was booed by

UNP lawmakers, who heckled her and tore copies of the new constitution.

The current parliament's six-year term was to end later in August, and elections would be required. In a move to attract UNP lawmakers to its side, the government approved electoral reforms to replace the current proportional representation system. A statement announcing the decision did not give details, but local media said the changes would increase the number of seats in parliament, allowing the government to accommodate breakaway UNP lawmakers in the next elections.

The UNP, after a meeting of its parliamentary group, said that it would withdraw from the debate on the constitution as it contained proposals contrary to a consensus reached with the government earlier this year. The party said that it also opposed the extension of the executive presidency that would keep Kumaratunga in place for another six years. The UNP wanted the presidency to be abolished immediately. The government wanted Kumaratunga to continue as president during the transition to the new constitution, which would become law only if approved in a referendum.

Beyond these disagreements, typical of the parliamentary sparring between the UNP and the SLFP since the 1950s, there was another sort of opposition. Influential Buddhist clergy and Sinhala nationalist groups opposed the new constitution, which in their opinion was not in the interests of the majority Sinhalese and could lead to the break up of the country. Some monks threatened to go on a hunger strike if the government went ahead with the reforms

In the end, the draft constitution was not approved. The government fell short by about ten votes of reaching the two-thirds majority needed. In the aftermath, Prime Minister Bandaranaike resigned, and several other ministers were replaced. Fighting resumed.

In the aftermath of the collapse of the constitutional revision project, the state-run media linked the opposition leader, Ranil Wickremesinghe, to a series of extra-judicial killings twelve years earlier. The allegations were made by a former senior police officer who said Wickremesinghe had links with groups involved in the suppression of a rebellion by the Marxist Janatha Vimukthi Peramuna party in the late 1980s. Official sources said that there was a possibility that Wickremesinghe could be arrested. His United National Party accused the government of a conspiracy to implicate their leader in torture and murder allegations instead of challenging him in an election.

When five JVP members were attacked and one was killed, Wickremesinghe joined a spokesman of the JVP, Wimal Weerawansa, in blaming the government. Wickremasinghe said he was worried that the upcoming election would not be free and fair. The winner of the election, whether the UNP or the Popular Alliance, would face the problem of finding a way out of Sri Lanka's long war. It remains unclear whether the devolution of power, proposed in various forms since the eighties, is a solution. Such a reform may be both too much for hard-liners among the Sinhalese Buddhists, and too little for the hard-line Tamils of the LTTE.

BIBLIOGRAPHY

Ajami, Fouad. "The Summoning." In *Foreign Affairs: Agenda 1994* New York: Council on Foreign Relations, 1994.

Bartholomeusz, Tessa J., and Chandra Richard De Silva, eds. *Buddhist Fundamentalism and Minority Identities in Sri Lanka.* Albany, N.Y.: State University of New York Press, 1998.

Buchanan, Allen. "Self-Determination, Secession, and the Rule of Law." In *Morality of Nationalism.* New York: Oxford University Press, 1997.

Bush, Kenneth. "Cracking Open the Ethnic Billiard Ball: Bringing the Intra-Group Dimension into Ethnic Conflict Studies—with Special Reference to Sri Lanka and Northern Ireland." In *Occasional Paper Series.* Notre Dame, Ind.: Joan B. Kroc Institute for International Peace Studies (University of Notre Dame), 1996.

Dharmadasa, K.N.O. *Language, Religion, and Ethnic Assertiveness: the Growth of Sinhalese Nationalism in Sri Lanka.* Ann Arbor, Mich.: University of Michigan Press, 1993.

Hannum, Hurst. *Autonomy, Sovereignty, and Self-Determination: The Accommodation of Conflicting Rights.* Philadelphia, Penn.: University of Pennsylvania Press, 1990.

Huntington, Samuel P. *Clash of Civilizations and the Remaking of World Order.* New York: Simon & Schuster, 1996.

Kloos, Peter. "Violent Youth Movements in Sri Lanka: the JVP and the LTTE Compared." *Antropologische Bijdragen*, 3 (1999).

Lipschutz, Ronnie, and Beverly Crawford. "'Ethnic' Conflict Isn't," *IGCC Brief (Institute on Global Conflict and Cooperation, University of California)*, 2 (1995): 4.

Marty, Martin E., and R. Scott Appleby, eds. *Religion, Ethnicity, and Self-Identity: Nations in Turmoil.* Hanover, N.H.: University Press of New England, 1997.

Rotberg, Robert I., ed. *Creating Peace in Sri Lanka: Civil War and Reconciliation.* Washington, D.C.: Brookings Institution, 1999.

Slater, Robert O., and Michael Stohl, eds. *Current Perspectives on International Terrorism.* New York: St. Martin's, 1988.

Stohl, Michael, and George A. Lopez, eds. *Terrible beyond Endurance? The Foreign Policy of State Terrorism.* Westport, Conn.: Greenwood, 1988.

Subramanian, L.N. *The Indian Army in Sri Lanka, 1987–90.* http://www.bharat-rakshak.com/CONFLICTS/Pawan (28 September 2000).

Tambiah, Stanley Jeyaraja. *Buddhism Betrayed?: Religion, Politics, and Violence in Sri Lanka.* Chicago: University of Chicago Press, 1992.

Young, Crawford, ed. *Rising Tide of Cultural Pluralism: the Nation-State at Bay?* Madison, Wisc.: University of Wisconsin Press, 1993.

Thomas Turner

TIBET: STRUGGLE FOR INDEPENDENCE

THE CONFLICT

Tibet, a land of Buddhists, currently is governed by the People's Republic of China. China discourages and actively interferes with religion. The controversy over Tibet's independence has become a media event with each side undertaking a public relations campaign.

Political

- Tibet has not been independent for much of known history.

- Tibet comprises unique people—dissimilar from Chinese in ethnicity and religion—who are seeking self-determination.

- Many Chinese have moved to Tibet, and it is not clear what would happen to them if China granted independence to Tibet.

- China fears that the ethnic separatism of Tibet—if allowed to lead to independence—could spread to other areas of China.

Religion

- Free religious expression in Tibet is denied.

In December 1999, Urgyn Trinley Dorje, a fourteen-year-old Tibetan Buddhist monk, left the Tsurphu monastery outside Lhasa, the capital of Chinese-occupied Tibet. He arrived in Dharamsala, India, the seat of the Tibetan government in exile on January 5, 2000. This boy was different from the thousands of Tibetans who have made the arduous trek over the Himalayas through Nepal and on to India since 1959, the year Tibet's highest spiritual figure, the Dalai Lama, went into exile. Both the Dalai Lama and the authorities of the People's Republic of China (PRC) recognized Urgyn Trinley Dorje as the seventeenth reincarnation of the Gyalwa Karmapa, head of the Kagyu or "Black Hat" sect of Tibetan Buddhism—a wealthy organization with hundreds of monasteries and meditation centers all over the world. This dual recognition caught the attention of the world's media. In a speech given on February 19, 2000, the young monk expressed his feeling about the Chinese occupation of Tibet: "Tibet, the Land of Snows, used to be a land where the sacred [Buddhist] faith and all aspects of intellectual and literary culture flourished. Over the last twenty to thirty years, Tibet suffered a great loss whereby Tibetan religious traditions and culture are now facing the risk of total extinction."

China was embarrassed by the boy's escape and his subsequent public statements. China had authorized the boy's enthronement in 1992 in the hopes that he might help Beijing exercise more influence over Tibetans' religious life. India was also disturbed by the events. It had hosted the Tibetan exiles for more than forty years, while simultaneously attempting to repair its relations with China. The two nations had fought a war in 1962 along their disputed Himalayan border.

CHRONOLOGY

200–100 B.C. Tibet is united under the Yarlung kings.

600s–800s A.D. The Tibetan empire dominates the region.

763 Tibet armies briefly overrun the Chinese Tang dynasty.

1271–1378 The Mongol Yuan dynasty dominates both China and Tibet.

1904 British India briefly gains control of Tibet with the Younghusband expedition. As the British withdraw, China attempts to regain control.

1913 China is expelled from Tibet; however, Tibet's independence is never recognized internationally.

1914 The Simla Conference gives Tibet autonomy within China.

1940 The fourteenth Dalai Lama is enthroned.

1950 Chinese troops occupy a Tibetan border town and kill thousands.

1959 The Dalai Lama and thousands of Tibetans flee Tibet.

1962 China and India fight a war over borders, including Tibet's borders.

1966–76 Thousands of Tibetan monasteries and nunneries are destroyed during the Cultural Revolution of China.

1982–84 The Dalai Lama and the People's Republic of China negotiate Tibet's status but fail to arrive at an agreement.

1999 A Tibetan monk, fourteen-year-old Urgyn Trinley Dorje, is recognized as the seventeenth reincarnation of Gyalwa Karmapa. He flees Tibet for India.

The escape also brought to light internal conflicts among Tibetan Buddhist sects. For example, in 1994 a rival boy was enthroned as the Karmapa in New Delhi, India, by the Sharmapa, another high Kagyu figure. This enthronement defied the Dalai Lama and the other regents entrusted with finding a reincarnation after the death of the sixteenth Karmapa in 1981. The Sharmapa claimed that the Dalai Lama, as head of the Gelug, or Yellow Hat sect, had no authority to recognize Kagyu incarnations. Western adherents have been disturbed by the internal squabbling and charges of corruption, deception, and even murder. The image of Tibetans as peaceful spiritualists levitating

above the world's problems has been tested by the ongoing Karmapa controversy and was perhaps irrevocably damaged when a well known Gelug monk and two disciples were murdered in Dharamsala, India, in 1997. Their deaths have generally been attributed to Tibetan followers of Dorje Shungden, a Gelug "protector god" whom the Dalai Lama officially renounced in 1996.

The Karmapa affair is not the first time that rival incarnations have been recognized. Enthronement has always been highly political. Such was the case when the Panchen Lama, the second-highest reincarnate figure after the Dalai Lama, suddenly died in Tibet in 1989. The Dalai Lama recognized a Tibetan boy, Gedhun Choekyi Nyima, as the Eleventh Panchen Lama in 1995. Soon after, however, Chinese authorities announced that they had enthroned Gyaltsen Norbu, whose parents were members of the Communist Party, as the new Panchen Lama. Although he had the devotion of most Tibetans, the Dalai Lama's chosen reincarnate disappeared; in May 1996 the Chinese government admitted they had taken the boy into custody. The Panchen Lama affair is written about extensively in Isabel Hilton's *The Search for the Panchen Lama.*

HISTORICAL BACKGROUND

Shangri-La: Real or Ideal?

Tibet's struggle for cultural survival and political independence is becoming more visible in the West. In recent decades, cause of Tibet's cause has been championed by movie stars like Richard Gere and Steven Seagal, who was recognized as a reincarnated Tibetan by the Nyingma sect; movie directors like Martin Scorcese, whose film *Kundun* told the story of the young Dalai Lama; and bands such as the Beastie Boys have helped organize Tibetan Freedom concerts. It has become fashionable to take up the Tibetan cause and "Free Tibet" bumper stickers are more common. Westerners who seek truth in the spiritual traditions of the East, are becoming troubled by news of human rights violations and the destruction of Tibet's environment.

The image of Tibet has not always been so positive. Until the Chinese occupation, many Westerners characterized Tibetan society as feudal and stagnant, its religion a degenerate and superstitious form of Buddhism, riddled with corruption and idol worship. During the nineteenth century, Western scholars portrayed the Tibetan political system as the dark mirror image of the rational British Indian administration, likening it to the church-dominated feudalism of Europe's Dark Ages. The image of traditional Tibet has since been revised as Western appreciation for the spiritual wisdom of "traditional" peoples has grown.

As Europeans and Americans became "disenchanted" with their "modern society" brought on by scientific and technological development, faraway Tibet, like other lands not fully mapped by Westerners, was imagined as a magical, sacred space where abominable snowmen and Himalayan gurus lived outside of history. This image was reinforced by the novel (and later film) *Lost Horizon*, in which the British writer James Hilton conjured up the secret Himalayan kingdom of Shangri-La, where peace reigns and no one grows old. Timelessness, harmony, and innocence of disappearing cultures are regular themes of coffee-table books, charitable solicitations, and travel advertisements. The alleged isolation of such societies makes them especially interesting to Western travelers precisely because they have not yet been contaminated by Western colonialism or tourism. This view fails to recognize accounts of internal violence and inequality that actually existed within most traditional societies and overlooks the impact of global politics and trade on even the most isolated peoples. For millions of New Age Westerners alienated from consumer society, an idealized and otherworldly Tibet has become a key symbol of spirituality that resists the twin onslaughts of modernism and materialism. New Age is a late twentieth century social movement drawing on concepts especially from Eastern traditions.

While scholars have begun to critically examine Western fantasies of Tibet, the Tibetan exiles and their supporters are concerned with countering propaganda from the People's Republic of China (PRC) about the evils of the old society. Chinese scholars emphasize old Tibet's technological underdevelopment, vast inequalities, and the alleged cruelty of its feudal system; while Tibetan activists tend to present idealized portraits of traditional Tibet both to foster nationalism within the refugee community and to elicit support from abroad. Tibetan activists have recently begun to appeal to the environmental consciousness of those in the West by portraying their culture as one that existed in harmony with nature before the Chinese occupation.

Like the idea of the Noble Savage—a mythic conception of non-Europeans as having innate simplicity and virtue uncorrupted by civilization— the myth of Shangri-La largely reflects Western desires, and it consequently places impossible expectations upon the Tibetans. The idealized,

THE 11TH PANCHEN LAMA, 6-YEAR OLD GYALTSEN NORBU, IS AT THE CENTER OF THE STRUGGLE BETWEEN THE EXILED DALAI LAMA AND THE CHINESE COMMUNISTS FOR THE LOYALTY OF THE BUDDHIST TIBETANS. *(AP/Wide World Photos. Reproduced by permission.)*

mythological image of Tibetans conflicts with their reality as flesh-and-blood people who are threatened with cultural extinction. The image of traditional Tibet as a completely isolated, spiritual, and peacefully unified nation is at odds with a historical record that reveals centuries of foreign alliances and sometimes violent power struggles among regional, religious, and aristocratic factions. Tibet's disputed history is at the heart of the "Tibet Question" as presented by Melvyn Goldstein's *The Snow Lion and the Dragon.*

Tibet Before the Storm

Tibet, on the "roof of the world," in the rain shadow of the Himalayan Mountains, attempted to remain aloof from global colonial and imperialist struggles. In name, Tibet was under Mongolian and Manchu imperial sovereignty for centuries, but it enjoyed a practical independence in its internal affairs, maintaining an imperfectly unified state under the dominance of Tibetan Buddhist monastic institutions. Although Tibet's recorded history presents no known cases of serious class conflict or peasant revolt, a short review of Tibetan society and history reveals enormous social, cultural, and political diversity, regional and religious conflict, and continuous foreign influences, both political and cultural.

At an average elevation of eleven thousand feet, the Tibetan plateau is dry, affords little arable land, and has a short growing season. The majority of Tibetan people live author had lived] in scattered agricultural valleys divided by mountain ranges and vast expanses of grasslands. Statistics on the Tibetan population are heatedly disputed. The Tibetan government-in-exile writes, "Although there is no independent census report of the Tibetan population in Tibet today, historical Tibetan sources show that their population before the Chinese invasion was at least six million." The exiles claim that about one million Tibetans have died as a result of the Chinese occupation. Geoffrey Samuel cited in the *Journal of Asian Studies.* the Chinese census of 1982, which estimated that there was a total of about five million culturally Tibetan people, of which only 1.79 million lived inside the Tibetan region. Indian, Nepalese, and Bhutanese sources supported these figures.

Tibetan settlements are linked by long-distance trading partners, Buddhist monastic networks, and nomadic pastoralists (herders) who tended herds of yak and sheep. The nomads trade meat and butter for barley, the staple grain of Tibet. Cities are few and relatively small, and industrial development is minimal. In rural areas the household is the basic unit of production. Families are organized into diverse forms to meet varied labor requirements and property rights. The most "exotic" and well-known Tibetan family arrangement is polyandry, the marriage of one woman to several men, usually brothers. Although the majority of Tibetan households are monogamous, some landholding families restricted their sons to having a single wife, so there would not be so many offspring to divide small farms among. Many households engage in diverse means of economic production, whereby members might specialize in agriculture, herding, or trade.

Tibetan people are ethnically distinct from the majority Han Chinese, and they speak a language that is only distantly related to Chinese languages. While there are fundamental similarities in the social structure, language, dress, and religion of all Tibetan people, there is also great regional and political variation and differences between agricultural and pastoral ways of life. Like the loosely structured pre-colonial Islamic societies of the Middle East, Tibet has a very low population density compounded by difficulties with communications and a heavy reliance on long-distance trade. These factors inhibit the development of a strong, centralized political authority. The presence of nearly autonomous monastic orders and waves of cultural and philosophical influences from China and India also has fostered the growth of a very rich and diverse set of Buddhist beliefs and practices, many of which retain significant elements of pre-Buddhist shamanism according to Geoffrey Samuel in *Civilized Shamans: Buddhism in Tibetan Societies.*

Tibet and Religion

Tibetans are devoutly religious people, and Buddhism permeates every aspect of a Tibetan's life. Before the Chinese occupation sparked nationalist feelings, Tibetans often identified themselves as *nangba*, or insiders (of the Buddhist community). Signs of their faith are visible everywhere, and prayer flags can be seen hanging from rooftops or strung across mountain passes. Many Tibetans make long pilgrimages to holy sites, walk around (circumambulate) temples daily, and offer prayers between snatches of conversation.

The vast Buddhist monasteries and nunneries, some of them virtual cities unto themselves, meet the Tibetan people's spiritual needs and provide the basis for the Tibetan socioeconomic system. According to Samuel in *Civilized Shamans*, monks account for approximately one-eighth of the Tibetan population, although some sources estimate up to one-fourth of the male population is made up of monks. Political power is shared between secular and religious figures, with the Dalai Lama, a sort of god-king, nominally above them all. Practical power and wealth is largely local, based on the manorial estates of aristocrats, incarnate lamas, and monastic institutions, which hold some fifty to sixty-two percent of the arable land in the twentieth century according to Melvyn Goldstein in *A History of Modern Tibet, 1913–1951.*

Historically, the central Tibetan state, which roughly corresponds to the present Tibetan Autonomous Region (TAR) of the People's Republic of China (PRC), governed less than half

DALAI LAMA

1935– The term "Dalai Lama" refers to the head of the *Gelug* (Yellow Hat) order of Tibetan Buddhists. The Dalai Lama is considered by many followers of the order to be the ruler of Tibet through reincarnation. Tibetan monks select a child they believe to be the physical manifestation of the previous Dalai Lama. Tibetans call the Dalai Lama *Rgyal-ba Rin-po-che,* which means Great Precious Conqueror.

The current Dalai Lama, Tenzin Gyatso (Ocean-like Guru) was born June 6, 1935. He was designated the fourteenth Dalai Lama in 1937, but his duties were exercised by a regent while he was being educated. As a child, the Dalai Lama was raised in a monastery and has recalled often being lonely.

After the unsuccessful revolt of the Tibetans against the Chinese forces in 1959, he disguised himself as a soldier, fled to India with one hundred thousand followers, and set up a government-in-exile. Known for his sense of humor and compassion, the Dalai Lama is the author of several books. He was awarded the 1989 Nobel Peace Prize for his commitment to the nonviolent liberation of Tibet. His life is the subject of the movie *Kundun.*

DALAI LAMA. *(AP/Wide World Photos. Reproduced by permission.)*

of the population. Much like feudal European kingdoms, the central state contained subordinate units, such as Sakya, that exercised considerable autonomy. Other Tibetan people lived under the political regimes of smaller agricultural states such as Bhutan, Sikkim, and Ladakh, and yet others lived under clan structures in pastoral areas such as in Kham and Amdo to the east, or were virtually self-governing, such as the Sherpas of Nepal. Many of these Tibetan peoples were incorporated into the modern nation-states of India, Nepal, and Pakistan, as well as into the PRC provinces of Sichuan, Yunnan, Gansu, and Qinghai that border the TAR. The annexation of Tibetan cultural regions into Chinese provinces is a continuing source of conflict.

The Rise and Fall of the Tibetan Nation

The early Tibetan political history is unclear. According to early Tibetan sources, rival chiefdoms and clans were first united under the Yarlung kings in the second century B.C. This period is also associated with a military expansion that continued for nine centuries. From the seventh to the mid-

ninth centuries, the Tibetan Empire dominated the Himalayas. In 763 A.D. Tibetan armies even overran and held the Tang dynasty capital of Chang'an (later Xian) for several weeks.

The unification of Tibet and the evolution of Tibetan Buddhism must be understood in the light of the political relationships that stretched beyond its borders. In 640 A.D. Tibetan king Songtsen Gampo married the Tang dynasty princess Wenchen. Tibetans interpreted the marriage as a tribute from the Chinese, while Chinese scholars insist that it was made based on the initiative of the Tang emperor. Wenchen took a statue of the Buddha with her to Tibet. Thus Wenchen and her Nepalese co-wife are credited with introducing Buddhism to Tibet.

Although they occasionally warred, Tibet traded with China and India. Tibet also came under the cultural, political, and religious influences of these civilizations. While Chinese scholars claim that Tang artisans took their refined skills to a less developed Tibet, Songsten Gampo, in fact, brought in artists from regents adjacent to Tibet, including what are now India, Nepal, and Pakistan. The Tibetan written script was developed in the seventh century and adapted from the Indian Gupta alphabet.

Tibetan Buddhist texts devote considerable attention to the historical competition between Chinese and Indian religious philosophies and styles. In 792 the Tibetan king Trisong Detsen organized a contest in which famed practitioners from the Chinese and Indian Buddhist traditions debated and engaged in a magical competition. The Indians were declared the victors and the Chinese delegation was banished from Tibet. Tibet's rejection of Chinese philosophical forms parallels its attempts to reject Chinese political influence. In early Tibetan Buddhism, Indo-Nepali influences in philosophy and art predominated.

Buddhism was institutionalized under King Trisong Detsen and the first monastery at Samye was established in 779. Monastic institutions grew into wealthy bureaucracies that controlled large agricultural estates and engaged in international trade, money lending, and tax collecting. Buddhism provided a language for cross-cultural communication during this period of Tibetan expansion. The conquest, or domestication, of Tibet by Buddhism is represented by the image of the nation as a pre-Buddhist demoness pinned on her back by nails in the form of monasteries as described by Janice Willis in *Feminine Ground: Essays on Women and Tibet.*

In the ninth century, King Ralpachen supported the growing Buddhist hierarchy who opposed the "old Bön" shamanic priests. The modern Bön religion is now generally considered a variant of Tibetan Buddhism. This threatened the legitimacy and influence of the priests and their patrons, the aristocratic rivals to the king. Along with the king's brother, Langdarma, they engineered the assassination of Ralpachen in 836. Langdarma was enthroned, and he reinstated Bön as the official state religion and began persecuting Buddhists. He was killed by a Buddhist monk a few years later. The Tibetan state then collapsed into warring principalities. This began what is often referred to as the four-hundred-year Dark Age, when Tibetan power in Central Asia shifted from the Tibetans to the Turks, then the Mongols, and finally the Manchus.

In the eleventh century, a Buddhist renaissance began in the western outskirts of Tibet. In 1042 the Indian Buddhist sage Atisha arrived in Tibet, and, after his death, his disciple Lama Drom systematized his teachings and founded the Kadampa

sect of Tibetan Buddhism. The Sakya and Kagyu sects also developed during this period. All three were rapidly transformed into monastic hierarchies. During this period, noble families and monasteries alike fielded armies in the contest for political supremacy. It was only under Mongol dominance that relative stability returned.

In 1207 the Mongol emperor Genghis Kahn threatened to invade Tibet unless it accepted vassal status and agreed to an annual tribute. A Tibetan delegation made payments until the Khan's death. The end of the annual monetary tributes provoked an invasion by the Khan's grandson, Godan Khan. Sakya Pandita, a Buddhist master, went to the Mongol court in 1244. He pacified the court and initiated a relationship between Tibetan clerics and Mongol rulers that Tibetans refer to as *yon-mChod*, or patron-priest. From 1271 to 1378, the Mongol Yuan dynasty dominated both China and Tibet, lending some credence to the Chinese claim that Tibet was a province of China at least since that time. Nevertheless Tibetan dynasties rejected the political or cultural union with the majority Han Chinese and both peoples lived under the loose foreign authority of Mongol and Manchu dynasties for centuries.

Under Kublai Khan, the first Yuan emperor, the Sakya sect was granted political authority over central Tibet and Kham and Amdo to the east. Mongol support of the Sakyas was the true beginning of Tibetan theocracy, a dual government of religion and politics, called *Cho Si Nyi Den* in Tibetan. In 1578 the abbot of Drepung monastery converted Altan Khan to the new reformist Gelug (Yellow Hat) sect, and received the Khan's military support as well as the title of Dalai Lama (Ocean of Wisdom). The Dalai Lama was believed to be an incarnation of Avalokitesvara, the Buddha of Compassion, and has remained a figure of reverence for all Tibetan peoples, including those living outside the political boundaries of the central Tibetan state. When the Third Dalai Lama died (the First and Second were recognized retroactively), the succeeding incarnation was found in the great grandson of Altan Khan.

The Great Fifth Dalai Lama faced resistance from aristocratic and monastic rivals to expanding Gelugpa power, and he turned to the Mongolian prince Gushri Khan for support. Gushri Khan supported the Dalai Lama as the spiritual and political head of Tibet. At the death of the Fifth Dalai Lama in 1682, however, Tibet again descended into chaos. The Sixth Dalai Lama, noted for his amorous adventures and love poetry, died or was killed under questionable circumstances. He was the first of many Dalai Lamas to meet an untimely demise. Stability was restored when Mongol power waned and the Manchu Qing dynasty of China sent troops into Lhasa, Tibet, in 1720 and installed the Seventh Dalai Lama.

The Qing dynasty made Tibet a relatively autonomous protectorate and generally attempted to direct Tibetan affairs only when it would benefit their interests. Despite the presence of two imperial representatives (*ambans*) and a small number of troops in Lhasa, Tibet maintained its own legal system and army according to Goldstein in *A History of Modern Tibet*. During this period, regents governed and exercised power because the Dalai Lamas was not of age. In order to counter the power of the Dalai Lama's regents in Lhasa, the Manchu emperors also supported the Gelug sect's second highest incarnation, the Panchen Lama in Shigatse, Tibet's second largest city.

Tibet's isolation during this period was not only a result of geography but also reflected the interests of Tibet's conservative elites who desired to hold foreign influences at bay. In the nineteenth century, the Tibetans refused to establish diplomatic or formal trade relations with British India to the south. The British sent the Pandits, Indians disguised as Tibetan pilgrims, on missions to investigate and map what the British perceived as "unknown" territory. These intrepid Indians, such as Sarat Chandra Das, painstakingly counted footsteps using Tibetan prayer beads to keep track of distances and hid compasses in handheld Tibetan prayer wheels to keep track of direction. Various European foreign adventurers vied to cross the Himalayas from the south, or traverse the great deserts from the north to reach the "forbidden city" of Lhasa. Few succeeded and most were turned back by Tibetan officials, bandits, or perished in the snows. Nevertheless, a French woman, Alexandra David-Neel, crisscrossed Tibet in disguise for years. Her book, *Magic and Mystery in Tibet*, contributed to a growing interest in Eastern spirituality, and fed the imaginations of less critical Western seekers. In the twentieth century, the books of Lobsang Rampa, such as *The Third Eye*, popularized many misconceptions about Tibet. Rampa claimed to be a Tibetan initiate but was in fact a British impostor, the son of a plumber.

Tibet and China

In the nineteenth century, the British and Russian empires were involved in a struggle for dominance over Central Asia, which was referred to as the Great Game. Britain never desired the unprofitable expense of incorporating Tibet into the empire: rather, it hoped to use Tibet as a buffer zone for its south Asian colonies. Lord Curzon, viceroy of India, sent the Younghusband military expedition to Lhasa in 1904. It brutally brushed aside the ragtag Tibetan army and its antiquated armaments. The Qing dynasty by this time was powerless to halt the intrusion. It had lost the Opium War (1839–42) to the British and was crumbling before a combination of European economic imperialism and internal discord.

The Younghusband mission had not been authorized by London, and the British soon reaffirmed Chinese power over Tibet. China, startled by the short-lived invasion, made attempts to reassert control over Tibetan affairs. This drove the independent, reform-minded Thirteenth Dalai Lama, the first to wield real and sustained power since the Great Fifth, into brief exile in India. The Qing dynasty, however, fell to a nationalist revolution in 1911, and China entered into decades of civil war and occupation by the Japanese.

In 1913 the Thirteenth Dalai Lama returned to Lhasa and expelled the Chinese from Tibet. Although Tibet enjoyed a de facto independence free from Chinese interference until 1950, Tibetan independence was never recognized by the Chinese Republic, Britain, the United States, or the League of Nations. Most nations acknowledged Chinese suzerainty (including another nation in international affairs but allowing the subject nation to have domestic sovereignty), but for all practical purposes dealt with Tibet as an independent nation. This is analogous to the current status of Taiwan, which exercises practical independence but is no longer recognized by the United States or the United Nations, both which adhere to a "one China" policy.

The Tibet question was addressed at the 1914 conference that brought together representatives of Britain, Tibet, and the new Chinese Republic at the Simla Conference. For the nationalist movement in China, reassuming control of Tibet and other border provinces was and remained a matter of great symbolic importance continues Goldstein in *A History of Modern Tibet*. The Simla Convention declared Tibet to be under Chinese suzerainty but autonomous in its internal affairs. The Chinese and Tibetans could not, however, reach consensus on Tibet's eastern borders, and ultimately the British and Tibetans signed the Convention without the consent of the Chinese Republic. The Tibetans also secretly agreed to accept British representative Arthur McMahon's map that for the first time clearly defined the boundaries of Tibet and British India from Bhutan to Burma, according to Warren Smith in *Tibetan Nation*. This boundary, known as the McMahon line, incorporated parts of Tibet into India in exchange for British support of Tibetan autonomy. Disputes over this border and China's refusal to recognize the legality of unequal and covert agreements eventually led to the 1962 war between India and China, in which India was defeated.

Despite problems with China, the Thirteenth Dalai Lama's worked to modernize Tibet and institute reforms. But these efforts, as well as his efforts to gain international recognition and organize a national army were sabotaged by conservative aristocrats and the monasteries, which deployed their own armies and were reluctant to pay taxes to the central government (Goldstein 1993). After the death of the Thirteenth Dalai Lama in 1933, the Fourteenth and current Dalai Lama was discovered in 1935 in eastern Tibet on the Chinese border. He was enthroned in Lhasa in 1940.

After the World War II, China was involved in a civil war that ended in 1949 with the founding of the People's Republic of China (PRC) under the rule of Mao Zedong and the Chinese Communist Party (CCP). The Nationalist Party, or Kuomintang (KMT), fled to exile in Taiwan. After its victory, the Peoples' Liberation Army (PLA) announced its intention to "liberate" all Chinese territories, including Taiwan and Tibet, which it claimed had been stolen from China during its previous weakness. On October 7, 1950, Chinese troops attacked and occupied the Tibetan border city of Chamdo, killing thousands of poorly armed Tibetan soldiers. On November 17, 1950, El Salvador requested that the Tibetan situation be addressed by the General Assembly of the United Nations. This request was tabled at the suggestion of the new Indian republic, which had gained independence in 1947 and was attempting to establish friendly relations with the PRC. The United States, already involved in a decades-long Cold War with the communist world, had little interest in confronting the PRC over the sparsely populated Tibet.

Confronted by imminent military defeat and occupation, the Tibetan government signed the Seventeen Point Agreement, meant to pave the way for the peaceful liberation of Tibet. The agreement stated that the Tibetan political-religious system would be preserved for the time being. It also stated, however, that Tibet was a province of China: this was the first time the Tibetan leadership had ever clearly consented to this proposition. Tibetan exiles have since argued that treaties imposed under the threat or use of force are invalid.

On September 9, 1951, some three thousand PLA troops entered Lhasa without resistance. The Dalai Lama was then just sixteen years old. Chairman Mao encouraged a policy of moderation in order to win over the Tibetans and to gradually institute reforms. At first these reforms appeared beneficial to many Tibetans, especially the poor. Improvements in roads and communications were made. The young Dalai Lama agreed that there were many faults with the old feudal system and had some sympathy for communist doctrines of equality. But during a face-to-face meeting with Mao Zedong, he was repulsed when Mao turned to him and said that "religion is poison."

Exile and Ethnocide

Friction in Tibet mounted, and in the late 1950s an armed resistance movement arose, particularly in Kham and Amdo, the eastern borderlands where more radical reforms had been instituted. The guerrillas obtained minor support from the U.S. Central Intelligence Agency (CIA). They fought for about twenty years and launched their relatively ineffective attacks from Nepal after 1959. The Dalai Lama, while sympathetic, never condoned the resistance movement, always adhering to a policy of nonviolence.

Things came to a head when thousands of refugees and guerrilla fighters from the countryside gathered in Lhasa in 1959. On March 10 the Dalai Lama was invited to a performance hosted by Chinese officials. He was told not to bring an escort or bodyguards, which fueled rumors that he was to be kidnapped. Thousands of Tibetans surrounded the Norbulingka, the Dalai Lama's summer palace, to protect him. In the ensuing chaos, the Dalai Lama escaped disguised as a soldier, fleeing to exile in India. The Chinese shelled the palace and crushed the revolt. The Tibetan exile administration claims that some eighty-seven thousand Tibetans were killed between 1959 and 1960.

About eighty thousand Tibetans, including members of the elite and ordinary farmers, artisans, and traders, followed the Dalai Lama into exile. Many became ill or died either from the passage over the Himalayas or from infectious diseases that swept through their ranks. In the following decades thousands more have fled the Chinese occupation, and today there are approximately 133,000 Tibetan refugees in India, Nepal, and Bhutan, as well as several thousand in the United States, Canada, and Switzerland. The majority of Tibetan refugees live in settlements administered from Dharamsala, India, by the Central Tibetan Administration (CTA).

TIBETANS PROTEST CHINA'S ACTIONS AGAINST TIBET BY TAKING PART IN A PUBLIC HUNGER STRIKE NEAR THE UNITED NATIONS AND VOW TO CONTINUE TO THE DEATH UNLESS THE UN MEETS THEIR DEMANDS. *(AP/Wide World Photos. Reproduced by permission.)*

With the help of host country governments, international aid agencies, and money made from treasure smuggled out with the Dalai Lama, the Tibetans have established a democratic state-in-exile that provides employment, education, and medical care for many of the refugees. In 1963 the CTA drafted the first ever Tibetan constitution. The Dalai Lama has made a commitment to democracy and nonviolence and has repeatedly hinted that he will be the last of his lineage.

Before the Chinese occupation, Tibetan elites attempted to keep foreign influences out of Tibet, and few Westerners were allowed to set foot in the capital city of Lhasa. In recognition of the new importance of international political and economic support, CTA offices have been opened in Delhi, India; New York, New York; Zurich, Switzerland; Budapest, Hungary; Canberra, Australia; Paris, France; Tokyo, Japan; Geneva, Switzerland; Moscow, Russia; Kathmandu, Nepal; Washington, D.C.; and London, England. Tibetan refugees have relied more on cultural resistance than direct action against the Chinese occupation. Sympathy and financial support for their cause has been generated as a result of their displays and promotions of art and ritual. Rather than directly competing with Indian and Nepali businesses, the exiles in India and Nepal produce traditional arts and crafts

for export and tourist markets. They have also profited from the surge of Western interest in Buddhism. Because so many Tibetans live in exile, they have been forced to adapt their traditional religious institutions. Over 117 monasteries have been reestablished in exile, in large part through Western donations. These echo the traditional *yon-mchod* relationships between Tibetan clerics and Mongol or Manchu elites. Tibetans in exile are extremely successful, and are often materially better off than their Indian and Nepali hosts.

In 1959, the situation in Tibet began to deteriorate. Under Chinese rule, the forced collectivization of agriculture in Tibet led to impoverishment and famine. Wheat, preferred by the Han Chinese, was planted in place of barley, and did poorly. The Tibetan government-in-exile claims that up to 1.2 million Tibetans died as a direct result of Chinese oppression and mismanagement. Destruction of the environment under Chinese rule has been rampant. There have been reports of Chinese soldiers machine-gunning wildlife. Some species unique to the Tibetan Plateau are now on the brink of extinction. China used Tibet for its nuclear testing and for dumping hazardous wastes. Because Tibet is the source of many Asian rivers and a watershed for China, India, and Bangladesh, the environmental damage will affect many including people outside Tibet's borders. Deforestation in the headwaters of the Yangze River may have contributed to the devastating floods in 1998 that killed thousands of people downstream. The PRC continues to construct massive hydropower plants, claiming it will provide power for Tibetan development. The scale of these projects, and the presence of military guards at construction sites, disrupts both the environment and the sensibilities of Tibetans who consider many lakes and rivers sacred.

During the Chinese Cultural Revolution (1966–76) rapid and ill-planned reforms were enforced by young communist zealots called the Red Guards who were encouraged by Chairman Mao to overturn the last vestiges of the old society and humiliate its representatives. Children were forced to denounce their parents, and religious figures were paraded through the streets, beaten, and spat upon. Tibetan religious expression, central to Tibetan identity, was forbidden, and the Tibetan language was banned in the schools. According to the exiles, in 1959 there were a total of over six thousand monasteries and some half a million monks and nuns. During the Cultural Revolution the great monasteries were shelled for target practice, religious texts were burned, and the Tsuglakhang, Tibet's most sacred temple, was used as a pigsty. By 1976 only eight monasteries and nunneries were left standing.

After the death of Mao in 1976 and the downfall of the ultra-leftist Gang of Four, the PRC made an about-face in social and economic policy under the leadership of Deng Xiaoping. Collectives were broken up and privatized, and the populace encouraged by the words, "enrich yourselves." Liberalization continues under the present leadership, which calls its policies "market socialism." Religious and cultural freedoms for Tibetans have expanded, many monasteries and temples are being rebuilt, and the Tibetan language has been reintroduced in the schools. Tibetans also now experience the (somewhat restricted) presence of sympathetic Western tourists.

Millions of ethnic Han Chinese, who are encouraged by the PRC to immigrate to Tibet, dominate much of political and commercial life. Tibetans are still discriminated against and subjected to what is referred to as the Great Han Chauvinism. Traditional neighborhoods are being pulled down and cities are being rapidly built in their place. Tibetan cities will soon be indistinguishable from Chinese cities. Under the PRC's family-planning policies, thousands of Tibetan women have been subjected to forced sterilizations and late-term abortions. Hundreds of cases of torture of political prisoners, many of them monks and nuns, have been documented by human rights organizations such as Amnesty International.

RECENT HISTORY AND THE FUTURE

A Future for Tibet?

Negotiations between representatives of the Dalai Lama and the PRC were conducted between 1982 and 1984 but little progress made. A key stumbling block has been the exiles' demand for a Greater Tibet that incorporates the ethnically Tibetan provinces of Qinghai, Sichuan, Gansu, and Yunnan. In 1987 the Dalai Lama announced a Five Point Plan, later reformulated in a well-publicized speech known as the Strasbourg Proposal that was delivered before the European Parliament. The Dalai Lama offered significant concessions to the PRC to the consternation of many exiles. He proposed Tibetan autonomy rather than full independence, and he envisioned a demilitarized "Zone of Peace" on the Tibetan Plateau. The Chinese rejected the inclusion of Tibetan ethnic regions in Chinese provinces and reiterated their demand that the Dalai Lama support the full integration of Tibet into the PRC. Chinese leadership seems to fear that the ethnic separatism of Tibet will spread to other regions of China where there is a Tibetan minority.

Negotiations are at a standstill, and the Tibetan exiles now have an international strategy to attract people and governments of the world to their in position who in turn will pressure the PRC. The Dalai Lama, who once lived in seclusion in the city of Lhasa, has become a globetrotter, addressing the U.S. Congress, meeting with presidents, and offering once-restricted Buddhist initiations to hundreds of thousands converts. His face can be seen advertising Apple computers, urging us to "Think Different." The Dalai Lama was awarded the Nobel Peace Prize in 1989.

Liberalization in Tibet has not softened Tibetan resentment. In September 1987, monks from Lhasa, Tibet's Drepung monastery were arrested after staging a protest in support of the Dalai Lama. When another small group of monks demonstrated on their behalf on October 1, the police took them into custody and beat them, sparking the first of several riots. Police fired into the crowds, killing an uncertain number of Tibetans. Much of our knowledge of these and other such incidents comes from the reports of Western tourists who have witnessed and sometimes covertly filmed these incidents. Riots in December 1988 and March 1989 provoked a declaration of martial law in Tibet and the expulsion of foreign tourists. Travel to Tibet is once again possible within strict limitations, and tourists remain a primary source of information about and sympathy for nationalist protests.

Despite the PRC's continuing violation of human rights accords and the feelings stirred by images of unarmed monks beaten by Chinese police, most nations are interested in maintaining good relations with the PRC and its vast and growing consumer market. The U.S. Congress has passed a number of resolutions calling for humans rights in China, and Presidents Bush and Clinton have met with the Dalai Lama on several occasions, to the great irritation of the PRC's leadership. Priority, however, is given to U.S. economic interests, and the Clinton administration succeeded in extending Most Favored Nation trading status to the PRC in 2000. President Clinton also supported its inclusion in the World Trade Organization (WTO). By the mid-1990s, many Tibetans and their supporters feared that the struggle had been lost. One recent bright spot for Tibetan nationalism was the cancellation of a controversial project supported by the World Bank that would have resettled some sixty thousand Chinese farmers in Tibetan regions.

More recently China may be hardening its stance. The Dalai Lama's visit to Taiwan in 1997 angered Beijing, and China now demands that the Dalai Lama recognize Chinese sovereignty over Taiwan as well as Tibet. In June, 2000, Taiwanese president Chen Shui-bian told an American delegation that he accepted the "one China" principle, although how that unitary China should be defined was still open to debate. Some Tibetan nationalists hope for the dissolution of the present Chinese state along the lines of the former Soviet Union in the early 1990s. The U.S. government and the Dalai LamaCwho made statements supporting China's membership in the WTOChope that by fully including the PRC in the global economy, it will gradually be reformed. In a democratic China, Tibetans might run their own affairs, and possibly hold a referendum on independence. In such a scenario, Tibet might return to the role it played in earlier centuries, as a buffer or "Zone of Peace" between larger nations, with its political and cultural autonomy recognized by nations and peoples from beyond the peaks. China appears to be waiting for the death of the Dalai Lama, now in his sixties, while Tibetans become a minority in much of their homeland.

BIBLIOGRAPHY

Avedon, John. *In Exile From the Land of Snows.* London: Wisdom Books, 1984.

Aziz, Barbara. *Tibetan Frontier Families.* New Delhi, India: Vikas, 1978.

Bishop, Peter. *The Myth of Shangri-La: Tibet, Travel Writing and the Western Creation of Sacred Landscape.* Berkeley, Calif.: University of California Press, 1989.

———. *Dreams of Power.* London: Athlone Press, 1993.

Chapela, Leonard. "Economic Institutions of Buddhist Tibet." *Tibet Journal* 18 (1992): 1–40.

David Neel, Alexandra. *Magic and Mystery in Tibet.* New York: Dover, 1971.

Ekvall, Robert. *Fields on the Hoof: Nexus of Tibtan Nomadic Pastoralism.* New York: Holt, Rinehart and Winston, 1968.

Forbes, Ann. *Settlements of Hope: An Account of Tibetan Refugees in Nepal.* Cambridge, Mass.: Cultural Survival, 1989.

Gilbert, Glen. Interview with Jamyang Norbu. *Tibet Brief* 3 (1992): 7.

Goldstein, Melvyn. *A History of Modern Tibet, 1913–1951.* Berkeley, Calif.: University of California Press, 1989.

———. *The Snow Lion and the Dragon: China, Tibet, and the Dalai Lama.* Berkeley, Calif.: University of California Press, 1997.

Gyatso, Tenzin (HH Dalai Lama XIV). *Freedom in Exile: The Autobiography of the Dalai Lama.* New York: Harper Collins, 1990.

Harrer, Heinrich. *Seven Years in Tibet.* Los Angeles: J. P. Tarcher, 1997.

Hilton, Isabel. *The Search for the Panchen Lama.* New York: W.W. Norton, 2000.

Hilton, James. *Lost Horizon.* New York: Pocket Books, 1933.

Hopkirk, Peter. *Trespassers on the Roof of the World: The Secret Exploration of Tibet.* Los Angeles: J. P. Tarcher, 1982.

Kleiger, Chrstiaan. *Tibetan Nationalism: The Role of Patronage in the Accomplishment of National Identity.* Berkeley, Calif.: Folklore Institute, 1992.

Knaus, John Kenneth. *Orphans of the Cold War: America and the Tibetan Struggle for Survival.* New York: Public Affairs, 1999.

Lopez, Donald. *Prisoners of Shangri-La: Tibetan Buddhism and the West.* Chicago: University of Chicago Press, 1998.

McGuckin, Eric. "Tibetan Carpets: From Folk Art to Global Commodity," *Journal of Material Culture* 2 (1997): 291–310.

———. "Serious Fun in Shangri-La: Gender, Tourism, and Interethnic Relations in a Tibetan Refugee Settlement," *Anthropology for a Small Plane* 21 (1996): 31–52.

Norbu, Dawa. *Red Star Over Tibet.* New Delhi, India: Sterling, 1987.

Norbu, Jamyang. *Illusion and Reality: Essays on the Tibetan and Chinese Political Scene from 1978 to 1979.* Dharamsala, Tibet: Tibetan Youth Congress, 1987.

Rampa, Lobsang (Cyril Hoskin). *The Third Eye.* New York: Ballantine, 1964.

Samuel, Geoffrey. "Tibet as a Stateless Society and Some Islamic Parallels," *Journal of Asian Studies* 41 (1982): 215–29.

———. *Civilized Shamans: Buddhism in Tibetan Societies.* Washington, D.C.: Smithsonian, 1993.

Schell, Orville. *Virtual Tibet: Searching for Shangri-La from the Himalayas to Hollywood.* New York: Henry Holt and Co., 2000.

Siebenschuh, William, Tashi Tsering, and Melvyn C. Goldstein. *The Struggle for Modern Tibet: The Autobiography of Tashi Tsering.* Armonk, N.Y.: M. E. Sharpe, 1997.

Smith, Warren. *Tibetan Nation: A History of Tibetan Nationalism and Sino-Tibetan Relations.* Boulder, Colo.: Westview, 1996.

Willis, Janice. *Feminine Ground: Essays on Women and Tibet.* Ithaca, N.Y.: Snow Lion Publications, 1989.

Eric A. McGuckin

UNITED NATIONS PEACEKEEPING FORCES: PEACE AND CONFLICT

The devastation of World War II (1939–45) led many world leaders to conclude that the best hope for the future of mankind lay in finding a peaceful means of managing disputes between nations and other warring parties. The creation of the United Nations Organization (UNO), or simply the United Nations (U.N.), in 1945 offered a forum for the settlement of international disputes. The concept of a global peace forum, however, had an unfortunate legacy. Although President Woodrow Wilson (1856–1924; president 1913–21) called for the creation of a League of Nations to govern international politics in at the end of World War I (1914–18), that institution fundamentally failed time and again to deter aggression by rising militaristic states. The outbreak of World War II, the bloodiest conflict in human history, spoke little for the League's efficacy as a peacemaker.

When the international community began to formulate a replacement for the League after the Second World War, it realized that the new body guaranteeing world peace needed to contain a mechanism for enforcing its decisions. In addition to the creation of an international justice system and the classification of international law and human rights, one of the approaches toward this goal was the concept of United Nations peacekeeping missions. These missions were intended to place troops of U.N.-member states into conflict situations in which both sides sought mediation for a peaceful solution. Since peacekeeping operations began in 1948, the United Nations has launched fifty-three missions involving troops from 111 countries. In 1988 the U.N. peacekeeping missions won the Nobel Peace Prize.

The efficacy of U.N. peacekeeping efforts has drawn some serious criticism, however. Despite the

THE CONFLICT

There is considerable conflict regarding the appropriateness, neutrality, and efficacy of United Nations (U.N.) peacekeeping forces. U.N. troops have prevented considerable bloodshed and provided a safe environment for non-combatants. They have also been taken hostage, killed, and accused of prolonging war.

Political

- The United Nations provides for peacekeeping operations in areas of extreme turmoil, where civilians are being killed, and where intervention seems appropriate and useful.

- The United Nations has been criticized for responding too slowly to situations, allowing, for example, half a million Rwandans to be killed before intervening.

- Regardless of their intent, U.N. peacekeeping missions have been criticized for being poorly armed and trained, for undertaking missions that precluded the use of force, and for allowing themselves to be used as shields against NATO bombs in Bosnia and being taken hostage.

- U.N. peacekeepers have been applauded for helping to stop war and restoring an environment where productive peace talks can take place.

CHRONOLOGY

1945 The United Nations Organizations (UNO), commonly known as the United Nations, is created.

1947 U.N. troops are sent into Palestine to prevent war following the end of the British mandate and the declaration of statehood by Israel.

1948 United Nations Truce Supervision Organization is established.

1949 United Nations Military Observer Group in India and Pakistan is established.

1956 First United Nations Emergency Force is established.

1958 United Nations Observation Group in Lebanon is established.

1964 United Nations Peacekeeping Force in Cyprus is established.

1965 Mission of the Representative of the Secretary-General in the Dominican Republic is established. United Nations India-Pakistan Observation Mission is established.

1973 Second United Nations Emergency Force is established.

1974 United Nations Disengagement Observer Force is established.

1978 United Nations Interim Force in Lebanon is established.

1988 United Nations Good Offices Mission in Afghanistan and Pakistan is established. United Nations

Iran-Iraq Military Observer Group is established. The U.N. peacekeeping missions win the Nobel Peace Prize.

1989 United Nations Transition Assistance Group is established. United Nations Observer Group in Central America is established.

1990 United Nations Iraq-Kuwait Observation Mission is established. United Nations Observer Mission in El Salvador is established. United Nations Advance Mission in Cambodia is established.

1992 United Nations Protection Force is established. United Nations Transitional Authority in Cambodia is established. U.N. attempts to organize famine relief efforts in Somalia are resisted by a local warlord. Eighteen American and twenty-four Pakistani peacekeepers are killed.

1993 United Nations Operation in Somalia II is established. United Nations Observer Mission Uganda-Rwanda is established. United Nations Assistance Mission for Rwanda is established, but troops do not enter Rwanda until more than five hundred thousand are already dead.

1995 United Nations Preventive Deployment Force is established. United Nations Mission in Bosnia and Herzegovina is established; peacekeepers are held hostage by Serbia and used as "human shields" to NATO's bombs.

2000 Five hundred peacekeeping soldiers are taken hostage in Sierra Leone.

good intentions of the international community toward resolving conflicts peacefully through the missions, history has shown that there are serious limitations to what they can accomplish. May 2000 headlines chronicled the abduction by a rebel force of more than five hundred international soldiers serving in the U.N. peacekeeping mission in the West African nation of Sierra Leone. Although most of the soldiers were released after a brief period of detention, some soldiers were reported to have been killed. Because so many were abducted, it became evident the peacekeeper role can be both ineffective and dangerous.

Indeed, the problems and limitations associated with peacekeeping missions have in many ways been caused by their definition. According to the United Nations itself, peacekeepers are restricted to entering and remaining in conflict situations when both warring parties agree to their presence while a peace settlement is being mediated. If one or both sides of a military conflict do not accept peace negotiations sponsored by the international community or the presence of peacekeepers as a component of such negotiations, the United Nations can do nothing to compel them to do so. The United Nations simply does not have the political authority to force nations or warring factions within nations to accept mediation.

A second major problem that peacekeeping operations have encountered is that peacekeeping forces are only lightly armed for their own self-defense. Since it was never intended for them to use force to compel warring parties to reach a settlement or even to act as a police force in the conventional sense, peacekeepers have often found themselves in dangerous situations, like the recent situation in Sierra Leone. As that case proves, peacekeepers are at considerable risk should one of the warring parties in a conflict change its mind about U.N. involvement.

These two serious structural weaknesses in peacekeeping operations have produced a third serious problem: growing indifference in the international community. Given the apparent problems with peacekeeping operations, many governments, lobbyist organizations, and private citizens have expressed dismay and disappointment with the United Nations' ability to resolve conflicts. Over time these attitudes have had fairly serious consequences for both the integrity of future peacekeeping operations themselves and for the working cohesion of the United Nations in general.

HISTORICAL BACKGROUND

Peacekeeping in the Middle East

An historical survey of peacekeeping operations reveals rather clearly why the current controversies about them have come about. Indeed, the first U.N. peacekeeping operation was directed at an international crisis yet to be resolved. The United Nation's November 1947 decision to replace the British mandate in Palestine with an independent Jewish state of Israel the following year destabilized the Middle East. Surrounded by hostile Arab neighbors and containing a minority population of Palestinian Muslims, Israel faced military challenges from the very day it gained independence in May 1948.

The United Nation's attempt to resolve the crisis and end the first Arab-Israeli War was the genesis of its peacekeeping efforts. A special resolution (Resolution 50) of the U.N. Security Council created the United Nations Troop Supervision Organization (UNTSO), establishing a liaison force to hold tentative peace arrangements between Israel and its Arab neighbors. Although the 1948 war was stopped by negotiations partly facilitated by the presence of these U.N. peacekeepers, the

fundamental problem of Arab-Israeli relations in the Middle East still remains a dominating factor in regional and world politics. On two subsequent occasions Israel has had to contend with Arab coalition attacks, and its Palestinian minority remains a source of unrest. Curiously, although the UNTSO mission continues today (with a staff of 153 and a budget of $23 million for the year 2000) there have been several additional U.N. deployments to stabilize peace in the Middle East.

Like the 1948 deployment, which inaugurated peacekeeping operations, subsequent U.N. involvement in the Middle East has enjoyed only mixed success. This was evidenced when the U.N. Security Council and strong American diplomatic pressure (both through the Security Council and on bilateral bases) established a cease-fire that stopped the Anglo-French-Israeli invasion of Egypt following that country's seizure of the Suez Canal in 1956. The United Nations Emergency Force (UNEF) that provided peacekeepers safety only lasted as long as peace was in the strategic interests of the Egyptian and Israeli forces. After building up his own forces and joining another anti-Israeli Arab coalition, Egyptian president Abdel Gamal Nasser simply ordered the UNEF peacekeepers to leave the buffer zone in May 1967. Although they had been there for nine years, the presence of the peacekeepers had failed to create a stable settlement. Nasser was able to treat them merely as a component of the truce, which he saw fit to discard. When U.N. forces left and after Nasser moved against Israel, Israel won and unexpectedly swift (six-day) victory—a military feat of considerable stature. In this incident, the United Nations peacekeeping had neither prevented the conflict nor had it reduced casualties or territorial losses. Indeed, it was in 1967 that Israel took control of the Sinai Peninsula (from Egypt, returned in 1975), of the Gaza Strip (also from Egypt), the West Bank (from Jordan), and Golan Heights (from Syria), the last three of which it still holds. In addition to the diplomatic problems associated with the territorial question, their acquisition and settlement by Israel has resulted in fractious Israeli rule over large Palestinian Muslim populations, which have loudly, and often violently, demanded their independence. Although the peacekeeping force deployed in 1956 may have delayed it, stability in the Middle East was not secured.

Nevertheless, peace agreements and peacekeeping operations in the region following the next Arab-Israeli confrontation in October 1973 were relatively more successful. A second U.N. Emergency Force (UNEF II) remained in place until

July 1979, following the conclusion of the Camp David Peace Accords between Egypt and Israel. A smaller peacekeeping force, the United Nations Disengagement Observer Force (UNDOF), has had a relatively easy time managing the tense situation between Israel and Syria in the Golan Heights since its original deployment in 1974, though the underlying issue of the Israeli occupation remains unresolved.

It is important to remember, however, that either of these deployments could have encountered serious difficulty if any party became (or in the case of the Golan Heights, becomes) dissatisfied. Israeli and Egyptian (after Nasser's death in 1971) adherence to peace has been predicated on a desire for American support. The United States' successive administrations tried to placate both sides, because they desired a pro-United States strategic consensus among the nations of the Middle East during the Cold War (tensions that existed between the United States and communist USSR from 1946 until 1991). Until his death in June 2000, longtime Syrian President Hafez al-Assad was reluctant either to engage Israel militarily or to antagonize the United States.

Significantly, a third peacekeeping force, the United Nations Interim Force in Lebanon (UNIFIL), was deployed in that country in 1978 and has in different circumstances met with less success. In June 1982 sporadic attacks against Israeli targets by militant Islamic forces based in Lebanon provoked the Israeli occupation of a "security zone" in the southern part of the country. Although Israel violated and remains in violation of U.N. Security Council resolutions calling for the withdrawal of foreign armies from Lebanese territory, Israeli security concerns in this case superceded the mandate of the peacekeepers. Since they were unable to prevent Israeli military action, UNIFIL's mission was altered to provide humanitarian aid to Lebanese civilians living under Israeli occupation. Only in April 2000 did the Israeli prime minister Ehud Barak inform the Security Council that his country's forces would withdraw by July of that year, though spontaneous violence against departing Israeli troops clouded the issue and resulted in talk of an additional U.N. peacekeeping deployment to monitor the situation.

Peacekeeping Missions in Asia

If peace in the Middle East has been less than guaranteed by peacekeeping operations, various other nations of the developing world had an equally mixed experience with U.N. peacekeeping. South Asia, another major trouble spot in the post–World War II world, has also been the site of decades of U.N. involvement, but has seen its stability decay rather than strengthen. After a short but extremely bloody war following the independence of India and Pakistan from Great Britain in 1947 (the religiously diverse British-ruled Indian Empire was divided into a Hindu state—India—and a Muslim state—Pakistan—at the time of independence), the U.N. Security Council established an office for the affairs of the subcontinent and decided to deploy a peacekeeping force to guard a negotiated cease-fire line in the disputed province of Kashmir. The arrival of this force, the U.N. Commission for India and Pakistan (UNCIP) in July 1949 and its successor, the U.N. Military Observer Groups in India and Pakistan (UNMOGIP), in March 1951, did help enforce observance of the cease-fire, but violations of the line continued. Further conflict was again averted not by a strong U.N. presence, but by the strategic decisions of the two parties, both of which desired to focus on their domestic development.

When a second Indo-Pakistani war broke out in December 1971, the UNMOGIP peacekeeping force could do relatively little to stop it or to prevent India's quick victory. Having established its main objective of securing East Pakistan's independence as Bangladesh in July 1972, India basically agreed to maintain the 1949 cease-fire line in Kashmir as a permanent Line of Control. Although the U.N. Security Council and Secretary General insisted that the peacekeeping force remain in place, India has consistently maintained that it is no longer necessary or even legal and has at times restricted the scope of its activities. Since the 1972 peace agreement, moreover, the province's permanent status is no closer to resolution and the Line of Control is subject to periodic violation by both sides. Most recently, in the fall of 1999, full-scale fighting broke out and the United Nations could do little to prevent it despite its fifty-year presence. The suspected acquisition of nuclear weapons technology by both nations in the summer of 1998 makes the situation all the more complicated and dangerous. U.N. involvement notwithstanding, strategic analysts regard the subcontinent as one of the most likely spots for a major war to break out in the near future.

Other parts of the developing world also experienced ambivalent outcomes from U.N. peacekeeping. During an era when European powers relinquished control of most of their colonial possessions, U.N. peacekeepers were often called upon to oversee the transfer of authority. This was especially true after the bloodshed that surrounded

BRITISH PEACEKEEPING SOLDIERS STAND GUARD FOLLOWING A GRENADE ATTACK IN KOSOVO. *(AP/Wide World Photos. Reproduced by permission.)*

Britain's unsupervised withdrawal from India. Also when turbulent nations—like India and Pakistan—entered their post-colonial periods with no U.N. assistance, violence oftentimes erupted within their borders. Many nations and regions with serious ethnic, religious, and political divisions exploded in violence shortly after achieving independence. Because all parties to a conflict have to agree to allow the entrance of peacekeeping mission, the United Nations could do nothing. Nowhere was this more true than in Indochina, where France's withdrawal in 1954 left a divided Vietnamese nation, each half of which breached the original independence settlement with attempts to dominate the other. This eventually caused a war that cost

the lives of a million Vietnamese and 58,000 American servicemen. At the same time the other new Indochinese nations of Laos and Cambodia experienced revolutions and wars that resulted in hundreds of thousands more deaths. Although the scale was smaller in terms of human casualties in southeast Asia than in south Asia, the same type of violent political instability affected many other nations in which U.N. peacekeepers played no role.

Peacekeeping Missions in Africa and Elsewhere

A U.N. peacekeeping presence in a newly independent country does not guarantee a successful transition from being ruled to self-rule. A U.N.

A JORDANIAN SOLDIER IS PART OF THE UNITED NATIONS PEACEKEEPING MISSION IN SIERRE LEONE AS THOUSANDS OF CIVILIANS, FEARING AN ATTACK BY THE REBEL REVOLUTIONARY UNITED FRONT, TRY TO REACH THE CAPITAL OF FREETOWN. *(Corbis Corporation. Reproduced by permission.)*

mission sent to oversee the transition to independence of the Belgian Congo (later Zaire and now the Democratic Republic of Congo) from 1960 through 1964 was unable to check either the rise or fall of Prime Minister Patrice Lumumba's Marxist regime and was unable to solve the problems associated with the attempted secession of the mineral-rich Katanga province. Despite its mandate to prevent other powers from influencing the outcome of the leadership struggle, the U.N. forces were unable to stop Soviet assistance from reaching Lumumba and were equally incapable of stopping the direct involvement of U.S. troops and other U.S. government agents who were sent to

help Lumumba's rival, Joseph Mobutu (also known as Mobutu Sese Seko). As a result of U.N. paralysis in this case, the emergence of a stable and democratic nation failed. After a rebellion ousted Mobutu in 1997, the political situation in the country was still far from stable, despite a renewed U.N. presence there since November 1999.

Other transitions have met with modest success. A U.N. peacekeeping mission serving in Cyprus, which became independent from Britain in 1960 and requested the Security Council's assistance in 1964, has met with some difficulties in managing ethnic strife between the island nation's Greek and Turkish populations. Its efforts have, however, prevented both Greece and Turkey, and their respective ethnic constituencies on the island, from carrying out plans to annex Cyprus to either country. A generally peaceful cease-fire has been maintained for twenty-five years. A peacekeeping force sent to facilitate the transfer of remaining Dutch possessions in Western New Guinea to Indonesia from 1962 through 1963 did so efficiently and without any casualties. Another observation mission successfully oversaw a democratic transition in the Dominican Republic in 1965 and 1966, although the political situation there had already been stabilized by President Lyndon Johnson's deployment of twenty-three thousand American combat troops in April 1965. Another, but much later, case of successful U.N. involvement in decolonization managed the peaceful transition of Namibia from South African control (as a League of Nations mandate in effect from after World War I) to an independent nation in 1989–90.

Peacekeeping at the End of the Cold War

The next and most prolific period of peacekeeping operations occurred as the Cold War began to wind down. As the superimposition of U.S.-Soviet antagonism became a less important factor in international relations, many parts of the world experienced turbulence that had been held in check for decades. There were also many places where Cold War-era struggles continued even as superpower tension eased. Indeed, forty of the fifty-three peacekeeping operations have been launched since 1988. Many of these missions have been successful. In the southwest African nation of Angola, torn by civil war since it won independence from Portugal in 1974, peacekeeping forces successfully oversaw the withdrawal of Cuban troops sent to back the nominally Marxist government of the country and then supervised free elections and a budding national reconciliation. Free elections and democratic government also came to Mozambique, another sub-Saharan nation torn by civil conflict rooted in Cold War tension, under the aegis of a U.N. peacekeeping mission that lasted from 1992 through 1994.

Other regions also benefited from a U.N. presence during this period. Peacekeeping operations in Central America were carried out in five countries (El Salvador, Guatemala, Nicaragua, Honduras, and Costa Rica) in the 1990s and generally succeeded in ending long periods of civil strife in each one. In Nicaragua and El Salvador these operations were especially important, as they oversaw both the end of the open and bloody civil wars in those countries and the return of democratic governments. Although there are still some questions

about human rights and democratic stability in the region, the worst problems seem to have been solved. In Southeast Asia, the long-term instability and violence in Cambodia was also ended under U.N. auspices. Although peacekeeping operations did not spare the nation the horrors of Pol Pot's genocidal regime in the 1970s or of the Vietnamese invasion of the country later in the decade, more recent involvement has contributed to ending the enduring civil conflict and restoring a stable government. U.N. monitoring of Saddam Hussein's Iraq, at war with a U.S.-led coalition in 1990 and 1991, has done a relatively effective job of preventing the dictator's acquisition of nuclear, chemical, and biological weapons and his violent persecution of the country's Kurdish and Shiite Muslim minorities.

Criticism of Peacekeeping Efforts

There have, however, been a number of critical failures in U.N. peacekeeping. Perhaps the most publicized in recent years has been the U.N.'s tortured involvement in the former Yugoslavia. A patchwork state of diverse ethnic and religious groups put together as a nation after World War I, Yugoslavia showed serious signs of collapsing as Cold War tensions came to a close. Several of its federal republics, loosely drawn along ethnic lines, declared independence in the early 1990s. Unlike the Yugoslavian state that was forced to recognize this reality, the multi-ethnic state of Bosnia-Herzegovina suffered from a bloody civil war among its three major ethnic groups: Roman Catholic Croats, Orthodox Christian Serbs, and Bosnian Muslims. Although U.N. peacekeepers (the United Nations Protection Force, or UN-PROFOR) first reached the country in February 1992, their original mission so undefined that their presence had little practical value. As the conflict accelerated over time, the world watched detailed press coverage of battlefield disasters, the horrible siege of the Bosnian capital city of Sarajevo, and repeated allegations of genocide and "ethnic cleansing" by and against all sides. The U.N. troops were powerless as negotiations dragged on and cease-fire agreements were broken. Only direct U.S. military involvement authorized by President Bill Clinton in December 1995 led to an effective cease-fire agreement. Although U.S. troops entered the country under the nominal authority of another U.N. peacekeeping mission, the weight of American involvement was the decisive factor in ending the military aspect of the crisis. When another ethnic conflict broke out in the Yugoslavian province of Kosovo in March 1999, an American-led NATO (North Atlantic Treaty Organization) occupation was a catalyst for a solution while the U.N. mission played a decidedly supporting role.

The need for unilateral solutions outside the traditional rubric of U.N. peacekeeping operations has manifested itself in other situations. In Africa, U.N. involvement in the ethnically-torn nation of Rwanda only came after the genocidal massacre of several hundred thousand Tutsis by the majority Hutu population of the country form 1993 to 1994. Although the U.N. mission did oversee the stabilization of the country by 1996, it had done little to save the victims. An earlier mission to organize and implement famine relief in Somalia in 1992 and 1993 also resulted in failure because one of the country's powerful "warlord" leaders, Mohammed Aidid, offered armed resistance to the peacekeepers. Constrained from using force against Aidid, the peacekeepers left Aidid and his forces undeterred and at large while eighteen American and twenty-four Pakistani peacekeepers were killed. The mass abduction of peacekeepers in Sierra Leone has also provoked a storm of criticism about the efficacy of U.N. peacekeeping on the continent.

RECENT HISTORY AND THE FUTURE

The 1998 Somalia incident in particular was a disaster. Film footage showing the bodies of dead American soldiers being dragged through the streets of Mogadishu, the capital city of Somalia, provoked serious domestic criticism of U.S. involvement in peacekeeping operations. After the mission ended in 1993, the Clinton administration adopted an official policy of non-participation in peacekeeping missions on the African continent. American reluctance to become involved in disputes in other parts of the world was influenced by the debacle in Somalia. Decisive American intervention like that in Bosnia and Kosovo has been absent from Rwanda, Congo, and, most recently, Sierra Leone. Worse still, the perception that the U.N. is inefficient and incapable of solving problems has led to principled domestic opposition to American financial contributions to its operations. For several years the U.S. Congress has withheld the United States's annual dues payments and, although a basic agreement to pay them has been reached, apparent objections to other U.N. policies have held up payment. A reckoning in May 2000 found that the United States owed $1.77 billion in back dues.

America's partial withdrawal from peacekeeping operations, caused by the process's inherent limitations, is symptomatic of a threat to the future of effective peacekeeping. Because of structural limitations, first of all, the world's most powerful country has become reluctant to involve its troops in U.N. operations. Many Americans bristle at the thought of placing U.S. troops under U.N. command, though the command and control structure of peacekeeping missions does not necessarily mean that this would always be the case. From a strategic standpoint, many object to U.S. involvement overseas when immediate U.S. interests are not at stake. Failed peacekeeping missions have reinforced that position.

In addition to the fact that the old rules have not changed with regard to the conditions of the missions, the current state of international affairs does not necessarily lend itself to consensus within the U.N. Crucially, many of the successful transition-era peacekeeping missions occurred in the late 1980s and early 1990s when the Soviet Union and its Russian successor state was collaborating with the West to end the continued arms race and prevent the destructively high military spending that caused the Soviet Union's collapse. Indeed, there was much enthusiasm about the emergence of a democratic Russia and the creation of a "strategic partnership" between the two Cold War antagonists. Unfortunately, neither of these early hopes has been fulfilled. In many ways, Cold War antagonism has continued and threatened to revive hostilities between the United States and Russia. As Russia struggles to find its place in the contemporary world, it has often found itself at odds with the United States. While this new antagonism reaches from finance to nuclear arms control to NATO expansion, it has affected peacekeeping as well. As U.S. involvement in the former Yugoslavia became increasingly pronounced in the mid-1990s, Russia, that nation's traditional ally, began to take exception. This was particularly true when NATO conducted military operations against the former Yugoslavia over the Kosovo issue in 1999. Some of the earlier partnership initiatives collapsed and the two governments became more suspicious of each other's motives. When a peacekeeping force was eventually deployed to the province, the Russian government would only agree to support it if Russian troops were included, thereby defusing a potential crisis.

Russia's confrontational approach to the Kosovo question in 1999 raises an important theoretical implication for peacekeeping. Since the U.N. Security Council must approve resolutions for peacekeeping operations, any of its five permanent members (the United States, Britain, France, Rus-

U.S. MARINES, PATROLLING DISPUTED TERRITORY IN MOGADISHU, SOMALIA, DRAW THEIR WEAPONS ON A SOMALI GUNMAN. *(AP/Wide World Photos. Reproduced by permission.)*

sia, and China) can veto them. Had Russia taken its objections to the Kosovo operation a step further, it could conceivably have blocked U.N.-sponsored action there. In other words, although it may have been in the Soviet interest to back U.N. peacekeeping operations in the past, Moscow may disrupt them in the future if it should find that they contradict Russian interests or if the Russian government's conditions for support are not met. This may also be true of China, which has found itself in opposition the United States on a number of international issues.

In a changing world, U.N. peacekeeping operations have at best an ambiguous legacy and an ambiguous future. Although they have enjoyed some important successes, especially in ensuring peaceful transitions to democracy, they have not dealt effectively with many other problems. The limited scope and powers of peacekeeping have remained consistent problems. Even though peacekeeping has worked in certain parts of the world, its failure in others has captured much more publicity and raised public doubt about its efficacy and desirability. Despite its controversial aspects, however, it is important to bear in mind that peacekeeping does demonstrate an institutionalized global awareness of the need to find peaceful solutions to violent conflict.

BIBLIOGRAPHY

Carpenter, Ted Galen, ed. *Delusions of Grandeur: The United Nations and Global Intervention.* Washington, D.C.: Cato Institute, 1997.

Diehl, Paul F. *International Peacekeeping: With a New Epilogue on Somalia, Bosnia, and Cambodia.* Baltimore, Md.: Johns Hopkins University Press, 1995.

Hillen, John F. *Blue Helmets: The Strategy of U.N. Military Operations.* Washington, D.C.: Brassey's, 1998.

Shawcross, William. *Deliver Us From Evil: Peacekeepers, Warlords, and a World of Endless Conflict.* New York: Simon and Schuster, 2000.

Paul du Quenoy

U.S. IMMIGRATION: SANCTUARY AND CONTROVERSY

THE CONFLICT

Each year, thousands of would-be immigrants from around the world apply to immigrate to the United States, others apply for asylum, and others immigrate illegally. The decision of who gets to stay is based on legislation that has established quotas and other regulations regarding immigration. Individuals and groups opposed to immigration—or to the immigration of certain groups—seek to limit immigration and sometimes perpetrate violence on immigrants.

Political

- Anti-immigration legislation has been very popular in some U.S. states, reflecting some people's frustration with rising costs and the changing ethnic demographics of the United States.

- Immigrants are an increasingly large political bloc that can influence elections and therefore command the attention of politicians.

Ethnic

- Some people want the United States to continue to have a majority of people of European ancestry and therefore want to limit immigration, especially from Central and South America, Asia, and Africa.

- Legislative regulations regarding immigration have, historically, been based on—at least partially—ethnicity or nationality.

Economic

- Anti-immigrants claim that immigrants, especially from non-European countries, put a heavy burden on society.

- Others claim that immigrants fill jobs that U.S. citizens will not take.

On Thanksgiving Day, November 1999, off the coast of Florida in the United States, a young Cuban boy, Elian Gonzalez, survived on an inner tube as his mother and other passengers disappeared with their sinking boat. Thus failed another desperate attempt to find refuge in America; ten died, including Elian's mother. For months afterwards, politicians and citizens alike debated the child's fate—should this six-year-old boy stay in the United States as his mother had wished or return to Cuba as his father asked. Finally he returned; although a refugee, he was a minor and thus not able to seek refuge on his own.

For others arriving in the United States, the debate is short, but the answer is that they too will not be allowed to stay. In March 2000, a boatload of illegal Dominican immigrants capsized in the surf off Puerto Rico. Ten died, twenty-seven were detained by the U.S. border patrol, and an unknown number disappeared into the hills, either to find work in Puerto Rico or somehow to make it to the United States mainland. In California, three illegal Latin American immigrants died in a winter storm in the mountains near San Diego, California, bringing the total deaths of illegal migrants crossing the California border to sixteen for the first quarter of 2000. In Oklahoma, the Immigration and Naturalization Service, local police, and citizens apprehended forty illegal Hispanic migrants trying to obtain drivers licenses. An unknown number of migrants fled, presumably to secure licenses in larger cities where they might be less conspicuous.

On the World Wide Web, the Emerald Isle Immigration Center is one of several country-specific sites that provide news and how-to information on acquiring citizenship, the diversity lot-

CHRONOLOGY

1798 The Alien and Sedition Acts authorized the president of the United States to deport any foreigner deemed to be dangerous and made it a crime to speak, write, or publish anything "of a false, scandalous and malicious nature" about the U.S. President or Congress.

1882 The Chinese Exclusion Act bars the immigration of Chinese, the first time the United States restricts immigration based on race.

1906 The first language requirement is adopted for naturalization: ability to speak and understand English.

1907–10 The Dillingham Commission reports on the inferiority of the new immigrants and recommends a slowdown in the rate of immigration. The Gentlemen's Agreement extends the ban on Chinese immigrants to other Asians, and identifies a new category of non-immigrant foreign workers, who can come to work but not to stay.

1917 The Immigration Act of 1917 establishes a literacy requirement for all prospective immigrants over the age of sixteen.

1919 The Red Scare results in the deportation of several hundred immigrants with radical political views.

1921 A quota system is introduced, permitting limited immigration based on a percent of the existing U.S. population by nationality. The quota system favors immigrants from Europe.

1943 A very small number of Chinese are permitted to immigrate, in order to appease China, an ally of the United States during World War II (1939–45). Japanese Americans are put in detention camps in the western United States because of fears that they will assist Japan in an invasion of the United States.

1950s During the Cold War, preference is given to potential immigrants requesting asylum from Communist regimes.

1965 The Immigration Reform and Control Act removes quotas based on race and nationality and adds criteria that favors family members and needed skills. The number of immigrants permitted into the United States is raised every subsequent year.

1980s A recession (economic slowdown) heightens tensions, new movements emerge, such as the English Only Movement, which agitates to require English as the language of government and business.

1986 Congress modifies the Immigration Reform and Control Act and gives amnesty to approximately three million undocumented residents. For the first time, the law punishes employers who hire persons who are in the United States illegally.

1996 Another recession and economic tension lead to the enactment of the Illegal Immigration Reform and Immigrant Responsibility Act, which toughens border enforcement and made it more difficult to gain asylum.

2000 In California, the most populous state in the United States, people of European ancestry officially become a minority.

---

tery, and helpful tips on how to acculturate, get a job and identification, and transition into American society. Additionally, there are law firms that specialize in immigration law, or corresponding subcategories of law, such as sanctuary for a particular class of refugee, or assistance for aliens facing deportation to homelands where they would be at risk. Some will wait years for legal entry; others attempt entry illegally and are willing to risk death or imprisonment to reside here.

For more than two centuries, the United States has struggled to establish an immigration policy with an equitable balance among interests within the U.S. community. The policy question is diffi-

cult, and there are no easy answers to decide who should live in United States and who should not. As the twentieth century ended, there was pressure to restrict further the number of annual legal immigrants from one million annual legal immigrants.

HISTORICAL BACKGROUND

The United States is a nation of immigrants, and from the beginning there has been an uneasy relationship between those already in the United States and those who came later. The ones already in the United States don't want to give up what they have to the later arrivals—no matter how much they might want what the newcomers bring. And they are concerned that the newcomers will change the old way of life and often assume that the change will be bad. In the eighteenth and nineteenth centuries, the early immigrants had qualms about Germans and both southern Catholic and northern Protestant Irish. Later, the old-timers (including the Germans and the Irish) became suspicious of Chinese, Japanese, and southern and eastern European immigrants. On the eve of the twenty-first century, the Latin Americans, Asians, and, increasingly, Africans, face opposition from early immigrants.

New immigrants provide labor that is needed, but at the same time, they are different. They bring strange customs and change the country the old-timers have come to know and love. There is a struggle to reconcile the basic decent impulse of humanitarianism and the fear of strange ideas. This reconciliation is especially hard when the immigrants are refugees—those running away from the old country instead of toward a new opportunity. Immigrants who come to the United States seeking new opportunities are generally ambitious, even if they are poor and unable to speak English. Refugees, especially those who come in the second or third wave of immigration from a particular country or region, are often completely alienated by their language, customs, level of sophistication, and understanding of Western ways. (The first wave of immigration from a particular country often includes the entrepreneurial, the wealthy, and the highly educated—individuals who can take advantage of the new country and send money home. Subsequent waves are family members, and, later, the poor and less educated.) And some politicians, analysts, and researchers would say that a mature America no longer needs immigrants and that it has reached the limits of responsible growth—at a certain point the United States cannot absorb more immigrants without hurting everyone's standard of living.

The First European Immigration

The first European arrivals in New England were refugees. The Puritans who settled there sought refuge from what they perceived as religious persecution; they also had concerns about undesirable cultural influences on their children, as well as economic motives. What they didn't have was a great deal of tolerance for those who were different.

The colonies quickly formed into three groups: colonies in New England and the southern areas were largely settled by the English and not a part of the immigration dispute; the middle colonies from New York to Maryland became the major ports of entry and became populated with people of varying ethnicity; recent immigrant populations, such as the Huguenots and Acadians, encountered animosity because they were French. The Huguenots took one path, absorption into the mainstream—including taking a new religion—and they ended up with above average wealth and political prominence. The Cajuns headed to a more tolerant climate in sparsely populated Louisiana. This pattern has continued—generally those who are more willing to assimilate American culture fare better.

In colonial times, the early Germans attempted to retain their customs when they settled in Pennsylvania and elsewhere. They generated distrust and attempts were made to make them more like English people. The Scots Irish retained their identity by moving to the frontier, where they served as a buffer between the English and the American Indians. The Catholic Irish didn't adjust as well initially and were forced to take bottom-level jobs due to discrimination and contempt. They gradually worked their way up economically and politically, but socially their inclusion was slower because of their religion. Anti-Catholic sentiment would be a problem into the late twentieth century. In the now-familiar pattern, America's love/hate relationship with immigrants produces periods of nativism and exclusion and occasionally, as in the 1920s, overpowers the myth of a land welcoming the world's "huddled masses."

Foreign politics also created friction. After the American Revolution (1775–83), there was conflict between the new United States and France. France had experienced major turbulence from 1789 through 1814—first with the revolution and then with the Napoleonic Wars. French refugees came to the United States and agitated for their political views, creating more friction. Compounding the problem, the United States government was split between pro-French and pro-English parties. In response to the controversy, the Untied States government in 1798 enacted the Alien and Sedition Acts, which made deportation easier and increased the length of residence required for U.S. citizenship. For the first time, America had a serious immigration policy.

Historians claim that international tensions were merely an excuse for the enactment of the Alien and Sedition Acts. When enforcing the Sedition Act, Federalist John Adams (president 1797–1801) targeted Republican newspaper editors, his rivals. The Sedition Act expired during Republican Thomas Jefferson's (president 1801–09) administration.

During the early nineteenth century, Ireland was in the middle of a population explosion and migration, even to an English country, was the solution. Since the slave trade was outlawed in England in 1808, the Irish were considered good labor for the ship captains and the English landowners in the United States. In the mid-1840s the potato famine hit Ireland causing even more Irish to immigrate. By the 1860s, there were 2.5 million Catholic Irish doing manual labor in the United States. By the 1850s, almost a million Germans displaced by industrialization began immigrating to the United States as well. Germans and Irish accounted for two-thirds of mid-nineteenth century immigrants. Some Germans who fled failed German 1848 uprisings brought with them radical ideas, including socialism. Many of them supported Victor Berger and Eugene Debs who co-founded the Social Democratic Party of America in 1897. Their support fostered the backlash known as the Red Scare. The Red Scare involved the deportation of several hundred immigrants with radical political views in 1919 and 1920; the deportation was driven by fears of communism.

In New England, the minority most despised were the French Canadians, primarily because they were Catholic, but there were fewer of them than of the Germans and Irish. Partially in response to the influx of immigrants, the American Party or the Know-Nothings came into being. It developed as a national party in the early 1850s and based its appeal on an anti-immigrant and anti-catholic stand. It enjoyed significant power during the 1950s. The Know-Nothings regarded Catholics as tools of a foreign power (Rome), prone to crime and disease, and morally depraved. The Know-Nothings also believed that Catholics took the jobs belonging by right to good (Protestant) Americans.

Asian Immigrants

In the 1850s there were around forty thousand Asian immigrants in the West. They were hired to build the railroads and provide services for those seeking to strike it rich during the gold rush. (In 1849 an estimated eighty thousand miners flocked to California in search of gold. They were known as "forty-niners.") The number of Asian immigrants was small, but the group was noticeably different and therefore unwanted. Some opportunity-seeking European immigrants moved to the West on the railroads the Asian immigrants built. They became prejudiced against Asians, because the Chinese worked for less money, which they said deprived a European immigrant of better paying jobs. This was one of many examples of two new immigrant groups fighting one another. Local and state governments enacted head taxes on Asians and other discriminatory legislation. The anti-Asian movement culminated in federal legislation, the Chinese Exclusion Act of 1882, that barred the immigration of Chinese. This was just the first law restricting immigration; later, the 1906 Gentlemen's Agreement excluded the Japanese as well. Filipinos, as colonial subjects (the Philippines was a colony of the United States), had special status in the eyes of the government, if not for the masses of older Americans.

Post-Civil War Immigration

At the same time that Americans were clamping down on Asians, they were running out of English, Irish, and Germans immigrants to fill unskilled jobs. The labor shortage, and industrialization, gave rise to an influx of new immigrants. From the 1880s, the type of work the United States had to offer changed to heavy industry—more unskilled, than skilled, labor. The need for craftsmen had been part of the attraction for the post-civil war immigrants from northern Europe, and the change in U.S. economy made immigration to the United States less desirable.

Furthermore, in 1890 the frontier officially closed—the land from coast to coast was largely claimed—and northern Europeans who wanted to be farmers could no find cheap homesteads. But the new immigrants from outside Europe were different. They included Jews fleeing from Russian pogroms (organized massacres) and Italians dislocated by overpopulation and industrialization. Economic, social, and political changes in their homelands brought Poles, Hungarians, Czechs, and Slavs. Between around 1900 and 1913, thirteen million immigrants came—in 1907 alone 1.28 million immigrants came to the United States. Italian immigration between 1890 and 1914 was nearly four million.

Social Darwinism and the White Man's Burden

These new immigrants came at a time when the United States was misconstruing the evolutionary theory of Charles Darwin into Social Darwinism and the white man's burden. One aspect of Social Darwinism included the creation of a racial ranking structure that put Nordic (northern European) people on top, with all others sorted in descending order. The 1907–10 Dillingham Commission reported on the inferiority of the new immigrants and recommended a slowdown in immigration to, at the very least, allow for acculturation. Presidents William Howard Taft and Woodrow Wilson vetoed several pieces of legislation to this effect up to 1915. Then the Americanization movement increased its influence. Subsequently, the Immigration Act of 1917 established a literacy requirement for all prospective immigrants over sixteen years of age, extended the ban on immigration from the Gentlemen's Agreement to other Asians, and defined a new category of non-immigrant foreign workers, who could come to work but not to stay.

World War I

During World War I (1914–18), newspaperman, muckraker, and presidential advisor George Creel headed the Committee on Public Information (CPI) under the Woodrow Wilson administration (1913–21). The committee was formed to encourage American patriotism. Tactics used by the committee were considered propaganda by critics. The committee created and atmosphere aroused intense suspicion of anyone not clearly patriotic. This put pressure on less recent immigrants, especially those who emigrated from the countries with which the United States was now at war. Through intimidation and coercion, patriots forced German immigrants to change their names and habits. Congress passed legislation comparable to the Alien and Sedition Acts of a century earlier. The anti-foreign fervor persisted through 1919, shifting focus to Russian Jews, Socialists, and labor groups. In 1918 the U.S. economy was in a shambles due to the disorganized demobilization of troops following the war and the overly speedy end of government controls over industry. Strikes by organized labor and racial strife from black veterans and others caused disruption and fear. Nearly hysterical, Americans reacted by lynching blacks, rioting, and suppressing labor groups. As for immigrants, many were accused of being disloyal or Communist. The U.S. government, pushed by the press and the ultrapatriotic groups, rounded up and deported several hundred aliens arbitrarily and without due process during 1919 in an event known as the Red Scare.

In the 1920s, Congress acted on the racial ideas that had been floating through America for several decades. In a mix of Social Darwinism, racism, and nativism, it set major restrictions on immigration and closed entry into the United States by new immigrant groups (African, Asian, and Latin American) in favor of the old immigrant groups that had come before the industrial age (European). Immigration dropped from 800,000 in 1921 to less than 150,000 in 1929. In 1933 only 23,000 new immigrants came to the United States. In the 1920s those who wanted to come didn't qualify due to the quotas, and those who did quality didn't want to come.

During the Great Depression of the 1930s, the immigrant problem seemed to solve itself. There were refugees, of course, but not in any great numbers, nowhere near what demand and humanity might have dictated (of the millions impoverished around the world in the 1930s and 1940s, only a handful came to the United States). In the United States there ran a strong undercurrent of anti-Semitism, and fascist and Nazi parties (fascism is a system characterized by belligerent racism) became more organized. Failure to change the 1920s immigration laws had made the migration of persecuted people—Jews and others—impossible. Some special accommodations were made for European intellectual exiles, some of whom remained after World War II. Especially noteworthy in this group were the nuclear physicists who put together the first atomic bomb.

World War II

World War II brought about increased tolerance. The Italian- and German-Americans, after initial accusations and questionable incarcerations, proved their loyalty by fighting—and dying—in the war. More important for immigration reform, Japanese-Americans proved loyal despite the unconstitutional deprivation of their rights and property. Japanese-Americans were wrongly suspected of disloyalty following the bombing of Pearl Harbor by Japan. About one hundred thousand Japanese-Americans were rounded up and put in detention camps in the western United States in order to prevent them from assisting in a Japanese invasion of the United States. And in the war against Japan, the Chinese were America's allies, making Chinese immigrants more acceptable. Besides, the obscene race policies of the Third Reich shifted world opinion and rendered persecution based on race or ethnicity unacceptable.

After World War II

During World War II, millions of British and other men went off to war. Millions of American GIs went to Britain and, later, to other parts of Europe and Asia. There they met young women brought into the workplace by the shortage of men. During and after the war, many fiancées and brides made their way to the United States. After the war, American policy gave special entry to these war brides, first from England, Australia, and Europe, and, by 1952, from Asia. The special legislation for Asian women was a reversal of the exclusionist immigration policy that had stood for seventy years.

THE IMMIGRATION DEBATE

Is immigration restriction necessary, beneficial, or appropriate to American tradition or interest? The debate is complex and ongoing. Both sides, those for and against restricting immigration, argue that banning it altogether is not the answer. Conditions in other countries and personal circumstance often make immigration into the United States a necessity. Most restrictionists today use ecological arguments instead of the traditional nativism argument to support their position. While there are people who still advocate extreme nativism, the movement is small and unrespectable.

A more applicable environmental argument for restrictionists rests on the U.S. Bureau of the Census population projections for the next fifty years. Unless there are radical changes in births, deaths, or immigration, the United States will have a population of 390 million to 520 million in 2050. Since 1970 the population has increased by sixty million, and over half of the increase is due to immigration—either the immigrants themselves or their children. The restrictionists point to environmental degradation in the United States as a sign that these statistics are problematic. Additionally, they feel that it makes no sense to ask Americans to sacrifice in the form of family planning and reduced consumption if, at the same time, the United States is allowing new people into the country, exacerbating the problem. On the other, anti-restricionists estimate that to maintain population levels of 1989 through 2010 will require five hundred thousand immigrants per year. Presently, the United States has more jobs than people as well as an aging home-grown population; it needs many immigrants to maintain the status quo.

Restrictionists rally around another central point: the zero-sum argument. It states that if one immigrant arrives in the United States, he or she takes American's job. Restrictionists argue that the United States already has enough economically disadvantaged people, and its economic strength must be maintained if it is to preserve its position. Immigrant workers depress the job market, especially at the low end where it affects the young and American minorities. Competition shuts the present American poor out of entry-level jobs, increases the income gap between haves and have-nots, and makes businesses dependent on cheap labor instead of innovation and modernization. Furthermore, even though the United States has tightened welfare and barred it to new immigrants and illegal aliens, restrictionists argue that immigrants are almost twice as likely to be on welfare as U.S. citizens.

Pro-immigrationists counter the zero-sum argument by citing the other side of the multiplier, its consumer impact. They maintain that there are still plenty of jobs to do, and each immigrant with a job is a potential buyer of house, car, and services. Working immigrants contribute to a booming economy. Furthermore, most immigrants today enter the United States under the family immigration provision. Immigrant families historically combine resources, cut corners, put everyone in the family to work, and rebuild deteriorated communities. From the new immigrants in New York City and San Francisco to others revitalizing slums into ethnic neighborhoods, immigrants display old American values of thrift, hard work, education, family, and upward mobility. While immigrants often take the low-end jobs and their pay is lower than natives, their household income is consistently higher than the average.

More reversals to exclusionist immigration policy came as the United States enacted refugee legislation in the early postwar years. In the anti-Communist fervor of the 1950s, the United States sought to protect dissenters of Communist regimes. Special legislation was enacted for specific groups adversely affected by Communist regimes, including Hungary in 1956, Cuba in 1958, Vietnam in 1973, Russia in the 1980s, and on into the 1990s.

There was a backlash to the increased influx immigrants, as there had been after World War I, and for similar reasons. With the seemingly large influx of refugees, as well as other groups specifically barred by the 1920s legislation, some "100-percent American groups"—groups of individuals who could trace their ancestors to the earliest settlers in the United States, including the Daughters of the American Revolution and the American Legion—wanted a moratorium placed on immigration. However, unlike after World War I, the climate of opinion in the United States was such that the 100-percent American groups had no influence on American policy. Instead there began a half-century of liberalizing U.S. immigration policy.

TWO CHILDREN WERE RETURNED TO THEIR MOTHER AFTER HAITIAN RESIDENTS MARCHED THROUGH MIAMI PROTESTING THE TREATMENT OF HAITIANS BY THE U.S. IMMIGRATION AND NATURALIZATION SERVICE. *(AP/Wide World Photos. Reproduced by permission.)*

One reason for the new receptivity was the propaganda war with a new enemy. In a display of Cold War unity against what was feared to be a monolithic Communist empire, anyone who sought refuge from a Communist regime was welcome. In addition, independent nations emerged from the former European colonial empires in Africa and Asia, and the Union of Soviet Socialist Republics and the United States competed to make alliances with the newly emerging nations. Foreign policy required tolerance for immigrants.

At that time, only a small portion of the American population had recently immigrated to the United States, and most immigrants were still from European countries. After two decades of stringent immigration policies, the Great Depression, and World War II, America came as close to being a homogeneous society in the 1940s through the 1960s as it would ever be. The religious animosities of an earlier age were submerged, if not gone; religion was in decline. The 1950s and 1960s were a boom time in the United States. For a quarter of a century, the United States was the world's envy due to its prosperity and power. It was good to be middle class, making a success of one's self economically, treating religion as one more trapping of new status.

RECENT HISTORY AND THE FUTURE

New Immigrants

The American idyll ended as an unforeseen consequence of the Immigration Reform and Control Act of 1965. President John F. Kennedy (served 1961–63) and others disliked immigration quotas by nationality, which by the 1960s had become a disadvantage to groups such as the Irish. Too many spaces were allotted to the English who didn't want or need them. The Civil Rights movement was influencing the United States to treat all groups of people more fairly. At the same time, the United States seemed to be running short of technical and scientific skills; immigrants with needed skills were not coming to the United States. Immigration reformers wanted to shift from national quotas to a system that brought in more family members and needed skills—a mix of humane and economic motives. Reformers assumed that, under their new law, most of the immigrants would come from the same places as they had for forty years, just in a different mix. And maybe there would be more from the places where the new immigrants of the 1890s had family, the places shut off by the 1920s legislation; by now the second and third generation immigrants had political clout. But in the 1960s, Europe—north and south—was experiencing an economic boom; therefore most Europeans chose to remain in their native countries and not immigrate.

Throughout the 1960s, although European immigration continued in significant numbers, the largest number of immigrants were from Latin American, Asia, and Africa, who were fleeing the political, economic, and social turmoil of their home nations. Over time, members of their extended family came one by one. During the ten years following the enactment of the Immigration Reform and Control Act of 1965, Asian immigration increased 663 percent while European immigration decreased thirty-eight percent. Total immigration increased sixty percent. At the same time, legal Latin American immigration increased to such an extent that quotas for immigrants from Latin American countries were reintroduced in 1976. There also seemed to be a great influx of illegal immigrants, so in 1986 Congress imposed penalties on people who employed illegal aliens but gave amnesty to illegal aliens who resided in the United States before 1982.

Beginning in 1980 the definition of refugee was broadened. Cubans had been coming since Fidel Castro's revolution of 1958. Cubans first came between 1959 and 1962 as refugees—primarily anti-Castro leaders and business leaders threatened by Castro's nationalization program. A second wave of Cuban immigrants—middle class and skilled labor—came between 1965 and 1973. In 1980 thousands of Cuban refugees came on the Mariel boatlift. The perception among some Americans was that Castro had opened the prisons and let all his prisoners and drug abusers go. The new influx created conflict and hardship and tested American commitment to welcoming all refugees from Communist regimes.

In the 1970s, ninety-nine percent of Haitians were denied asylum, because they were not fleeing persecution. The rule was that refugees from communist countries had political motives, while those who fled rightist regimes were economic immigrants. Economic immigrants had quotas, and those who came without American consent were illegal and sent back.

Compounding American concern regarding the immigrants were the Vietnamese. Like the Cubans, the first wave of Vietnamese was the elite that left in 1973 following the pullout of American troops and the collapse of Saigon. The next wave was less advantaged and, finally, the very poor immigrated. These last were sometimes called boat people. (The poorest refugees are often called boat people because they arrive in over-crowded, frequently unsafe, rafts or boats.) Even during the second wave, there was conflict regarding the Vietnamese immigrants, especially in Louisiana and Texas in 1975. The economies of Louisiana and Texas were suffering, and the cost of living was rising rapidly. The Gulf of Mexico had been over-shrimped, reducing the income that could be made from shrimping. The Vietnamese immigrants—with different culture and values—were perceived

by some to be undercutting the natives in a tight economy. Alienated shrimpers felt frustrated at a government that brought in unnecessary competition. Perceived government favoritism toward Vietnamese, as elsewhere toward Cubans, created friction and led to violence against the new immigrants.

Illegal Immigration

Between 250,000 to 750,000 illegal immigrants are coming to the United States annually. Most of them are from Latin America via Mexico; California and the American southwest has an indefensible two-thousand-mile-long border. These illegal immigrants continue the Bracero tradition of filling the need in California and the southwest for cheap labor—first to harvest the crops, later to maintain the lawns and gardens. They also move into the cities of the midwestern United States.

Efforts designed to deter illegal immigration have proven futile. Amnesties for illegal immigrants in 1982, 1986, and the late 1990s failed to stem the tide or to reform the process. The amnesties legitimated large numbers of illegal immigrants, while at the same time leaving larger numbers illegitimate. At the same time, the amnesties provoked opposition from those who felt that America already had too many people.

Conflict Regarding Contemporary Immigration

As Americans increasingly recognized that they were in a period of economic stagnation, there was a backlash against immigration in the early 1980s. As in Louisiana and Texas earlier, there was a slow stirring of resentment and opposition. One indicator was the English Only Movement, which attempted to require English as the language of government and business. In California, politicians noted that Americans faced an increasing income gap, crime, moral breakdown, community breakdown, rising racial tension, and cynicism, which they attributed in part to an influx of immigrants. California led the way in anti-immigrant legislation; the federal government followed with new immigration laws. California set the terms of the debate that would soon become national. Proponents of limiting immigration cited the cost of bilingual education, the welfare burden, and increased competition for jobs. In Iowa in 2000, where anti-immigrationists sought to create barriers for immigrants, others sought to promote Iowa as the "Ellis Island of the Midwest." Opponents to the legislation to limit immigration claimed that immigrants took jobs Americans could not or would not do, filling an unmet need, moving quickly to self-

CHENIDU ANIKWATA AND HER MOTHER VIRGINIA ARE CONCERNED THAT VIRGINIA'S POSSIBLE EXTRADITION TO NIGERIA WOULD DOOM HER DAUGHTER, A U.S. CITIZEN, TO FEMALE CIRCUMCISION. MOST AMERICANS AGREE THAT THE ANIKWATAS ARE EXAMPLES OF ACCCEPTABLE IMMIGRANTS. *(AP/Wide World Photos. Reproduced by permission.)*

sufficiency and turning a profit for the system. The evidence was inconclusive. The debate regarding what to do about illegal immigrants continued. As the demand grew for more reform, Congress passed on average one reform law per year in the 1990s.

Restrictionist groups, such as Federal Agricultural Improvement and Reform Act (FAIR), Carrying Capacity Network, Californians for Population Stabilization, Population-Environment Balance, and American Immigration Control Foundation express concern about problems of assimilation, define a possible shortfall of land and or jobs, note the increase in pollution due to increased numbers, decry the poorly run INS and America's leaky borders, and note that refugees and immigrants include criminals and terrorists. Some of the groups focus on social and environmental issues, unlike earlier anti-immigrant groups such as the Daughters of the American Revolution and American Legion.

The new restrictionists had some impact in the 1980s and 1990s in both California and nationally. Tighter rules became easier to enforce in 1996 when Congress authorized more money for border patrols, tighter asylum rules, and increased deportations of alien criminals. In addition, during the same year, welfare reform hit immigrants especially hard by denying them food stamps and disability.

While pressure led state and federal governments to restore some welfare benefits for pre-1996 immigrants, the U.S. Supreme Court ultimately upheld the welfare restriction laws in 2000. The tightened immigration and welfare rules convinced many aliens to become citizens, with a fourfold increase in new citizens between 1990 and 1996. The government responded by tightening citizenship rules in 1998, but all those new citizens were firmly on the voter registration rolls, and new immigrants are expected to play a key role in future elections.

With immigration to the United States exceeding one million people per year, anti-immigrant agitation appears likely to continue into the future. Nobody knows how many people—immigrant or native—the United States can handle without negatively impacting its quality of life. Nobody even knows whether less consumption would actually improve quality. What is known is that the United States and the American people have been working for thirty-five years to develop immigration policies that balance the United States' promise of sanctuary with economic and political reality. Congress modified the immigration rules in 1965, 1976, 1978, 1980, 1986, and 1990— each time expanding the numbers of immigrants eligible to come to the United States. In the 1990s the diversity lottery (an immigration program) specifically targeted the underrepresented, including Africans. Asylum law got more liberal just about every year in the 1990s. The Immigration and Naturalization Service sought ways to eliminate a large backlog, establish a streamlined process, and give petitioners a quick and fair decision, a marked departure from the approach of the Red Scare era. On the other hand, the INS tightened enforcement, border patrols intensified, and the number of deportations grew. Still, many more immigrants await entry into the United States.

Recently, the United States has experienced a change in the relative American homogeneity that had developed after World War II. In 2000 in California, the most populous U.S. state, people of European ancestry officially became a minority within their state. In 1970 only 4.8 percent of Americans were not native born; by 1996 the foreign-born represented 9.3 percent of the population. However the United States chooses to proceed with immigration restrictions and allowances, the importance of its immigrant population will only increase over time.

BIBLIOGRAPHY

Bennett, David. *The Party of Fear: From Nativist Movements to the New Right in American History.* Chapel Hill, N.C.: The University of North Carolina Press, 1988.

Bodnar, John. *The Transplanted.* Bloomington, Ind.: Indiana University Press, 1985.

Countryman, Edward. *Americans, A Collision of Histories.* New York: Hill & Wang, 1996.

Dinnerstein, Leonard and David M. Reimers. *Ethnic Americans.* 4th ed. New York: Columbia University Press, 1999.

Fleming, Donald and Bernard Bailyn, eds. *The Intellectual Migration; Europe and America, 1930–1960.* Cambridge, Mass.: The Belknap Press of Harvard University Press, 1969.

Takaki, Ronald. *A Different Mirror.* Boston, Mass.: Little, Brown and Company, 1993.

John H. Barnhill

ZIMBABWE'S LAND REFORM: RACE AND HISTORY

THE CONFLICT

In 2000 in Zimbabwe, black Africans began occupying the farms of the white minority (who owned most of the land), terrorizing the families living there and threatening to take the land for black Africans. The occupying forces were encouraged by Zimbabwe's president, Robert Mugabe.

Political

- The white minority owns much of the land in Zimbabwe, a remnant of the colonial times.

- Some of the land was to have been redistributed—with reparations to the current owners—following independence. But little land was redistributed to the masses of people (most went to the army and supporters of the president).

- Mugabe is encouraging the activities and threatening wider redistribution—with no reparations—in order to secure electoral support.

- The United Kingdom, the United States, and South Africa have offered to contribute to reparations funds in the interests of a peaceful resolution.

Economic

- Many black Zimbabweans are impoverished and frustrated at the lack of land for farming.

Recently, many news headlines have focused on the unequal distribution of land in developing countries such as South Africa, Peru, Honduras, Brazil, and Zimbabwe. Although land reform is not new to the politics of these countries, the issue has been receiving increasing attention due to the negative impact the uneven distribution of land has on the lives and the livelihoods of so many of the poor in these countries. The result of years of inequity is often frustration, which then boils over into political action and even violence and war.

Land reform is generally defined as the redistribution of property or rights in the land for the benefit of those who do not own land: the tenants and farm laborers. The issue of land reform in Zimbabwe is an instructive case study in the politics of land, revolution, and development in southern Africa and elsewhere. Zimbabwe, formerly known as Rhodesia, achieved its independence from British colonial rule in 1965 and its independence from white minority rule in 1980. Land has been the central issue in Zimbabwean politics ever since the British colonists arrived in 1890. The British colonists appropriated the majority of land from the native tribes living in Zimbabwe prior to the 1890 invasion. By independence in 1980 about forty-two hundred white farmers (less than one percent of the population) controlled over seventy percent of the arable land, while twelve million black inhabitants of Zimbabwe had to eke out a living on the rest. Despite promises of land reform by President Robert Mugabe (the only president since independence in 1980), very little has changed. Some land has been bought by the state for redistribution, but this land has been given primarily to loyal supporters and government officials. In February 2000 a referendum calling for the seizure of white lands without compensation for the

CHRONOLOGY

1830 Ndebele tribes enter Matabeleland in southern Zimbabwe.

1890 Cecil Rhodes and the British South Africa Company invade Mashonaland.

1893 British defeat the Ndebele and occupy Matabeleland.

1895 Mashonaland and Matabeleland are renamed Rhodesia.

1923 Rhodesia rejects union with South Africa and opts for self-rule.

1930 Land Apportionment Act divides Rhodesia into European and African areas.

1951 Native Land Husbandry Act significantly changes African land tenure practices.

1961 Zimbabwe African People's Union (ZAPU) is formed.

1963 Zimbabwe African National Union (ZANU) is formed.

1965 Unilateral Declaration of Independence by white government of Rhodesia.

1966 Armed struggle by black Africans in Rhodesia begins.

1969 Land Tenure Act detrimentally impacts those living on reserves.

1975 Mugabe becomes leader of ZANU.

1979 Lancaster House Agreements are signed, ending white minority rule in Rhodesia.

1980 Mugabe wins presidential elections and declares independence.

1992 Land Acquisition Act passes that allowing the government to set price for land reform.

1997 Mugabe targets fifteen hundred white farms for resettlement and the economy collapses.

February 2000 Referendum to seize land fails. War veterans occupy white-owned farms.

April 2000 Land Acquisition Bill passes allowing the government to seize farms for resettlement without compensation.

June 2000 MDC opposition makes significant gains in parliamentary elections.

---

purposes of redistribution failed. This was an embarrassment to the government of President Mugabe, which supported the referendum. Shortly after the referendum failed, war veterans began occupying the white-owned commercial farms and intimidating or killing the white minority and other supporters of the opposition party. In the face of such unrest over land and racial issues, Zimbabwe held parliamentary elections in June 2000 in which the opposition made substantial gains, though the extent of future land reform is unclear.

HISTORICAL BACKGROUND

Pre-Colonial Society

The current land claims fueling the call for land reform in Zimbabwe are rooted in the pre-colonial experiences in the land now called Zimbabwe. It is difficult to be certain about what life was like prior to colonial experience because the indigenous tribes were largely oral cultures that did not leave much written history. Nevertheless, historians and anthropologists have pieced together a useful picture of the two major ethnic groups occupying Zimbabwe prior to colonization, the Shona and the Ndebele. These ethnic groupings are still highly relevant to politics in contemporary Zimbabwe.

The Shona people lived in Zimbabwe for at least one thousand years before the British entered in 1890. They lived in both regions of Zimbabwe, Mashonaland in the north and Matabeleland in the south. To suggest that the Shona were all one tribe is very misleading: the Shona ethnic identity has more to do with shared linguistics and cultural traits than with a command structure. In fact the Shona, with a few noted exceptions, tended to be politically decentralized, making most decisions at a familial or village level. There are two notable dynasties among the Shona prior to British colonization. The first great dynasty, the Mwene Mutapa, ruled from the fifteenth to the seventeenth century. This dynasty largely became a puppet figure ma-

ROBERT MUGABE

1924– Robert Gabriel Mugabe was born February 21, 1924, in what is now Zimbabwe. At the time, the area was known as Northern and Southern Rhodesia, and ruled by whites in a system similar to apartheid. As a student, Mugabe attended the local Catholic mission school before studying at the University of Fort Hare in South Africa, where he was introduced to African nationalism and socialism. He graduated in 1951 and earned subsequent degrees in economics and education.

After spending several years abroad, Mugabe returned home in 1960. By 1963 he had cofounded the Zimbabwe African People's Union (ZANU). Arrested for denouncing the white-ruled Rhodesian government in 1964, he spent the next decade in prison, earning a law degree through correspondence. He was released in 1975 and joined the leadership of the Patriotic Front of Zimbabwe in the civil war of 1975–79.

At the war's end, Mugabe's party swept the 1980 elections, and he became Zimbabwe's first prime minister. By 1987 Mugabe established one-party (ZANU-PF) rule, and became Executive President. He was reelected in 1990. By the end of the decade, economic crises caused many problems in Zimbabwe. Mugabe reestablished his popularity by encouraging forcible occupation of white-owned farms. Although this caused some political backlash, he retained power in the May 2000 parliamentary elections.

nipulated by the Portuguese colonists in neighboring Mozambique.

The second dynasty, the Rowzi Mumbos, drove the Portuguese out of Zimbabwe and built the Great Zimbabwe, a seventeenth- and eighteenth-century walled city now in ruins. They seem to have been highly organized and remained largely peaceful and prosperous. This dynasty was destroyed in the 1830s when the Zulu (later renamed the Ndebele) invaded after being chased out of South Africa. The Shona were primarily agricultural and egalitarian. They decided most issues through popular discussion and consent. They were very religious and the dead ancestors played a vital function in punishing or rewarding the living. Shrines and offerings were plentiful.

For the Shona, land had a sacred quality. Land was held in trust by the chiefs and elders and owned by the community as a whole, including the ancestors. Land could not be sold or taken without great offense to the ancestors and ensuing punishment for their displeasure. Consequently, the Shona could not comprehend the British demands to sell the rights to the land or to abandon ancestral lands and move to some other location even if it were still within Zimbabwe. They also thought that the ancestors would join them in defense of the land against the white usurpers. The concept of land rights to the pre-colonial Shona was more aptly described as guardianship rather than ownership. (Guardianship of the land means that the Shona believed they were to care for and protect the land for their people and ancestors.)

The Ndebele ethnic group arrived in Zimbabwe rather late in 1830 as a result of defeat by other Zulu tribes in South Africa. Unlike the Shona, the Ndebele were hierarchically organized with the king controlling the land, cattle, and military regiments. The Ndebele were pushed north into Zimbabwe by a combination of Zulu forces and Boer Trekkers (Dutch colonists) entering the Transvaal region of northern South Africa. Their economy was based on a mix of agriculture and the raiding of neighboring Shona villages where tribute was demanded. Their most prominent king was a man named Lobengula. Lobengula exercised arbitrary and often brutal power from his court. He was heavily involved in negotiations with the white colonists and consequently became the chief focus of the British colonial invasion in 1890. The Ndebele held the most fertile lands and became the greatest dissenters of redistribution of lands to British colonists. They were also hurt the most by the rapid urbanization that took place in the later half of the twentieth century.

Colonialism

The Portuguese were the first Europeans to come to Zimbabwe. They established a foothold in eastern Mozambique in 1505, and Antonio Fernandez was the first white explorer of Zimbabwe. In 1569 the Portuguese launched an expedition to crush local resistance to colonial rule, but soon found it more expedient to manipulate local tribal leadership. By 1607 the Shona dynasty of the Mutapa struck a deal with the Portuguese to Christianize Zimbabwe and establish trade in return for military aid. By 1629 the Portuguese installed a puppet regime, but the Rowzi Mambo dynasty drove them out, effectively ending Portuguese influence in Zimbabwe.

The British initially interacted with the people of Zimbabwe by sending a series of missionar-

MAP OF ZIMBABWE. (© *Maryland Cartographics. Reprinted with permission.*)

ies from the London Missionary Society led by Robert Moffat in 1816. By 1860 Moffat had established the first white settlement in Matabeleland, at Inyati. The missions made little headway for the next thirty years, although Moffat negotiated a series of treaties with the Ndebele king, Lobengula, granting the British access to mining rights in Matabeleland. Lobengula signed the most decisive of these treaties in 1885, essentially ceding all mining rights to the British. (Lobengula also signed a similar treaty with the Boer government in the Transvaal Republic in 1887.) Lobengula later renounced this treaty as a trick, claiming he would never have ceded away the land if he understood the terms of the treaty. He claimed the translators, including Moffat himself, misrepresented the treaty's terms to him. British colonist and entrepreneur Cecil Rhodes continued to claim rights ceded by this treaty as the justification for British invasion five years later.

In the 1880s the Boers and the British were competing for spheres of influence in the Ndebele kingdom. Rhodes, then governor of the British Cape Town Colony in South Africa, saw the Boer treaty with Lobengula as a threat to British interests in the region and pushed to have Mashonaland and Matabeleland declared British protectorates. Interest in Mashonaland and Matabeleland were fueled by rumors of huge gold reserves in the regions. The British were also concerned about resurgent Portuguese influence in the area that, combined with their power in Angola, would effectively isolate South Africa from the rest of British Africa. The Germans also threatened to cut off South Africa by unifying Namibia and Tanzania through Zimbabwe.

Rhodes proposed to use the British South Africa Company police and settler posses to take possession of both Mashonaland and Matabeleland.

This had the added appeal to the British government of gaining another colony with little expense. In September 1890, Rhodes and his posses entered Mashonaland and stopped near the present-day capital of Harare. The Shona had not been consulted at all. They initially greeted the British settlers, but after realizing the loss of land this entailed, they resisted. The colonists sought cheap African labor and a seizure of prime farming land. In 1893 the British South African Company promised six thousand acres of land to each of the settler recruits who would help drive the Ndebele out of Matabeleland. The settlers were also promised mining shares and cattle as the spoils of war. Lobengula was defeated and later died in retreat. The Ndebele and Shona united to resist the colonial invasion in 1896, but the British bought off the Ndebele leadership and scatter the disorganized, nonhierarchical Shona. The British took control of Mashonaland and Matabeleland and named the territory Rhodesia, after Governor Rhodes.

Rumors of gold originally enticed Rhodes and the white settlers into Zimbabwe but these rumors were largely unfounded. When mining riches were not found, the focus of the invasion shifted to long-term agricultural development and the redistribution of land from the indigenous people to white settlers in the form of large commercial tracts. In 1907 the British began land redistribution and moved the native population to reserves set aside for them. These reserves were of marginal agricultural potential even at the outset, a situation that was made worse by rising population pressures on the reserves. As the population grew, the land was less able to feed and provide for the population. In order to be competitive, the British colonists instituted a number of policies that favored white commercial farmers over Africans. This was achieved by giving the Africans marginal lands away from transportation networks such as railroads and roads so they could not get their crops to market. In 1931 the colonial government passed the Land Apportionment Act designating 17.5 million acres as European-purchase lands, while only 7.5 million acres were designated as native-purchase lands.

The British also increased the rent on African agricultural land and imposed a series of hut and poll taxes on the native population. These taxes were waged on each indigenous household and, later, on each native person. This had two fundamental effects on African agriculture. First, much of the reinvestable surplus went to the tax instead of the improvement of African farms. Second, the 1894 hut tax drew labor into the market as the subsistence African farmers needed to sell their labor

to mines and commercial white-owned farms to pay the tax. The poll tax provided 41.4 percent of the government revenues by 1904 and 1905.

Political power was also concentrated in the hands of the white colonists. Property ownership was a requirement for voting, and a literacy test in English only further limited the Africans' ability to vote and control their destiny. Africans were also stripped of any rights while residing in European towns and urban areas. The white minority designated some towns as European, even though they were on the African continent, and Africans living there had few, if any rights. White-owned farms were heavily subsidized by the state. Ninety-nine percent of all infrastructure money was invested in European-purchase areas only. The reserves created a pool of unemployed African workers (estimates as high as thirty percent of the African population) for the labor markets in commercial farms and mines. Despite all of these tactics, African agriculture was initially prosperous and fed much of the mining population until the 1920s. By this time white-owned commercial farms replaced African agriculture in the market and the demise of African farms forced increasing numbers of Africans into the labor market. By the time the white government declared an independent Rhodesia in 1965, over eighty percent of all arable land was in the hands of the white minority. These farmers made up less than one-half a percent of the overall population of the country.

The colonists would also maintain control over the land and the people of Zimbabwe by finding willing collaborators among the indigenous population. These people were invested with recognized authority by the colonial government and given administrative tasks to perform. These tribal members, the *bhuku* or the "keepers of the book," maintained records of the land and its ownership for the colonial government. This role of land administrator commodified the relationship of the people to the land by putting a price on the land. Another tactic of the colonial government was to endow certain tribal leaders with control over the dispersal of the land, giving rise to tribal factions and war. Legitimacy of authority became tied to the control over territory.

In 1951 the colonial government passed the Native Land Husbandry Act, which forced African farmers to radically change their land tenure practices. Under this new law, Africans were only allowed to own five head of cattle and all the rest were to be immediately sold off. The white commercial farmers bought most of the excess stock at sub-market prices. This change had huge cultural implications because cattle ownership was critical to one's prestige and to the passage from adolescence to adulthood among the indigenous cultures. Under the Native Land Husbandry Act, Africans were also limited to the ownership of only eight acres of land. This virtually eliminated the possibility of significant African contribution to commercial farming in colonial Rhodesia (Zimbabwe). The Act made way for a huge influx of white settlers arriving after World War II for the promise of land and livestock. The white population of Rhodesia doubled from 1946 to 1955. One hundred ten thousand additional Africans were forced to resettle in the reserves from 1950 to 1960.

Such absolute colonial control over the resources of Zimbabwe led to growing resentment among the Africans themselves and they began to organize. In 1961 the Zimbabwe African People's Union (ZAPU) was formed as the first black African political party in Zimbabwe. Although the Africans agreed that they wanted the end of colonial rule and a return of the land, they disagreed about the tactics of such a change. In August 1963 a splinter group of ZAPU formed a new political party known as the Zimbabwe African National Union (ZANU). The leadership of these political parties, including Joshua Nkomo (ZAPU) and Robert Mugabe (ZANU), were arrested and imprisoned for ten years for their role in the indigenous opposition. ZANU would later win power in a post-independence struggle with ZAPU and control politics in Zimbabwe almost without opposition from 1980 until the elections in June 2000.

These colonial legacies play heavily in the politics of land reform in contemporary Zimbabwe. In colonial Zimbabwe, land had become a status symbol of power, and today, when the majority of the land is in the hands of the white minority opposition, Mugabe and ZANU-PF feel they must seize control of the land to solidify their power base. Elements of tribalism, ethnicity, class, and racism is still present whenever the subject of land is brought up.

Rhodesian Rule

The black Africans were not the only members of the population disillusioned with British colonial rule. Taking their cue from the white minority government in neighboring South Africa, the white Rhodesian local government declared independence from Britain in April 1965 under the leadership of Prime Minister Ian Smith. This Unilateral Declaration of Independence (UDI) followed a white-only referendum in Rhodesia in which independence won by a ten-to-one margin.

IAN SMITH

1919– Ian Douglas Smith was born April 8, 1919, in Selukwe, Rhodesia (now Shurugwi, Zimbabwe). He grew up among the ruling white elite and attended private schools. After his high school graduation, Smith enrolled in Rhodes University in South Africa, but interrupted his studies to become a pilot during World War II (1939–45). He resumed his studies after the war, and returned to Rhodesia in 1946.

Smith was elected to the Southern Rhodesian Assembly in 1948 and continued to gain power within the parliament. In Rhodesia, whites controlled the government and economy, and only a small number from the black majority were allowed to vote.

In 1961 Smith founded the Rhodesian Front. Relying on white-supremacist support and violent repression of the black population, Smith led his party to victory by promising independence from Britian and a government based on continued white rule. Smith became prime minister in 1964, and immediately authorized the arrest and banishment of black African nationalists, including now-president Robert Mugabe. He further suppressed civil rights through officially sanctioned police violence.

In November 1965, Smith declared Rhodesia's independence from Britain, and in March 1970, declared Rhodesia a republic. Although he was forced to transfer power to the black majority of what became Zimbabwe in 1979, Smith continued to represent whites in parliament until 1987.

Limited British sanctions immediately followed as the government of Rhodesia under Ian Smith was declared illegitimate and racist. Smith responded by declaring a state of emergency in Rhodesia that remained in effect until black majority independence in 1980. The United Nations joined in sanctions in 1968. The sanctions hurt commercial agriculture, especially tobacco. However, the government responded by increasing subsidies given to white-owned commercial agriculture, a policy that also helped these farms after independence because it encouraged diversification of crops. Even with diversification the control the white minority had over land ensured that much of the land they controlled was underutilized. In fact, of all the land held by the white farmers, only 3.5 percent of the usable land was under cultivation at the time of independence.

SUPPORTERS OF PRESIDENT ROBERT MUGABE GREET HIM AT HARARE AIRPORT IN ZIMBABWE WHERE HE TOLD THEM HE WOULD NOT FORCE THE WAR VETERANS TO LEAVE THE WHITE-OWNED FARMS THEY OCCUPY. *(Corbis Corporation. Reproduced by permission.)*

The white Rhodesian government continued the unequal distribution of land developed under British colonial rule and the racially driven policies regarding almost every aspect of life including agriculture, education, health care, and property rights. The Land Tenure Act passed in 1969 had a significant impact on the lives of black Africans living on the government reserves (later renamed Tribal Trust Lands). Under the banner of greater local autonomy and democracy on the reserves, much of the day-to-day administration of the lands was handed over to local black leaders. Unfortunately the government also forced the locals to raise the revenue needed to cover such expenditures as schools and other services. The result of this act was a massive decrease in national spending for education and the closing of many reserve schools due to a lack of resources. The decline in services to the millions of blacks living on the reserves was then used by the white government as proof that the Africans were incompetent and couldn't be trusted to govern themselves. In reality the plan was doomed from the start due to overpopulation, high unemployment, and the lack of resources or arable land to be found in the reserves.

Independence and Land Reform

Although political control had changed from British to white Rhodesian hands, life for the black Africans did not improve. In fact, many would argue that it declined because the British had been committed to the blacks—at least in rhetoric and principle. Realizing that the UDI was not a revolution from colonialism but an exchange of one master for another, rebel movements began to organize and train in neighboring Mozambique and Botswana. The armed struggle began in 1966. After Robert Mugabe was released from prison in 1975 he became the unquestioned head of the ZANU party and a key revolutionary leader. Although forces associated with ZANU and ZAPU were involved in the struggle, the ZANU forces had the greatest success and brought the Rhodesian government to the negotiating table in 1977. According to Mugabe, the struggle was always about land. In 1979 the Rhodesian government, the British government, and the rebels met in England at Lancaster House to sign an agreement that paved the way for black majority rule in a newly independent Zimbabwe. In 1980 Robert Mugabe and the ZANU party (renamed ZANU-PF for the Zimbabwe African National Union-Patriotic Front) won a resounding electoral victory. When Robert Mugabe, the first (and only) president, declared independence in 1980, sanctions were dropped and foreign aid began to pour in from both sides of the Cold War, despite the declared Communist ideology of ZANU-PF.

As part of the Lancaster House agreement, Britain pledged financial support for a land resettlement scheme based on willing buyers and willing sellers. The Zimbabwe government was to compensate white commercial farmers who sold their land to the government to resettle the millions who had been living on the reserves. Mugabe made land reform a central tenant of his campaign and his first major promise upon election. An ambitious plan was devised for the government to buy 3.2 million hectares to resettle 160,000 black families within the first five years. By the year 2000, 3.5 million hectares have been purchased, but only 60,000 families have been resettled. Whites—less than one percent of the population—still own 11.2 million hectares. Immediately after independence in 1980 the economy boomed due to increases in foreign and domestic demand after the sanctions were lifted. Mugabe claimed that this newfound prosperity was a direct result of his land reform programs, but the prosperity proved short-lived and land reform efforts stalled.

RECENT HISTORY AND THE FUTURE

Failure of Land Reform

There were several factors involved in the failure of land reform in Zimbabwe during its twenty years of independence. First, rising debt to fund the land distribution schemes and other expensive government social programs promised by ZANU-PF have crippled the economy. The debt service ratio (the amount of money earned from exports that is required to pay interest payments on a country's debt) rose from ten percent in 1981 to thirty-five percent in 1986-87. Other government expenditures such as the Zimbabwean army's participation in the civil war in the Democratic Republic of the Congo (with whom they share no border) have increased defense spending by $1 million a day. This increase in military spending will help members of the ZANU-PF leadership to secure lucrative cobalt mining contracts, but at the expense of most social programs, including land reform. There is simply no money left to pay a fair price for land. In 1992 the government passed a Land Acquisitions Bill that allowed the government—not the seller—to set the price for land purchased to resettle blacks on the reserves. This "deal" was to be paid over five years in local (inflationary currency) and the white owners had no recourse in court to government seizures of their land.

Another contributing factor to the failure of land reform is the poor performance of the economy that limits government revenue to pay for land redistribution. The poor economy is caused in part by escalating inflation. Inflation rates peaked in November 1999 at 70.4 percent per year. The inflation level is currently at sixty percent per year. An individual would expect to pay $49 (dollar amounts are in U.S. dollars) to buy the same food that they could have purchased for $2.60 in 1990. The costs of medical care have risen at similar rates. In the ten-year period from 1990 to 2000 the cost of bread, milk, and cereal have increased twenty times. Unemployment is estimated at fifty-five percent, leading to political unrest and protest. The United Nations estimates that seventy-six percent of the population lives below the poverty level.

Government inefficiency, corruption, and poor planning have also contributed to the failure of land reform. To date, the government has acquired nine hundred farms through the land reform programs, but has settled peasants on only two hundred of them, according to the *World Press Review*. Due to poor planning and a lack of follow up those that have been resettled remain desperately poor. They were granted land, but no supporting infrastructure was developed. Under Mugabe's socialist policies the settlers can't own the title to their new plots, and thus are unable to borrow money to improve the land. The typical experience of farmers on communally held lands is one of overcrowding, marginalized production, and environmental and socioeconomic degradation. Bureaucratic incompetence has also been blamed for the failure of land reform initiatives. The Land Acquisition Act of 1992 clearly spells out the procedures necessary for the compulsory taking of land; however, the bureaucracy has ignored these stipulations and many of the acquisitions have been thrown out in court.

While very few Zimbabweans have benefited from the land reform initiatives, there are exceptions. The members of the ruling ZANU-PF party have received a disproportionate number of the new farm plots. In 1990 a new program was introduced to use land reform as a vehicle for getting blacks into large-scale commercial agriculture. Four hundred thousand hectares of the resettlement land were diverted to four hundred people connected to the ruling party, including cabinet ministers, judges, and army commanders. Without much farming experience among the privileged recipients, the lands remain underutilized at the end of the century. Another exception is the war veterans who fought the white Rhodesians from 1966 to 1980. These veterans have received substantial pensions and recently the right to squat (occupy land without being the legitimate owner) on white-owned commercial farms in return for their unwavering support of the ZANU-PF party and Robert Mugabe personally. The issues of land reform and the participation of war veterans in land seizures and occupations played a pivotal role in the June 2000 elections.

While the return of land to its "rightful" owners before colonial domination sounds attractive in theory, land reform in Zimbabwe has failed because of several practical concerns about the economics of the process. These consequences were unforeseen or ignored by the Mugabe government in the initial excitement over land reform. The fourteen hundred white-owned farms that have been targeted for redistribution owe commercial banks more than $2.6 billion in collateral debt. This debt would have to be paid if the land was seized, and the debt would presumably have to be paid by the government that has taken over the farms. The resettlement programs have distinct disadvantages to the whites that lose their land beyond the denial of their personal property rights. Once a farm is designated for purchase, the farmer

looses all rights to it. The title is gone, he can't sell it or borrow on it or grow anything on it, but the government can take its time paying for the land, if it pays for it at all.

The land issue highlights a larger practical issue of the security of any personal property. If the government can't guarantee property rights, investors in all sectors will flee, as they did in 1997 when the government listed fifteen hundred farms for redistribution. The economy hasn't even been able to begin recovering from this loss of international investment confidence. Additionally, land reform is not always profitable for the country's economy. White farmers raise eighty percent of Zimbabwe's export crop. These farmers claim they are more efficient and provide more jobs to black workers than if the same land was redistributed in smaller plots proposed by reform schemes. The white-dominated Commercial Farm Union of Zimbabwe suggests that the proposed land reform would drop national farm production and exports by one-third. Such a decrease would further cripple an already beleaguered economy.

Zimbabwe's international credit has been deteriorating, undermining any chance for successful land reform in the early twenty-first century. The World Bank promised $5 million in new loans to help with a land reform plan known as the "Inception Phase Framework Plan." This plan will experiment with a variety of techniques to resettle thirty-four hundred farmers onto one million hectares of land. Unfortunately, in May 2000 Zimbabwe defaulted on $1.6 billion in other loans to the World Bank. The International Monetary Fund and the World Bank, the two largest multilateral lending agencies in the world, have frozen all future financial aid to Zimbabwe because of the poor performance of the Zimbabwean economy, their poor track record on debt servicing, and their continued participation in the civil war in the Democratic Republic of the Congo. On April 6, 2000 the United States also suspended assistance to any land reform plans due to the illegal land seizures and lawless behavior in Zimbabwe.

If the multiple man-made factors weren't enough to doom the hopes of successful land reform in Zimbabwe, nature has also contributed to the dismal results. Recurrent droughts in 1984 and 1992 forced Zimbabwe to rely on imports of food and agricultural supplies at the very time that exports had been destroyed due to lost crops. Zimbabwe is particularly vulnerable to such natural disruptions because of its heavy reliance on agriculture for any earnings. In 1999 Cyclone Eline dis-

FARMER ANDREAO MALUS FOUND A GROUP OF UNEMPLOYED MEN AND BOYS ON HIS FARM, PART OF AN INVASION OF WHITE-OWNED FARMS BY THE UNEMPLOYED IN ZIMBABWE. *(AP/Wide World Photos. Reproduced by permission.)*

placed 250,000 people and destroyed much of Zimbabwe's crop. Relief efforts were slowed because all of the country's helicopters were one thousand miles away, fighting in a civil war in the Democratic Republic of Congo. The land given to the black Africans during colonialism and the Rhodesian rule was more drought prone than the fertile white-owned lands.

Election Politics and Land Reform

Although land reform dominates political discussions and rallies in Zimbabwe, there is little money or will to pay the price for successful land reform. There are simply too many conflicting priorities for the Mugabe government despite the heavy reliance on the issue every election cycle. The February 2000 referendum and the June 2000 parliamentary elections are instructive in how the issue of land reform is manipulated in the political process.

Concerned with decreasing popularity in the polls for the ZANU-PF ruling party, President Mugabe called for a referendum vote to substantially change the constitution. The referendum encompassed a number of issues beyond land reform, including an increase in the powers of the president; however, the land issue has always proved to

be popular politics. Mugabe focused on Clause 57 of the referendum that granted the government the power to seize targeted white-owned commercial farms needed for resettlement. There would be no compensation for the land, only for improvements such as buildings and irrigation. The growing opposition movement organized under the coalition political party, known as the Movement for Democratic Change (MDC). The MDC lobbied heavily against the referendum. The white-dominated Commercial Farmer's Union (CFU) also opposed the referendum. The commercial farmers argued that many of the targeted farms had been purchased after the 1980 independence at fair market prices: they should not be held responsible for the sins of the past. They also argued that they were more efficient at production, and that Mugabe was manipulating the seizures as a smokescreen for popular discontent over the state of the economy, high unemployment, and costly troop deployment in the Democratic Republic of the Congo. The referendum was rejected by fifty-five percent of the voters.

Mugabe and his government seemed determined not to take "no" for an answer. The ZANU-PF controlled all but three seats of the 150-seat parliament. This was clearly enough to pass constitutional amendments by the needed two-thirds

MEMBERS OF THE ZIMBABWE NATIONAL LIBERATION WAR VETERANS ASSOCIATION SING REVOLUTIONARY SONGS AFTER INVADING ONE OF MORE THAN 420 WHITE-OWNED FARMS. *(AP/Wide World Photos. Reproduced by permission.)*

majority. In April 2000 the Zimbabwe parliament passed the "Land Acquisition Bill," which allows the government to seize commercial farms without compensation. Mugabe promised the seizure of four thousand white farms covering forty-six thousand square miles. Mugabe and the ZANU-PF leadership saw a greater threat in the defeated referendum than the loss of land reform. They saw an organized opposition that stood in their way for the first time in the history of the independent Zimbabwe. This was of great concern because parliamentary elections were scheduled for April 2000. What followed the defeat of the referendum can only be described as orchestrated chaos. The

parliamentary elections were postponed until the end of June as a wave of terror descended upon Zimbabwe.

President Mugabe, fearing a powerful opposition, turned once again to the popular issue of land resettlement. He supported a growing number of independence war veterans and others in their occupation of white commercial farms. They moved onto the land and intimidated both workers and owners alike to support the ZANU-PF party in the upcoming elections and to surrender control of their land. At the height of the occupations, nearly fifty thousand war veterans and their supporters, including unemployed urban youth, had occupied thirteen hundred farms. Mugabe fanned the flames of unrest by refusing to carry out a High Court order to remove the squatters from the farms. Instead he declared, "I will say to the white farmers, today is your day too. We have also liberated you from thinking that this country is yours alone. You now know that the country belongs to its rightful owners." Mugabe also gave $600,000 to the leader of the war veterans, Chenjerai Hunzvi (whose nickname, "Hitler," he received proudly during the independence war), to help ensure ZANU-PF's victory in the upcoming elections. The veterans' tactics were often quite violent. The targets of this violence were not only white commercial farmers, but also all political opposition, especially the MDC. Members of the opposition were routinely raped, beaten, and sometimes murdered. Many went into hiding in fear for their lives. Since the referendum, four white farmers and nineteen black members of the MDC opposition have been killed, while hundreds more have been injured. Journalists were detained and tortured regularly. The political districts were redrawn to favor the ruling ZANU-PF in a process known as gerrymandering. These new district maps were withheld from the opposition. The war veterans promised to return to civil war if ZANU-PF was defeated in the June parliamentary elections.

There is some evidence that Mugabe not only turned a blind eye to the terror created by the war veterans but he may have actually helped them. The *Financial Gazette,* an independent Zimbabwe newspaper, reported that unemployed youth were receiving between $1.30 and $5.25 each day to join the war veterans in the occupation of white-owned commercial farms. Mugabe also turned over to the veterans a shipment of AK-47 assault rifles that arrived from Russia on April 28. Some farmers cut a deal with the veterans allowing them to stay and promising not to support the opposition MDC in exchange for an end to the violence and destruction. The occupations have wreaked havoc on the agricultural exports of Zimbabwe, further harming the economy. When the High Court tried Hunzvi on contempt of court charges for refusing to end the occupations, the court was mobbed by ZANU-PF and war veteran supporters who became so unruly that the court had to be temporarily shut down. In the four months between the referendum and the June parliamentary elections, the rule of law was a shambles in Zimbabwe. The veterans promised to end the occupations if Parliament passed a law allowing the uncompensated seizure of the farms. Parliament passed such a law in April, but the veterans refused to leave the farms. This has led the

opposition to suggest that land is not the issue at all. They argue that this entire ordeal was a campaign of political intimidation to undermine the opposition in the June elections and to help the ZANU-PF party to cling to power. The MDC opposition also supports land reform schemes, but calls on these reforms to be compensated and transparent (the documents and process must be done publicly). Foreign governments such as Britain and the United States have also called for such a process.

Parliamentary Election Results

Despite months of intimidation, district manipulation, reports of election fraud, and some MDC candidates having to campaign in hiding, the MDC did exceptionally well in the June elections. Of the 120 seats up for election, the MDC and other opposition parties won fifty-seven of seats, just five less than the ruling ZANU-PF party. President Mugabe is allowed to select twenty additional members of parliament and tribal chiefs appoint the remaining ten. Although ZANU-PF will be able to continue a ruling majority with the help of Mugabe's appointments, they will not have the two-thirds majority needed to change the constitution at will. They will need to cooperate with the opposition to pass important legislation such as the budget. Most of the MDC's success was in the urban areas, while ZANU-PF did well in the rural areas where an appeal to redistribution of farm land is likely to play better among the millions still living on reserves.

What is perhaps more critical for the future of politics and land reform in Zimbabwe are a few of the significant winners and losers in the June elections. "Hitler" Hunzvi, leader of the war veterans, was elected as a ZANU-PF party member. After the elections Hunzvi sounded uncharacteristically conciliatory, calling for an end to the violence. The occupations of farmland continued, however. Morgan Tsuangirai, leader of the MDC opposition, lost in a rural district, but he has already declared his intention to run against Mugabe for the presidency in 2002. Roy Bennett, a white commercial farmer whose land was occupied, won as a member of the MDC. Perhaps the most important outcome of the elections was that seven members of Mugabe's ruling cabinet were defeated, signaling popular discontent with the ruling regime. Perhaps the most prominent of the cabinet ministers to be defeated was Emmerson Munagagwa, the Justice Minister and Mugabe's expected successor. Munagagwa was defeated by a two-to-one margin in a rural district by an MDC opponent who had been in hiding for the previous three months in fear for his life. Mugabe accepted the results, calling for national unity and reconciliation. After the election, the chairman of ZANU-PF, John Nkomo, said that the government would press ahead with uncompensated land seizures according to the April Land Acquisition Bill. It may be some time before the impact of these elections is felt in the area of Zimbabwe land reform.

The MDC has said they are willing to work with the Mugabe government but they will not take any cabinet posts and they wish to offer a constructive opposition. The MDC still intends to challenge a few close votes where there are questions about the authenticity of the election results. Because of their strong support in the urban areas, their agenda will be driven more by unemployment than land reform. The government has said that it intends to push ahead with land seizures and redistribution. The CFU reports that several more farms have been occupied since the elections, seeming to indicate that the disputes remain largely unresolved by the democratic process.

Prospects for the Future

If land reform is to be meaningfully and successfully instituted, Mugabe and the ruling ZANU-PF are going to have to live up to their calls for reconciliation and an end to intimidation and violence. If they do not, the MDC opposition is likely to gain even more ground in the 2002 presidential elections. This might come at the cost of renewed civil war initiated by the war veterans. The rule of law and the courts are almost completely ignored in Zimbabwe. It is critical that some semblance of law and order are restored to Zimbabwe. Without this, foreign investors are unlikely to make any more loans to or investments in the country, though it is desperately in need of foreign help. During the 1990s, out-of-control inflation, spending, and unemployment have destroyed the economy. If the squatter occupations are allowed to continue, then commercial agriculture in Zimbabwe, its leading export earner, will be devastated. This suggests that there would be little in the way of money flowing into the economy from any direction.

With a growing population living in poverty, Zimbabwe is poised for significant unrest unless things change dramatically. Mugabe is a shrewd politician and is unlikely to wish to alienate himself further from the voters prior to his own election in 2002 and may try to reconcile with the MDC members of Parliament and encourage the war veterans to end their occupations of farmland without driving them back into the bush for a civil war. Mugabe's empire has been built on patron-client relationships in which numerous favors are exchanged, bonding individuals to the government. As long as he is still in charge of land reform schemes, one could expect to see favoritism for the recipients of "returned" land. Mugabe is also not likely to pay any compensation for land acquisition for three reasons: his government can't afford to pay anything; the constitution no longer required him to after April 2000; and he believes the British should pay because they were in charge when the problem occurred and they did not compensate black Africans when their land was taken.

For land reform to succeed, it is essential that the government be concerned about more than the mere purchase (or seizure) of land to be resettled. Without training, the new occupants will be helpless to feed themselves or anyone else. Resources need to be allocated for infrastructure, roads, irrigation, schools, and clinics. The current government is unwilling or unable to do that. Without such investment, land reform plans appear doomed to failure. Foreign nations, particularly Britain, the United States, and South Africa, have agreed to help provide funding for some of the land reform if it is a transparent process. The IMF and World Bank are ready to start funds flowing again if Zimbabwe's economy should show any sign of recovery and if Zimbabwe pulls out of the civil war in the Democratic Republic of Congo. South Africa is going through a similar transition from white racist rule to black majority rule. They also face issues of very unevenly distributed land segmented along racial lines. The South African solution is a land reform bill that grants tenant farmers rights to settle themselves permanently on white farm property. If Mugabe does not find a way to stop the downward spiral of the economy and, at the same time, distribute land to the poor, Zimbabwe stands to reverse all the gains it has made since independence. If it does not reverse its direction, the stability of the entire southern Africa subcontinent is in jeopardy.

Land reform is not an issue isolated to Zimbabwe. The colonial treatment of native people in Zimbabwe—which includes taking land, cattle, and minerals—and the United States treatment of the Native American tribes are somewhat similar. The issue of land reform not only encompasses Zimbabwe and the Native Americans in the United States; it also includes the Zapatista movement in Chiapas Mexico, the Indians of Ecuador and Peru, the rubber tappers in the Brazilian rain forest, and the Maori of New Zealand. The specific circumstances may differ, but the consequences of an unequal distribution of land in the developing world are very similar. Poverty, hunger, exploitation of laborers, and the destruction of culture are all potential consequences of a lack of commitment to meaningful land reform.

BIBLIOGRAPHY

"The Black and White Divide in Southern Africa: Race Relations After Colonialism," *World Press Review* 47 (2000): 17–21.

Gordon, April, and Donald L. Gordon. *Understanding Contemporary Africa.* 2d ed. Boulder, Colo.: Lynne Rienner Publishers, 1996.

Loney, Martin. *Rhodesia: White Racism and Imperial Response.* Harmondsworth, England: Penguin, 1975.

Martin, David, and Phyllis Johnson. *The Struggle for Zimbabwe: The Chimurenga War.* Boston, Mass.: Faber and Faber, 1981.

Meldrum, Andrew. "The Land Scandal," *Africa Report* 40 (1995): 28–31.

O'Flaherty, Michael. "Communal Tenure in Zimbabwe: Divergent Models of Collective Land Holding in the Communal Areas," *Africa* 68 (1998): 537–55.

Owen, Ken. "Bloody Mugabe," *New Republic* 220 (1999): 21–23.

"Peasants' Revolt: Zimbabwe," *Economist,* 27 June 1998.

Ranshod-Nilsson, Sita. "Zimbabwe: Women, Cultural Crisis, and the Reconfiguration of the One-Party State." In *The African State at a Critical Juncture: Between Disintegration and Reconfiguration.* Boulder, Colo.: Lynne Rienner Publishers, 1998.

Skalnes, Tor. "The State, Interest Groups and Structural Adjustment in Zimbabwe," *Journal of Development Studies* 29 (1993): 401–29.

"Your Land Will be My Land," *Economist,* 15 February 1992.

T. Timothy Casey

CONTRIBUTORS

John H. Barnhill has a Ph.D. in American history from Oklahoma State University, Stillwater. His primary field is the twentieth century American South. His dissertation topic was Brooks Hays, congressman from Arkansas and president of the Southern Baptist Convention. He currently works for the Department of Defense in Oklahoma as a writer and analyst, as well as reviewing books and writing encyclopedia articles.

ENTRIES: U.S. Immigration: Sanctuary and Controversy

Michael P. Bobic earned his B.A. in Political Science from Berea College (1985) in Kentucky. He earned his M.A. in 1992 and Ph.D. in 1996 in Political Science from the University of Tennessee, specializing in national institutions and research methods. Dr. Bobic is currently employed at Emmanuel College in Franklin Springs, Georgia, as an Assistant Professor of Political Science and as the Director of Institutional Research. He and his wife live in upstate South Carolina.

ENTRIES: The Iranian Revolution: Islamic Fundamentalism Confronts Modern Secularism; Peru's Shining Path: Revolution's End

Dallas L. Browne is Chairman of the Department of Anthropology at Southern Illinois University-Edwardsville. He is also president of the St. Louis Council on Foreign Relations and Chairman of the CFR Board of Directors. He is under consideration to become Honorary Counsel for the Republic of Tanzania. He is completing a book-length biography of Allison Davis, the first African American ever awarded tenure on any faculty in the United States.

ENTRIES: Mexican-U.S. Border Relations: Opportunities and Obstacles; Mozambique: Independence and a Dirty War

T. Timothy Casey is an Assistant Professor of Political Science at Mesa State College in Grand Junction, Colorado. His teaching and research interests include international relations and political theory.

ENTRIES: Zimbabwe's Land Reform: Race and History

Anthony Q. Cheeseboro is an Assistant Professor at Southern Illinois University-Edwardsville. He has published in *Northeast African Studies* and the *Journal of the Illinois State Historical Society*, as well as the *Historical Encyclopedia of World Slavery*. He received his B.A. from the University of Georgia, his M.A. from the University of South Carolina, and his Ph.D. from Michigan State University.

ENTRIES: Algeria's Post-Colonial War

Jeffrey S. Cole is an Assistant Professor of History at King College in Bristol, Tennessee. He earned his Ph.D. from Bowling Green State University (Ohio) with emphases in American, Asian, Latin American, and Policy History.

ENTRIES: The Colombian U'wa Indians: Sacred Land and Oil

Guillaume de Syon teaches European history and the history of technology at Albright College in Reading, Pennsylvania. He is the author of *Zeppelin! Germany and the Airship Experience* from Johns Hopkins University Press.

ENTRIES: The Basques: The ETA and Separatism

Paul du Quenoy is a doctoral candidate in History at Georgetown University.

ENTRIES: European Union Conflict: The British Beef Controversy; United Nations Peacekeeping Forces: Peace and Conflict

James Frusetta is a doctoral candidate in modern European history at the University of Maryland-College Park, focusing on Southeastern Europe in the early twentieth century. He has been an NSEP Graduate Fellow holder in both the Republic of Macedonia and in Bulgaria, and is currently working on the dissertation, "Bulgaria in Macedonia: Intersection between Bulgarian and Macedonian National Identity."

ENTRIES: Kosovo: Ethnic Tensions and Nationalism

Richard C. Hanes earned a B.S. in Aerospace Engineering from Texas A&M University and a Ph.D. in Anthropology from the University of Oregon. He has worked in the field of historic preservation for more than twenty-five years in the American West and associated contemporary socio-economic issues, such as American Indian exercise of treaty rights, traditional economies, and interactions with dominant society social structures. He has been adjunct professor at the University of Nevada-Reno and University of Oregon. He has published work on applied anthropology and prehistory of the American West in addition to contributions to Gale Group volumes on constitutional law, multiculturalism, civil rights, and U.S. economic history.

ENTRIES: Cyprus: An Island Divided; Native Americans: Centuries of Struggle in North America

Charles Hauss teaches political science at George Mason University in Fairfax, Virginia, and is Political Science Guide at About—The Human Internet.

ENTRIES: Jerusalem: Divided City

David L. Kenley (Ph.D., University of Hawaii) specializes in modern Chinese history, and is particularly interested in overseas Chinese communities and Chinese intellectual history. His publications include such articles as "The May Fourth Movement in Singapore: Studying May Fourth from a Diaspora Perspective" and "Publishing the New Culture: Singapore's Newspapers and Diaspora Literature, 1919–1933." Dr. Kenley is currently an Assistant Professor of History at Marshall University where he teaches courses on modern Asia.

ENTRIES: China and Religious Protest: The Falun Gong

Keith A. Leitich received his bachelor's degree from Iowa State University and a master's and educational specialist degrees from Arkansas State University. He is a past recipient of a Korea Foundation Fellowship and is an author of published works focusing on Central Asian politics, Chinese history and Korean history and education. He has contributed articles to *Contemporary Education, Education* and *International Education Forum* as well as entries to the *Encyclopedia of Asia, Encyclopedia USA, Encyclopedia of World War II Pacific War, Magill's Guide to Military History, ABC-Clio's World Military Leaders* and the *World Social Leaders* series.

ENTRIES: The Korean Peninsula: A Fifty-Year Struggle for Peace and Reconciliation

Alynna Lyon is an Assistant Professor of Political Science at Southeast Missouri State University. She received a Ph.D. in Political Science from the University of South Carolina (1999) and her research focuses on the relationship between ethnic conflict and international politics. Her recent publications include "Separatism in Chechnya: The Role of the *Jihad*," in Rolin G. Mainuddin's (ed.), *Religion and Politics: An Examination of the Explosive Interactions.* In 1999, she was awarded the Ethnicity, Nationalism and Migration Section of the International Studies Association Graduate Student Paper Competition winner for her work entitled: "Rethinking Intervention in Ethnic Conflict: Blueprint for Assistance or Aggravation?" Dr. Lyon's other teaching and research interests

include the United Nations, conflict resolution, Third World politics, and human rights.

ENTRIES: East Timor: The Path of Democracy for the World's Newest Nation

Antoinette M. Mannion is Senior Lecturer in the Department of Geography, University of Reading, in the United Kingdom. She received her B.S. Honors in Geography from the University of Liverpool in 1972 and a Ph.D. in Geography from the University of Bristol in 1975 where her research focused on environmental change during the last twelve thousand years. She is the author of *Global Environmental Change*, (Longman, 1st ed., 1991; 2d ed., 1997), *Agriculture and Environmental Change* (Wiley, 1995) and *Natural Environmental Change* (Routledge, 1999). She also authored numerous journal papers and was editor of Routledge's *Introduction to Environment Series.*

ENTRIES: Romania's Cyanide Spill

Eric A. McGuckin is Assistant Professor of Anthropology and Global Studies at the Hutchins School of Liberal Studies at Sonoma State University. In addition to travels in Nepal and Tibet, Dr. McGuckin conducted ethnographic research on Tibetan refugees in Dharamsala, India, 1992–94. His published work includes articles on Tibetan craft production, tourism, and interethnic relationships.

ENTRIES: Tibet: Struggle for Independence

Eugene O'Brien teaches Irish Studies at the University of Limerick in the Republic of Ireland. His research interests include critical and cultural theory, deconstruction and the writings of Yeats, Joyce and Heaney. He is the author of two books, *The Question of Irish Identity in the Writings of William Butler Yeats and James Joyce* and *The Epistemology of Nationalism.* He has published some twenty articles on literary and cultural theory and Irish literature, and is the commissioning editor of the Edwin Mellen Press's Irish Studies Series *Ireland in Theory.*

ENTRIES: Northern Ireland: The Omagh Bomb, Nationalism, and Religion

Carlos Pérez received a Ph.D. in History from the University of California, Los Angeles, in 1998, for his dissertation "Quinine and Caudillos: Manuel Isidoro Belzu and the Cinchona Bark Trade in Bolivia, 1848–1855." He is currently an Assistant Professor in the Department of Chicano and Latin American Studies at California State University, Fresno. He has published numerous articles, including "Caudillos, comerciantes y el Estado-Nacional en la Bolivia decimonovena" and "The Export Roots of Bolivian Caudillo Politics: The Cinchona Bark Boom and Belzu's Jacquerie." He also contributed to the following books: *Encyclopedia of Historians and Historical Writing, A Global Encyclopedia of Historical Writing, Historical Dictionary of the Spanish Empire*, and *Historical Dictionary of European Imperialism.* He received a Fulbright Fellowship, 1988–89, to conduct research at the Archivo y Biblioteca Nacionales de Bolivia, Sucre, Bolivia, the Archives of La Paz, and other Bolivian archives.

ENTRIES: Guatemala: Indian Testimony to a Genocidal War

Jonathan T. Reynolds (Ph.D., Boston University, 1995) is an Assistant Professor of African History at Northern Kentucky University. He previously taught at Livingstone College (North Carolina), where he was the recipient of the 1997–1998 Teacher of the Year Award. He was a Fulbright Scholar at Bayero University, Kano, Nigeria from 1992–1993. He was awarded a West African Research Association Fellowship in the spring of 2000. He is the author of *The Time of Politics (Zamanin Siyasa): Islam and the Politics of Legitimacy in Northern Nigeria, 1950–1966* (University Press for West Africa, 1999) and several works on African History in texts and Journals. With Dr. Erik Gilbert of Arkansas State University, he is the co-author of the forthcoming text, *Africa in World History*.

ENTRIES: Nigeria and *Shari'a*: Religion and Politics in a West African Nation

Christopher Saunders is a Professor of History at the University of Cape Town in South Africa. Born in England, he has lived in South Africa almost all his life. Educated at the University of Cape Town and Oxford University, where he obtained his doctorate, he has published widely on topics in South African and Namibian history. The book he is most proud of is *The Making of the South African Past* (Barnes and Noble, New York, 1988).

ENTRIES: South Africa's Truth and Reconciliation Committee

Ximena Sosa-Buchholz was born and raised in Quito, Ecuador. She earned her undergraduate degree in history from the Catholic University of Ecuador and where she taught history. She was the recipient of the CEHILA scholarship to study church history in Brazil. She was then awarded a Fulbright-LASPAU scholarship to study history at the University of New Mexico in Albuquerque. There she earned her M.A. and Ph.D. in Latin American History. She returned to Ecuador and the Catholic University to teach in the history department. She is the author of numerous articles in both English and Spanish, the latest being the chapter, "The Strange Career of Populism in Ecuador," in Michael Conniff's volume, *Populism in Latin America*. Currently she teaches at the University of Kansas.

ENTRIES: The Ecuadorian Indigenous People's Movement: Autonomy and the Environment

George Thadithil is an Associate Professor of History and Political Science at Paul Quinn College in Dallas. Prior to joining Paul Quinn he had taught at Mountain View College (Dallas, Texas) and St. Thomas College, Kerala, India. He lives in Mesquite, Texas, with his wife and three children. His areas of interest include Asian Collective security, international organizations, South Asia, and minority studies.

ENTRIES: Myanmar: The Agony of a People

Michael Tkacik earned his Ph.D. in Political Science from the University of Maryland. His M.A. in Political Science is from Columbia University. He also holds a J.D. from Duke University School of Law. His publications include: *Nuclear Deterrence, Arms Control, and Multipolarity: An Argument for Incremental Policy, Change Armed Forces and Society, World Trade Organization Dispute Settlement: Substance, Strengths, Weaknesses, and Causes for Concern, International Legal Perspectives, Islam and Democracy: Toward Creating a User-Friendly Environment,* and *An Evolutionary Approach Toward Drafting Autonomy Agreements: Applying Theory to Reality in the Search for the Resolution of Ethnic Conflict.* Tkacik is currently an Assistant Professor of Political Science at Stephen F. Austin State University in Texas. His research and teaching interests include international relations, international security, international law, and ethnic conflict resolution.

ENTRIES: China and the World Trade Organization: Values in Conflict

Emily Turner-Graham, B.A., Graduate Diploma of Arts (History), M.A. (History), M.A. (Public History), is an Australian historian who specializes in the historical study of fascism. Her M.A. thesis was entitled "True Comrades in Struggle? Women of the Far Right: A Study of Leaders in Fascism and Sympathetic Movements in Inter-War Britain." She is presently researching German National Socialist attitudes towards the natural environment.

ENTRIES: Austria's Shunning by the Global Community

Thomas Turner earned a Ph. D. in Political Science and a Certificate in African Studies from the University of Wisconsin-Madison. He has taught in universities of the Congo (formerly Zaire), Kenya, and Tunisia. He is the author of *Ethnogenèse et nationalisme en Afrique centrale: aux racines de Patrice Lumumba* (*Ethnogenesis and Nationalism in Central Africa: The Roots of Patrice Lumumba*) and co-author of *Rise and Decline of the Zairian State*.

ENTRIES: Angola: Civil War and Diamonds; Sri Lanka: Civil War and Ethno-Linguistic Conflict

GENERAL BIBLIOGRAPHY

This bibliography contains a list of sources, primarily books and articles, that will assist the reader in pursuing additional information on the topics contained in this volume.

A

Amstutz, Mark R. *International Conflict and Cooperation: An Introduction to World Politics.* New York: McGraw-Hill Companies, 1998.

Arrighi, G. *The Long Twentieth Century.* New York and London: Verso, 1994.

Atlas of World History. New York and London: Oxford University Press, 1999.

Avruch, Kevin. *Culture and Conflict Resolution.* Washington, D.C.: U.S. Institute of Peach Press, 1998.

B

Bairoch, Paul. *The Economic Development of the Third World since 1900.* Berkeley, Calif.: University of California Press, 1975.

Bartlett, C. J. J. *The Global Conflict: The International Rivalry of the Great Powers.* New York: Addison-Wesley Longman, 1994.

Bercovitch, Jacob and Richard Jackson. *International Conflict: A Chronological Encyclopedia of Conflict Management, 1945–1995.* Washington D.C.: Congressional Quarterly, 1997.

Best, Geoffrey. "Where Rights Collide with Duties," *Times Literary Supplement* (22 September 1995): 11–12.

Bothe, Michael and Horst Fischer, et al. *The Handbook of Humanitarian Law in Armed Conflict.* New York and London: Oxford University Press, 1999.

Brown, Michael E. *Ethnic Conflict and International Security.* Princeton, N.J.: Princeton University Press, 1993

———. *The International Dimensions of Internal Conflict.* Cambridge, Mass.: MIT Press, 1995.

C

Clark, Robert P. *The Global Imperative.* Boulder, Colo.: Westview Press, 1997.

Costello, Paul. *World Historians and Their Goals: Twentieth-Century Answers to Modernism.* De Kalb, Ill.: Northern Illinois University Press, 1994.

D

Deudney, Daniel H. and Richard A. Matthew, eds. *Contested Grounds: Security and Conflict in the New Environmental Politics.* Albany, N.Y.: State University of New York Press, 1999.

Diamond, Jared. *Guns, Germs and Steel.* New York: W.W. Norton & Co., 1997.

Diehl, Paul and Nils Gleditsch. *Environmental Conflict.* Boulder, Colo.: Westview Press, 2000.

E

Encyclopedia of World History. New York and London: Oxford University Press, 1999.

F

Fukuyama, Francis. "Rest Easy. It's Not 1914 Anymore," *New York Times,* 9 February 1992.

G

Gall, Susan B., ed. *Worldmark Chronology of the Nations.* Farmington Hills, Mich.: Gale Group, 2000.

Gall, Timothy L., ed. *Worldmark Encyclopedia of Cultures and Daily Life.* Farmington Hills, Mich.: Gale Group, 1997.

Ganguly, Rajat and Raymond C. Taras. *Understanding Ethnic Conflict: The International Dimension.* New York: Longman, 1998.

Goldstone, Jack A., Ted Robert Gurr and Farrakh Mashiri. *Revolutions of the Late Twentieth Century.* Boulder, Colo.: Westview Press, 1991.

Gottlieb, Gidon. *National Against State: A New Approach to Ethnic conflicts and Sovereignty.* Washington, D.C.: Council on Foreign Relations, 1994.

H

Haass, Richard N. *Conflicts Unending: the United States and Regional Disputes.* New Haven, Conn.: Yale University Press, 1990.

Hobsbawm, Eric. *Nations and Nationalism Since 1780: Programme, Myth, Reality.* Cambridge, England: Cambridge University Press, 1993.

Hodgson, Marshall G. S. "World History and a World Outlook." In *Rethinking World History: Essays on Europe, Islam and World History.* New York: Cambridge University Press, 1993.

Hoffman, Stanley. *World Disorders:Troubled Peace in the Post Cold War Era.* Lanham, Md.: Rowman & Littlefield, Publishers, 2000.

Homer-Dixon, Thomas F. *Environment, Scarcity, and Violence.* Princeton, N.J.: Princeton University Press, 1999.

J

Jones, E. L. *Growth Recurring: Economic Change in World History.* New York and London: Oxford University Press, 1993.

K

Kakar, Sudhir. *The Colors of Violence: Cultural Identities, Religon, and Conflict.* Chicago, Ill.: University of Chicago Press, 1996.

Kanet, Roger E. *Resolving Regional Conflicts.* Urbana, Ill.: University of Illinois Press, 1998.

Katz, Richard S. *Democracy and Elections.* New York and London: Oxford University Press, 1998.

Keegan, J. *A History of Warfare.* New York: Vintage Books, 1994.

King, Anthony, ed. *Culture, Globalization and the World-System: Contemporary Conditions for the Representation of Identity.* Minneapolis, Minn.: University of Minnesota Press, 1997.

Khalilzad, Zalmay and Ian O. Lesser, eds. *Sources of Conflict in the 21st Century.* Santa Monica, Calif.: Rand, 1998.

Kohn, Hans. "Nationalism," *International Encyclopedia of the Social Sciences* 11: 63–39.

L

Lambert, Richard D., Alan W. Heston, and William Zartman. *Resolving Regional Conflicts: International Perspectives.* London: Sage Publications, 1991.

Landes, David S. *The Wealth and Poverty of Nations: Why Some are So Rich and Some are So Poor.* New York: W.W. Norton, 1999.

M

Mazlish, Bruce and Ralph Buultjens, eds. *Conceptualizing Global History.* Boulder, Colo.: Westview Press, 1993.

McNeill, W. H. *Plagues and Peoples.* New York: Anchor Books/Doubleday & Co, Inc., 1998.

Meadows, et al. *Beyond the Limits: Confronting Global Collapse, Envisioning a Sustainable Future.* Mitts, Vt.: Chelsea Green Publishing, 1992.

Miall, Hugh and Tom Woodhouse, et al. *Contemporary Conflict Resolution: The Prevention, Management and Transformations of Deadly Conflict.* Malder, Mass.: Blackwell Publishers, 1999.

Mitchell, C. R. *The Structure of International Conflict.* New York: St. Martin's Press, 1990.

N

Nash, Gary B., Charlotte Crabtree, and Ross E. Dunn. "In the Matter of History." In *History on Trial: Culture Wars and the Teaching of the Past.* New York: Alfred A. Knopf, 1998.

Nye, Joseph S. *Understanding International Conflict: An Introduction to Theory and History.* New York: Addison-Welsey Longman, 1999.

P

Prendergast, John. *Frontline Diplomacy: Humanitarian Aid and Conflict in Africa.* Boulder, Colo.: Lynne Rienner Publishers, 1996.

R

Ramsbotham, Oliver and Tom Woodhouse. *Humanitarian Intervention in Contemporary Conflict: A Reconceptualization.* Oxford, England: Blackwell Publishers, 1996.

Ratcliffe, Peter. *Race, Ethnicity, and Nation: Ethnicity and Nation International Perspectives on Social Conflict.* London: UCL Press, 1994.

Ray, James Lee and Charles W. Kegley, et al., eds. *Democracy and International Conflict: An Evaluation of the Democratic Peace Proposition.* Columbia, S.C.: University of South Carolina Press, 1995.

Rayner, Caroline, ed. *Encyclopedic World Atlas: Country-by-Country Coverage.* New York and London: Oxford University Press, 1994.

Rieff, David. "A Just War is Still a War," *Newsweek,* 14 June 1999.

Rochards, Andrew. "Meaning of 'Genocide'," *Times Literary Supplement,* 15 May 1998.

Rothchild, Donald and Dave A. Lake, eds. *The International Spread of Ethnic Conflict: Fear, Diffusion, and Escalation.* Princeton, N.J.: Princeton University Press, 1998.

S

Sachs, Wolfgang. *Global Ecology: A New Arena of Political Conflict*. London: St. Martin's Press, 1993.

Schlesinger, Arthur Meier. *The Disuniting of America: Reflections on a Multicultural Society*. New York: W.W. Norton, 1998.

Schnaiberg, Allan and Kenneth Alan Gould. *Environment and Society: The Enduring Conflict*. New York: St. Martin's Press, 2000.

Shawcross, William. *Deliver Us from Evil: Peacekeepers, Warlords and a World of Endless Conflict*. New York: Simon and Schuster, 2000.

Shrire, C. *Past and Present in Hunter-Gatherer Societies*. London: Academic Press, 1985.

Simmons, I. G. *Changing the Face of the Earth: Culture, Environment, History*. 2d ed. New York and London: Oxford University Press, 1993.

Smith, David A. and Steven Topik, eds. *States and Sovereignty in the Global Economy*. New York: Routledge, 1999.

Snooks, Graeme Donald. *The Dynamic Society: Exploring the Sources of Global Change*. New York: Routledge, 1996.

Stearns, Peter N. "Nationalisms: An Invitation to Contemporary Analysis," *Journal of World History* (Spring 1997): 57–74.

Strayer, Robert. *Why Did the Soviet Union Collapse? Understanding Historical Change*. San Diego, Calif.: Greenhaven Press, 1994.

Sulimann, Mohamed. *Ecology, Politics and Violent Conflict*. New York: St. Martin's Press, 1998.

V

Van Evera, Stephen. *Causes of War: Power and the Roots of Conflict*. Ithaca, N.Y.: Cornell University Press, 1999.

W

Walter, Barbara F. *Civil Wars, Insecurity, and Intervention*. New York: Columbia University Press, 1999.

Waterfield, Larry W. *Conflict and Crisis in Rural America*. New York: Praeger, 1986.

Weart, Spencer R. *Never at War*. New Haven, Conn.: Yale University Press, 2000.

Wippman, David. *International Law and Ethnic Conflict*. Ithaca, N.Y.: Cornell University Press, 1998.

Worldmark Encyclopedia of Nations. Farmington Hills, Mich.: Gale Group, 1998.

Wolfe, Patrick. "Imperialism and History: A Century from Marx to Postcolonialism," *The American Historical Review* 102 (April 1997): 388–420.

Worsley, Peter. *The Three Worlds: Culture and World Development*. Chicago, Ill.: University of Chicago Press, 1989.

INDEX

Page numbers in boldface refer to a topic upon which an essay is based. Page numbers in italics refer to illustrations, figures, and tables. A number followed by a colon refers to the volume in which you will find the given page reference(s).

A

Abkhazian, 1:263
Accra Acceptance and Accession Agreement and Accra Clarification (1994), 1:180
Act of Union (1801, Great Britain), 2:226
Acteal Massacre (1997), 1:68, 69
Activism, 2:193, 210–211
Activists, 2:210–211
    Belo, Carlos Filipe Ximenes, 2:92–93
    Freitas, Terence, 2:69–70
    Gay, Lahe'ena'e, 2:69–70
    Mandela, Nelson, 2:257
    Menchú Tam, Rigoberta, *2:125*
    Peltier, Leonard, 2:207
    Suu Kyi, Aung San, 2:189, *2:194*
    Tutu, Desmond, 2:258
    Washinawatok, Ingrid, 2:69–70
Adams, Gerry, 2:232
Addis Ababa agreement (1972), 1:272
AFDL (Armed Forces for the Liberation of Congo-Zaire), 1:82
Afghanistan, **1:1–11**, *4*
    chronology, 1:2
    civil war, 1:4–5
    Communism, 1:3–4
    demography, 1:2
    drug trade, 1:9
    ethnic groups, 1:2
    maps, *1:7, 8, 9, 10*
    Muslims, 1:2–3
    westernization, 1:3
Afghan-Soviet conflict (1978-1989), 1:3–4
AFL (Armed Forces of Liberia), 1:179–180
African Association for the Defense of Human Rights in Congo-Kinshasa (ASADHO), 1:87
African National Congress (ANC), 2:253, 254–256, 258, 261
African slaves. *See* Slavery
"African World War," **1:78–88**
African-Americans, 1:174–176, *1:176*
Africanizing, 1:80
Agrarian reform. *See* Land reform
Agriculture

Amazon rainforest, 1:16–17, 20
    coca leaf, 1:71
    France, 2:120
    Great Britain, 2:112, 120
    Guatemala, 2:123–124
    Peru, 2:241
    sugar, 1:91, 92
Aguablanca, Gustavo Bocota, 2:71
Aguirre y Lecuba, José Antonio, 2:36
Ahmad, Muhammad, 1:269
AIM (American Indian Movement), 2:204
AIS (Islamic Salvation Army), 2:5–7
Ajuba II Peace Accord (1996), 1:180
Alaska, 1:202
Alaska Native Claims Settlement Act (1971), 2:206–207
Alaskan Natives, 2:206–208
Albanians
    Kosovo, 1:246–247, *1:247*, 2:157–166
    Macedonia, 2:166–168
    relations with Serbs, 1:26, 241–242
    See also Kosovo
Algeria
    chronology, 2:2
    civil war, 1991-present, **2:1–8**, *5, 6*
    colonization by France, 2:2–3
    geography/demography, 2:1–2
    map, *2:3*
Alien and Sedition Acts of 1798, 2:294
Alliance of Democratic Forces for Liberation of the Congo, 1:81
All-India Muslim League, 1:156–157
Alvor Agreement (1975), 2:12
Amazon rainforest, *1:17*
    carbon dioxide processing, 1:18
    deforestation, **1:12–23**, *18*
    development, 1:13–15, 16–17, 19–20
    indigenous people, 1:19
    preservation, 1:19–22
American Colony hotel (Jerusalem), 2:146
American Indian Movement (AIM), 2:204
American Party (U.S.), 2:295
American Popular Revolutionary Alliance (APRA, Peru), 2:238
Americo-Africans. *See* African-Americans

Amnesty
    Algeria, 2:7–8
    South Africa, 2:255–256, 260
Amnesty International, 1:142
Andrade, Venusemar, 1:39
Angola
    chronology, 2:10
    civil war, 1960-present, **2:9–24**
    colonization by Portugal, 2:11–12
    geography/demography, 2:9–11
    map, *2:13*
    relations with Congo, 1:84
    relations with Cuba, 1:99–100, 2:12–15, 16–21
Anschluss, 2:26–28
Anti-Catholicism, 2:294–295
Anti-communism, 1:206–207
Anti-Fascist People's Freedom League, 2:194
Anti-Semitism, 2:30–31
Apartheid, South Africa, 2:184, 253
APF (Azerbaijan Popular Front), 1:191
Arab-Israeli conflict, **1:112–123, 2:141–148**, 2:285
Arabs
    Algeria, 2:1–4
    relations with British, 1:113–114
    relations with Israel, 1:115, 116–117, 118, 279
    relations with United States, 1:120
    Sudan, 1:267–268
Arafat, Yasir, 1:116, 119
Arévalo, Juan José, 2:124–125
Argentina
    human rights violations, 1:211
    working class, 1:304–305
Arias Cárdenas, Francisco, 1:304, 309
Arizmendi, Felipe, 1:69
Armed Forces for the Liberation of Congo-Zaire
    (AFDL), 1:82
Armed Forces of Liberia (AFL), 1:179–180
Armed Islamic Group (GIA), 2:5
Armed Revolutionary Forces of Colombia (FARC), 2:66,
    69–71
Armenia
    genocide, World War I, 1:165
    independence, 1:192
    nationalism, 1:187–188
    relations with Nagorno-Karabakh, **1:184–195,**
        1:261–262
    relations with Russia, 1:185, 186–192
    relations with United States, 1:195
Arms dealing. *See* Weapons traffic
Aryan Nations Liberty Net, 1:301
ASADHO (African Association for the Defense of
    Human Rights in Congo-Kinshasa), 1:87
Asian financial crisis (1998), 1:15
Assassinations
    Aung San, U, 2:194
    Blanco, Carrero, 2:38
Assimilation
    Native Americans, 2:201–203
    United States, 2:299–300
Asylum laws, 1:127–128
Ataturk, 1:168, *1:169*
ATF (United States Bureau of Alcohol, Tobacco, and
    Firearms), 1:295
Aung San, U, 2:192, 193–194
Aurul mine incident (2000, Romania), **2:246–252**

Austria
    Anschluss, 2:26–28
    chronology, 2:26
    map, *2:28*
    right-wing politics, **2:25–33**
    World War II, 2:29
Austrian Nazis (World War II), 2:26–28
Austrian People's Party, 2:25, 29
Authoritarian government, 2:3–4
Automobiles, 1:200–201
Ayatollah Ali Hoseini-Khamenei, 2:133
Ayatollah Khomeini, 2:136–137
Azad Kashmir. *See* Kashmir
Azerbaijan
    nationalism, 1:187, 191
    relations with Nagorno-Karabakh, **1:184–195,**
        1:261–262
    relations with Russia, 1:185, 186–192
    relations with United States, 1:195
Azerbaijan Popular Front (APF), 1:191

B

Badme, Ethiopia, 1:107–108
Balfour Declaration (1917)
    Jews in Israel, 1:113
    Palestinian nationalism, 1:114
Balkan conflict, **1:24–38**
    See also Bosnia-Herzegovina
Banana exports, 2:123–124
Bandaranaike, Sirimavo, 2:265–266, 267
Bandaranaike, Solomon, 2:265, 267
Banyarwandans, 1:79, 82
Baqqara, 1:269, 273–274
Barak, Ehud, 1:114, 121, 282
"Basque Homeland and Freedom" (political party). *See*
    ETA (Euskadi Ta Askatasuna)
Basque Nationalist Party (PNV). *See* PNV
Basque region
    chronology, 2:35
    demography, 2:34–35
    militant separatist movement, **2:34–41**
Batista, Fulgencio, 1:94–96
"Battle in Seattle" (1999), **1:311–320,** *2:56*
Battle of Kosovo Polje (1389), 2:159–160
Battle of Krajina (1995), 1:33
Battle of the Bogside (1969), 2:229
Bay of Pigs Invasion (1961), 1:97–98
Beam, Louis, 1:301
Belaúde Terry, Fernando, 2:240, 242
Belgian Congo. *See* Congo
Belgium
    Congo colony, 1:79
    Rwanda colony, 1:228, 229
Bella, Ahmed Ben, 2:3, 4
Belo, Carlos Filipe Ximenes, 2:92–93, 94
Berbers, 2:1–2
Biafran movement, 2:215
"Big business," 1:198–199
"Big government," 1:296, 297
Biko, Steve, *2:256,* 2:260
bin Laden, Osama, 1:6–8
Bissel, George, 1:197–198
Black September (1970), 1:280

Blackfeet, 2:209
Blanco, Carrero, 2:38
Bolivar University, 2:102–103
Bolsheviks, 1:50–51
Bombs. *See* Terrorism
Bön (religion), 2:276
Bonner, Elena, 1:190
Borders
    African countries, 1:87
    Ethiopia and Eritrea, **1:103–111**, *105, 110*
    Kashmir, **1:151–162**
    Mexico and U.S., **2:169–178**, *176*
    Nagorno-Karabakh, 1:189, 261–262
    Palestine, 1:116
    Tibet, 2:277–278
    Yugoslavia, 1:31
Borja, Rodrigo, 2:103
Bosnia-Herzegovina
    chronologies, 1:25, 239
    civil war, **1:24–38**, *28*
    demography, 1:29
    ethnic cleansing, 1:30–31, 245
    ethnic groups, 1:29, *1:37*
    map, *1:30*
    Muslims, 1:30–31
    partitioning of, 1:31
    Serbs, 1:246
    United Nations peace keepers in, 1:29, 245
    See also Yugoslavia
Bouteflicka, Abdelaziz, 2:7–8
Bove, Jose, 2:120
Boxers United in Righteousness (China), 2:43
Boyne, Battle of (1690), 2:225
Branch Davidians, 1:298–299
Brazil
    abolition of slavery, 1:42
    Amazon rainforest deforestation, **1:12–23**
    Asian financial crisis, 1:15
    chronologies, 1:13, 40
    economic development, 1:14–15
    government programs for Amazon rainforest,
        1:13–15, 16–17, 19–20
    race relations, **1:39–45**, *44*
    slavery, 1:40–41, *1:41, 42*
    social system, 1:40–42
Brewe, Dr. Francis, 1:197
Briceño, German, 2:70–71
British East India Company, 1:155
British South African Company, 2:305–306
Bucaram, Abdalá, 2:108
Buddhism, 2:43
    Myanmar, 2:191–192
    Tibet, 2:274, 275–277
Burma. *See* Myanmar
Burundi
    map, *1:227*
    relations with Congo, 1:84

C

Cabinda Enclave Liberation Front (FLEC), 2:11
Cacuango, Dolores, 2:109
Cali drug cartel, *1:72*, 1:75
California, 1:249

Camarillas, 2:175–176
Camp David negotiations (2000), 2:147
Caño Limon pipeline, 2:65, 66
Carajas Iron Ore Project (1982), 1:15
Carbon dioxide processing, 1:18
Cárdenas, Lázaro, 1:62
Cardoso, Fernando, 1:14
Carnation Revolution (1974-1975), 2:183
Cartels
    Colombian drugs, *1:72*, 1:75, 2:174
    Mexican drugs, 2:174–177
    OPEC, 1:196, 200
Carter, Jimmy, 2:137
de las Casas, Bartolomé, 2:73
Cash crops. *See* Agriculture
Castillo Armas, Carlos, 2:127
Castillo, Rene, *2:173*
Castro, Fidel, 1:94–101, *1:95*
Catechists, 1:63–64
Catholic Church
    Chiapas, 1:59–60, 63–64
    China, 2:45
    East Timor, 2:92–93
    Ecuador, 2:100, 103
    Northern Ireland, 2:223–225, 223–228
    Peru, 2:237
Cattle industry, 1:16, 2:112, *2:118*
Caucasus. *See* Armenia; Azerbaijan; Nagorno-Karabakh
Caudillos, 1:304
CCP (Chinese Communist Party), 1:286, 2:44–45
Central Intelligence Agency. *See* United States Central
    Intelligence Agency
Central Tibetan Administration (CTA), 2:278–279
Ceylon. *See* Sri Lanka
CFU (Commercial Farmer's Union, Zimbabwe), 2:311
Chávez Frías, Hugo, 1:303–304, *1:305,* 1:307–309,
    1:309
Chechen-Ingush Republic. *See* Chechnya
Chechens, 1:51–52
Chechnya
    chronology, 1:47
    demography, 1:48–50
    elections, 1:53, 54
    ethnic groups, 1:48–49
    human rights violations, 1:47–48, 56–57
    independence from Russia, **1:46–57**, *55, 259,*
        1:263–264
    map, *1:48*
    mass media, 1:52
    oil industry, 1:49–50, 54, 56
Chen Shui-bian, 1:284, 292
Chernobyl Disaster (1986), 2:251
Cherokee Nation v. Georgia (1831), 2:201
Chiang Ching-kuo, 1:291
Chiang Kai-shek, 1:286–287, *1:287*
Chiapas, Mexico. *See* Mexico
Chile
    chronology, 1:205
    drug trade, 1:75
    economy, 1:204–208
    elections, 1:206, 208
    human rights violations, 1:208–209
    map, *1:212*
    nationalist politics, 1:206–207
    relations with United States, 1:206–207

China
    chronologies, 1:285, 2:43, 52
    civil war, 2:278
    Cultural Revolution (1966-1976), 2:45, 280
    economy, 2:54–62
    emigration to United States, 2:295
    Falun Gong, **2:42–50**
    involvement in Angola, 2:16, 19
    involvement in Korea, 2:152
    maps, *1:288, 2:44*
    "One nation, two systems," 1:290, 292
    relations with Republic of China (ROC), 1:287–291
    relations with Taiwan, **1:284–294**, *293*, 2:281
    relations with Tibet, 2:276–281
    relations with United States, 1:289, 292
    religious oppression, 2:44–45, 47–49
    Tibet, 2:45
    "two Chinas," 1:288
    World Trade Organization involvement, **2:51–63**
Chinese Communist Party (CCP), 1:286, 2:44–45
Ching-kuo, Chiang, 1:291
Christian Identity (organization), 1:298
Christian Social Party, 2:25, 29
Christians
    Jerusalem, 2:142–143
    Myanmar, 2:191–192
    Nigeria, 2:214–220
Church of Cyprus, 2:77
CIA. *See* United States Central Intelligence Agency
CIS. *See* Commonwealth of Independent States (CIS);
        Russia
Citizenship rights
    Ecuador, 2:106–107
    Mexican Americans, 2:172
    Native Americans, 2:203
Civil rights
    Native Americans, 2:203, 204–205
    women, *1:5*, 1:5–6 (*See also* Human rights violations)
Civil Rights Act of 1964 (U.S.), 2:205
Civil war
    Afghanistan, 1:4–5
    Algeria, **2:1–8**
    Angola, **2:9–24**
    Bosnia-Herzegovina, **1:24–38**
    China, 2:278
    Congo, **1:78–88**, *85*
    Georgia, 1:262–263
    Lebanon, 1:280
    Liberia, **1:174–183**, *181*
    Serbia, **1:238–251**
    Sri Lanka, **2:262–270**
    Sudan, **1:266–275**
    Taiwan, 1:286–287
    Turkey, **1:163–173**
    Yugoslavia, **1:238–251**
    Zimbabwe, 2:309
Civilians, attacks on, 2:5–7
Clark Amendment (1975), 2:17
Clerides, Glafkos, 2:85–86
Clinton, Bill, 2:211
Cobraria, Roberto, 2:67–68, 71
Coca leaf farming, 1:71
    See also Drug trade
Cocaine
    Colombia, 1:71

crack, 1:75
    Mexico, 2:174
    United States, 1:72–73, 75
    See also Drug trade
Coffee industry
    Guatemala, 2:123–124
Coffee production, 1:65
Coke. *See* Cocaine
Cold War, 2:289
    Angola, 2:15–17, 19–21
    British involvement, 2:118–119
    Cuba, 1:97
    Guatemala, 2:127
    Korean Peninsula, 2:149–154
Colleges. *See* Universities and colleges
Colombia, 2:67
    chronologies, 1:71, 2:65
    coca leaf farming, 1:71
    drug trade, **1:70–77**
    guerrilla movements, 1:75–76
    map, *1:74*
    political reform, 1:72
    U'wa-Occidental Petroleum controversy, **2:64–74**
Colonization
    Brazil, 1:40
    Congo, 1:79
    Cuba, 1:92
    Eritrea, 1:105
    India, 1:155
    Mexico, 1:58–59, 63
    Taiwan, 1:286
    Zimbabwe, 2:304, 305–307
Commercial Farmer's Union (CFU, Zimbabwe), 2:311
Common Market, 2:114–119
Commonwealth of Independent States (CIS)
    formation, 1:252–253
    Georgia, 1:263
    map, *1:265*
    See also Russia
Communism
    Afghanistan, 1:3–4
    China, 1:286, 2:44–45, 54–57
    Cuba, 1:96–97
    Guatemala, 2:124, 127
    Russia, 1:254–255
    Tito, Josep, 1:26
    United States immigration, 2:298
    Yugoslavia, 1:243
Communist Party of the Soviet Union (CPSU), 1:254,
        255–258
Concentration camps, 1:138–139, 217–218
    See also Holocaust
Confederation of Indigenous Nationalities of Ecuador
        (CONAIE), **2:99–111**
Confederation of Indigenous Nationalities of the
        Ecuadorian Amazon (CONFENIAE), 2:101
Confederation of Quichua Communities in Ecuador
        (ECUARUNARI), 2:101
Confucianism, 2:43
Congo
    Africanizing, 1:80
    Belgian colonization, 1:79
    chronology, 1:79
    civil war, **1:78–88**, *85*
    democratization, 1:86

Congo (con't)
    demography, 1:78–79
    ethnic groups, 1:78–79, 80–83
    human rights violations, 1:86, 87
    independence, 1:79–80, 87
    kleptocracy, 1:80
    refugees, 1:82–83, 86
    relations with Angola, 2:15
    relations with regional African governments, 1:84, 87
    United Nations peacekeeping forces, 2:287–288
Congo-Kinshasa. *See* Congo
Congo-Leopoldville. *See* Congo
Constitutional rights and militant separatist movements,
    1:297, 298, 300–301
Constitutions
    Ecuador, 2:102
    Germany, 1:126
    Sri Lanka, 2:268–269
    Venezuela, 1:308
Contonou Agreement (1993), 1:179–180
Convention 169 (International Labor Organization),
    2:106
Copper industry, 1:204–205
Corruption, political
    China, 2:60–61
    Mexico, 2:174–177
Council of Europe, 1:47–48
Coup d'etat. *See* Rebellion
Covenant communities, 1:301
Covenant, Sword and Arm of the Lord (CSA), 1:299–300
CPSU (Communist Party of the Soviet Union), 1:254,
    255–258
    See also Communism
Crack cocaine, 1:75
    See also Cocaine; Drug trade
CRD (Defense of the Republic, Rwanda), 1:231–232
Creoles (Angola), 2:21–23
Creutzfeldt-Jakob Syndrome, 2:112
Crimes against humanity. *See* Human rights violations
Criollos (Guatemala), 2:122–123
Croatia
    armed forces, 1:32
    ethnic cleansing, 1:248
    independence, 1:29
    relations with Serbs, 1:26, 242
    United Nations ceasefire, 1:244–245
    See also Yugoslavia
Crop production. *See* Agriculture
Crude oil. *See* Oil industry
CSA (Covenant, Sword and Arm of the Lord), 1:299–300
CTA (Central Tibetan Administration), 2:278–279
Cuba
    chronology, 1:90
    Communism, 1:96–97
    economy, 1:91, 99
    elections, 1:95
    emigration, 1:100–101
    Great Depression (1929-1939), 1:93
    independence, 1:93
    map, *1:98*
    nationalism, 1:91
    nuclear weapons, 1:98–99
    relations with Angola, 1:99–100, 2:12–15, 16–21
    relations with Ethiopia, 1:100
    relations with Russia, 1:96, 97–99

    relations with United States, **1:89–102**, *97*
    Socialism, 1:96
    Spanish colonization, 1:92
Cuban Missile Crisis (1962), 1:98–99
CUC (Peasant Unity Committee, Guatemala), 2:128–129
Cults. *See* Religious groups
Cultural identity
    Ecuador, 2:102–103
    Georgia, 1:262–263
    Great Britain, 2:119–120
    Mexico, 2:171
    Rwanda, 1:229–230
    See also Nationalism
Cultural Revolution (1966-1976, China), 2:45, 280
Cultural Survival (organization), 1:21
Cyanide, 2:247–249
Cyprus
    chronology, 2:76
    conflict between Greek and Turkish Cypriots,
        2:75–87, *78, 81*
    constitution of 1960, 2:80–81
    demography, 2:84–85
    map, *2:77*
    United Nations peacekeeping forces, 2:288–289
Czech Republic
    map, *1:221*
    relations with Roma, **1:214–224**, *222*

D

Dalai Lama, *2:275*, 2:276–278
D'Almeida, Jackie, *2:185*
Daoism, 2:43
Dark Age (Tibet), 2:276
Daud, Muhammed, 1:3
Dawes Act (1887, U.S.), 2:203
Dayton Accords (1995), 1:34–35, 36
de Klerk, F. W., 2:254, 261
Defense of the Republic (CRD, Rwanda), 1:231–232
Deforestation. *See* Amazon rainforest
Democracy
    China, 2:57–58
    Congo, 1:86
    Russia, 1:254, 264
Democratic People's Republic of Korea. *See* North Korea
Democratic Progressive Party (DPP) (Taiwan), 1:291
Democratic Republic of Congo (DRC). *See* Congo
Deng Xiaoping, 1:290–291
Denktash, Rauf, 2:83, 84, 85–86
Dhlakama, Afonso, 2:185
Diamonds, 2:9
Die Freiheitlichen in Österreich. *See* Freedom Party of
    Austria
Dinka, 1:269, 273
Disasters, 2:248–249, 251
Discrimination
    Roma, **1:214–224**, *222*
    Rwanda, 1:230
    See also Elitism
Doctors Without Borders, *1:136*
Doe, Samuel K., 1:177–178
Dole-Lieberman Amendment (1994), 1:32
Dollarization, 2:99, 101
Dostum, Abdul Rashid, 1:4

DPP (Democratic Progressive Party) (Taiwan), 1:291
Drake, Edwin L., 1:198
DRC (Democratic Republic of Congo). *See* Congo
Drought, 2:310–311
Drug cartels. *See under* Cartels
Drug control agencies, Mexico, 2:173–177
Drug trade
    Afghanistan, 1:9
    Chile, 1:75
    Colombia, **1:70–77**, 2:66
    Mexico-U.S., 2:173–177
Drug-related violence, 2:175–177
Dudayev, Dzhokhar, 1:53–54
Dunant, Henry, 1:135–136, 137
DVU (German People's Union), 1:130–132

E

Earth Summit (1992), 1:13–14, 22
East Germany. *See* Germany
East Timor
    chronology, 2:89–90
    conflict with Indonesia, **2:88–98**
    demography, 2:89–90
    independence from Indonesia (1999), 2:95–96
    independence from Portugal (1975), 2:90–91
EC (European Community), 1:243–244
Ecological disasters, 2:248–249, *2:249*, 2:251
Economic Community of West African States
    (ECOWAS), 1:178–179
Economic recession
    Brazil, 1:15
    Ecuador, 2:104
    Great Britain, 2:116, 117–118
    Guatemala, 2:124
    Myanmar, 2:195
    Nigeria, 2:215
    North Korea, 2:154–155
    Peru, 2:241–242
Economic sanctions, **1:143–150**, *147, 150,* 2:9
ECSC (European Coal and Steel Community), 2:114
Ecuador
    chronology, 2:100
    demography, 2:100
    indigenous people's movement, **2:99–111**, *110*
    map, *2:102*
ECUARUNARI (Confederation of Quichua
    Communities in Ecuador), 2:101
Education
    independent of governments, 2:109
    indigenous peoples in Ecuador, 2:102–103
    Kosovo, 2:163–164
    Macedonia, 2:168
EEC (European Economic Community), 2:114–119
Egypt
    control of Gaza Strip, 1:115
    relations with Syria, 1:278–279
    United Nations peacekeeping forces, 2:285
Elchibey, Abulfz, 1:193
Elections
    Algeria, 2:4
    Chechnya, 1:53, 54
    Chile, 1:206, 208
    Cuba, 1:95

East Timor, 2:88
Ecuador, 2:107–108
Germany, 1:125, 129–131
India, 1:158–159
Iran, 2:132–133, 132–134, 139–140
Liberia, 1:178, 180–181
Mexico, 1:64, 67–68, 69
Myanmar, 2:195–196
Russia, 1:254
Taiwan, 1:284–285, 291–292
United States, 2:71–72
Venezuela, 1:303, 307–309, *1:309*
Yugoslavia, 1:243
Zimbabwe, 2:313
Elitism, 1:60, 61–62, 64
    See also Discrimination
ELN (National Liberation Army, Colombia), 2:66, 71–73
Embargo
    impact on Iraqis, 1:149–150, *1:150*
    oil, 1:201–202
    United Nations against Iraq, **1:143–150**, *147*
    United Nations against Yugoslavia, 1:31
    United States against Cuba, 1:97
England, settlers in Ireland, 2:223–225
    See also Great Britain
English Only Movement, 2:299–300
enosis (Cyprus), 2:78–83
Environmental issues
    Amazon rainforest, 1:15, 19, 21–22
    China, 2:59
    Colombia, 2:66, 68, 72
    Earth Summit (1992), 1:13–14, 22
    Ecuador, 2:105–106
    Native American, 2:208
    Romania, 2:248–249
    Tibet, 2:279–280
EOKA (National Organization of Cypriot Fighters), 2:80,
    82
EPRDF (Ethiopian People's Revolutionary Democratic
    Front), 1:106
Eritrea
    border war, **1:103–111**, *105, 110*
    chronology, 1:104
    economy, 1:106–107
    funding to rebel groups, 1:110
    independence, 1:103
    Italian colonization, 1:105
    map, *1:108*
    military spending, 1:109
Esmeralda Exploration (mining company), 2:247
ETA (Euskadi ta Askatasuna), **2:34–41**
ETA-m (ETA-military), 2:38–39
Etarras. See ETA (Euskadi ta Askatasuna)
Ethiopia
    border war, **1:103–111**, *105*
    chronology, 1:104
    economy, 1:106–107
    map, *1:108*
    military spending, 1:109
    relations with Cuba, 1:100
Ethiopian People's Revolutionary Democratic Front
    (EPRDF), 1:106
Ethnic cleansing
    Bosnia-Herzegovina, 1:30–31
    Croatia, 1:248

Ethnic cleansing (con't)
    Holocaust, 1:30–31
    See also Human rights violations
Ethnic conflict. *See* Civil war
Europe
    integration as political body, 2:113–114
    reconstruction after World War II, 2:113–117
European Coal and Steel Community (ECSC), 2:114
European Commissioners. *See under* European Union
European Community (EC), 1:243–244
European Convention on Human Rights, 2:119–120
European Economic Community (EEC), 2:114–119
European Union (EU)
    anti-E.U. sentiment, 2:30
    Austria, 2:32–33
    Cyprus, 2:86
    European Commissioners, 2:119
    Great Britain, **2:112–121**
    involvement in World Trade Organization, 2:54
    membership, 2:119
    Turkey, 1:173, 2:86
Euskadi Ta Askatasuna. *See* ETA
Exile, 2:278, 280
Extradition, 1:76, **1:204–213,** *2:300*
Exxon Valdez Oil Spill (1989), 2:251
EZLN (Zapatista National Liberation Army), 1:66–69

F

Falun Gong, **2:42–50,** 2:43, *2:47*
Famine, 1:137–138, 2:154
FAR (Revolutionary Armed Forces, Guatemala),
    2:127–129
FARC (Armed Revolutionary Forces of Colombia), 2:66,
    69–71
Farming. *See* Agriculture
Farooq Abdullah, 1:158–159
Fatah (organization), 1:116
FBI. *See* United States Federal Bureau of Investigation
    (FBI)
Federal Republic of Yugoslavia. *See* Serbia
Federation of Shuar Centers, 2:100–101
Fidelity Investments, 2:72
Final Solution, 1:218–219
    See also Concentration camps; Holocaust
FIS (Islamic Salvation Front), 2:4–7
Fishing industry, 2:249–250
FLEC (Cabinda Enclave Liberation Front), 2:11
FLN (National Liberation Front (FLN) of Algeria), 2:2–3
FNLA. *See* National Liberation Front of Angola
Forced relocation
    Native Americans, 2:201–203
FPÖ. *See* Freedom Party of Austria
FR Yugoslavia. *See* Serbia
France
    colonization of Algeria, 2:2–3
    involvement in EEC, 2:116–119
    relations with Great Britain, 2:112, 116–117
    relations with United States, 2:294
    See also Basque region
"Free" presses, 1:299
Free trade. *See* International trade
Freebase. *See* Cocaine
Freedom Party of Austria, 2:25, 29–33

Freeman (militant separatist movements), 1:300–301
Frei, Eduardo, 1:206
Freitas, Terence, 2:69–70
FRELIMO (Mozambique Liberation Front), 2:181–186
FRETILIN (The Revolutionary Front for an Independent
    East Timor), 2:90–91
Freyre, Gilberto, 1:42–43
Front Line States, 2:18–19
FSLN (Sandinista National Liberation Front), 1:100
Fujimori, Alberto, 2:244
FZLN (Zapatista Front of National Liberation), 1:67, 68

G

Gambling, 2:208–210
Gamsakhurdia, Zviad, 1:262–263
García, Alan, 2:242
GATT (General Agreement on Tariffs and Trade, 1947),
    1:316–317, 2:52
de Gaulle, Charles, 2:116–117
Gay, Lahe'ena'e, 2:69–70
Gaza Strip
    Egyptian control, 1:115
    Palestinian-Israeli conflict, 1:118, *1:119,* 2:145
Gelug sect (religion), 2:276
General Allotment Act of 1887 (U.S.), 2:203
Geneva Conventions, 1:140
Genocide, 1:233
    Armenia, 1:165, 187–188
    East Timor, 2:95
    Guatemala, 2:128–129
    Rwanda, 1:82–83, **1:225–237**
Georgia, Cherokee Nation v. (1831), 2:201
Georgia (nation), 1:262–263
Georgia, Worcester v. (1832), 2:201
German People's Union (DVU), 1:130–132
Germany
    asylum laws, 1:127–128
    chronology, 1:125
    colonization of Rwanda, 1:228–229
    constitution, 1:126
    elections, 1:125, 129–131
    emigration to United States, 2:295
    military, 1:132
    neo-Nazism, 1:125–126
    political parties, 1:129–133
    reconstruction after World War II, 2:114
    relations with Slovenia, 1:244
    right wing extremism, **1:124–133**
    Roma, 1:217–220
    Third Reich, 2:26–29
GIA (Armed Islamic Group), 2:5
Glasnost, 1:189, 257
Globalization, 1:318–319
Gold mining. *See* Mining
Gonzalez, Elian, 1:89–90, *1:91,* 2:292
Good Friday Agreement (1997, Northern Ireland),
    2:234
Gorbachev, Mikhail, 1:189, 190–191, *1:255,* 1:255–258,
    260
Gore, Al, 2:71–72
Gossens, Salvador Allende, 1:206, 207–208
Government programs for the Amazon rainforest,
    1:13–15, 16

Government reform
    Colombia, 1:72
    Guatemala, 2:124–126
    Iran, **2:132–140**
    Mexico, 1:60, 62, 63
    Russia, 1:255–258
    Rwanda, 1:230
    Sri Lanka, 2:265, 268
    Tibet, 2:278
Government subsidies
    European Union, 2:117–118
    Native American, 2:209–210
Grannobles, 2:70–71
Grau, Ramon, 1:94
Great Britain
    chronology, 2:113
    Cyprus colony, 2:78–83
    extradition of Augusto Pinochet, 1:210, *1:211*
    India colony, 1:155–157
    involvement in European Union, **2:112–121**
    Jerusalem, 2:143–144
    Myanmar colony, 2:192–194
    Nigeria colony, 2:215
    partition plan for India, 1:157–158
    relations with Iraq, 1:149
    relations with Ireland, 2:223–230
    relations with Sudan, 1:269–271
    relations with Tibet, 2:277
    relations with United States, 2:115–116, 118–119
    relations with Zimbabwe, 2:304–307
    Sri Lanka colony, 2:264
Great Depression (1929-1939), 1:93
Greece
    conflict between Greek and Turkish Cypriots,
        2:75–87
    relations with Macedonia, 2:168
Gritz, James "Bo," 1:298
Grivas, George, 2:79, 82–83
Guardian Council (Iran), 2:133, 139–140
Guatemala
    chronology, 2:123
    conflict with indigenous peoples, **2:122–131**
    map, *2:126*
    National Democratic Revolution (1944-1954),
        2:124–126
Guerrilla warfare
    Angola, 2:9–24
    Basque region, 2:36–41
    Colombia, 1:75–76, 2:66, 69–73
    East Timor, 2:88, 92, 95–96
    Guatemala, 2:127–129
    Kosovo, 2:161, 162, 165–166
    Kurds, 1:170
    Mozambique, 2:181–186
    Myanmar, 2:188–189
    Peru, 2:242–244
    Santa Cruz Massacre (1991, East Timor),
        2:93–94
    Sri Lanka, 2:262–263, 266, 268
Gun control laws, 1:296, 298
Guomindang, 1:286–287
Gusmao, Jose Xanana, 2:92, 96
Gutiérrez, Lucio, 2:99, 108
Gúzman Reynoso, Abimael, 2:236–237, 240, *2:243*,
    2:243–244

Gyaltsen Norbu, *2:273*
Gypsies. *See* Roma

H

Habyarimana, Juvenal, 1:229–232
Haciendas (Peru), 2:239–240
Haider, Jörg, 2:25, 29–33
Haitians, *2:298*
Hapsburg dynasty, 1:216
Hawaiian Natives, 2:208
Health care
    Iraq, 1:149
    Liberia, 1:183
Hekmatyar, Gulbuddin, 1:4
Heroin, *1:73*
Herzegovina. *See* Bosnia-Herzegovina
Hijacking, 1:1–2, 8–9
Hikmatyar, Gulbuddin, 1:4
Himmler, Heinrich, 1:218
Hindus
    India, 1:155–156
    relations with Muslims, 1:154–155, 156–157
Hitler, Adolf, 1:217, 2:26–29, *2:27*
Hizballah, 1:281–282
Holbrooke, Richard, 1:32
Holland, 2:90
Holocaust
    comparison to ethnic cleansing in Bosnia-
        Herzegovina, 1:30–31
    humanitarian aid, 1:138–140
    International Red Cross, 1:139
    Jerusalem, 2:143
    Roma, 1:218–219
Holy Land. *See* Jerusalem
Home Rule (Ireland), 2:226, 227
Hong Kong, 1:290–291
Hong Xiuquan, 2:43
Htoo, Johnny and Luther, 2:188–189, *2:191*
Human rights violations
    Afghanistan, *1:5*, 1:5–6
    Argentina, 1:211
    Basque region, 2:37–38
    Chechnya, 1:47–48, 56–57
    Chile, 1:208–209
    China, 2:58, 59
    Congo, 1:86, 87
    Falun Gong, 2:48
    Guatemala, 2:122, 129–130
    International Criminal Court (ICC), 1:234
    Nagorno-Karabakh, 1:194
    South Africa, 2:257–258
    Tibet, 2:281
    See also Ethnic cleansing
Humanitarian aid, **1:134–142**
    Africa, 1:87
    chronology, 1:135
    international politics, 1:140–141
    mass media, 1:136–137
    military technology, 1:135–137
    Mozambique, 2:186
    Nazi Germany, 1:139–140
    Russia to Chechnya, 1:46–47
Humanitarian aid organizations, *1:136*, 1:141–142, 274
    See also International Red Cross

Hume, John, 2:230
Hung Hsiu-ch'uan, 2:43
Hussein, Abdul ibn, 1:280
Hussein, Saddam, 1:144, 146
Hutu
    Congo, 1:82, 84
    genocide, **1:225–237**, *235*
    Interahamwe, 1:82
    refugees, 1:225, 234–235
    Rwanda, 1:82

I

ICC (International Criminal Court), 1:234
ICTFY (International Crime Tribunal for the Former
        Yugoslavia), 1:234
ICTR (International Crime Tribunal for Rwanda), 1:234
IIPF (Islamic Iran Participation Front), 2:132–133
Illegal immigration
    Mexico-U.S., 2:172–173
    United States, 2:292, 299
Illegal logging, 1:15–16
IMF. *See* International Monetary Fund (IMF)
Immigration
    Austria, 2:30–31
    extradition, *2:300*
    Mexico-U.S., 2:170–173
    United States, **2:292–301**, *2:295, 296–297, 2:298*
Implementation Force (IFOR) (organization), 1:35
Import restrictions. *See* International trade
INC (Indian National Congress), 1:156–157
Independence
    Abkhazian, 1:263
    Chechnya, *1:259*, 1:263
    Congo, 1:79–80, 87
    Croatia, 1:29
    Cuba, 1:93
    East Timor, 2:88
    Eritrea, 1:103
    Mexico, 1:60
    Nagorno-Karabakh, **1:184–195**, 1:262
    Russian republics, 1:261
    Rwanda, 1:229
    Serbia, 1:24
    Slovenia, 1:29
    Sri Lanka, 2:264
    Taiwan, 1:291, 292–293
    Zimbabwe, 2:307
India
    British colonization, 1:155–158
    chronology, 1:152
    elections, 1:158–159
    ethnic groups, 1:155–157
    government, 1:153
    map, *1:156*
    nuclear weapons, 1:151, 160
    relations with Kashmir, **1:151–162**
    relations with Pakistan, 1:151–152, 158–160, *1:161*,
        2:286
    relations with Sri Lanka, 2:266–267
    relations with United States, 1:160
Indian Civil Rights Act of 1968 (U.S.), 2:205
Indian Country, 2:200, 204, 211
Indian Gaming Regulatory Act (1988, U.S.), 2:208–209

Indian National Congress (INC), 1:156–157
Indian Peace Keeping Force (IPKF, Sri Lanka), 2:266
Indian Self-Determination and Education Assistance Act
        (1975, U.S.), 2:205
Indian Trade and Intercourse Act (1790, U.S.), 2:201
Indians. *See* Indigenous peoples
Indigenous Congress (1974), 1:63
Indigenous peoples, 2:206
    Amazon rainforest, 1:19
    Ecuador, **2:99–111**
    Guatemala, **2:122–131**
    labor, 1:60, 61–62
    Liberia, 1:175, 177, 182
    localism, 1:62–63
    Mexico, **1:58–69**
    Native Americans, **2:198–213**
    U'wa (Colombia), 2:64–74
    World Trade Organization (WTO), 1:318
    See also Land reform; Self-determination
Indochina, 2:286–287
Indonesia, **2:88–98**
Indo-Sri Lankan Peace Accord (1987), 2:266
Inflation, 2:309
Institute of Indigenous Cultures, 2:101–102
Institutional Revolutionary Party. *See* Partido
        Revolucionario Institucional (PRI) (Mexico)
Intellectual property, 2:54
Interahamwe, 1:82
Intercontinental Encounter on Humanity and Against
        Neo-Liberalism (1996), 1:67
International Crime Tribunal for Rwanda (ICTR),
        1:234
International Crime Tribunal for the Former Yugoslavia
        (ICTFY), 1:234
International Criminal Court (ICC), 1:234
International drug trade. *See* Drug trade
International Labor Organization (Convention 169),
        2:106
International Monetary Fund (IMF)
    aid to Zimbabwe, 2:310
    assistance to Brazil, 1:15, 20
    humanitarian aid, 1:141
International Red Cross, 1:135–136, 137, *1:138*, 1:139,
        1:141
International relief. *See* Humanitarian aid
International relief organizations. *See* Humanitarian aid
        organizations; International Red Cross
International trade, 1:315, 318–319
    Central America, 2:124
    European organizations, 2:114–120
    non-tariff barriers (NTBs), 1:316
    Peru, 2:238, 241–242
    tariffs, 1:315–316
    trade deficits, 2:58
    U.S.-Mexico, 2:170–172
    World Trade Organization, 2:52–63
International Trade Organization (ITO), 1:315–316
International Tropical Timber Organization (ITTO,
        Brazil), 1:21–22
Internet, 2:189–190, 193
Interventionism, 1:99–100
Intifada, 1:117, 118
IP. *See* Intellectual property
IPKF (Indian Peace Keeping Force, Sri Lanka), 2:266
IRA. *See* Irish Republican Army

Index

Iran
    chronology, 2:133
    demography, 2:134
    Iran Hostage Crisis (1979-1980), 2:137
    Iran-Contra Affair (1983-1986), 2:138
    Iran-Iraq War (1980-1990), 1:144, 2:137–139
    map, *2:135*
    recent political reform, **2:132–140**
    Revolution of 1979, 2:136–137
Irani, Ray, 2:72
Iraq
    chronology, 1:144
    economic sanctions against, **1:143–150**
    economy, 1:149–150
    health care, 1:149
    Iran-Iraq War (1980-1990), 1:144, 2:137–139
    Kurd uprisings, 1:146
    map, *1:145*
    oil industry, 1:143–144
    relations with United States, 1:144
    United Nations Special Commission (UNSCOM)
        inspections, 1:143–144
    weapons of mass destruction (WMD), 1:147–149
Ireland
    chronology, 2:222
    emigration to United States, 2:295
    map, *2:223*
    Troubles, **2:221–235**
Irish Republican Army (IRA), 2:227, *2:231*
    See also Provisional Irish Republican Army; Real
        Irish Republican Army
Islam, 1:157–158
    Afghanistan, 1:2–3
    Bosnia-Herzegovina, 1:30–31
    Iran, 2:134
    Jerusalem, 2:142–143, *2:144*
    Kashmir, 1:152, 153–154
    Myanmar, 2:192
    Nigeria, 2:214–220
    radicalism, 1:264
    relations with Hindus, 1:154–155, 156–157
Islamic Iran Participation Front (IIPF), 2:132–133
Islamic law
    Afghanistan, 1:5
    Nigeria, **2:214–220**, *218*
    Sudan, 1:268, 269, 273
Islamic policical movements
    Algeria, 2:4–9
    Nigeria, **2:214–220**
Islamic Revolution of 1979 (Iran), 2:136
Islamic Salvation Army (AIS), 2:5–7
Islamic Salvation Front (FIS), 2:4–7
Islamic Students Association, 2:133
Isolation, political, 2:154
Israel
    chronologies, 1:113, 277, 2:142
    conflict with Palestine, **1:112–123**
    conflict with Syria, **1:276–283**, *282*
    control of Jerusalem, 1:116
    independence (1947), 2:144
    map, *1:117*
    Palestinian refugees, 1:115, *1:120*
    relations with Arabs, 1:115, 116–117, 118, 279
    relations with Lebanon, 1:280, 2:286
    relations with Palestinians, **2:141–148**
    relations with United States, 1:279, 283
    United Nations peacekeeping force, 2:285–286
    See also Jerusalem
Issayas Afeworki, 1:108
ITO (International Trade Organization), 1:315–316
ITTO (International Tropical Timber Organization,
    Brazil), 1:21–22

J

Jackson-Vanik legislation (1974), 2:53, 59
Jadid, Saleh, 1:278
James II (England), 2:225
Jammu and Kashmir Liberation Front (JKLF), 1:159
Janatha Virmukthi Peramuna (JVP, Sri Lanka), 2:265,
    266
Japan, 1:286, 2:193–194
Japanese-American interment, 2:296
Jayawardene, R., 2:266
Jerusalem
    chronology, 2:142
    claims by Jews, 1:117
    control by Israel, 1:116
    demography, 2:145
    Palestinian-Israeli conflict, **2:141–148**
    See also Israel
Jewish refugees
    emigration to United States, 2:296
Jews
    Austria, 2:30–31
    claims to Jerusalem, 1:117
    immigration to Palestine, 1:113, 114
    Jerusalem, 2:142–144
Jiang Jieshi, 1:286–287, *1:287*
Jiang Jingguo, 1:291
JKLF (Jammu and Kashmir Liberation Front), 1:159
JNA (Yugoslavian army), 1:28–29
Johnson v. McIntosh (1823), 2:201
Jordan, 1:280
Journalism. *See* Mass media
Junta. See Military government
JVP (People's Liberation Front, Sri Lanka), 2:265, 266

K

Kabila, Laurent Desire, 1:81, 82–84, 87
Kahl, Gordon, 1:297–298
Karabakh. *See* Nagorno-Karabakh
Karabakh Committee (KC), 1:190–191
Kashmir, **1:151–162**, *154*
    British partition plan, 1:157–158
    chronology, 1:152
    demography, 1:152–153
    Muslims, 1:152, 153–154, 157–158
    resolution with India, 1:160–161
    United Nations peacekeeping force, 2:286
Katanga. *See* Congo
Katangans, 1:81–82
    See also Congo
Kemal, Mustafa, 1:168, *1:169*
Khamenei, Ayatollah Ali Hoseini-, 2:133
Khatami, Hojjatoleslam Mohammed, 2:132–133, 138
Khomeini, Ayatollah, 2:136–137
Kidnappings
    Americans in Colombia, 1999, 2:69–71

Kim Dae Jung, 2:149, 152, 154–155
Kim Il Sung, 2:150–151, 154–155
Kim Jong Il, 2:149, 154–155
KLA. *See* Kosovo Liberation Army
KLA (Kosovo Liberation Army), 1:247, 2:165–166
Kleptocracy, 1:80
KMT (Kuomintang), 1:286–287
Know-Nothing Party, 2:295
Kongo (Angola), 2:10
Korean Peninsula, **2:149–156**
    chronology, 2:150
    map, *2:151*
    See also North Korea; South Korea
Korean People's Republic (KPR), 2:150–151
Korean War (1950-1953), 2:152–153
Kosovo, *1:242*
    chronology, 1:239, 2:158
    ethnic groups, 1:241–242
    independence, 1:241, 246
    regional relations, 1:250
    relations with Serbia, **1:238–251**
    Roma, 1:221–223
    Serb-Albanian conflict, **2:157–168**
    United Nations peacekeeping forces, *2:287*
Kosovo Liberation Army (KLA), 1:247, 2:165–166
Ku Klux Klan, 1:296–297
Kumaratunga, Chandrika Bandaranaike, 2:267, 268–269
Kuomintang (KMT), 1:286–287
Kurdish Workers Party (PKK), 1:163–164, 170–171
Kurdistan, 1:164
Kurds, *1:172*
    chronology, 1:164
    guerrilla movements, 1:170
    language, 1:166
    patriotism to Turkey, 1:171–173
    Persian Gulf War, 1:170–171
    Turkish civil war, **1:163–173**
    uprisings in Iraq, 1:146
Kuwaru'wa, Berito. *See* Cobraria, Roberto

L

Labor force
    China, 2:59
    Mexican, 2:170–173
    United States, 2:295
Labor unions
    Guatemala, 2:124–125
    Mexican immigrants to the US, 2:171–172
    Peru, 2:238
    United States, 2:59
Ladinos, 1:59, 60, 61, 62, 2:122–123
Lancaster House agreement, 2:309
Land Acquisition Bills, 2:311–312, 314
Land mines, 1:104, *2:22, 185*
Land reform
    Agrarian Reform Law of 1952 (Guatemala),
        2:125–126
    Ecuador, 2:104–105
    Peru, 2:241
    Zimbabwe, **2:302–315**, *311*
Land rights
    Mexico, 1:64–65
    Native American, 2:202–204, 206, 208

Land Tenure Act (1969), 2:308
Langdarma, 2:276
Law enforcement, 2:175–177
"Law of the Wheel" (religious group). *See* Falun Gong
"Leaderless resistance," 1:300, 301
Lebanon, 1:279–280, 2:286
Lee Teng-hui, 1:291
Lenin, Vladimir Ilyich, 1:137
Leninism, 2:242
Leopold II, King, 1:79
Les patriotes (Algeria), 2:6
Li Denghui, 1:291
Li Hongzhi, 2:45–46
Liberation Theology, 1:63, 2:237
Liberation Tigers of Tamil (LTTE), 2:262, 266–269
Liberia
    chronology, 1:175
    civil war, **1:174–183**, *181*
    economy, 1:183
    elections, 1:178, 180–181
    health care, 1:183
    indigenous people, 1:175, 177, 182
    map, *1:180*
    mulattos, 1:175–176
    refugees, 1:182–183
Line of Control (LOC) (Kashmir), 1:152–153
The Little War, 1:92
Lobengula, 2:304–305
LOC (Line of Control) (Kashmir), 1:152–153
Localism, 1:62–63
Logging, 1:15–16
LTTE (Liberation Tigers of Tamil), 2:262, 266–269
Luba, 1:81–82
Lumumba, Patrice, 1:79–80, *1:80*
Lunda, 1:80–81
Lusaka Accords (1998), 1:85–86

M

Maastricht Treaty (1992), 2:119
Macao, 1:290–291
MacArthur, Douglas, 2:152
Macas, Luís, 107
Macedonia, 2:166–168
Machado, Gerardo, 1:93
Machel, Samora Moises, 2:183, 186
Macmillan Plan (1958, Cyprus), 2:80
"Mad cow disease," 2:112, *2:118*
Mahuad, Jamil, 2:108
Mai-Mai (military group), 1:84
Major, John, 2:119
Makarios II, 2:79
Makarios III, 2:79, 82–84
Mandela, Nelson, 2:256, 257
Mao Tse-tung, 1:286, *1:289*
Mao Zedong, 1:286, *1:289*, 2:278
Maoism, 2:236, 240, 242
Maquiladores, 2:171–172
Marcos, Subcomandante, 1:64, *1:66, 68*
Mariel boatlift, 1:100–101
Marshall Trilogy, 2:201
Marti, Jose, 1:92
Marxism, 1:137
    Angola, 2:13, 14, 20–21
    Peru, 2:240, 242

Index

Mashantucket Pequots, 2:209
Maskhadov, Aslan, 1:54
Mass media
    Chechnya, 1:52
    Colombia, 1:76
    East Timor, 2:93–94
    Iran, 2:140
    Nigeria, 2:218–219
    Radio Free Europe, 1:34
    reports on human suffering, 1:136–137
    Serbs, 1:31, 249
Massoud, Ahmad Shah, 1:5
Mas'ud, Ahmad Shah, 1:5
Mbundu (Angola), 2:10
McIntosh, Johnson v. (1823), 2:201
McKinney, Cynthia, 2:72
McMahon line (Tibet), 2:277–278
MDC (Movement for Democratic Change, Zimbabwe),
    2:311–314
Médécins Sans Frontieres, *1:136*
Medellin drug cartel, 1:75
Meles Zenawi, 1:108
Menchú Tam, Rigoberta, *2:125*, 2:129–130
Mendes, Francisco "Chico," 1:19–20
Meriage, Larry, 2:72
Mexico
    chronologies, 1:59, 2:170
    colonization of jungles, 1:63
    elections, 1:64, 67–68, 69
    elitism, 1:60, 61–62, 64
    indigenous people, **1:58–69**
    land seizure, 1:64–65
    Mexican Revolution (1911-1920), 1:61–62
    missionaries, 1:59–60, 63–64
    Spanish colonization, 1:58–60
    U.S. border relations, **2:169–178**, *176*
MFN (Most-favored nation) status. *See under* World
    Trade Organization (WTO)
Middle East, 2:285–286
    United Nations peacekeeping forces,
        2:285–286
Middle East Peace Conference, 1:281–282
Militant separatist movements, *1:299*
    Basque, **2:34–41**
    chronology, 1:296
    constitutional rights, 1:297, 298, 300–301
    Kosovo, 2:164–166
    "leaderless resistance," 1:300
    Mozambique, **2:179–187**
    Palestinian, 2:142, 147
    religious beliefs, 1:296, 297–298, 299
    technology use, 1:299
    United States, **1:295–302**
    United States Bureau of Alcohol, Tobacco, and
        Firearms (ATF), 1:295
    United States Federal Bureau of Investigation (FBI),
        1:295
Military government
    Algeria, 2:3–7
    Cuba, 1:93
    Guatemala, 2:124–130
    Korean Peninsula, 2:153
    Myanmar, **2:188–197**
    Nagorno-Karabakh, 1:191
    Nigeria, 2:215

Peru, 2:241
South America, 1:305–306
Military separatism. *See* Militant separatist movements
Military trials. *See* Trials
Militia movements. *See* Militant separatist movements
Millenarian movement, 1:60, 61
Milosevic, Slobodan, 1:28–29, 222, 242, 243, 2:164–165
Mining industry
    Amazon, 1:16
    Chile, 1:204–205
    Romania, 2:246, 247–248
    Zimbabwe, 2:306
Missionaries, 1:59–60, 63, 2:304–305
Mobutu, Joseph Desire, 1:80, *1:83*, 1:86
Mobutu Sese Seko, 1:80, *1:83*, 1:86
Moffat, Robert, 2:304–305
Moldova, 1:261
Mondlane, Eduardo, 2:181
Mongolia, 2:276–277
Montenegro. *See* Serbia
Mossadeq, Muhammed, 2:135–136
Most-favored nation (MFN) status. *See under* World
    Trade Organization (WTO)
Movement for Democratic Change (MDC, Zimbabwe),
    2:311–314
Mozambique
    chronology, 2:180
    map, *2:182*
    relations with South Africa, 2:184–186
    relations with Zimbabwe, 2:184–186
    war for independence, **2:179–187**
Mozambique Liberation Front (FRELIMO), 2:181–186
Mozambique National Resistance (RENAMO), 2:184
MPLA. *See* Popular Movement for Liberation of Angola
Mugabe, Robert Gabriel, 2:304, *2:308*, 2:309, 311–314
Mughal empire, 1:154–155
Mujadin, 1:3–4, 6
Mulattos, 1:40–41, 175–176
Multiethnicity, 2:102
Munhumutapa, 2:180
Museum of the Seam (Jerusalem), 2:141
Muslims. *See* Islam
Myanmar
    chronology, 2:189
    demography, 2:190–191
    map, *2:190*
    military government, **2:188–197**

N

NAFTA (North American Free Trade Agreement), 2:169
Nagorno-Karabakh
    chronology, 1:185
    civil war, **1:184–195**
    demography, 1:185–187
    ethnic groups, 1:186, 187, 262
    human rights violations, 1:194
    independence, 1:262
    map, *1:194*
    refugees, 1:184
    relations with Russia, 1:187–192, 191
Namibia, 2:18–19
Narcotics trade. *See* Drug trade
Nasser, Abdel Gamal, 2:285

National Council of State (2000, Nigeria), 2:218
National Democratic Convention (Mexico), 1:66–67
National Democratic Party (NPD) (Germany), 1:129–130
National Guard (Cyprus), 2:82
National Islamic United Front for Afghanistan (NIUFA), 1:9–10
National League for Democracy (NLD, Myanmar), 2:195–196
National Liberation Army (ELN, Colombia), 2:66, 71–73
National Liberation Front (FLN) of Algeria, 2:2–3
National Liberation Front of Angola (FNLA), 2:11–12, 15–17, 19–21, 23–24
National Organization of Cypriot Fighters (EOKA), 2:80, 82
National Party (South Africa), 2:253
National Patriotic Front of Liberia (NPFL), 1:179–180
National Socialists (Nazi) Party, 2:26–28
National Union for the Total Independence of Angola (UNITA), 2:9–24, *2:18*
Nationalism, 1:186
    Arabs, 1:278
    Armenians, 1:187–188
    Azerbaijanis, 1:187, 191
    Congolese, 1:80
    Cubans, 1:91, 92
    Georgians, 1:262–263
    Indians, 1:156
    Ireland, 2:226–228
    Palestinians, 1:114, 117
    Russians, 1:263–264
    Serbs, 1:28, 242
    Sri Lanka, 2:265
    Tibet, 2:281
    Turks, 1:168–169, 172–173
    United States, 2:296
    Yugoslavians, 1:26, 240
    See also Nationalist politics
Nationalist politics
    Argentina, 1:304–305
    Chile, 1:206–207
    China, 1:286
    Russia, 1:261
    See also Nationalism
Native American reservations. *See* Indian Country
Native Americans, 1:197
    chronology, 2:199
    demography, 2:200
    relations with U.S. government, **2:198–213**
Native Land Husbandry Act, 2:306–307
NATO (North Atlantic Treaty Organization)
    air campaign against Serbia, **1:238–251**
    expansion, 1:37
    Yugoslavian civil wars, 1:33–34
Nazi Party (World War II), 2:26–28
Nazism
    concentration camps, 1:138–139
    Germany, 1:133
    Humanitarian aid, 1:139–140
    Roma, 1:217–219
    See also Neo-Nazism
Ndebele, 2:304
Ne Win, 2:194–195
Neo-liberalism, 1:64, 307
Neo-Nazism
    comparison to Nazis, 1:126–127

    Germany, 1:125–126
    United States, 1:298
    See also Nazism
Netanyahu, Benjamin, 1:121
The Netherlands, 2:90
Neto, Antonio, 2:11–12
New Age movement, 2:273
New Right. *See* Right wing extremism
New Spain. *See* Mexico
News media. *See* Mass media
NGOs. *See* Humanitarian aid organizations
Nicaragua, 2:138
Nigeria, 1:180
    demography, 2:215
    map, *2:215*
    Shari'a (code of Islamic law), **2:214–220**, *218*
an-Nimieri, Jafaar Mohommad, 1:268, 271
NIUFA (National Islamic United Front for Afghanistan), 1:9–10
Nobel Peace Prize
    Belo, Carlos Filipe Ximenes, 2:94
    de Klerk, F. W., 2:257
    Hume, John, 2:234
    Mandela, Nelson, 2:257
    Menchú Tam, Rigoberta, *2:125,* 2:129–130
    Ramos-Horta, José, 2:94
    Suu Kyi, Aung San, *2:194,* 2:196
    Trimble, David, 2:234
    Tutu, Desmond, 2:258
Noboa, Gustavo, 2:99, 111
Nomadism, 1:217
Non-Aligned movement, 2:3
Normal trade relations (NTR). *See* World Trade Organization (WTO)—most-favored nation status
North American Free Trade Agreement (NAFTA), 2:169
North Atlantic Treaty Organization. *See* NATO
North Korea
    chronology, 2:150
    conflict with South Korea, **2:149–156**
    map, *2:151*
Northern Ireland
    chronology, 2:222
    map, *2:223*
    Troubles, **2:221–235**
    See also Great Britain
Northwest Ordinance (1787, U.S.), 2:200–201
NPD (National Democratic Party) (Germany), 1:129–130
NPFL (National Patriotic Front of Liberia), 1:179–180
NTBs (Non-tariff barriers), 1:316
Nuclear reactors, 2:251
Nuclear weapons
    Cuba, 1:98–99
    India, 1:151, 160
    Pakistan, 1:151, 160
Nuremberg Laws, 1:218

O

OAS (Organization of American States), 2:68
Obasanjo, Olesegun, 2:215, 217
Ocalan, Abdullah, 1:163–167, *1:166, 167,* 1:171
Occidental Petroleum Corp., **2:64–74**
Occupation by foreign armies
    Korean Peninsula, 2:149–153

Index

O'Donnell, Hugh, 2:224
Odría, Manuel, 2:238–240
Office of the High Representative (OHR) (Bosnia-
    Herzegovina), 1:36
Oil industry, **1:196–203**, *199*
    Angola, 2:10, 13
    "Big business," 1:198–199
    Chechnya, 1:49–50, 54, 56
    chronology, 1:197
    Colombia, **2:64–74**
    Ecuador, 2:105–106
    embargo, 1:201–202
    Iran, 2:135–136
    Iraq, 1:143–144, *1:148*
    pricing, 1:199–200, 202
    quotas, 1:201
    Sudan, 1:272
    United States, 1:198, 202
    Venezuela, 1:304, 306–307
Oil pipelines. *See* Oil industry
Oil spills
    Ecuador, 2:105–106
    Exxon Valdez (1989), 2:251
Oklahoma City Bombing, 1:299–300
Olvera, Gustavo, *2:173*
Omagh bombing (1998, Northern Ireland), 2:221–222,
    234
Omar, Mohammed, 1:5
"One nation, two systems" (China), 1:290, 292
O'Neill, Hugh, 2:224
OPEC (Organization of Petroleum Exporting Countries)
    embargo, 1:201–202
    formation, 1:199–200
    limited oil production, 1:196, 200
    oil production rates, 1:201, 202
"Operation Intercept" (1969), 2:173–174
The Order (militant separatist movements), 1:298
Organization of American States (OAS), 2:68
Organization of Petroleum Exporting Countries. *See* OPEC
Organization on Security and Cooperation in Europe
    (OSCE), 1:35–36
Oslo Accords (1993), 1:120–121, 2:146–147
Ottoman Empire
    Algeria, 2:2
    Cyprus, 2:77–78
    Jerusalem, 2:143
    Serbia, 2:159–161
Ovimbundu (Angola), 2:10
Owen, Lord David, 1:31

P

Pachakutik, 2:107–108
Paisley, Ian, 2:229
Pakistan, *1:154*
    chronology, 1:152
    formation, 1:157
    government, 1:153
    map, *1:156*
    nuclear weapons, 1:151, 160
    relations with India, 1:151–152, 158–160, *1:161*,
        2:286
    relations with Kashmir, **1:151–162**
    relations with United States, 1:160

Pakistan-Occupied Kashmir. *See* Kashmir
Palace of Justice, 1:76
Palestine, 2:143–144
    borders, 1:116
    chronology, 1:113
    conflict with Israel, **1:112–123**, 1:278, **2:112–123**
    economic dependence, 1:117
    immigration of Jews, 1:113, 114
    nationalism, 1:114, 117
    refugees, 1:115, *1:120*
    statehood, 1:117–119, 121, 122
Palestinian Authority, 1:116
Palestinian Council, 1:120–121
Palestinian Liberation Organization (PLO). *See* PLO
Palma, Hector, 2:176
Panchen Lama, 2:45, *2:273*
Paramilitary groups, 1:75–76
Partido Revolucionario Institucional (PRI) (Mexico), 1:62,
    64, 67, 68
Passports and Permits Ordinance (Sudan), 1:270–271
Patriotism. *See* Nationalism
PCP (Peruvian Communist Party), 2:240
Peace negotiations
    Bosnia, 1:34–35, 36
    Israeli-Palestinian, 1:120–121, 2:146–147
    Korean Peninsula, 2:153–155
    Northern Ireland, 2:221, 233–235
    Rwanda, 1:85–86
    South Africa, 2:254–256
    Sri Lanka, 2:266
Peacekeeping forces. *See* United Nations peacekeeping
    forces
Peasant Unity Committee (CUC, Guatemala),
    2:128–129
Peltier, Leonard, *2:207*
People's Liberation Front (JVP, Sri Lanka), 2:265, 266
People's Party (Austria), 2:25, 29
People's Politics (PP) (Mexico), 1:63–64
People's Redemption Council (PRC) (Liberia),
    1:177–178
People's Republic of China (PRC). *See* China
Perestroika, 1:257
Pérez, Carls Andrés, 1:307
Perez, Roberto, 2:72–73
Perón, Eva Duarte de, 1:305
Perón, Juan Domingo, 1:304–305
Persian Gulf War, 1:26, 144–145
    effects on oil industry, 1:202
    Kurds, 1:170–171
    Palestinian support, 1:119–120
Peru
    chronology, 2:237
    demography, 2:237
    map, *2:239*
    Shining Path, **2:236–245**
Peruvian Communist Party (PCP), 2:240
Petroleum. *See* Oil industry
PIDE (Portugal International and State Police), 2:181
Pinochet, Augusto, **1:204–213**, *209*
PIRA. *See* Provisional Irish Republican Army
PKK (Kurdish Workers Party), 1:163–164, 170–171
Plantation system, Northern Ireland, 2:224–225
Platt Amendment, 1:93
PLO (Palestinian Liberation Organization)
    creation by Arab states, 1:115

PLO (Palestinian Liberation Organization) (con't)
    Fatah (organization), 1:116
    relations with Israel, 1:280, 2:142, 145–148
Plundered art, 1:258
PNV (Basque Nationalist Party), 2:36–41
Police. *See* Law enforcement
Political corruption. *See* Corruption, political
Political isolation, 2:154
Political prisoners
    Basque region, 2:37–38
    Falun Gong, 2:48
Political reform. *See* Government reform
Pollution, 2:246, 248–250
Polyandry, 2:274
Pope John Paul II, 2:93
Popular Movement for Liberation of Angola (MPLA),
    2:11–17, 19–21, 23–24
Populism, **1:303–310**
Porfiriato, 1:61
Portugal, 1:40
    Angola colony, 2:11–12
    East Timor colony, 2:90–91
    Mozambique colony, 2:179–183
    Zimbabwe colony, 2:304
Portugal International and State Police (PIDE), 2:181
Posse Comitatus, 1:297
PP (People's Politics) (Mexico), 1:63–64
Prado, Manuel, 2:240
Prazeros, 2:180
PRC (People's Redemption Council) (Liberia),
    1:177–178
PRC (People's Republic of China). *See* China
Presidential elections. *See* Elections
Press. *See* Mass media
PRI. *See* Partido Revolucionario Institucional (PRI)
    (Mexico)
Privatization in Russia, 1:259–261
Promotion of National Unity and Reconciliation Act
    (1995, South Africa), 2:256
Property rights. *See* Land rights
Proposition 187 (1994, California), 2:172
Protestants, 1:63, 2:223–230
Protests. *See* Public demonstrations
Provisional Irish Republican Army (PIRA), 2:221–222,
    230, 231–235
Public demonstrations
    Austria, *2:32*
    Ecuador, *2:103, 104*
    Falun Gong, 2:42, *2:46,* 2:46–49
    France, *2:117,* 2:120
    Great Britain, *2:115*
    Guatemala, 2:128–129
    Internet protests, 2:193
    Jerusalem, 2:145
    Kosovo, *2:162,* 2:164–165
    Mozambique, 2:181
    Myanmar, 2:195
    Northern Ireland, 2:226, 228–229, 231–232
    Peru, *2:244*
    Tibet, *2:279*
    U'wa (Colombia), *2:68,* 2:72–73
    against World Trade Organization (WTO),
        1:311–320, *313, 314, 317,* 2:56
Puritans, 2:294
Putin, Vladimir V., 1:46, 47–48, *1:260*

Q

Qing dynasty, 2:277
Quichua, 2:102–103
Quiwonka, Thomas, 1:177–178
Quotas, immigration to United States, 2:295, 296–297,
    298

R

Rabbani, Burhanuddin, 1:4
Rabin, Yitzhak, 1:282
Race relations, 1:300
    Brazil, **1:39–45**, *44*
    United States, 1:43–44, 2:296
Racial discrimination. *See* Race relations
Racial equality. *See* Race relations
Racism. *See* Race relations
Radio Free Europe, 1:34
Railroads, 1:16
Reagan, Ronald, 2:138
Real Irish Republican Army (RIRA), 2:222
Rebellion
    Argentina, 1:304–305
    Chile, 1:208
    Cuba, 1:92, 94–96
    East Timor, 2:92
    Ecuador, 2:99, 100–101, 108
    Georgia, 1:261
    Iran, 2:136–137
    Israel, 2:144–145
    Jerusalem, 2:145
    Kosovo, *2:167*
    Muslims, 1:157–158
    Myanmar, 2:194, 195
    Nigeria, 2:217
    Northern Ireland, 2:229
    Peru, 2:238
    South Africa, 2:258–259
    Tibet, 2:280–281
    Venezuela, 1:304, 307
Red Cross. *See* International Red Cross
Red Scare, 2:295
Referendum for independence, 2:88, 95–96
Refugees, 2:294, 297
    Albania, *2:159*
    Congo, 1:82–83, 86
    Cuba, 1:89–90, 100–101
    Cuban, 2:299
    Hutu, 1:225, 234–235
    Jewish, 2:296
    Liberia, 1:182–183
    Nagorno-Karabakh, 1:184
    Palestinians, 1:115, *1:120*
    Roma, 1:223
    Rwanda, 1:141
    Tibetan, 2:278–279
    Tutsi, 1:225, *1:232*
Reiss-Passer, Susanne, 2:31
Religious beliefs, 1:296, 297–298
Religious conversion, 1:59–60
Religious extremism, 2:49
Religious groups, 2:49
    Boxers United in Righteousness (China), 2:43
    Falun Gong, **2:42–50**

Religious groups (con't)
    Gelug sect, 2:276
    Taipings, 2:43
    Yellow Hat sect, 2:276
Religious influence in government
    Iran, 2:132–134
    Nigeria, **2:214–220**
    Northern Ireland, 2:223–224
Religious oppression, 2:44–45, 47–49
Remin (mining company), 2:247
RENAMO (Mozambique National Resistance), 2:184
Republic of China (ROC), **1:286–291**
    nationalist politics, 1:286
    relations with China, 1:287–291
    relations with United States, 1:286, 287–288
    "two Chinas," 1:288
Republic of Cyprus, 2:83, 84–85
    See also Cyprus
Republic of Korea. *See* South Korea
Republic of Serbia. *See* Serbia
Republican Sinn Féin (RSF), 2:222
Republikaner Party, 1:130–132
Resettlement programs, 2:309–310
Resolution 181 (U.N. Special Committee on Palestine),
    2:144
Reunification, Korean Peninsula, 2:154–155
Revolt. *See* Rebellion
Revolution. *See* Rebellion
Revolutionary Armed Forces (FAR, Guatemala),
    2:127–129
Revolutionary Front for an Independent East Timor
    (FRETILIN), 2:90–91
Reza Shah Pahlavi (1878-1944), 2:135
    See also Shah Pahlavi, Mohammad Reza (1919-1980)
Rhee, Syngman, 2:150–151
Rhodes, Cecil, 2:304–306
Right wing extremism
    among youth, 1:128, 131
    Austria, **2:25–33**
    eastern Germany, 1:128–129
    German military, 1:132
    Germany, **1:124–133**
Riots. *See* Rebellion
RIRA (Real Irish Republican Army), 2:222
River Boyne, Battle of, 2:225
Roads
    Amazon rainforest, 1:16
    United States, 1:200–201
Roberto, Holden, 2:11, 15–16
Rockefeller, John D., 1:198–199
Roma
    chronology, 1:215
    discrimination in Czech Republic, **1:214–224**, *222*
    Holocaust, 1:217–220
    population, *1:216*
    refugees, 1:223
    relations with Kosovo, 1:221–223
Roman Catholic Church. *See* Catholic Church
Romania
    chronology, 2:247
    cynanide spill, **2:246–252**, *249*
    map, *2:248*
Roosevelt, Theodore, 1:198–199
Routier, Nicholas, *2:117*
Royal Ulster Constabulary, 2:229

RPF. *See* Rwandan Patriotic Front (RPF)
RSF (Republican Sinn Féin), 2:222
Rubber tapping, 1:13, 19–20
Ruby Ridge (ID) incident, 1:295–296
Ruckus Society, 1:316
Ruiz, Samuel, 1:63
"Rule of law," effect on World Trade Organization, 2:53,
    60
Russia
    censure by Council of Europe, 1:47–48
    chronologies, 1:47, 253
    Communism, 1:254–255
    cultural revival, 1:257–258
    demography, *1:256*
    disintegration of USSR, 1:26, 27, 52–53, 185,
    1:252–265
    economic reform, 1:254–256, 259–261
    elections, 1:254
    ethnic groups, *1:256*, 1:261, 263–264
    famine, 1:137–138
    Media Ministry, 1:52
    nationalism, 1:263–264
    peacekeeping missions, 2:290–291
    political reform, 1:255–258
    privatization, 1:259–261
    relations with Afghanistan, 1:3–4
    relations with Angola, 2:12, 16, 19–21
    relations with Chechnya, **1:46–57**, *50, 259*
    relations with Cuba, 1:96, 97–99
    relations with Korea, 2:149–154
    relations with Syria, 1:278–279
    relations with United States, 1:98–99, 137–138, 257
    relations with Western countries, 1:256–257
    statehood for republics, 1:261
    trophy art, 1:258
Russian czars, 1:50–51
Russian Federation, 1:48
    See also Russia
Russification, 1:187
Rwanda
    chronology, 1:226
    colonization, 1:228–229
    demography, 1:226–227
    ethnic groups, 1:227–228
    genocide, 1:82–83, **1:225–237**
    Interahamwe, 1:82
    mythology, 1:228
    political reform, 1:230
    relations with Congo, 1:84
    United Nations peacekeeping forces, *1:231,*
    1:231–232, 235, 2:290
Rwandan Patriotic Front (RPF), 1:230, 232, 233–234

S

Sabotage, 2:184–186
Samoré Block, 2:64, 65, 68–69
San Andrés Accord on Indigenous Rights and Culture,
    1:67
San Remo Peace Conference, 1:114
Sandinista National Liberation Front (FSLN), 1:100
Santa Cruz Massacre (1991, East Timor), 2:93–94
Savimbi, Jonas Malheiro, 2:11–12, 14–15
School of Andean Education and Culture, Bolivar
    University, 2:102–103

Schuessel, Wolfgang, 2:31
von Schuschnigg, Kurt, 2:26–28
Scientific racism, 1:42
    See also Race relations
Scottish in Ireland, 2:223–225
Secularization, Turkey, 1:169, 171
Self-determination, 2:106–107
Self-rule. *See* Independence
Sellassie, Haile, 1:106
Sellers, John, 1:316
Sendero Luminoso. *See* Shining Path
Sepoy Rebellion, 1:155–156
September Laws. *See* Islamic law
Serbia
    chronology, 1:239
    economy, 1:249
    independence, 1:24
    medieval Serbia, 2:159–160
    NATO air campaign, **1:238–251**
    Roma, 1:222
    Serbians in Kosovo, 2:157–166
    Yugoslavian army (JNA), 1:28–29
    See also Kosovo; Yugoslavia
Serbs
    Bosnia, 1:246
    ethnic cleansing, 1:248
    Kosovo, 1:241–242, *1:244*, 1:246–248
    nationalism, 1:28, 242
    portrayal in media, 1:31, 249
    relations with Albanians, 1:26, 241–242
    relations with Croats, 1:26, 242
    relations with Muslims, 1:30–31
Seventeen Point Agreement, 2:278
SFOR (Stabilization Force), 1:35
SFRY (Socialist Federal Republic of Yugoslavia). *See*
    Yugoslavia
Shah Pahlavi, Mohammad Reza (1919-1980), 2:134,
    135
Shamil, Iman Aver, 1:49
Shangri-La, 2:273
Shari'a law. *See* Islamic law
Sharif, Nawaz, 1:160
Shining Path (Maoist organization), **2:236–245**
Shona, 2:303–304
Sierre Leone, *2:288*
Simla Convention, 2:277–278
Singh, Hari, 1:157
Sinhalese (Sri Lanka), 2:263–269
Sinn Féin, 2:226, 232–235
Six-Day War (1967), 1:116–117, 278–279, *1:281*, 2:145
Slash-and-burn clearing technique, *1:14*, 1:16, 17
Slavery
    Brazil, 1:40–41, *1:41, 42*
    Cuba, 1:92
    Sudan, **1:266–275**, *270*
    United States, 1:40, 41–42
Slovenia, 1:243, 244
    See also Yugoslavia
Smith, Ian Douglas, 2:307
Smuggling, 2:172, 174–177
Sobradinho regulating dam, 1:15
Social classes
    Brazil, 1:40–42
    Chile, 1:206
Social Darwinism, 2:295–296

Socialism
    Chile, 1:206
    Cuba, 1:96
    East Timor, 2:90–91
    Mozambique, 2:183
Socialist Federal Republic of Yugoslavia (SFRY). *See*
    Yugoslavia
Socialist Republic of Yugoslavia. *See* Yugoslavia
Soil erosion, 1:17–18
Somalia, 2:290, *2:291*
Soros, George, 1:34
South Africa
    chronology, 2:254
    map, *2:255*
    relations with Angola, 2:12–15, 17–19
    relations with Mozambique, 2:184–186
    Truth and Reconciliation Commission, **2:253–261**
    war with Front Line States, 2:18–19
South Korea
    chronology, 2:150
    conflict with North Korea, **2:149–156**
    map, *2:151*
South West Africa. *See* Namibia
Southern Rhodesia. *See* Zimbabwe
Sovereign National Conference (SNC, Nigeria),
    2:217–218
Soviet Union. *See* Russia
Spain
    Basque conflict, 2:36–41
    colonization of Cuba, 1:92
    colonization of Guatemala, 2:122–123
    colonization of Mexico, 1:58–59
    extradition of Augusto Pinochet, 1:210
    See also Basque region
Spanish Civil War (1936), 2:36
Spanish-American War, 1:92–93
Species loss, 1:18–19, *1:21*
Spirituality, 2:272–273
SPLA (Sudan Peoples Liberation Army), *1:273*
Sri Lanka
    chronology, 2:263
    civil war, **2:262–270**
    demography, 2:263–264
    independence (1948), 2:264
    Indo-Sri Lankan Peace Accord (1987), 2:266
Stabilization Force (SFOR), 1:35
Stalin, Joseph, 1:137–138, 189
Standard Oil, 1:198–199
Starovoitova, Galina, 1:188
Statehood
    Palestine, 1:117–119, 121, 122
    Russian republics, 1:261
State-of-exile, 2:279
State-owned enterprises (China), 2:55–57
Strikes, 2:230
Sucres (Ecuador), 2:101
Sudan, *1:274*
    chronology, 1:267
    communism, 1:272
    demography, 1:267–269
    ethnic groups, 1:266–269
    Islamic law, 1:268
    map, *1:269*
    political parties, 1:271–272
    slavery, **1:266–275**, *270*

Sudan Peoples Liberation Army (SPLA), *1:273*
Suez Canal crisis (1956), 1:115, 2:116
Suharto, 2:91
Sun Yat-sen, 1:286
Sun Yixian, 1:286
Suu Kyi, Aung San, 2:189, *2:194*, 2:195–196
Syria
    chronology, 1:277
    map, *1:278*
    relations with Palestine, 1:277, 278
    relations with Turkey, 1:163
    relations with United States, 1:281

T

Taipings, 2:43
Taiwan
    chronology, 1:285
    civil war, 1:286–287
    elections, 1:284–285, 291–292
    Japanese colonization, 1:286
    map, *1:288*
    relations with China, **1:284–294**, *290, 293*, 2:281
    relations with United States, 1:287–288, 292
    ruled by Republic of China (ROC), 1:286–291
Taiwanization, 1:291
Taliban, **1:1–11**, *3*
    drug trade, 1:9
    education, 2:109
    Islamic law, 1:5
    leadership, 1:4–5
    treatment of women, *1:5*, 1:5–6
Tamils (Sri Lanka), 2:263–269
Tang dynasty, 2:275–276
Taoism. *See* Daoism
Tariffs. *See* International trade
Taylor, Charles, 1:178, 179
Technology
    humanitarian aid, 1:135–137
    militant separatist movements, 1:299
Ten Years War, 1:92
Ter-Petrosyan, Levon, 1:191–192
Terrorism
    Algeria, *2:7*
    Basque region, 2:37–41, *2:39*
    Colombia, 2:69–71
    Iran, 2:137
    Mexico, 2:175–177
    Northern Ireland, 2:221–222, 230, 232–235
    Peru, 2:236
    Sri Lanka, 2:268
Texaco Petroleum Co., 2:105–106
Thatcher, Margaret, 2:118–119
Third Reich. *See under* Germany
Tibet, **2:271–282**
    chronology, 2:272
    human rights violations, 2:281
    nationalism, 2:281
    political system, 2:275–277
    relations with China, 2:276–281, *2:279*
    religious oppression, 2:45
Tiblisi, 1:263
Timor, 2:90
    See also East Timor

Tito, Josip Broz, 1:26, 2:162–163
TMT. *See* Turkish Resistance Organization
Tolbert, William Richard, Jr., *1:177*
Tourism industry, 2:85
Toxic waste
    Ecuador, 2:105–106
    Romania, **2:246–252**
Trade Act of 1974 (U.S.), 2:53
Trade deficits. *See* International trade
Trail of Tears (U.S.), 2:201–202
Transcaucasus. *See* Armenia; Azerbaijan; Nagorno-
    Karabakh
Treaties, Native American, 2:200–203, 208
Treaty negotiations. *See* Peace negotiations
Treaty of Alliance (1960, Cyprus), 2:80–81
Treaty of Establishment (1960, Cyprus), 2:80–81
Treaty of Guarantee (1960, Cyprus), 2:80–81
Treaty of Lausanne (1923), 2:78
Trench warfare, 1:103–104, 107
Trials
    East Timor, 2:96
    Former Yugoslavia, 1:234
    Guatemala, 2:122, 129–130
    Rwanda, 1:234
    South Africa, 2:256–261, *2:259*
Tribal government, 2:203–204, 205, 207–208, 210
Tribal sovereignty, 2:200–205, 208, 209–210, 211
Trimble, David, 2:234
Trophy art, 1:258
Truth and Reconciliation Commission (TRC, South
    Africa), **2:253–261**, *259*
Tudjman, Franjo, 1:35
Turabi, Hasan al, 1:271–272
Turkey
    chronology, 1:164
    civil war, **1:163–173**
    conflict between Greek and Turkish Cypriots,
      2:75–87
    European Union membership, 1:173
    military, 1:166, 170
    nationalism, 1:168–169, 172–173
    relations with United States, 1:171
    secularization, 1:169, 171
Turkish Republic of Northern Cyprus, 2:84, 85
    See also Cyprus
Turkish Resistance Organization (TMT), 2:80
The Turner Diaries, 1:300
Tutsi
    Congo, 1:82
    genocide, **1:225–237**, *235*
    refugees, 1:225, *1:232*
    Rwanda, 1:82, 84
Tutu, Desmond, 2:258
Twa (Rwanda), 1:227
"Two Chinas," 1:288

U

U Nu, 2:193–194
Ubico, Jorge, 2:124
Uganda
    relations with Congo, 1:84
    relations with Rwanda, 1:230
ULIMO (United Liberation Movement of Liberia),
    1:179–180

Ulster, 2:223–226
    See also Northern Ireland
Ulyanov, Vladimi Ilyich, 1:137
UNATAET (East Timor). *See under* United Nations
Undocumented workers. *See* Illegal immigration
UNIFIL (United Nations Interim Force in Lebanon),
    2:286
Unilateral Declaration of Independence (UDI), 2:307
Union Carbide Disaster (1984), 2:251
Union of Soviet Socialist Republics (USSR). *See* Russia
Union Treaty, 1:258
Unionism (Ireland), 2:226
UNITA (National Union for the Total Independence of
    Angola), 2:9–24
United Fruit Company (UFCO), 2:123–124, 125–126,
    127
United Irish Rebellion (1798), 2:225
United Kingdom. *See* Great Britain
United Liberation Movement of Liberia (ULIMO),
    1:179–180
United National Party (Sri Lanka), 2:264–265, 269
United Nations
    Angola, 2:14–15, 19
    Bosnia-Herzegovina, *1:27,* 1:29, 31, 36
    chronology, 2:284
    Congo, 1:86, 87
    Croatia, 1:244–245
    Cyprus, 2:82, 86
    East Timor, 2:95–96
    Eritrea, 1:109
    Ethiopian, 1:109
    Iraq, **1:143–150,** *147*
    Jerusalem, 2:143–144
    Liberia, 1:179–180
    Palestine, 1:114–115
    Rwanda, 1:231–232, 235
    Yugoslavia, 1:31, 244–245
United Nations Interim Force in Lebanon (UNIFIL),
    2:286
United Nations peacekeeping forces, **2:283–291**
    Angola, 2:15
    Cyprus (UNFICYP), 2:82, 84
    East Timor (UNAMET), 2:95, 97
    Korean Peninsula, 2:152
    Kosovo, 2:166, *2:287*
    Mozambique, 2:186
    Sierre Leone, *2:288*
United Nations Special Commission (UNSCOM),
    1:147–149
United Nations Special Committee on Palestine, 2:144
United Nations Temporary Commission for Korea
    (UNTCOK), 2:151–152
United Nations Troop Supervision Organization
    (UNTSO), 2:285
United States
    aid to Europe after World War II, 2:113–114
    chronologies, 2:170, 199, 293
    cocaine, 1:72–73, 75
    foreign policy, 2:17–18
    gun control laws, 1:296, 298
    immigration, **2:292–301**
    map, *1:98*
    Mexican border relations, **2:169–178,** *176*
    militant separatist movements, **1:295–302**
    Native Americans, **2:198–213**

oil industry, 1:196, 198, 200–202
peacekeeping missions, 2:289–290
race relations, 1:43–44
relations with Afghanistan, 1:6–7
relations with Angola, 2:12–19
relations with Bosnia-Herzegovina, 1:29–35
relations with Chile, 1:206–207
relations with Colombia, 1:76, 77, 2:71
relations with Congo, 1:80
relations with Cuba, **1:89–102,** *97*
relations with East Timor, 2:91, 95
relations with France, 2:294
relations with Great Britain, 2:115–116, 118–119
relations with Guatemala, 2:127–129
relations with India, 1:160
relations with Iran, 2:135–139
relations with Iraq, 1:144, 149
relations with Korea, 2:149–153
relations with Kosovo, 1:248, 250
relations with Mozambique, 2:185–186
relations with Myanmar, 2:190, 196
relations with Pakistan, 1:160
relations with Russia, 1:98–99, 137–138, 257
relations with Serbs, 1:238, 246
relations with Taliban, 1:7–8
relations with Yugoslavia, 1:246
road development, 1:200–201
slavery, 1:40, 41–42
World Trade Organization (WTO), 1:319, 2:54,
    57
United States Army Military Government in Korea (US-
    AMGK), 2:150–151
United States Bureau of Alcohol, Tobacco, and Firearms
    (ATF), 1:295
United States Central Intelligence Agency
    activity in Iran, 2:136
    aid to Angolan insurrgents, 2:12, 15–17
    aid to Guatemalan guerillas, 2:127
United States Constitution, 1:297, 2:201
United States Federal Bureau of Investigation (FBI)
    Branch Davidians, 1:298–299
    militant separatist movements, 1:295
    Ruby Ridge (Idaho) incident, 1:295–296
Universal Declaration on the Rights of Indigenous
    Peoples, 2:106
Universities and colleges
    Ecuador, 2:110–111
    Kosovo, 2:163–164
    Macedonia, 2:168
University of Prishtina, 2:164
University of Tetovo, 2:168
Urbanization, 2:200, 204
Urbina, Ernesto, 1:62
Urgyn Trinley Dorje, 2:271–272
USSR (Union of Soviet Socialist Republics). *See* Russia
U'wa (Colombia)
    chronology, 2:65
    conflict with Occidental Petroleum, **2:64–74**
U'wa Defense Working Group, 2:68

V

Vale of Kashmir. *See* Kashmir
Vance, Cyrus, 1:31
Vatican. *See* Catholic Church

Venezuela
  chronology, 1:304
  constitution, 1:308
  elections, 1:303, 307–309, *1:309*
  map, *1:306*
  oil industry, 1:304, 306–307
  Populism, **1:303–310**
  relations with Cuba, 1:307
  working class, 1:303
Vietnam, 2:299
Vigilantism, 2:6
Vincente, Rafael Sebastin Guillen, 1:64, *1:66, 68*
Voigt, Udo, 1:130

W

Wahid, Abdurrahman, 2:96–97
War. *See* Civil war; specific wars
War brides, 2:296
War crimes tribunals. *See* Trials
War veterans, 2:311–312
Washinawatok, Ingrid, 2:69–70
Water
  Ecuador, 2:105–106
  Native American, 2:208
  Romania, **2:246–252**
Weapons of mass destruction (WMD), 1:147–149
Weapons traffic, 1:96
  Angola, 2:16, 20
  Iran, 2:138
Weaver, Randy, 1:295–296
West Bank, 1:118, *1:120,* 2:145
West Germany. *See* Germany
Western influence, 1:3, 2:139–140
White supremacy
  Germany, **1:124–133**
  United States, 1:297–298
Wickremesinghe, Ranil, 2:269
William II (England), 2:225
WMD (Weapons of mass destruction), 1:147–149
Women's rights issues, *1:5,* 1:5–6, 2:5–6, 6, *2:139, 218*
Worcester v. Georgia (1832), 2:201
Working class, 1:303–305
World Bank
  aid to Zimbabwe, 2:310
  assistance to Brazil, 1:20
  humanitarian aid, 1:141
World Trade Organization (WTO), **1:311–320**
  China's involvement, **2:51–63**, *61*
  chronology, 2:52
  Jackson-Vanik legislation (1974), 2:53, 59
  most-favored nation status, 2:52–53, 59
  protests against, *1:313, 314, 317,* 2:56
  "rule of law," 2:53, 60
World War I, 2:161–162
World War II, 2:296
  Austria, 2:29
  Cyprus, 2:29
  India, 1:157
  Iran, 2:135–136
  Kosovo, 2:162
  Timor, 2:90
  Yugoslavia, 1:26

X

Xenophobia, 1:125, 2:30–31

Y

Yamoussoukro IV Agreement, 1:179
Year 2000, 1:301
Yellow Hat sect (religion), 2:276
Yelstin, Boris Nikolaevich, 1:53, 54, 257, 258–259
Y2K, 1:301
Yom Kippur War (1973), 1:117, 279
Yugoslavia
  arms embargo, 1:31
  chronology, 1:239
  civil war, **1:24–38, 238–251**
  Communism, 1:243
  economy, 1:27, 241
  elections, 1:243
  ethnic groups, 1:24, 26, 240
  films, 1:249
  formation, 1:24, 26
  Kosovo, 2:161–166
  Macedonia, 2:166–168
  nationalism, 1:26, 240
  United Nations peacekeeping forces, 2:289
  World War II, 1:26
  See also Bosnia-Herzegovina; Croatia; Kosovo;
    Serbia; Slovenia
Yugoslavian army (JNA), 1:28–29

Z

Zacarias, General, *2:14*
Zahir Shah, Mohammed, 1:3
Zaire, 1:80
  See also Congo
Zamfara State (Nigeria), 2:214, 215–217
Zapata, Emiliano, *1:65*
Zapatista Front of National Liberation (FZLN), 1:67, 68
Zapatista National Liberation Army (EZLN), 1:66–69
Zapatistas. *See* Zapatista National Liberation Army
    (EZLN)
Zedong, Mao, 2:278
Zeroual, Lamine, 2:6–7
Zhongnanhai protest (1999), 2:47
Zimbabwe, **2:302–315**, *311*
  British missions, 2:304–305
  chronology, 2:303
  civil war, 2:309
  elections, 2:313
  ethnic groups, 2:303–304
  map, *2:305*
  Portuguese colonialism, 2:304
  relations with British, 2:304–307
  relations with Congo, 1:84
  relations with Mozambique, 2:184–186
Zimbabwe African National Union (ZANU), 2:307
Zimbabwe African National Union-Patriotic Front
    (ZANU-PF), 2:309–314
Zimbabwe African People's Union (ZAPU), 2:307
Zimbabwe National Liberation War Veterans Association,
    2:312